Handbook of Research on Automated Feature Engineering and Advanced Applications in Data Science

Mrutyunjaya Panda
Utkal University, India

Harekrishna Misra
Institute of Rural Management, Anand, India

A volume in the Advances in Data Mining and Database Management (ADMDM) Book Series

Published in the United States of America by
   IGI Global
   Engineering Science Reference (an imprint of IGI Global)
   701 E. Chocolate Avenue
   Hershey PA, USA 17033
   Tel: 717-533-8845
   Fax: 717-533-8661
   E-mail: cust@igi-global.com
   Web site: http://www.igi-global.com

Library of Congress Cataloging-in-Publication Data

Names: Panda, Mrutyunjaya, editor. | Misra, Harekrishna, editor.
Title: Handbook of research on automated feature engineering and advanced
  applications in data science / Mrutyunjaya Panda and Harekrishna Misra,
  editors.
Description: Hershey, PA : Engineering Science Reference, [2021] | Includes
  bibliographical references and index. | Summary: "This edited book will
  start with an introduction to feature engineering and then move onto
  recent concepts, methods and applications with the use of various data
  types that includes : text, image, streaming data, social network data,
  financial data, biomedical data, bioinformatics etc. to help readers
  gain insight into how features can be extracted and transformed from raw
  data"-- Provided by publisher.
Identifiers: LCCN 2020026646 (print) | LCCN 2020026647 (ebook) | ISBN
  9781799866596 (hardcover) | ISBN 9781799866619 (ebook)
Subjects: LCSH: Data mining. | Big data--Industrial applications. |
  Automatic data collection systems. | Automatic classification.
Classification: LCC QA76.9.D343 H395 2021 (print) | LCC QA76.9.D343
  (ebook) | DDC 006.3/12--dc23
LC record available at https://lccn.loc.gov/2020026646
LC ebook record available at https://lccn.loc.gov/2020026647

This book is published in the IGI Global book series Advances in Data Mining and Database Management (ADMDM) (ISSN: 2327-1981; eISSN: 2327-199X)

British Cataloguing in Publication Data
A Cataloguing in Publication record for this book is available from the British Library.

All work contributed to this book is new, previously-unpublished material. The views expressed in this book are those of the authors, but not necessarily of the publisher.

For electronic access to this publication, please contact: eresources@igi-global.com.

Advances in Data Mining and Database Management (ADMDM) Book Series

David Taniar
Monash University, Australia

ISSN:2327-1981
EISSN:2327-199X

MISSION

With the large amounts of information available to organizations in today's digital world, there is a need for continual research surrounding emerging methods and tools for collecting, analyzing, and storing data.

The **Advances in Data Mining & Database Management (ADMDM)** series aims to bring together research in information retrieval, data analysis, data warehousing, and related areas in order to become an ideal resource for those working and studying in these fields. IT professionals, software engineers, academicians and upper-level students will find titles within the ADMDM book series particularly useful for staying up-to-date on emerging research, theories, and applications in the fields of data mining and database management.

COVERAGE

- Heterogeneous and Distributed Databases
- Data Analysis
- Web Mining
- Text Mining
- Data Mining
- Profiling Practices
- Cluster Analysis
- Database Testing
- Educational Data Mining
- Quantitative Structure–Activity Relationship

IGI Global is currently accepting manuscripts for publication within this series. To submit a proposal for a volume in this series, please contact our Acquisition Editors at Acquisitions@igi-global.com or visit: http://www.igi-global.com/publish/.

Titles in this Series

For a list of additional titles in this series, please visit: www.igi-global.com/book-series

Multidisciplinary Functions of Blockchain Technology in AI and IoT Applications
Niaz Chowdhury (The Open University, Milton Keynes, UK) and Ganesh Chandra Deka (Ministry of Skill Development and Entrepreneurship, New Delhi, India)
Engineering Science Reference • © 2021 • 255pp • H/C (ISBN: 9781799858768) • US $245.00

Handbook of Research on Engineering, Business, and Healthcare Applications of Data Science and Analytics
Bhushan Patil (Independent Researcher, India) and Manisha Vohra (Independent Researcher, India)
Engineering Science Reference • © 2021 • 583pp • H/C (ISBN: 9781799830535) • US $345.00

Advanced Deep Learning Applications in Big Data Analytics
Hadj Ahmed Bouarara (Tahar Moulay University of Saida, Algeria)
Engineering Science Reference • © 2021 • 351pp • H/C (ISBN: 9781799827917) • US $245.00

Opportunities and Challenges for Blockchain Technology in Autonomous Vehicles
Amit Kumar Tyagi (Vellore Institute of Technolgy, Chennai, India) Gillala Rekha (K. L. University, India) and N. Sreenath (Pondicherry Engineering College, India)
Engineering Science Reference • © 2021 • 316pp • H/C (ISBN: 9781799832959) • US $245.00

Cross-Industry Use of Blockchain Technology and Opportunities for the Future
Idongesit Williams (Aalborg University, Denmark)
Engineering Science Reference • © 2020 • 228pp • H/C (ISBN: 9781799836322) • US $225.00

Applications and Developments in Semantic Process Mining
Kingsley Okoye (University of East London, UK)
Engineering Science Reference • © 2020 • 248pp • H/C (ISBN: 9781799826682) • US $195.00

Handling Priority Inversion in Time-Constrained Distributed Databases
Udai Shanker (Madan Mohan Malaviya University of Technology, India) and Sarvesh Pandey (Madan Mohan Malaviya University of Technology, India)
Engineering Science Reference • © 2020 • 338pp • H/C (ISBN: 9781799824916) • US $225.00

IGI Global
PUBLISHER of TIMELY KNOWLEDGE

701 East Chocolate Avenue, Hershey, PA 17033, USA
Tel: 717-533-8845 x100 • Fax: 717-533-8661
E-Mail: cust@igi-global.com • www.igi-global.com

Editorial Advisory Board

List of Contributors

Table of Contents

Detailed Table of Contents

Chapter 1

    Nilesh Kumar Sahu, Birla Institute of Technology, Mesra, India
    Manorama Patnaik, Birla Institute of Technology, Mesra, India
    Itu Snigdh, Birla Institute of Technology, Mesra, India

The precision of any machine learning algorithm depends on the data set, its suitability, and its volume. Therefore, data and its characteristics have currently become the predominant components of any predictive or precision-based domain like machine learning. Feature engineering refers to the process of changing and preparing this input data so that it is ready for training machine learning models. Several features such as categorical, numerical, mixed, date, and time are to be considered for feature extraction in feature engineering. Datasets containing characteristics such as cardinality, missing data, and rare labels for categorical features, distribution, outliers, and magnitude are currently considered as features. This chapter discusses various data types and their techniques for applying to feature engineering. This chapter also focuses on the implementation of various data techniques for feature extraction.

Chapter 2

    Bhanu Chander, Pondicherry University, India

High-dimensional data inspection is one of the major disputes for researchers plus engineers in domains of deep learning (DL), machine learning (ML), as well as data mining. Feature selection (FS) endows with proficient manner to determine these difficulties through eradicating unrelated and outdated data, which be capable of reducing calculation time, progress learns precision, and smooth the progress of an enhanced understanding of the learning representation or information. To eradicate an inappropriate feature, an FS standard was essential, which can determine the significance of every feature in the company of the output class/labels. Filter schemes employ variable status procedure as the standard criterion for variable collection by means of ordering. Ranking schemes utilized since their straightforwardness and high-quality accomplishment are detailed for handy appliances. The goal of this chapter is to produce complete information on FS approaches, its applications, and future research directions.

Chapter 3

Hocine Chebi, Faculty of Electrical Engineering, Djillali Liabes University, Sidi Bel Abbes, Algeria

In this chapter, the authors propose two algorithms based on the device of attributes for tracking of the abnormal behavior of crowd in the visual systems of surveillance. Previous works were realized in the case of detection of behavior, which uses the analysis and the classification of behavior of crowds; this work explores the continuity in the same domain, but in the case of the automatic tracking based on the techniques of filtering one using the KALMAN filter and particles filter. The proposed algorithms he the technique of filter with particle is independent from the detection and from the segmentation human, so is strong with regard to (compared with) the filter of Kalman. In conclusion, the chapter applies the method for tracking of the abnormal behavior to several videos and shows the promising results.

Chapter 4

Eugenio Vocaturo, DIMES, University of Calabria (UNICAL), Italy & CNR-NANOTEC National Research Council, Italy
Ester Zumpano, DIMES, University of Calabria (UNICAL), Italy

The development of performing imaging techniques is favoring the spread of artificial vision systems as support tools for the early diagnosis of skin cancers. Epiluminescence microscopy (ELM) is currently the most adopted technique through which it is possible to obtain very detailed images of skin lesions. Over time, melanoma spreads quickly, invading the body's organs through the blood vessels: an early recognition is essential to ensure decisive intervention. There are many machine learning approaches proposed to implement artificial vision systems operating on datasets made up of dermatoscopic images obtained using ELM technique. These proposals are characterized by the use of various specific features that make understanding difficult: the problem of defining a set of features that can allows good classification performance arises. The aim of this work is to identify reference features that can be used by new researchers as a starting point for new proposals.

Chapter 5

Diwakar Naidu, BRSM College of Agricultural Engineering and Technology and Research Station, Chatarkhar, India & Indira Gandhi Agricultural University, Raipur, India
Babita Majhi, Guru Ghashidas Vishwavidyalaya, Central University, Bilaspur, India
Surendra Kumar Chandniha, BRSM College of Agricultural Engineering and Technology and Research Station, Chatarkhar, India & Indira Gandhi Agricultural University, Raipur, India

This study focuses on modelling the changes in rainfall patterns in different agro-climatic zones due to climate change through statistical downscaling of large-scale climate variables using machine learning approaches. Potential of three machine learning algorithms, multilayer artificial neural network (MLANN), radial basis function neural network (RBFNN), and least square support vector machine (LS-SVM) have been investigated. The large-scale climate variable are obtained from National Centre for Environmental

Prediction (NCEP) reanalysis product and used as predictors for model development. Proposed machine learning models are applied to generate projected time series of rainfall for the period 2021-2050 using the Hadley Centre coupled model (HadCM3) B2 emission scenario data as predictors. An increasing trend in anticipated rainfall is observed during 2021-2050 in all the ACZs of Chhattisgarh State. Among the machine learning models, RBFNN found as more feasible technique for modeling of monthly rainfall in this region.

Chapter 6

Hadeer Elziaat, Future University in Egypt (FUE), Egypt
Nashwa El-Bendary, Arab Academy for Science, Technology, and Maritime Transport
    (AASTMT), Smart Village, Egypt
Ramadan Moawad, Future University in Egypt (FUE), Egypt

Freezing of gait (FoG) is a common symptom of Parkinson's disease (PD) that causes intermittent absence of forward progression of patient's feet while walking. Accordingly, FoG momentary episodes are always accompanied with falls. This chapter presents a novel multi-feature fusion model for early detection of FoG episodes in patients with PD. In this chapter, two feature engineering schemes are investigated, namely time-domain hand-crafted feature engineering and convolutional neural network (CNN)-based spectrogram feature learning. Data of tri-axial accelerometer sensors for patients with PD is utilized to characterize the performance of the proposed model through several experiments with various machine learning (ML) algorithms. Obtained experimental results showed that the multi-feature fusion approach has outperformed typical single feature sets. Conclusively, the significance of this chapter is to highlight the impact of using feature fusion of multi-feature sets through investigating the performance of a FoG episodes early detection model.

Adem Assfaw Mekonnen, Addis Ababa Science and Technology University, Ethiopia
Hussien Worku Seid, Addis Ababa Science and Technology University, Ethiopia
Sudhir Kumar Mohapatra, Addis Ababa Science and Technology University, Ethiopia
Srinivas Prasad, GITAM University, India

The timely prognosis of brain tumors is gambling a great role within the pretreatment of patients and keep the life of suffers. The manual classification of brain tumors is a difficult task for radiologists due to the intensity variation pixel information produced by the magnetic resonance machine and it is a very tedious task for a large number of images. A deep learning algorithm becomes a famous algorithm to conquer the problems traditional machine learning algorithms by automatically feature extraction from the input spaces and accurately detect the brain tumors. One of the most important features of deep learning is transferred a gain knowledge strategy to use small datasets. Transfer learning is explored by freezing layers and fine-tuning a pre-trained model to a recommended convolutional neural net model. The proposed model is trained using 4000 real magnetic resonance images datasets. The mean accuracy of the proposed model is found to be 98% for brain tumor classifications with mini-batch size 32 and a learning rate of 0.001.

    Esraa Elhariri, Faculty of Computers and Information, Fayoum University, Egypt
    Nashwa El-Bendary, Arab Academy for Science, Technology, and Maritime Transport
        (AASTMT), Smart Village, Egypt
    Shereen A. Taie, Faculty of Computers and Information, Fayoum University, Egypt

Feature engineering is a key component contributing to the performance of the computer vision pipeline. It is fundamental to several computer vision tasks such as object recognition, image retrieval, and image segmentation. On the other hand, the emerging technology of structural health monitoring (SHM) paved the way for spotting continuous tracking of structural damage. Damage detection and severity recognition in the structural buildings and constructions are issues of great importance as the various types of damages represent an essential indicator of building and construction durability. In this chapter, the authors connect the feature engineering with SHM processes through illustrating the concept of SHM from a computational perspective, with a focus on various types of data and feature engineering methods as well as applications and open venues for further research. Challenges to be addressed and future directions of research are presented and an extensive survey of state-of-the-art studies is also included.

    Judith Justin, School of Engineering, Avinashilingam Institute for Home Science and Higher
        Education for Women, Coimbatore, India
    Vanithamani R., School of Engineering, Avinashilingam Institute for Home Science and
        Higher Education for Women, Coimbatore, India

In this chapter, a speech enhancement technique is implemented using a neuro-fuzzy classifier. Noisy speech sentences from NOIZEUS and AURORA databases are taken for the study. Feature extraction is implemented through modifications in amplitude magnitude spectrograms. A four class neuro-fuzzy classifier splits the noisy speech samples into noise-only part, signal only part, more noise-less signal part, and more signal-less noise part of the time-frequency units. Appropriate weights are applied in the enhancement phase. The enhanced speech sentence is evaluated using objective measures. An analysis of the performance of the Neuro-Fuzzy 4 (NF 4) classifier is done. A comparison of the performance of the classifier with other conventional techniques is done for various noises at different noise levels. It is observed that the numerical values of the measures obtained are better when compared to the others. An overall comparison of the performance of the NF 4 classifier is done and it is inferred that NF4 outperforms the other techniques in speech enhancement.

    Shashwati Mishra, B.J.B. College (Autonomous), Bhubaneswar, India
    Mrutyunjaya Panda, Utkal University, Vani Vihar, Bhubaneswar, India

Feature plays a very important role in the analysis and prediction of data as it carries the most valuable information about the data. This data may be in a structured format or in an unstructured format. Feature engineering process is used to extract features from these data. Selection of features is one of the crucial steps in the feature engineering process. This feature selection process can adopt four different approaches.

On that basis, it can be classified into four basic categories, namely filter method, wrapper method, embedded method, and hybrid method. This chapter discusses about different techniques coming under these four categories along with the research work on feature selection.

  Partha Sarathi Mishra, North Orissa University, India
  Debabrata Nandi, North Orissa University, India

Weather prediction has gained a point of attraction for many researchers of variant research communities. The emerging deep learning techniques have motivated many researches to explore hidden hierarchical pattern in the great mass of weather dataset for weather prediction. In this chapter, four different categories of computationally efficient deep learning models—CNN, LSTM, CNN-LSTM, and ConvLSTM—have been critically examined for improved weather prediction. Here, emphasis has been given on supervised learning techniques for model development by considering the importance of feature engineering. Feature engineering plays a vital role in reducing dimension, decreasing model complexity as well as handling the noise and corrupted data. Using daily maximum temperature, this chapter investigates the performance of different deep learning models for improved predictions. The results obtained from different experiments conducted ensures that the feature engineering based deep learning study for the purpose of predictive modeling using time series data is really an encouraging approach.

  Dwiti Krishna Bebarta, Gayatri Vidya Parishad College of Engineering for Women, India
  Birendra Biswal, Gayatri Vidya Parishad College of Engineering (Autonomous), India

Automated feature engineering is to build predictive models that are capable of transforming raw data into features, that is, creation of new features from existing ones on various datasets to create meaningful features and examining their effect on planned model performances on various parameters like accuracy, efficiency, and prevent data leakage. So the challenges for experts are to plan computationally efficient and effective machine, learning-based predictive models. This chapter will provide an imminent to the important intelligent techniques that could be utilized to enhance predictive analytics by using an advanced form of the predictive model. A computationally efficient and effective machine learning model using functional link artificial neural network (FLANN) is discussed to design for predicting the business needs with a high degree of accuracy for the traders or investors. The performance of the models using FLANN is encouraging when scientifically analyzed the experimental results of the model using different statistical analyses.

  Rajesh K. V. N., Department of Computer Science and Systems Engineering, Andhra University
  College of Engineering (Autonomous), Andhra University, Visakhapatnam, India
  Lalitha Bhaskari D., Department of Computer Science and Systems Engineering, Andhra
  University College of Engineering (Autonomous), Andhra University, Visakhapatnam, India

Plants are very important for the existence of human life. The total number of plant species is nearing 400 thousand as of date. With such a huge number of plant species, there is a need for intelligent systems for plant species recognition. The leaf is one of the most important and prominent parts of a plant and is available throughout the year. Leaf plays a major role in the identification of plants. Plant leaf recognition (PLR) is the process of automatically recognizing the plant species based on the image of the plant leaf. Many researchers have worked in this area of PLR using image processing, feature extraction, machine learning, and convolution neural network techniques. As a part of this chapter, the authors review several such latest methods of PLR and present the work done by various authors in the past five years in this area. The authors propose a generalized architecture for PLR based on this study and describe the major steps in PLR in detail. The authors then present a brief summary of the work that they are doing in this area of PLR for Ayurvedic plants.

Chapter 14

Rabindranath Jana, Indian Statistical Institute, Kolkata, India
P. Vdhyarani, Sri Parasakthi College for Women, India
R. Maruthakutti, M. S. University, India

In the past few years, it is being observed that there is a wake-up call for creating one economic India, one market place with free movement of goods and people. Again, for creating one economic India, the needs of creating one economic India, it needs to preserve sovereignty for the Indian states. However, it is very pertinent to ask how much internal integration India has achieved through trade between states within India. Under such brief backdrop, the author has tried, as an initial attempt, to apply social network analysis (SNA) for studying empirically reciprocation/cohesiveness of Indian states using the data on inter-firm and intra-firm trade flows between states for the financial year 2015-2016. On the basis of reciprocity counts for weighted social networks on inter-states trade relation, the standardized reciprocity measures have been adopted for the chapter. The outcomes of the chapter seem to offer important implications for understanding cooperation and integration on inter-states trade interactions and to exhibit the equilibrium and circularity of inter-state trade flows.

Chapter 15

Babita Majhi, Guru Ghasidas Viswavidyalaya, Bilaspur, India
Sachin Singh Rajput, Guru Ghasidas Vishwavidyalaya, Bilaspur, India
Ritanjali Majhi, National Institute of Technology, Karnataka, India

The principle objective of this chapter is to build up a churn prediction model which helps telecom administrators to foresee clients who are no doubt liable to agitate. Many studies affirmed that AI innovation is profoundly effective to anticipate this circumstance as it is applied through training from past information. The prediction procedure is involved three primary stages: normalization of the data, then feature selection based on information gain, and finally, classification utilizing different AI methods, for example, back propagation neural network (BPNNM), naïve Bayesian, k-nearest neighborhood (KNN), support vector machine (SVM), discriminant analysis (DA), decision tree (DT), and extreme learning machine (ELM). It is shown from simulation study that out of these seven methods SVM with polynomial based kernel is coming about 91.33% of precision where ELM is at the primary situation with 92.10% of exactness and MLANN-based CCP model is at third rank with 90.4% of accuracy. Similar observation is noted for 10-fold cross validation also.

Ajit Kumar Behera, Department of Computer Science and Application, Utkal University,
India & Silicon Institute of Technology, Bhubaneswar, India
Mrutyunjaya Panda, Department of Computer Science and Application, Utkal University, India

Determining appropriate software reliability prediction technique is a challenging task for the software development process. So, it is essential for software engineers to develop good quality software product. Though several prediction models are in use for small size data, the estimation of the reliability of software system is crucial. Inadequate data may lead sub-optimal solution. This chapter proposes a technique of increasing training dataset by generating virtual data points original data. For improving the prediction of cumulative failure time in software, multilayer perceptron (MLP)-based virtual data positions (DEVDP) exploration techniques have been proposed. The parameters of the network are optimized by evolutionary algorithm differential evolution (DE). For validation of the model in presence of virtual data point (VDP), eight failure datasets from different sources has been used. The results obtained from the simulation studies indicate that proposed DEVDP exploration technique outperformed traditional models.

K. Abhimanyu Kumar Patro, National Institute of Technology, Raipur, India
Mukesh Drolia, National Institute of Technology, Raipur, India
Akash Deep Yadav, National Institute of Technology, Raipur, India
Bibhudendra Acharya, National Institute of Technology, Raipur, India

In this present era, where everything is getting digitalized, information or data in any form, important to an organization or individual, are at a greater risk of being attacked under acts, commonly known as cyber-attack. Hence, a proper and more efficient cryptosystem is the prime need of the hour to secure the data (especially the image data). This chapter proposes an efficient multi-point crossover operation-based chaotic image encryption system to secure images. The multi-point crossover operation is performed on both the rows and columns of bit-planes in the images. The improved one-dimensional chaotic maps are then used to perform pixel-permutation and diffusion operations. The main advantage of this technique is the use of multi-point crossover operation in bit-levels. The multi-point crossover operation not only increases the security of cipher images but also increases the key space of the algorithm. The outcomes and analyses of various parameters show the best performance of the algorithm in image encryption and different common attacks.

Gyana Ranjana Panigrahi, Sambalpur University, India
Nalini Kanta Barpanda, Sambalpur University, India
Madhumita Panda, Gangadhar Meher University, India

Cybersecurity is of global importance. Nearly all association suffer from an active cyber-attack. However, there is a lack of making cyber policy violator more resilient for analysts in proportionately analyzing security incidents. Now the question: Is there any proper technique of implementations for assisting automated decision to the analyst using a comparison study feature selection method? The authors take multi-criteria decision-making methods for comparison. Here the authors use CICDDoS2019 datasets consisting of Windows benign and the most vanguard for shared bouts. Hill-climbing algorithm may be incorporated to select best features. The time-based pragmatic data can be extracted from the mainsheet for classification as distributed cyber-policy violator or legitimate benign using decision tree (DT) with analytical hierarchy process (AHP) (DT-AHP), support vector machine (SVM) with technique for order of preference by similarity to ideal solution (SVM-TOPSIS) and mixed model of k-nearest neighbor (KNN AHP-TOPSIS) algorithms.

Foreword

A reader holding this book might think what is a feature and why we need the engineering of it? Feature engineering is an emerging discipline gaining widespread attention of researchers from the academia, and industry. Feature engineering efforts deals with the preparation of proper input dataset, compatible with the machine learning algorithm requirements and thereby improving the model performance. Under the umbrella of Industry 4.0, big data analytics play a major role and from an application perspective there is a need to deal with diverse datasets which are mostly generated real-time and online. Due to the tremendous growth in machine learning, data analytics field, the demand for improving feature engineering is ever increasing. Typically, a data scientist would spend 40-60% of the project time in identifying good techniques for data pre-processing, mining data patterns and finding suitable algorithms, etc.

This edited Volume comprising of 18 chapters has succeeded in bringing together data scientists working in the area of feature engineering to showcase various frameworks and data science applications including environment, cybersecurity and agro-climatic applications. Besides providing a nice literature about various feature engineering techniques, the book illustrates practical case studies and real-world applications.

I am sure that this book will serve as a useful reference as it provides an in-depth analysis on both theoretical and latest empirical research findings. The Volume will be useful for graduate students, big-data scientists, researchers, data analysts, etc. as the primary text for courses on feature engineering or a supplement to the course like data mining, big data analytics etc.

The editors are internationally recognized experts in the field, and this makes the work authoritative. Equally important is the fact that they have carefully chosen a set of contributions that highlight the state of the art of feature engineering. In view of the depth and breadth of the coverage and the usefulness of the techniques and applications, I am convinced that the readers will enjoy reading the contents. All the best!

Ajith Abraham
Machine Intelligence Research Labs (MIR Labs), USA
September 5, 2020

Preface

AN OVERVIEW OF THE SUBJECT MATTER

With the advancement of technologies, innovative skills abound to predict business behaviour through intelligent data management. Intelligent data management seeks collaborative networks of data science, data engineering, and data models. It is evident that no emerging data model is good enough to meet every dynamic and market-driven business requirement, and yet if not adequately addressed, the failure in predictive decisions will only increase. In contemporary digital world, it is quite natural a phenomenon for organizations to capture data and strive to make effective use to hasten provocative and predictive decisions. Due to emerging low-cost computing infrastructure, computing skills and cloud-based services, including software as a service (SaaS), platform as a service (PaaS) and computing tools and models, the huge amount of data is at the disposal of the organization to churn. Big data concepts are very typical today for any organization to take pride in not only to acquire but also to invest in managing for garnering business advantages over competitors or enhancing customer experience. Managerial decisions are no more limited to intuitive analyses and also are not expert-driven because of such advancements in handling big data. This computing transformation has enabled common users to assess problems having study multi-disciplinary dimensions and feature engineering isn emphatic support in this direction. The emergence of machine learning (ML), artificial intelligence (AI), fog computing, industry 4.0 and web 4.0 environment is likely to make the big data scenario very complex. This is because various data formats, data types, and modes of data management will likely be machine-driven. Machine-driven data management will continue to gain importance as business complexities grow. The role of data science, engineering and modelling is also likely to grow complex. It is a new trend to argue that ML and AI will pave the way for quick decision making. However, data science and data engineering are not entirely modern as their underlying principles are experienced in the era of enterprise data interchange (EDI), data warehousing and data mining to support business decisions. These principles seek qualitative and quantitative data management tools and techniques to size data received. However, automating data engineering to qualitatively support data models for the effective use of ML and AI for business decisions is a challenge.

It is essential to appreciate that feature engineering is a process in the direction to support data models and ML tools. This stems from the fact that data generated and received are generally unstructured, different types, messy, chaotic and is not under the control of user in real life. Feature engineering is used as a process to organize these data sets to bring to a meaningful form in order to develop effective and transparent ML models. This way, the transformed data will be more transparent to the machine learning models for better prediction and analysis of results. Data science helps the data scientist to assess the trade-offs of their decision regarding the effectiveness of the machine learning model implemented.

Feature engineering is a process engineering at work to support the data science discipline and statistical modeling. Feature engineering provides the necessary environment to arrange data sets irrespective of its sources. This approach is beneficial for any data-driven problem-solving modeling exercises and across all sectors, including business, government, health, transport, market, energy, and climate etc. through which innovative insights are likely to help improve products, services and the society. The purpose of feature engineering is thus to support this endeavor, not through intuitive skills of the managers and administrators alike, but with adequate professionally managed data inputs to the predictive models. Feature engineering approach, in turn, will create an environment for building systems to display fact-based predictions and outcomes.

The demand for feature engineering to deliver is ever increasing. Yet there are fewer academic examples and cases available to present best practices that academia could cater to the needs of industry and society. The motivation behind this edited book is to bring together data scientists working in the area of feature engineering to showcase various sector-based work.

A DESCRIPTION OF THE TARGET AUDIENCE

As feature engineering aims to provide organized inputs to the ML oriented mathematical and predictive models, it is important to note that the features engineered sit between data and the models. Thus it is imperative to note that the audience for this edited book will be threefold. First, it would provide a gamut of supporting literature in the areas of ML, AI, and feature engineering. The second, the book will provide insights to case-based algorithms to learn from and make use of. This edited book will be an ingredient to graduate students, post-graduate students, research scholars, big-data scientists, academia, project developers, data analysts, etc. The book will be useful as the primary text for courses on feature engineering, or a supplement to the course like data mining, machine learning, and big data analytics.

OBJECTIVE

This book is useful as a reference, which aims to provide an insight how features can be extracted and transformed from the raw data. It will provide an in-depth analysis on both theoretical and latest empirical research findings.

CHAPTER SCHEME

The book is organized into 18 chapters. A brief description of each of the chapters follows:

Chapter 1 provides an in-depth compilation of advances in feature engineering and its relationship with data science. It also discusses the implementation of data techniques for feature extraction. It is argued in this chapter that the precision of any ML algorithm depends on the data set, its suitability, and its volume. Therefore data and its characteristics have currently become the predominant components of any predictive or precision-based domain like machine learning. Feature Engineering refers to the process of changing and preparing this input data so that it is ready for training machine learning models. Thus it needs several features such as Categorical, Numerical, Mixed, date, and time for feature extraction. Datasets containing characteristics such as cardinality, missing data, and rare labels for categorical features, distribution, outliers, and magnitude are currently considered as features. Considering all these contours of feature engineering, and its utilities, this chapter discusses various data types and their techniques for applications. The chapter also focuses on the implementation of different data techniques for feature extraction.

Chapter 2 discusses high-dimensional data inspection as one of the major disputes for researchers and engineers in domains of Deep learning (DL), ML and data mining. In this chapter authors present feature selection (FS) that deals with difficulties in eradicating unrelated and outdated data, to be capable of reducing calculation time, learning with precision, and smoothening the progress of an enhanced understanding of the learning representation or information. The chapter focuses on FS and its utility to eradicate an inappropriate feature, and advocates that FS standard was essential to determine the significance of every feature in a business set up and to provide duce complete information on FS approaches, its applications and future research directions.

Chapter 3 proposes two algorithms based on the device of attributes for tracking of the abnormal behavior of crowd in the visual systems of surveillance. Authors presents their on filtering algorithms and compared with KALMAN filter and particles filter algorithms by relating to previous works on behavior detection, analysis and classification of crowds. The proposed algorithms presented the improvd results when compared with the filter of KALMAN. This aproposed algorithms showcased the method for tracking abnormal behavior in practical applications like videos.

Chapter 4 discusses development of imaging techniques using artificial vision systems as support tools for the early diagnosis of skin cancers. Authors recognizing Epiluminescence microscopy (ELM) as currently the most adopted technique to obtain very detailed images of skin lesions argied that over time, melanoma spreads quickly, invading the body's organs through the blood vessels. Thus authors presented an early recognition which is essential to ensure decisive intervention through ML to implement artificial vision systems. Authors used datasets made up of dermatoscopic images obtained using ELM technique and presented proposals that are characterized by the use of various specific features which otherwise make understanding difficult and restricting classification performance.

Chapter 5 focuses on the modelling the changes in rainfall patterns in different Agro-climatic zones (ACZ) due to climate change through statistical downscaling of large scale climate variables using ML approaches. The study investigated three ML algorithms, Multilayer Artificial Neural Network (MLANN), Radial Basis Function Neural Network (RBFNN) and Least Square Support Vector Machine (LS-SVM) by using large scale climate data obtained from National Centre for Environmental Prediction (NCEP) reanalysis product and used as predictors for model development. Proposed ML models are applied to generate projected time series of rainfall for the period 2021-2050 using the Hadley Centre Coupled model (HadCM3) with B2 emission scenario data as predictors. An increasing trend in anticipated rainfall was observed during 2021-2050 in all the ACZs of Chhattisgarh State. Among the machine learning models, RBFNN was found as more feasible technique for modeling of monthly rainfall in this region.

Chapter 6 recognized freezing of gait (FoG) as a common symptom of Parkinson's Disease (PD) that causes intermittent absence of forward progression of patient's feet while walking. Accordingly, FoG momentary episodes are always accompanied with falls. This chapter presents a novel multi-feature fusion model for early detection of FoG episodes in patients with PD. In this chapter two feature engineering schemes are investigated; namely, time-domain hand-crafted feature engineering and Convolutional Neural Network (CNN) based spectrogram feature learning. Data of tri-axial accelerometer sensors for patients with PD is utilized to characterize the performance of the proposed model through several experiments with various Machine Learning (ML) algorithms. Experimental results showed that the multi-feature fusion approach outperformed typical single feature sets. Conclusively, the significance of this chapter is to highlight the impact of using feature fusion of multi-feature sets through investigating the performance of a FoG episodes early detection model.

Chapter 7 discusses that timely prognosis of brain tumors is gambling a great role within the pre-treatment of patients. The manual classification of brain tumors is a difficult task for radiologists due to the intensity variation pixel information produced by the magnetic resonance machine and it is a very tedious task for a large number of images. A DL algorithm approach aims to conquer the problems as it is a superior approach to traditional ML by automatically feature extraction from the input spaces and accurately detect the brain tumors. Authors argued that DL has one of the most important features using small datasets. In this work, transfer learning (TL) is explored by freezing layers and fine-tuning a pre-trained model to a recommended convolutional neural net model. The proposed model was trained using 4000 real magnetic resonance images datasets . The mean accuracy of the proposed model was found to be 98% for brain tumor classifications with mini-batch size 32 and a learning rate of 0.001.

Chapter 8 considers feature engineering a key component contributing to the performance of the computer vision pipeline which includes object recognition, image retrieval, and image segmentation. However, the emerging technology of structural health monitoring (SHM) paved the way for spotting continuous tracking of structural damage. Damage detection and severity recognition in the structural buildings and constructions are issues of great importance as the various types of damages represent an essential indicator of building and construction durability. In this chapter, authors attempted to connect the feature engineering with SHM processes through illustrating the concept of SHM from a computational perspective, with a focus on various types of data and feature engineering methods as well as applications and open venues for further research. The chapter discusses challenges and future directions of research with an extensive survey of state-of-the-art studies.

Chapter 9 presents a speech enhancement technique using a neuro-fuzzy classifier. Noisy speech sentences from NOIZEUS and AURORA databases are taken for the study. Feature extraction is implemented through modifications in amplitude magnitude spectrograms. A four class Neuro-fuzzy classifier splits the noisy speech samples into a) noise-only, b) signal only, c) more noise-less signal and d) more signal-less noise classes of the time-frequency units. Appropriate weights are applied in the enhancement to each class. The enhanced speech sentence is evaluated using objective measures. An analysis of the performance of the Neuro-fuzzy 4 (NF 4) classifier along with the performance of the classifier with other conventional techniques at different noise levels. The experimentation and anlyss observed that the numerical values of the measures obtained were better when compared to the others. An overall comparison of the performance of the NF 4 classifier was done and it was inferred that it outperformed the other techniques in speech enhancement.

Chapter 10 considers that feature plays a vital role in the analysis and prediction of data as it carries the most valuable information about the data irrespective of its structuredness. Feature engineering process can be used to extract features from these data. Authors argue that the selection of features is one of the crucial steps in the feature engineering process. This feature selection process can adopt four different approaches. On that basis, it can be classified into four basic categories, namely, filter method, wrapper method, embedded method and hybrid method. This chapter discusses about different techniques coming under these four categories along with the research work on feature selection.

Chapter 11 discusses the importance of weather prediction by using DL techniques to explore hidden hierarchical pattern in the great mass of weather datasets. Authors use four different categories of computationally efficient deep learning models like CNN, LSTM, CNN-LSTM and ConvLSTM and have critically examined for improved weather prediction. The research emphasis is on supervised learning ML for model development with the support of feature engineering. Authors argued that feature engineering played a vital role in reducing the dimension, decreasing model complexity as well as handling the noise and corrupted data. Research further investigates the performance of different DL models for improved predictions using the daily maximum temperature, The results obtained from various experiments conducted, ensured that the feature engineering based DL study for predictive modeling using time series data is really an encouraging approach.

Chapter 12 describes that automated feature engineering is to build predictive models that are capable of transforming raw data into features. Authors explained that the creation of new features from existing ones on various datasets would help create the meaningful features, and examining their effect on planned model performances on various parameters like accuracy, efficiency and prevent data leakage. Thus, the challenges for experts are to plan computationally efficient and effective ML-based predictive models. This work of authors aims at providing important intelligent techniques to enhance predictive analytics by using an advanced form of the predictive model. A computationally efficient and effective ML model using Functional Link Artificial Neural Network (FLANN) to design for predicting the business needs with a high degree of accuracy for the traders or investors. Authors claim the performance of the models using FLANN is really encouraging when scientifically analyzed the experimental results of the model using different statistical analyses.

Chapter 13 recognizes that plants are very important for the existence of human life. The authors argued that the total number of plant species is nearing four hundred thousand as on date. With such a huge number of plant species, there is a need for intelligent systems for plant species recognition. The leaf is one of the most important and prominent parts of a plant and is available throughout the year. Leaf plays a major role in the identification of plants. Plant Leaf Recognition (PLR) is the process of automatically recognizing the plant species based on the image of the plant leaf. Many researchers have worked in this area of PLR using image processing, feature extraction, machine learning, and convolution neural network techniques. As a part of this chapter, the authors review several such latest methods of PLR and present the work done by various authors in the past five years in this area. The authors propose a generalized architecture for PLR based on this study and describe the major steps in PLR in detail. The authors then present a summary of the work that they are doing in this area of PLR for Ayurvedic plants.

Chapter 14 presents a scenario for India in which there are attempts to creating one economic India, one market place with free movement of goods and people. The authors argue that, for creating one economic India, there is a need to preserve sovereignty for the Indian states. In this research, the authors seek to apply social network analysis (SNA) to study empirically reciprocation/cohesiveness of Indian states using the data on intra-firm trade flows between states. On the basis of reciprocity counts for weighted social networks on inter-states trade relations, the standardized reciprocity measures have been adopted. The outcomes of the paper seem to offer important implications for understanding cooperation and integration on inter-states trade interactions and to exhibit the equilibrium and circularity of inter-state trade flows.

Chapter 15 seeks to build up a churn prediction model to support telecom administrators to foresee agitating clients. Authors argued that much research affirmed AI innovation to predict this circumstance through training from past data. The prediction procedure is involved three primary stages: normalization of the data followed by feature selection based on information gain and finally classification utilizing different AI methods. Authors provide an examples of Back Propagation Neural Network(BPNNM),

Naïve Bayesian, K-Nearest Neighborhood(KNN), Support Vector Machine(SVM), Discriminant Analysis(DA), Decision tree(DT) and Extreme learning machine(ELM) to support this claim. Authors showed through this simulation study that out of these seven methods SVM with polynomial based kernel presented 91.33% of precision where ELM is at the primary situation with 92.10% of exactness and MLANN based CCP model is at third rank with 90.4% of accuracy. Similar observation is noted for 10-fold cross-validation as well.

Chapter 16 devotes to determine appropriate software reliability prediction techniques which is a challenging task for the software development process. Authors argue that software engineers need to develop good quality software products and processes to support the creation of prediction models. Many such models are in use for small size data to estimate the reliability of the software system. These models showcase the sub-optimal solution with limted datasets. This article proposes a technique of increasing training dataset by generating virtual data points of the original data. The authors propose multilayer perceptron (MLP) based virtual data positions (DEVDP) exploration techniques with the use of evolutionary algorithm differential evolution (DE) for improving the prediction of cumulative failure time in software. The technique uses eight failure datasets from different sources for validation of the model in presence of the virtual data point (VDP). The results obtained from simulation studies indicate that the proposed DEVDP exploration technique outperformed traditional models.

Chapter 17 discusses that in the contemporary digital world, where everything is getting digitalized, information, or data in any form, is essential to an organization or the individual. This digitalization process poses a greater risk for the organization and the individuals as well, despite many benefits. Hence a proper and more efficient cryptosystem is the prime need of the hour to secure the data (especially, the image data). This chapter proposes an efficient multi-point crossover operation based chaotic image encryption system to secure images. The multi-point crossover operation is performed on both the rows and columns of bit-planes in the images. The improved one-dimensional chaotic maps are used to perform pixel-permutation and diffusion operations. The main advantage of this technique is the use of multi-point crossover operation in bit-levels. The multi-point crossover operation not only increases the security of cipher images but also increases the key space of the algorithm. The outcomes and analyzes of various parameters show the best performance of the algorithm in image encryption and different common attacks.

Chapter 18 recognizes the importance of cybersecurity in the digitalized world. In the absence of cyber policy, the violators are likely to be more active. Thus there is a need for resilient analytical methods for tracking security breach incidents. The authors argued for identifying any proper techniques of an automated decision model for the analysts using a feature selection method. The authors take multi-criteria decision-making methods for comparison. The authors used CICDDoS2019 datasets consisting of Windows benign and the most vanguard for shared bouts and also examined the use of Hill-Climbing algorithm to select the best features. The authors also claimed the time-based pragmatic data can be extracted with various approaches like a) the mainsheet for classification as a distributed cyber-policy violator, b) legitimate benign using Decision Tree (DT) with Analytical Hierarchy Process (AHP) (DT-AHP), c) support Vector Machine (SVM), d) Similarity to Ideal Solution (SVM-TOPSIS) and e) mixed model of K Nearest Neighbor (KNN AHP-TOPSIS) algorithms.

A CONCLUSION OF HOW YOUR BOOK IMPACTS THE FIELD AND CONTRIBUTES TO THE SUBJECT MATTER

Feature engineering is an emerging discipline and has gained the attention of researchers, academia, and industry. Its importance is growing as it creates a scope to support ML and AI models for creating an optimized proactive and predictive decision-making environment. This environment is necessary for the organizations in the contemporary business world where predictions are rather implicit to understand the market. Empirical analyses using quantitative methods and techniques, data science, and data engineering-driven tools are not uncommon. The main challenge for the data scientists and model developers, however, has been around extracting and validating datasets despite advancements in data warehousing and adat mining tools. This challenge is increasing manifold with the innovations in technologies around internet protocols leading prolific growth in data acquisition points, which are now based on the internet of things (IoT) devices supported by the cloud, and fog computing. Such diverse datasets are now mostly generated realtime and online with varied data types. Sourcing varied datasets with diverse data types and time-independent data acquisitions provide the scope for using automated feature engineering. The automated feature engineering stems from the principles of software engineering and has multi-disciplinary dimensions as it has strong alignment with data architectures, data engineering, and data models. Because of the architectural principles, feature engineering has ubiquitous applications. This edited book, therefore, aimed to bring varied contributions to the field of automated feature engineering.

Market studies indicate that data scientists devote a lot of time and spend lot of their resources in identifying good techniques for data preparation, cleaning datasets, mining data patterns through extractions and data marts, and finding suitable algorithms. The effort through this edited book is to provide cases, gather supporting literature and populate various emerging models for comparison and validations in varying environments. This edited book has 18 chapters chosen by critically examining the appropriateness in terms of providing overviews and contemporary advancements in automated feature engineering and showcasing sector-specific applications of the automated feature engineering process models and techniques. The sectors that this edited book covers in which automated feature engineering process models are applied include health, plants, environment, cybersecurity, and agro-climatic applications. More prominently, few chapters include critical analyses and comparisons of various feature engineering models to support ML and AI models effectively. Thus the book is expected to support the practitioners to use the feature engineering-driven models, support researchers to further their contributions to sector-based ML and AI modeling with automated feature engineering tools. This book will also be useful to the students seeking a career in software engineering process models, emerging areas in feature engineering, modeling with focus on ML, DL and AI.

Mrutyunjaya Panda
Utkal University, India

Harekrishna Misra
Institute of Rural Management, Anand, India
September 2, 2020

Acknowledgment

The Editors are grateful to IGI Global, USA for accepting our proposal to come up with this edited book volume, "Automated Feature Engineering and Advanced Applications in Data Science". Special thanks to Ms. Jan Travers of IGI Global for her constant support throughout this project.

We are thankful to the authorities of Utkal University, Bhubaneswar and Institute of Rural Management Anand, Gujarat for support and encouragement to carry out this edited book project successfully.

Also, we are extremely thankful to the editorial advisory board for their suggestions and guidance; contributors for their contribution and the reviewers for their constructive suggestions to improve the quality of the chapters.

We wish to thank all colleagues and friends those who directly or indirectly motivated us during this project.

Mrutyunjaya Panda
Utkal University, India

Harekrishna Misra
Institute of Rural Management, Anand, India

Chapter 1
Feature Engineering for Various Data Types in Data Science

Nilesh Kumar Sahu
https://orcid.org/0000-0003-1675-7270
Birla Institute of Technology, Mesra, India

Manorama Patnaik
https://orcid.org/0000-0003-4035-2468
Birla Institute of Technology, Mesra, India

Itu Snigdh
Birla Institute of Technology, Mesra, India

ABSTRACT

The precision of any machine learning algorithm depends on the data set, its suitability, and its volume. Therefore, data and its characteristics have currently become the predominant components of any predictive or precision-based domain like machine learning. Feature engineering refers to the process of changing and preparing this input data so that it is ready for training machine learning models. Several features such as categorical, numerical, mixed, date, and time are to be considered for feature extraction in feature engineering. Datasets containing characteristics such as cardinality, missing data, and rare labels for categorical features, distribution, outliers, and magnitude are currently considered as features. This chapter discusses various data types and their techniques for applying to feature engineering. This chapter also focuses on the implementation of various data techniques for feature extraction.

INTRODUCTION

The process of changing and preparing input data trained to be ready for machine learning models is called Feature Engineering. Features such as Categorical, Numerical, Mixed and date and time are to be considered for feature extraction in feature engineering. Datasets containing features such as cardinality, missing data and rare labels for categorical features, distribution, outliers and magnitude are being

DOI: 10.4018/978-1-7998-6659-6.ch001

considered as features. This chapter discusses about various data types and their techniques applied in feature engineering. This chapter also focuses on implementation of various data techniques for feature extraction.

Feature Engineering is a process of transforming the raw data from one form to another such that it can be represented in a better way (Kuhn & Johnson, 2019). In a short we can say creating new features from the existing list of features such that it will help in the improvement of learning model performance (Ruder et.al, 2019). Feature engineering became out of the desire to change linear regression inputs that are not typically distributed (Bengio et.al., 2013). Such change can be useful for liner regression. The original work by George Box and David Cox in 1964 presented a technique for figuring out which of a few force capacities may be a valuable change for the result of Linear Regression (Box, 1964). This is now known as the Box-Cox change (Tommaso, 2011). Linear regression isn't the main machine learning model that can benefit from highlight building and different changes. In 1999, it was shown that element building could improve the presentation of rules learning for text classification (Heaton, 2016).

Feature engineering is the assignment of improving prescient demonstrating execution on a dataset by changing its component space (Coates, et.al, 2011). Existing ways to deal with mechanize this procedure depends on either changed component space investigation through assessment guided hunt, or unequivocal extension of datasets with every single changed element followed by include determination (Scott & Matwin, 1999). Such methodologies acquire high computational expenses in runtime and additionally memory. A novel procedure for learning Feature Engineering (LFE) is presented, for robotizing feature building in classification errands which depends on learning the adequacy of applying a change (e.g., number-crunching or total administrators) on numerical highlights, from past component designing encounters. Given another dataset (Nargesian, et.al, 2017), LFE prescribes resource of helpful changes to be applied on highlights without depending on model assessment or express component development and determination (Krasanakis, et.al, 2018). Utilizing an assortment of datasets, we train a lot of neural systems, which target anticipating the change that impacts classification execution decidedly (Jiang, et.al, 2008).

This chapter is presenting section 1 as Introduction, section 2 is discussing on data types in data Science, section 3 is focussing on Different Techniques of applying Feature Engineering, section 4 illustrates Different Techniques of applying Feature Engineering, section 5 presents conclusion and section 6 describes the future work .

Goal of Feature Engineering in Data Science

The main goal of feature engineering is to remove unwanted features from the given raw dataset while keeping the main and important features, which will help us to derive some useful and important information's (Khurana, et.al, 2016).

Why Feature Engineering Is Needed?

Feature Engineering is needed for increasing the accuracy of the learned model such that the model which is being trained on the given data can also achieve better accuracy on the unseen data too (Weiss, et.al, 2016) .

According to the latest survey in Forbes, Data Scientist spend around 75% of their time, just on data preparation (Dong, et.al, 2018).

Figure 1. Time spent by data scientist

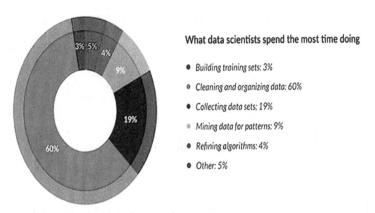

Thus, Figure 1 represents this survey which proves the importance of feature engineering in the field of data science.

Advantage of Feature Engineering

- The main advantage of feature engineering is that it reduces the training time of the learning model as number of feature decreases and also increases the accuracy of the Learning Model (Bruna, & Mallat, 2013).
- The features collected from data will impact the outcomes that our predictive model can accomplish.
- Designing great features will permit us to most precisely speak to the fundamental structure of the information and consequently make the best model.
- Features in feature engineering can be designed by parting of features, from outer feature sources, or totalling or consolidating features to make new features.
- Feature selection lessens the calculation time and assets expected to make models just as forestalling overfitting which would corrupt the exhibition of the model. The adaptability of good features permits less unpredictable models, which would be quicker to run and more obvious, to deliver practically identical outcomes to the perplexing ones.

Data Types in Data Science

Each variable in data science has an associated data type. Each data types are handled in a different way while applying feature engineering in data science (Roh, 2019). Fig.2 is describing the hierarchical data types in data science. Each and every data type is divided into either Numerical or Categorical data types. Each Numerical data type is further categorised into continuous or discrete data type. Similarly categorical data type can be categorised in to ordinal, nominal and binary data type.

1. Numerical Data: The information that is measurable and is represented as numbers.
   a. Continuous Data: Continuous data is a quantitative data that can be measure but can't be counted. It has an infinite no. of possible values within a given range (Dougherty, 1995). Ex: - Height of a child, Length of a leaf, Speed of a train, Temperature range etc.

Figure 2. Data type classification in data science

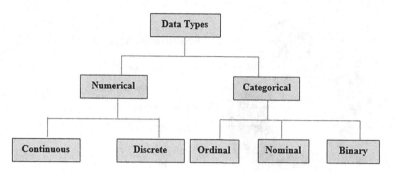

b.   Discrete Data: Discrete data is a quantitative data that can be counted (Bhardwaj, 2014). Ex: - Number of students in a class, No. of books on a shelf, Number of languages spoken etc.

2.   Categorical Data: The information that neither can be measured nor be represented as a number, but represent characteristics. These information's are string of text (Bhardwaj, 2014).

a.   Ordinal Data: The data which can be ordered are called as Ordinal Data. In this type of data, order is meaningful. Ex: -Grading of marks as A, B, C and F. Educational background of a student as Elementary, High School, Under graduate and Graduate. Ranking of race as First, Second and Third etc.

b.   Nominal Data: The data which represent discrete units but don't have any quantitative values. These data are just opposite of Ordinal data and here ordering doesn't convey any meanings (Bhardwaj, 2014). It is similar to labelling of data. Ex: - What languages do you speak? English, Hindi, French, German. Variables like Country, Martial Status etc.

c.   Binary Data: As name suggest it has only two labels. The data which only have two values – True and False. This type of data can also be represented in a different way like Yes and No or 1 and 0. Ex: - A person bought a car or not, Do I have subscription of the magazine or not. Etc.

Different Techniques of Applying Feature Engineering

The different techniques available for applying Feature Engineering are (Schmitz, 2012): -

1.   Imputation
2.   Handling Outliers using Statistical methods
3.   Binning
4.   Encoding
5.   Log Transform
6.   Feature Splitting
7.   Scaling

Imputation

Imputation is the process of replacing missing data or values with a substituted data or values. Real world data consist of missing information for many various reasons and are written as blanks, NA, NaN, or any other identity and training a learning model with a dataset containing lots of missing values will affect the model's performance and quality. So, to handle this problem, either the tuple consisting of missing data are dropped or replaced with substituted values.

As said above, the most trivial solution to handle the missing data is to drop the rows or the entire column. We can consider some threshold value for dropping and if any row or columns which have missing data higher than the considered threshold, than these rows and columns will be dropped. Figure 3 is representing the python codes dropping missing values for a certain threshold.

Figure 3. Python code for dropping missing values for a certain threshold

```
#Python code

threshold = 0.80
#Dropping columns with missing value higher than 80%
dataset = dataset[dataset.columns[dataset.isnull().mean() <
  threshold]]

#Dropping rows with missing value higher than 80%
dataset = dataset.loc[dataset.isnull().mean(axis=1) < thres
hold]
```

Another option for handling the missing values is replacing them with the substituted values.

1. Using Mean or Median Values: In this method, first either mean or median of the non-missing values present in a column is calculated and then those missing values present in a column are replaced with the calculated mean / median. This method can only be applied in numeric data. Figure 4 is showing an example in Mean Imputation where as Figure 5 is showing Python Codes for Mean and Mode Imputation.

Figure 4. Mean imputation

SNo.	col1	col2	col3
0	2 NA	NA	
1	5	8	5
2 NA	NA	NA	
3	11	12 NA	

SNo.	col1	col2	col3
0	2	10	5
1	5	8	5
2	6	10	5
3	11	15	5

2. Using Most Frequent or Zero/Constant Values: In this method, the missing data are replaced by most frequent appeared data within each column. This method works with both Numerical and categorical variables. Figure 6 is representing an example of Imputation using most frequent items.

Figure 5. Mean and mode imputation

```
#Python Code for Mean and Mode Imputation
# Taking care of missing data
from sklearn.preprocessing import Imputer
imputer = Imputer(missing_values = 'NaN', strategy = 'mean'
, axis = 0)
imputer1 = Imputer(missing_values = 'NaN', strategy = 'medi
an', axis = 0)
imputer = imputer.fit(dataset1[:, 1:3])
dataset[:, 1:3] = imputer.transform(dataset[:, 1:3])
imputer1 = imputer1.fit(dataset1[:, 1:3])
dataset1[:, 1:3] = imputer1.transform(dataset1[:, 1:3])
```

Figure 6. Imputation using most frequent items

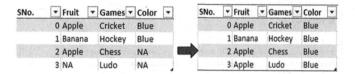

While in the case of Zero/Constant values, as the name suggest, we either replace the missing values with some constant k or replace the missing values with zero. Figure 7 is stating one example with filling missing values with Zeros.

Figure 7. Filling missing values with zeros

SNo.	col1	col2	col3	
0	2 NA		NA	
1	5	8		5
2 NA	NA		NA	
3	11	12 NA		

SNo.	col1	col2	col3	
0	2	0	0
1	5	8	5
2	0	0	0
3	11	15	0

Handling Outliers Using the Statistical Approach

Outlier detection is the way toward recognizing and in this manner barring outliers from a given arrangement of information.

An outlier might be characterized as a bit of information or perception that strays radically from the given standard or normal of the dataset collection. An exception might be caused just by some coincidence, yet it might likewise show estimation mistake or that the given dataset has a substantial followed appropriation. Figure 8 is presenting a graph of outlier detection.

Outliers are the data point which doesn't fall in the given range of population or sample. Ex: -

[2, 4, 6, 8, 10, 12, 14, 16, 18, 20, **400**, 24, 26, 28, 30,**900**, 34, 36]

Figure 8. Outlier detection

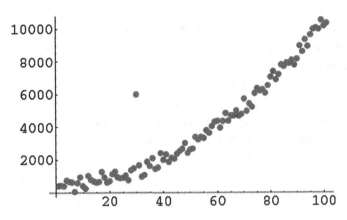

1. Mean Deviation: It helps us to know how far the data points from the central mean and using this plot or variation we can decide which points are the outliers.
2. Standard Deviation: This method works same as mean deviation except here we consider Standard deviation instead of mean deviation. Here, if we have any data points which are more than 3 times the standard deviation, then those points are very likely to be outliers.
3. Percentile: In this method we consider a certain percent of the data from the top and bottom of the dataset as an outlier.
4. Boxplots: This method is same as percentiles method, except box plots is a graphical depiction of numerical data through their quantiles.

Maximum (Upper whiskers) and Minimum (lower whiskers) are the boundaries of data distribution and if any data point lies beyond these boundaries are considered to be outliers. Figure 9 is presenting Boxplot diagram.

Figure 9. Boxplot

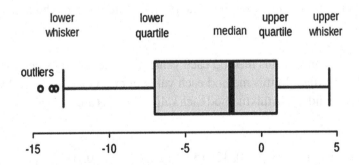

Binning

Binning is also known as bucketing. Binning method is used for handling noisy data. The main motive behind binning method is to prevent our learning model from over fitting. Instead of having a large data we will divide these data into smaller groups.

There are two methods used for binning:

1. Equal Frequency Binning: In this method, data are divided into k different group where each group consist of approximately same number of data points.
2. Equal width Binning: In this method, data are divided into k intervals of equal sizes.

The width of interval is defined as: -

W=(max-min) / k

Interval boundaries are defined as: -

min + w, min + 2w, ..., min + (k-1) w

Ex: -
- Data: 0, 2, 4, 7, 11, 15, 17, 19, 21, 24, 27, 28.
- Equal Frequency Binning
  - Bin 1: 0, 2, 4, 7
  - Bin 2: 11, 15, 17, 19
  - 21, 24, 27, 28
- Equal Width Binning
  - Bin 1: 0, 2, 4, 7
  - Bin 2: 11, 15, 17
  - Bin 3: 19, 21, 24, 27, 28

Binning Method is used for smoothing the data and there are three methods to perform smoothing using binning methods.

1. Smoothing by bin Means: In this method each value in bucket are replaced by its mean value.
2. Smoothing by bin Median: In this method each value in bucket are replaced by its median value.
3. Smoothing by bin Boundary: In this method each value in bucket are replaced by it closest boundaries.

Ex: -
Consider the following data: 2, 5, 7, 10, 12, 15, 19, 22, 24, 27, 30, 31
Step1: - Sort the data
Step 2: - Perform Equal frequency binning
Step 3: - Perform smoothing
Bin 1: [2, 5, 7, 10]
Bin 2: [12, 15, 19, 22]
Bin 3: [24, 27, 30, 31]

- Smoothing by bin means
  - Bin 1: [6, 6, 6, 6]
  - Bin 2: [17, 17, 17, 17]
  - Bin 3: [28, 28, 28, 28]
- Smoothing by bin median
  - Bin 1: [6, 6, 6, 6]
  - Bin 2: [17, 17, 17, 17]
  - Bin 3: [29, 29, 29, 29]
- Smoothing by bin boundaries
  - Bin 1: [2, 2, 10, 10]
  - Bin 2: [12, 12, 22, 22]
  - Bin 3: [24, 24, 31, 31]

Binning can be applied on both numerical data as discussed above and categorical data. Table 1 and Table 2 are representing a corresponding Numerical and Categorical binning example.

Table 1. Numerical binning example

Value	Bin
0-50	Low
51-100	Medium
101-150	High

Table 2. Categorical binning example

Value	Bin
India	Asia
Sri Lanka	Asia
Spain	Europe
Brazil	South America

Encoding

Encoding is the most general approach for handling categorical data present in our dataset. Two of the most basic approach for handling categorical data is Label Encoding and One hot Encoding.

1. Label Encoding: In this technique, the categorical data are labelled with numerical. It is mainly used for the output or say final variable. Table 3 is stating an example of before label encoding example while Table 4 is presenting after label encoding example.

Table 3. Before label encoding example

Salary (in Rs.)	Class
10000	Low
20000	High
15000	Mid
25000	High

Table 4. After label encoding example

Salary (in Rs.)	Class
10000	0
20000	2
15000	1
25000	2

This class variable can be encoded as given in Table 4.

2.   One hot Encoding: Data Science is purely a statistical model so to use categorical data we need to encode those data. One hot encoding is one of the most basic encoding techniques.

In this technique, a new column is created for each of the distinct category present in the feature and 1 or 0 is assigned to indicate the presence of category in the data. Table 5 is showing one example of how one hot encoding is applied so that it can be encoded as shown in Table 6. At the same time Fig. 10 is showing Python Codes for Label Encoding and One-hot encoding.

Table 5. Before one hot encoding

User_id	Fruit
1	Apple
2	Banana
3	Mango
4	Apple
5	Papaya

Table 6. After applying one hot encoding to data set

User_id	Fruit (Apple)	Fruit (Banana)	Fruit (Mango)	Fruit (Papaya)
1	1	0	0	0
2	0	1	0	0
3	0	0	1	0
4	1	0	0	0
5	0	0	0	1

Figure 10. Python code label encoding and one-hot encoding

```
#Python Code Label Encoding and One-hot encoding

# Taking care of missing data
from sklearn.preprocessing import Imputer
imputer = Imputer(missing_values = 'NaN', strategy = 'mean'
, axis = 0)
imputer1 = Imputer(missing_values = 'NaN', strategy = 'medi
an', axis = 0)
imputer = imputer.fit(dataset1[:, 1:3])
dataset[:, 1:3] = imputer.transform(dataset[:, 1:3])
imputer1 = imputer1.fit(dataset1[:, 1:3])
dataset1[:, 1:3] = imputer1.transform(dataset1[:, 1:3])
```

Now, this table can be encoded as shown in Table 6.

Log Transform

Logarithmic transformation is one of the commonly use mathematical function for feature engineering. It is mainly used to make highly skewed data into less skewed. Log transformation helps to make a clear image regarding the relationship between variables.

Figure 11. Scatter plot of brain weight vs body.

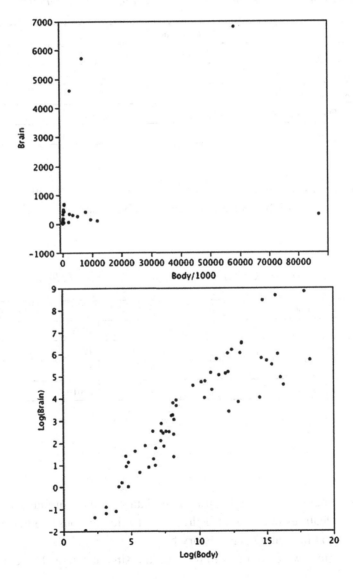

Figure 11 shows Scatter plot of brain weight vs body. The log transform helps to learn the relationship between brain and body weight which is not clear in first part of the figure.

Feature Splitting

In this technique, we extract only the utilizable parts of a column to make a new feature. This helps in improving the performance of the learning model. It is mainly used in case if our dataset consists of string column. Table 7 showing one set of data having name of books and year published in a same column.

Table 7. Data consisting name of books and year published in a same column

Book Name
Jumanji (1995)
Harry Potter and the Philosopher's Stone (1997)
Harry Potter and the Chamber of Secrets (1998)
Fantastic Beasts and Where to Find Them (2001)
The Cuckoo's Calling (2013)

Ex: - Data consisting name of books and year published in a same column.

This feature could be split into two different features as book name and year published as given in Table 8.

Table 8. Data consisting name of books and year published in a same column

Book Name	Year Published
Jumanji	1995
Harry Potter and the Philosopher's Stone	1997
Harry Potter and the Chamber of Secrets	1998
Fantastic Beasts and Where to Find Them	2001
The Cuckoo's Calling	2013

Scaling

Scaling is the process of making sure that feature in our data set are on similar scale.

Ex: - If there are two features like, No. of bedroom and Price of house so Price feature will totally dominate our dataset so feature scaling is necessary here.

Scaling helps in bringing two or more column data in a similar range. There are two different approaches for scaling.

1. Normalization: This technique is also known as min-max normalization. Normalization scale all values in a column within a fixed range of 0 and 1. This transformation doesn't change any distribution of our data as normalization is done on all the features.

$$X_{norm} = \frac{X - X_{min}}{X_{max} - X_{min}}$$

2. Standardization: Standardization is also known as Z score Normalization. Standardization too scales the value but it considers standard deviation while scaling. The con of Normalization was that it decreases the Standard deviation because of which number of outliers increases but Standardization reduces the effect of outliers. Table 9 is stating one example before standardisation. Fig. 3.9 is presenting Python Code Label Encoding and One-hot encoding and Table 9 is showing final data after standardisation. Formula is shown as follows;

$$z = \frac{x - \mu}{\sigma}$$

Table 9. Before standardisation

No. of Bedroom	Price of House (in $)
2	10000
3	16000
5	27000
7	35000
4	21000

Normalized table for the above given table is given in Table 10.

Standardized table for the above un scaled table is given below in Table 10 and Figure 12 is showing Python Codes for Standard Scaling

Table 10. After standardisation

No. of Bedroom	Price of House (in $)
0	0
0.2	0.24
0.6	0.68
1	1
0.4	0.44

Table 10. Standardisation for un scaled table

No. of Bedroom	Price of House (in $)
-1.28	-1.36
-0.70	-0.67
0.47	0.60
1.63	1.52
-0.17	-0.09

Figure 12. Python codes for standard scaling

```
#Python Code for Standard Scaling
# Taking care of missing data
from sklearn.preprocessing import StandardScaler
sc = StandardScaler()
dataset = sc.fit_transform(dataset)
imputer1 = imputer1.fit(dataset1[:, 1:3])
dataset1[:, 1:3] = imputer1.transform(dataset1[:, 1:3])
```

CONCLUSION

As machine learning becomes more widely used, it becomes more important to acquire large amounts of data and label data, quintessentially for state-of-the-art Feature Engineering. Traditionally, the machine learning, natural language processing, and computer vision communities has contributed to this problem – primarily on data labelling techniques including semi-supervised learning and active learning. Recently, in the era of Big data, the data management community is also contributing to numerous sub problems in data acquisition, data labelling, and improvement of existing data. In this chapter, we have investigated the research landscape of how all these technique complement each other and have provided guidelines on deciding which technique can be used when feature engineering applied. Finally, we have discussed interesting data collection challenges that remain to be addressed as a broader part of Feature Engineering.

FUTURE WORK

Quantum based feature engineering is a developing research field, which is committed to formulating and implementing quantum calculations that could empower artificial intelligence with machine learning quicker than that of traditional data types.

In future, feature engineering based quantum theory may have a lot of utilizations: physics of elementary particles, science of rudimentary particles, atomic weapon and vitality, and the most recent years additionally - quantum data, processing, cryptography, and teleportation. It must be underlined that the last uses of quantum theory (quantum data, etc) are basically more grounded identified with stronger establishments.

REFERENCES

Bengio, Y., Courville, A., & Vincent, P. (2013). Representation learning: A review and new perspectives. *IEEE Transactions on Pattern Analysis and Machine Intelligence, 35*(8), 1798–1828. doi:10.1109/TPAMI.2013.50

Bhardwaj, A., Bhattacherjee, S., Chavan, A., Deshpande, A., Elmore, A. J., Madden, S., & Parameswaran, A. G. (2014). *Datahub: Collaborative data science & dataset version management at scale.* arXiv preprint arXiv:1409.0798

Box, G. E., & Cox, D. R. (1964). An analysis of transformations. *Journal of the Royal Statistical Society. Series B. Methodological, 26*(2), 211–243. doi:10.1111/j.2517-6161.1964.tb00553.x

Bruna, J., & Mallat, S. (2013). Invariant scattering convolution networks. *IEEE Transactions on Pattern Analysis and Machine Intelligence, 35*(8), 1872–1886. doi:10.1109/TPAMI.2012.230

Coates, A., Ng, A., & Lee, H. (2011, June). An analysis of single-layer networks in unsupervised feature learning. In *Proceedings of the fourteenth international conference on artificial intelligence and statistics* (pp. 215-223). Academic Press.

Dong, G., & Liu, H. (Eds.). (2018). *Feature engineering for machine learning and data analytics.* CRC Press.

Dougherty, J., Kohavi, R., & Sahami, M. (1995). Supervised and unsupervised discretization of continuous features. In Machine learning proceedings 1995 (pp. 194-202). doi:10.1016/B978-1-55860-377-6.50032-3

Guyon, I., Gunn, S., Nikravesh, M., & Zadeh, L. A. (Eds.). (2008). *Feature extraction: foundations and applications* (Vol. 207). Springer.

Heaton, J. (2016, March). An empirical analysis of feature engineering for predictive modeling. In SoutheastCon 2016 (pp. 1-6). IEEE. doi:10.1109/SECON.2016.7506650

Jiang, Y., Cukic, B., & Menzies, T. (2008, July). Can data transformation help in the detection of fault-prone modules? In *Proceedings of the 2008 workshop on Defects in large software systems* (pp. 16-20). 10.1145/1390817.1390822

Khurana, U., Turaga, D., Samulowitz, H., & Parthasrathy, S. (2016, December). Cognito: Automated feature engineering for supervised learning. In *2016 IEEE 16th International Conference on Data Mining Workshops (ICDMW)* (pp. 1304-1307). IEEE.

Krasanakis, E., Spyromitros-Xioufis, E., Papadopoulos, S., & Kompatsiaris, Y. (2018, April). Adaptive sensitive reweighting to mitigate bias in fairness-aware classification. In *Proceedings of the 2018 World Wide Web Conference* (pp. 853-862). 10.1145/3178876.3186133

Kuhn, M., & Johnson, K. (2019). *Feature engineering and selection: A practical approach for predictive models.* CRC Press. doi:10.1201/9781315108230

Nargesian, F., Samulowitz, H., Khurana, U., Khalil, E. B., & Turaga, D. S. (2017, August). *Learning Feature Engineering for Classification* (pp. 2529–2535). IJCAI.

Roh, Y., Heo, G., & Whang, S. E. (2019). A survey on data collection for machine learning: A big data-ai integration perspective. *IEEE Transactions on Knowledge and Data Engineering*, 1. doi:10.1109/TKDE.2019.2946162

Ruder, S., Peters, M. E., Swayamdipta, S., & Wolf, T. (2019, June). Transfer learning in natural language processing. In *Proceedings of the 2019 Conference of the North American Chapter of the Association for Computational Linguistics: Tutorials* (pp. 15-18). Academic Press.

Schmitz, M., Soderland, S., Bart, R., & Etzioni, O. (2012, July). Open language learning for information extraction. In *Proceedings of the 2012 Joint Conference on Empirical Methods in Natural Language Processing and Computational Natural Language Learning* (pp. 523-534). Academic Press.

Scott, S., & Matwin, S. (1999). Feature engineering for text classification. In *ICML* (Vol. 99, pp. 379–388). Citeseer.

Tommaso, P., & Helmut, L. (2011). Does the Box-Cox transformation help in forecasting macroeconomic time series? Academic Press.

. Weiss, K., Khoshgoftaar, T. M., & Wang, D. (2016). A survey of transfer learning. *Journal of Big Data, 3*(1), 9.

Chapter 2
Feature Selection Techniques in High Dimensional Data With Machine Learning and Deep Learning

Bhanu Chander

iD https://orcid.org/0000-0003-0057-7662

Pondicherry University, India

ABSTRACT

High-dimensional data inspection is one of the major disputes for researchers plus engineers in domains of deep learning (DL), machine learning (ML), as well as data mining. Feature selection (FS) endows with proficient manner to determine these difficulties through eradicating unrelated and outdated data, which be capable of reducing calculation time, progress learns precision, and smooth the progress of an enhanced understanding of the learning representation or information. To eradicate an inappropriate feature, an FS standard was essential, which can determine the significance of every feature in the company of the output class/labels. Filter schemes employ variable status procedure as the standard criterion for variable collection by means of ordering. Ranking schemes utilized since their straightforwardness and high-quality accomplishment are detailed for handy appliances. The goal of this chapter is to produce complete information on FS approaches, its applications, and future research directions.

INTRODUCTION

It is the era of big data, where vast amount of high-dimensional data turn out to be omnipresent in a mixture of fields like online education, social media, bioinformatics, and healthcare. The rapid enlargement of data show disputes for effectual and proficient data organization. It is advantageous to concern data-mining and machine-learning practices to involuntarily determine facts from data of different sorts. But in Data mining and ML fields, while dimensionality of data elevates, the size of data required offering consistent analysis raises exponentially. From the past two decades data demanding appliances

DOI: 10.4018/978-1-7998-6659-6.ch002

demand has increased more and more in terms of capacity, superiority and the extraction of valuable knowledge from such a huge amount of data is not an easy assignment. With this tremendous development, new modern technologies and internet technology applications create a huge amount of data which is unpredicted such as audio, video, text documents, voice conversations, etc, These collected data may restrain high characteristics of measurements that pose a dispute to data scrutiny and result making. With the service of some machine learning (ML) techniques it is possible to reduce, compress the data however still the high dimensional section is momentous issues in mutually supervised and unsupervised ML techniques, now it turns to even more essential with an explosion of available data with the size of data samples along with many relevant features in each sample (Phinyamork et al., 2012; kendall et al., 2015; Barry et al., 2015).

Feature Selection (FS) is the procedure of choosing the most correlated feature points in a data sample, which is essential in ML as well as data mining techniques. Since unimportant or unnecessary features reduce the training speed, interoperability, more importantly, shrinks the generalization performances on the data set. The foremost enthusiasm in dimensionality reduction is to decrease the number of features as low as possible that diminish the training time and increase the taxonomy techniques precision. In detail, feature selection means it is the process of automatically obtaining a subset of features according to employed feature criteria that contribute most to the predicted output which is interested in us. The feature is a variable from the given input data that efficiently express the input at the same time as individual computable belongings of any progression being observed, utilizing those feature sets any ML techniques can perform classification. The focal point of FS is to choose a subset of eliminating noise-related information and produce good prediction results. Feature selection methods able to preprocess learning algorithms, high-quality feature selection consequences which can develop learning precision, condense learning time as well as make things easier to learning results (Bolon et al., 2015; Hira et al., 2015; Pui et al., 2017).

Based on various literature surveys, feature selection techniques foundation on statistics, rough set information theory, and manifold. Numerous techniques are come into action to resolve the problems generated by inappropriate and unneeded variables which are trouble with challenging responsibilities. Depend on the characteristics of feature selection, it applicable in many appliances such as text mining, information retrieval, fault diagnosis, image recognition, bio-metrical data analysis, outlier detection, pattern recognition, data mining, machine learning, and natural language processing, etc. In most of these scenarios feature selection applied at data preprocessing before apply any classification training algorithm. Hence, it also acknowledged as variable selection, variable subset selection, or feature reduction. Standardized data contain thousands of variables where lots of them might be highly associated with additional variables when there two variables are associated with every other merely solitary feature is enough to illustrate the data. Here, the dependent relative variables do not offer any further information regarding the data classes means the entire substance can be acquired from a smaller number of exclusive features that hold the utmost intolerance information on the data classes. Thus removing the reliant variables, the quantity of data can be condensed direct to improvising the categorization performance. In a few situations variables that don't contain a relationship to the classes supply as uncontaminated noise which may initiate bias in the forecaster and diminish the taxonomy presentation. Elimination of irrelevant data needs not to compare with other dimension reduction methods, for the reason that good features independent from the rest of data classes (Jin et al., 2011; Girsh et al., 2017; Han et al., 2011; Song et al., 2007; Starogzyk et al., 2012; Aravjo et al., 2017).

BACKGROUND: ML AND DL

Machine learning (ML) initiate as a skill on behalf of Artificial Intelligence. It is course of action with the intention of automatically find out possession of trained data, without being exclusively planned or programmed. Purely apply computational models to develop machine performance by determine and describing the unpredictability in existing data. ML models produce and analyze more composite data proficiently and precisely. ML takes care of training data and attempts to discover various representations like a set of decisions positioned on the input of one-by-one feature moreover this validation set concern as indication set to approve effectiveness of training models. End-results useful to adjust learning, training parameters to boost ultimate precision. Numerous ML practices develop into exceedingly complex when train data dimensioning is high. With the assist of static training samples, the projecting power of ML will first amplify but amplified features dimensions will lessen ML performance. Nearly every ML algorithms make use of manually calculated features, it means features of real-world records have to be acknowledged, progressed by humans then only it will grant most excellent precision cost. Furthermore, ML has time-consuming in design and validation, takes deficient records, most of ML appliance cannot be globalised effortlessly to other appliances, and handcrafted features are precious and composite practice.

Machine learning is an action/learning where computational methodologies assume to progress machinery work via detecting furthermore concerning the constancy, discrimination in testing/training datasets. Just you train a process what to achieve with composed data it will do it robotically without planned or programmed. Deep learning (DL) efforts to study a huge number of representations by a hierarchy of multiple layers moreover it initiate to recognize, reply in a functional way. ML integrates ample range of performances although not a single of them shows taxonomy performance as DL. Statistical, Bayesian algorithms, as well as gathering approximations like linear, logistic, decision trees are influential ML practices but constrained in exact appliance activities, capacity to trained key features from exceptionally composite data representation. DL progressed from cognitive with information theories, imitate knowledge from the human brain in addition create a complicated interrelated neuron formation. DL learns from multiple levels of features to discover rich hierarchical features by design. Hierarchical representations discover soaring levels of notions where every layer is train with a non-linear feature phase.

More About Feature Selection

Hypothetically, having a huge amount of information might be attractive but the annoyance of dimensionality is one of the essential troubles in high dimensionality information moreover identifying appropriate algorithms for particular data is one more issue. In the late 1960s, Hughes started research on Bayesian classifier as efficacy for the measure of features and proposed a statement that selection, combination, and reduction are not acknowledged as improved techniques, rather than this they must illustrate further investigation. From that research on a feature, selection has come into action. After that 1990 tremendous change has taken place in feature selection with the inclusion of machine learning because ML can develop the accuracy of the learning techniques, feature selection has fascinated in ML filed in proceedings such as classification, clustering, and regression, etc (Zahavy et al., 2016; Tang et al., 2014; Li et al., 2016; Tang et al., 2014; Tuv et al., 2009; Wang et al., 2003)

Feature selection organizes according to a mixture of principles like as according to revolution criteria feature selection described from information measure, Euclidean distance, and correlations. Most importantly FS approaches classified into two categories based on the availability of label information and search stratagems. Again these label information base FS divided into supervised, unsupervised, and semi-supervised models. Supervised FS algorithm with the help of available label information efficiently select discriminative and relevant features to distinguish samples from dissimilar classes. Semi-supervised FS utilizes small part of labeled data and unlabeled data, most of these models build comparison matrix and pick best fit the similarity matrix. Coming to unsupervised models, due to the nonexistence of labels those plays major function in demonstrating the search for discriminative features is a tough issue. FS on dissimilar search tactics categorized into Filter approaches, wrapper approaches, and embedded approaches. The filter approaches go for a good number of discriminative features through the character of data. The wrapper approach employs the anticipated learning algorithm itself to guesstimate the features. Embedded perform FS in the succession of model building.

FEATURE SELECTION METHODS

As stated above feature selection techniques define as a procedure of detecting and describing important features at the same time discarding irrelevant, redundant data. The final objective is to attain the subset of features that represent a specified problem with the least degradation of performance. This feature selection procedure contains many advantages like as make use of simple methods to gain speed; Data understanding as well as acquire knowledge and visualizes data from applied methods; reduce data usage, storage for help to reduce costs; advances machine learning performances, etc Table 2. FS techniques developed in various ways, all of them classified into Filters, Wrappers, Embedded and Harmony methods Table 1.

Filter Method

Filter methods regard as the oldest feature selection techniques where filtering of various features is complete previous to the execution of any learning procedure. Features are ranked pedestal on certain progression standards. Modeling algorithms utilize features after finding them in proper formation. The ranking mechanism used to grad the features and those features removed by making a threshold value. And the main reason to call them as filters, because of filters the features before feeding them to any learning model. Most of the filter methods based on relevance – an association of features with target and redundancy – whether the features shared redundant information. Filter methods produce fast and efficient outcomes on execution. Limitations of these methods are that they disregard interactions between classifiers and dependence of one feature above others and may perhaps not succeed to choose the majority valuable features. But the issue raises in the relevancy of a feature, on what base we consider the measure the relevancy feature of data. More definitions mentioned in various literature reviews, mainly its states as "feature must be considered when it conditionally independent of the class labels means the feature that has no authority on the class labels can be useless or deleted". (Barry et al., 2015; Dessi et al., 2015; Girsh et al., 2017; Jilang et al., 2016; Jain et al 2018; Khiabani et al., 2015; Mohammad et al., 2015; Pui et al., 2017; Hira et al., 2015; Zahavy et al., 2016; T li et al., 2016).

Chi-squared: It is a univariate filter method based on Chi-squared statistics. This method implements the evolution of features individually with the help of measuring their chi-squared statistic concerning the class. How much high the assessment of chi-squared, the more fitting feature concerning class, suppose it is less than a pre-defined threshold, the feature not more needed. This method was mostly applicable to cases where the target and features can take only distinct fixed values. Here (p) denotes the number of intervals, the number of classes (q), amount of occurrences (N), the cost of Chi-squared for a feature is designed as

$$\chi 2 = \sum_{i=1}^{V} \sum_{j=1}^{B} \frac{\left(A_{ij} - \frac{R_i - B_j}{N} \right)^2}{\frac{R_i - B_j}{N}}$$

where Ri symbolize the quantity of examples in the range ith, Bj quantity of examples in-class jth, as well as Ai j the quantity of instances in the range ith and jth class.

- **Symmetrical Uncertainty (SU):** It based on entropy perception to estimate the relationship flanked by a feature X plus class C. The information grow linked with a feature, stabilize by taking into consideration of essential entropy of the feature along with the entropy of class. In a further aspect, it is achieved as a result of:
- **Correlation Criteria:** It also acknowledged as Dependence measure (DM), depending on the prediction of each feature. This predictive value calculated through finding the association among the independent feature, target vector. Higher predictive valued features more useful ranked with the help of some heuristic evolution function. Pearson coefficient correlation is the best example.
- **Information Gain (IG):** It also pronounced as Mutula information and information-theoretic ranking criteria (ITRC). It measures dependence or shared information among two random variables. Here we need to take full advantage of the shared information among the feature and the target variable. The mutual information (MI), which was the relative entropy among the joint distribution and product distribution is shown as

$$MI\left(X; T \right) = \sum_{X} \sum_{T} p\left(x^j, t \right) \log \frac{p\left(x^j, t \right)}{p\left(x^j \right), p\left(t \right)}$$

Here p(xj,t) is the combined possibility density function of feature xj along with target t. the p(xj) and p(t) are the trivial density tasks. MI will be zero or superior than zero if X and Y are independent or reliant, respectively. To maximization, a greedy step-wise selection algorithm is adopted.

- **Consistency Based Filter**: It employs a consistency measure which was based on both relevance and redundancy as well as it has a selection criterion that aims to retain the intolerance influence of the data definite by unique features. From the given data of features, it creates a random subset S in every iteration. In case S holds very smaller quantity features compare to existing most excellent subset, the unpredictability index of the data illustrated by S is evaluate with the index of unpredictability in the most excellent subset. If S is further reliable than the best subset, then S turns to be the best subset. Means consistency is the key triumph for this algorithm, which defines how great the decline of dimension in the data.

- **OneR (OR):** It obtains the level of implication of every feature with a trouble-free rule-based classifier. For every point in training data, model constructs one rule by shaping majority recurrent class on behalf of every point significance. Then the categorization precision of each rule is designed, along with the attributes are ranked based on the precision of the subsequent regulations.

- **Interact:** Algorithms that are employed for feature selection consider the association metrics to find out which features correlates for most of the target. But coming to interact algorithms considers single out features and ignore the two or more features with the target. These algorithms contain two foremost steps. In the initial step, features are ranked in downward order found on their symmetrical uncertainty, which utilized to evaluate the correlation of individual features with the target. Coming to second step, features estimated one by one starting from the backward ranked feature record. Features consistency contribution less than the estimated threshold, that features deleted or else selected. Utilizing cross-validation suitable predefined threshold value assigned. Interact method has the benefit of being high-speed.

$$CC\ (x_i, X) = ICR\ X/x_i - ICRX$$

Where Xi is the feature for which cc is being calculated, and ICR stands for inconsistency rate X/xi means X excluding the feature Xi.

- **Markov Blanket:** Feature selection with Markov Blanket (MB) is a graphical model perspective based on relevance. MB nodes described as parents, children, and spouses of that node. In MB methods, the target MB mode found, nodes in MB are sufficed to estimate that target node. Then the features of MB node selected, rest are removed. Dissimilar methods are employed to choose MB of target those are GrowShirnk, Koller-Sahami, Max-Min MB, and Incremental Association MB, etc.

- **Fisher Score:** In the Fisher score method, features those have high superiority must allocate alike standards to instances in a similar class furthermore dissimilar standards to instances from dissimilar classes. Fisher score defined as

$$S_i = \frac{\sum_{k=1}^{K} n_j \left(\mu_{ij} - \mu_i \right) 2}{\sum_{k=1}^{K} n_j p_{ij}^2}$$

Here nj is the quantity of instances in the Jth class, μij, ρij are mean as well as a variance of ith feature in jth class correspondingly. μi is the mean of ith feature.

- **Minimal Redundancy and Maximal Relevance (mRMR):** The Minimal redundancy and Maximal relevance is a multivariate filter method that take full advantage of the application and minimize the redundancy of features. Means preferred features must have the largest relevance with the target t for having better discrimination, chooses features those maximally disparate to every other.
- **ReliefF:** Filter ReliefF handles multiclass problems and capable to handle with incomplete noised data. It calculates the significance of features pedestal on their respective capabilities to differentiate among instances that are surrounded by all others. Simply, for a given instance the weight w of feature x acquired by calculating how the instances adjacent hit (same class) dissimilar from its nearest miss (other class).

RF efforts to estimate the following dissimilarity of possibilities:

$w(X) = P$(dissimilar value of X| nearest instance from dissimilar class)
$-P$(dissimilar value of X| nearest instance from similar class)

Initially define for two-class difficulties, technique later on widespread to hold noise plus multi-class datasets. The RF filter is capable of familiar with weight adjacent neighbors by their distance.

- **Gain Ratio:** It is developed with a small modification of Information Gain (IG), it approves the IG gain of a feature X with information split.

$$\text{Infosplit} = -\sum_{i=1}^{r} \frac{|x_i|}{N} \log \frac{|x_i|}{N}$$

Here $|X_i|$ is amount of examples where X obtains a value of X_i, r is quantity of discrete values of X, and moreover N is overall amount of examples in dataset. The GR gain of a feature achieves as InfoSplit, which was sensitive to how frequently, continually feature rips the information.

- **Md:** Md is extension work to Minimal redundancy and Maximal relevance; it employs a measure of monotone confidence to access significance, inappropriateness because it is trouble-free to estimation from data. Moreover, it consists of the most preferred properties of a measure of dependence and reaches its utmost if two arbitrary variable shares a monotonic association.

Wrapper Method

Wrapper methods reflect feature subsets as a result of superiority performance of a modeling technique, which is taken as black box reviewer. As discussed above filter methods chooses the optimal features to be passed to the learning model. Besides, wrapper methods integrate the model within the feature subset search. In the same process, dissimilar subsets of features are initiates or created and calculated through the model. By train and test, it on the model feature subsets fitness levels are evaluated. However, wrappers slower than filters in the process of judgment in suitable high-quality subsets since they depend on source demands of modeling technique. Moreover, feature subsets are biased en route to modeling schemes on which they are estimated. So there is a need for an autonomous rationale sample furthermore one more modeling algorithm utilized after the final subset initiating. Nonetheless, many authors' work proved that wrappers brought best subsets with the best performance than filters since the subsets are calculated using a genuine modeling technique. Wrappers broadly classify into sequential selection algorithms and Metaheuristic search algorithms (Chakraorty and Das et al.,2018; (Ji et al., 2013; Amorim and Mirkin et al., 2016; Hancer et al., 2018; Hancer et al., 2020).

- **Sequential Selection Algorithms:** In sequential feature selection (SFS), the model initiates with a blank set furthermore includes one feature for the primary step which provides utmost significance for the object utility. In second step, remained features included independently to existing subset along with a fresh subset are calculated. This individual feature eternally integrated with the subset if it gives the highest categorization precision. This practice recurring until the mandatory amount of features be added. Moreover, a SBS scheme could be assembled which was alike to SFS with small variation, it starts with the entire set of variables plus get rid of one feature at an instance whose exclusion provides the lowest reduction in forecasted production. Even though both SFS and SBS switch between including and excluding features, both are base on dissimilar algorithms according to the leading direction of the search. SFS, as well as SBS, pay no heed to the dependence of features, some explicit features perform better than along some other features. For this reason, Sequential forward selection and Sequential floating backward selection come into act. In SFFS, after adding a feature same as in SFS, each feature was tested for being excluded if the performance improves. The same procedure is performed in SFBS but in the opposite direction.
- **Meta-Heuristic Search Algorithms:** Metaheuristic algorithms also acknowledged as Evolutionary algorithms, which have low implementation complexity and can able to adapt to a wide variety of problems. Compare to other techniques these have less prone to get stuck in a local optimum as compared to sequential methods. Many metaheuristic methods applied for feature selection such as binary dragonfly algorithm, particle swarm optimization, Genetic algorithm, and whale optimization algorithm. The novel version of PSO urbanized for continuous optimization issues whose probable solutions are symbolized by particles. Coming to GA, the potential solutions are represented by chromosomes. For feature selection process the genes in chromosome corresponded to features and take values 1 or 0 for selection or not a selection of features correspondingly.

Feature selection for Wrapper methods: In comparison with other feature selection models, wrapper models are best suited and designed for clustering algorithms, moreover they produce great results in clustering performance in contrast with other modules.

1. **Feature Selection for K-Means:** The k-means algorithm has its popularity in ML and Data mining techniques but at the same time it also has some deficiencies. Some of the k-means performances dependent on primary cluster set, some clusters K must be preferred by an abuser, it performs greedy search which may converge to local minima, it imagines every feature uniformly essential rather than considering the definite degree of their significance. Every feature determined as less relevant, unrelated, or outmoded has a similar contribution to the clustering procedure. (Chakraorty and Das et al.,2018) tackled by transfer weights to each feature as feature weighting, here FS believes that all related features in the preferred subset have the same degree. Feature weighting presume

that each feature in elected subset cannot have similar degree of relevance. (Ji et al., 2013) authors come up with an advanced edition of the k-prototypes clustering technique which endeavor to reduce the WKmeans decisive factor. Here authors use Manhattan distance and frequency-based distances, the proposed approach showed better results. (Amorim and Mirkin et al., 2016) extended WK-means, the smart WK-means (iMWKmeans) were proposed that automatically identify the number of clusters or the cluster formation in the data with the help of the Minkowski score, at the same time shapes feature weights.

2. **Feature Selection for Model-based Clustering:** In model-based clustering approaches complexity high because every part of available features consider for design modeling. But the issue is some of the features might not be favorable and some might be harmful to the clustering procedure. Even though the entire collection of features is presumed to incorporate in the clustering process, it may be awkward due to the general phrase, referred to as the bother of dimensionality. (Ratery and dean et al., 2006) propose a model-based feature selection for clustering, they separated two sets: one set holds both relevant and irrelevant features that carry cluster information, sensor set holds redundant features conditionally independent of the other set. Bayes techniques with greedy search utilized to compare both of the sets. (Zeng and Cheung et al., 2006) designed a rival penalized expectation-maximization algorithm (RPEM) through feature weighting (FW-RPEM) to concomitantly execute clustering as well as feature selection. Moreover, the authors use a Markov blanket filter to eliminate redundant features.

3. **Feature Selection for Evolutionary clustering (EC):** Evolutionary clustering addressed various clustering as well as data mining issues. Various studies proved that EC techniques show better results than other eminent cluster techniques. But, unrelated and unnecessary features and datasets might change the performance of EC techniques. To overcome these issues feature selection techniques for EC divided into single-objective and multi-objective. In single-objective techniques, (Sheng et al., 2015) authors present a variable-length GA, called NMA-CFS, which chooses features while performing clustering at similar time. (Lensen et al, 2017) build a multi-staged PSO based model, they employed Gaussian function to choose the feature subset from available features. (Hancer et al., 2018) initiate a DE-based method to concurrently execute clustering and FS. In this method, a comparable plan based discrete DE variant is employed to develop results. Coming to multi-objective schemes both clustering as well as feature selection treated at the same time (Prakash and Singh et al., 2019) authors' presents Inspired Multi-objective Binary Gravitational Search based simultaneous Clustering and FS technique (IMBGSAFS). In this feature subset search utilized to construct non-dominated resolution sets and K-means applied on reduced selected features. Simulation results show that it has good results. (Hancer et al., 2020) established a variable-string length based multi-objective DE-based model (MODE-CFS). For each explanation, a mutant result is produced using a specific two-case mutation plan, and next the existing solution and its mutant additional to a union set. According to the consequences, it out-performed a mixture of usual and newly introduced multi-objective clustering models.

Embedded Method

Coming to an embedded feature selection process, the learning process guides the search operation. This kind of procedure is also acknowledged as a Nested subset technique, which habitually procedures the helpfulness of feature subsets as well as achieves FS as an element of the training procedure. These methods made enhanced handling of accessible data moreover produce faster solutions as they do not involve separation of training data into training, validation sets. Here operations are computationally economical and fewer levels to over-fitting compared to wrapper procedures. Most interestingly, embedded methods have enhanced computational complication than wrapper methods (Girsh et al., 2017; Jilang et al., 2016; Jain et al 2018; Khiabani et al., 2015; Mohammad et al., 2015; Pui et al., 2017)

There are three kinds of embedded systems. The primary one is pruning techniques that principally make exploit of every features to teach a representation plus then endeavor to get rid of various features via setting the consequential coefficients to 0, even maintain representation concert like recursive feature exclusion with support vector machine (SVM). The second kind of model contains an integrated system for FS as ID3 and C4.5. The third kind is regularization optimization tasks that reduce fitting faults along with in the meantime power the co-efficients to be diminutive or to be precisely zero. Features with co-efficient that close 0 abolished. Because of high-quality performance, regularization models magnetize rising consideration. Sparse learning models are the most suited to embedded approaches due to their interpretability and performance; moreover it measures similarity among a quantity of goodness and sparsity of the end-result. For suppose, in sparse learning cluster process, we are not only considering the quality of a cluster or some other typical measurement performances, but we also take care of the non-expert abuser point of view. Most importantly these techniques first find the cluster labels with the help of clustering advances and after that convert the unsupervised feature selection into a supervised environment through the generated cluster labels. Hence, embedded methods computationally lesser expensive than wrapper methods. Numerous issues deteriorate the embedded model's performance, one of them is noise to overcome this author in (Qian and Zhai et al., 2013) designed a spectral learning FS model in favor of clustering entitled as robust unsupervised FS (RUFS). Here cluster labels resolved by local learning nonnegative matric factorization and robust Joint L1,2-norms for feature selection. Authors in (Du et al., 2017) extend the RUFS by adding matrix factorization and they use cluster centroids in place of cluster labels. (Wang et al., 2017) designed a new embedded technique that straightforwardly embeds feature selection into the clustering model without the transformation. The authors employed the K-means algorithm by minimizing the reconstruction error to find the cluster labels along with features. (Zhu and Yang et al 2018) address the discriminative embedded unsupervised feature selection technique and it obtains the cluster labels by maximizing the heterogeneity among clusters to model the cluster structure of data. Simulation results show better than (Wang et al., 2017) model.

Hybrid Method

Hybrid methods come into the act to unite the most excellent possessions of filters and wrappers. At the initial stage, filter system utilized to decrease feature measurement space, probably obtain numerous contestant subsets. Now, wrapper applied to find-out finest contestant subset. Hybrid approaches classically accomplish elevated precision that is distinctive to wrappers and higher competence characteristics to filters. Various combinational methodologies were recently presented such as hybrid ant colony optimization, fuzzy random forest-based feature selection, mixed gravitational search algorithm, and hybrid genetic algorithm. In the present era, it is one of the most extensively utilized procedures by the researchers to apply on FS. Hybrid techniques comprehensives more than one approach collectively to acquire benefit of the merits of a dissimilar approach to get the best consequences.

A hybrid feature selection model based on an enhanced particle swarm optimization method was offered by the authors in (Chikkara et al., 2015). Researchers employed both filter and wrapper methods collectively for image steganalysis. It was originate from the tentative results that the projected hybridized techniue drastically condensed the amount of features and improved the taxonomy precision as compared to further prior FS methods. Additionally, computational expenditure and time also got condensed with the projected method. A hybrid genetic approach based FS models consisting filter and wrapper model developed by the authors in (Huang and Cai et al., 2013). Selection of most favorable subset of features was made with the inclusion of profits of both filter and wrapper methods in two optimization phases. The wrapper method for the large-scale search and filter method for the limited search was applied to get the most excellent subset of features in external and internal phases correspondingly. When both optimizations were functional jointly, the consequences accomplished were formed with very high predictive accurateness and high limited search competence. in (Peng and Wu et al., 2010) authors introduced a feature pre-selection pace and employed Receiver Operating Characteristics (ROC) curves to compact with the concerns of high dimensional biomedical data and to progress the performance of the SVM classifier. The tentative outcomes with biomedical databases exposed that the anticipated model extensively enhanced the classification presentation and the results of this approach better than the results of Sequential Forward Floating Search (SFFS) process.

Auto-encoders Feature Representation

Auto-encoders (AE) is one style of deep neural networks that fabricate or purely copy input to the output means auto-encoder find out representations of features from uncooked data which know how to shape training data. Auto-encoders internally have hidden layer h that demonstrate the unique set of laws to signify input data to output. It has two mechanisms encoder: mapping input data to hidden code, decoder: which maps data from hidden code to reconstruction output. However if auto-encoders minimally successful, to learn copy input to output it is not so handy. As a substitute of this, it designed in a explicit way where it will copy correctly means copy input data which only look a lot like training data, for these auto-encoders severely enforced to prioritize definite data and then learns functional records from that data (Barry et al., 2015; Dessi et al., 2015; Girsh et al., 2017; Jilang et al., 2016; Jain et al 2018; Khiabani et al., 2015; Mohammad et al., 2015).

- **Denoising Autoencoder (DAE):** A DAE is proposed as an AE with self-determining input-hidden as well as hidden-output weights. AE educated with noise inside the input data and then recreate innovative unaffected data at output layer. Noise may be pepper noise, masking noise, Gaussian noise. Denoising AE is educated by bringing in noise to the input data after that minimize appropriate reconstruction error. After training, the initial autoencoder, hidden to output weights are redundant and input to hidden weights is exploit to initialize the input to initial hidden layer weights of deep neural network. hidden representation of primary DAE representations uses as input for training next coming to denoising AE. The input to the hidden weights of second DAE is used to initialize the first hidden layer to the second hidden layer weights of the Deep neural network (DNN). As mention above various DAE's are educated and the input to hidden weights of DAE is exploited to initialize weights in DNN. Finally, the output layer is connected to the DNN and the complete system is educated via minimize classification fault with backpropagation which is pronounced as fine-tuning.
- **Predictive Sparse Decomposition (PSD):** As the name imply it is a mixture of sparse coding along with parametric auto-encoders. It is extensively utilized in image, video detection, and un-

supervised learning process typically inside the framework of the multistage convolutional deep structural design. Sparse coding could be sight as one type of AE which exploits a linear decoder with a squared reconstruction error, however, encoder achieves nontrivial and reasonably expensive iterative minimization. PSD capable to work as a type of AE, where the codes h are specified various independence that can help to advance progress renovation. One can also analyze the encoding results affixed on top of sparse coding as a type of regularizer that strengthens the sparse codes to be almost calculable in a soft as well as a well-organized encoder.

Deep Belief Network Feature Selection

Deep learning (DL) is the subfield of Machine learning (ML), it attracts a wide range of attention in industrial as well as research institutes since the start of this decade. Because of visual cortex learning, the brain consists of several layers and signals run from layer to layer, to gain dissimilar stages of generalization. As a result of replicate the task of the deep structural design of the brain, DL develops various techniques in ML to attempt toward model high-level generalization in data through make use of model structure composed of multiple nonlinear renovation learning. The DL method of the DBN holds two levels: those are layer-wise feature generalization - here DBN uses Restricted Boltzmann Machines to evaluate the rebuilding weights layer-wise. And restoration weight fine-tuning – DBN execute a backpropagation to adjust the weights obtain from the original point.

Table 1. Feature selection methods, filters classes, application fields

Filters	**Chi-squared** **Interact** **mRMR** **CC** **IG** **CBF** **OR** **GR** *Md* *ReliefF* *FS* *Markov Blanket* *FCBF* *SU*	Univariate Univariate Multivariate Univariate Univariate Univariate Univariate Univariate Univariate Univariate Univariate Univariate Multivariate Univariate	Text classification, medical imaging, action recognition Network intrusion detection, fry eye detection, classification Health monitoring, gene prediction Network intrusion detection, advertisement, action management, process learning medication, prototype selection credit scoring, fault detection, Gaussian mixture clustering, intelligent tutoring, medication, prototype selection, face recognition, speech recognition, process learning, internet traffic, network fault diagnosis prototype selection, face recognition, Health monitoring, gene prediction medication, prototype selection Network intrusion detection, internet traffic, network fault diagnosis speech recognition, process learning,
Wrappers	**SS** **Metaheuristic**	Multivariate Univariate	Satellite images, medical images, hospital operations, disease classification, image classification
Embedded	**Decision trees** **SVM** **LASSO** **Sequential forward** **Elastic net**	Multivariate Univariate	Gaussian mixture clustering, intelligent tutoring, medication, prototype selection, face recognition, medical images, hospital operations, disease classification, image classification
Hybrid	**Ant colony** **GA** **Fuzzy set**	Multivariate Univariate	Network intrusion detection, internet traffic, network fault diagnosis, speech recognition, process learning

Table 2. Feature selection methods, Advantages/Disadvantages, Evolution, Limitations and Characteristics

FS Approaches	Advantage /Disadvantage	Evolution/Search Strategy	Limitation	Characteristics	References
Filter	**Advantages** 1. high-speed 2. Computationally less expensive 3. Scalable 4. Good generality 5. Independent of classifier 6. Produce fast outcomes on completing 7. Works well with huge data **Disadvantages** 1. ignore iteration with classifier	1. correlation based FS 2. Chi-square test 3. Fisher score 4. Gain ratio 5. Inconsistency norm 6. Mutual information 7. Minimum redundancy, Maximum relevance 8. Symmetrical uncertainty 9. Markov blanker filter 10. FOCUS algorithm 11. Forward selection	1. Does not promise accurateness 2. Not consider enslavement of one feature over another 3. pay no attention to interactions between classifiers	1. measure the best relevant features 2. employees statistical approaches for evaluation 3. choose features independent of any classifier 4. provides rank for features 5. Elects subset of features 6. Depend on intrinsic characteristics of data	(Barry et al., 2015; Dessi et al., 2015; Girsh et al., 2017; Jilang et al., 2016; Jain et al 2018; Khabani et al., 2015; Pui et al., 2017; Bolon et al., 2015; Hira et al., 2015; Zahavy et al., 2016; T li et al., 2016; Kendall et al., 2015
Wrapper	**Advantages** 1. Simple 2. Best performance of predictive accuracy 3. Feature dependencies 4. Best classifier interactions 5. interrelate through classifier 6. optimize the classifier **Disadvantages** 1. classifier dependent selection 2. Risk of over-fitting	1. Branch and Bound 2. Genetic algorithm 3. Sequential forward selection 4. Beam sech method 5. Stepwise selection 6. Backward elimination 7. Best-fit 8. Recursive selection	1. Highest execution time 2. Less scalable for large datasets 3. Needs greater computation sources 4. Greater complexity 5. Over=fit on small training data	1. Use bias of induction model 2. Score mentioned on accurateness model 3. Employs special classifier to estimate the quality of features 4. It provides optimal features for the learning model.	Chakraorty and Das et al.,2018; (Ji et al., 2013; Amorim and Mirkin et al., 2016; Hancer et al., 2018; Hancer et al., 2020
Embedded	**Advantages** 1. Best usage of available data provides faster solutions 2. Lesser complexity than the wrapper 3. Better classification interaction 4. Models feature dependencies 5. Less prone to overfitting than a wrapper **Disadvantages** 1. Classifier dependent selection	1. Sequential forward 2. Decision trees 3. Ridge regression 4. SVM 5. Artificial neural networks 6. Lasso method	1. Computationally costlier than wrapper and filter models 2. Poor generality 3. Specific to the learning machine 4. collection of appropriate features due consideration of classifier	1. performs FS in the process of training 2. utilizes a supervised approach 3. frequently specific to the learning model 4. performs optimization 5. Aggregates the advantages of filter and wrapper 6. Search models guided by learning algorithms	Peng and Wu et al., 2010) Chikkara et al., 2015 Huang and Cai et al., 2013

APPLICATIONS

There are a wide variety of applications for feature selection some of them presented below

- **Face Recognition:** From the past years, human face detection has raised as an active research field because of its wide variety of commercial and legal appliances. one major problem in the field is how to calculate which part of features or which image features are the largest part instructive for the recognition principle. It is not a petty assignment because the facial database contains a large number of features with a strong correlation. The introduction of feature selection techniques provides suggestions to solve issues in face recognition, a discrete cosine transform (DST) for face recognition, principal feature selection (PFS) to choose original features and suggested a sequential floating forward search (SFFS) to select optimal color components from color face images.
- **Microarray Analysis:** DNA based Microarray analysis holds information regarding gene expression differentiation on cell issues that may helpful for illness diagnosis and used for identifying the definite type of tumors. From 2000 onwards univariate and multivariate based microarray feature selection take into place. Compare to multivariate, univariate analysis produce best results in terms of scalable, fast but issue is it ignores the dependencies among features. Numerous researchers proposed a wide variety of methodologies in the filter, wrapper, and embedded models. At last with a lot of literature surveys realized that combine algorithms or ensemble methods may produce the best results.
- **Text Classification:** Text classification mainly categorizes documents, files into predetermined groups or labels which is mainly applicable in spam discovery in shopping and websites. Here each word visualizes as a feature. Preprocessing applied at the primary stage to remove the duplicate, repeated words, and combine the words such as plurals and verbs into a single word. After the preprocessing stage, the word limit may high so feature selection is a supreme technique. High-quality techniques developed and applied to text taxonomy problems. Developed genuine feature selection techniques for text clustering, come with successions of filter methods concern to binary, multi as well as hierarchical text taxonomy problems.
- **Image Classification:** Image categorization recently gained tremendous attention in the research community. As a result of technological developments such as smartphones, internet services a huge quantity of images available but image processing and computer vision needs lots of memory as well as power. Feature selection facilitates to lessen the number of features for proficiently classify the images. Various properties of features of images analyze and conclude which class the images fit in. feature selection can also apply for automatic image annotation.

FOCAL POINTS

- **Scalability:** Scalability defined as the impact of increased training data on the computational complexity of algorithms in provisions of precision, training occasion as well as allocation of memory. Various existing techniques applied on a small amount of data and produce best results, however at present dissimilar problems will raise if the same techniques applied on large scale information because of computational complications of the learning techniques. Moreover the largest part of these algorithms manufactured under the hypothesis of single memory residents, so data size is one of the scaling machine learning algorithms. Model and algorithm complexity, inference time complexity, prediction cascades, and model selection, as well as parameter sweeps, are some of the scaling machine learning algorithms. Scaling up is popular since a rising amount of training size increases the accurateness of algorithms. Feature selection research community also focused on the stability, few training sets with huge quantity feature sets, modifications on existing approaches, online and parallel approaches, combinations of feature selection strategies, etc. univariate feature selection algorithms produce some advantages in scalability but they over-look dependencies. Multivariate feature selection produces great performance but the scalability cost reduced.

- **Model Preference:** For most FS models in particular for feature weighting techniuess, we have to indicate amount of preferred features. Still, it is mysterious what is the best possible number of preferred features. A big quantity of selected features will amplify the jeopardy in noisy, and inappropriate features, which may possibly jeopardize the learning act. On the otherhand, it is also not excellent to incorporate various too-small sized elected features, because a few appropriate features may abolished. In practice, we frequently assume a heuristic way to grid search the quantity of elected features and choose the number that has the finest taxonomy or clustering, however the whole practice is computationally costly. It is still an open and tricky trouble to determine finest number of features. In addition need to need to denote quantity of clusters or pseudo-classes for unsupervised FS approaches. In real-world issues, we generally have imperfect facts about clustering formation of data. Preferring diverse numbers of clusters can unite dissimilar small clusters into solitary full-size cluster or divide into lesser ones. From above consequence, it may effect in finding special subsets of features.

- **Large Range Dimensions:** As a result of technology improvement, day by day the amount of data increasing continuously. After that machine learning, Big data come into the act with this exceptional range of data. At the early timcs in the 1980's the maximum quantity of data is only 100, in the 1990's it goes to 2000, at present some data repositories may contain data dimensionality above 4 million. Same as in LIBSVM maximum data dimensionality is 62000 in the early 1990s and it raised to 30 million in 2010. Some other data repositories like image analysis and DNA microarray classifications. Most of the offered FS practices deal with strong correlation among features but when dealing with millions of features which raises enormous challenges that are still questionable to ML experts.

- **Computational Complexity:** In any ML, Big data, and Data mining model, computational complexity is an uneliminated concern and it follows the same as feature selection methods because they involve a high amount of datasets and processing. In some works filter models produce better results than wrapper models hence there is a need for unique effectual and well-organized feature selection models. FS for clustering, mainly wrapper models, is very costly due to every evaluation involve to execute a clustering procedure to test the integrity of the preferred feature subset. Even though FS for clustering can decrease the execution time for future appliances. there is a need for developing a resourceful, well-organized search method for FS or fast evaluation actions.

- **Real-Time Processing:** Accumulation of data continuous and fast, according to that data processors must be done. Data from social media and internet sources generate huge quantities of data so the refined techniques were capable to deal with this vast amount of data in real-time. The online learning process applied to realtime learning problems, which can continue modifying and refined models by integrating fresh data on requiring because it solves major problems that occur in realtime. Most of the online-based feature selection deals with individual basis much like pre-selecting features in an independent online ML step or else online FS devoid of successive online taxonomy. Consequently, attain concurrent scrutiny, computation for high-dimensional datasets stay as a confront for computational intellect.

- **Distributed Feature Processing:** From the above study, it concluded that data is collectively in a solitary very huge data set. Most of the classical feature selection schemes applied on centralized, solitarily solves its problem. At present days data maintain a distributed manner, an equivalent feature learning applied on each of them and the results combined. The dataset is not principally outsized but dissimilar FS schemes should be functional to detect unnoticed instances moreover merge results. One more open line of research is utilization of graphics dispensation units (GPUs) to distribute and as a consequence speed up results completed in FS algorithms. Applicable with several appliances to physics simulations, parallel algorithms, signal processing, financial modeling, neural networks along with numerous new grounds.

- **Feature Interoperability:** Model or techniques are first-rate only if they have good features means features continuously plays the most important key role in any representation interoperability. For instance feature selection for decision trees, instead of agents simulating human resources in an association to model sustainability behaviors during a proficient review of their hypothetical reliability. Mechanical enhancement scheme, in which the FS step chooses the finest distinctiveness automatically.

- **Evolution Measure:** The evolution measure is important for any feature selection or extraction approach. It strikes classification precision, search time, and computation space. However in some models of wrapper and filter have high computational costs, to overcome this there exist some speedy evaluation measures like mutual information that evaluate features separately and do not consider features dependencies that produce redundant features in a subset of features. In some cases, other measurements might compact with feature dependencies, which may show high computational complexities. Multivariate feature selection approaches may work well in feature dependency but the correlations do not scale well if it holds big datasets. So there is a need for new evolution measures to adapt extensive scale feature selection issues.

- **Feature Cost:** Feature selection cost related to various models. Computational expenditure of mining each feature differs entails dissimilar computational epochs. In real-time appliances, the space complication is minor, while the time complication is vital. Reduction of the cost related to feature selection methods has gain attention in research groups. Tremendous research is going on by dissimilar researchers to build innovative feature selection techniques that can compact with comprehensive, real-time appliances.

- **Stability or Sensitivity:** While design an efficient feature selection technique, considering the stability of that particular technique is also one of the measurable parameters. In most of the techniques, features selected and the majority of them obtained form new samples in the presence of little quantity of disorder. If not it is hard to trust algorithm when they deal with dissimilar sets of features even though the data sets drained for similar troubles. Hence, stability or sensitivity becomes more attention in the feature selection community. Developing feature selection with high taxonomy precision and steadiness is still a demanding assignment.

- **Linked Data:** Existing techniques assume available data as generic, independent, and identically distributed. Linked data has some omnipresent in real-world appliances as chats, Facebook, Twitter, etc. feature selection techniques for linked data solve following issues how to classify associations between data samples and how to catch benefit of these associations while selecting features. Linked data improves the feature selection but some noted issues like handling noise, unfinished as well as unlabeled links of social media information

FUTURE WORKS

1. When we work on high dimensional datasets the main goal is to find the optimal feature subset. In some cases, we also apply feature weighting or feature ranking for better results. But it still

2. needs to decide the subset from ranking outcome. If the amount of essential features is identified, this fortitude is extremely simple, we just require opting the essential features one after one from the ranking set in anticipation of the number of features meets preferred requisite. Unluckily, without any preceding information, the quantity of essential feature is anonymous. In that case, the alteration of feature ranking to feature subset is still an open model selection concern in FS.

3. **Feature Selection with Large Dimensional Data:** In real-world appliances, the quantity of data collection is amplified in the shape of audio, video, images, medical data, and text documents. Numerous FS approaches have advanced time complexity regarding dimensionality. Filter approaches have lesser computational complexity than wrapper approaches at the same time filter approaches have more scalable than the wrapper. The above-mentioned argument concludes that upcoming research must be rigorous on small time complication with high scalability FS techniques.

4. The investigation development of FS very much directly goes next to the progress of ML. When any innovation takes place on ML background techniques then the consequent feature selection themes also will be calculated. At present most of the researchers working on hybrid ML techniques and Adversarial ML then automatically shifted to hybrid FS and adversarial FS. Moreover, most FS approaches focus on classification, clustering performance but there is a need for the attention of stability, security, and scalability of the FS approach.

5. **Feature Selection with a Sparse Data Matrix:** Sparse data contains a reasonable entitlement of variables that were no genuine data in it. Sparse data available in two varieties: controlled sparsity, which holds one or more than one dimension that has no data. Random sparsity, blank values spread all through the data variable. Market base analysis, healthcare, direct-mail marketing, insurance in addition to computer plus internet web expertise like news, HTML, emails, XML, and customer assessments. In recent times, video stream data is also growing at a fast rate with high dimensionality through scrutiny cameras, sensors, kas well as web streaming. FS from labeled or unlabelled sparse data is a hard assignment since countless FS procedures are not proper for soaring dimensional sparse data. As a result, it is a prerequisite of future research to extend proficient FS approaches on behalf of sparse data.

6. **Sub-Space Searching and Instance Selection:** In literature, most of the clustering approaches implemented with special subspaces for small size data with over-lapped or else non-overlapped magnitude. Here, subspace searching is not only the FS trouble, it is also like creating numerous subspaces in which FS discover solitary subspace. Hence, there is a requisite for proficient subspace search model for cluster/classification. Coming to instance selection, sampling models has been implemented to search for a set of examples that can execute in a focused manner.

7. **Forward and Backward Selection:** Some recent works of FS build on backward elimination and forward selection, here backward elimination has fewer proficient results compared to forward FS.

Reasons are forward FS has lower computational complications and it employs greedy FS which does not overfit, however, the mistakes made at initial stages will not approve afterward stages. In backward elimination, errors are remodeled but it begins with the non-over-fit techniue. If the combinational method of forwarding greedy and backward greedy will computationally effectual and error-corrected so for expectations research fault correction, over-fitting as well as computational value can measured as features of efficient approaches.

8. **Structured and Dynamic Feature:** In a few real datasets, features demonstrate as spatial/temporal correlations, tree or graph-like structures but some of them are not dependent. If we consider the specific dependencies among features that may increase the performances of the models. For this, recent approaches apply feature structures with the help of Lasso regularization to work with dissimilar structures. Coming to dynamic features that are unknown in size, they arrived in streamed form and the modeling algorithms have to reach whether they useful for the model formation or not. Sometimes unexpected features irrelevant, those must be rejected, this kind of situation frequently happens in the twitter network.

9. In feature selection, evaluation actions are essential parts that establish the speed and the absolute performance of any technique. Compare to classification, clustering is harder and it is an unsupervised scheme, numerous clustering evaluation measures exist some of the compactness, inside or between cluster distances, division, and connectedness. But, dissimilar estimation measures show a diverse level of righteousness for similar set of clustering consequences, in addition, to advise dissimilar models as most excellent algorithms. For that reason, it is tough for abusers to formulate a conclusion. It is extremely tough assignment to build authoritative and comprehensive valuation procedures.

CONCLUSION

Feature selection (FS) techniques illustrate that huge raw information is not always first-rate in ML appliances. Authors exploit dissimilar methods on the data at hand along with baseline taxonomy presentation morals and finally select an ultimate FS technique. For the appliance at hand, a feature FS technique can be preferred pedestal on the subsequent reflections: straightforwardness, immovability, amount of concentrated features, taxonomy precision, storage space, and computational necessities. Taken as a whole concern FS will at all times supply reimbursement like afford insight into the information, enhanced classifier representation, develop simplification and credentials of inappropriate variables.

REFERENCES

Araujo, T., Aresta, G., Castro, E., Rouco, J., Aguiar, P., Eloy, C., ... Campilho, A. (2017). Classification of breast cancer histology images using convolutional neural networks. *PLoS One*, *12*(6), e0177544. doi:10.1371/journal.pone.0177544

Bennasar, Hicks, & Setchi. (2015). Feature selection using Joint Mutual Information Maximisation. *Expert Systems With Applications*.

Bolón-Canedo, V., Sánchez-Maroño, N., & Alonso-Betanzos, A. (2015). (2015). Recent advances and emerging challenges of feature selection in the context of Big Data. *Knowledge-Based Systems*, *86*, 33–45. doi:10.1016/j.knosys.2015.05.014

Chakraborty, S., & Das, S. (2018). Simultaneous variable weighting and determining the number of clusters—A weighted Gaussian means algorithm. *Statistics & Probability Letters*, *137*, 148–156. doi:10.1016/j.spl.2018.01.015

Chandrashekar, G., & Sahin, F. (2017). A survey on feature selection methods. *Computers & Electrical Engineering*, *40*(1), 16–28. doi:10.1016/j.compeleceng.2013.11.024

Chhikara, R.R., Sharma, P., & Singh, L. (n.d.). A hybrid feature selection approach based on improved PSO and filter approaches for image steganalysis. *Int J Mach Learn Cybern*, 1–12.

Dessì, N., & Pes, B. (2015). Similarity of feature selection methods: An empirical study across data intensive classification tasks. *Expert Systems with Applications*.

Du, S., Ma, Y., Li, S., & Ma, Y. (2017). Robust unsupervised feature selection via matrix factorization. *Neurocomputing*, *241*, 115–127.

Han, J., Pei, J., & Kamber, M. (2011). *Data mining: concepts and techniques*. Elsevier.

Hancer, E. (2018) A diferential evolution approach for simultaneous clustering and feature selection. *International conference on artifcial intelligence and data processing*, 1–7.

Hancer, E. (2020). A new multi-objective diferential evolution approach for simultaneous clustering and feature selection. *Engineering Applications of Artificial Intelligence*, *87*, 103307. doi:10.1016/j.engappai.2019.103307

Hancer, E., Xue, B., & Zhang, M. (2020). A survey on feature selection approaches for clustering. *Artificial Intelligence Review*, *53*(6), 4519–4545. doi:10.100710462-019-09800-w

Hira & Gillies. (2015). *A Review of Feature Selection and Feature Extraction Methods Applied on Microarray Data*. Hindawi Publishing Corporation Advances in Bioinformatics. . doi:10.1155/2015/198363

Huang, J., Cai, Y., & Xu, X. (2007). A hybrid genetic algorithm for feature selection wrapper based on mutual information. *Pattern Recognition Letters*, *28*(13), 1825–1844. doi:10.1016/j.patrec.2007.05.011

Ji, J., Bai, T., Zhou, C., Ma, C., & Wang, Z. (2013). An improved k-prototypes clustering algorithm for mixed numeric and categorical data. *Neurocomputing*, *120*, 590–596. doi:10.1016/j.neucom.2013.04.011

Jin, C., & Yang, C. (2011). Integrating hierarchical feature selection and classifier training for multi-label image annotation. In *Proceedings of the 34th international ACM SIGIR conference on Research and development in Information Retrieval*, (pp. 515–524). ACM 10.1145/2009916.2009987

Kendall, A., Grimes, M., & Cipolla, R. (2015). Posenet: A convolutional network for real-time 6-dof camera relocalization. *Proceedings of the IEEE international conference on computer vision*, 2938–2946.

Khiabani, F. B., Ramezankhani, A., Azizi, F., Hadaegh, F., Steyerberg, E. W., & Khalili, D. (2015). A tutorial on variable selection for clinical prediction models: Feature selection methods in data-mining could improve the results. *Journal of Clinical Epidemiology*. doi:10.1016/j.jclinepi.2015.10.002

Lee, P. Y., Loh, W. P., & Chin, J. F. (2017). feature selection for multimedia: A state of the art. *Image and Vision Computing*, *67*, 29–42. doi:10.1016/j.imavis.2017.09.004

Lensen, A., Xue, B., & Zhang, M. (2017). Using particle swarm optimisation and the silhouette metric to estimate the number of clusters, select features, and perform clustering. In G. Squillero & K. Sim (Eds.), *Applications of evolutionary computation* (pp. 538–554). Berlin: Springer. doi:10.1007/978-3-319-55849-3_35

Li, T., Meng, Z., Ni, B., Shen, J., & Wang, M. (2016). Robust geometric p-norm feature pooling for image classification and action recognition. *Image and Vision Computing*, *55*(Part 2), 64–76. doi:10.1016/j.imavis.2016.04.002

O'Sullivan, B., & Wooldridge, M. (2015). *Artificial intelligence foundations theory and applications. Feature selection for high dimensional data*. Springer.

Peng, Y., Wu, Z., & Jiang, J. (2010). A novel feature selection approach for biomedical data classification. *Journal of Biomedical Informatics*, *43*(1), 15–23. doi:10.1016/j.jbi.2009.07.008

Phinyomark, A., Hu, H., Phukpattaranont, P., & Limsakul, C. (2012). Application of linear discriminant analysis in dimensionality reduction for hand motion classification. *Measurement Science Review*, *12*(3), 82–89. doi:10.2478/v10048-012-0015-8

Prakash, J., & Singh, P. K. (2019). Gravitational search algorithm and k-means for simultaneous feature selection and data clustering: A multi-objective approach. *Soft Computing*, *23*(6), 2083–2100. doi:10.100700500-017-2923-x

Qian, M., & Zhai, C. (2013). Robust unsupervised feature selection. In: Proceedings of the twenty-third international joint conference on artifcial intelligence. *IJCAI (United States)*, *13*, 1621–1627.

Raftery, A. E., & Dean, N. (2006). Variable selection for model-based clustering. *Journal of the American Statistical Association*, *101*(473), 168–178. doi:10.1198/016214506000000113

Song, L., Smola, A., Gretton, A., Borgwardt, K., & Bedo, J. (2007). Supervised feature selection via dependence estimation. *Proceedings of the 24th International Conference on Machine Learning*, 823-830.

Staroszczyk, T., Osowski, S., & Markiewicz, T. (2012). Comparative Analysis of Feature Selection Methods for Blood Cell Recognition in Leukemia. *Proceedings of the 8th International Conference on Machine Learning and Data Mining in Pattern Recognition, MLDM 2012*, 467-481. 10.1007/978-3-642-31537-4_37

Tang, Alelyani, & Liu. (2016). Feature selection for classification: A Review. *Egyptian Informatics J.* doi:10.1016/j.eij.2018.03.002

Tang, J., Alelyani, S., & Liu, H. (2014). *Feature selection for classification: a review*. Data Classification Algorithm Applications.

Tang, J., Alelyani, S., & Liu, H. (2014). Feature Selection for Classification: A Review. In C. C. Aggarwal (Ed.), *Data Classification: Algorithms and Applications* (pp. 37–64). CRC Press.

Tuv, E., Borisov, A., Runger, G., & Torkkola, K. (2009). Feature selection with ensembles, artificial variables, and redundancy elimination. *Journal of Machine Learning Research, 10*, 1341–1366.

Wang, H., Jing, X., & Niu, B. (2017). A discrete bacterial algorithm for feature selection in classifcation of microarray gene expression cancer data. *Knowledge-Based Systems, 126*, 8–19. doi:10.1016/j.knosys.2017.04.004

Wang, X., & Paliwal, K. K. (2003). Feature extraction and dimensionality reduction algorithms and their applications in vowel recognition. *Pattern Recognition, 36*(10), 2429–2439. doi:10.1016/S0031-3203(03)00044-X

Zahavy, T., Ben-Zrihem, N., & Mannor, S. (2016). Graying the black box: Understanding dqns. *International Conference on Machine Learning*, 1899–1908.

Zhu, Q. H., & Yang, Y. B. (2018). Discriminative embedded unsupervised feature selection. *Pattern Recognition Letters, 112*, 219–225. doi:10.1016/j.patrec.2018.07.018

Chapter 3
Hybrid Attributes Technique Filter for the Tracking of Crowd Behavior

Hocine Chebi

Faculty of Electrical Engineering, Djillali Liabes University, Sidi Bel Abbes, Algeria

ABSTRACT

In this chapter, the authors propose two algorithms based on the device of attributes for tracking of the abnormal behavior of crowd in the visual systems of surveillance. Previous works were realized in the case of detection of behavior, which uses the analysis and the classification of behavior of crowds; this work explores the continuity in the same domain, but in the case of the automatic tracking based on the techniques of filtering one using the KALMAN filter and particles filter. The proposed algorithms he the technique of filter with particle is independent from the detection and from the segmentation human, so is strong with regard to (compared with) the filter of Kalman. In conclusion, the chapter applies the method for tracking of the abnormal behavior to several videos and shows the promising results.

INTRODUCTION

The security of the people and the goods is one of major problems in the public zones such as airports, subway stations, shopping malls or squares. The automatic processing of videos resulting from security cameras is more and more used to present relevant information to the operators who have to act in the critical, dangerous or unusual situations. These last year's saw the integration in the systems of video surveillance of algorithms of detection of movements, events, abandoned luggage or follow-up of people. However, seen the complexity of the problem, few systems dealt with the situations implying crowds of people.

The analysis of the flows of people consists in detecting the unusual behavior in the watched zones. She becomes necessary when the follow-up of individual objects fails; what is often the case in a scene of crowd. This analysis is made by handling the information of movement through successive images, and then to make follow-up the behavior by technique of filtering. The detection of events is defined

DOI: 10.4018/978-1-7998-6659-6.ch003

as being the detection of the situations which draw the attention of a person (Chebi 2015; Chebi 2017; Chebi 2018; Chebi 2020).

In this article, we introduce techniques of tracking of behavior by attributes to allowing following the behavior to represent in a scene. This model manages effectively the complexity of the scenarios and the unpredictability of the behavior.

These approaches were applied to a selection of events and experimented on the sample of videos of the workshop PETS'2009 (Dataset 2009).

This article is organized as follows. First of all, the section II presents some previous works dealing with the problem of the analysis of crowd and tracking of behavior of crowds. The section III details the techniques of attributes (KALMAN filter and particles Filter). The results of the experiment on the sample of videos PETS'2009 are presented in the section IV. The section V concludes this article and describes the future potential works.

STATE OF THE ART OF TRACKING

Tracking methods propose to recognize and locate over time objects present in a temporal sequence of images (Gabriel 2003). In the context of crowds, they find a particular interest in video surveillance where the tracking of individuals makes it possible to automatically control the comings and goings in a space. Like image recognition, tracking can rely on graphic properties such as colors or outlines (Mathes 2006; Yang 2005). The added temporal dimension also makes it possible to assume continuity in the presence and position of people in the scene, despite the occlusions (Rabaud 2006).

In this part, we will therefore explore four main approaches: follow-up by regional approach, follow-up using a model, follow-up by contours approach, follow-up using attributes. For each of these methods, it must be kept in mind that a good monitoring method must be robust, precise and above all fast to be able to follow a person in real time. The quality of monitoring is also dependent on good detection of people on the move. We will present the different monitoring techniques, in order to draw the different advantages and disadvantages:

Follow-up by Regional Approach

The region approach is one of the most classic: people have been segmented in the image, and tracking consists of matching regions between two consecutive images. One of the simplest follow-ups is that of recovery (McKenna 2000). It does not require a position prediction; the objects are matched by box overlap between the image t −1 and the image t. This method requires that the movement is not too large for there to be overlap.

The advantage is that the amount of movement between two images can be greater since it is based on color information. Any tracking technique can be improved by combining other information such as texture, shape, speed of the person, etc. The follow-up of regions is not limited to that of people; it can sometimes be interesting to follow a characteristic element of the person.

1.   Tracking using a template

Another tracking method is to fit a model to the person. These models can be classified into two categories: 2D models and 3D models. A 2D model fits quite easily but can be wrong depending on the point of view of the camera (Gabriel 2003; Serajeh 2013). A 3D model will be more precise but also more complicated to determine (Horain 2002). Adjusting a model does not necessarily require several images, the information in the current image may be sufficient. However, we can improve a model by using temporal information which will allow us to impose constraints on the latter.

2.   Contour approach monitoring

The contour approach consists in following an object by its contours. For example, for the Advisor project (Gao 2004; Yang 2005), the system follows the shape of the person approximated by a B-spline using a Kalman filter. The advantage of following an outline is that the model is often simple, which makes the method quick in computation time. Also this technique requires a robust and automatic initialization, which is not necessarily always obvious.

3.   Tracking using attributes

This approach involves following attributes such as lines or points, which are, in general, easy to extract. For example, it is possible to follow a driver's eyes using infrared lighting (Ji 2002): the driver's pupils appear very clear in the image, and using a Kalman filter, the system is able to follow the pupils and see the driver's waking state. An advantage of this method is that even in the event of partial occlusion, the rest of the visible characteristics can make it possible to continue monitoring.

Synthesis

The advantages and disadvantages of people-tracking approaches are summarized in Table 1.

Table 1. Comparison of monitoring methods.

Methods	Advantage	Disadvantages
KALMAN filter	Track vehicles or people.	It becomes inadequate in the presence of occlusions or multi-target follow-up.
Particle filter	They are well suited to follow a trajectory with abrupt changes. This tracking method looks very promising.	Provided you have enough particles to have a good maximum likelihood for the estimated state.
Follow-up by regional approach	The amount of movement between two images may be greater since we are based on color information.	Rarely used in crowd monitoring.

Mathematical Tracking Tools

While the time derivative quantifies the variation in the appearance of each pixel considered individually in the case of motion detection, the optical flow is modeled by a two-dimensional vector field representing the projection on the image plane of the actual motion observed. (3D). In this perspective, many methods (Fradi 2015; Mehran 2009; de Almeida 2013; Chen 2011; Andrade 2006) have been proposed since the precursor article of Horn and Schunck (Gabriel 2003; Mathes 2006; Yang 2005; Rabaud 2006) in order to improve the implementation of the latter.

Segmentation is an approach that consists of splitting the image successively by estimating the apparent motion of untagged areas and then detecting areas that do not conform to this pattern of motion (Chebi 2015). The principle of this method is based on the taking into account of a global image on which the dominant movement and the zones conforming to this movement forming a first region of the score are estimated.

This estimation and detection method is iterated on the non-conforming zones until all the pixels are classified (Chebi 2015; Chebi 2017).

The learning method for a classification phase generates a function that maps an input image to a specific label. There are several methods of learning in literature, such as decision trees, neural networks, fuzzy logic, AdaBoost (Adaptive Boosting), or support vector machines. (SVM) ... etc.

The tracking methods propose to recognize and locate over time objects present in a temporal sequence of images. In the context of human crowds, they find a particular interest in video surveillance where tracking individuals can automatically control the comings and goings in a space. Like image recognition, tracking can rely on graphic properties such as colors or outlines (Chebi 2018; Chebi 2020). The added temporal dimension also allows supposing a continuity of the presence and the position of the objects in the scene, in spite of occultation's. The temporal and spatial consistency of the monitored characteristics can in some cases be obtained by means of clustering methods.

In this party of tracking, we are thus going to explore four big approaches: followed by approach region, followed by means of a model, followed by approach outlines, followed by means of attributes. Our work was concerned the use of technique attribute, it is necessary to guard in head that a good method of follow-up must be strong, precise and especially rapids to be able to follow a real time person. The quality of the follow-up is also dependent on a good detection of the people in movement.

The proposed approaches contribute to the detection and followed major in a complex scene. She also contributes in the detection of events in the crowd by following groups of nobody instead of following every person individually, what facilitates the detection of events occurring on crowds.

FILTERING TECHNIQUE

This approach consists in following attributes such as lines or points, which are, generally, easy to extract. For example, it is possible to follow the eyes of a driver thanks to an infrared lighting (Ji 2002; Bishop 2001): the pupils of the driver seem very clear on the image, and by means of a filter of KALMAN, the system is capable of following wards and of seeing the state of awakening of the driver. An advantage of this method is that even in case of partial occlusion, the rest of the visible characteristics can allow to tracking the follow-up.

Filter de KALMAN

Le filtre de Kalman est utilisé dans une large gamme de domaines technologiques (radar, vision électronique, communication ...). C'est un thème majeur de l'automatique et du traitement du signal. Un exemple d'utilisation peut être la mise à disposition, en continu, d'informations telles que la position ou la vitesse d'un objet à partir d'une série d'observations relatives à sa position, incluant éventuellement des erreurs de mesures (Funk 2003; Isard 1998).

$$\begin{cases} X_t = A_t X_{t-1} + B_t U_t + v_t \\ \quad Z_t = C_t X_t + w_t \end{cases} \tag{1}$$

X_t: The vector of state, U_t: the vector of command, A_t and B_t is two matrices of size (n x n) and (n x m) respectively, n: the size of the vector of state, m is: the size of the vector of command is. The gaussian noise of process v_t models the random transition of state, its average is nil and its covariance is a matrix R_t. Z_t: The vector of measure of size k, C_t: a matrix of size (k x n) is. The noise of measure is modelled by a vector w_t, his distribution is also a gaussienne of average worthless and of covariance Q_t.

The entrance of this filter is the credibility of the state of the system represented by its average and its covariance $\left(\mu_{t-1}, \Sigma_{t-1} \right)$ at the moment (t–1).

$$\bar{\mu}_t = A_t \mu_{t-1} + B_t U_t \tag{2}$$

$$\bar{\Sigma}_t = A_t \sum_{t-1} A_t^T + R_t \tag{3}$$

The equation 2 and the equation 3 of the algorithm determine estimated values $\left(\mu_t, \bar{\Sigma}_t \right)$ .before the incorporation of the measure.

$$K_t = \bar{\Sigma}_t C_t^T \left(C_t \Sigma_t C_t^T + Q_t \right)^{-1} \tag{4}$$

The third stage presents 4 the calculation of the gain of KALMAN which decides on the degree of importance of the incorporation of the vector of measure.

$$\mu_t = \bar{\mu}_t + K_t (Z_t - C_t \bar{\mu}_t) \tag{5}$$

$$\Sigma_t = \left(I - K_t C_t \right) \bar{\Sigma}_t \tag{6}$$

Particulate Filter

Initialization: pull a sample of particles $\left\{ x_0^1, \ldots x_0^N \right\}$ according to a gaussienne law centered on the vector of initial state and associate with every particle an equal weight à 1/N.

Stage of prediction: generate a new sample $\left\{ x_k^1, \dots x_k^N \right\}$ by a gaussienne among which the average and the variance are calculated by the equations of KALMAN from the sample $\left\{ x_{k-1}^1, \dots x_{k-1}^N \right\}$.

Stage of correction: at the moment k, the weights of every particle w_k^i are updated w_k^i via the formula 7 there:

$$w_k^i = w_{k-1}^i \frac{f\left(y_k - H_k\left(x_k^i\right)\right) p\left(x_k^i / x_{k-1}^i\right)}{q\left(x_k^i / x_{1,\dots k-1}^i, y_{1,\dots k}\right)} \tag{7}$$

Normalization of the weights:

$$w_k^i = \frac{w_k^i}{\sum_{i-1}^{N} w_k^i} \tag{8}$$

Calculate:

$$Neff = \sum_{i-1}^{N} \left(w_k^i\right)^2 \tag{9}$$

Choose a threshold (*N*th). And we test the condition of discrete; if (*Neff* >*N*th): make a multinomial edition of the particles. Otherwise go worm the next stage 10.

Calculation of the vector of estimated state

$$\hat{x}_k = \sum_{i-1}^{N} w_k^i x_k^i \tag{10}$$

SIMULATION RESULTS

In this section, the proposed model on both synthetic data and real data is evaluated. The videos are mainly collected from the UMN dataset and the PETS2009 dataset (Dataset 2009), which have been widely used for performance evaluation. Firstly, results based on the gradient-based acceleration algorithm for estimating the acceleration and velocity on synthetic and real vector fields are showed. Next, the UMN dataset and the PETS2009 dataset are adopted in anomalous frame behavior detection experiments.

Of our application that is the analysis of behavior of crowds, the prediction is chosen according to the characteristic of position of the people (position of the people in the image of individual), to manage to predict the behavior of crowds in an automatic way and to avoid any confusion of behavior. We wish to make the tracking of the people moving according to a rectilinear movement uniformly varied on a plan embellish with images (*X,Y*).

Algorithm 1. Filter particles hybrid Algorithm

1.   Initialization: to draw a sample from particles $\left\{x_0^1, \ldots x_0^N\right\}$

2.   Stage of prediction: to generate a new sample $\left\{x_k^1, \ldots x_k^N\right\}$

3.   Stage of correction: of each particle w_k^i :

$$w_k^i = w_{k-1}^i \frac{f\left(y_k - H_k\left(x_k^i\right)\right) p\left(x_k^i / x_{k-1}^i\right)}{q\left(x_k^i / x_{1,\ldots k-1}^i, y_{1,\ldots k}\right)}$$

4.   Standardization of the weights: $\qquad w_k^i = \dfrac{w_k^i}{\sum_{i-1}^N w_k^i}$

5.   To calculate $Neff = \sum_{i-1}^N \left(w_k^i\right)^2$

6.   To choose a threshold of rééchantillannage $\left(Nth\right)$

7.   To test the condition of rééchantillannage $\left(Neff > Nth\right)$

8.   Calculation of the vector of estimated state: $\qquad \hat{x}_k = \sum_{i-1}^N w_k^i x_k^i$

The vector of state consists of address and phone coordinates x and y there of the center of gravity of nobody in the image, and the speeds according to X which we shall note v_y and according to Y that we shall note v_y in figure 1 (Person in the mark embellishes with images for the tracking). The measures are address and phone coordinates on the image x and it of every point of the trajectory.

We shall thus have the model of following state:

$$\begin{cases} X\left(k+1\right) = AX\left(k\right) + BW\left(k\right) \\ \quad Y\left(k\right) = CX\left(k\right) + V\left(k\right) \end{cases} \tag{11}$$

Such as:

The vector of state at the moment k is $X\left(k\right) = \begin{bmatrix} x\left(k\right) \\ y\left(k\right) \\ v_x\left(k\right) \\ v_y\left(k\right) \end{bmatrix}$, and the vector of measures or observation at

the moment k is $Y\left(k\right) = \begin{bmatrix} x\left(k\right) \\ y\left(k\right) \end{bmatrix}$.

$$A = \begin{bmatrix} 1 & 0 & T & 0 \\ 0 & 1 & 0 & T \\ 0 & 0 & 1 & 0 \\ 0 & 0 & 0 & 1 \end{bmatrix}, B = \begin{bmatrix} \dfrac{T^2}{2} & 0 \\ 0 & \dfrac{T^2}{2} \\ T & 0 \\ 0 & T \end{bmatrix}, C = \begin{bmatrix} 1 & 0 & 0 & 0 \\ 0 & 1 & 0 & 0 \end{bmatrix}$$

T being the period of sampling.

During this simulation, we used a noise of measure of matrix of covariance $R = \begin{bmatrix} 16 & 0 \\ 0 & 16 \end{bmatrix}$, with $x(0)=$ [301515].

Having made the algorithm of filter of KALMAN, we obtain the following results (figure 2 Illustration of the tracking results with filter of KALMAN).

We notice after the results of the tracking one using the filter of KALMAN, that the hypothesis of gaussian models (KALMAN filter) not being still verified in practice. This favors the use of the stochastic techniques based on the simulation of random variables by approximations of Gone Up Carlo, known under the name of the particles filtering. This technique gives us the figure 3 (Illustration of the initialization tracking results with particles filter), such as the blue point represents the initialization of particles before the follow-up of the normal behavior.

We obtain a positive convergence in the case of abnormal behavior (to see figure 4 Illustration of the tracking results with particles filter in the case of abnormal behavior), we notice that particles stacked on the people subjected of an abnormal behavior with the aim of the visual tracking.

We summarize has appear by the advantages and the inconveniences of the approaches of follow-up of the people in the Table 2.

Table 2. Comparison tracking methods

Methods	Advantages	Inconveniences
KALMAN filtre	Follow vehicles or people.	He becomes inadequate in the presence of occlusions or in the presence of follow-up multi-target.
Particules filtre	they are adapted well to follow a trajectory with sudden changes. this method of follow-up seems very promising.	Condition of credit note enough particles to have a good maximum of credibility for the estimated state.

CONCLUSION

This work concerns the use of the pursuit of behavior of crowds in a video by the prediction of the future events of a known behavior based on visual observations. The prediction of the behavior is partially useful to explain the gap from the partial observations due to intermittent visual observations and strongly made sound effects, we have watch that the pursuit by the filter of KALMAN becomes inadequate in the presence of occlusions or in the presence of follow-up multi-target.

REFERENCES

Andrade, E. L., Blunsden, S., & Fisher, R. B. (2006, August). Modelling crowd scenes for event detection. In *18th international conference on pattern recognition (ICPR'06)* (Vol. 1, pp. 175-178). IEEE. 10.1109/ICPR.2006.806

Bishop, G., & Welch, G. (2001). An introduction to the kalman filter. *Proc of SIGGRAPH, Course, 8*(27599-23175), 41.

Chebi, H., & Acheli, D. (2015, December). Dynamic detection of anomalies in crowd's behavior analysis. In *2015 4th International Conference on Electrical Engineering (ICEE)* (pp. 1-5). IEEE. 10.1109/INTEE.2015.7416735

Chebi, H., Acheli, D., & Kesraoui, M. (2017, October). Intelligent Detection Without Modeling of Behavior Unusual by Fuzzy Logic. In *International Conference on Model and Data Engineering* (pp. 300-307). Springer. 10.1007/978-3-319-66854-3_23

Chebi, H., Acheli, D., & Kesraoui, M. (2018). Crowd events recognition in a video without threshold value setting. *International Journal of Applied Pattern Recognition, 5*(2), 101–118. doi:10.1504/IJAPR.2018.092518

Chebi, H., Tabet-Derraz, H., Sayah, R., Meroufel, A., Acheli, D., Benaissa, A., & Meraihi, Y. (2020). Intelligence and Adaptive Global Algorithm Detection of Crowd Behavior. *International Journal of Computer Vision and Image Processing, 10*(1), 24–41. doi:10.4018/IJCVIP.2020010102

Chen, D. Y., & Huang, P. C. (2011). Motion-based unusual event detection in human crowds. *Journal of Visual Communication and Image Representation, 22*(2), 178–186. doi:10.1016/j.jvcir.2010.12.004

Dataset. (2009). *Unusual crowd activity dataset of University of Minnesota.* Available from http://mha.cs.umn.edu/movies/crowdactivity-all.avi

de Almeida, I. R., & Jung, C. R. (2013, August). Change detection in human crowds. In *2013 XXVI Conference on Graphics, Patterns and Images* (pp. 63-69). IEEE. 10.1109/SIBGRAPI.2013.18

Fradi, H., & Dugelay, J. L. (2015). Towards crowd density-aware video surveillance applications. *Information Fusion, 24*, 3–15. doi:10.1016/j.inffus.2014.09.005

Funk, N. (2003). A study of the Kalman filter applied to visual tracking. *University of Alberta, Project for CMPUT, 652*(6).

Gabriel, P. F., Verly, J. G., Piater, J. H., & Genon, A. (2003, September). The state of the art in multiple object tracking under occlusion in video sequences. In Advanced Concepts for Intelligent Vision Systems (pp. 166-173). Academic Press.

Gao, J., Hauptmann, A. G., Bharucha, A., & Wactlar, H. D. (2004, August). Dining activity analysis using a hidden markov model. In *Proceedings of the 17th International Conference on Pattern Recognition, 2004. ICPR 2004* (Vol. 2, pp. 915-918). IEEE.

Horain, P., & Bomb, M. (2002, December). 3D model based gesture acquisition using a single camera. In *Sixth IEEE Workshop on Applications of Computer Vision, 2002.(WACV 2002). Proceedings* (pp. 158-162). IEEE.

Isard, M., & Blake, A. (1998). Condensation—Conditional density propagation for visual tracking. *International Journal of Computer Vision, 29*(1), 5–28. doi:10.1023/A:1008078328650

Ji, Q., & Yang, X. (2002). Real-time eye, gaze, and face pose tracking for monitoring driver vigilance. *Real-Time Imaging, 8*(5), 357–377. doi:10.1006/rtim.2002.0279

Mathes, T., & Piater, J. H. (2006, September). Robust non-rigid object tracking using point distribution manifolds. In *Joint Pattern Recognition Symposium* (pp. 515-524). Springer. 10.1007/11861898_52

McKenna, S. J., Jabri, S., Duric, Z., Rosenfeld, A., & Wechsler, H. (2000). Tracking groups of people. *Computer Vision and Image Understanding, 80*(1), 42–56. doi:10.1006/cviu.2000.0870

Mehran, R., Oyama, A., & Shah, M. (2009, June). Abnormal crowd behavior detection using social force model. In *2009 IEEE Conference on Computer Vision and Pattern Recognition* (pp. 935-942). IEEE. 10.1109/CVPR.2009.5206641

Rabaud, V., & Belongie, S. (2006, June). Counting crowded moving objects. In *2006 IEEE Computer Society Conference on Computer Vision and Pattern Recognition (CVPR'06)* (Vol. 1, pp. 705-711). IEEE.

Serajeh, R., Faez, K., & Ghahnavieh, A. E. (2013, March). Robust multiple human tracking using particle swarm optimization and the Kalman filter on full occlusion conditions. In *2013 First Iranian Conference on Pattern Recognition and Image Analysis (PRIA)* (pp. 1-4). IEEE. 10.1109/PRIA.2013.6528450

Yang, T., Pan, Q., Li, J., & Li, S. Z. (2005, June). Real-time multiple objects tracking with occlusion handling in dynamic scenes. In *2005 IEEE Computer Society Conference on Computer Vision and Pattern Recognition (CVPR'05)* (Vol. 1, pp. 970-975). IEEE. 10.1109/CVPR.2005.292

Chapter 4
Useful Features for Computer-Aided Diagnosis Systems for Melanoma Detection Using Dermoscopic Images

Eugenio Vocaturo

https://orcid.org/0000-0001-7457-7118

DIMES, University of Calabria (UNICAL), Italy & CNR-NANOTEC National Research Council, Italy

Ester Zumpano

DIMES, University of Calabria (UNICAL), Italy

ABSTRACT

The development of performing imaging techniques is favoring the spread of artificial vision systems as support tools for the early diagnosis of skin cancers. Epiluminescence microscopy (ELM) is currently the most adopted technique through which it is possible to obtain very detailed images of skin lesions. Over time, melanoma spreads quickly, invading the body's organs through the blood vessels: an early recognition is essential to ensure decisive intervention. There are many machine learning approaches proposed to implement artificial vision systems operating on datasets made up of dermatoscopic images obtained using ELM technique. These proposals are characterized by the use of various specific features that make understanding difficult: the problem of defining a set of features that can allows good classification performance arises. The aim of this work is to identify reference features that can be used by new researchers as a starting point for new proposals.

INTRODUCTION

The analysis of images for dermatoscopy (DIA) is a very active area of research. The abundance of publications is likely to confuse new researchers who have objective difficulties in identifying new directions to explore.

DOI: 10.4018/978-1-7998-6659-6.ch004

Skin cancer is related to an abnormal development of skin cells and arises when DNA induces a change in skin cells or hereditary deformities. One of the main reasons for the onset of skin cancer are the ultraviolet (UV) radiation of both UVA and UVB sunlight. Melanoma is a particularly aggressive form of skin cancer, which can easily spread from one part of the body to another.

Practically, the doctor who examines the patient's skin takes the first step in diagnosing melanoma. If the specialist notices some significant variation in the size, color, shape and texture of the mole, the patient is referred to as pathologist or dermatologist, which by biopsy confirms or not the presence of skin cancer. Biopsy is a clinical method that involves the excision of portions of skin tissues subsequently used to diagnose skin cancer. The biopsy is invasive and involves up to 12 weeks of awaiting for the results.

Dermatoscopy or epiluminescence microscopy (ELM) is an increasingly used technique for detecting skin cancer because it allows the analysis of enlarged images (usually × 20) being also a non-invasive skin imaging technique. Dermatologists acquire the image of the affected skin through a particular tool called dermatoscopy, and discriminate the nature of the skin lesion, applying clinical protocols such as the ABCDE rules (AAD 2019) (Asymmetry, Border, Color, Diameter and Evolution), 7-point checklist (Argenziano et al., 1998), CASH (Color, Architecture, Symmetry and Homogeneity) (Henning et al., 2007) and the Menzies method (Menzies et al., 1996).

The medical scientific community looks with increasing interest to artificial vision systems for the classification of skin lesions. Early diagnosis and removal become essential when the tumor is in the early stages. This justifies the common interest in providing solutions that support early and accurate diagnosis, facilitating both the work of specialists and effective self-diagnosis through mobile applications.

The diagnosis of melanoma through automated analyzes is not yet reliable and the diagnostic accuracy still depends on the experience of dermatologists: the current interest is directed towards a solution capable of offering a second opinion to the specialist.

The World Health Organization reports that in 2018 more than 60.000 persons died due to melanoma and the new cases are over 28.0000 (International Agency for Research on Cancer, 2019). Melanoma is affecting both male and female populations of the whole world, and in particular that of North America, Australia and Europe (Figure 1).

If on one hand the cutaneous melanoma is fearful for its aggressiveness and for its ability to spread quickly to other organs, on the other hand when it is diagnosed in the initial stages it can be simply managed. Unfortunately, however, in the early stages melanoma appears similar to other benign lesions. These assumptions amplify the need to create automatic systems capable of supporting the diagnosis of melanoma from the initial stage. In general, these solutions provide a series of steps including: image acquisition, image pre-processing, segmentation, features extraction and finally classification.

Among the different phases of a CAD system, the most relevant is that of features extraction. The aim of this work is to identify reference features that can be used as a starting point for new proposals.

In Section II, to help the reader understand visual differentiation, the optical properties of skin layers are addressed. In Section III, referring to the literature, the general aspects of image acquisition, pre-processing and segmentation are introduced while in Section IV an overview on useful features that can be taken in considerations by new researchers as profitable starting set on dermoscopic images is reported. Finally, some conclusions are drawn.

Figure 1. Statistics on Melanoma in 2018
(International Agency for Research on Cancer, 2019)

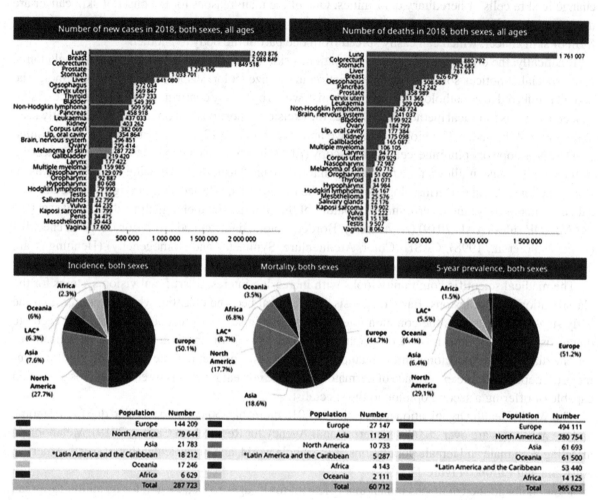

BACKGROUND

Optical Properties of Skin Layers

The optical properties of the skin layers vary according to their composition. If the skin is exposed to a source of white light, only a part penetrates the superficial layers being absorbed, while the majority is reflected. This behavior on exposure to light allows the resulting signal to be recorded using suitable digital equipment.

The epidermis is the outermost layer visible to the naked eye (Figure 2), and constitutes an impermeable barrier that protects our body from bacteria and all other microorganisms that are present in the surrounding environment. The epidermis is composed of connective tissues and also contains melanocytes a particular type of cell capable of producing melanin.

Figure 2. Skin Layers
[depositphtos.com]

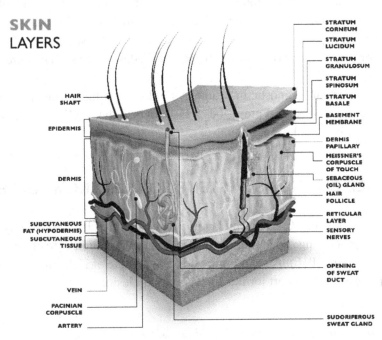

Melanin is a pigment that strongly absorbs light in the blue part of the visible spectrum, effectively acting as a protective filter against UV radiation; not all light is absorbed by melanin: excess light can harmfully pass through the dermis which contains sensors, receptors, blood vessels and nerve ends.

Visually, pigmented skin lesions appears like darker spots often due to an excessive concentration of melanin in the skin. Melanin plays a fundamental role as regards the nature of the skin lesions (Figure 3). In fact, while in benign lesions (common nevi), melanin deposits are normally found in the epidermis, in melanoma, melanocytes reproduce melanin at a higher rate, invading the dermis.

Figure 3. Melanin's role in the nature of skin lesions
[depositphtos.com]

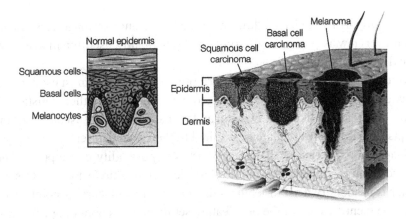

These triggers fibrosis or the thickening of collagen fibers typically occurs with the increase in the blood supply to the periphery of the lesion (erythematic reaction) together the lack of blood inside the lesion. The presence of melanin in the dermis is indicative of melanoma in situ, although some benign nevi can manifest dermal deposits of melanin but with a more regular structure.

Color is a first indicator of melanoma, as characteristic shades can be seen that are not found in other skin conditions.

This provides an important diagnostic indication for a doctor. If the visual approach corroborates a suspicion of skin cancer, the specialist prescribes a histology analysis (Claridge et al., 2003) to dispel the doubt about the nature of the lesion.

COMPUTER AIDED DIAGNOSIS SYSTEMS FOR MELANOMA DETECTION

Tipically, the proposals of every CAD for melanoma detection are characterized by the same phases (Figure 4): image pre-processing, image segmentation, feature selection/extraction, and finally classification (Kasmi & Mokrani, 2016). Also in Figure 4 is an example of instrumentation equipped with a dermatoscope for professional support for the analysis of skin lesions.

Figure 4. Fundamental steps of Computer Aided Diagnosis Systems.

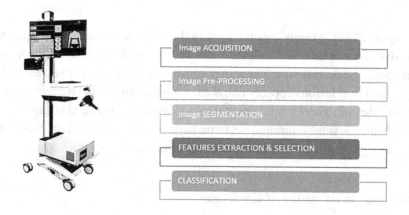

In order to give support for understanding the issue of melanoma image classification, in the following section an overview is presented of some methods mainly used for image acquisition, image pre-processing and segmentation.

In a dedicated section focus is made on the description of the features most used for CAD implementations. Color, texture, shape, and also histogram, geometric and many other statistical features as well as clinical dermoscopic features like ABCD, local and global patterns are used for melanoma detection. Each author adopts sets of features that are best suited to their own dataset.

Several challenges arise: a first challenge concerns the possibility of supporting new researchers who undertake studies on the issue of automatic classification of skin lesions. In this sense, the objective of this chapter is to identify a set of features that can be a valid starting point. Another important challenge regards the identification of the best feature set that allows obtaining good classification and computational time results. An absolute valid choice is not easily identifiable depending on the specific choices of each case (Alkawaz et al., 2018; Khan et al., 2017; Sharif et al., 2017).

Image Acquisition Methods

Many are the techniques used for the acquisition of skin digital images, each of which has strengths and weaknesses, being more or less suitable for the specific case. Among the most adopted technique for Computer Aided Diagnosis (CAD) systems must be considered total cutaneous photography, confocal scanning laser microscopy (CSLM), multifrequency electrical impedance, dermoscopy, ultrasound, optical coherence tomography (OCT), magnetic resonance imaging (MRI), computed tomography (CT), multispectral imaging, positron emission tomography (PET), Transmission electron microscopy (TEM) and Raman spectra. Recent overviews which compare some of the existing screening techniques are (Vocaturo et al., 2018; Giuffrida et al., 2020).

Transmission electron microscopy (TEM), is used to screen the melanoma's development when the lesion is in the dermis (Aberg et al., 2004). The light source via the lateral transillumination makes translucent the superficial and the sub-surface layers of the skin, allowing to ascertain the vascularization of the lesion and the colorimetric variations of the pigmentation.

Another aspect strongly indicative of the presence of melanoma is the variation of the texture of the skin. The Epiluminescence microscopy (ELM, or dermoscopy) it is establishing itself as one of the most popular techniques because in addition to allowing the evaluation of color, permits an in-depth analysis of the surface texture of skin.

To evaluate the evolution of melanoma and patient's response Computed tomography (CT) images have been used (Sigurdsson et al., 2004).

When it is suspected that melanoma has spread to the various layers of the skin must be adopted a useful diagnostic method for examining the potential metastatic of cutaneous melanoma. In this case Positron Emission Tomography (PET) is often adopted. PET, using fluoro-deoxyglucose, allows to evaluate the rate of proliferation and the degree of malignancy of a given tumor (Loane et al., 1997).

Techniques that well support the screening stages are multi-frequency electrical impedance (Singh et al., 2001) and Raman spectra (Maier et al., 2015). The electrical impedance of a biological material is associated with the physical properties of the tissue. Raman spectra are obtained by aiming a laser beam at a sample of skin lesion. The laser beam excites the molecules in the sample and a dispersion effect returns useful information on the physical structure of skin lesion.

Framework designed for professional use as well as end-user mobile applications require the development of new image classification algorithms capable of operating on unlabeled data that do not require manual segmentation by experts.

Various type of Machine Learning approaches have been applied for automated melanoma detection (Vocaturo et al., 2019a). New classification approaches, such as Multiple Instance Learning, Active Learning and Transfer Learning, are currently being studied (Cheplygina et al., 2019; Quellec et al., 2017; Gaudioso et al., 2019). In particular, very recent MIL applications provide interesting results regarding the classification of melanoma from benign nevi (Astorino et al., 2020; Fuduli et al., 2019), melanoma from dysplastic nevi (Vocaturo & Zumpano, 2019) and dysplastic nevi from common ones (Vocaturo & Zumpano, 2020).

The developments of increasingly high-performance cameras with which smartphones are equipped, together with the usability of the internet connection, fuel the possibility of creating mobile applications aimed at self-diagnosis of skin lesions. What has been said is in line with the affirmation of new patient-led healthcare models, capable of supporting the decision-making and responsibility processes of the medical component also through predictive aspects approaches (Vocaturo & Veltri, 2017).

Image Pre-Processing

The pre-processing phase is fundamental to optimize the quality of the images, removing all the artifacts and causes of noise that can invalidate the automatic diagnosis.The presence of hair or of irregular lighting on dermoscopic images, for example, make difficult the separation of the lesion area from healthy skin. For this reason, anything that influences the image has to be traced and then removed, masked or replaced.

In literature, we find many proposals such as image resizing, masking, cropping, hair removal and the conversion from RGB to grayscale images.

To easily remove unwanted traces it is useful to use different filters such as peer group filter (Malinski & Smolka, 2016), medium filters, median filter (Maglogiannis et al., 2005) or Gaussian filters (Anantha et al., 2004). These filters are directly applied on grayscale images, while on color images they are separately applied on each channel according to marginal filtering approach.

There is no single prescription that can eliminate all causes of noise: a good system would be to use purposeful solutions for each type of unwelcome traces. Among the most valuable techniques, the transformation of color space via change of color coordinates and the quantization of color are often used to minimize the number of colors to be managed in the image analysis.

Even less contrast complicates the detection of edges in dermoscopic images; this problem has been addressed with the independent histogram search (IHP) (Gomez et al., 2007), which provides for the determination of an elongation histogram which expands the pixel values on the interval [0, 255], and the use of the equalization histogram, to obtain a uniform distribution of the pixel values.

Monomorphic filtering, (FFT) and high-pass filter were used to highlight the maximum contrast between lesion and healthy skin to make up for irregular illumination. In literature, other authors faced problems concerning removing air bubbles and dermoscopic gels, often adopting medial filter, even in an adaptive and recursive weighted manner (Tafti & Mirsadeghi, 2012). The processing of a local portion of image is carried out, considering a square neighborhood, usually named *blob*, of certain pixels with the aim to assign the median value to the central one: the point noise at very high frequencies are so eliminated containing the variations in the image.

Another element that disturbs the analysis based on dermoscopic images is the presence of hairs. Different proposals have been made for cleaning images but most of these techniques often leave undesirable blurring, so it becomes difficult to use them for further differentiation of skin cancer.

Among the most referred ones some approaches refer to the use of morphological operators applied to images (Schmid, 1999) while others use curvilinear structures (Fleming et al., 1998), and others have foreseen the use of inpainting (Wighton et al., 2008).

Zhou et al. in 2009 presented an algorithm focusing on the detection of curvilinear traces concerning the structure of the lesion (Zhou et al., 2009). This approach allows the removal of hair marks but needs high computational requirements.

All the referred strategies, like the ones present in literature, aim to simplify the segmentation phase allowing to valid features extraction operations. Recent studies focus on pre-processing techniques used for automatic image analysis in various machine learning approaches, showing how the adoption of pre-processing steps effectively improve the classification performances (Vocaturo et al., 2018; Vocaturo et al., 2019b).

Image Segmentation

Image segmentation is a fundamental step in the implementation of systems for the automatic diagnosis of skin lesions. Some recent interesting proposals present automatic tools through which an effective segmentation phase could be obtained.

In (Jain & Pise, 2015) a computer aided method for the detection of Melanoma Skin Cancer using Image Processing tools was presented, by applying novel image processing techniques. The combination of an automatic threshold and masking operation in the R, G and B planes is adopted to perform image segmentation. The automatic thresholding proposed by Otsu is applied to each single plane and the final mask of the lesion is obtained by juxtaposing the masks of the single planes.

In (Pennisi et al., 2016), the authors present "Delaunay Triangulation", a very rapid automated algorithm capable of generating a binary mask of the lesion, without the need for training phases.

More precisely, the authors conduct a quantitative experimental evaluation on a publicly available database, by taking into account well-known state-of-the-art segmentation methods.

In order to effectively determine the characteristics it is necessary to isolate the lesion from the surrounding normal skin. In fact, typically, the various proposals of Computer Aided Diagnosis systems use the segmentation phases to separate skin lesion from healthy skin (Figure 5).

The black and white mask is used to face an accurate edge detection of skin lesion: this operation is essential to quantify the geometric features of the lesion like area, perimeter and maximum diameter and features for evaluating lesion symmetry of the melanoma. Among the most adopted types of segmentation methods have to be mentioned:

- **Threshold Base:** Which includes methods like the Otsu method, maximum entropy, the local and global threshold, and histogram based methods.
- **Region-Based:** Which includes growth of the sown region, and watershed segmentation methods.
- **Pixel-Based:** Including various methods like fuzzy c-means clustering, random field Markov and artificial neural network.
- **Model-Based:** Methods used for specific application contexts such as the deformable parametric or layer sets models.

The simultaneous use of features of different types such as color, structure, shape, size favors an early diagnosis of malignant melanoma and other types of skin cancer (Tanaka et al., 2008).

Figure 5. (a) original image (b) segmented image
(Mendonça et al., 2013)

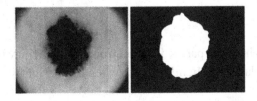

Once the skin lesion is separated from healthy skin, it's possible to apply various algorithms (Astorino et al., 2017, 2018, 2019) to extract both globally and locally features through which it's possible to classify lesion as benign or malignant.

MAIN FOCUS OF THE CHAPTER

Features for Melanoma Detection

Segmentation steps have like main goal the separation of skin lesion from healthy regions allowing the successive features evaluation useful for melanoma detection. When dealing with automatic classification of medical images, one of the most delicate aspects is related to the choice of features.

The scientific community is trying to realize Computer Vision System able to pull out the features borrowing them from the traditional diagnostic analysis protocols. The aim is to obtain a reliable classification of skin lesions identifying cases of malignant melanoma, dysplastic nevi or common nevi. The already mentioned ABCD system, the 7-point checklist, CASH and Menzies method are protocols that inspired the researchers for the choice of features in CAD.

In the ABCD rule clinical diagnosis is highly reliable, also with little computational implication. Therefore, a lot of automated decision support systems are based on the ABCD rule or the 7-point checklist for features extraction step. On the other hand, the best sensitivity conduct is reached with solutions based on Menzies method as shown in different studies (Dolianitis et al., 2005). Several studies have also revealed the effectiveness of the edge shape descriptors for the noticing of malignant melanoma both in clinical and in computerized assessment methods (Maglogiannis & Doukas, 2009; Zumpano et al., 2018).

Features extraction is the most important step among the various phases of the CAD systems, for which in literature there is a great variety of proposals. In (Celebi et al., 2015) the authors focus on edge detection of the lesion in dermoscopic images, while in (Barata et al., 2018) the authors analyze the use of different types of features, highlighting their relevance and limitations.

An exhaustive categorization of the most referenced features for melanoma classification includes features of four principal categories:

- Asymmetry,
- Border,
- Color,
- Texture.

The goal of this work is to refer to the features that are most suitable as a starting configuration for the study of new proposals for automated melanoma detection. In particular, reference will be made to features that can be used considering datasets of dermatoscopic images.

Asymmetry

Asymmetrical skin growths, where one part is different from the other, may indicate melanoma. In Figure 6, the left side of the mole is dark and slightly raised, whereas the right side is lighter in color and flat.

Figure 6. Asymmetry of Melanomas
(Sawatsky et al., 2010)

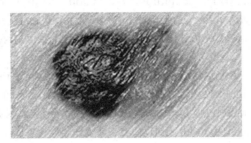

Asymmetry features were immediately used in CAD implementations inspired by the protocol of seven-point checklist (7-PCL) (Argenziano et al. 1998; Betta et al., 2005). 7-PCL is an identification protocol made up of seven criteria that consider both the colorful characteristics and those related to the shape and structure of the lesion. The dermoscopic image of a melanocytic skin lesion is examined looking at the presence of standard criteria, and if the total score obtained is more than three, that indicates that the injury is malignant, leading the patient to a professional visit.

Asymmetry index is used to measure the asymmetry by folding the outline of the lesion about its chord of the best-fit ellipse, evaluating the difference and the percentage of the difference over the area of lesion is calculated:

$$AS = \frac{\Delta T}{T} * 100\%$$

where, ΔT is the number of pixels in area of difference (Moussa et al., 2016).

Figure 7. Asymmetry axes for Melanomas detection

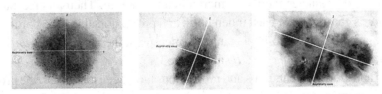

To assess asymmetry, the melanocytic lesion is bisected by two 90° axes that were positioned to produce the lowest possible asymmetry score. If both axes dermoscopically show asymmetric contours with regard to shape, colors and/or dermoscopic structures, the asymmetry score is 2, while the score is 1 when asymmetry involves on one axis. If asymmetry is absent with regard to both axes the score is 0 (Figure 7).

Typically, dermatologists judge asymmetry by comparing the two halves of the lesion according to the principal axis. Stoecker et al., presented an algorithm able to judge an asymmetry index of the lesion, looking at principal axis: if a symmetric lesion occurs the principal axis matches with the symmetry ones (Stoecker et al., 2005). This index is obtained by defining a percentage of asymmetry, considering the smallest difference between the image area of the lesion and the image of the reflected lesion from the main axis. In (Cudek et al., 2011), the authors take in consideration the center of gravity of the lesion, and calculate the asymmetry index starting from the differences between the areas defined by the 180 axes. Then, an array of radii is created to assess the potential axis of symmetry, based on which the lesions are classified.

Lengthening index is another used features which describe the lengthening and the anisotropy degree of the lesion. This index is related to eigenvalues λ', λ'' of the inertia matrix, and is defined according the relationship between the moment of inertia around the principal axis λ' and the moment of inertia around the secondary axis λ'' (Celebi et al., 2007).

$$A = \frac{\lambda'}{\lambda''} \ with \ \lambda' = \frac{m_{20} - m_{02} - \sqrt{\left(m_{20} - m_{02}\right) + 4\left(m_{11}\right)^2}}{2}$$

$$\lambda'' = \frac{m_{20} + m_{02} + \sqrt{\left(m_{20} - m_{02}\right)^2 + 4\left(m_{11}\right)^2}}{2}$$

where m_{11}, m_{20} and m_{02} represent respectably the standard moment, quadratic moment according to the horizontal Cartesian axis and quadratic moment according to the vertical Cartesian axis. Asymmetry is a quantifiable property, that can be used to distinguish and characterize melanomas.

Border

One of the important clinical features that differentiates benign melanocytic nevi from malignant melanomas is the irregularity of the lesion border. Referring to structure irregularities, the global indentations and protrusions are associated with how far a skin lesion moves away from a regular and rounded shape.

In (Lee & Atkins, 2000), the author proposed an approach for measuring the structure irregularities in the border. More in particular, the proposed algorithm first locates all the local and global indentations and protrusions and organizes them in a hierarchical structure. Then an area-based index, called the *irregularity index*, is computed for each indentation and protrusion along the border (Figure 8). From the individual irregularity indices, two important new measures, the *most significant irregularity index (MSII)* and the *overall irregularity index (OII)* are derived.

Once all the local and global indentations and protrusions have been identified, the proposed algorithm calculates for each of them an *irregularity index* based on the area (Figure 7). The *Most Significant Irregularity Index (MSII)* and the *Overall Irregularity Index (OII)* derive from the individual irregularity indices.

$$MSII = \max\{I_1, I_2, ..., I_n\}$$

$$OII = \sum_{j=1}^{n} I_j$$

where,

$$I_j = \frac{\Delta_j}{R_j}$$

These two new indices provide a measure of the degree of irregularity along the lesion border. The user study showed that both of the new indices vastly outperformed the other shape descriptors.

Figure 8. MSII e OII
(Lee & Atkins, 2000)

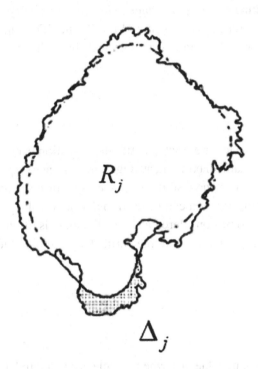

Among the most used shape factors have to be mentioned, referring to the seminal works: the larger diameter, area, edge irregularity, thinness ratio (Argenziano & Giorgy, 2002), aspect ratio (Nathanson, 2012), circularity index (CIRC), variance of the distance between points of the frontal lesions to the centroid position (Schindewolf et al.,1994), the compactness shape factor (Grana et al., 2003), the fractal analysis (Lee et al., 1997) and Simmetry Distance (Stanley et al., 2007).

Aspect ratio is a function that relates the largest diameter and the smallest diameter orthogonal to it. The normalized aspect ratio is approaching zero for a very elongated particle, such as a grain in a cold-worked metal, to near unity for an equiaxed grain. An alternative used index is the reciprocal of the right side of the above equation; in this case the index varies from one to approaching infinity.

$$A_R = \frac{d_{min}}{d_{max}}$$

Circularity index or isoperimetric quotient is defined as a function of perimeter P and area A. The circularity index for a circle is equal to 1, and it is much less than one for a starfish footprint. An alternative used index is the reciprocal of the circularity index; in this case the index varies from one to infinity.

$$Circ = \frac{4A\pi}{P^2}$$

Simmetry Distance (SD) calculates the average displacement between a number of vertices when a transformation is applied making the original shape symmetrical. The symmetrical form closest to the original form P is called the symmetry transform (ST) of P. The SD of an object depends on the effort required to transform the original shape into a symmetrical shape. It's calculated as follows:

$$SD = \frac{1}{n}\sum_{i=0}^{n-1}\left\|P_i - \widehat{P}_i\right\|$$

Emphasis is also placed on the features that quantify the transition from the lesion to the skin (Stanley et al., 2007). Features like minimum, maximum, average, and variance responses of the gradient operator applied on the intensity image along the lesion border are used for these measures.

Thinness Ratio (TR) and polygon area can be used to define how large or small the gap or overlapping area can be in order for it to be considered a sliver. Thinness is often used to define the regularity of an object. After calculating the area (A) and the perimeter (P) of an object, the thinness ratio can be defined as:

$$TR = 4\pi\frac{A}{p^2}$$

This measure takes a maximum value of 1 when a circle is considered. Objects of regular shape have a higher TR than similar irregular ones. Generally, TR's value is less than 1.

In image segmentation a very critical task is the identification of the border of the lesions that aims at separating the skin lesion from the healthy skin. Innovative approaches use algorithms capturing active contours (Psaty et al., 2009) and combine color transformation and edge detection techniques. An interesting comparison of some of the most popular methods is reported in (Nakariyakul et al., 2008).

Color

A recurring approach of the first CAD proposals involved the analysis of lesions in a clinical perspective similarly to that of dermatologists (Celebi et al., 2008; Barata et al., 2008; Sadeghiet al., 2013). Considering that one of the more relevant dermoscopic characteristics is color, dermatologists usual can either count the number of colors in the lesion or search for relevant color structures. Both approaches have been investigated, and CAD systems have been proposed that perform the former (Celebi & Zornberg, 2014) or the latter (Di Leo et al., 2009; Madooei et al., 2013). For that matter, a common approach is to extract statistical parameters from color channels as color features. Typically, basic statistical measures such as mean, standard deviation, the ratio of these (which is the same as the signal-to-noise ratio), variance, skewness, kurtosis, and entropy of each channel as color features are computed (Celebi et al., 2015). Each of the above-mentioned statistical measures is a scalar, calculated separately for each color channel.

Even in recent CAD proposals, which also tend to follow different approaches than the clinical ones, color variations constitute a discriminating element for the classification of the lesion between benign and malignant melanoma (Oliveira et al., 2019; Afza et al., 2019; Nasir et al., 2018) as well as statistical parameters are adopted to describe color features (Barata et al., 2014; Rastgoo et al., 2015; Ma & Tavares, 2017).

The skin lesion can present itself in different ways depending on how the melanin deposit in the different skin layers. More precisely, melanin appears as black in the upper epidermis, slate blue in the papillary dermis, steel blue in the reticular dermis and light brown-brown in the dermo-epidermal junction. Any red tinge is indicative of bleeding, and of an increased vascularization in a tumor.

Typically dermatoscopic images are in RGB format and are usually managed through the individual red, green and blue color channels. In many proposals, images have been used in different color spaces using different color channels like cyan, magenta, yellow (CMY) or hue, saturation, value (HSV). The evaluation of the change of colors can be appreciated by enhancing the chromatic differences within the lesion and by measuring the minimum deviations, maximum, averages and standards of the values of the selected channels and through the intensity of the color. An alternative method, presented in (Stanley et al., 2007) estimates the skin colors based on the normal skin structure model.

A color space is a geometrical and mathematical representation of color. There is no general method that is applicable to all domains; the number of variables involved make for complexity such that a complete theoretical analysis is not feasible in most practical applications. In any problem of color quantification, the first step toward a solution is to define the color space. Historically, many different representations have been defined, but each was developed for a specific purpose. Since color information plays an inevitable role in skin cancer detection systems, researchers try to extract the more closely related color of images for further processing.

RGB, HSV, HSI, CIE LAB and CIE-XYZ are the most adopted color spaces. RGB, as can easily be deduced from its acronym, is a color space which comprises the red, green, and blue spectral wavelength. The most frequent presentation of colors in image processing is RGB, which however has some limitation in high level processing; for these reasons other color space representations have been developed as reported in the seminal work (Umbaugh et al., 1991). The HSV and HSI color spaces are also very popular in the application field since they have been obtained by imitating the human visual perception of color in terms of hue, saturation and intensity, translating it in terms of average wavelength of the color, the amount of white in color and brightness.

One of the steps that must be taken into account optimizing an image, is a correct evaluation of the color space most appropriate to the context of interest. Image transformations in different color spaces may be necessary.

In view of the purposes of this chapter, new researchers can effectively refer to situations involving the use of RGB images that can be managed through the individual red, green and blue color channels. Subsequent attempts to refine the search can consider the transformation of an image into a different color space defining the values of the new channels starting from the values of the RGB channels. Considering for example the transformation from RGB to HIS color space which follows (Umbaugh, et al., 1991):

$$
\begin{cases}
I = \dfrac{(R + G + B)}{3} \\[2mm]
S = 1 - \dfrac{3}{(R + G + B)} \cdot \min(R + G + B) \\[2mm]
W = \arccos \dfrac{R - \dfrac{1}{2}(G + B)}{\sqrt{(R - G)^2 - (R - B)(G - B)}}
\end{cases}
$$

where hue is defined as follow:

$$
H \begin{cases}
W \longrightarrow if \ \ G > B \\[1mm]
(2\pi - W) \longrightarrow G < B \\[1mm]
0 \longrightarrow if \ \ G = B
\end{cases}
$$

The change of colors can be appreciated by measuring the minimum deviations, maximum, averages and standards of the values of the selected channels and through the intensity of the color, enhancing the chromatic differences within the lesion (Sheha et al., 2016).

Texture Analysis

Skin texture withholds the native property and information of skin itself. Texture introduces the connection between spatial neighborhood pixels and gray values of image space, having both regular and statistical peculiarities. So, one single method is not enough to efficiently analyze all texture features.

In literature, four kinds of methods are mainly used to analyze texture: (1) statistical techniques, (2) model-based techniques, (3) structural techniques, and (4) transform-based techniques.

Statistical methods include descriptors like gray level co-occurrence matrix (GLCM) which is the classical second-order statistics method, edge frequency, run-length matrices (RLM) and gray level histogram. The statistical method is used where a texture primitives or texture elements are not easily recognized.

Structural methods are frequently used for pattern identification applications based on topological and geometrical properties.

Model-based methods contained fractal and stochastic models such as Gaussian Markov random field (GMRF), autoregressive (AR) model and fractional Brownian motion (fBm).

Transform based methods used spatial frequency properties to interpret the image into a new form like Fourier, Gabor, and wavelet transforms (Chatterjee et al., 2018).

To reduce the useless data, most researchers use gray level co-occurrence matrix (GLCM) (Jaworek-Korjakowska & Kłeczek, 2016; Mohanaiah et al., 2013), decision boundary feature extraction (Woo & Lee, 2018), principal component analysis (PCA), Gaussian derivative kernels, wavelet packet transform (WPT) (Clausi & Deng 2005) and Fourier power spectrum for extraction of skin texture features.

The information that concerns lesion plot is taken by analyzing the textures; the features extracted are typically statistical and structural. Statistical methods describe the plot as regards to local statistics by concentrating on the gray levels that, in a particular area of the lesion, can remain constant or differ more or less slowly. An initial set of features to consider includes (Anantha et al., 2004):

Neighboring gray-level dependence matrix (NGLDM) is adopted for the detection of the pigmented network on skin lesions (Anantha et al., 2004). To detect the contrast, the measure called dissimilarity *d* is introduced. This measure becomes concrete when moving away from the diagonal of the co-occurrence matrix of the gray level (GLCM). A formulation of dissimilarity is as follows:

$$d = \sum_{i,j=0}^{N-1} P_{i,j} \left| i - j \right|$$

in which *i* indicates the row number, *j indicates* the column number, *N* is the total number of rows and columns of the GLCM matrix, and

$$P_{i,j} = V_{i,j} \Big/ \sum_{i,j=0}^{N-1} V_{i,j}$$

indicates the normalization equation in which $V_{i,j}$ is the current gray-scale pixel value or more formally the digital number (DN) value of the cell *i, j* in the image window.

Angular second moment (ASM), is a measure related to orderliness, where $P_{i,j}$ is used as a weight to itself, and is given by:

$$ASM = \sum_{i,j=0}^{N-1} i \cdot P_{i,j}^{\,2}$$

GLCM mean, μ_i, is a measure that denotes the frequency of the occurrence of one pixel value in combination with a certain neighbor pixel value, and is given by:

$$\mu_i = \sum_{i,j=0}^{N-1} i \cdot (P_{i,j})$$

GLCM standard deviation, σ_i which gives a measure of the dispersion of the values around the mean, and is given by:

$$\sigma_i = \sqrt{\sum_{i,j=0}^{N-1} P_{i,j} (i - \mu_i)^2}$$

From the studies presented in literature it has been possible to appreciate how various proposals for computer skin lesions identification, often adopt color and texture features by resorting to what is presented in this paragraph, or rather deriving specific features from those referred to here or presenting new approaches.

For example, in (Ruela et al., 2017), the authors presented a very interesting approach that combines both global and local features. Starting from the original image, the authors evaluate as local features a bag of features while global features are shape and geometric-based. Local and global features are fused using an early and late fusion steps obtaining good results on PH_2 dataset (Mendonça, et al., 2013).

DISCUSSION AND CONCLUSION

Even according to recent literature, there is no fix efficient features set which is dedicated for skin lesion segmentation (Oliveira et al., 2019) and melanoma classification: various features gave different results on different datasets. In (Shoieb et al. 2016), the authors carried out a comparison among hand-crafted features and deep learning showing that the adoption of hand-crafted features gave better results on a certain number of datasets. In (Abbes & Sellami, 2016), the authors demonstrate that using high level features (asymmetric, border, color, texture) it's possible to obtain better results in term of sensitivity (92%) and a specificity (95%) on more than 200 datasets as compared to low level features. Ma and Tavares, presented a comparative study exploring a list of features along with 36 colors, and 14 shape features tested by 250 classifications task, verifying extremely long computational time (Ma & Tavares 2017). In general, numerous researches are conducted considering specific features sets for automatic detection of melanoma (Abuzaghleh et al., 2015).

In this chapter Computer Aided Diagnosis systems for melanoma detection are referred, calling the main issues for acquisition, pre-processing and segmentation steps. Regarding the particular context of DIA (Dermatoscopy Image Analysis) several proposals omit the meaning and formulation of features.

Today again, there is no definitive set of features that can be applied to any context: researchers who approach CAD issues are not clear which features to start using and why, thus the problem of indicating the most recurrent and significant features useful to analyze dermoscopic images arises. Our intent was to provide a clear, quick and streamlined view to address the issues of automatic classification of melanoma.

ACKNOWLEDGMENT

Sincere thanks to Mrs Sonia Fortino for her precious support.

REFERENCES

AAD. (n.d.). *Melanoma: Signs and symptoms*. https://www.aad.org/public/diseases/skin-cancer/melanoma

Abbes, W., & Sellami, D. (2016, November). High-level features for automatic skin lesions neural network based classification. In *2016 International Image Processing, Applications and Systems (IPAS)* (pp. 1-7). IEEE.

Aberg, P., Nicander, I., Hansson, J., Geladi, P., Holmgren, U., & Ollmar, S. (2004). Skin cancer identification using multifrequency electrical impedance-a potential screening tool. *IEEE Transactions on Biomedical Engineering*, *51*(12), 2097–2102. doi:10.1109/TBME.2004.836523 PMID:15605856

Abuzaghleh, O., Faezipour, M., & Barkana, B. D. (2015, May). A comparison of feature sets for an automated skin lesion analysis system for melanoma early detection and prevention. In *2015 Long Island Systems, Applications and Technology* (pp. 1-6). IEEE.

Afza, F., Khan, M. A., Sharif, M., & Rehman, A. (2019). Microscopic skin laceration segmentation and classification: A framework of statistical normal distribution and optimal feature selection. *Microscopy Research and Technique*, 82(9), 1471–1488. doi:10.1002/jemt.23301 PMID:31168871

Alkawaz, M. H., Sulong, G., Saba, T., & Rehman, A. (2018). Detection of copy-move image forgery based on discrete cosine transform. *Neural Computing & Applications*, 30(1), 183–192. doi:10.100700521-016-2663-3

Anantha, M., Moss, R. H., & Stoecker, W. V. (2004). Detection of pigment network in dermatoscopy images using texture analysis. *Computerized Medical Imaging and Graphics*, 28(5), 225–234. doi:10.1016/j.compmedimag.2004.04.002 PMID:15249068

Argenziano & Giorgy. (2002). Interactive Atlas of Dermoscopy. Dermoscopy Tutorial: Vascular Structures. EDRA Medical Publishing & New Media.

Argenziano, G., Fabbrocini, G., Carli, P., De Giorgi, V., Sammarco, E., & Delfino, M. (1998). Epiluminescence microscopy for the diagnosis of doubtful melanocytic skin lesions: Comparison of the ABCD rule of dermatoscopy and a new 7-point checklist based on pattern analysis. *Archives of Dermatology*, 134(12), 1563–1570. doi:10.1001/archderm.134.12.1563 PMID:9875194

Astorino, A., Fuduli, A., Gaudioso, M., & Vocaturo, E. (2018, June). A multiple instance learning algorithm for color images classification. In *Proceedings of the 22nd International Database Engineering & Applications Symposium* (pp. 262-266). 10.1145/3216122.3216144

Astorino, A., Fuduli, A., Gaudioso, M., & Vocaturo, E. (2019, June). Multiple Instance Learning algorithm for medical image classification. In CEUR Workshop Proceedings (Vol. 2400). Academic Press.

Astorino, A., Fuduli, A., Veltri, P., & Vocaturo, E. (2017, November). On a recent algorithm for multiple instance learning. Preliminary applications in image classification. In *2017 IEEE international conference on bioinformatics and biomedicine (BIBM)* (pp. 1615-1619). IEEE.

Astorino, A., Fuduli, A., Veltri, P., & Vocaturo, E. (2020). Melanoma detection by means of multiple instance learning. *Interdisciplinary Sciences, Computational Life Sciences*, 12(1), 24–31. doi:10.100712539-019-00341-y PMID:31292853

Barata, C., Celebi, M. E., & Marques, J. S. (2018). A survey of feature extraction in dermoscopy image analysis of skin cancer. *IEEE Journal of Biomedical and Health Informatics*, 23(3), 1096–1109. doi:10.1109/JBHI.2018.2845939 PMID:29994234

Barata, C., Marques, J. S., & Rozeira, J. (2012). A system for the detection of pigment network in dermoscopy images using directional filters. *IEEE Transactions on Biomedical Engineering*, 59(10), 2744–2754. doi:10.1109/TBME.2012.2209423 PMID:22829364

Barata, C., Ruela, M., Mendonça, T., & Marques, J. S. (2014). A bag-of-features approach for the classification of melanomas in dermoscopy images: The role of color and texture descriptors. In *Computer vision techniques for the diagnosis of skin cancer* (pp. 49–69). Berlin: Springer. doi:10.1007/978-3-642-39608-3_3

Betta, G., Di Leo, G., Fabbrocini, G., Paolillo, A., & Scalvenzi, M. (2005, May). Automated Application of the "7-point checklist" Diagnosis Method for Skin Lesions: Estimation of Chromatic and Shape Parameters. In *2005 IEEE Instrumentationand Measurement Technology Conference Proceedings* (Vol. 3, pp. 1818-1822). IEEE. 10.1109/IMTC.2005.1604486

Celebi, M. E., Iyatomi, H., Stoecker, W. V., Moss, R. H., Rabinovitz, H. S., Argenziano, G., & Soyer, H. P. (2008). Automatic detection of blue-white veil and related structures in dermoscopy images. *Computerized Medical Imaging and Graphics*, *32*(8), 670–677. doi:10.1016/j.compmedimag.2008.08.003 PMID:18804955

Celebi, M. E., Kingravi, H. A., Uddin, B., Iyatomi, H., Aslandogan, Y. A., Stoecker, W. V., & Moss, R. H. (2007). A methodological approach to the classification of dermoscopy images. *Computerized Medical Imaging and Graphics*, *31*(6), 362–373. doi:10.1016/j.compmedimag.2007.01.003 PMID:17387001

Celebi, M. E., Mendonca, T., & Marques, J. S. (Eds.). (2015). *Dermoscopy image analysis* (Vol. 10). CRC Press. doi:10.1201/b19107

Celebi, M. E., Wen, Q., Iyatomi, H., Shimizu, K., Zhou, H., & Schaefer, G. (2015). A state-of-the-art survey on lesion border detection in dermoscopy images. *Dermoscopy Image Analysis*, *10*, 97-129.

Chatterjee, S., Dey, D., & Munshi, S. (2018). Optimal selection of features using wavelet fractal descriptors and automatic correlation bias reduction for classifying skin lesions. *Biomedical Signal Processing and Control*, *40*, 252–262. doi:10.1016/j.bspc.2017.09.028

Cheplygina, V., de Bruijne, M., & Pluim, J. P. (2019). Not-so-supervised: A survey of semi-supervised, multi-instance, and transfer learning in medical image analysis. *Medical Image Analysis*, *54*, 280–296.

Claridge, E., Cotton, S., Hall, P., & Moncrieff, M. (2003). From colour to tissue histology: Physics-based interpretation of images of pigmented skin lesions. *Medical Image Analysis*, *7*(4), 489–502. doi:10.1016/S1361-8415(03)00033-1 PMID:14561553

Clausi, D. A., & Deng, H. (2005). Design-based texture feature fusion using Gabor filters and co-occurrence probabilities. *IEEE Transactions on Image Processing*, *14*(7), 925–936. doi:10.1109/TIP.2005.849319 PMID:16028556

Cudek, P., Paja, W., & Wrzesień, M. (2011). Automatic system for classification of melanocytic skin lesions based on images recognition. In *Man-Machine Interactions 2* (pp. 189–196). Berlin: Springer. doi:10.1007/978-3-642-23169-8_21

Di Leo, G., Fabbrocini, G., Paolillo, A., Rescigno, O., & Sommella, P. (2009, March). Towards an automatic diagnosis system for skin lesions: estimation of blue-whitish veil and regression structures. In *2009 6th International Multi-Conference on Systems, Signals and Devices* (pp. 1-6). IEEE.

Dolianitis, C., Kelly, J., Wolfe, R., & Simpson, P. (2005). Comparative performance of 4 dermoscopic algorithms by nonexperts for the diagnosis of melanocytic lesions. *Archives of Dermatology, 141*(8), 1008–1014. doi:10.1001/archderm.141.8.1008 PMID:16103330

Fleming, M. G., Steger, C., Zhang, J., Gao, J., Cognetta, A. B., & Dyer, C. R. (1998). Techniques for a structural analysis of dermatoscopic imagery. *Computerized Medical Imaging and Graphics, 22*(5), 375–389. doi:10.1016/S0895-6111(98)00048-2 PMID:9890182

Fuduli, A., Veltri, P., Vocaturo, E., & Zumpano, E. (2019). Melanoma detection using color and texture features in computer vision systems. Advances in Science. *Technology and Engineering Systems Journal, 4*(5), 16–22. doi:10.25046/aj040502

Gaudioso, M., Giallombardo, G., Miglionico, G., & Vocaturo, E. (2019). Classification in the multiple instance learning framework via spherical separation. *Soft Computing*, 1–7.

Giuffrida, R., Conforti, C., Di Meo, N., Deinlein, T., Guida, S., & Zalaudek, I. (2020). Use of noninvasive imaging in the management of skin cancer. *Current Opinion in Oncology, 32*(2), 98–105. doi:10.1097/CCO.0000000000000611 PMID:31850969

Gomez, D. D., Butakoff, C., Ersboll, B. K., & Stoecker, W. (2007). Independent histogram pursuit for segmentation of skin lesions. *IEEE Transactions on Biomedical Engineering, 55*(1), 157–161. doi:10.1109/TBME.2007.910651 PMID:18232357

Grana, C., Pellacani, G., Cucchiara, R., & Seidenari, S. (2003). A new algorithm for border description of polarized light surface microscopic images of pigmented skin lesions. *IEEE Transactions on Medical Imaging, 22*(8), 959–964. doi:10.1109/TMI.2003.815901 PMID:12906250

Henning, J. S., Dusza, S. W., Wang, S. Q., Marghoob, A. A., Rabinovitz, H. S., Polsky, D., & Kopf, A. W. (2007). The CASH (color, architecture, symmetry, and homogeneity) algorithm for dermoscopy. *Journal of the American Academy of Dermatology, 56*(1), 45–52. doi:10.1016/j.jaad.2006.09.003 PMID:17190620

International Agency for Research on Cancer. (2019). *Global cancer observatory*. World Health Organization. http://gco. iarc. fr

Jain, S., & Pise, N. (2015). Computer aided melanoma skin cancer detection using image processing. *Procedia Computer Science, 48*, 735–740. doi:10.1016/j.procs.2015.04.209

Jaworek-Korjakowska, J., & Kłeczek, P. (2016). Automatic classification of specific melanocytic lesions using artificial intelligence. *BioMed Research International*. PMID:26885520

Kasmi, R., & Mokrani, K. (2016). Classification of malignant melanoma and benign skin lesions: Implementation of automatic ABCD rule. *IET Image Processing, 10*(6), 448–455. doi:10.1049/iet-ipr.2015.0385

Khan, M. A., Sharif, M., Javed, M. Y., Akram, T., Yasmin, M., & Saba, T. (2017). License number plate recognition system using entropy-based features selection approach with SVM. *IET Image Processing, 12*(2), 200–209. doi:10.1049/iet-ipr.2017.0368

Lee, T., Ng, V., Gallagher, R., Coldman, A., & McLean, D. (1997). Dullrazor®: A software approach to hair removal from images. *Computers in Biology and Medicine, 27*(6), 533–543. doi:10.1016/S0010-4825(97)00020-6 PMID:9437554

Lee, T. K., & Atkins, M. S. (2000, June). New approach to measure border irregularity for melanocytic lesions. In Medical Imaging 2000: Image Processing (Vol. 3979, pp. 668-675). International Society for Optics and Photonics.

Loane, M. A., Gore, H. E., Corbett, R., Steele, K., Mathews, C., Bloomer, S. E., ... Wootton, R. (1997). Effect of camera performance on diagnostic accuracy: Preliminary results from the Northern Ireland arms of the UK Multicentre Teledermatology Trial. *Journal of Telemedicine and Telecare, 3*(2), 83–88. doi:10.1258/1357633971930913 PMID:9206278

Ma, Z., & Tavares, J. M. R. (2017). Effective features to classify skin lesions in dermoscopic images. *Expert Systems with Applications, 84*, 92–101. doi:10.1016/j.eswa.2017.05.003

Madooei, A., Drew, M. S., Sadeghi, M., & Atkins, M. S. (2013, September). Automatic detection of blue-white veil by discrete colour matching in dermoscopy images. In *International Conference on Medical Image Computing and Computer-Assisted Intervention* (pp. 453-460). Springer. 10.1007/978-3-642-40760-4_57

Maglogiannis, I., & Doukas, C. N. (2009). Overview of advanced computer vision systems for skin lesions characterization. *IEEE Transactions on Information Technology in Biomedicine, 13*(5), 721–733. doi:10.1109/TITB.2009.2017529 PMID:19304487

Maglogiannis, I., Pavlopoulos, S., & Koutsouris, D. (2005). An integrated computer supported acquisition, handling, and characterization system for pigmented skin lesions in dermatological images. *IEEE Transactions on Information Technology in Biomedicine, 9*(1), 86–98. doi:10.1109/TITB.2004.837859 PMID:15787011

Maier, T., Kulichova, D., Schotten, K., Astrid, R., Ruzicka, T., Berking, C., & Udrea, A. (2015). Accuracy of a smartphone application using fractal image analysis of pigmented moles compared to clinical diagnosis and histological result. *Journal of the European Academy of Dermatology and Venereology, 29*(4), 663–667. doi:10.1111/jdv.12648 PMID:25087492

Malinski, L., & Smolka, B. (2016). Fast averaging peer group filter for the impulsive noise removal in color images. *Journal of Real-Time Image Processing, 11*(3), 427–444. doi:10.100711554-015-0500-z

Mendonça, T., Ferreira, P. M., Marques, J. S., Marcal, A. R., & Rozeira, J. (2013, July). PH 2-A dermoscopic image database for research and benchmarking. In *2013 35th annual international conference of the IEEE engineering in medicine and biology society (EMBC)* (pp. 5437-5440). IEEE.

Menzies, S. W., Ingvar, C., & McCarthy, W. H. (1996). A sensitivity and specificity analysis of the surface microscopy features of invasive melanoma. *Melanoma Research, 6*(1), 55–62. doi:10.1097/00008390-199602000-00008 PMID:8640071

Mohanaiah, P., Sathyanarayana, P., & GuruKumar, L. (2013). Image texture feature extraction using GLCM approach. *International Journal of Scientific and Research Publications, 3*(5), 1.

Moussa, R., Gerges, F., Salem, C., Akiki, R., Falou, O., & Azar, D. (2016, October). Computer-aided detection of Melanoma using geometric features. In *2016 3rd Middle East Conference on Biomedical Engineering (MECBME)* (pp. 125-128). IEEE. 10.1109/MECBME.2016.7745423

Nakariyakul, S., & Casasent, D. P. (2008, August). Improved forward floating selection algorithm for feature subset selection. In *2008 International Conference on Wavelet Analysis and Pattern Recognition* (Vol. 2, pp. 793-798). IEEE 10.1109/ICWAPR.2008.4635885

Nasir, M., Attique Khan, M., Sharif, M., Lali, I. U., Saba, T., & Iqbal, T. (2018). An improved strategy for skin lesion detection and classification using uniform segmentation and feature selection based approach. *Microscopy Research and Technique*, *81*(6), 528–543. doi:10.1002/jemt.23009 PMID:29464868

Nathanson, L. (Ed.). (2012). *Basic and clinical aspects of malignant melanoma* (Vol. 35). Springer Science & Business Media.

Oliveira, R. B., Pereira, A. S., & Tavares, J. M. R. (2019). Computational diagnosis of skin lesions from dermoscopic images using combined features. *Neural Computing & Applications*, *31*(10), 6091–6111. doi:10.100700521-018-3439-8

Pennisi, A., Bloisi, D. D., Nardi, D., Giampetruzzi, A. R., Mondino, C., & Facchiano, A. (2016). Skin lesion image segmentation using Delaunay Triangulation for melanoma detection. *Computerized Medical Imaging and Graphics*, *52*, 89–103. doi:10.1016/j.compmedimag.2016.05.002 PMID:27215953

Psaty, E. L., & Halpern, A. C. (2009). Current and emerging technologies in melanoma diagnosis: The state of the art. *Clinics in Dermatology*, *27*(1), 35–45. doi:10.1016/j.clindermatol.2008.09.004 PMID:19095152

Quellec, G., Cazuguel, G., Cochener, B., & Lamard, M. (2017). Multiple-instance learning for medical image and video analysis. *IEEE Reviews in Biomedical Engineering*, *10*, 213–234.

Quellec, G., Cazuguel, G., Cochener, B., & Lamard, M. (2017). Multiple-instance learning for medical image and video analysis. *IEEE Reviews in Biomedical Engineering*, *10*, 213–234. doi:10.1109/RBME.2017.2651164 PMID:28092576

Rastgoo, M., Garcia, R., Morel, O., & Marzani, F. (2015). Automatic differentiation of melanoma from dysplastic nevi. *Computerized Medical Imaging and Graphics*, *43*, 44–52. doi:10.1016/j.compmedimag.2015.02.011 PMID:25797605

Ruela, M., Barata, C., Marques, J. S., & Rozeira, J. (2017). A system for the detection of melanomas in dermoscopy images using shape and symmetry features. *Computer Methods in Biomechanics and Biomedical Engineering. Imaging & Visualization*, *5*(2), 127–137. doi:10.1080/21681163.2015.1029080

Sadeghi, M., Lee, T. K., McLean, D., Lui, H., & Atkins, M. S. (2013). Detection and analysis of irregular streaks in dermoscopic images of skin lesions. *IEEE Transactions on Medical Imaging*, *32*(5), 849–861. doi:10.1109/TMI.2013.2239307 PMID:23335664

Sawatsky, A. P., Rosenman, D. J., Merry, S. P., & McDonald, F. S. (2010, August). Eight years of the Mayo International Health Program: What an international elective adds to resident education. *Mayo Clinic Proceedings*, *85*(8), 734–741. doi:10.4065/mcp.2010.0107 PMID:20675512

Schindewolf, T., Schiffner, R., Stolz, W., Albert, R., Abmayr, W., & Harms, H. (1994). Evaluation of different image acquisition techniques for a computer vision system in the diagnosis of malignant melanoma. *Journal of the American Academy of Dermatology, 31*(1), 33–41. doi:10.1016/S0190-9622(94)70132-6 PMID:8021369

Schmid, P. (1999). Segmentation of digitized dermatoscopic images by two-dimensional color clustering. *IEEE Transactions on Medical Imaging, 18*(2), 164–171. doi:10.1109/42.759124 PMID:10232673

Sharif, M., Khan, M. A., Akram, T., Javed, M. Y., Saba, T., & Rehman, A. (2017). A framework of human detection and action recognition based on uniform segmentation and combination of Euclidean distance and joint entropy-based features selection. *EURASIP Journal on Image and Video Processing, 2017*(1), 89. doi:10.118613640-017-0236-8

Sheha, M. A., Sharwy, A., & Mabrouk, M. S. (2014, December). Pigmented skin lesion diagnosis using geometric and chromatic features. In *2014 Cairo International Biomedical Engineering Conference (CIBEC)* (pp. 115-120). IEEE. 10.1109/CIBEC.2014.7020931

Shoieb, D. A., Youssef, S. M., & Aly, W. M. (2016). Computer-aided model for skin diagnosis using deep learning. *Journal of Image and Graphics, 4*(2), 122–129. doi:10.18178/joig.4.2.122-129

Sigurdsson, S., Philipsen, P. A., Hansen, L. K., Larsen, J., Gniadecka, M., & Wulf, H. C. (2004). Detection of skin cancer by classification of Raman spectra. *IEEE Transactions on Biomedical Engineering, 51*(10), 1784–1793. doi:10.1109/TBME.2004.831538 PMID:15490825

Singh, S., Stevenson, J. H., & McGurty, D. (2001). An evaluation of Polaroid photographic imaging for cutaneous-lesion referrals to an outpatient clinic: A pilot study. *British Journal of Plastic Surgery, 54*(2), 140–143. doi:10.1054/bjps.2000.3507 PMID:11207125

Stanley, R. J., Stoecker, W. V., & Moss, R. H. (2007). A relative color approach to color discrimination for malignant melanoma detection in dermoscopy images. *Skin Research and Technology, 13*(1), 62–72. doi:10.1111/j.1600-0846.2007.00192.x PMID:17250534

Stoecker, W. V., Gupta, K., Stanley, R. J., Moss, R. H., & Shrestha, B. (2005). Detection of asymmetric blotches (asymmetric structureless areas) in dermoscopy images of malignant melanoma using relative color. *Skin Research and Technology, 11*(3), 179–184. doi:10.1111/j.1600-0846.2005.00117.x PMID:15998328

Tafti, A. D., & Mirsadeghi, E. (2012, November). A novel adaptive recursive median filter in image noise reduction based on using the entropy. In *2012 IEEE International Conference on Control System, Computing and Engineering* (pp. 520-523). IEEE. 10.1109/ICCSCE.2012.6487201

Tanaka, T., Torii, S., Kabuta, I., Shimizu, K., & Tanaka, M. (2008). Pattern classification of nevus with texture analysis. *IEEJ Transactions on Electrical and Electronic Engineering, 3*(1), 143–150. doi:10.1002/tee.20246

Umbaugh, S. E., Moss, R. H., & Stoecker, W. V. (1991). Applying artificial intelligence to the identification of variegated coloring in skin tumors. *IEEE Engineering in Medicine and Biology Magazine, 10*(4), 57–62. doi:10.1109/51.107171 PMID:18238392

Vocaturo, E., Perna, D., & Zumpano, E. (2019a, November). Machine Learning Techniques for Automated Melanoma Detection. In *2019 IEEE International Conference on Bioinformatics and Biomedicine (BIBM)* (pp. 2310-2317). IEEE. 10.1109/BIBM47256.2019.8983165

Vocaturo, E., & Veltri, P. (2017). On the use of Networks in Biomedicine. *FNC/MobiSPC, 2017*, 498-503.

Vocaturo, E., & Zumpano, E. (2019, November). Dangerousness of dysplastic nevi: a Multiple Instance Learning Solution for Early Diagnosis. In *2019 IEEE International Conference on Bioinformatics and Biomedicine (BIBM)* (pp. 2318-2323). IEEE. 10.1109/BIBM47256.2019.8983056

Vocaturo, E., & Zumpano, E. (2020). A Multiple Instance Learning Solution for Automatic Detection of Dysplastic Nevi. *Proceedings of the 28th Italian Symposium on Advanced Database Systems, Villasimius (Sud Sardegna).*

Vocaturo, E., Zumpano, E., & Veltri, P. (2018, December). Image pre-processing in computer vision systems for melanoma detection. In *2018 IEEE International Conference on Bioinformatics and Biomedicine (BIBM)* (pp. 2117-2124). IEEE. 10.1109/BIBM.2018.8621507

Vocaturo, E., Zumpano, E., & Veltri, P. (2019b, June). On the Usefulness of Pre-Processing Step in Melanoma Detection Using Multiple Instance Learning. In *International Conference on Flexible Query Answering Systems* (pp. 374-382). Springer. 10.1007/978-3-030-27629-4_34

Wighton, P., Lee, T. K., & Atkins, M. S. (2008, March). Dermascopic hair disocclusion using inpainting. In Medical Imaging 2008: Image Processing (Vol. 6914, p. 691427). International Society for Optics and Photonics. doi:10.1117/12.770776

Woo, S., & Lee, C. (2018). Incremental feature extraction based on decision boundaries. *Pattern Recognition, 77*, 65–74. doi:10.1016/j.patcog.2017.12.010

Zhou, H., Schaefer, G., Sadka, A. H., & Celebi, M. E. (2009). Anisotropic mean shift based fuzzy c-means segmentation of dermoscopy images. *IEEE Journal of Selected Topics in Signal Processing, 3*(1), 26–34. doi:10.1109/JSTSP.2008.2010631

Zumpano, E., Iaquinta, P., Caroprese, L., Dattola, F., Tradigo, G., Veltri, P., & Vocaturo, E. (2018, December). Simpatico 3d: A medical information system for diagnostic procedures. In *2018 IEEE International Conference on Bioinformatics and Biomedicine (BIBM)* (pp. 2125-2128). IEEE. 10.1109/BIBM.2018.8621090

Chapter 5
Development of Rainfall Prediction Models Using Machine Learning Approaches for Different Agro–Climatic Zones

Diwakar Naidu

BRSM College of Agricultural Engineering and Technology and Research Station, Chatarkhar, India & Indira Gandhi Agricultural University, Raipur, India

Babita Majhi

Guru Ghashidas Vishwavidyalaya, Central University, Bilaspur, India

Surendra Kumar Chandniha

BRSM College of Agricultural Engineering and Technology and Research Station, Chatarkhar, India & Indira Gandhi Agricultural University, Raipur, India

ABSTRACT

This study focuses on modelling the changes in rainfall patterns in different agro-climatic zones due to climate change through statistical downscaling of large-scale climate variables using machine learning approaches. Potential of three machine learning algorithms, multilayer artificial neural network (MLANN), radial basis function neural network (RBFNN), and least square support vector machine (LS-SVM) have been investigated. The large-scale climate variable are obtained from National Centre for Environmental Prediction (NCEP) reanalysis product and used as predictors for model development. Proposed machine learning models are applied to generate projected time series of rainfall for the period 2021-2050 using the Hadley Centre coupled model (HadCM3) B2 emission scenario data as predictors. An increasing trend in anticipated rainfall is observed during 2021-2050 in all the ACZs of Chhattisgarh State. Among the machine learning models, RBFNN found as more feasible technique for modeling of monthly rainfall in this region.

DOI: 10.4018/978-1-7998-6659-6.ch005

INTRODUCTION

Climate comprises a general pattern of weather conditions, seasons and weather extremes like drought, flood, heat wave and cold wave situations. Climate study is a very complicated phenomenon which contains various climatic variables, and their behaviors are also different. Climate of any region varies with space and time on account of various atmospheric forcing. Long-term systematic changes of statistical properties of the climate variables are referred to as "climate change". The statistical distribution of weather patterns with a particular long-term or extended period (decades or longer time span) indicates the climate change (Yang et al. 2010; 2015; 2017; Shi et al. 2016). In another word, climate change also refers to a shift in climate from its average weather condition eventually for the long-term period. According to United Nations Framework Convention on Climate Change (UNFCCC), climate change is directly or indirectly associated with human interventions, which alter the composition of atmospheric balance (IPCC, 2007). However, it may be caused by a hydrological cycle imbalance, phytochemical effects, biotic manners, variation in solar radiations, geological inequality, volcanic eruptions, anthropogenic activities, etc. During the recent past, the intervention of anthropogenic activities such as urbanization, population growth, industrialization, deforestation, settlements, burning of fossil fuels, etc., has increased the greenhouse gases (GHG) emission (Kumar and Sharma, 2017). Intergovernmental Panel on Climate Change (IPCC, 1996) reported that global warming is mainly due to the enhanced GHG radiation and is likely to have a significant impact on the hydrological cycle and future climate change. Alarming effects of climate change viz. severe floods, droughts and other extreme hydrological events catch the attention of the entire world to think and assess its future impact on global climate. In the recent past, various severities of adverse climatic events have been identified. Climate change seems to be more pronounced, if assessed at local and regional scale compared to global scale because globally its effects are more generalized.

In an agrarian country like India, uneven rainfall distribution may disrupt food availability and results in reduced agricultural productivity. Hence, precise knowledge about the past, present and future rainfall pattern over a region can play an important role in planning cropping pattern, finalizing the schedule of the farm operation and designing irrigation structures for effective utilization of available water resources for enhancing the agricultural production. Hence, in order to assess the climate change impacts on rainfall distribution and its future trends, the present investigation is carried out using long term monthly rainfall time series to develop an appropriate technique for the rainfall modeling in the three distinct Agro-climatic Zones (ACZs) viz., Chhattisgarh Plains, Bastar Plateau and Northern Hills ACZs of Chhattisgarh state in east central India.

In a recent decade study about possible changes in rainfall pattern over a region due to climate change is being assessed using statistical downscaling of general circulation models (GCM) products from global to local scale. Statistical downscaling methodologies are based on transfer functions, which highlight relationships between global scale predictors and local scale response variable using linear/non-linear regression equations (Wilby et al. 2002, 2004; Murphy and Timbal, 2008). GCM products provide the required the long period global scale data of various large scale climate variables, which is used as predictors for rainfall prediction. Multi-linear regression (MLR), principal component analysis (PCA) and canonical correlation analysis (CCA) are outdated statistical downscaling regression methods (Dibike and Coulibaly, 2005). Conversely, machine learning techniques such as artificial neural network (ANN), least square support vector machine (LS-SVM) and least square support vector regression (LS-SVR) are gaining popularity during the past two decades and considered under nonlinear regression models. Among them most of the researchers have demonstrated the potential of MLR, LS-SVM (Benestad et al. 2007; Cannon and Whitfield 2002; Chen et al. 2010; Najafi et al. 2011; Ojha 2013; Cheng et al. 2008; Maheras et al. 2004; Kostopoulou et al. 2007; Schoof et al. 2007; Huth 1999, 2002, 2004), PCA (Wetterhall et al. 2005; Tolika et al. 2006), CCA (Huth 1999, 2002, 2004; Kostopoulou et al. 2007; Tomezeiu et al. 2006; Landman et al. 2001; Tolika et al. 2006), ANN (Goyal and Ohja 2012; Kostopoulou et al. 2007; Samadi et al. 2013; Tisseuil et al. 2010; Trigo and Palutikof, 2001; Tripathi et al. 2006), and SVM (Anandhi et al. 2009; Chen et al. 2010; Ghosh and Mujumdar 2008; Tripathi et al. 2006; Najafi et al. 2011; Chen et al. 2012) for modelling climate variables. Out of all discussed downscaling techniques, ANN has gained broad credit (Cannon and Whitfield, 2002; Tisseuil et al. 2010). In climate impact studies, SVM has theoretically proved better than other techniques in transfer functions (Tripathi et al. 2006). Sachindra et al. (2013) stated that LS-SVM is found to be the proper technique for statistical downscaling of General Circulation Model (GCM) outputs to stream flow than multiple linear regressions. Besides this, recently, Xu et al. (2020) developed a multiple machine learning (MML) downscaling models, based on a Bayesian model average (BMA), to downscale the precipitation simulation of 8 Coupled Model Inter comparison Project Phase 5 (CMIP5) models using model output statistics (MOS) in the upper Han River basin. Ahmed et al. (2020) developed Multi-Model Ensembles (MMEs) using machine learning algorithms; ANN, K-Nearest Neighbor (KNN), SVM and Relevance Vector Machine (RVM) for rainfall prediction over Pakistan. Vandal et al. (2018) compared Perfect Prognosis (PP) approaches, Ordinary Least Squares, Elastic-Net, and SVM, along with two machine learning methods Multitask Sparse Structure Learning (MSSL) and Autoencoder Neural Networks for downscaling of daily and extreme precipitation. Sachindra et al. (2018) also investigated four machine learning techniques, Genetic Programming (GP), ANNs, SVM, and RVM for statistical downscaling of precipitation.

Literature review motivated the authors to conduct the present investigations and therefore an attempt has been made to develop appropriate machine learning models for monthly rainfall predictions in different ACZs of Chhattisgarh state of east-central India. Potential of most popular and conventional machine learning models, such as multi-layer artificial neural network (MLANN), radial basis function neural network (RBFNN) and least Square support vector machine (LS-SVM) are investigated to model the monthly rainfall pattern in different ACZs. These, machine learning techniques are based on transfer functions and model the relationships between predictors and the target variable. These regression techniques are mainly based on a set of supervised learning methodologies that can analyze historical long term observed rainfall time series and recognize patterns. The developed machine learning models are then applied for future rainfall trend using appropriate GCM projections. However, successful implementation of such models are highly dependent on the appropriateness of future climatic projection(s) at a regional level. Future rainfall time series obtained through these machine learning models, will be beneficial for future prospectives like sustainable planning and mitigation. The present investigation demonstrated some alternate machine learning approach for statistical downscaling of long term monthly rainfall time series and its application for future rainfall projections using appropriate climate change scenarios over Chhattisgarh state of India.

MATERIAL AND METHODS

Study Area

The Chhattisgarh state of east central India is acknowledged as "Bowl of Rice" with the geographical area of about 135,190 km^2 (Kansal et al. 2015). It contributes about 12% forest to the Indian sub-continent. However, 44% contribution itself in Chhattisgarh. The aerial extent of Chhattisgarh state lies between 17.78°N to 24.11°N and 80.24°E to 84.39°E. A total of 27 districts come under the administrative boundary of Chhattisgarh state which is located in a tropical zone due to its location near to the tropic of cancer. The Chhattisgarh state is divided into three distinct ACZs viz. Chhattisgarh Plains, Bastar Plateau and Northern Hills as depicted in Figure 1. Chhattisgarh state is a mono-cropped state with rice (*Oryza sativa*) being the main crop cultivated in 3/5th of the total area during the *Kharif* season. More than 80% of the population are dependent upon agriculture for its livelihood.

Figure 1. Location map of the study area

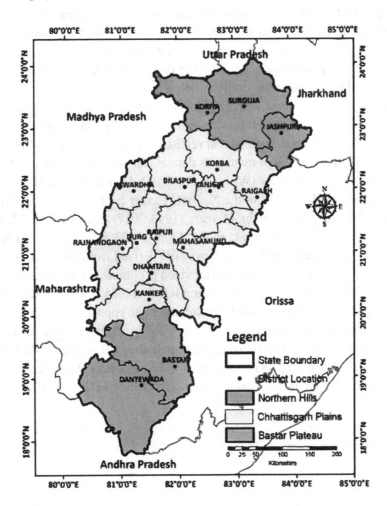

Rainfall Data Collection

Long-term daily rainfall data are obtained from the fine resolution (0.25° x 0.25°) time series released by India Meteorological Department (IMD). Further, daily time series from 1948 to 2017 has been converted into monthly/annual time series using area weighted-average technique with the help of geographic information system (GIS) platform for all the 27 districts of Chhattisgarh region. Descriptive statistics of annual rainfall has been computed for finding the behavior or variability of rainfall in different ACZs. Location of meteorological stations and its spatial distribution of average annual rainfall along with descriptive statistics are shown in Table 1. No missing evidence is found in the time series. The outliers have been removed using the standard ratio method (ratio between the highest peak and the mean value of the correlation plane) as indicated by Raffel (2007). District wise monthly rainfall time series is averaged to obtain monthly rainfall time series for respective ACZs and used as target variable for calibration and validation of the proposed machine learning models.

Selection of Predictors for Rainfall Modeling

The selection of appropriate predictors is one of the most essential and complex steps in a downscaling procedure. The selection of predictors varies with space and time, which is based on the target variable characteristics under large-scale atmospheric circulation. A different scenario provides a wide range of predictors and each and every predictor is important in downscaling techniques. It is very necessary to develop strong relationships between the target variable and predictors (Wetterhall et al., 2005). According to guidelines for use of climate scenarios developed from statistical downscaling methods the predictors should be selected as per the following criterion: (1) The large-scale predictors should be physically relevant to the local-scale features and realistically simulated by GCMs, (2) the predictors are readily available from the archives of reanalysis datasets and GCMs output and, (3) predictors have strongly correlated with target variables (Wilby et al., 2004). Hence, the monthly observed predictor data of climatic variables are derived from the National Center for Environmental Prediction (NCEP) reanalysis data on 2.5° x 2.5° grid-scale for 41 years (1948-2017) (Mishra et al. 2014). The extracted data range between 17.50°N - 24.33°N latitude and 80.11°E - 84.73°E longitude, which covers the entire Chhattisgarh state. The large-scale monthly predictors are derived from Hadley Center Coupled GCM Model, version-3 (HadCM3) for B2 future scenario which is obtained from the Climate Change Severity Index (CCSI) from 2021 to 2050 on grid resolution is 2.5° x 3.75° for future rainfall prediction. The HadCM3 B2 GCM scenario defines the world with intermediate population and its growth of economic condition under consideration of sustainability through social, economic and environmental factors, therefore, B2 scenarios is considered for Indian condition. In India, HadCM3 GCM B2 has been chosen while studying the climate change impact because of its widespread acceptance. The 26 NCEP predictors of different atmospheric pressure levels used for rainfall modelling in this study are shown in Table 2.

Table 1. Location of meteorological stations and average annual rainfall distribution in different ACZs of Chhattisgarh state and its descriptive statistics (data base 1948-2017)

Districts	Long.	Lat.	Alt.	Average RF	SD	CV
Balod	81.21	20.73	324	1210.0	251.5	20.8
Balodabazar	82.16	21.66	254	1127.7	263.8	23.4
Bemetra	81.54	21.71	278	1119.2	234.3	20.9
Bilaspur	82.13	22.07	264	1271.1	233.5	18.4
Dhamtari	81.54	20.70	305	1267.5	277.6	21.9
Durg	81.28	21.18	289	1179.8	254.9	21.6
Gariabandh	82.30	20.26	292	1226.9	245.8	20.0
Janjgir-Champa	82.57	22.00	256	1296.8	264.7	20.4
Kanker	81.49	20.27	388	1379.2	276.9	20.1
Kawardha	81.23	22.01	353	1126.5	231.2	20.5
Korba	82.70	22.34	316	1376.8	284.3	20.7
Mahasamund	82.09	21.10	318	1213.5	266.5	22.0
Mungeli	81.69	22.07	288	1203.3	225.2	18.7
Raigarh	83.39	21.89	215	1363.8	288.6	21.2
Raipur	81.62	21.25	298	1153.7	281.6	24.4
Rajnandgaon	81.03	21.09	307	1210.4	243.2	20.1
Chhattisgarh Plains				**1232.9**	**257.7**	**20.9**
Bastar	81.93	19.20	552	1502.0	228.3	15.2
Bijapur	80.82	18.79	592	1516.0	302.8	20.0
Dantewada	81.35	18.90	362	1498.9	281.8	18.8
Kondagaon	81.66	19.59	593	1356.2	231.5	17.1
Narayanpur	81.25	19.72	408	1408.6	256.0	18.2
Sukma	81.66	18.39	210	1468.9	277.0	18.9
Bastar Plateau				**1458.5**	**262.9**	**18.0**
Balrampur	83.61	23.61	441	1199.8	257.0	21.4
Jashpur	83.85	22.90	753	1422.0	272.9	19.2
Koriya	82.54	23.25	700	1214.3	253.4	20.9
Surajpur	82.87	23.21	528	1258.4	283.8	22.6
Surguja	83.19	22.95	623	1374.1	290.5	21.1
Northern Hills				**1293.7**	**271.5**	**21.0**
Chhattisgarh				**1318.9**	**185.2**	**14.0**

Long., Lat., Alt., RF, SD and CV denotes longitude(°N), latitude(°E), altitude(m), rainfall (mm), standard deviation (mm) and coefficient of variation(%) respectively

Table 2. Description of all NCEP predictors used for rainfall modelling.

S. No.	Atmospheric Pressure Level	NCEP Variables Descriptions	Code	Units
A	1013.25 hPa	Mean sea level pressure	ncepmslpas	Pa
B	1000 hPa	Surface airflow strength	ncepp__fas	m/s
		Surface zonal velocity	ncepp__uas	m/s
		Surface meridional velocity	ncepp__vas	m/s
		Surface vorticity	ncepp__zas	s^{-1}
		Surface wind direction	ncepp_thas	degree
		Surface divergence	ncepp_zhas	s^{-1}
C	850 hPa	850 hPa airflow strength	ncepp8_fas	m/s
		850 hPa zonal velocity	ncepp8_uas	m/s
		850 hPa meridional velocity	ncepp8_vas	m/s
		850 hPa vorticity	ncepp8_zas	s^{-1}
		850 hPa wind direction	ncepp8thas	degree
		850 hPa divergence	ncepp8zhas	s^{-1}
		850 hPa geopotential height	ncepp850as	m
		Relative humidity at 850 hPa	ncepr850as	%
D	500 hPa	500 hPa airflow strength	ncepp5_fas	m/s
		500 hPa zonal velocity	ncepp5_uas	m/s
		500 hPa meridional velocity	ncepp5_vas	m/s
		500 hPa vorticity	ncepp5_zas	s^{-1}
		500 hPa wind direction	ncepp5thas	
		500 hPa divergence	ncepp5zhas	s^{-1}
		500 hPa geopotential height	ncepp500as	m
		Relative humidity at 500 hPa	ncepr500as	%
E	Near surface	Surface specific humidity	ncepshumas	g/kg
		Mean temperature at 2m	nceptempas	^0C
		Near surface relative humidity	nceprhumas	%

Machine Learning Models

Radial Basis Function Neural Network (RBFNN)

RBFNN is a category of feed forward network with a single hidden layer and an output layer formulated by Broomhead and Lowe (1988). Pictorial representation of the RBFNN is given in Figure 2. Each processing unit termed as a neuron in the hidden layer is associated with centers $c = c_1, c_2, c_3, \ldots, c_h$, and its width $\sigma = \sigma_1, \sigma_2, \sigma_3, \ldots, \sigma_h$, where h is the number of neurons in the hidden layer. Each neuron in hidden layer receives the same set of input data (x= $x_1, x_2, x_3, \ldots, x_n$). Centers of every hidden neuron have the same dimension as that of the input data, i.e. $c_i \in R^n, x \in R^n$. The output of each hidden layer neurons

$(\varnothing_1, \varnothing_2, \varnothing_3 \ldots \varnothing_h)$ is associated with synaptic weight (w1,w_2,w_3,...,wh). Output $\varnothing_i$ of it$h$ ^{h}idden layer neuron is basically a Gaussian function and is represented by:

$$\varnothing_i(z) = e^{\frac{-z^2}{2\sigma_i^2}}$$

(1)

where, $z = \left\| x - c_i \right\|$, represents the Euclidian distance between input data and corresponding centers and $\varnothing_i = \varnothing(\left\| x - c_i \right\|)$. The Gaussian function used in the each hidden layer neuron is actually a category of radial basis function. Finally the response of the RBFNN for a given set of input data at the output layer neuron is linear in terms of weights and computed using the following expression.

$$y = \sum_{i=1}^{h} w_i \varnothing_i$$

(2)

Calibration of the RBFNN network for each instant of input data and its corresponding output $\{x,y\}$ is done in a recursive manner, by updating the network parameters $\{w_i, c_i, \sigma i_j$ to minimize the following instantaneous error cost function.

$$e = \frac{1}{2}\left(y^d - y\right)^2$$

(3)

The weight update rules to optimize the network parameters $\{w_i, c_i, \sigma i_j$ at time t is given by following equations which are derived using a gradient descent algorithm.

$$w_i(t+1) = w_i(t) + \eta_1\left(y^d - y\right)\varnothing_i$$

(4)

$$c_{ij}(t+1) = c_{ij}(t) + \frac{\eta_2}{\sigma_i^2}\left(y^d - y\right)w_i\varnothing_i\left(x_j - c_{ij}\right)$$

(5)

$$\sigma_i(t+1) = \sigma_i(t) + \frac{\eta_3}{\sigma_i^3}\left(y^d - y\right)w_i\varnothing_i z_i^2$$

(6)

where,

y^d = desired output or target value

c_{ij} = j^{th} element of ith center

η_1, η_2, η_3 = learning rate for network parameters $\{w_i, c_i, \sigma i_j$ respectively.

Figure 2. Block diagram of RBFNN based estimator

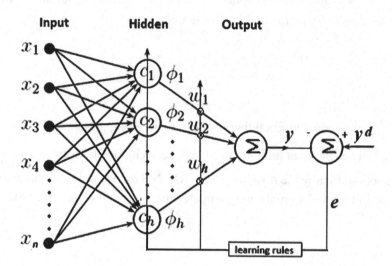

Least Square Support Vector Machine (LS-SVM)

Least squares support vector machines (LS-SVM) is another statistical downscaling machine learning technique. Least square version of support vector machine has been also utilized for this study. LS-SVM is based on a set of supervised learning methodology that can analyze data and it recognizes patterns which are used for categorization as well as regression analysis. In this method, the solution can be found by solving a set of linear equations instead of a convex quadratic programming (QP) problem for classical SVMs. LS-SVM classifiers (Suykens and Vandewalle, 1999; Suykens et al., 2001). LS-SVMs are a class of kernel-based learning methods. Consider a finite training sample of N patterns $\{(x_i, y_i), i = 1, ..., N\}$, where x_i denote the ith pattern in N-dimensional space (i.e. $x_i = [x_{1i}, ..., x_{Ni}] \in \Re N^)$ constitutes input to LS-SVM and $Y_{i\in} \Re N$ is the corresponding value of the desired model output. Further, let the learning machine be defined by a set of possible mappings $x \rightarrow f(x, w)$, where $f(\cdot)$ is a deterministic function which for a given input pattern x and adjustable parameters w ($w \in \Re N$), always gives the same output. Calibration phase of the learning machine involves adjusting the parameters w. The parameters are estimated by minimizing the cost function $\Psi L_{(w}, e)$. The LS-SVM optimization problem for function estimation is formulated by minimizing the cost function.

$$\Psi_L\left(w, e\right) = \frac{1}{2} w^T w + \frac{1}{2} C \sum_{i=1}^{N} e_i^2 \qquad (7)$$

Subject to the equality constraint

$$y_i = \hat{y}_i = e_i, i = 1, ..., N \qquad (8)$$

Where C is a positive real constant and $\hat{y}$ is the actual model output. The first term of the cost function represents weight decay or model complexity-penalty, function. It is used to regularize weight sizes and to penalize large weights. This helps in improving generalization performance. The second term of the cost function represents a penalty function. The solution of the optimization problem is obtained by considering the Lagrangian as

$$L\left(w,b,e,\alpha\right)=\frac{1}{2}w^{T}w+\frac{1}{2}C\sum_{i=1}^{N}e_{i}^{2}-\sum_{i=1}^{N}\alpha_{i}\left\{\hat{y}_{i}+e_{i}-y_{i}\right\}+b \qquad (9)$$

Where α_i are Lagrange multipliers and b is the bias term. The conditions for optimality are given by

$$\begin{cases} \dfrac{\partial L}{\partial w}=w-\sum_{i=1}^{N}\alpha_{i}\varphi\left(x_{i}\right)=0 \\[2mm] \dfrac{\partial L}{\partial b}=\sum_{i=1}^{N}\alpha_{i}=0 \\[2mm] \dfrac{\partial L}{\partial e_{i}}=\alpha_{i}-Ce_{i}=0,i,\ldots\ldots..N \\[2mm] \dfrac{\partial L}{\partial \alpha_{i}}=\hat{y}_{i}+e_{i}-y_{i}=0,i=1,\ldots\ldots..N \end{cases} \qquad (10)$$

The elimination of w and e will yield a linear system instead of a quadratic programming problem. The above conditions of optimality can be expressed as the solution to the following set of linear equations after elimination of e and e_i.

$$\begin{bmatrix} 0 & \vec{1}^{T} \\ \vec{1} & \Omega+C^{-1}I \end{bmatrix}\begin{bmatrix} b \\ \alpha \end{bmatrix}=\begin{bmatrix} 0 \\ y \end{bmatrix} \qquad (11)$$

$$where,\, y=\begin{bmatrix} y_{1} \\ y_{2} \\ \vdots \\ y_{N} \end{bmatrix};\vec{1}=\begin{bmatrix} 1 \\ 1 \\ \vdots \\ 1 \end{bmatrix}_{N\times N} \qquad (12)$$

$$\alpha=\begin{bmatrix} \alpha_{1} \\ \alpha_{2} \\ \vdots \\ \alpha_{N} \end{bmatrix};I=\begin{bmatrix} 1 & 0 & \cdots & 0 \\ 0 & 1 & \cdots & 0 \\ \vdots & \vdots & \vdots & \vdots \\ 0 & 0 & \cdots & 1 \end{bmatrix}_{N\times N} \qquad (13)$$

Here, I_N is an N×N identity matrix, and $\Omega \in R^{N \times N}$ is the kernel matrix defined by Ω is obtained from the application of Mercer's theorem.

$$\Omega_{i,j} = K\left(x_i, x_j\right) = \varphi\left(x_i\right)^T \varphi\left(x_j\right) \cdots \forall i, j \tag{14}$$

Where $\varphi(\cdot)$ represents the nonlinear transformation function defined to convert a nonlinear problem to a linear problem in a higher dimensional feature space. The resulting LS-SVM model for function estimation is:

$$f\left(x\right) = \sum \alpha_i^* K\left(x_i, x\right) + b^* \tag{15}$$

$K(\mathbf{x}_i \mathbf{x})$ is the inner product kernel function defined in accordance with Mercer's theorem (Courant and Hilbert, 2008) and b^* is the bias. There are several possibilities for the choice of the kernel function, including linear, polynomial and radial basis function (RBF). The linear kernel is a special case of RBF (Keerthi and Lin, 2003). Further, the signed kernel behaves like RBF for certain parameters (Lin and Lin, 2003). They are defined as follow.

Linear kernel:

$$K\left(x_i, x_j\right) = x_i^T x_j \tag{16}$$

Polynomial kernel:

$$K\left(x_i, x_j\right) = \left(x_i^T x_j + t\right)^d, t \geq 0 \tag{17}$$

Radial Basis Function kernel:

$$K\left(x_i, x_j\right) = e^{-\frac{\left\|x_i - x_j\right\|^2}{2\sigma^2}} \tag{18}$$

Where, t is the intercept and d is the degree of the polynomial, σ is the width of RBF kernel, which can be adjusted to control the expressivity of RBF.

Multi-Layer Artificial Neural Network (MLANN)

MLANN is a feed forward neural network suggested by Haykin (1998) with an input layer, one or more hidden layer and an output layer. A N-5-1 structure of MLANN (N=26 represents the number of input data, 5 neurons in hidden layer and one neuron at the output layers) is used in this study with different input combinations. The training of the network is done by back-propagation algorithm which is based on the error-correcting learning rule to update the weights and biases of each neuron in different layers. Hyperbolic tangent (tanh) is used as the activation function.

Performance Evaluation Measures

The performance of the predictive models is evaluated by computing root mean square error (RMSE), coefficient of determination (R^2) and Nash and Sutcliffe efficiency factor (NSE) (Kim and Kim 2008; Zhang and Govindaraju 2000; Nash and Sutcliffe 1970) between desired (FAO-PM) and estimated ET_0. The mathematical formula for the different evaluation measures are as follows.

$$RMSE = \sqrt{\frac{1}{T}\sum_{i=1}^{T}(Out_{est} - Out_{obs})^2} \tag{19}$$

$$R^2 = \frac{\left[\sum_{i=1}^{T}\left(Out_{obs} - \overline{Out_{obs}}\right)\left(Out_{est} - \overline{Out_{est}}\right)\right]^2}{\sum_{i=1}^{T}\left(Out_{obs} - \overline{Out_{obs}}\right)^2 \sum_{i=1}^{T}\left(Out_{est} - \overline{Out_{est}}\right)^2} \tag{20}$$

$$NSE = 1 - \frac{\sum_{i=1}^{T}\left(Out_{est} - Out_{obs}\right)^2}{\sum_{i=1}^{T}\left(Out_{obs} - \overline{Out_{obs}}\right)^2} \quad (-\infty \leq EF \leq 1) \tag{21}$$

where, Out_{obs} and Out_{est} represent the observed and estimated values, respectively. T is the total number of validation patterns and i denotes the number of particular instances. Low RMSE values represent the close association between desired and estimated output. Similarly, R^2 and EF values close to 1 are also an indicator of superior predictive ability of the model. (Duhan and Pandey 2015).

Stepwise Algorithm for Model Development and Its Application

Monthly Rainfall data are considered as the target variable and climatic variables (n=26) as predictors. First of all, screening of variables has been chosen based on partial correlation coefficients. Highly positive and negative correlated variables have been selected for the same. MLANN, RBFNN, LS-SVM machine learning technique have been adopted for downscaling of monthly rainfall. There techniques are non-parametric downscaling techniques which are based on convex quadratic programming (QP) and Kernel-based learning functions. The entire downscaling process is completed by the regression/transform function. The overall methodology is based on a set of supervised approaches which provide better results compared to traditional statistical based approach (Suykens and Vandewalle, 1999). Proposed methodology for rainfall downscaling is shown in Figure 3. The stepwise algorithm used to carry out the future projection of rainfall is as follows:

1. Obtain the monthly rainfall time series from a reliable source.
2. Check missing values and consistency for all the meteorological stations.
3. For calibration and validation purpose, NCEP data for the period 1948-2017 are utilized. However, the calibration and validation periods are taken as 1948-2010 and 2011-2017 respectively.
4. For possible future projection of the target variable (rainfall), HadCM3 B2 future scenarios is used.
5. Select the potential predictors using the screen of variables by partial correlation (Duhan and Pandey 2014).
6. Run the MLANN, RBFNN, LS-SVM machine learning models with potential NCEP predictors (Keerthi and Kin 2003; Courant and Hilbert 2008).
7. Calibrate the model by fine tuning the parameters of transfer function. (Keerthi and Kin 2003) to by minimizing the error cost function.
8. After calibrating of the machine learning models to a satisfactory level, validate the model with remaining data, which is kept reserved for validation of the models.
9. The performance of model efficiency is checked by the root mean square error (RMSE), coefficient of determination (R^2), Nash-Sutcliffe efficiency coefficient (NSE) (Kim and Kim 2008; Zhang and Govindaraju 2000; Nash and Sutcliffe 1970).
10. Further developed machine learning models have been applied using the predictor variables of HadCM3 B2 scenario (Chandniha and Kansal 2016) and projection of future rainfall scenarios for study locations for the period of 2021 to 2050.

RESULTS AND DISCUSSION

Calibration and Validation of Machine Learning Models

In this study potential of three machine learning models, namely MLANN, RBFNN and LS-SVM are investigated for rainfall modeling. Simulation studies are carried out for modeling monthly rainfall time series for different ACZs of Chhattisgarh using NCEP predictor variables. Long term monthly NCEP predictors from 1948-2010 is considered for calibration of different machine learning models as per the methodology described in the previous section. Recent 7 years of NCEP predictors and monthly rainfall data from 2011-2017 is used for model validation in different ACZs.

To calibrate the model, NCEP predictors and desired target data is normalized between -1 to 1. Model parameters of the MLANN, RBFNN and LS-SVM i.e., learning rate, weights are initialized to random numbers between -1 to 1. Input patterns are given to the input layer of the model in a sequential manner and corresponding estimated output is obtained at the output layer after completion of the forward pass for each set of input patterns. Estimated output is compared with the target output to compute the instantaneous error which is the cost function for the proposed model. Real time update of the model parameters is done in each instance to minimize the squared error. The process continues till all the available input patterns for model calibration gets exhausted. This completes one cycle called epoch. At the end of each epoch, mean square error is computed. The iterative process is repeated several times until RMSE is minimized to a desired low value. This completes the supervised calibration process and model parameters are then fixed to constitute proposed model.

Figure 3. Proposed methodology for rainfall downscaling

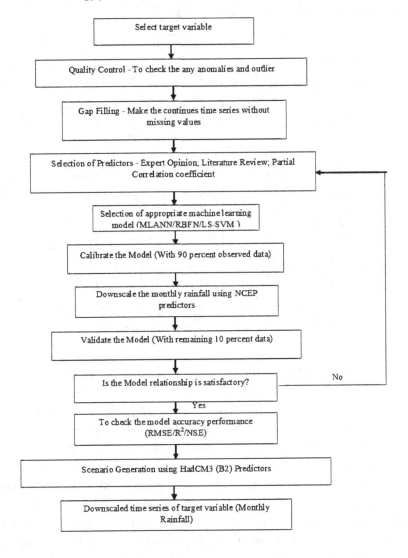

After completion of the model calibration process, validation data sets are used and corresponding monthly rainfall estimates are obtained using the developed models. For model comparison and selection, performance evaluation measures i.e., RMSE (mm/week), NSE and R^2 are computed for each model under consideration and the results are presented in Table 3. It is can be easily seen that, the calibration and validation performance in terms of R^2, RMSE and NSE values are comparatively better in case of Chhattisgarh Plains as compared to Northern Hills and Bastar Plateau ACZs. This may be associated with a different topographic situation of respective ACZs. Also, the difference between R^2, RMSE and NSE values during calibration and validation phase is less in Chhattisgarh Plains with different machine learning approaches, whereas the validation performance of these machine learning models are comparatively inferior to calibration performance and the difference is more in Bastar Plateau and Northern Hills ACZs.

Table 3. Calibration and validation performance of MLANN, RBFNN and LS-SVM machine learning techniques for monthly rainfall estimation using NCEP predictors

Zone	Model	Calibration Performance (1948-2010)			Validation Performance (2011-2017)		
		R^2	RMSE	NSE	R^2	RMSE	NSE
Chhattisgarh Plains zone	MLANN	0.936	39.20	0.925	0.930	39.82	0.913
	RBF	**0.938**	**36.14**	**0.936**	**0.931**	**39.75**	**0.913**
	LS-SVM	0.907	43.72	0.907	0.923	43.30	0.897
Bastar Plateau zone	MLANN	0.921	46.10	0.914	0.888	60.26	0.853
	RBF	**0.924**	**43.35**	**0.924**	**0.894**	**51.39**	**0.893**
	LS-SVM	0.891	52.63	0.889	0.876	58.00	0.864
Northern hills zone	MLANN	0.934	38.29	0.934	0.890	49.00	0.879
	RBF	**0.939**	**38.17**	**0.934**	**0.911**	**42.80**	**0.908**
	LS-SVM	0.896	48.64	0.893	0.870	54.30	0.852
Chhattisgarh state	MLANN	0.930	41.20	0.925	0.902	49.70	0.882
	RBF	**0.934**	**39.20**	**0.932**	**0.912**	**44.70**	**0.905**
	LS-SVM	0.898	48.30	0.896	0.889	51.90	0.871

It is observed that, RBFNN models performed better in terms of R^2, RMSE and NSE in all the three ACZs as well as in the Chhattisgarh state and ranked first. Lower RMSE and higher R^2 and NSE values are highlighted by bold numbers in the Table 3. In Chhattisgarh plains, low RMSE values of 39.75 and 39.82 are obtained with RBFNN and MLANN models during the validation phase, whereas the same for LS-SVM are obtained 43.30, which is comparatively higher. At Bastar Plateau zone, RMSE ranges from a low of 51.39 for RBFNN to a high of 58.00 and 60.26 for LS-SVM and MLANN respectively. Similarly, in the Northern hills zone too, the validation performance of RBFNN models is superior (RMSE = 42.88) as compared to MLANN (RMSE =49.00) and LS-SVM (54.37).

Two more performance evaluation measures, R^2 and NSE are also computed for each model as model selection based on R^2 alone may mislead sometimes. In general, R^2 and NSE value close to one indicates higher prediction accuracy of any regression model. It can be seen from the Table 3 that in most of the cases, higher R^2 values close to 0.9 or above is obtained and hence, it becomes difficult to choose a particular model based on R^2 alone.

It can be seen that both R^2 and NSE in different ACZs during calibration and validation phase computed close to 0.9 or more with different machine approaches. This indicates that all the selected machine learning models have the potential of modeling monthly rainfall in different ACZs. However, among the machine learning approaches R^2 and NSE values obtained with RBFNN model is found superior as compared to MLANN and LS-SVM in all the three ACZs.

A comparison between estimated and observed monthly rainfall for different machine learning models under investigation in Chhattisgarh Plains, Bastar Plateau and Northern Hills ACZs are illustrated in Figure 4 (a to i). It can be seen that, estimated monthly rainfall during the validation period (2011-2017) in respectively ACZs matches closely with the observed monthly rainfall in all locations. However, as compare to MLANN and LS-SVM rainfall estimates, RBFNN rainfall estimates overlapped more precisely with observed rainfall in all the ACZs.

Figure 4. Comparison of observed and predicted monthly rainfall using machine learning models (MLANN, LS-SVM and RBFNN) during validation phase (2011-2017) in different ACZs of Chhattisgarh state

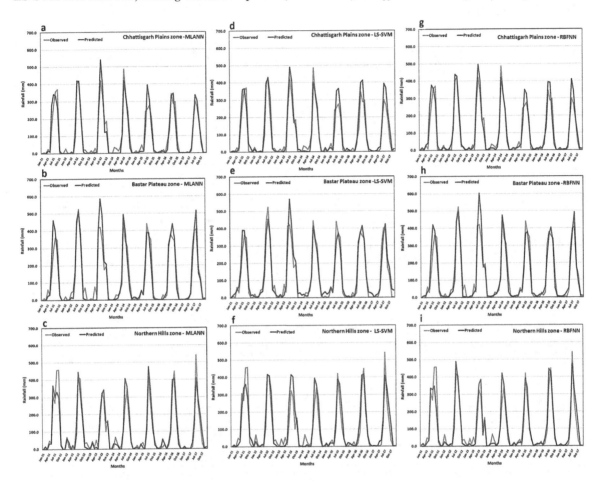

Future Projections of Rainfall Using Hadcm3 B2 Emission Scenario

After the calibration and validation of the RBFNN, MLANN and LS-SVM models, model experiments are carried using large scale climate variables obtained through GCM outputs. For this purpose the feature vectors of predictor variable are prepared from HadCM3 GCM for B2 emission scenarios and simulations are carried out to obtain a downscaled result of future projected monthly/annual rainfall using the developed RBFNN, MLANN and LS-SVM machine learning models. The anticipated trend of future annual rainfall of Chhattisgarh Plains, Bastar Plateau and Northern hills ACZs for the period from 2021 to 2050 are obtained through RBFNN, MLANN and LS-SVM machine learning models and are shown in Figure 5 (a to i). The projected values of annual rainfall are represented as box plot arrangements to describe the decadal changes in future rainfall time series. The box plots of decadal rainfall pattern for the period 2021-2033, 2031-2040 and 2041-2050 are shown in Figure 6 (a to i). The middle line of the box plot signifies the median value while the upper and lower edges signify the 75% and the 25% of the data set respectively. The highest and lowest limits of the upper and lower vertical

Figure 5. Linear trend of possible annual rainfall estimated by different machine learning models (MLANN, LS-SVM and RBFNN) for the period 2021-2050 using HadCM2-B2 predictors in different ACZs of Chhattisgarh state

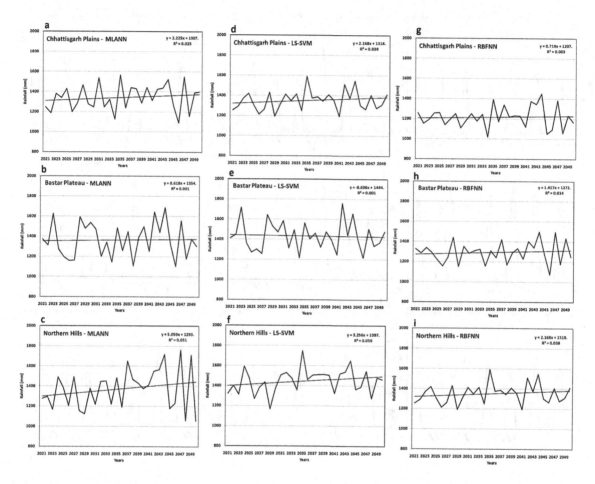

lines indicate highest and lowest values respectively. The black square depicts the simulated mean, and the straight-line shows the observed mean. The Figures, 5 & 6 and ultimate result show an increasing pattern in the future rainfall with some variations of increase and decrease within decades with most of the machine learning approaches in different ACZs. Considering the superiority of RBFNN model over MLANN and LS-SVM, future rainfall trends obtained with RBFNN model can be used for planning of regional level agricultural policies as well as for efficient water resource management under the changing climate of the region.

CONCLUSION

In the present investigation the impact of climate change on rainfall pattern is assessed in three distinct ACZs in Chhattisgarh region of India. For this purpose the MLANN, RBFNN and LS-SVM machine learning techniques are used for statistical downscaling of the large scale climate variable from global

Figure 6. Box plot of decadal changes in expected annual rainfall estimated by different machine learning models (MLANN, LS-SVM and RBFNN) for the period 2021-2050 using HadCM2-B2 predictors in different ACZs of Chhattisgarh state

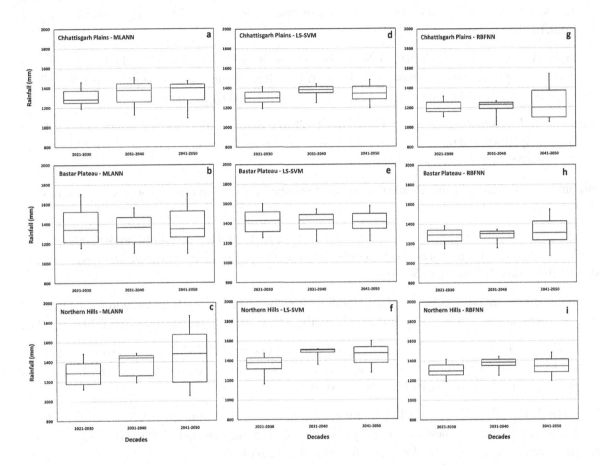

to local scale. For model development, calibration and validation of different machine learning approach are done using the long term NCEP variables as predictor variable and local scale rainfall time series as the target variable in different ACZs. The efficiency of the MLANN, RBFNN and LS-SVM models are evaluated by model performance criteria, i.e., R^2, RMSE and NSE, which shows the an excellent agreement between observed and estimated monthly rainfall during calibration and validation periods with all the machine learning approaches in different ACZs. Among the machine learning approaches considered for investigation, results obtained with RBFNN model is found superior over MLANN and LS-SVM models. The projected rainfall time series are obtained using HadCM3 GCM predictors for B2 emission scenarios with the help of proposed machine learning models. The changes in the rainfall pattern in different ACZs are discussed for the future periods i.e. 2030s, 2040s and 2050s. The projected rainfall time series shows an overall increasing trend of rainfall during the period 2021-2050 for all the ACZs. Despite uncertainties and bias always associated with the projected time series, but these machine learning models proved to be more feasible for downscaling rainfall as compared to other statistical downscaling techniques used in the past. Therefore, the present investigation will provide useful insight for planning better strategies for the management of water resources.

REFERENCES

Ahmed, K., Sachindra, D. A., Shahid, S., Iqbal, Z., Nawaz, N., & Khan, N. (2020). Multi-model ensemble predictions of precipitation and temperature using machine learning algorithms. *Atmospheric Research, 236.* doi:10.1016/j.atmosres.2019.104806

Anandhi, A., Srinivas, V. V., Kumar, D. N., & Nanjundiah, R. S. (2009). Role of predictors in downscaling surface temperature to river basin in India for IPCC SRES scenarios using support vector machine. *International Journal of Climatology, 29*(4), 583–603. doi:10.1002/joc.1719

Benestad, R. E., Hanssen-Bauer, I., & Førland, E. J. (2007). An evaluation of statistical models for downscaling precipitation and their ability to capture long-term trends. *International Journal of Climatology, 27*(5), 649–665. doi:10.1002/joc.1421

Broomhead, D. (1988). Multivariable functional interpolation and adaptive networks. *Complex Systems, 2,* 321–355.

Cannon, A. J., & Whitfield, P. H. (2002). Downscaling recent streamflow conditions in British Columbia, Canada using ensemble neural network models. *Journal of Hydrology (Amsterdam), 259*(1–4), 136–151. doi:10.1016/S0022-1694(01)00581-9

Chandniha, S. K., & Kansal, M. L. (2016). Rainfall estimation using multiple linear regression based statistical downscaling for Piperiya watershed in Chhattisgarh. *Journal of Agrometeorology, 18*(1), 106–112.

Chen, H., Guo, J., Xiong, W., Guo, S., & Xu, C.-Y. (2010). Downscaling GCMs using the Smooth Support Vector Machine method to predict daily precipitation in the Hanjiang Basin. *Advances in Atmospheric Sciences, 27*(2), 274–284. doi:10.100700376-009-8071-1

Chen, H., Xu, C. Y., & Guo, S. (2012). Comparison and evaluation of multiple GCMs, statistical downscaling and hydrological models in the study of climate change impacts on runoff. *Journal of Hydrology (Amsterdam), 434–435,* 36–45. doi:10.1016/j.jhydrol.2012.02.040

Chen, S. T., Yu, P. S., & Tang, Y. H. (2010). Statistical downscaling of daily precipitation using support vector machines and multivariate analysis. *Journal of Hydrology (Amsterdam), 385*(1–4), 13–22. doi:10.1016/j.jhydrol.2010.01.021

Cheng, C. S., Li, G., Li, Q., & Auld, H. (2008). Statistical downscaling of hourly and daily climate scenarios for various meteorological variables in South-central Canada. *Theoretical and Applied Climatology, 91*(1–4), 129–147. doi:10.100700704-007-0302-8

Courant, R., & Hilbert, D. (2008). *Methods of Mathematical Physics. In Methods of Mathematical Physics* (Vol. 2, pp. 1–830). Wiley Blackwell. doi:10.1002/9783527617234

Dibike, Y. B., & Coulibaly, P. (2005). Hydrologic impact of climate change in the Saguenay watershed: Comparison of downscaling methods and hydrologic models. *Journal of Hydrology (Amsterdam), 307*(1–4), 145–163. doi:10.1016/j.jhydrol.2004.10.012

Duhan, D., & Pandey, A. (2015). Statistical downscaling of temperature using three techniques in the Tons River basin in Central India. *Theoretical and Applied Climatology, 121*(3–4), 605–622. doi:10.100700704-014-1253-5

Ghosh, S., & Mujumdar, P. P. (2008). Statistical downscaling of GCM simulations to streamflow using relevance vector machine. *Advances in Water Resources, 31*(1), 132–146. doi:10.1016/j.advwatres.2007.07.005

Goyal, M. K., & Ojha, C. S. P. (2012). Downscaling of surface temperature for lake catchment in an arid region in India using linear multiple regression and neural networks. *International Journal of Climatology, 32*(4), 552–566. doi:10.1002/joc.2286

Haykin, S. (1999). *Neural Networks: A Comprehensive Foundation (3rd Edition). The Knowledge Engineering Review* (Vol. 13, p. S0269888998214044). Prentice-Hall, Inc. Retrieved from http://www.journals.cambridge.org/abstract_S0269888998214044

Huth, R. (1999). Statistical downscaling in central Europe: Evaluation of methods and potential predictors. *Climate Research, 13*(2), 91–101. doi:10.3354/cr013091

Huth, R. (2002). Statistical downscaling of daily temperature in central Europe. *Journal of Climate, 15*(13), 1731–1742. doi:10.1175/1520-0442(2002)015<1731:SDODTI>2.0.CO;2

Huth, R. (2004). Sensitivity of local daily temperature change estimates to the selection of downscaling models and predictors. *Journal of Climate, 17*(3), 640–652. doi:10.1175/1520-0442(2004)017<0640:SOLDTC>2.0.CO;2

IPCC. (1996). Intergovernmental Panel on Climate Change (IPCC), 1996. Report of the Twelfth Season of the Intergovernmental Panel on Climate Change, Mexico City.

IPCC. (2007). The physical science basis. Summary for policymakers. Contribution of working group I to the fourth assessment report. The Intergovernmental Panel on Climate Change. *Climatic Change.*

Keerthi, S. S., & Lin, C. J. (2003). Asymptotic behaviors of support vector machines with gaussian kernel. *Neural Computation, 15*(7), 1667–1689. doi:10.1162/089976603321891855 PMID:12816571

Kim, S., & Kim, H. S. (2008). Neural networks and genetic algorithm approach for nonlinear evaporation and evapotranspiration modeling. *Journal of Hydrology (Amsterdam), 351*(3–4), 299–317. doi:10.1016/j.jhydrol.2007.12.014

Kostopoulou, E., Giannakopoulos, C., Anagnostopoulou, C., Tolika, K., Maheras, P., Vafiadis, M., & Founda, D. (2007). Simulating maximum and minimum temperature over Greece: A comparison of three downscaling techniques. *Theoretical and Applied Climatology, 90*(1–2), 65–82. doi:10.100700704-006-0269-x

Kumar, A., & Sharma, M. P. (2017). Estimation of green house gas emissions from Koteshwar hydropower reservoir, India. *Environmental Monitoring and Assessment, 189*(5). doi:10.100710661-017-5958-7 PMID:28451962

Lal Kansal, M., Chandniha, S. K., & Tyagi, A. (2015). Distance based water sustainability assessment using SPI for the state of Chhattisgarh in India. In *World Environmental and Water Resources Congress 2015: Floods, Droughts, and Ecosystems - Proceedings of the 2015 World Environmental and Water Resources Congress* (pp. 2300–2319). American Society of Civil Engineers (ASCE). https://doi.org/10.1061/9780784479162.227

Landman, W. A., Mason, S. J., Tyson, P. D., & Tennant, W. J. (2001). Statistical downscaling of GCM simulations to streamflow. *Journal of Hydrology (Amsterdam)*, *252*(1–4), 221–236. doi:10.1016/S0022-1694(01)00457-7

Lin, H., & Lin, C. (2003). A study on sigmoid kernels for SVM and the training of non-PSD kernels by SMO-type methods. *Neural Computation*, (2): 1–32. https://doi.org/10.1.1.14.6709

Maheras, P., Tolika, K., Anagnostopoulou, C., Vafiadis, M., Patrikas, I., & Flocas, H. (2004). On the relationships between circulation types and changes in rainfall variability in Greece. *International Journal of Climatology*, *24*(13), 1695–1712. doi:10.1002/joc.1088

Mishra, P. K., Khare, D., Mondal, A., & Kundu, S. (2014). *Multiple Linear Regression Based Statistical Downscaling of Daily Precipitation in a Canal Command. In Climate Change and Biodiversity* (pp. 73–83). Tokyo: Springer. doi:10.1007/978-4-431-54838-6_6

Murphy, B. F., & Timbal, B. (2008). A review of recent climate variability and climate change in Southeastern Australia. *International Journal of Climatology*, (28): 859–879. doi:10.1002/joc.1627

Najafi, M. R., Moradkhani, H., & Jung, I. W. (2011). Assessing the uncertainties of hydrologic model selection in climate change impact studies. *Hydrological Processes*, *25*(18), 2814–2826. doi:10.1002/hyp.8043

Nash, J. E., & Sutcliffe, J. V. (1970). River flow forecasting through conceptual models part I - A discussion of principles. *Journal of Hydrology (Amsterdam)*, *10*(3), 282–290. doi:10.1016/0022-1694(70)90255-6

Ojha, C. S. P. (2013). Downscaling of Precipitation for Lake Catchment in Arid Region in India using Linear Multiple Regression and Neural Networks. *The Open Hydrology Journal*, *4*(1), 122–136. doi:10.2174/1874378101004010122

Raffel, M., Willert, C. E., Wereley, S. T., Kompenhans, J., Willert, S., Wereley, S. T., & Kompenhans, J. (2007). Particle Image Velocimetry: A Practical Guide. In Particle Image Velocimetry (Vol. 2, p. 448). Springer. https://doi.org/ doi:10.1097/JTO.0b013e3182370e69

Sachindra, D. A., Ahmed, K., Rashid, M. M., Shahid, S., & Perera, B. J. C. (2018). Statistical downscaling of precipitation using machine learning techniques. *Atmospheric Research*, *212*, 240–258. doi:10.1016/j.atmosres.2018.05.022

Sachindra, D. A., Huang, F., Barton, A., & Perera, B. J. C. (2013). Least square support vector and multi-linear regression for statistically downscaling general circulation model outputs to catchment streamflows. *International Journal of Climatology*, *33*(5), 1087–1106. doi:10.1002/joc.3493

Samadi, S., Carbone, G. J., Mahdavi, M., Sharifi, F., & Bihamta, M. R. (2013). Statistical Downscaling of River Runoff in a Semi Arid Catchment. *Water Resources Management, 27*(1), 117–136. doi:10.100711269-012-0170-6

Schoof, J. T., Pryor, S. C., & Robeson, S. M. (2007). Downscaling daily maximum and minimum temperatures in the midwestern USA: A hybrid empirical approach. *International Journal of Climatology, 27*(4), 439–454. doi:10.1002/joc.1412

Shi, P., Yang, T., Zhang, K., Tang, Q., Yu, Z., & Zhou, X. (2016). Large-scale climate patterns and precipitation in an arid endorheic region: Linkage and underlying mechanism. *Environmental Research Letters, 11*(4). doi:10.1088/1748-9326/11/4/044006

Suykens, J. A. K., & Vandewalle, J. (1999). Least squares support vector machine classifiers. *Neural Processing Letters, 9*(3), 293–300. doi:10.1023/A:1018628609742

Suykens, J. A. K., Vandewalle, J., & De Moor, B. (2001). Optimal control by least squares support vector machines. *Neural Networks, 14*(1), 23–35. doi:10.1016/S0893-6080(00)00077-0 PMID:11213211

Tisseuil, C., Vrac, M., Lek, S., & Wade, A. J. (2010). Statistical downscaling of river flows. *Journal of Hydrology (Amsterdam), 385*(1–4), 279–291. doi:10.1016/j.jhydrol.2010.02.030

Tolika, K., Maheras, P., Flocas, H. A., & Arseni-Papadimitriou, A. (2006). An evaluation of a general circulation model (GCM) and the NCEP-NCAR reanalysis data for winter precipitation in Greece. *International Journal of Climatology, 26*(7), 935–955. doi:10.1002/joc.1290

Tomozeiu, R., Cacciamani, C., Pavan, V., Morgillo, A., & Busuioc, A. (2007). Climate change scenarios for surface temperature in Emilia-Romagna (Italy) obtained using statistical downscaling models. *Theoretical and Applied Climatology, 90*(1–2), 25–47. doi:10.100700704-006-0275-z

Trigo, R. M., & Palutikof, J. P. (2001). Precipitation scenarios over Iberia: A comparison between direct GCM output and different downscaling techniques. *Journal of Climate, 14*(23), 4422–4446. doi:10.1175/1520-0442(2001)014<4422:PSOIAC>2.0.CO;2

Tripathi, S., Srinivas, V. V., & Nanjundiah, R. S. (2006). Downscaling of precipitation for climate change scenarios: A support vector machine approach. *Journal of Hydrology (Amsterdam), 330*(3–4), 621–640. doi:10.1016/j.jhydrol.2006.04.030

Vandal, T., Kodra, E., & Ganguly, A. R. (2019). Intercomparison of machine learning methods for statistical downscaling: The case of daily and extreme precipitation. *Theoretical and Applied Climatology, 137*(1–2), 557–570. doi:10.100700704-018-2613-3

Wetterhall, F., Halldin, S., & Xu, C. Y. (2005). Statistical precipitation downscaling in central Sweden with the analogue method. *Journal of Hydrology (Amsterdam), 306*(1–4), 174–190. doi:10.1016/j.jhydrol.2004.09.008

Wilby, R. L., Charles, S. P., Zorita, E., Timbal, B., Whetton, P., & Mearns, L. O. (2004). *Guidelines for use of climate scenarios developed from statistical downscaling methods. In IPCC Data Distribution Centre Report* (p. 27). Norwich, UK: UEA.

Wilby, R. L., Dawson, C. W., & Barrow, E. M. (2002). SDSM - A decision support tool for the assessment of regional climate change impacts. *Environmental Modelling & Software, 17*(2), 145–157. doi:10.10161364-8152(01)00060-3

Xu, R., Chen, N., Chen, Y., & Chen, Z. (2020). Downscaling and Projection of Multi-CMIP5 Precipitation Using Machine Learning Methods in the Upper Han River Basin. *Advances in Meteorology, 2020.* doi:10.1155/2020/8680436

Yang, T., Cui, T., Xu, C. Y., Ciais, P., & Shi, P. (2017). Development of a new IHA method for impact assessment of climate change on flow regime. *Global and Planetary Change, 156,* 68–79. doi:10.1016/j.gloplacha.2017.07.006

Yang, T., Shao, Q., Hao, Z. C., Chen, X., Zhang, Z., Xu, C. Y., & Sun, L. (2010). Regional frequency analysis and spatio-temporal pattern characterization of rainfall extremes in the Pearl River Basin, China. *Journal of Hydrology (Amsterdam), 380*(3–4), 386–405. doi:10.1016/j.jhydrol.2009.11.013

Yang, T., Wang, C., Chen, Y., Chen, X., & Yu, Z. (2015). Climate change and water storage variability over an arid endorheic region. *Journal of Hydrology (Amsterdam), 529*(P1), 330–339. doi:10.1016/j.jhydrol.2015.07.051

Zhang, B., & Govindaraju, R. S. (2000). Prediction of watershed runoff using Bayesian concepts and modular neural networks. *Water Resources Research, 36*(3), 753–762. doi:10.1029/1999WR900264

Chapter 6

Multi–Feature Fusion and Machine Learning:
A Model for Early Detection of Freezing of Gait Events in Patients With Parkinson's Disease

Hadeer Elziaat
Future University in Egypt (FUE), Egypt

Nashwa El-Bendary
https://orcid.org/0000-0001-6553-4159
Arab Academy for Science, Technology, and Maritime Transport (AASTMT), Smart Village, Egypt

Ramadan Moawad
Future University in Egypt (FUE), Egypt

ABSTRACT

Freezing of gait (FoG) is a common symptom of Parkinson's disease (PD) that causes intermittent absence of forward progression of patient's feet while walking. Accordingly, FoG momentary episodes are always accompanied with falls. This chapter presents a novel multi-feature fusion model for early detection of FoG episodes in patients with PD. In this chapter, two feature engineering schemes are investigated, namely time-domain hand-crafted feature engineering and convolutional neural network (CNN)-based spectrogram feature learning. Data of tri-axial accelerometer sensors for patients with PD is utilized to characterize the performance of the proposed model through several experiments with various machine learning (ML) algorithms. Obtained experimental results showed that the multi-feature fusion approach has outperformed typical single feature sets. Conclusively, the significance of this chapter is to highlight the impact of using feature fusion of multi-feature sets through investigating the performance of a FoG episodes early detection model.

DOI: 10.4018/978-1-7998-6659-6.ch006

Figure 1. The main consequences related to elderly falling

BACKGROUND

Parkinson's Disease (PD) is a degenerative disorder, which affects patient's movements. It is marked by decreased dopamine levels in the brain and considered as the second most common symptom after Alzheimer's Disease (AD). A lack of dopamine, which results in abnormal nerve functioning, causes a loss in the ability to control body movements. The PD has influenced about 1% or 2% of elderly people worldwide (Nilashi, 2016). This study aimed to detect Freezing of Gait (FoG) attacks in patients with PD, using different features and classifiers, for increasing the detection performance and decreasing the social costs that face the patients with PD symptoms. The PD patients usually spend almost two more days in hospitals, 43 more days in care institutions, and fill more than 20 medical therapies than the non-PD subjects do. The total cost for PD patients is more than a double of the non-PD subjects. On the other hand, the productivity loss recorded for PD patients reaches 49.4% (Dua et al., 2006). Furthermore, as shown in Figure 1, among several consequences related to elderly falling, the loss of independence risk represents a significant social consequence. That is, the PD patient will constantly be dependent on one of the family members or a medical center caregiver (El-Bendary et al., 2013). According to the World Health Organization (WHO), the percentage of Global Disability Adjusted Life Years (DALYs) by 2030 will increase by 0.13% for patients with PD, coming after the percentage of Alzheimer's Disease that has been predicted to increase by 1.2%. Also, the deaths for PD patients will reach 23% by 2030 as the total deaths globally for neurological disorders will reach 12.22% (Dua et al., 2006).

Parkinson's Disease contains two types of symptoms that affect the quality of daily life; namely, motor and non-motor symptoms. Motor symptoms or cardinal symptoms contain resting tremor, rigidity, bradykinesia (movement slowness), postural instability (balance problems), and Freezing of Gait (FoG). Whereas non-motor symptoms contain cognitive impairment, sleep behavior disorder, olfactory loss, constipation, speech & swallowing problems, unexplained pains, drooling, low blood pressure when standing, and rapid eye movement. Freezing of Gait occurs in most patients with PD in early stages, as patients suddenly feel an inability to step forward while walking. During the FoG episodes that are characterized by a short period of inability to initiate a gait, PD patients intermittently feel that their feet are stuck to the floor as being held by magnets when trying to walk. Accordingly, FoG momentary episodes are always accompanied by patients falling, the case that affects activities in daily life, and quality of life by having a significant negative impact on PD patients with FoG symptoms (Sveinbjornsdottir, 2016). The FoG could be observed in some patients who experience brief trembling in their feet followed by short small steps. Other PD patients may experience total immobility in body movements and are unable to move at all for a few seconds.

For proposing state-of-the-art solutions to soundly handle the problem of detecting/predicting Parkinson's Disease, various studies were proposed using Machine Learning (ML) techniques. In (Kumar, 2016), the author aimed to predict PD using Random Forest classification algorithm with 20 different features using a dataset of a range of biomedical voice measurements from 31 subjects, 23 with PD. Also, the authors in (Sujatha & Rajagopalan, 2017) aimed to classify the patients as healthy and PD subjects using fundamental frequency, amplitude, hitter, noise-to-harmonic ratio, harmonic-to-noise ratio, Detrended Fluctuation Analysis (DFA), and spread biomedical voice features. Machine Learning algorithms such as ZeroR, OneR, Bayes Net, Radial Basis Function (RBF), Hidden Markov Model, Naïve Bayes, Logistic Regression, Multilayer Perceptron, AdaBoost, Decision Tree, J48, and Random Forest were used for classification of PD patients.

The authors in (Karan et al., 2020) proposed a model based on empirical mode decomposition for PD detection using two speech datasets. Different features were extracted; namely, acoustic features, mel-frequency cepstral coefficients (MFCC), statistical features, spectral entropy, energy, entropy, and intrinsic mode function-cepstral coefficient, with Support Vector Machine (SVM) and Random Forest ML classifiers.

Furthermore, the SVM classification algorithm with recursive feature elimination was used in (Senturk, 2020) for early PD diagnosis. Feature importance and recursive features elimination methods were used for feature selection. The dataset used in this study consists of 31 PD subjects, with 8 of them representing the control group.

In (Abdulhay et al., 2018) the goal was to diagnose PD using the gait cycle that consisted of various phases to determine and differentiate between normal and abnormal gait patterns. Vertical ground reaction force dataset was used, which contains 279 gait recordings from 93 patients with PD and 73 healthy subjects. The data was recorded based on 8 sensors placed under the patients' feet. Stride time, stance time, swing time, and foot strike profile features were used with medium Gaussian SVM to classify normal and PD subjects.

On the other hand, numerous image classification methods were also proposed for solving the problem of PD early detection. In (Astorino et al., 2019), the authors focused on multiple instance learning (MIL) approach based on SVM classifier. The aim was to identify images containing color pattern based on a dataset containing images of melanoma and common nevi. In (Zumpano et al., 2018) the authors proposed Sistema Informativo Medico PATologIe COmplesse (SIMPATICO 3D) to provide facilities to organizations by designing a software platform suited for those organizations. It uses Model-View-View-Model (MVVM) that allows the direct binding of medical information with 3D graphic objects.

More studies also worked on images like in (Challa et al., 2016), where the authors used DataScan SPECT imaging obtained from PPMI imaging centers with boosted Logistic Regression classifier. In that study, different non-motor features have been used such as sleep behavior disorder and olfactory loss. The University of Pennsylvania Smell Identification Test (UPSIT), REM sleep Behavior Disorder Screening Questionnaire (RBDSQ), Cerebrospinal Fluid Biomarkers, and Neuroimaging markers were the features used for PD prediction. Moreover, the authors in (Chakraborty et al., 2020) utilized MRI scanned images for early PD detection of 637 PD patients, 66 prodromal subjects and 203 healthy controls. A multi-layer perceptron ML algorithm was used with 107 extracted features from segmented 3D voxels of interest.

In this chapter, various state-of-the-art ML models for Freezing of Gait episodes' early detection are presented through investigating the utilization of different extracted feature sets; namely, time-domain statistical features, time-frequency spectrogram CNN-learned features, and fusion of time-domain and time-frequency features. Spectrogram images based on time-series data of tri-axial accelerometer sensors have been used as the models' input instead of using the raw data signals. The proposed models are also tested using Principle Component Analysis (PCA) algorithm for achieving feature set dimensionality reduction. The implemented ML classifiers in this chapter are Random Forest, Logistic Regression, AdaBoost, K-Nearest Neighbor (K-NN), Decision Tree, Bagging, SVM with (Linear, RBF, and sigmoid Kernel functions), Ensemble Stacking SVMs classifier, and Ensemble Stacking of all the implemented ML classifiers. All the stated ML algorithms are tested for subject-dependent and subject-independent modes, using accelerometer sensor-independent (Ankle, Knee, and Trunk) sensor schemes.

LITERATURE REVIEW

This section describes relevant state-of-the-art studies and discusses the corresponding algorithms, aims, features, and approaches. Different types of assessment, such as clinical and non-clinical are also presented. Moreover, this section provides guidance for identifying many important features and approaches in order to help selecting the most effective ones.

For clinical assessments, in (Suppa et al., 2017) the authors' aim was to compare and examine the gait clinically and objectively for PD patients with and without FoG. The study included 28 PD patients with FoG, 16 without FoG, and 16 healthy subjects. The gait was evaluated clinically by using the Hoehn and Yahr (H&Y) scale and the Movement and Disorder Society Unified Parkinson's Disease Rating Scale (MDS-UPDRS) part III. The gait was also measured objectively by using Timed Up and Go (TUG) test video recording. The results are 93.41% for sensitivity and 98.51% for specificity. Furthermore, the authors in (Capecci et al., 2016) tried to detect FoG for PD patients by using a smartphone-based architecture. To verify the acceptance of this method and its reliability at detecting FoG in real-time by preforming a TUG test video recording while wearing a smartphone, the authors used also the smartphone-based accelerometer. By applying a sliding window with 256 samples, the Fast Fourier Transform (FFT) and the power spectrum are calculated. Also, the FI and step cadence, computed as the second harmonic in the power spectrum, gait features are extracted. This architecture used two different algorithms, the first one was the Freeze Index (FI) and the second one was Energy Index (EI). The achieved sensitivity and specificity are 87.57% and 94.97%, respectively.

On the other hand, for the non-clinical assessment approach, FoG detection has been proposed in many research studies using different types of Inertial Measurement Unit (IMU) sensors and features.

The authors in (Mazilu et al. 2016) used a new sensor placement style at patient's wrist and both ankles with a 3D accelerometer, 3D magnetometer and 3D gyroscope to from the CuPiD dataset for detecting FoG episodes. The proposed approach in that study based on C4.5 classifier with statistical features and frequency features. In that research, the authors have achieved 0.9 hit rate and specificity of 66% and 80%. On the other hand, the authors in (Xu et al. 2017) aimed at detecting FoG episodes, however through using template matching methods as an approach for comparing two sequences of time. Accordingly, the authors have proposed an improved subsequence Dynamic Time Wrapping (IsDTW) method using time and frequency domain features from the Daphnet dataset. The proposed model has achieved an accuracy of 92%.

In (Ahlrichs et al., 2016), the main objective has been developing a waist-worn device for detecting FoG episodes based on acceleration measurements, magnetometer and gyroscope sensors. The proposed system has used frequency and time domain features. A windowing mechanism of 128 samples has been applied. The output of linear SVM classifier has been aggregated over time in seconds for achieving the highest accuracy of 98.7% and a geometric mean of 96.1%. Also, in (Rodrıguez-Martın et al., 2017), the authors have proposed a method that used frequency-domain features for detecting FoG episodes. The SVM classifier has been used with the leave-one-out technique. The achieved results were 88.1%, 80.1, and 84%% for sensitivity, specificity, and geometric mean, respectively.

Moreover, the aim in (Shah et al., 2018) was to detect the absence or presence of FoG for PD patients based on 2 body-mounted acceleration sensors. Using the Daphnet dataset, the authors have proposed two algorithms; namely, the Constrained optimization- based Extreme Learning Machine (C-ELM) and the C-ELM with bagging (C-ELMBG). The achieved accuracy was 93% and 93.9% for C-ELM and C- ELMBG, respectively. Furthermore, in (Mazilu et al. 2013), the aim was detection of FoG with 64 samples data windowing based on the 3D accelerometers features extracted with 3 seconds windowing using a Decision Tree classifier. Applied frequency domain, time domain, statistical features, and sensor features were extracted from the Daphnet dataset.

In (De Sousa, 2018) the author has utilized the accelerometer based readings in the Daphnet dataset. The proposed approach used Random Forest and SVM with RBF kernel classifiers for detecting the motor symptoms in PD patients; namely, the pre-FoG episode and pre-FoG patterns. The model achieves a specificity of 82%, a sensitivity of 85.1%, and an F1-score of 58.9%, with different frequency domain features, in addition to the features from (Mazilu et al. 2013). In (Rezvanian & Lockhart, 2016), identifying Freezing of Gait was based on the use of Continuous Wavelet Transform (CWT) with a 3D accelerometer sensor on patient's shank, thigh, and lower back. The sensor based features, which are the x, y, and z readings from each sensor placement with 1 sec., 2 sec., 3 sec., and 4 sec. windowing was applied. The obtained results are 82.1% and 77.1% for sensitivity and specificity, respectively. The authors in (Tahafchi et al., 2017) used 3 accelerometers, 3 gyroscopes, and 3 magnetometers, which were attached to the thigh, shank, and foot to extract different types of features like time-frequency domain, spatial, frequency, and time domain features. Those features were used for FoG detection using SVM classifier with Gaussian kernel. The authors in (Mazzetta et al., 2019) used a combination of surface Electromyography (EMG) and a 3D gyroscope and a 3D accelerometer integrated in a wearable device that senses the actions and movements simultaneously of the leg muscles, for real-time FoG detection. Also, fusion of gyroscope with EMG readings for remote assistant patients was used by distinguishing the trembling in place and the shuffling forward FoG subtypes. For classifying gait, the authors in that study used the ratio between the maximum value of the normalized absolute value of the averaged angular velocity (ABS) and the corresponding sEMG value. Experiments were applied on seven patients with a very wide variety of disease features.

Also, in (Polat, 2019), the authors used statistical features with a Logistic Regression classifier to detect the FoG events. Using Daphnet dataset with a single sensor that was placed on the patient's ankle achieved an accuracy of 81.3%. An integration of features technique was adopted in (El Attar et al., 2018) by fusing a (1D DWT) Discrete Wavelet Transform, and Fast Fourier Transform (FFT) for the analysis of acceleration sensor signals. Then, features were extracted from the signal transformation. A feature vector of fifteen extracted features was used for classification using Artificial Neural Network (ANN). The achieved accuracy was 96.28% using the vertical acceleration signal of the sensor placed on the ankle from Daphnet dataset. The authors in (Ghosh & Banerjee, 2019) used a classification method based on Grey Relational Analysis (GRA) for FoG detection with bagging ensemble method with an achieved accuracy of 90.62%.

Then again, in (Ashour et al., 2018), the authors aimed to detect FoG based on patient-dependent model using SVM classifier with linear kernel with the use of infinite feature selection (IFS) as a ranked features method to differentiate between freezing and non-freezing events and Eigenvector feature selection. Nine types of signals were extracted from three accelerometer body sensors with three signals; namely, horizontal, vertical, and lateral, with two different sets of features extracted using Discrete Wavelet Transform (DWT) and FFT experimented on patients of the Daphnet dataset. The extracted features were fused to present a new feature vector of DWT and FFT features together. The most significant experimental results are the ones obtained on Patient 2 with and achieved accuracy of 94.4%.

MULTI-FEATURE FUSION FOR EARLY DETECTION OF FOG EVENTS USING MACHINE LEARNING

This section introduces the four phases of the proposed model, as illustrated in Figure 2.

1. Data Preparation
2. Feature Extraction
3. Feature Fusion and Dimensionality Reduction
4. Classification

The section starts with introducing the dataset used in this study for validating the proposed model.

Dataset Description

The benchmark Daphnet FoG dataset, which is a publicly available dataset from the UCI Machine Learning Repository (B"achlin et al., 2010), has been used for validating the proposed approach. The data readings were collected from ten participants with PD as shown in Table 1. While performing several walking tasks in the lab, eight subjects have experienced FoG episodes. The dataset has been recorded using three wearable tri-axial accelerometer sensors attached to the shank (ankle), the thigh (above the knee), and to the trunk (lower back) of each subject. During the stufy, 237 FoG events have been identified by professional physiotherapists over eight hours of the recorded data. The length of FoG events ranged from 0.5 to 40.5 seconds. Almost half of the FoG episodes have lasted for less than 5.4 seconds.

Figure 2. General structure of the FoG early detection model

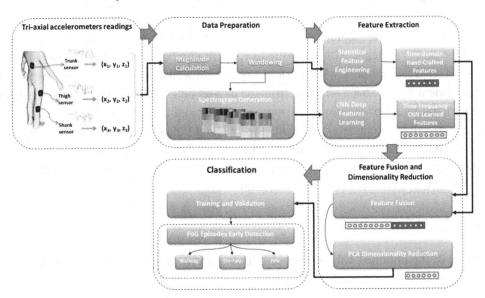

Data samples have been originally labeled as 0, 1, and 2 corresponding to out-of-experiment, no-FoG, and FoG events, respectively. Subjects completed sessions of 20-30 minutes each, consisted of three basic walking tasks in order to represent different characteristics of daily walking, as follows (B¨achlin et al., 2010):

- Straight-line walking back and forth with several 180-degrees turns.
- Random walking with a series of initiated stops and 360-degrees turns.
- Walking with simulating activities of daily living, including entering and leaving rooms, walking to the kitchen, getting something and returning to the starting room.

Table 1. Detailed patient characteristics with FoG attacks of each patient after windowing

Patient	Gender	Age	Disease Duration	H&Y Score	FoG Attacks With 1 Second Windowing	FoG Attacks With 4 Seconds Windowing
1	Male	66	16	2	109	34
2	Male	67	7	2	180	49
3	Male	59	30	2.5	289	86
4	Male	62	3	3	-	-
5	Male	75	6	2	482	130
6	Female	63	22	2	130	35
7	Male	66	2	2.5	90	29
8	Female	68	18	4	201	51
9	Male	73	9	2	271	71
10	Female	65	24	3	-	-

Data Preparation

As previously mentioned, the Daphnet dataset is consisted of time-series readings from 3 tri-axial accelerometers for ten PD patients, with two patients (patient number 4 and patient number 10) who have not experienced any FoG episodes while performing several walking tasks. Wherefore, data for patient number 4 and patient 10 have been removed from the dataset before starting our experiments and during the data preparation phase of the proposed approach. The original data samples have been labeled as 0, 1 and 2 corresponding to out-of-experiment, no-FoG, and FoG event, respectively. Thus, the dataset has been edited by neglecting the data records labeled as 0 before starting the implementation of the data preparation phase. Accordingly, the data preparation phase includes the three steps of magnitude calculation, windowing, and spectrogram generation.

Magnitude Calculation

The magnitude of the obtained values has been derived from each record of the three accelerometer values x, y, and z, according to equation (1).

$$Magnitude = \sqrt{(x_s^2 + y_s^2 + z_s^2)} \tag{1}$$

Where *s* refers to the used ankle's (shank), knee's (lower thigh), or trunk's (lower back) sensor.

Windowing

During the windowing step, the calculated magnitudes for each sensor have been sliced into partially overlapping dynamic and fixed sized windows based on the data labels for testing different windowing mechanisms. To select the most efficient slicing method with the best performance, two methods of windowing have been employed.

Windowing scheme-1: A windowing method of 1 second window size (15 msec. each, 67 samples), as shown in Figure 3 (a). For this method, data readings with a very short duration (less than 1 sec.), which are assumed as accidental appearing of FoG similar behaviors, have been neglected. Thus, windows containing less than 67 similarly labeled samples, between other windows of samples with a different label, have been neglected. Partial overlapping also has been applied in case of having a window or a sequence of windows with similarly labeled samples, followed by a group of remaining samples (less than 67 samples) of the same label. In that case, an additional group of samples from the last complete window will be duplicated and added to the incomplete group of samples in order to formulate a new complete window of 67 similarly labeled samples.

The described scheme-1 method of windowing is used for guarantee generating spectrogram images of the same size. Feature engineering for generating time-domain statistical features should produce a group of feature vectors of the same number equals to the feature vectors produced by spectrograms. For fulfilling the requirements of validating the baseline approach using multi-feature fusion between statistical features (time-domain) and spectrogram based CNN features (time-frequency), the previous windowing method is implemented.

Windowing scheme-2: A windowing method of window sizes between 4 seconds (268 samples) and 1 second (67 samples), as shown in Figure 3 (b). On the other hand, in this method based on the data labels, a partially overlapping windowing method of dynamic-sized windows has been applied. In this method, for each group of 67 to 268 similarly labeled samples, a new generated window has been generated. Similar to the first windowing scheme, windows contain less than 67 similarly labeled samples, between other windows of samples with a different label, have been neglected. The same partial overlapping methodology has been followed in the case of having a group of remaining samples (less than 268 samples) of the same label. This scheme-2 windowing is not used with the feature fusion model because the generated spectrogram images will not be of the same size. For that reason, the CNN based feature vectors will not be of the same size as the statistical feature vectors.

Figure 3. Windowing schemes: (a) 1 second (67 samples) windowing and (b) 4 seconds (268 samples) windowing

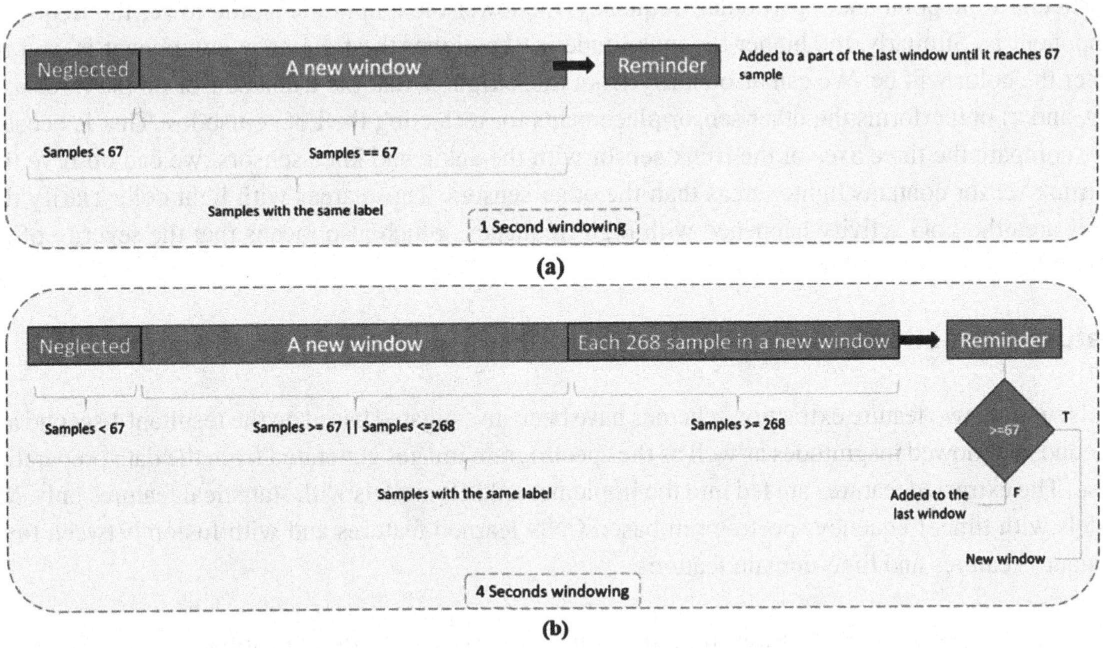

Spectrogram Generation

The conventional frequency-domain or time-domain analysis cannot fully describe non-stationary and non-periodic signals, whose frequency content varies with time (Boualem, 2015). So, in order to gain frequency-domain as well as time-domain related information of real life signals, it is recommended to use time-frequency analysis. For displaying the time-frequency analysis information, the spectrogram is used as it is one of the basic visual tools. (Astrid et al., 2015). The spectrogram is a 2D map where the horizontal axis represents the time of the signal and the vertical axis represents the frequency. Time-frequency spectrogram features that contain three-dimensional information; namely, time, frequency, and amplitude, are presented as follows:

- **Time:** Is a 1D array of time corresponding to the columns in spectrum (amplitude).
- **Frequency:** Is also a 1D array of frequencies corresponding to the rows in spectrum.
- **Amplitude:** Is a 2D array of a period-grams of successive segments.

In this chapter, Short-Time Fourier Transform (STFT) has been used for generating the corresponding spectrograms as the time-frequency analysis algorithm of windowed sensors readings (Wang et al., 2018). The spectrogram parameters are the window size, noverlap, nfft, and fs. The input to the spectrogram is a data signal x and the output will be a matrix of 2D array q that will have (nfft/2+1) rows if nfft is even and (nfft+1)/2 rows if nfft is odd. For columns, the equation will be (the length of q – noverlap) / (length (window-noverlap)).

Figures 4, 5, and 6 present three different samples of spectrogram images generated for each of the 3D accelerometer axes (x, y and z) for the FoG activity detected by each of the three sensors ankle, knee, and trunk, respectively. The same portion of data has been used for generating the spectrograms for the three figures. From Figures 4, 5, and 6, we can also observe that dark colors with the indication that for a particular time point and a particular frequency, the lower the amplitude is, the lower the frequency component is. Similarly, the higher the magnitude is, the higher the frequency component is, and the lighter the color will be. We can also clarify from those figures that the trunk sensor on the three axes (x, y, and z) outperforms the other sensor placements for reflecting the FoG episodes. That is because if we compare the three axes of the trunk sensor with the ankle and knee sensors, we can observe that the trunk sensor contains lighter areas than the other sensors. Those areas with light color clarify that in this area the FoG activity happened with high frequency, which also means that the severity of the FoG in the same area is high.

Feature Extraction

In this section, two feature extraction schemes have been investigated based on the resultant 1 second and 4 seconds windowed magnitudes as well as the spectrogram images generated from the data preparation phase. The extracted features are fed into the implemented ML models with statistical features only, ML models with time–frequency spectrogram based CNN learned features and with fusion between time-frequency features and time-domain features.

1. Feature engineering for various time-domain features (hand-crafted features).

The generated feature set is a time-domain statistical features that involves features manually engineered/calculated based on measures typically used in motion or human activity pattern recognition problems. The extracted statistical features in this study are *Variance, Standard deviation, Median, Mean, Maxima, Minima,* and *Range,* as shown in Table 2.

2. Deep feature learning for time-frequency analysis of spectrogram images.

The generated feature set reflecting the time and frequency analysis of spectrogram images. Recently, for outstanding performance in image processing and feature learning, CNN is the most widely used in deep learning models (Ahn et al., 2018). Various CNN models are capable of automatically learning features to capture complicated visual variations. The CNN consists of several layers; namely, convolu-

Figure 4. Spectrogram images of the x, y, and z axes for FoG activity on ankle sensor

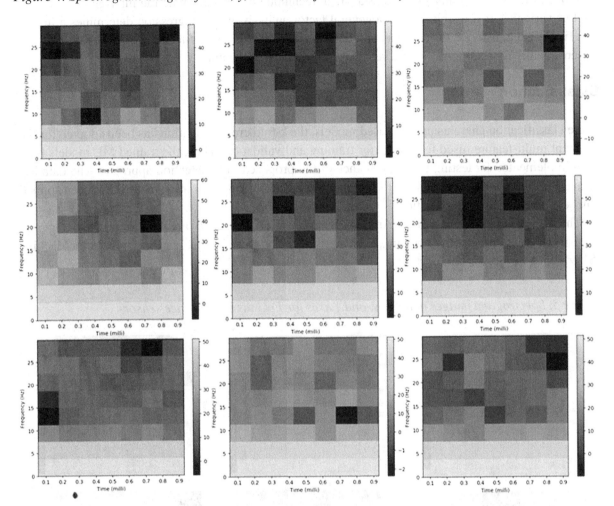

tional layers, pooling layers, and fully-connected layers. The automatic and adaptive learning of spatial hierarchies of useful features from low level to high level patterns is the main aim of CNN. In this phase, as shown in Figure 7 a 2D CNN conventional model has been used for feature learning. Table 3 clarifies the 2D CNN structure used for extracting time-frequency features from spectrograms. The full feature vector size extracted from each image is 128 features.

After the feature extraction phase, each pair of the resultant feature vectors from the extracted time-domain and time-frequency analysis feature sets are fused to form a higher dimensionality fusion feature set, as depicted in Figure 8. Normalization has been performed to transform the features into a unified range of [0, 1] in order to avoid incompatibility due to fusion of different features.

Furthermore, the Principal Component Analysis (PCA) algorithm has been adopted for reducing the dimensionality of the fused feature vectors that leads to the problems of higher computation complexity and time consumption. The PCA is a statistical procedure that uses an orthogonal transformation, which converts a set of correlated variables to a set of uncorrelated variables, as described in Figure 9. The PCA is one of the most widely used tools in exploratory data analysis and in ML for predictive models.

Moreover, the PCA is an unsupervised statistical technique used to examine the interrelations among a set of variables. It is also known as a general factor analysis, where regression determines a line of best fit. It also transforms the columns of a dataset into fewer new set of features. After using PCA for dimensionality reduction, the feature vector is minimized to 14 features.

Classification

In the classification phase using ML based models, the k-fold cross validation has been adopted for the resultant multi-feature fused feature set for training and validation. Then, the trained ML models have been implemented for testing the performance of the proposed FoG detection approach. The data has been divided into 80% training and 20% for testing. The k-fold cross validation method has been applied with *k=5* for training and validation of the ML models.

The implemented ML classifiers (Amalina et al., 2016; Trivedi, 2016) are: Random Forest, Bagging, Logistic Regression, Adaptive boosting, K-Nearest Neighbor, Decision tree, and Support Vector Machine (SVM) with various kernel functions.

Figure 5. Spectrogram images of the x, y, and z axes for FoG activity on knee sensor

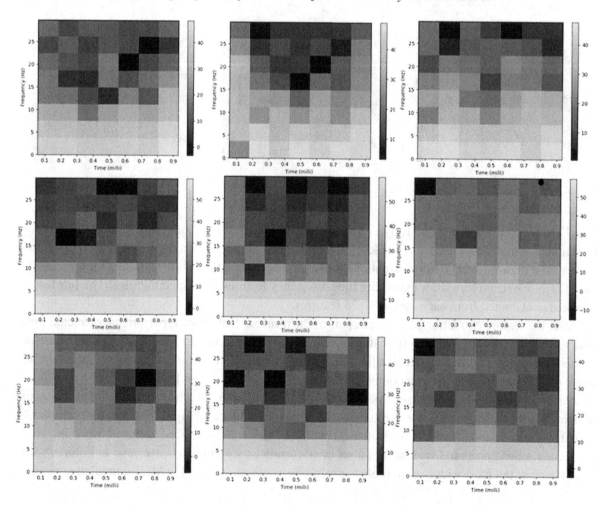

Figure 6. Spectrogram images of the x, y, and z axes for FoG activity on trunk sensor

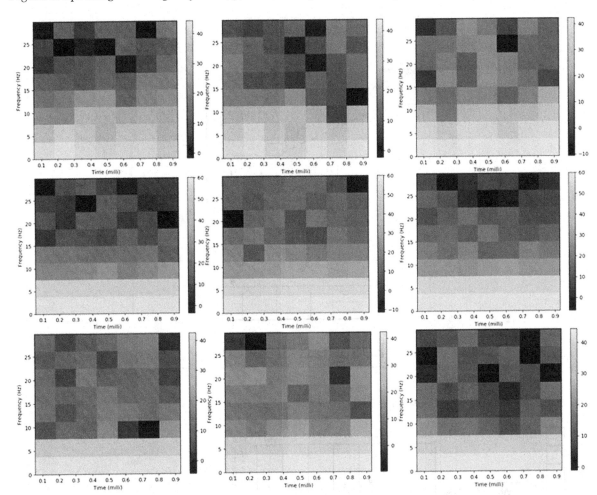

Table 2. Time-domain statistical features (handcrafted features)

Feature	Description	Formula
Mean	The average value of the magnitude over time	$\sum_{i=1}^{T} \dfrac{y_i}{T}$
Standard deviation	The square root of the average of the squared deviations from mean over time	$\left(\sum_{i=1}^{T} \dfrac{y_i - \mu_y}{T} \right)^{\frac{1}{2}}$
Variance	The average of the squared differences of the mean value over time	$\sum_{i=1}^{T} \dfrac{y_i - \mu_y}{T}$
Median	Median value of a signal over time	$median_{yi}(y_i)$
Range	The difference between the maximum and minimum signal over time	$\lvert \max y_i(y_i) - \min y_i(y_i) \rvert$
Maxima	The maximum value of the signal over time in window	$\max_{yi}(y_i)$
Minima	The minimum value of the signal over time in window	$\min_{yi}(y_i)$

Figure 7. 2D Convolutional Neural Network (CNN) structure

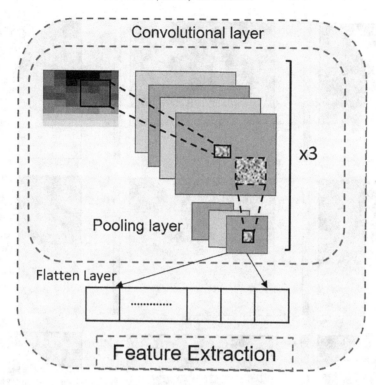

Figure 8. Time-domain and time-frequency feature fusion mechanism

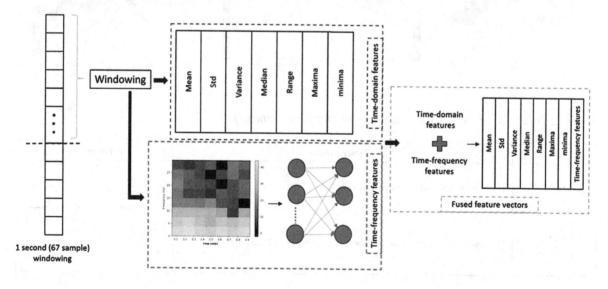

1. **Decision Tree (DT):** Decision trees are trees that classify instances by sorting them based on feature values. Each node in a decision tree represents a feature in an instance to be classified, and each branch represents a value that the node can assume. Instances are classified starting at the root node and sorted based on their feature values.

Table 3. Description and values of the CNN layers

Layer Description	Value
Convolutional layers	3
Max-pooling	3
Flatten	1
Activation function	ReLU
Optimizer	Adadelta

Figure 9. The PCA algorithm

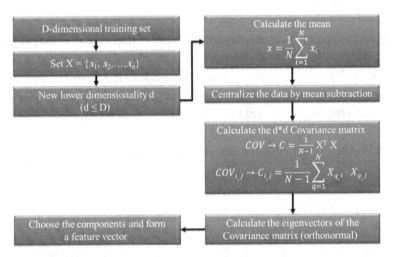

2. **Adaptive Boosting (AdaBoost):** The basis of boosting methods is bootstrapping. The bootstrapping is to re-assess the accuracy of some estimate. It is a statistical sample based method consists of randomly drawing with replacement from the dataset. Adaptive boosting works to re-weight the data rather random sampling. This method builds ensembles for performance improvement of the classifiers.

3. **Logistic Regression (LR):** This is a statistical classification method for modeling binary data. It makes use of linear regression model and the output of which is transformed to the range 0 and 1.

4. **Bagging:** This is an ensemble method like AdaBoost, however the algorithm of bagging is based on combining predictions from multiple models. When constructing models in bagging, these models are random but they are distributed. The final result of the prediction of the bagged model is based on the average of the individual predictions of the ensemble members.

5. **K-Nearest Neighbor (KNN):** For this classifier the entire training set is stored in the memory. To classify a new instance, the Euclidean distance is computed between the instance and each stored training instance, and the new instance is assigned the class of the nearest neighboring instance.

6. **Random Forest (RF):** This kind of ensemble classifier used many decision tree models, so a different subset of training data is selected each time with the replacement of each tree for training.

7. **Support Vector Machine (SVM):** This is a well-known classifier in the field of classification that works under the concept of "statistical learning theory and structural maximization principal". It

can deal with high dimensional data by the help of distinctive Kernel function, so it is a popular classifier in the research field. A linear kernel works fine if the dataset linearly separable and it is a parametric model. The Radial Basis Function (RBF) kernel creates a non-linear combination of features. A sigmoid kernel is equivalent to a two-layer perceptron neural network.

8. **Stacked Ensemble:** The stacked ensemble is a technique for using multiple classifiers or regression models via a meta-classifier or a meta-regressor. The combined classifiers are trained based on complete training set, then the meta-model is trained through treating the outputs of those combined classifiers as features.

RESULTS AND DISCUSSION

This section presents and discusses the experimental outcomes of implementing the proposed multi-feature fusion scheme for early detection of FoG episodes. The metrics that have been used for performance evaluation are Accuracy, Recall, Precision, F−score, and Specificity, which have been calculated according to equations (2), (3), (4), (5), and (6), respectively. The terms TP, FP, TN, and FN refer to True Positive, False Positive, True Negative, and False Negative, respectively.

- *Accuracy* (Acc.) is the overall effectiveness of the classifier.

$$Accuracy = \frac{TP + TN}{TP + FN + FP + TN} . \tag{2}$$

- *Precision* is the guarantee of the data labels with the classifier positive labels.

$$Precision = \frac{TP}{TP + FP} . \tag{3}$$

- *Recall* (Sensitivity) is the effectiveness of the classifier to identify the positive labels (true positive rate).

$$Recall = \frac{TP}{TP + FN} . \tag{4}$$

- *F-score* is the relation between precision and recall.

$$F\text{-}score = 2\frac{Precision * Recall}{Precision + Recall} . \tag{5}$$

- *Specificity* is the effectiveness of the classifier to identify the negative labels (true negative rate).

$$Specificity = \frac{TN}{\left(TN + FP\right)}. \tag{6}$$

Subject-independent FoG Early Detection

Generally, Figure 12 shows the classification accuracy of FoG early detection using the proposed multi-feature fusion approach when applying PCA for dimensionality reduction. From Figure 12, the Random Forest, Bagging, and KNN ML classifiers outperform the other tested ML classifiers with an accuracy of 87.5% for FoG detection. Moreover, Figure 10 and Figure 11 show that Random Forest and Bagging ensemble learning classifiers once more outperform the other tested ML classifiers with an accuracy of 80.5% and 81.2%, using the statistical features set, and 85.5% and 85.2%, using the CNN learned time-frequency analysis features sets, respectively. It is observed that the enhancement in FoG detection performance is clearly noticeable when using the multi-feature fusion approach with applying PCA dimensionality reduction against using the time-domain statistical feature engineering or the CNN learned time-frequency features.

Figure 10. FoG detection accuracy using time-domain statistical features extraction scheme, with and without using PCA

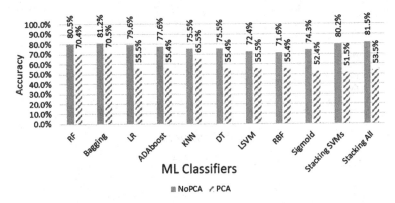

Moreover, Table 4 summarizes the most significant F-score results for 67 samples (1 second window-ing) multi-feature fusion subject-dependent/sensor-dependent FoG early detection. Furthermore, as shown in Figure 13 and Figure 14, we can observe that the use of CNN learned features outperforms the use of the statistical features. Also, from Figure 13 and Figure 14, the enhancement on ankle sensor when using CNN features against statistical features was 5.4% and 5%, respectively, and the enhancement on knee sensor was 4.4% and 4%, respectively. The performance increased also when using trunk sensor with a recorded enhancement of 4.3% and 5.7% for the two schemes, respectively. For the sensor-independent mode, the enhancement using CNN learned features against the statistical features is 5.1%.

Additionally, from Figure 13 and Figure 14, we can clarify the enhancement achieved by implement-ing FoG detection episodes with 1 second (67 samples) windowing against 4 seconds (268 samples) windowing. First, on ankle sensor the performance increased by 5.7% and 5.3% for CNN learned features and statistical time-domain features, respectively. Second, on the knee sensor the enhancement was 5.2%

and 4.8% for the two modes, respectively. Third, the enhancement on trunk sensor achieves 5.1% and 6.5% for the two modes, respectively. Finally, when implementing the sensor-independent mode, the performance increases by 4.7% and 4.9% for the two modes, respectively.

Comparative Analysis

Table 5 proposes a comparative analysis of the achieved performance by the proposed model against the state-of-the-art related studies using different ML algorithms and feature sets. The proposed approach of time-domain and time-frequency feature fusion with PCA based dimensionality reduction outperformed the other surveyed state-of-the art studies. The proposed model achieves an F-score of 90.5% and a sensitivity of 91.5%.

Figure 11. FoG detection accuracy using time-frequency spectrogram based CNN learned features extraction scheme, with and without using PCA

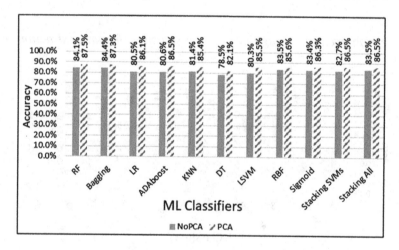

Figure 12. FoG detection accuracy using multi-feature fusion scheme, with and without using PCA

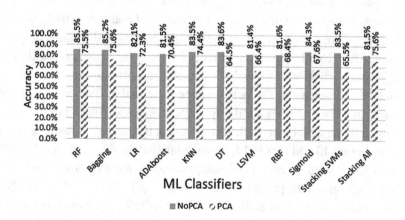

Table 4. The F-score performance measure for 67 samples window (1 second windowing) multi-feature fusion subject-dependent/sensor-dependent FoG early detection

Subject	No. Samples	Ankle		Knee		Trunk		All Sensors	
		Classifier	F-Score	Classifier	F-Score	Classifier	F-Score	Classifier	F-Score
#1	1838	LR	94.3%	LR	93.6%	RF	94.6%	SVM-RBF	93.9%
#2	1371	LR	92.5%	Bagging	86.6%	AdaBoost	82.6%	AdaBoost	89.3%
#3	1658	RF	85.5%	Bagging	81.7%	Bagging	80.7%	SVM-RBF	82.9%
#5	2058	Bagging	91.8%	LR	82.6%	LR	80.2%	Bagging	84.6%
#6	1614	DT	90.4%	Bagging	92.7%	RF	93.4%	AdaBoost	90.8%
#7	1561	Bagging	92.5%	Bagging	91.7%	SVM-RBF	91.7%	RF	93.8%
#8	752	RF	76.1%	Bagging	72.8%	LR	70.8%	RF	82.2%
#9	1692	Bagging	86.5%	DT	85.6%	DT	87.3%	RF	89.3%

Figure 13. Accuracy of FoG detection with 1 second windowing (67 samples)

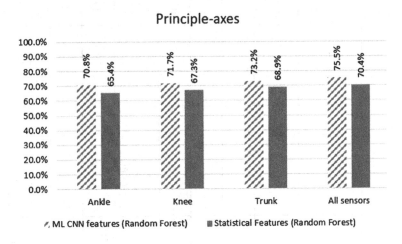

Figure 14. Accuracy of FoG detection with 4 seconds windowing (268 samples)

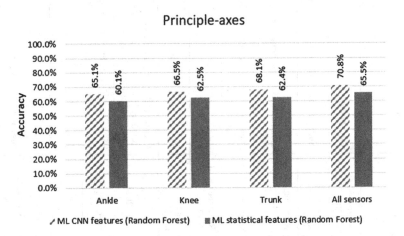

Table 5. Performance measurements of the proposed model compared to different state-of-the- art studies

Ref.	Classifier	Accuracy	Precision	Recall	F-Score	Specificity
Mazilu et al., 2013	Decision tree	-	-	77.15% for unsupervised features 67.8% for supervised features	78.2% for unsupervised features 70.94% for supervised features	86.71% for unsupervised features 84.75% for supervised features
Mazilu et al., 2016	C4.5 classifier	-	-	-	-	66% ~ 80%
Ahlrichs et al., 2016	Support Vector Machine (SVM) - Linear kernel	90%	-	89%	-	91%
Rezvanian & Lockhart, 2016	Continuous Wavelet Transform (CWT)	-	-	82.1%	-	77.1%
Xu et al. 2017	Improved subsequence Dynamic Time Wrapping (IsDTW)	92%	-	-	-	-
Rodrnguez et al. 2017	SVM	-	-	7.2% geometric mean.	-	7.2%. geometric mean
Tahafchi et al 2017	SVM - Gaussian kernel	-	95%	90%	92%	-
Shah et al. 2018	Constrained optimization based Extreme Learning Machine (C- ELM) and C-ELM with bagging (C-ELMBG) classifiers	93.11% for C-ELM and 93.97% for C- ELMBG	-	99.37% for C-ELM and 100% for C-ELMBG	0.9402 for C-ELM and 0.9476 for C- ELMBG	85.59% for C-ELM and 86.73% for C-ELMBG
De Sousa, 2018	SVM - Radial Basis Function (RBF) kernel and Random Forest	-	-	90.7%	45%	72.56%
El Attar et al. 2018	ANN	96.28%	-	-	-	-
Polat 2019	Logistic Regression	81.3%	72.72%	100%	-	62.5%
Ghosh & Banerjee, 2019	Grey Relational Analysis (GRA) with Bagging ensemble	90.62%	-	-	-	-
Ashour et al. 2018	Linear SVM kernel	94.4%	-	97.26%	91.89%	82.68%
Proposed model	**Multi-feature fusion with RF classiffier and PCA dimensionality reduction**	**87.6%**	**89.5%**	**91.5%**	**90.5%**	**92.8%**

CONCLUSION AND FUTURE CHALLENGES

In this chapter, several feature extraction schemes were investigated for early FoG detection. The time-domain features, time-frequency spectrogram based CNN-learned features, and fusion feature of time-domain and time-frequency features schemes were implemented. The tested models were implemented with the use of PCA algorithm for dimensionality reduction, and were tested for two windowing techniques; namely, 1 second (67 samples) and 4 seconds (268 samples) windowing. Several Machine Learning models using multi-feature fusion were tested. Based on the obtained experimental results, it's noticed that the ML based multi-feature fusion model along with the Random Forest classifier and the PCA based dimensionality reduction method outperformed the other surveyed state-of-the art studies.

For future work several challenges could be considered in the domain of predicting the FoG episodes via pre-FoG behavior detection as well as predicting FoG attacks severity. Also, working on new feature fusion sets, in addition to building new benchmark datasets should be applied and investigated.

REFERENCES

Abdulhay, E., Arunkumar, N., Kumaravelu, N., & Vellaiappan, E. (2018). Gait and tremor investigation using machine learning techniques for the diagnosis of Parkinson disease. *Future Generation Computer Systems, 83*, 366–373. doi:10.1016/j.future.2018.02.009

Ahlrichs, C., Samà, A., Lawo, M., Cabestany, J., Rodríguez-Martín, D., Pérez-López, C., ... Rodríguez-Molinero, A. (2016). Detecting freezing of gait with a tri- axial accelerometer in Parkinson's disease patients. *Medical & Biological Engineering & Computing, 54*(1), 223–233. doi:10.100711517-015-1395-3 PMID:26429349

Ahn, J., Park, J., Park, D., Paek, J., & Ko, J. (2018). Convolutional neural network-based classification system design with compressed wireless sensor network images. *PLoS One, 13*(5), e0196251. doi:10.1371/journal.pone.0196251 PMID:29738564

Amalina, F., Feizollah, A., Anuar, N., & Gani, A. (2016). Evaluation of machine learning classifiers for mobile malware detection. *Soft Computing, 20*(1), 343–357. doi:10.100700500-014-1511-6

Ashour, A. S., Attar, A. E., Dey, N., & Abd Elnaby, M. M., & Abd elkader, H. A. A., (2018). Patient-dependent freezing of gait detection using signals from multi-accelerometer sensors in Parkinson's disease. *9th Cairo International Biomedical Engineering Conference (CIBEC)*, 171-174. 10.1109/CIBEC.2018.8641809

Astorino, A., Fuduli, A., Gaudioso, M., & Vocaturo, E. (2019). Multiple instance learning algorithm for medical image classification. *SEBD, 2400*.

Astrid, R., Mohieddine, J., & Dirk, S. (2015). A brief review and a first application of time- frequency-based analysis methods for monitoring of strip rolling mills. *Journal of Process Control, 35*, 65–79. doi:10.1016/j.jprocont.2015.08.010

B¨achlin, M., Plotnik, M., Roggen, D., Maidan, I., Hausdorff, J. M., Giladi, N., & Tr¨oster, G. (2010). Wearable assistant for Parkinson's disease patients with the freezing of gait symptom. *IEEE Transactions on Information Technology in Biomedicine, 14*(2), 436–446. doi:10.1109/TITB.2009.2036165 PMID:19906597

Boualem, B. (2015). *Time-frequency signal analysis and processing: A comprehensive reference.* Academic Press.

Capecci, M., Pepa, L., Verdini, F., & Ceravolo, M. (2016). A smartphone-based architecture to detect and quantify freezing of gait in Parkinson's disease. Gait & amp. *Posture, 50,* 28–33. doi:10.1016/j. gaitpost.2016.08.018 PMID:27567449

Chakraborty, S., Aich, S., & Kim, H. (2020). 3D textural, morphological and statistical analysis of voxel of interests in 3T MRI scans for the detection of Parkinson's disease using artificial neural networks. *Multidisciplinary Digital Publishing Institute, 8*(1), 34. PMID:32046073

Challa, K., Pagolu, V., Panda, G., & Majhi, B. (2016). An improved approach for prediction of Parkinson's disease using machine learning techniques. *International Conference on Signal Processing, Communication, Power and Embedded System (SCOPES),* 1446-1451. 10.1109/SCOPES.2016.7955679

De Sousa, S. P. (2018). *Real-time detection of FOG episodes in patients with Parkinson's disease* (PhD Dissertation). Engineering Faculty, The University of Porto, Porto, Portugal.

Dua, T., Cumbrera, M., Mathers, C., & Saxena, S. (2006). Neurological disorders public health challenges. World Health Organization (WHO).

Dua, T., Janca, A., Kale, R., Montero, F., Muscetta, A., & Peden, M. (2006). Neurological disorders public health challenges. World Health Organization (WHO).

El Attar, A., Ashour, A. S., Dey, N., Abdelkader, H. A., Abd Elnaby M. M., & Fuqian, S., (2018). Hybrid DWT-FFT features for detecting freezing of gait in Parkinson's disease. *ITITS,* 117-126.

El-Bendary, N., Tan, Q., Pivot, F., & Lam, A. (2013). Fall detection and prevention for the elderly: A review of trends and challenges. *International Journal on Smart Sensing and Intelligent Systems, 6*(3). doi:10.21307/ijssis-2017-588

El-Bendary, N., Zawbaa, H., Hassanien, A., & Snasel, V. (2011). PCA-based home videos annotation system. *International Journal of Reasoning-based Intelligent Systems, 3*(2), 71–79. doi:10.1504/ IJRIS.2011.042202

Ghosh, N., & Banerjee, I. (2019). IoT-based freezing of gait detection using grey relational analysis. Elsevier. doi:10.1016/j.iot.2019.100068

Karan, B., Sahu, S., & Mahto, K. (2020). Parkinson disease prediction using intrinsic mode function based features from speech signal. *Biocybernetics and Biomedical Engineering, 40*(1), 249–264. doi:10.1016/j.bbe.2019.05.005

Kumar, A. (2016). Machine learning based approaches for prediction of Parkinson's disease. *Machine Learning and Applications: An International Journal, 3*(2), 33–39. doi:10.5121/mlaij.2016.3203

Mazilu, S., Blanke, U., Calatroni, A., Gazit, E., Hausdorff, J., & Tro¨ster, G. (2016). The role of wrist-mounted inertial sensors in detecting gait freeze episodes in Parkinson's disease. *Pervasive and Mobile Computing*, *33*, 1–16. doi:10.1016/j.pmcj.2015.12.007

Mazilu, S., Calatroni, A., Gazit, E., Roggen, D., Hausdorff, J. M., & Ro¨ster, G. T. (2013) Feature learning for detection and prediction of freezing of gait in Parkinson's disease. In *Proceedings: The International Workshop of Machine Learning and Data Mining in Pattern Recognition*. Springer. 10.1007/978-3-642-39712-7_11

Mazzetta, I., Zampogna, A., Suppa, A., Gumiero, A., Pessione, M., & Irrera, F. (2019). Wearable sensors system for an improved analysis of freezing of gait in Parkinson's disease using electromyography and inertial signals. *Sensors (Basel)*, *19*(4), 948. doi:10.339019040948 PMID:30813411

Nilashi, M. (2016). Accuracy improvement for predicting Parkinson's disease progression. Scientific Reports. *Nature*, *6*, 34181. PMID:27686748

Polat, K. (2019). Freezing of gait (FoG) detection using logistic regression in Parkinson's disease from acceleration signals. Scientific Meeting on Electrical-Electronics & Biomedical Engineering and Computer Science (EBBT), 1-4.

Rezvanian, S., & Lockhart, T. E. (2016). Towards real-time detection of freezing of gait using wavelet transform on wireless accelerometer data. *Sensors (Basel)*, *16*(4), 475. doi:10.339016040475 PMID:27049389

Rodrıguez-Martın, D., Sama, A., Pérez-López, C., Catala, A., Moreno Arostegui, J. M., Cabestany, J., ... Rodríguez-Molinero, A. (2017). Home detection of freezing of gait using support vector machines through a single waist- worn triaxial accelerometer. *PLoS One*, *12*(2), e0171764. doi:10.1371/journal.pone.0171764 PMID:28199357

Senturk, Z. (2020). Early diagnosis of Parkinson's disease using machine learning algorithms. *Medical Hypotheses*, *138*, 109603. doi:10.1016/j.mehy.2020.109603 PMID:32028195

Shah, S., Iqbal, K., & Riaz, A. (2018). Constrained optimization-based extreme learning machines with bagging for freezing of gait detection. *Big Data and Cognitive Computing*, *2*(4), 31. doi:10.3390/bdcc2040031

Sujatha, J., & Rajagopalan, S. (2017). Performance evaluation of machine learning algorithms in the classification of parkinson disease using voice attributes. *International Journal of Applied Engineering Research*, *12*(21), 10669–10675.

Suppa, A., Kita, A., Leodori, G., Zampogna, A., Nicolini, E., Lorenzi, P., ... Irrera, F. (2017). l-DOPA and freezing of gait in Parkinson's disease: Objective assessment through a wearable wireless system. *Frontiers in Neurology*, *8*, 406. doi:10.3389/fneur.2017.00406 PMID:28855889

Sveinbjornsdottir, S. (2016). The clinical symptoms of Parkinson's disease. *Journal of Neurochemistry*, *139*, 318–324. doi:10.1111/jnc.13691 PMID:27401947

Tahafchi, P., Molina, R., Roper, J., Sowalsky, K., Hass, C. J., Gunduz, A., . . . Judy, J. W. (2017). Freezing-of-gait detection using temporal, spatial, and physiological features with a support- vector-machine classifier. *39th Annual International Conference of the IEEE Engineering in Medicine and Biology Society (EMBC),* 2867-2870.

Trivedi, S. (2016). A study of machine learning classifiers for spam detection. In *Proceedings: The 4th International Symposium on Computational and Business Intelligence, ISCBI,* 176-180. 10.1109/ISCBI.2016.7743279

Wang, L., Wang, C., & Chen, Y. A. (2018). Fast three-dimensional display method for time- frequency spectrogram used in embedded fault diagnosis devices. *Applied Sciences, 8*(10), 1930. doi:10.3390/app8101930

Xu, C., He, J., Zhang, X., Wang, C., & Duan, S. (2017). Detection of freezing of gait using template-matching-based approaches. *Journal of Sensors,* 1–8.

Zumpano, E., Iaquinta, P., Caroprese, L., Cascini, G., Dattola, F., Franco, P., ... Vocaturo, E. (2018). 3D: A medical information system for diagnostic procedures. *IEEE International Conference on Bioinformatics and Biomedicine,* 2125-2128. 10.1109/BIBM.2018.8621090

Chapter 7
Developing Brain Tumor Detection Model Using Deep Feature Extraction via Transfer Learning

Adem Assfaw Mekonnen

Addis Ababa Science and Technology University, Ethiopia

Hussien Worku Seid

Addis Ababa Science and Technology University, Ethiopia

Sudhir Kumar Mohapatra

https://orcid.org/0000-0003-3065-3881

Addis Ababa Science and Technology University, Ethiopia

Srinivas Prasad

GITAM University, India

ABSTRACT

The timely prognosis of brain tumors is gambling a great role within the pretreatment of patients and keep the life of suffers. The manual classification of brain tumors is a difficult task for radiologists due to the intensity variation pixel information produced by the magnetic resonance machine and it is a very tedious task for a large number of images. A deep learning algorithm becomes a famous algorithm to conquer the problems traditional machine learning algorithms by automatically feature extraction from the input spaces and accurately detect the brain tumors. One of the most important features of deep learning is transferred a gain knowledge strategy to use small datasets. Transfer learning is explored by freezing layers and fine-tuning a pre-trained model to a recommended convolutional neural net model. The proposed model is trained using 4000 real magnetic resonance images datasets. The mean accuracy of the proposed model is found to be 98% for brain tumor classifications with mini-batch size 32 and a learning rate of 0.001.

DOI: 10.4018/978-1-7998-6659-6.ch007

INTRODUCTION

Recently, cancer is considered one of the highest crisis diseases that affect the lives of humans in the world. According to the International Agency for Research on Cancer (IARC), the latest news about the brain and other nervous system cancers are published by GLOBOCAN, 296, 851 new cases and 24, 1037 cancer in death were diagnosed in 2018 (Bray et al.,2018). MR image is one of the methods to identify cancer. Cancer is a fast and uncontrollable boom of ordinary tissues that damages the nearby healthy tissues of the brain (Rindi et al., 2018). A brain tumor will be treated by surgery, radiation therapy, and chemotherapy. The prevention of neoplasm will rely upon several factors just like the size, type, and grade of the tumor. But MR images are critical in neoplasm treatment by showing the characteristics of brain tumors throughout the method of the medical process to assist the specialists in the identification of it.

Timely diagnosis of brain tumor is playing a great role in the pretreatment of patients and save the life of patients. The classification of brain tumors is still a challenging area for researchers. The manual classification of brain tumors is accomplished by medical radiologist. The manual classification of the brain is a tedious task for radiologists when the MR images have a similar structure. The tasks performed by a radiologist is to discover to identify the brain MR image is tumors or non-tumors and detect the abnormal stages of tumors. A large quantity of time was spent by radiotherapists and doctors for the identification of tumors and segmenting it from different brain tissues. So, the manual classification of brain tumors is very tedious for a huge quantity of MR images data, non-reproducible and time-wasting due to the range of the patient become increases from day today. To mitigate the issue, autonomous classification is the best approach to analyze brain MR images with a minimum time for a radiologist. In this chapter, we have to focus on the classification of brain MR images into normal and abnormal images. A real MR image dataset is utilized in this study that collected from the pioneer diagnosis center.

The classic methods are used for the detection of brain tumors into different stages from MR images. The main steps used by conventional methods are preprocessing, segmenting, feature extraction, dimension reduction and classification of brain tumor MR images. The traditional machine-learning algorithm uses handcrafted feature extraction methods (Machhale et al., 2015). The handcrafted feature extraction method is depending on the knowledge experts of the domains. The handcrafted method is a laborious task for non - experts to use conventional algorithms. The performance of the model is depending on the feature extraction methods. There are numerous classic algorithms proposed for brain neoplasm identification using feature extraction methods (Balan et al, 2018). The feature extraction methods are low level feature (Duron et al., 2019), first-order statics (Tong et al., 2019), second-order statics (Padlia et al., 2019), wavelet (Devi et al., 2018), Gabor (Vidyarthi et al., 2015) and fisher vector extractions (Cheng et al., 2016). There are numerous methodologies proposed for brain tumor classifications using handcrafted feature extractions in machine learning algorithms (Kumar et al., 2016; Praveen et al., 2016; Sonavane et al., 2016;Panda et al., 2019; Mathew et al.,2017).

Recent works on medical image analysis on brain tumor classification focuses on deep learning algorithms due to its good performance classification results. The deep learning algorithm is a type of classic algorithms that use automatic feature extraction methods (Talo et al., 2019). Deep learning algorithms overcome the problems of classic algorithms due to its hand-crafted feature extraction methods (Greenspan et al.,2016).The foremost distinction between machine learning and deep learning approach is handcrafted feature extraction is executed manually using feature engineers or humans but in case of deep learning approach, the feature extraction is done automatically without feature engineers (Moolayil, 2019).

The CNN algorithm is one kind of deep studying algorithm that is mostly applicable to brain tumor classification and segmentation for radiology (Hemanth et al., 2018). The structure of CNN algorithms has two stack blocks of convolution feature learning and classification layers. The feature learning layers extracted automatically during the training process rather than design manually by users in classic algorithms. The component extraction of ConvNet is a special type of neural network in which the weights are determined during the training process. The features of the input image extracted by the feature extraction net and recognized by the classification layers (Shin et al., 2016). The classification layers operate based on the feature extraction of the image to detect the given MR images is Normal or abnormal images (Benzebouchi et al.,2019).The structure of the CNN algorithms is a series of Convolutional layers, maxpooling, ReLU activation functions, and output layers shown in figure 1.

Figure 1. Example of CNN
(Krizhevsky et al., 2012)

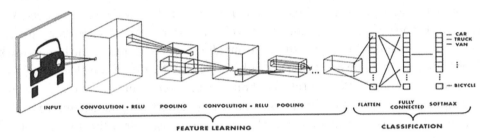

Recently, CNN becomes a popular algorithm in image recognition by showing a good performance in computer visions after trained on millions of ImageNet on large image visual recognition (Karpathy et al., 2015). However, it is a laborious challenge to apply a CNN algorithm inside the detection of the tumor within the scientific diagnosis center because of the necessity of a massive wide kind of MR images. Additionally, the datasets of MR images are limited in the health care center due to requiring domain experts to label the image, manually examine identify the MR images, keep confidentiality, take time, and costly. To train CNN algorithm from scratch using small datasets that show overfitting, convergence problems and not efficiently detect the given tumor images.

Therefore, the CNN is a laborious task to train brain tumor image datasets from the scratch due to requiring a huge variety of images, to adjust the parameters and hyperparameters want domain professionals to revise the model operation during training time to gain the fine overall performance accuracy results.

To overcome the limitation of small MR image datasets to apply CNN algorithms via transfer learning. Transfer learning is the most important feature of deep learning algorithms (Shao et al., 2014) that use pre-trained deep learning algorithms that trained on millions of ImageNet on large image visual recognition datasets. The most important Transfer learning techniques are ConvNet as fixed feature extraction and fine-tuning (Shu,2019) . Among the CNN pre-trained model, the VGG 16 model is selected to modify the original CNN architectures due to it uses small size filters that uniform throughout the layers of VGG 16 models. In this chapter, a CNN model is proposed for brain tumor classification via deep transfer learning. The proposed CNN model is trained on real MR image datasets collected from the Pioneer diagnosis center. Additionally, the proposed CNN model is evaluated using different metrics.

The remainder of this chapter is sorted as related work, proposed methodology, experiment and results, discussion, conclusion, and recommendations.

The reminder of the chapter is organized as follow: the next section we discussed some of the important recent related works. Section 3 discuss the method followed for brain tumor detection. In this section the parameter and tuning of convolutional neural network is also discussed. Section 4 discussed about the data set and details of the experiment conducted. The results are discussed in a separate section i.e section 5. Finally we conclude the chapter.

RELATED WORKS

There are several various methodologies have been developed during the last years ago to create arobotized brain tumor classification from MR images. There are several researchers who proposed the algorithms from the traditional machine learning algorithms via sequential steps from preprocessing MR images, image segmentation, feature extraction, dimension reduction and classify the brain tumors. Mathew et al. (2017) developed brain neoplasm segmentation and classification via machine learning algorithms. In preprocessing step use a median filter and Ostu's Thresholding to segmentation brain tumors use k means algorithm. The authors used future extraction algorithms like GLCM, Gabor wavelet, and DWT and use for future reduction algorithms by PCA and classify brain tumors using a supportive vector machine. They have achieved an accuracy rate is 70% for classification brain tumors but poor accuracy results and the process is complex. Karaddi et al. (2018) proposed Otsu-Region Based algorithm to segment and detect the brain tumor MR images. The author used 50 MR images to experiment. After segmentation brain tumor MR images used GLCM to extract features and gives to ANN to analyze brain tumors. The overall performance result is 83.3%. The authors proposed a future work to combine two or more algorithms in segmentation and classification brain tumors but the feature extraction process is the handcrafted method and poor accuracy results. Atanu et al. (2018) proposed automatic brain tumor detection via the SVM classifier. The authors used for image segmentation k-means clustering algorithms and for future extraction via GLCM using SVM classifiers.Theyused 64 MR images to experiment. The overall accuracy result achieved by the proposed algorithm is 99.9%but the process is very tedious in segmentation and hand-crafted future extraction that prone to errors. Singh et al. (2016) proposed the algorithm for brain tumor segmentationand classification . They have used different preprocessing techniques and segment using k means algorithm via SVM classifiers. The authors achieved an accuracy result accurate result for SVM classification 91.49% and for Bayes 87.23% but the proposed method is not accurate for poor MR images used quality images as future work. Singh(2015) proposed a combination of fuzzy c means and SVM algorithmsto identifybrain tumors. The authors use preprocessing, segmentation, feature extraction, and classification of a brain tumor. The authors used 70 MR images for experiments and achieved the accuracy rate is 93.5% and proposed a data mining techniqueto classify brain tumors but the author didn't specify the type of image type used and used conventional future extraction methods.

Seetha et al. (2018) proposed a simple CNN architecture to detect brain tumors into tumors and non-tumors fromMR images by training the algorithm from scratch. The authors collect the datasets from different online sources like Radiopaedia, BRATS) 2015 andachieved the accuracy result 97.5% but the model is not accurate due to the requirement a lot of data.Lorenzo et al.(2019) developed a fully CNN to segment brain tumors on flair images. In this chapter, the authors used in the preprocessing stage is data normalization and data augmentations. The author used11 patient data during this experiment. But the author didn't include all types of different modality MR images during this study. Talo et al.(2019) proposed deep learning to automate brain tumor abnormality classifications via transfer learning. The authors used in the preprocessing stage uses data augmentations. The authors used 613 T2-weightedMR images for training and validations during the experiment. Among these images, 27 were abnormal images and 513 were normal images. They have achieved an accuracy rate of 98.2% but the number of the dataset is small that not include all variety of MR images and data imbalance that leads to overfitting and the selected architecture is complex. Deepak et al. (2019) proposed GoogLeNet pre-trained model to classify different stages of brain tumors from MR images. The author only fine-tuning the fully connected layers and train all convolutional layers of GoogLeNet architectures. The author used fig share datasets that trained the pre-trained model using 3064 brain MR images from 233 patients but the authors did not consider all types of MRimages.

Generally, In the above traditional machine learning algorithms are used for brain tumor detection. But the accuracy of the classifier model depends on the future extraction methods. The future extraction techniques in the conventional method are handcrafted and the process is complex that starts from the preprocessing, segmentation, future extraction, dimensional reduction, and classifications. In our study, we have used deep learning algorithms for brain tumor classification via transfer learning. But, the previous related works on brain tumor detection, the researchers used one type of MR image variety, heterogeneous datasets and a limited number of MR images. So, in this research, we have proposed a CNN model for brain tumor detection via transfer learning using a real grayscale different variety ofMR images compared to previous work.

METHODS

In this chapter, the general structure of the proposed CNN model is shown in Figure 2. The proposed CNN architecture shows the classification of brain tumor MR images. The datasets are split into a training set, validation set, and test sets. The dataset can be preprocessed by resizing the original image size and data augmentation before applying to the proposed CNN models. The preprocessed MR image dataset is trained using the proposed CNN model. The training model is evaluated using validation datasets to provide an unbiased evaluation of the proposed model on training datasets and at the same time tuning the model hyper-parameters. After trained the proposed CNN model is saved. Finally, the trained model is evaluated using unseen test datasets to classify brain tumors.

Transfer Learning and Fine-Tuning VGG 16

The VGG16 model has 13 convolutional layers, 5 pooling layers, and 3 fully connected layers. It also has 138 million parameters. To select the pre-trained model for brain tumor classification is very difficult due to the CNN architecture deployed on large scale applications such as ImageNet

Large Scale Visual Recognition Challenge (ILSVRC)which train on million image datasets and thousand classification scores by requiring large memory storage and computational powers. The VGG16 pre-trained model is selected to modify the original CNN architectures according to our new datasets due to its simple architectures and use uniform small size filter in all layers. The proposed methodology for brain tumor detection is a CNN model. The original input layers of the pre-trained VGG16model require RGB images with a size of 244 x 244x3. But in our proposed CNN model, the input layer required 128

Figure 2. Proposed structure CNN model

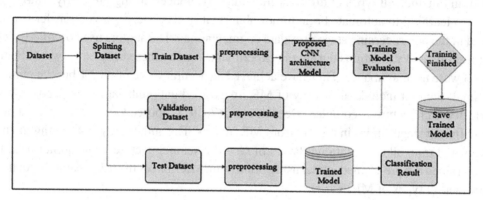

x 128 x 1 grayscale MR images brain tumor images. Most of the researchers use by converting the MR grayscale images as RGB images in the pre-trained model due to the input layer requires RGB images. So, the conversion of grayscale MR images into an RGB image creates dummies. So, the input layers of the VGG16 model is modified from RGB images to grayscale images. The original pre-trained VGG16 model fully connected layers 4096 nodes but in our proposed CNN model the fully connected layers are 128 nodes to reduce the computational costs and the number of parameters is reduced. The output classification layer is modified from 1000 classes in the VGG16 model to two classes in the proposed CNN models. In this chapter, the number of image datasets is limited and only two class task classifications problems. The pre-trained VGG16 model is modified by freezing the block's convolutional and fully connected layers. After several experiments are done by freezing different blocks of convolutional layers and fully connected layers, the best performance is gotten by freezing the first three blocks of Conv. layers and train the remain the fourth, the fifth blocks and the fully connected layers. The activation function used for the proposed CNN model in the hidden layer is ReLU. Because ReLU is most widely and less computationally expensive other than Tanh and sigmoid because it performs on simple mathematical operations.

Proposed CNN Model

The proposed CNN model contains input layers, convolutional layers, ReLu activation functions, pooling layers, and fully connected layers. Figure 3 shows the proposed CNN model by freezing and fine-tuning different blocks of CNN.

Input Layers

The input layer of our proposed CNN algorithm accepts grayscale image with size 128 * 128* 1 with two different classes normal and abnormal brain tumor MR images.

Convolutional Layers

In the proposed CNN model, the first convolutional layers 128*128*64 with the kernel filter 3*3*64 to produce the output size of the Convolutional layers 128*128*64 activation map. The proposed CNN

Figure 3. Proposed CNN model

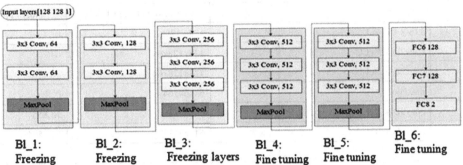

model has five convolutional blocks of convolutional layers. By fine-tuning, the classification layers of the pre-trained VGG16 model to get the best accuracy of the proposed CNN models.

Pooling Layers

We have used five max-pooling layers to reduce the dimension of the images that come from the output dimension of the convolutional layers. The filter size of pooling layers is 2x2 kernel filters and 2x2 stride applied on the output of convolutional images.

Fully Connected Layers

In the proposed model, we have used three fully connected layers including the output layers. The number of nodes in the fully connected layers used in the proposed CNN model is 128 nodes because the number of the parameter is reduced. The last output layers used in the proposed CNN model are softmax layers with 1 output node.

Output Layers

The output layer is the last fully-connected layer which has two nodes. the softmax activation function is used to classify normal and abnormal brain tumor MR images.

The number of parameters for the proposed CNN model has 15,799,010 parameters shown in Table 1. The number of parameters is reduced from 138 million to 15,799,010 and to reduce the computational cost and use efficient memory to use CNN architectures for small datasets. In the developed CNN algorithm, the number of weights trains only 14,044,674 parameters form the total parameters 15,799,010 of the proposed CNN layers by freezing some layers from the top of VGG 16 architectures and the number of non-trainable parameters is 1,754,336 which have fixed number of weights. So, the VGG 16 pre-trained model is modified according to our new datasets by freezing the Conv layers of different blocks and fully connected layers.

Table 1. Number of parameters of the proposed CNN model

Layer		Filter	Size of the Output Image	No. of Parameter
Input	$128 \times 128 \times 1$	-	128 x128x1	0
1	conv2D + ReLU	3×3	128x128x64	640
2	conv2D + ReLU	3×3	128x128x64	36,928
	maxPool2D	3×3	64x64x64	0
3	conv2D + ReLU	3×3	64x64x128	73,856
4	conv2D + ReLU	3×3	64x64x128	147,584
	maxPool2D	2×2	32x32x128	0
5	conv2D + ReLU	3×3	32x32x256	295,168
6	conv2D + ReLU	3×3	32x32x256	590,080
7	conv2D + ReLU	3×3	32x32x256	590,080
	maxPool2D	2×2	16x16x256	0
8	conv2D + ReLU	3×3	16x16x512	1,180,160
9	conv2D + ReLU	3×3	16x16x512	2,359,808
10	conv2D + ReLU	3×3	16x16x512	2,359,808
	maxPool2D	2×2	8x8x512	0
11	conv2D + ReLU	3×3	8x8x512	2,359,808
12	conv2D + ReLU	3×3	8x8x512	2,359,808
13	conv2D + ReLU	3×3	8x8x512	2,359,808
	maxPool2D	2×2	4x4x512	0
	Flatten	-		0
14	FC + ReLu	-	128	1048704
	Dropout	-		0
15	FC + ReLu	-	128	16,512
	Dropout	-		0
Output	FC + Softmax	-	2	258
Total Number of Parameters				15,779,010
Trainable parameters				14,044,674
Non-Trainable parameters				1,734,336

EXPERIMENTS AND RESULTS

Datasets

The dataset used in this study is real MR images that consist of normal and abnormal images collected from the Pioneer diagnosis center. The medical image format is DICOM (digital image and communication in medicine). The importance of the DICOM format is to keep the patient confidentiality that packs the patient information with header and data file. The header file contains the patient information and the data file contains the patient MR images. To use the image data, the Dicom format is converted into

Figure 4. Preprocessing steps of MR images

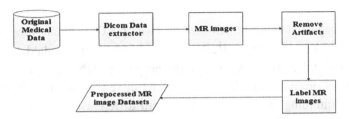

jpg format and clean patient information to keep the patient confidentiality data. To extract the image from Dicom format and clean patient information by using radiant Dicom viewer tools. To visualize the collected patient medical data using a radiant Dicom viewer to see the slices of MR image variety of each patent. The patents have T1 weighted, T2 weighted and Fluid-attenuated inversion recovery slices are labeled by medical radiologist doctors into normal and abnormal images of each patient. The total number of images in the MR image datasets are 4000 images extracted from 88 patients.

The preprocessed MR image dataset is split into training datasets and testing datasets with a ratio of 80% and 20% respectively as the principle . The dimension of the MR image is 256 by 256 image width and height of matrix pixels. The image resizes function is applied to the MR imagedataset to reduce the complexity of the network during training time. The MR images are resized from 256 by 256 images to 128 by 128 image width and height of matrix pixels to reduce the network complexity.CNN requires a large quantity of data to train the network from scratch. The data augmentation technique is implemented to boom the sample size of the dataset. The basic data augmentations techniques are rotation, translation, and reflection concerning different angles of the input images. Some of the sample images are in the class of datasets shown in Figure 5 and Figure 6.

Figure 5. a) T1 Weighted b) T2 Weighted C) Flair abnormal MR images.

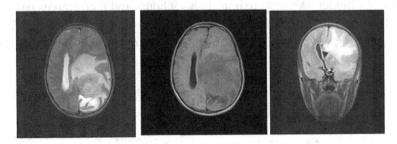

Figure 6. a) T1 Weighted b) T2 Weighted c) Flair MR normal images.

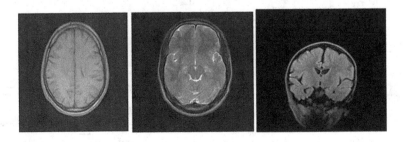

Experimental Setup

The programming language and environment used to develop a CNN brain tumor classification model via transfer learning in MATLAB version R2018b_win64 MATLAB (Vedaldi et al.,2015). MATLAB tool is used to check and analyze the efficiency of the proposed CNN model and algorithm. MATLAB is a fourth-era high-level programming language and intuitive condition for numerical computation, visualization, and programming. MATLAB is rich with different built-in toolboxes such as Image Processing Toolboxes, and Deep Learning Toolbox provides functions and apps to produce, measure, convert, filter, and visualize images.The code for the prototype was written in MATLAB script m-files. MATLAB is preferred to this study due to its basic features to implement the experiment such as image processing and deep learning toolboxes. In addition to this, it has a vast library, interactive environment, and built-in graphics for visualizing data. The experiment was run on Intel(R) Core (TM) i7-4510 CPU @ 2.60GHz processor, and memory 8 GB.

Training and Parameter Optimizations

Hyper-parameters are a parameter that sets the value before the training process started. There are no standard rules to choose the best hyper-parameters for the given problems. The hyper-parameters are chosen by try and error of conducting a different experiment on the Proposed CNN model that gives the best performance of the models. The best hyper-parameters to converge the proposed CNN model during the training process depends on the initial learning rate 0.001, maximum epoch 30,Adam optimizers and mini-batch size 32 images into the network rather than the whole datasets to reduce the complexity of the network. Most of the freezing and fine-tuning the Proposed CNN models converge between 20 and 30 epochs. The validation set is used to evaluate the proposed CNN model to predict correctly and prevent the network from overfitting during training time. After several experiments were done by changing the learning rate, we have got the best classification result at the learning rate is 0.001 with Adam solver optimization algorithms and softmax activation functions. By freezing and fine-tuning to train the proposed CNN model takes approximately 8 - 9 hours and it converges based on the selected hyper-parameters. If the training and validation accuracy is not good during training time after a certain time, the hyper-parameter of the proposed CNN model is adjusted by stopping the training progress.

Figure 7. Training and validation accuracy of proposed CNN model one and proposed CNN model two

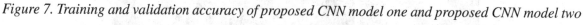

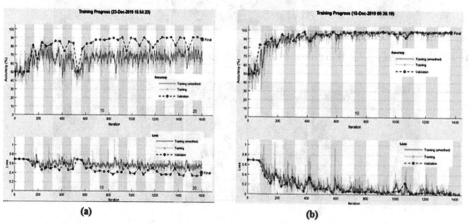

(a)   (b)

Figure 8. Training and validation accuracy the proposed CNN model three Seven.

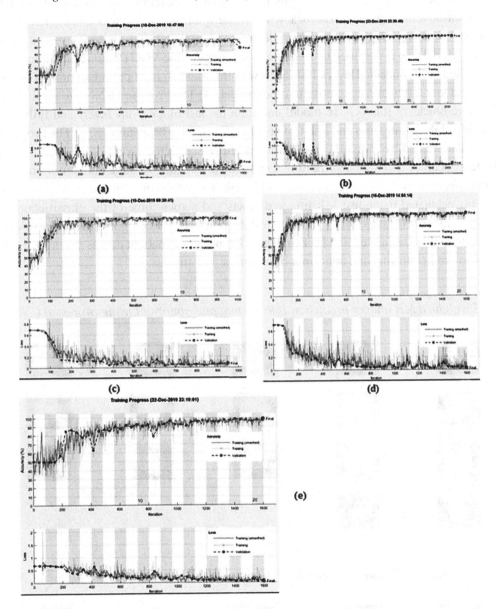

Figure 7 shows the proposed model one is obtained by freezing all the convolutional layers and train only the fully connected layers of the pre-trained VGG16 model but it shows over-fitting and the training and validation loss is high that not classify brain tumors correctly. b) The proposed CNN model two is obtained by Freezing one blocks of the VGG16 model and train the remain convolutional layers and fully connected layers. It shows the test dataset less accuracy and it takes a long time to train the convolutional layers and needs a lot of data because it has a high number of parameters. Figure 8 The Proposed CNN Model three is obtained by Freezing two blocks of the VGG16 model and train the remain convolutional layers and fully connected layers but it shows high training and low validation accuracy. The validation loss is high- and low-test accuracy. d) The Proposed CNN model four is obtained Freezing three blocks of the VGG16 model and train the remain convolutional and classification layers. It shows high training accuracy, validation accuracy, and test accuracy. The training and validation loss is low relative to another proposed model. It shows a high probability of detecting normal and abnormal MR images correctly. e) The Proposed Model five is obtained by freezing four blocks of the VGG16 model and train the remain convolutional and fully connected layers. It shows low training and high validation accuracy. The validation loss is high- and low-test accuracy relative to other models. f) The Proposed CNN Model six is obtained by freezing five blocks of the VGG16 model and train the last block Conv layers and fully connected layers. It shows high training loss and low-test accuracy to classify brain tumors. g) The Proposed CNN Model seven is obtained by train all convolution and fully connected layers of the VGG 16 model. It shows less test accuracy and high loss training data because it requires a large number of images to train from scratch. Because our MR image dataset is different from the natural image dataset. The proposed CNN model is evaluated using test MR image datasets and shows some of the classifications of MR images. Some patient MR images are utilized to test the proposed CNN algorithms to classify the given patient T1 weighted, T2 weighted and flair images. The individual patient data is given to the proposed CNN model to predict normal and abnormal brain tumor MR images.

Figure 9. T1 weighted MR images prediction into normal and abnormal using proposed CNN model.

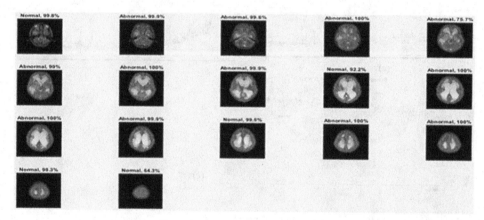

Figure 10. T2 weighted MR images prediction into normal and abnormal using proposed CNN model

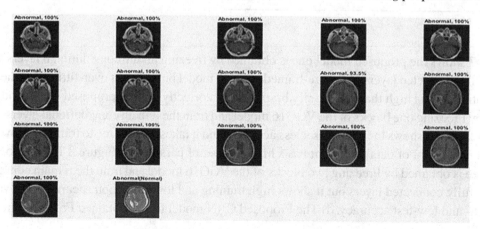

Figure 11. Flair MR images prediction into normal and abnormal using proposed CNN model.

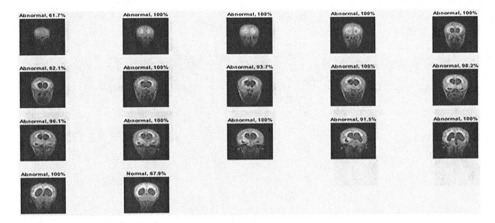

Figure 12. T1 weighted MR images prediction into normal and abnormal using proposed CNN model

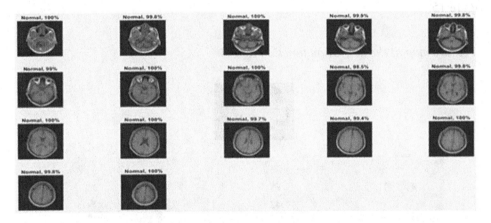

Figure 13. T2 weighted MR images prediction into normal and abnormal using proposed CNN model

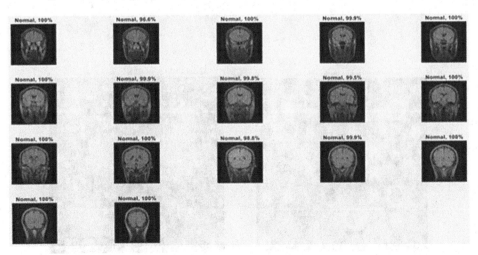

Figure 14. Flair MR images prediction into normal and abnormal using proposed CNN model

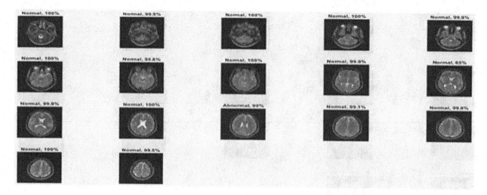

The feature extraction of the convolutional layers from the input image in the proposed CNN model is shown in the activation from the convolutional layers and the feature map of the activation function RELU in figure 15.

Figure 15. Feature map of the activation function RELU

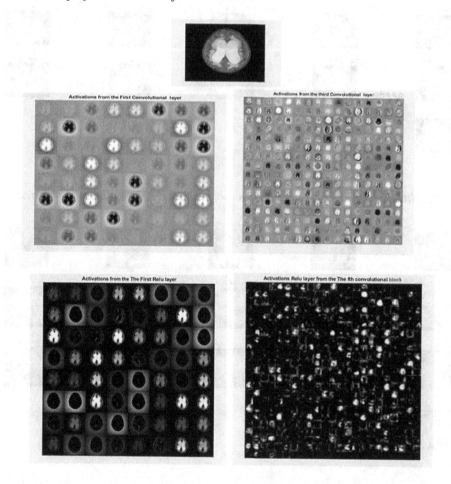

Result Analysis and Comparisons

In this chapter, the experiment result is conducted using real MR image datasets. So, we have compared the experiment results by freezing layers and fine-tuning the VGG 16 model. The best performance is obtained by freezing the three blocks and train the remain convolutionaland classification layers for the proposed CNN models. But the freezing layers and fine-tuning the other blocks and fully connected layers we obtain fewer performance metrics concerning the freezing the first three blocks of convolutional layers in Table 2.

Table 2. Comparative result by freezing and fine-tuning VGG 16 model

Freezing and Fine-tuning Blocks	Training Accuracy	Validation Accuracy	Test Accuracy	Training Loss	Validation Loss
Block 1 - Block 6	96.00%	95.91%	80.09%	3.95	8.19%
Block 2 - Block 6	93.75%	87.34%	81.24%	9.89%	21.65%
Block 3 - Block 6	**99.0%**	**98.91%**	**88.86%**	**1.43%**	**2.29%**
Block 4 - Block 6	96.88%	97.81%	80.66%	5.38%	8.10%
Block 5 - Block 6	93.88%	94.81%	77.66%	35.00%	12.70%
Block 6 - Block 6	75.00%	88.91%	68.09%	51.95	42.19%

DISCUSSION

In this chapter, we focus on brain tumor type into tumors and non-tumors From MR images. Transfer learning is explored in this research by freezing and fine-tuning the pre-trained VGG16 model to get the best classification results using small MR IMAGES datasets. By freezing and fine-tuning the VGG16 model, we have proposed CNN models to classify brain tumors into normal and abnormal MR images. The CNN algorithms learn high-level features from low-level features. The low-level information is curves, edges, shapes, and textures. The earlier layers learn the low-level information in convolutional layers and the high-level information combines the low-level information and produces the activation features. The classification layers learn high-level abstract information on CNN. Fine-tuning the last fully connected layers in a CNNare not achieved good performance because the MR IMAGES datasets differ from the natural images. Therefore, it is difficult to modify the classification layers in CNN algorithms in medical images because the CNN model is not learning the medical MR images from the natural images. The proposed CNN model learns the low-level information in the earlier layers and combines the low-level information to learn the high-level abstraction information of the medical images. We adopt the VGG 16 pre-trained model to freezing and fine-tuning because its architecture is suitable to feature extraction to learn specific information and use a uniform filter in all convolutional layers.

This research focuses on brain tumor classification into normal and abnormal on 2D MR images because CNN models are 2D in natures. But we didn't focus on other body organs and a variety of medical images like CT scan and mammography. Additionally, we have not to focus on three-dimensional images due to the medical images are 2D grayscale images. Therefore, the proposed CNN model is trained on real 2D MR image datasets that collected from the pioneer diagnosis center.

CONCLUSION AND RECOMMENDATIONS

In this chapter, a CNN model is proposed for brain tumor type into tumors and non-tumors from MR images using a deep learning approach via transfer learning. By freezing and fine-tuning the layers of the VGG16 model, we have achieved good performance classification results. The proposed CNN model may be used to other body organs like CT scan, X-rays and PET when the data is available. The proposed CNN model train on real 2D MR grayscale image datasets collected from the pioneer diagnosis center. The main advantage of the CNN algorithm is transferred a gain knowledge from the natural image to medical images. The proposed CNN model is generic because it doesn't need more preprocessing and handcrafted feature extraction techniques. The performance of the proposed CNN model is evaluated using different metrics. The recommended metrics used to evaluate the proposed CNN model using training, validation and test accuracy. The mean accuracy of the proposed CNN model is found to be 98% for brain tumor classifications. Therefore, the proposed model is used to classify brain MR images into tumors and non-tumors. In the future work we will add different stages of brain tumors MR images and segment the region of brain abnormal tumors.

ACKNOWLEDGMENT

This research did not receive any specific grant from funding agencies in the public, commercial, or not-for-profit sectors.

REFERENCES

Balan, P. S., & Sunny, L. E. (2018). Survey on Feature Extraction Techniques in Image Processing. [IJRASET]. *International Journal for Research in Applied Science and Engineering Technology*, 6(3).

Benzebouchi, N. E., Azizi, N., & Ayadi, K. (2019). A computer-aided diagnosis system for breast cancer using deep convolutional neural networks. In *Computational Intelligence in Data Mining* (pp. 583–593). Singapore: Springer. doi:10.1007/978-981-10-8055-5_52

Bray, F., Ferlay, J., Soerjomataram, I., Siegel, R. L., Torre, L. A., & Jemal, A. (2018). Global cancer statistics 2018: GLOBOCAN estimates of incidence and mortality worldwide for 36 cancers in 185 countries. *CA: a Cancer Journal for Clinicians*, 68(6), 394–424. doi:10.3322/caac.21492 PMID:30207593

Cheng, J., Yang, W., Huang, M., Huang, W., Jiang, J., Zhou, Y., ... Chen, W. (2016). Retrieval of brain tumors by adaptive spatial pooling and fisher vector representation. *PLoS One*, 11(6), e0157112. doi:10.1371/journal.pone.0157112 PMID:27273091

Deepak, S., & Ameer, P. M. (2019). Brain tumor classification using deep CNN features via transfer learning. *Computers in Biology and Medicine*, 111, 103345. doi:10.1016/j.compbiomed.2019.103345 PMID:31279167

Devi, T. M., Ramani, G., & Arockiaraj, S. X. (2018, March). Mr brain tumor classification and segmentation via wavelets. In *2018 International Conference on Wireless Communications, Signal Processing and Networking (WiSPNET)* (pp. 1-4). IEEE. 10.1109/WiSPNET.2018.8538643

Duron, L., Balvay, D., Perre, S. V., Bouchouicha, A., Savatovsky, J., Sadik, J. C., ... Lecler, A. (2019). Gray-level discretization impacts reproducible MRI radiomics texture features. *PLoS One, 14*(3).

Greenspan, H., Van Ginneken, B., & Summers, R. M. (2016). Guest editorial deep learning in medical imaging: Overview and future promise of an exciting new technique. *IEEE Transactions on Medical Imaging, 35*(5), 1153–1159. doi:10.1109/TMI.2016.2553401

Hemanth, D. J., Anitha, J., Naaji, A., Geman, O., Popescu, D. E., & Hoang Son, L. (2018). A modified deep convolutional neural network for abnormal brain image classification. *IEEE Access: Practical Innovations, Open Solutions, 7*, 4275–4283. doi:10.1109/ACCESS.2018.2885639

Karaddi, S. H., Babu, A., & Reddy, R. K. (2018), Detection of Brain Tumor Using Otsu-Region Based Method of Segmentation. *Proc. 2nd Int. Conf. Comput. Methodol. Commun. ICCMC 2018*, 128–134. 10.1109/ICCMC.2018.8488013

Karpathy, A., & Fei-Fei, L. (2015). Deep visual-semantic alignments for generating image descriptions. In *Proceedings of the IEEE conference on computer vision and pattern recognition* (pp. 3128-3137). 10.1109/CVPR.2015.7298932

Krizhevsky, A., Sutskever, I., & Hinton, G. E. (2012). Imagenet classification with deep convolutional neural networks. In Advances in neural information processing systems (pp. 1097-1105). Academic Press.

Kumar, P. S., & Chatteijee, S. (2016, December). Computer aided diagnostic for cancer detection using MRI images of brain (Brain tumor detection and classification system). In *2016 IEEE Annual India Conference (INDICON)* (pp. 1-6). IEEE. 10.1109/INDICON.2016.7838875

Lorenzo, P. R., Nalepa, J., Bobek-Billewicz, B., Wawrzyniak, P., Mrukwa, G., Kawulok, M., ... Hayball, M. P. (2019). Segmenting brain tumors from FLAIR MRI using fully convolutional neural networks. *Computer Methods and Programs in Biomedicine, 176*, 135–148. doi:10.1016/j.cmpb.2019.05.006 PMID:31200901

Machhale, K., Nandpuru, H. B., Kapur, V., & Kosta, L. (2015, May). MRI brain cancer classification using hybrid classifier (SVM-KNN). In *2015 International Conference on Industrial Instrumentation and Control (ICIC)* (pp. 60-65). IEEE.

Mathew, A. R., & Anto, P. B. (2017, July). Tumor detection and classification of MRI brain image using wavelet transform and SVM. In *2017 International Conference on Signal Processing and Communication (ICSPC)* (pp. 75-78). IEEE. 10.1109/CSPC.2017.8305810

Mathew, A. R., Anto, P. B., & Thara, N. K. (2017, July). Brain tumor segmentation and classification using DWT, Gabour wavelet and GLCM. In *2017 International Conference on Intelligent Computing, Instrumentation and Control Technologies (ICICICT)* (pp. 1744-1750). IEEE. 10.1109/ICICICT1.2017.8342834

Moolayil, J. (2019). An Introduction to Deep Learning and Keras. In *Learn Keras for Deep Neural Networks* (pp. 1–16). Berkeley, CA: Apress. doi:10.1007/978-1-4842-4240-7_1

Padlia, M., & Sharma, J. (2019). Fractional Sobel filter based brain tumor detection and segmentation using statistical features and SVM. In *Nanoelectronics, circuits and communication systems* (pp. 161–175). Singapore: Springer. doi:10.1007/978-981-13-0776-8_15

Panda, B., & Panda, C. S. (2019). *A Review on Brain Tumor Classification Methodologies*. Academic Press.

Praveen, G. B., & Agrawal, A. (2016, March). Multi stage classification and segmentation of brain tumor. In *2016 3rd International Conference on Computing for Sustainable Global Development (INDIACom)* (pp. 1628-1632). IEEE.

Rindi, G., Klimstra, D. S., Abedi-Ardekani, B., Asa, S. L., Bosman, F. T., Brambilla, E., ... Fernandez-Cuesta, L. (2018). A common classification framework for neuroendocrine neoplasms: An International Agency for Research on Cancer (IARC) and World Health Organization (WHO) expert consensus proposal. *Modern Pathology*, *31*(12), 1770–1786. doi:10.103841379-018-0110-y PMID:30140036

Samanta, A. K., & Khan, A. A. (2018, February). Computer aided diagnostic system for automatic detection of brain tumor through MRI using clustering based segmentation technique and SVM classifier. In *International Conference on Advanced Machine Learning Technologies and Applications* (pp. 343-351). Springer. 10.1007/978-3-319-74690-6_34

Seetha, J., & Raja, S. S. (2018). Brain tumor classification using convolutional neural networks. *Biomedical & Pharmacology Journal*, *11*(3), 1457–1461. doi:10.13005/bpj/1511

Shao, L., Zhu, F., & Li, X. (2014). Transfer learning for visual categorization: A survey. *IEEE Transactions on Neural Networks and Learning Systems*, *26*(5), 1019–1034. doi:10.1109/TNNLS.2014.2330900 PMID:25014970

Shin, H. C., Roth, H. R., Gao, M., Lu, L., Xu, Z., Nogues, I., ... Summers, R. M. (2016). Deep convolutional neural networks for computer-aided detection: CNN architectures, dataset characteristics and transfer learning. *IEEE Transactions on Medical Imaging*, *35*(5), 1285–1298. doi:10.1109/TMI.2016.2528162 PMID:26886976

Shu, M. (2019). *Deep learning for image classification on very small datasets using transfer learning*. Academic Press.

Singh, A. (2015, February). Detection of brain tumor in MRI images, using combination of fuzzy c-means and SVM. In *2015 2nd International Conference on Signal Processing and Integrated Networks (SPIN)* (pp. 98-102). IEEE.

Singh, G., & Ansari, M. A. (2016, August). Efficient detection of brain tumor from MRIs using K-means segmentation and normalized histogram. In *2016 1st India International Conference on Information Processing (IICIP)* (pp. 1-6). IEEE.

Sonavane, R., & Sonar, P. (2016, December). Classification and segmentation of brain tumor using Adaboost classifier. In *2016 International Conference on Global Trends in Signal Processing, Information Computing and Communication (ICGTSPICC)* (pp. 396-403). IEEE. 10.1109/ICGTSPICC.2016.7955334

Talo, M., Baloglu, U. B., Yıldırım, Ö., & Acharya, U. R. (2019). Application of deep transfer learning for automated brain abnormality classification using MR images. *Cognitive Systems Research*, *54*, 176–188. doi:10.1016/j.cogsys.2018.12.007

Tong, J., Zhao, Y., Zhang, P., Chen, L., & Jiang, L. (2019). MRI brain tumor segmentation based on texture features and kernel sparse coding. *Biomedical Signal Processing and Control*, *47*, 387–392. doi:10.1016/j.bspc.2018.06.001

Vedaldi, A., & Lenc, K. (2015, October). Matconvnet: Convolutional neural networks for matlab. In *Proceedings of the 23rd ACM international conference on Multimedia* (pp. 689-692). 10.1145/2733373.2807412

Vidyarthi, A., & Mittal, N. (2015, December). Performance analysis of Gabor-Wavelet based features in classification of high grade malignant brain tumors. In *2015 39th National Systems Conference (NSC)* (pp. 1-6). IEEE. 10.1109/NATSYS.2015.7489135

Chapter 8

Feature Engineering for Structural Health Monitoring (SHM):
A Damage Characterization Review

Esraa Elhariri

Faculty of Computers and Information, Fayoum University, Egypt

Nashwa El-Bendary

ⓘ https://orcid.org/0000-0001-6553-4159

Arab Academy for Science, Technology, and Maritime Transport (AASTMT), Smart Village, Egypt

Shereen A. Taie

Faculty of Computers and Information, Fayoum University, Egypt

ABSTRACT

Feature engineering is a key component contributing to the performance of the computer vision pipeline. It is fundamental to several computer vision tasks such as object recognition, image retrieval, and image segmentation. On the other hand, the emerging technology of structural health monitoring (SHM) paved the way for spotting continuous tracking of structural damage. Damage detection and severity recognition in the structural buildings and constructions are issues of great importance as the various types of damages represent an essential indicator of building and construction durability. In this chapter, the authors connect the feature engineering with SHM processes through illustrating the concept of SHM from a computational perspective, with a focus on various types of data and feature engineering methods as well as applications and open venues for further research. Challenges to be addressed and future directions of research are presented and an extensive survey of state-of-the-art studies is also included.

DOI: 10.4018/978-1-7998-6659-6.ch008

Figure 1. General architecture of standard SHM system

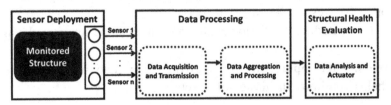

INTRODUCTION

In recent years, Structural Health Monitoring (SHM) is an emerging field that received remarkable attention from many researchers, and its techniques have been noteworthy improved by integrating advancements in communication and sensing technology. The focus of SHM is on the condition assessment, especially structures durability, of different structure types; including civil structures, mechanical, and aerospace, using a dense deployment of various sensors. Thus, SHM is a substantial method of estimating the integrity of structures through detection, localization of damages, and estimation of structures durability, based on the appropriate analysis of the measured data in situ. The goal of SHM is not solely monitoring the integrity of structures, but also is providing an estimation for the damage at earlier stages, which results in determining the ideal repair strategies before the structural damage results in failure, increasing safety, and decreasing maintenance cost (Dorvash, Pakzad & Cheng, 2013; Fang, Liu & Teng, 2018; Bolandi et al., 2019; Abdulkarem et al., 2020).

A standard SHM system comprises three major components (Dorvash, Pakzad & Cheng, 2013; Zhou & Yi, 2013; Fang, Liu & Teng, 2018; Bolandi et al., 2019; Abdulkarem et al., 2020), as depicted in Figure 1.

1. Sensor Deployment: This component aims to use the different sensors to measure the required data parameters of a structure, such as acceleration, images, stress, and displacement. Moreover, the influential environmental parameters (e.g., humidity, temperature, and wind speed) are measured. These parameters provide necessary data for structural health assessment.
2. Data Processing: This component comprises data acquisition and transmission, data aggregation and processing, and storage modules. Data acquisition and transmission module is responsible for data collection from various SHM sensors and achieved by sensor nodes. Data aggregation and processing module is necessary for extracting features of SHM algorithms and can be allocated in different units such as sensor nodes and base stations. It also can take place before or after data transmission, according to the network topology and data processing strategy.
3. Structural Health Evaluation: The main task of this component is to estimate the overall stability and safety of the structure.

Accordingly, having an SHM system helps at the following domains (Yan, Chen & Mukhopadhyay, 2017):

1. **Enhancement of Structural Integrity:** The weak structure can be enhanced based on the conditional information of SHM.

2. **Avoidance of Catastrophic Failures:** Early detection of structure damages can hinder the structure from catastrophic failures and secondary defects.

3. **Maintenance Costs Reduction:** Periodical maintenance can be substituted with condition-based maintenance.

4. **Further Development Support:** Studying the dynamic behavior of the structures over the periods of time may help to optimize the design of structures.

On the other hand, considering the rapid progress in digital cameras as well as computer vision-based sensing and monitoring technologies, major research fields are opened and attracted the attention of the structural health monitoring research community. The main reason for this is its unique characteristics and applicability in the past few years such as long-distance, high accuracy, non-contact nature, and electromagnetic interference immunity in multipoint, and structural measurement /monitoring over large-range (Ye, Dong & Liu, 2016).

Up to now, many researchers have developed several computer vision-based analysis techniques for measurement of structural displacement, monitoring of stress/strain, vibration response, crack detection, inspection, and characterization. Most of these techniques are based on both Machine Learning (ML) and Deep Learning (DL) models. The performance of these techniques is highly affected by various factors like the algorithm parameters, the dataset size, the features number, and the nature of the underlying problem. Moreover, it is heavily influenced by the representation of the feature vector. As a result, feature engineering is the major component of the ML applications, which is one of the most time-consuming components, that highly contributes to the performance of ML models. Much of the actual effort in building the ML applications is spent on designing preprocessing pipelines and feature engineering (Zheng & Casari, 2018). Thus, this chapter highlights and discusses the usage of feature engineering for Structural Health Monitoring (SHM) applications.

This chapter presents a contemporary review with an entire picture for intelligent damage detection, feature engineering for SHM, and the major challenges and open research issues related to feature engineering for SHM to help the researchers understand the obstacles and suitability of implementing intelligent SHM systems based on different feature engineering methods with a focus on feature extraction methods. The remaining of this chapter is organized as follows: In the "Intelligent Damage Detection" section, the general structure of the damage detection system is illustrated. The "Feature Engineering" section presents the basics of feature engineering by explaining the concepts of feature extraction and feature selection, in addition to providing a comprehensive comparison between the different feature selection methods. In the "Feature Engineering Methods in Structural Health Monitoring" section, a survey of feature engineering methods that are most utilized in SHM applications is introduced. In the "Recent Studies on Structural Health Monitoring" section, state-of-the-art ML models and algorithms used for feature engineering in SHM applications are discussed. The "Challenges and Open Issues in SHM" section provides key challenges of SHM and suggests future open research issues from SHM as well as feature engineering perspectives. Finally, the chapter is concluded with the "Summary" section.

INTELLIGENT DAMAGE DETECTION

Any structure is expected to sustain damage and still operate satisfactorily. To describe deficient in structures and systems in a consistent way, the following terms need to be defined:

- **Defect** when a flaw is ingrained in the material. Statistically speaking, all materials include defects at the level of atomic microstructural such as inclusions, hollow spaces, and impurities, this implies that the structure can operate, be safe, and stable at its design condition even if the constitutive materials include defects.
- **Fault** when the structure can no more be safe, stable, or satisfactorily operate. If the quality of a structure is defined as its fitness for purpose, safety, and stability, it is enough to define a fault as a change in the structure that results in an unsatisfactory quality downgrading.
- **Damage** when the structure is no longer in its perfect condition but is still safe, stable, and operating satisfactorily.

Structure monitoring and damage detection at the possible early stages help at supporting maintenance strategies and providing precise predictions. The objective of structure monitoring is to collect information about the damage for taking proper regenerative actions to restore the system or structure to the high-quality operation or at least to guarantee safety. Damage diagnosis in structural systems firstly includes damage detection, followed by damage localization, category, and severity. This section aims to describe the general framework of intelligent damage detection. The intelligent damage detection framework comprises three main phases; namely, data acquisition and preprocessing, feature engineering, and classification as depicted in Figure 2 (Worden & Dulieu-Barton, 2004; Worden, 2010; Sun et al., 2020).

- **Data Acquisition and Preprocessing Phase:** It constitutes a very important phase of any intelligent damage detection system and has a significant influence on the capability for damage detection and assessment. It is responsible for data collecting using various sensors and preprocessed the collected data for the feature engineering phase. Preprocessing includes data cleaning, data transformation, and dimension reduction.
- **Feature Engineering Phase:** This phase is the key component of a successful ML algorithm, contributing to their performance. It aims to extract features that better represent the underlying problem from raw data and transform them into a proper format for machine learning models.
- **Classification Phase:** This phase is responsible for classifying patterns into various categories using ML algorithms. These algorithms can be divided into three categories; namely, supervised learning, semi-supervised learning, and unsupervised learning based on the amount of required labeled data (Worden & Dulieu-Barton, 2004; Worden, 2010; Sun et al., 2020).

Figure 2. General framework of intelligent damage detection

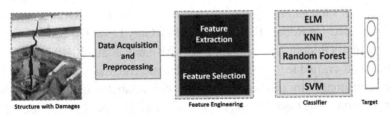

FEATURE ENGINEERING

Feature engineering is defined as the task of extracting features that better represent the underlying problem from raw data and transforming them into a proper format for ML models, resulting in improving the performance of a trained model on unseen data.

Feature engineering can be categorized into the two groups of feature extraction and feature selection, as depicted in Figure 3. The main aim of feature extraction and selection is to 1) reduce high-dimensional feature space to low-dimensional representation, 2) focus on the most relevant data, 3) avoid overfitting the data, and 4) enhance the quality of feature space and hence the performance of machine learning algorithms such as learning time and accuracy (Nargesian et al., 2017; Zheng & Casari, 2018).

Figure 3. Feature engineering categories

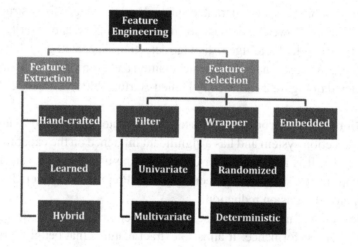

Feature Extraction

Feature extraction is the process of extracting a set of new features from the original features through some mapping functions. Feature extraction methods can be classified into three groups: 1) the hand-crafted features, 2) the learned ones, and 3) hybrid features. Hand-crafted features are the ones that are extracted from an image or an input data source via following some specific hand-engineered predefined algorithms and based on expert knowledge. There are a wide variety of state-of-the-art algorithms for the hand-crafted features such as Histogram of Oriented Gradients (HOG), Scale Invariant Features Transform (SIFT), Speeded-Up Robust Features (SURFs), Grey Level Co-occurrence Matrix (GLCM), and several others (Nanni, Ghidoni & Brahnam, 2017; Alshazly et al., 2019).

In contrast to the hand-crafted features, the learned features are the set of descriptors that are learned directly from raw input images by training a network with a labeled dataset to accomplish a specific task (e.g., face recognition). The Convolutional Neural Network (CNN) is considered as the main class of Deep Neural Networks (DNNs), used to extract learned features. The main idea behind the learned features approach is to discover data representations with multiple levels of abstraction to enable higher-level features of representing the semantics of the data, which provides better robustness to intra-class variability. Finally, hybrid features are the set of features that integrate both hand-crafted and learned ones. In this chapter, we will briefly discuss some of the popular learned features and hand-crafted features used in building the SHM systems (Nanni, Ghidoni & Brahnam, 2017; Alshazly et al., 2019).

Feature Selection

Selecting the optimal subset of distinct features plays a key role in improving the performance of a classification model with lower computational effort, shorter learning time, data visualization, refined understanding of computational models, low risk of data overfitting, and lower dimensions of the problem. Feature selection picks out the subset of the features with maximum relevance to the target class and minimal redundancy from the original set to increase the classification accuracy (Biswas, Bordoloi & Purkayastha, 2017; Manikandan & Abirami, 2018). As shown in Figure 3, feature selection can be broadly classified into three categories: 1) the filter methods, which select features from the data regardless of the involved learning algorithm, 2) the wrapper methods that employ learning algorithms to evaluate which features are most powerful, and 3) the embedded methods, which insert the feature selection step into the classifier construction. The FS methods can be also classified into: 1) supervised learning, class labels are specified beforehand, and the algorithms maximize some functions to pick out the relevant features, which are extremely correlated with the class and 2) unsupervised learning, class labels are not given resulting in difficulty in finding relevant features simultaneously (Ang et al., 2016; Biswas, Bordoloi & Purkayastha, 2017; Manikandan & Abirami, 2018; Faisal, et al., 2019).

Filter Methods

Filter methods are independent of learning algorithms and select the optimal subset of features based on examining the relevance of features by considering the substantial properties criteria of the data e.g. using Statistical ranking methods. Filter methods keep high-scoring features and remove low-scoring features. In other words, the feature with no effect on the class labels can be ignored. Filter methods are divided into univariate and multivariate methods. In the univariate filter methods, each feature is evaluated individually; thereby feature dependencies are neglected that may result in misclassification. To overcome the problem of disregard feature dependencies, multivariate filter methods are presented, aiming at the incorporation of the relationships among the features. Filter methods are computationally simple and scalable. Filter-based feature selection approach is shown in Figure 4 (Ang et al., 2016; Biswas, Bordoloi & Purkayastha, 2017; Manikandan & Abirami, 2018; Faisal, et al., 2019).

Wrapper Methods

Unlike filter methods, wrapper methods are dependent on learning algorithms in evaluating the worth of features to find the optimized feature subset. Wrapper methods utilize one or more of learning algorithm performance metrics such as accuracy as a criterion for feature evaluation. The wrapper methods pick out the most discriminative features subset by minimizing the prediction error of a specific learning algorithm. That makes them give superior performance than the filter methods because they consider the feature dependencies and directly merge bias in the learning algorithm. On the other hand, wrapper methods are less general than the filter ones because they are learning algorithm dependent. So, there is no assurance that the obtained solution-based specific learning algorithm is optimal for other algorithms.

Figure 4. Filter-based feature selection approach

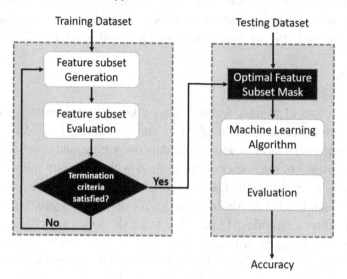

Moreover, the wrapper methods have a higher overfitting risk than filter methods. Wrapper methods are classified as Randomized and Deterministic. Randomized methods include randomization into their search space to scape local minima. They use Simulated Annealing, Scatter Search, and Evolutionary Computation Algorithms (e.g., Genetic Algorithm (GA), Particle Swarm Optimization (PSO), Artificial Bee Colony (ABC), Cuckoo-Search Algorithm (CSA), Whale Optimization Algorithm (WOA), Ant Colony Optimization (ACO), Firefly Algorithm (FA), Bat Algorithm (BA), Grey Wolf Optimization (GWO), Salp Swarm Algorithm (SSA), etc. While deterministic methods search through the space of available features either backward or forward using Sequential Forward Selection (SFS) or Sequential Backward Elimination (SBE). Wrapper-based feature selection approach is shown in Figure 5 (Ang et al., 2016; Biswas, Bordoloi & Purkayastha, 2017; Manikandan & Abirami, 2018; Hancer, Xue & Zhang, 2018; Faisal et al., 2019; Hammami et al., 2019; Zhang et al., 2020).

Embedded Methods

Embedded methods combine both filter and wrapper methods, where they are a built-in feature selection method embedding the feature selection in the learning algorithm and utilizing its properties to lead feature assessment. That makes them more efficient and tractable than the wrapper one, with similar performance and a lower risk of overfitting. Similar to the wrapper method, they consider the dependencies among features but are dependent on a given learning algorithm. Figure 6 shows the embedded feature selection approach (Ang et al., 2016; Biswas, Bordoloi & Purkayastha, 2017; Manikandan & Abirami, 2018; Faisal et al., 2019).

Table 1 illustrates a comprehensive comparison of the different feature selection methods (Ang et al., 2016; Biswas, Bordoloi & Purkayastha, 2017; Manikandan & Abirami, 2018; Faisal, et al., 2019).

Figure 5. Wrapper-based feature selection approach

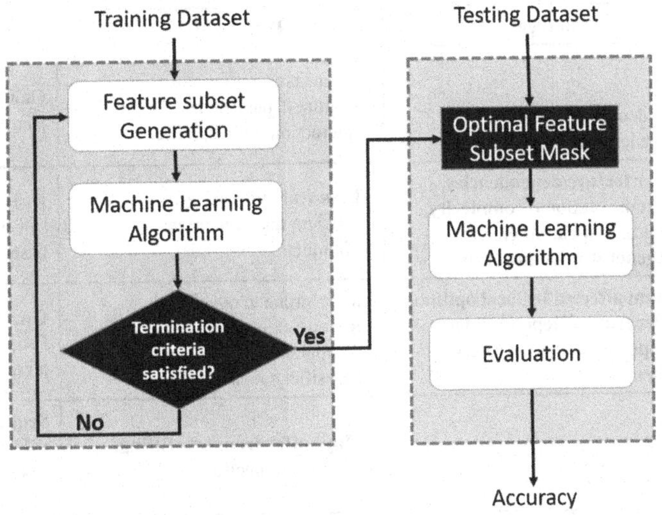

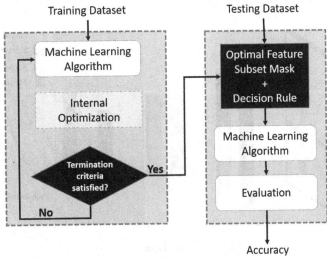

FEATURE ENGINEERING METHODS IN STRUCTURAL HEALTH MONITORING

Convolutional Neural Network (CNN)

Among various DL models, CNN is the most widely used model for image classification. Standard CNN comprises various convolutional layers, max-pooling layers, and fully-connection (FC) layers. The major aim of CNN is to automatically and adaptively learn the spatial hierarchies of useful features, from low- to high-level patterns. Figure 7 depicts a sample CNN architecture with the corresponding layers (Cha, Choi & Büyüköztürk, 2017; Silva & Lucena, 2018; Maeda at al., 2018).

Figure 6. Embedded feature selection approach

Table 1. Comparison of feature selection methods

Method	Advantages	Disadvantages	Examples
Univariate Filter	- Fast - Scalable - Independent of classifier - Better generalizable property	It neglects: - Feature dependencies. - Interaction with classifier	Gain ratio, Euclidean distance, Entropy, i-test,
Multivariate Filter	**- Consider feature dependencies,** **- Better computational complexity,** **- Independent of classifier** **- Better generalizable property**	**- Less scalable and less** - efficient than univariate techniques	Fast correlation-based feature selection (FCBF), Correlation based feature selection (CFS)
Wrapper Randomized	**- Minimum affected by local optima,** **- Consider feature dependencies** **- Higher performance accuracy** - than filter	- More prone to overfitting - Require expensive - computation - Classifier specific	GA, PSO, FA, GWO, etc. Estimation of distribution algorithm
Wrapper Deterministic	- Simple. - Better interaction with classifier. - Consider feature dependencies.	**- May suffer from overfitting,** **- Classifier specific**	**Sequential Forward Selection (SFS), Beam Search, Sequential Backward Elimination** (SBE)
Embedded	**- Better computational complexity than wrapper approaches;** - Consider interaction with classifier and feature dependencies	- Classifier specific	**Weighted SVM, Weighted Naive Bayes, Decision Tree Algorithm**

Convolutional Layer

The convolutional layer is the key aspect of CNN. It operates by applying three steps. The first step is an element-by-element multiplication between a sub-array of the input array and a receptive field. The second step is summing the multiplied values, then adding bias to the summed values. The last step is to add them to the output array. The weight values of a receptive field/ (filter or kernel) are randomly initialized. It works as shown in Algorithm 1 (Cha, Choi & Büyüköztürk, 2017; Silva & Lucena, 2018; Maeda et al., 2018).

Figure 7. An example of the CNN architecture

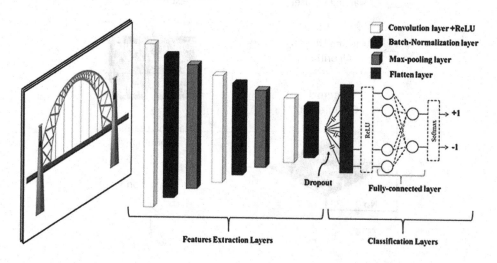

Algorithm 1. Convolution layer

```
Input: Array A of size I, receptive field, and stride step N
Output: Down-sampled array
Step 1: Multiply sub-array of A and a receptive field element-by-element (both
of size N × N)
Step 3: Sum all of the multiplied values
Step 4: Add bias to the output values of step 3
Step 5: Add the output values of step 4 to the output array
```

Pooling Layer

Another key aspect of CNN is the down-sampling process performed by the pooling layer. It aims to obtain spatial invariance by decreasing the resolution of the input feature map. Each pooled feature map corresponds to one feature map of the previous layer. Max- pooling and mean-pooling are two types of pooling. The maximum values from an input array's sub-arrays are taken in max-pooling, while in mean-pooling the mean values are taken. From the survey, max-pooling performance in image datasets outperforms mean-pooling. Process of pooling layer operates as shown in Algorithm 2 (Cha, Choi & Büyüköztürk, 2017; Silva & Lucena, 2018; Maeda et al., 2018).

Algorithm 2. Pooling layer

```
Input: Array A of pool size I and stride step N
Output: Down-sampled array
Step 1:  For each sub-array of A of pool size I
•          Select the maximum value of the pool (Max-pooling), or
•          Compute the mean value of the pool (Mean-pooling)
Step 2: Add the computed value to the output array
```

Activation Layer

The activation layer is a non-linear transformation function, which is widely used in the standard Artificial Neural Networks (ANN). There are many various activation functions like hyperbolic tangent (tanh), sigmoid, Rectified Linear Unit (ReLU), etc. It is applied after the convolution operation is completed to enable CNN to avoid learning trivial linear combinations of inputs. All non-linear functions are restricted to output values except ReLU, which has only restricted outputs for its negative inputs. The features of ReLU make computation faster and more accurate. ReLU is computed according to equation (1) (Cha, Choi & Büyüköztürk, 2017; Silva & Lucena, 2018; Maeda et al., 2018).

$$R(x) = \max(0, x), \tag{1}$$

Where x is the input to a neuron.

Softmax Layer

To classify an input image, it is essential to include a layer for prediction. This layer is responsible for classifying input images and is located at the end of the CNN model. Any ML algorithm can be used like Support Vector Machines (SVMs), Multi-Layer Perceptron (MLP), etc. To date, using the Softmax function is the most outstanding method. The Softmax function is given by equation (2) (Cha, Choi & Büyüköztürk, 2017; Silva & Lucena, 2018; Maeda et al., 2018).

$$y_k = \frac{\exp\left(\phi_k\right)}{\sum_j^C \exp\left(\phi_j\right)}, \tag{2}$$

Where ϕ the neural network output and y is the probability of belonging to a class.

Histogram of Oriented Gradients (HOG)

Histogram of oriented gradients (HOG) is a widely used local features descriptor in the field of computer vision for various tasks like object detection, face recognition, human detection, pose estimation, etc., with attaining outstanding accuracy due to its high ability to describe shape and texture strongly. Using orientation intensity distribution and edges gradient, the HOG descriptor is capable of preserving image local information. HOG is computed using magnitude and orientation. Equations (3) and (4) are used to compute vertical and horizontal gradients (Wang et al., 2018; Elhariri, El-Bendary & Taie, 2019; Elhariri, El-Bendary & Taie, 2020).

$$Gx = I_f *[-1,0,1] \tag{3}$$

$$G_y = I_f *[-1,0,1]^T \tag{4}$$

The obtained gradients are then used to compute gradient magnitude and angular orientations using equations (5) and (6).

$$m\left(x,y\right) = \sqrt{G_x^2 + G_y^2} \tag{5}$$

$$\theta\left(x,y\right) = \tan^{-1}\left(\frac{G_x}{G_y}\right) \tag{6}$$

After dividing the image into N blocks, the histogram of gradient directions is computed for each block. Finally, the histograms of the four blocks are combined to form the final feature vector. HOG can be computed using Algorithm 3 (Wang, Zhao, Gao, Zhang & Wang, 2018; Elhariri, El-Bendary & Taie, 2019; Elhariri, El-Bendary & Taie, 2020).

Algorithm 3. HOG feature vector computation

```
Input: Grayscale image
Output: Final HOG feature vector
Step 1: Compute vertical and horizontal gradients according to equations (3)
and (4)
Step 2: Compute gradient magnitude and angular orientations according to equa-
tions (5) and (6)
Step 3: Segment image into cells and blocks
Step 4: Build the HOG features vector for each cell
Step 5: Normalize HOG features vector for each block
Step 6: Concatenate all blocks histograms to obtain the final HOG feature vec-
tor
```

Local Binary Pattern (LBP)

Local Binary Pattern (LBP) is a widely used feature descriptor for texture features extraction in various computer vision tasks, with excellent performance, in terms of both discrimination performance and speed. The main strength LBP feature descriptor is its robustness to rotation variation and illumination. For a given center pixel p, the LBP model compares its intensity value with the 8 immediately neighboring pixels to generate a binary code according to equation (7) (Wang et al., 2018; Elhariri, El-Bendary & Taie, 2019; Elhariri, El-Bendary & Taie, 2020).

$$s\left(i\right) = \begin{cases} 1, \left(g_i - g_c\right) \geq 0 \\ 0, \left(g_i - g_c\right) < 0 \end{cases}, \tag{7}$$

Where g_c and g_i are the gray levels of the center pixel of the circle, and the surrounding pixels, respectively.

To obtain the LBP value of pixel p, the generated binary code is converted into a decimal format according to equation (8) and different textures around the p pixel can be represented by different LBP values. Finally, a histogram is computed over the output LBP values as the feature vector. The LBP feature vector can be computed according to Algorithm 4 (Wang, Zhao, Gao, Zhang & Wang, 2018; Elhariri, El-Bendary & Taie, 2019; Elhariri, El-Bendary & Taie, 2020).

$$LBP_{P,R} = \sum_{i=0}^{7} s\left(i\right) * 2^i \tag{8}$$

Where P is the number of surrounding pixels of the central pixel located on a circle of radius R.

Algorithm 4. LBP feature vector computation

```
Input: Grayscale image
Output: Final LBP feature vector
Step 1: Segment image into N cells
Step 2: For each pixel in a cell, compare the pixel with its 8 neighbors and
compute 8-bit binary vector S according to equation (7)
Step 3: Convert each 8-bit vector into its corresponding decimal value and re-
place the intensity value by the obtained decimal value using equation (8)
Step 4: For each cell, extract the histogram, containing only values (0 to 255)
Step 5: Concatenate all histograms of all cells to obtain the final LBP fea-
ture vector
```

Scale Invariant Feature Transform (SIFT)

Scale Invariant Feature Transform (SIFT) is the most popular method for extracting interest points and feature descriptors that are invariant to scale, translation, rotation, noise, change in illumination, affine distortion, perspective, and similarity transform. It is widely used for various computer vision applications, like scene detection, object detection, image matching, etc. The SIFT feature descriptor is computed through four main stages; namely, Scale-space extrema detection, Key-point localization, Orientation assignment, and Key-point descriptor. The SIFT feature descriptor can be computed using Algorithm 5 (Li, Liu, Li, Huang & Li, 2014; Qu, Lin, Ju & Liu, 2015).

Scale-Space Extrema Detection

At the first stage, a Gaussian scale-space is constructed from the input image using equation (9):

$$L(x,y,\sigma) = G(x,y,\sigma) * I(x,y) \tag{9}$$

Where $G(x, y, \sigma)$, $I(x, y)$, and σ represent a variable-scale Gaussian, the input image, and the factor of scale-space, respectively. Then, the difference of Gaussian (DoG) $D(x, y, \sigma)$ is computed as the difference between two filtered images using equation (10):

$$D(x,y,\sigma) = L(x,y,k\sigma) - L(x,y,\sigma) \tag{10}$$

To detect the candidate extreme keypoints of $D(x, y, \sigma)$, each point is compared with the pixels of all its 8 neighbors of the same scale factor and 18 neighbors of the adjacent scale factors. If the value of the point is maximum or minimum, then this point is the extrema. Then, a second-order Taylor series expansion is used to refine the localization of the keypoint to subpixel accuracy. The true extrema location is given by equation (11):

$$z = -\left(\frac{\partial^2 D}{\partial x^2}\right)^{-1} \frac{\partial D}{\partial x},$$ (11)

Where D and its derivatives are evaluated at the sample point and x = (x, y, σ)T is the offset from the sample point.

Keypoint Elimination

During this stage, the poorly localized points on an edge or points with low contrast are eliminated from the candidate list of keypoints. The value of the keypoint in the DoG pyramid at the extrema is computed using equation (12):

$$D(z) = D + \frac{1}{2} \frac{\partial D^1}{\partial x} z$$ (12)

To eliminate points having low contrast, if the value at the extrema is less than a threshold value, it is rejected. While for eliminating unstable keypoints laying on edges, a second-order Hessian matrix is used.

Orientation Assignment

The main aim of this stage is a consistent orientation assignment to the keypoints based on local image properties. To form an orientation histogram, the gradient orientations of sample points within a region around the keypoint is calculated using equation (13):

$$\theta(x,y) = \tan^{-1}\left[\frac{L(x,y+1) - L(x,y-1)}{L(x+1,y) - L(x-1,y)}\right]$$ (13)

Afterward, the dominant orientation is assigned as the orientation of the keypoint.

Keypoint Descriptor

Finally, the feature descriptor is built using the following steps:

- Divide the region around the keypoint into 16 sub-regions of size 4×4 pixels.
- For each sub-region, an 8-bin histogram is computed.
- All the histograms are concatenated to generate the final 128-values descriptor.
- Normalize the final descriptor to eliminate the effect of the illumination change (Li, Liu, Li, Huang & Li, 2014; Qu, Lin, Ju & Liu, 2015).

Algorithm 5. SIFT features extraction

```
Input: Grayscale image
Output: SIFT feature vector
Step 1: Construct a Gaussian scale-space using equation (9)
Step 2: Compute the Difference of Gaussians (DoG) using equation (10)
Step 3: Find the candidate extreme keypoints
Step 4: Refine candidate keypoints location with sub-pixel precision using a
second-order Taylor series expansion
Step 5: Eliminate points having low contrast or localized on the edge
Step 6: Compute the gradient orientations θ(x,y) using equation (13)
Step 7: Assign the dominant orientation as the orientation of the keypoint
Step 8: Build the feature descriptor
Step 9: Normalize the final descriptor
```

Speeded-Up Robust Features (SURF)

Speeded-Up Robust Features (SURF) is a local feature detector and descriptor, which is widely used in various computer vision tasks like object recognition, classification, image registration, or 3D reconstruction. It is a fast and efficient scale and rotation invariant descriptor. The purpose of the SURF descriptor is to reduce the computational complexity of the SIFT descriptor. In SURF, the Difference of Gaussian (DoG) filters are replaced by the Haar box filters to approximate the Laplacian of Gaussian. Integral images are utilized to rapidly compute a convolution with these box filters. The SURF descriptor is obtained using the Wavelet responses in the horizontal and vertical directions (Bay, Tuytelaars & Van Gool, 2006; Kim at al., 2019).

The process of SURF descriptor extraction works as follow:

For the fast computation of pixel intensities in a square region, the integral image is used. Each pixel in the integral image I_Σ is computed using equation (14):

$$I_\Sigma(x,y) = \sum_{x=1}^{X}\sum_{y=1}^{Y} I(x,y),\tag{14}$$

Where X and Y are image width and height, respectively. Then, the second-order Gaussian filter among x, y and xy directions is utilized for the Hessian matrix computation as given by equation (15):

$$H(x,\sigma) = \begin{bmatrix} L_{xx}(x,\sigma) & L_{xy}(x,\sigma) \\ L_{xy}(x,\sigma) & L_{yy}(x,\sigma) \end{bmatrix},.\tag{15}$$

Where x is a given point in the input image I, is the convolution of the middle point X with the Gaussian filter, and is defined as scale.

Although Gaussians are optimal for scale-space analysis, they are continuous. They need to be discretized to be used in practice. For this reason, the approximations of convolutions of the Gaussian filter D_{xx}, D_{yy}, and D_{xy} in the x-direction, y-direction, and xy-direction, respectively, are used instead to compute the determinant of Hessian matrix using equation (16):

$$\Delta x = D_{xx}D_{yy} - (wD_{xy})^2. \tag{16}$$

Where w is the relative weight of the filter responses utilized to balance the impact of box filter approximation usage. After computing the determinant of the Hessian matrix, the determinant responses are normalized to scale. Afterward, the non-maximal suppression is computed via finding the maximum determinant value within 3x3x3 neighbors present in the lower, and upper scale. To reserve the strongest interest point only, the obtained values are filtered with a predefined threshold. For the orientation assignment, Haar wavelets of size 4σ in x and y directions are computed for pixels located within a radius of 6σ around the interest point. The dominant orientation is computed by summing the vertical and horizontal responses. Finally, the descriptor is calculated using Haar wavelets in a square of 20σ size area centered at the interest point and oriented along the dominant direction. Algorithm 6 summarizes the process of extracting the SURF descriptor (Bay, Tuytelaars & Van Gool, 2006; Kim at al., 2019).

There are many variations on the SURF descriptor such as Upright-SURF (U-SURF), Modified-SURF (M-SURF), Modified Upright-SURF (MU-SURF), Gauge-SURF (G-SURF), GU-SURF, Modified Gauge-SURF (MG-SURF), and No Gaussian Weighting-SURF (NG-SURF). The G-SURF methods are of particular interest. Unlike the standard SURF descriptors, which use the standard local first-order derivatives, they use second-order multiscale gauge derivatives. Since the building process of G-SURF descriptors uses the integral images, G-SURF descriptors are fast to compute similar to the standard SURF descriptors. In addition to the extra matching robustness resulting from the extra invariance provided by gauge derivatives (Alcantarilla, Bergasa & Davison, 2013; Krig & Krig, 2014).

Harris Corner Detector (Harris)

The Harris corner detector is a common corner detector, widely used in various computer vision tasks due to its strong invariance to image noise, rotation, scale, and illumination variation. Harris depends on the pixels' gradient. Whereas, the pixel is declared as a corner if the absolute of the gradient value changes in all directions significantly. Image corners can be detected using Algorithm 7 (Mahesh & Subramanyam, 2012; Cui et al., 2014).

RECENT STUDIES ON STRUCTURAL HEALTH MONITORING

Recently, many studies developed SHM systems; however, a limited number of studies considered using feature selection and fusion methods for attaining improved recognition rate. This section provides a discussion of some state-of-the-art research work that investigated feature engineering for SHM.

Algorithm 6. SURF features extraction

```
Input: Grayscale image
Output: SURF feature vector
Step 1: Convert image I into an integral image I_Σ
Step 2: Compute the Hessian matrix
Step 3: Compute the approximation of convolutions of the Gaussian filter D_xx,
D_yy, and D_xy
Step 4: Compute the determinant of the Hessian matrix
Step 5: Normalize the determinant responses to scale
Step 6: Calculate the non-maximal suppression
Step 7: Filter the obtained values with a predefined threshold
Step 8: Form a square area of size 20s centered on the interest point, where s
is the scale at which the interest point is detected
Step 9: Divide the formed square area into 4x4 sub-region squares
Step 10: For each region, compute interest point orientations using Haar Wave-
lets in x and y directions
Step 11: Compute interest point descriptors using the obtained Haar Wavelet
responses
```

Hand-Crafted Features Based SHM

Figure 8 shows a schematic framework of damage detection systems based on hand-crafted features. It comprises four phases; namely, preprocessing, feature extraction, feature selection, and classification.

Figure 8. Schematic framework of damage detection systems based on hand-crafted features

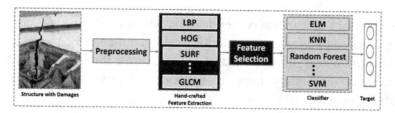

To overcome the limited representation problem caused by using one type of features, Wang et al. presented an effective crack detection model integrating the power of using multiple visual features, and the strength of multi-task learning. The LBP and the HOG were combined as two complementary features of texture and edges. The combined extracted feature vectors were fed into an ELM-based multi-task learning classification for crack detection. A total of 350 raw concrete images taken from some experimental concrete structures at Shijiazhuang Tiedao University were used to evaluate the proposed model. The results of the conducted experiment proved that the proposed crack detection method outperformed the other traditional methods and achieved an accuracy of 92% (Wang et al., 2018).

Algorithm 7. Harris corner detection

```
Input: Grayscale image I
Output: Interest (corner) points
Step 1:  Apply image smoothing using an averaging filter
Step 2: Compute the magnitude of the x and y gradients at each pixel
Step 3: Construct the autocorrelation matrix in a window around each pixel
using equation (17):
```

$$C = \begin{bmatrix} \sum I_x^2 & \sum I_x I_y \\ \sum I_x I_y & \sum I_y^2 \end{bmatrix} = \begin{bmatrix} \lambda_1 & 0 \\ 0 & \lambda_2 \end{bmatrix},$$

(17)

```
Where C and I_x and I_y represent the autocorrelation matrix, the derivatives of
an image I in the x-direction and y-direction. While λ_1 and λ_2 are the eigen-
values of matrix C
Step 4: Compute corner response measure (R) using equation (18):
```

$$R = Det\left(C\right) - K * T\left(C\right)^2 = \lambda_1 \lambda_2 - k * \left(\lambda_1 + \lambda_2\right)^2,$$

(18)

```
Where Det and T are the determinant and the trace of matrix C, respectively. K
is a constant
Step 5: Threshold the value of R based on λ_1 and  λ_2 to determine the slow
changes of areas, corners, and edge through the following three cases:
1.          If λ_1 ≈ 0 and λ_2 ≈ 0, then this pixel (x, y) has no feature interest
2.          If λ_1 ≈ 0 and λ_2 has some large positive value, then an edge is found
3.          If λ_1 and λ_2 have large positive values, then the corner is found
```

Kabir et al. proposed a ML-based crack detection method for concrete surface crack. The proposed method utilized texture features extracted from GLCM. After extracting texture features from images, ANN with MLP architecture was utilized to classify crack into three classes; namely, no crack, narrow crack, and wide crack. The used datasets for evaluation consists of many of thermographic, grayscale, and visual color images of concrete blocks. Based on the obtained results, the three types of images achieved reasonable performance. However, the infrared thermography obtained more precise results compared to others by achieving an accuracy of 83.5% (Kabir, 2010).

Another ML-based crack detection method for pavement surface crack was proposed by HU et al. The used dataset for evaluating the proposed method is a total of 287 pavement images. The proposed method utilized texture features extracted from GLCM and two translation-invariant shape descriptors for building the feature vector. Feeding SVM with the obtained feature vector achieved an average accuracy, sensitivity, specificity of 98.28%, 88.31%, and 98.53% (Hu, Zhao & Wang, 2010).

Learned Features Based SHM

Figure 9 shows the framework of the basic end-to-end DL-based damage detection system. Unlike damage detection systems based on hand-crafted features, there is no need for the preprocessing phase, as DL has the ability to learn features from raw data. Thus, it comprises only the two phases of feature extraction and classification.

Figure 10 shows the framework of the basic damage detection system based on DL. Unlike the end-to-end DL-based damage detection system, it comprises only three phases; namely, feature extraction, feature selection, and classification.

Figure 9. Structure of the end-to-end DL-based damage detection system

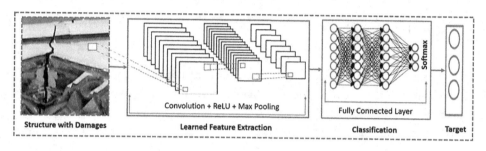

Figure 10. Framework of the basic damage detection system based on DL

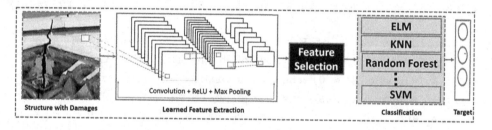

With the aim of both improving crack detection rate and reducing false alarms, Keunyoung et al. presented a hybrid approach based on DL for crack detection (Jang, Kim & An, 2019). The presented approach combines the advantages of both vision and laser IR thermography images. Time-Spatial-Integrated (TSI) coordinate transform was used for image reconstruction. After reconstructing the image, a pre-trained GoogLeNet CNN architecture was utilized for extracting features from the images. The presented system was evaluated using a total of 200 raw images that increased to 20,000 images by segmentation and augmentation. The experimental results showed that there was an improvement of 38.56% and 1.97% in the precision and recall of the presented crack detection system using hybrid images.

Maeda et al. presented CNN-based approach for road crack detection. The used dataset is a total of 500 pavement images, which are captured using a smartphone at the campus of Temple University (Maeda et al., 2018). All images are cropped into patches of 99×99 pixel using sampling strategy capable of increasing the number of crack samples via rotating each sample by random angle and minimizing the similarity between the samples in training data, resulting in datasets of 640,000, 160,000 and 200,000 samples are used as the training, validation, and testing data sets, respectively. The training dataset was used to train the proposed CNN model using 5-fold cross-validation. Finally, a comparative study among the proposed method, SVM, and Boosting methods was conducted. The obtained results proved that the proposed CNN model outperformed both SVM and Boosting methods, through improving the F-measure by 0.1606.

In a similar vein, Silva et al. developed a deep learning-based concrete crack detection system (Silva & Lucena, 2018). The pre-trained VGG16 CNN architecture using transfer learning schema was utilized for extracting features. Besides the system development, the effect of various training parameters on the proposed system performance was studied. A balanced dataset consists of 3500 images of concrete surfaces, was used to evaluate the proposed system with 80% and 20% used for training and testing. An accuracy of 92.27% was achieved using the proposed system.

Most edge detectors generate residual noise in the final binary images. To reduce this noise and to improve crack detection accuracy, Dorafshan et al. developed a new hybrid crack detector that combined an edge detection method with a DCNN model. Besides the detector development, a comparative study between traditional edge detectors and DL models for crack detection is presented. On evaluating the proposed method with a dataset of 100 raw concrete images, the LoG technique performed well by accurately detecting about 53-79% of crack pixels, but it generated noise in the binary images. AlexNet in TL mode attained an accuracy of about 98% against 97% for both FT and classification modes. The noise was reduced by a factor of 24 (Dorafshan, Thomas & Maguire, 2018a).

A new crack detection benchmark dataset called SDNET2018 was presented with benchmark results using a deep learning model by Dorafshan et al. The used dataset is of 230 raw images of cracked and intact concrete surfaces, including several challenges such as scaling, edges, surface roughness, and shadows. This dataset contains three different types of concrete surfaces, which are bridge decks, walls, and pavements. Each image was segmented into patches of size (256×256 pixels) to generate more than 56,000 sub-images, which then divided into training, validation, and testing datasets. After that, AlexNet DCNN architecture was used for crack detection. Based on the depicted experimental results, AlexNet in full training (FT) mode beat the one in transfer learning (TL) mode by achieving an accuracy of 91.92% against 90.45%, 89.31% against 87.54%, and 95.52% against 94.86% for TL mode with bridge deck, walls, and the pavement surfaces, respectively (Dorafshan, Thomas & Maguire, 2018b).

Due to the deep learning capability to learn features automatically from raw data, Cha et al. proposed an automatic crack detection method based on DL to minimize the impact of noise raised by various reasons on the classification algorithm. The proposed method utilized a CNN architecture consisting of four convolution layers, two max-pooling layers, and a Softmax layer following the fourth convolution layer for classification purposes. A total of 332 raw images captured from a complex engineering building with various image variations using a DSLR camera were used for evaluating the proposed method. After cropping the images into sub-images of size 256×256 pixels, sub-images were divided into training and validation datasets. The experimental results showed that the proposed method attained an accuracy of 97.95%, compared to other traditional methods (Cha, Choi & Büyüköztürk, 2017).

Xu et al. developed a crack detection model based on DL to improve the accuracy of crack detection. The proposed model combined the power of the Atrous Spatial Pyramid Pooling (ASPP) module, Atrous convolution, and depth-wise separable convolution in obtaining a multi-scale image feature and denser feature map. The proposed model can avoid details loss caused by the process of pooling and reduce computational complexity. Dataset of total 2068 bridge crack images was used to evaluate the proposed model. Based on the conducted results, it was observed that the proposed crack detection model outperformed the traditional DL models by attaining a reasonable performance with an accuracy of 96.37%, a precision of 78.11%, a sensitivity of 100%, a specificity of 95.83%, and F-measure of 0.8771, respectively (Xu et al., 2019).

Zhang et al. developed a unified crack detection approach based on DCNN for pavement and sealed cracks. The main strength of the proposed approach is its ability to solve the crack extraction difficulty and budgeting inaccurate caused by sealed cracks, noises, and cracks with identical width and intensity, respectively. The images were passed through a preprocessing step to eliminate the illuminance unbalance. After the preprocessing step, a two-step Deep CNN model in transfer learning mode was utilized to categorize images into 3 classes that are background, crack, and sealed crack. The binary image was then generated using a thresholding-based segmentation. The final crack region was extracted by applying a tensor voting-based curve detection method. The used dataset for evaluating the proposed approach is a total of 800 images of size (2000×4000 pixels) for sealed cracks. Based on the experimental results, a reasonable performance with recall and precision of 0.951 and 0.847, respectively was obtained using the proposed approach (Zhang, Cheng & Zhang, 2018).

A pixel-level end-to-end trainable deep CNN for road crack detection, able to handle strong non-uniformity, compound topology, and intensive noise-like problems in road images was proposed by Song et al. Multiscale dilated convolution module was used to obtain more bountiful information about crack texture. To reclaim the crack boundary details, a pixel-level dense prediction mapping was then generated by fusing the up-sampling module of low-level features. Datasets of total 4736, 1036, and 2416 crack images were used as training, validation, and testing sets, respectively. The experimental results showed that the proposed method achieved high performance with a recall of 97.85%, F-measure of 97.92%, a precision of 98.00%, and a mIoU of 73.53% (Song, Jia, Zhu, Jia & Gao, 2020).

Kim et al. developed a ML-based crack identification approach comprising of two major processes: 1) the generation of crack candidate regions (CCR) and 2) classification based on SURF and CNN. The proposed approach aims to resolve the challenge of identifying crack-like patterns such as stains, holes, dark shadows, and lumps as a crack. After extracting crack candidates using image binarization and annotation as crack or non-crack, crack candidates were utilized to construct the classification model based on both SURF and CNN features obtained from the CCR. The used dataset is a total of 487 images captured from concrete surfaces using a digital camera. Based on the experimental results, the proposed crack identification approach based on CNN attained accuracy and F-measure of 98% and 0.95, respectively (Kim at al., 2019).

Elhariri et al. developed a crack detection system for identifying cracks in the historical building using three types of features sets; namely, hand-crafted features, CNN learned features, fused features. The first utilized both HOG and LBP for generating hybrid hand-crafted features vector. The second utilized a pre-trained VGG16 DL model for generating CNN learned features vector. Finally, the third combined the two vectors to generate the fused features vector. After that, Principle Component Analysis (PCA) was applied for features dimensionality reduction. Several ML classifiers with 3-fold cross-validation and two datasets for crack images were used to validate the proposed system. The obtained experimental results showed that both Support Vector Machine (SVM) and stacked ensemble classifiers achieved the highest accuracy of 98% for crack detection using the reduced CNN-learned features (Elhariri, El-Bendary & Taie, 2019).

Moreover, Elhariri et al. proposed a novel system able to recognize crack severity degrees using a hybrid filter-wrapper feature selection method. The proposed system consists of two main phases of feature extraction and feature selection. Both hand-crafted features and CNN-based features were used to recognize crack severity. HOG and LBP were utilized to extract hand-crafted features vector, while, pre-trained VGG-16 deep learning model was utilized to extract learned features vector. After that, a hybrid filter-wrapper feature selection with a multi-objective improved binary Salp Swarm Optimization algorithm was used for picking out the optimal subset of features to improve performance and reduce the dimensionality of the features. Ten representative UCI datasets and four datasets of crack images were used to evaluate the proposed system. Based on the conducted experiments, the proposed system improved the performance of crack severity recognition with an average recognition rate of ≈ 37% and F-measure of ≈ 31%. Also, it achieved an average feature reduction rate of 67% with all the used datasets compared to the traditional classification methods using the original set of features. In addition to this, using VGG-16 learned features outperformed using the hand-crafted features by an increase of 17.7%, 15.9%, and 23.5% in fine, moderate, and severe crack recognition, respectively (Elhariri, El-Bendary & Taie, 2020).

CHALLENGES AND OPEN ISSUES

Despite the great advancement in recent SHM technologies, there still various challenges and open issues that need to be addressed.

Challenges: SHM Methods Perspective

1. The SHM implementation cost: the SHM is still in the transformation stage from lab research work to the industry norm.
2. The reliability and robustness of installed sensors: the functionality of sensors themselves may need to be monitored to avoid any possibility of failure. Besides, the damage detection algorithms need to be adaptable to the new sensor networks in case of sensors failure.
3. The SHM systems sensitivity: the SHM systems are very sensitive to various environmental and operational conditions, it has an impact on obtaining optimal results.
4. Optimal sensor placement: as accurate placement of sensors is a major step in developing a successful SHM system based on Wireless Sensor Network (WSN).
5. Damage allocation in both civil and mechanical structures: as it requires a lot of database comparison and experience to identify parameters resulting in damage initiation.

Challenges: Feature Engineering Methods Perspective

1. Limited benchmark datasets and accordingly limited multimodal datasets (e.g. both time series and image) available to build SHM systems-based multimodal neural network.
2. Poor sensor data quality as it may contain noise.
3. Complex damage detection due to the difficulty in detecting complex/composite damages such as CrackTree.
4. Novel feature selection modules that significantly affects stiffness as well as mass and energy dissipation properties of the entity that is being monitored.
5. Handling variety and veracity characteristics of SHM data types.
6. Handling the SHM images containing noise generated by several factors, such as imaging environments, capabilities of cameras, and scanners. etc.

SUMMARY

This chapter presents a survey of state-of-the-art feature engineering methods and their usage for SHM through conducting a comprehensive survey of three main parts. First, background information related to SHM technologies and intelligent damage detection has been clarified. Second, special attention has been devoted to the details of feature engineering methods. The basic concepts of the current popular feature engineering methods are introduced, and the categories in each method were reviewed. Third, the key challenges related to SHM systems and feature engineering for SHM systems were presented. We believe that the presented insights in this chapter will motivate further research towards optimizing SHM systems and invent new feature engineering methods for SHM.

REFERENCES

Abdulkarem, M., Samsudin, K., Rokhani, F. Z., & Rasid, A. (2020). Wireless sensor network for structural health monitoring: A contemporary review of technologies, challenges, and future direction. *Structural Health Monitoring*, 19(3), 693–735. doi:10.1177/1475921719854528

Alcantarilla, P. F., Bergasa, L. M., & Davison, A. J. (2013). Gauge-SURF descriptors. *Image and Vision Computing*, 31(1), 103–116. doi:10.1016/j.imavis.2012.11.001

Alshazly, H., Linse, C., Barth, E., & Martinetz, T. (2019). Handcrafted versus CNN features for ear recognition. *Symmetry*, 11(12), 1493. doi:10.3390ym11121493

Ang, J. C., Mirzal, A., Haron, H., & Hamed, H. N. A. (2016). Supervised, unsupervised, and semi-supervised feature selection: A review on gene selection. *IEEE/ACM Transactions on Computational Biology and Bioinformatics*, 13(5), 971–989. doi:10.1109/TCBB.2015.2478454 PMID:26390495

Bay, H., Tuytelaars, T., & Van Gool, L. (2006). SURF: Speeded up robust features. Lecture Notes in Computer Science, 3951, 404-417.

Biswas, S., Bordoloi, M., & Purkayastha, B. (2017). Review on feature selection and classification using neuro-fuzzy approaches. *International Journal of Applied Evolutionary Computation*, 7(4), 28–44. doi:10.4018/IJAEC.2016100102

Bolandi, H., Lajnef, N., Jiao, P., Barri, K., Hasni, H., & Alavi, A. H. (2019). A novel data reduction approach for structural health monitoring systems. *Sensors (Basel)*, 19(22), 4823. doi:10.339019224823 PMID:31698686

Cha, Y., Choi, W., & Büyüköztürk, O. (2017). Deep learning-based crack damage detection using convolutional neural networks. *Computer-Aided Civil and Infrastructure Engineering*, 32(5), 361–378. doi:10.1111/mice.12263

Cui, J., Xie, J., Liu, T., Guo, X., & Chen, Z. (2014). Corners detection on finger vein images using the improved Harris algorithm. *Optik (Stuttgart)*, 125(17), 4668–4671. doi:10.1016/j.ijleo.2014.05.026

Dorafshan, S., Thomas, R., & Maguire, M. (2018a). Comparison of deep convolutional neural networks and edge detectors for image-based crack detection in concrete. *Construction & Building Materials*, *186*, 1031–1045. doi:10.1016/j.conbuildmat.2018.08.011

Dorafshan, S., Thomas, R., & Maguire, M. (2018b). SDNET2018: An annotated image dataset for non-contact concrete crack detection using deep convolutional neural networks. *Data in Brief*, *21*, 1664–1668. doi:10.1016/j.dib.2018.11.015 PMID:30505897

Dorvash, S., Pakzad, S., & Cheng, L. (2013). An iterative modal identification algorithm for structural health monitoring using wireless sensor networks. *Earthquake Spectra*, *29*(2), 339–365. doi:10.1193/1.4000133

Elhariri, E., El-Bendary, N., & Taie, S. (2019). Performance analysis of using feature fusion for crack detection in images of historical buildings. *11th International Conference on Management of Digital EcoSystems, MEDES 2019* (pp. 308-315). New York, NY: Association for Computing Machinery, Inc. 10.1145/3297662.3365800

Elhariri, E., El-Bendary, N., & Taie, S. (2020). Using hybrid filter-wrapper feature selection with multi-objective improved-salp optimization for crack severity recognition. *IEEE Access: Practical Innovations, Open Solutions*, *8*, 84290–84315. doi:10.1109/ACCESS.2020.2991968

Faisal, A. I., Majumder, S., Mondal, T., Cowan, D., Naseh, S., & Deen, M. J. (2019). Monitoring methods of human body joints: State-of-the-art and research challenges. *Sensors (Basel)*, *19*(11), 2629. doi:10.339019112629 PMID:31185629

Fang, K., Liu, C., & Teng, J. (2018). Cluster-based optimal wireless sensor deployment for structural health monitoring. *Structural Health Monitoring*, *17*(2), 266–278. doi:10.1177/1475921717689967

Fatemeh, N., Horst, S., Udayan, K., Elias, B. K., & Deepak, T. (2017). Learning feature engineering for classification. In *Proceedings of the 26th International Joint Conference on Artificial Intelligence* (pp. 2529-2535). Melbourne, Australia: AAAI Press.

Hammami, M., Bechikh, S., Hung, C., & Ben Said, L. (2019). 61). A Multi-objective hybrid filter-wrapper evolutionary approach for feature selection. *Memetic Computing*, *11*(2), 193–208. doi:10.100712293-018-0269-2

Hancer, E., Xue, B., & Zhang, M. (2018). Differential evolution for filter feature selection based on information theory and feature ranking. *Knowledge-Based Systems*, *140*, 103–119. doi:10.1016/j.knosys.2017.10.028

Hu, Y., Zhao, C., & Wang, H. (2010). Automatic pavement crack detection using texture and shape descriptors. *IETE Technical Review, 27*(5), 398-405.

Jang, K., Kim, N., & An, Y.-K. (2019). Deep learning–based autonomous concrete crack evaluation through hybrid image scanning. *Structural Health Monitoring*, *18*(5-6), 1722–1737. doi:10.1177/1475921718821719

Kabir, S. (2010). Imaging-based detection of AAR induced map-crack damage in concrete structure. *NDT & E International*, *43*(6), 461–469. doi:10.1016/j.ndteint.2010.04.007

Kim, H., Ahn, E., Shin, M., & Sim, S.-H. (2019). Crack and noncrack classification from concrete surface images using machine learning. *Structural Health Monitoring, 18*(3), 725–738. doi:10.1177/1475921718768747

Krig, S., & Krig, S. (2014). Interest point detector and feature descriptor survey. In Computer Vision Metrics (pp. 217-282). Apress. doi:10.1007/978-1-4302-5930-5_6

Li, Y., Liu, W., Li, X., Huang, Q., & Li, X. (2014). GA-SIFT: A new scale invariant feature transform for multispectral image using geometric algebra. *Information Sciences, 281*, 559–572. doi:10.1016/j.ins.2013.12.022

Maeda, H., Sekimoto, Y., Seto, T., Kashiyama, T., & Omata, H. (2018). Road damage detection and classification using deep neural networks with smartphone images. *Computer-Aided Civil and Infrastructure Engineering, 33*(12), 1127–1141. doi:10.1111/mice.12387

Mahesh, & Subramanyam, M. (2012). Automatic image mosaic system using steerable Harris corner detector. *2012 International Conference on Machine Vision and Image Processing, MVIP 2012*, 87-91.

Manikandan, G., & Abirami, S. (2018). A survey on feature selection and extraction techniques for high-dimensional microarray datasets. *Knowledge Computing in Specific Domains, 2*, 311–333.

Nanni, L., Ghidoni, S., & Brahnam, S. (2017). Handcrafted vs. non-handcrafted features for computer vision classification. *Pattern Recognition, 71*, 158–172. doi:10.1016/j.patcog.2017.05.025

Qu, Z., Lin, S.-P., Ju, F.-R., & Liu, L. (2015). The improved algorithm of fast panorama stitching for image sequence and reducing the distortion errors. *Mathematical Problems in Engineering*, 2015.

Silva, W., & Lucena, D. (2018). Concrete cracks detection based on deep learning image classification. *Proceedings, 2*(8), 489. doi:10.3390/ICEM18-05387

Song, W., Jia, G., Zhu, H., Jia, D., & Gao, L. (2020). Automated pavement crack damage detection using deep multiscale convolutional features. *Journal of Advanced Transportation*.

Sun, L., Shang, Z., Xia, Y., Bhowmick, S., & Nagarajaiah, S. (2020). Review of bridge structural health monitoring aided by big data and artificial intelligence: From condition assessment to damage detection. *Journal of Structural Engineering (United States), 146*(5).

Wang, B., Zhao, W., Gao, P., Zhang, Y., & Wang, Z. (2018). Crack damage detection method via multiple visual features and efficient multi-task learning model. *Sensors (Basel), 18*(6), 1796. doi:10.339018061796 PMID:29865256

Worden, K. (2010). Structural health monitoring using pattern recognition. In *New Trends in Vibration Based Structural Health Monitoring* (pp. 183–246). Vienna: Springer. doi:10.1007/978-3-7091-0399-9_5

Worden, K., & Dulieu-Barton, J. M. (2004). An overview of intelligent fault detection in systems and structures. *Structural Health Monitoring, 3*(1), 85–98. doi:10.1177/1475921704041866

Xu, H., Su, X., Wang, Y., Cai, H., Cui, K., & Chen, X. (2019). Automatic bridge crack detection using a convolutional neural network. *Applied Sciences, 9*(14), 2867. doi:10.3390/app9142867

Yan, R., Chen, X., & Mukhopadhyay, S. C. (2017). Advanced signal processing for structural health monitoring. In *Structural Health Monitoring* (pp. 1–11). Cham: Springer. doi:10.1007/978-3-319-56126-4_1

Ye, X. W., Dong, C. Z., & Liu, T. (2016). A review of machine vision-based structural health monitoring: Methodologies and applications. *Journal of Sensors*.

Zhang, K., Cheng, H., & Zhang, B. (2018). Unified approach to pavement crack and sealed crack detection using preclassification based on transfer learning. *Journal of Computing in Civil Engineering*, *32*(2), 04018001. doi:10.1061/(ASCE)CP.1943-5487.0000736

Zhang, Y., Gong, D., Gao, X., Tian, T., & Sun, X. (2020). Binary differential evolution with self-learning for multi-objective feature selection. *Information Sciences*, *507*, 67–85. doi:10.1016/j.ins.2019.08.040

Zheng, A., & Casari, A. (2018). *Feature engineering for machine learning: principles and techniques for data scientists*. Academic Press.

Zhou, G.-D., & Yi, T.-H. (2013). The nonuniform node configuration of wireless sensor networks for long-span bridge health monitoring. *International Journal of Distributed Sensor Networks*.

Chapter 9
Speech Enhancement Using Neuro-Fuzzy Classifier

Judith Justin

School of Engineering, Avinashilingam Institute for Home Science and Higher Education for Women, Coimbatore, India

Vanithamani R.

School of Engineering, Avinashilingam Institute for Home Science and Higher Education for Women, Coimbatore, India

ABSTRACT

In this chapter, a speech enhancement technique is implemented using a neuro-fuzzy classifier. Noisy speech sentences from NOIZEUS and AURORA databases are taken for the study. Feature extraction is implemented through modifications in amplitude magnitude spectrograms. A four class neuro-fuzzy classifier splits the noisy speech samples into noise-only part, signal only part, more noise-less signal part, and more signal-less noise part of the time-frequency units. Appropriate weights are applied in the enhancement phase. The enhanced speech sentence is evaluated using objective measures. An analysis of the performance of the Neuro-Fuzzy 4 (NF 4) classifier is done. A comparison of the performance of the classifier with other conventional techniques is done for various noises at different noise levels. It is observed that the numerical values of the measures obtained are better when compared to the others. An overall comparison of the performance of the NF 4 classifier is done and it is inferred that NF4 outperforms the other techniques in speech enhancement.

INTRODUCTION

The autonomous, computer-driven translation of spoken language into readable text in real-time can be termed as Automatic Speech Recognition (ASR). In short, ASR is a technique that permits a computer to recognize the speech conversed into a microphone or telephone and translate it to written text (Stuckless, R., 1994). The composition of a characteristic continuous-speech recognizer comprises a feature examination block as front-end, followed by a statistical pattern classifier (Thomas Eisele et al. 1996). The interface connecting these two, should ideally hold all the relevant data of the speech signal appro-

DOI: 10.4018/978-1-7998-6659-6.ch009

priate to succeeding classification, be insensitive to irrelevant variations and simultaneously have a low dimensionality to reduce the computational burden of the classifier (Shigeru Katagiri & Chin-Hui Lee, 1993). The objective of speech recognition is to build up mechanisms to make improvements in the static representation of input speech. Nowadays, ASR has extensive applications that need a human-machine interface like automatic call processing (Reddy, D.R, 2009).

The field of ASR (Young.S, 1996 & Nurul Huda et al., 2010) mainly depends on statistical techniques, retreating from approaches that were primarily put forward such as template matching, dynamic time warping, and non-probabilistically motivated distortion measures. Consequently, methods for robust ASR have been developed to accomplish a near-perfect allocation of the acoustic mixture into contributions from constituent sources (Martin Cooke et al., 2001). The Hidden Markov Model (HMM) (Rojathai. S. & Venkatesulu. M., 2013) is one of the well-known algorithms and has proved to be an efficient technique of dealing with large units of speech amongst numerous categories of speech recognizers utilized in ASR products, implemented as well as proposed (Rabiner L.R. & B.-H. Juang, 1993, Bahl L.R, 1993). ASR has been employed for purposes like business dictation and particular requirements accessibility and the market presence for language learning has improved noticeably in recent years (In –Seok Kim, 2006). There are ASR systems that are based on stochastic replicas of speech acoustics that take out a set of major acoustic features from the speech signal and make use of statistical models to symbolize the distribution of these features for speech objects such as vocabulary, syllables or phonemes. Typical scalable signal processing methods are employed by a speech feature extractor to gather feature vectors from input audio forms (Jike Chong et al. 2010).

Speech Recognition is a pattern identification system (Ben Nasr, et al. 2013). Training and Testing are the two phases of pattern recognition (Santosh K. Gaikwad, et al. 2010). The modification caused by room reverberation is particularly unsafe for ASR systems (Nakamura.S & Shikano. K, 1997, Couvreur. L, et al. 2000, Y. Pan and A. Waibel, 2000). To minimize the inconsistency between the training conditions (close-talking / anechoic speech) and the operating conditions (distant-talking/reverberated speech) because of room reverberation, several approaches have been proposed (Laurent Couvreur & Christophe Couvreur, 2014). The illustration of the speech signal performs a significant role in the noisy speech recognition (Gong. Y, 1995). A person could speak slow or fast. It influences both the sequential and spectral uniqueness of the signal, upsetting the acoustic models. Specific models of frequency warping (which depends on vocal tract length differences) as well as more universal characteristic compensation and model alteration techniques, relying on Maximum Likelihood or Maximum a Posteriori criteria have been presented earlier. These model adaptation methods recommend a universal formalism for re-estimation based on reasonable amounts of speech data (Benzeghiba. M., 2007).

The proposed technique aims to enhance the speech quality in a noisy signal using a weighted mask and neuro-fuzzy classifier. The enhancement technique is divided into three phases. In the initial phase, the feature selected from the input noisy signal is the Modified Amplitude Magnitude Spectrogram (MAMS). Here, the noisy speech is split into 25 Time-Frequency (TF) units using a bandpass filter. The resultant channel is rectified and decimated by a factor of three. The envelope is segmented and windowed and then, Discrete Cosine Transform (DCT) is applied and multiplied with a triangular function to obtain the feature set. In the training phase, the estimated signal is computed and the ratio of the estimated to the original signal is obtained. Based on the values obtained, the respective training is implemented. In the third and the final phase, the noisy signal is filtered and windowed. Here, the weight of the mask is determined with the help of the probability function of feature vectors in the respective class. Weights are assigned based on the class having the maximum probability function. The signal is then weighted by the mask value and summed up to obtain the enhanced waveform.

RELATED WORK

Dramatic advances have been made in ASR technology and a number of methods have been proposed by researchers. A brief review of some of the recent results published is presented here.

Gibak Kim & Philipos C.Loizou (2010) discussed a binary mask for evaluating speech simplicity based on magnitude spectrum constraints. The planned binary mask was intended to retain TF units of the mixture signal convincing a magnitude constraint while discarding TF units violating the constraint. An algorithm was proposed that decayed the input signal into TF units and made binary decisions, based on a Bayesian classifier, as to whether each TF unit satisfies the magnitude constraint or not. Speech corrupted at low Signal-to-Noise (SNR) levels using dissimilar types of maskers was synthesized by that algorithm and presented to normal-hearing listeners for identification. Miao Chen Klaus Zechner (2011) proposed a method for mining and evaluating features related to the syntactic complexity of impulsive spoken responses. Their goal was to find efficient features selected from a large set of features. New features were designed in analogous ways from a syntactic complexity perspective that associated well with human ratings of the same spoken responses and automatic scoring models were constructed using machine learning methods. On human transcriptions with manually explained clause and sentence boundaries, their best scoring model accomplished overall Pearson correlation with human rated scores on an unnoticed test set.

Ghania Droua-Hamdani *et al.* (2010) presented the Algerian Arabic Speech Database (ALGASD), a Modern Standard Arabic (MSA) speech corpus arranged with utterances well-defined by 300 Algerian native speakers selected from eleven regions of Algeria. One of the goals of this corpus design was to represent the local accents of MSA spoken in Algeria. Useful information associated to the speakers, such as gender, age, and education level was presented. The paper produced the results of ASR application of the corpus and sketched an original global monophonic recognition model to handle linguistic changeability. The global phone recognition rate for the ASR reference system was reasonable and contained a useful baseline ASR system dedicated to MSA.

Tsuo-Lin Chiu *et al.* (2007) discussed a computer-assisted language learning technique as an application of ASR technology in order to help learners to engage in meaningful speech communication. In this study, a web-based conversation environment called Candle Talk, which permitted learners to apparently talk with the computer, was developed. It helped learners to speak English as a Foreign Language (EFL) which led to better oral competence. Candle Talk was prepared with an ASR engine that judged whether learners offer appropriate input. Six speech acts were presented as the foci of the materials with local cultural information incorporated as the content of the dialogues to develop student motivation. Oral ability assessment using the format of the Discourse Completion Test (DCT) was given before and after the use of Candle Talk. An estimation questionaire was used for data gathering.

Ibrahim Patel & Dr. Y. Srinivas Rao (2010) proposed a method for the recognition of speech signal using frequency spectral information with Mel frequency for the development of speech feature illustration in an HMM-based recognition approach. Frequency spectral information was integrated into the conventional Mel spectrum-based speech recognition approach. The Mel frequency approach demoralized the frequency observation for speech signal in a given resolution which resulted in resolution feature overlapping resulting in recognition limit.

Bushra Naz *et al.* (2011) proposed that visual speech information could play an important role in lip-reading under noisy conditions or for listeners with hearing impairment. The paper reported a review of the technology and development used in Lip Reading to appreciate and find the growth of technology for the basic energy minimizing model, ASR and some aspects of intelligent technology like Artificial Neural Network. They presented the hierarchical development of technology. The image-based and model-based Lip-Reading techniques typically used for that task was presented in detail.

Dipanwita Paul & Dr. Ranjan Parekh (2011) put forth a methodology for automated recognition of isolated words independent of speakers. It employed a feature vector consisting of a combination of the first three formant frequencies of the vocal tract and the mean Zero Crossing Rate (ZCR) of the audio signal. Formant frequencies were approximated by simulating the vocal tract by a Linear Prediction Coefficients (LPC) filter and calculating its resonant frequencies. ZCR was figured by partitioning the audio signal into segments and calculating the number of times the signal crosses the zero-amplitude level within each segment. A neural network (multi-layer perception) was used as a classifier for identifying the spoken word. The network was guided by using a set of specific words expressed by nine speakers (both male and female) and experimented for the same words expressed by a different set of speakers. A. El Ghazi *et al.* (2011) proposed a system for automatic speech recognition in the Moroccan dialect. HMM was used to model the phonetic units matching words obtained from the guiding base. To reveal the flexibility of the HMM they carried out a comparison of results obtained at the end.

Parchami et al. 2016 presented an overview on noise reduction in the short-time Fourier transform (STFT) domain. They reviewed the single and multi-channel cases separately. In the single-channel case, the focus is on the spectral subtractive methods, Wiener filter-based methods, speech amplitude estimators and estimators of the complex STFT coefficients. In the multi-channel scenario, a selection of key beamforming approaches as well as conventional post-filtering methods is detailed. A survey of the most recent advances in the STFT-based noise reduction methods is presented. Finally, conclusions are drawn on each of the investigated topics.

Ram & Mohanty (2017) specified that a number of algorithms based on Neural Network and its modifications are used for the purpose of speech enhancement and classification. In this paper, Deep Neural Network (DNN) based speech enhancement method is used to increase the Signal-to-Noise Ratio of the speech signal. Hidden layers are altered to test the results. The audio features are extracted by using the short time Fourier transforms and these features assisted in improving the speech enhancement performance of DNN. Segmental Signal-to-Noise Ratio (SegSNR) and Perceptual Evaluation of Speech Quality (PESQ) are used to assess the quality of speech signal.

Samui *et al.* (2019) stated that deep learning based supervised speech enhancement methods have gained consideration over the statistical signal processing-based methods. For speech enhancement, the authors have deliberated the time–frequency masking based deep learning framework and the performance of these methods. They identified that significant performance improvement can be achieved if the Deep Neural Network (DNN) is pre-trained by using Fuzzy Restricted Boltzmann Machines (FRBM) instead of Restricted Boltzmann Machines (RBM). This is due to the fact that the performance of FRBM is more robust and effective when the training data is noisy. From the experimental results they have concluded that the approach proposed by them ensures a consistent improvement in various objective measure scores of perceived speech quality and intelligibility compared to DNN-based speech enhancement methods which use regular RBM for unsupervised pre-training.

Anil Garg & Sahu (2019) proposed a hybrid method. In this hybrid method, speech signal is taken from the database and pre-reconstruction of the speech signal is done using empirical mode decomposition. Bionic wavelet transform (BWT) is used for de-noising and subsequently Butterworth filter is used. An inverse BWT is used to obtain the final de-noised signal. The recommended methodology is implemented in the MATLAB platform. This method is assessed utilizing a large number of noises.

PROPOSED METHOD

In the previous technique (Gibak Kim et al., 2009), the input signals were broken down into TF units and the features were extracted by the AMS feature extraction technique. The decisions as to whether each TF unit is ruled by the target or the masker were taken based on the Bayesian classifier. Speech corrupted at low SNR levels using different types of maskers are synthesized by the technique and was presented to normal-hearing listeners for identification. An improvement is attempted over the previous technique to enhance the speech signals using i) Weighted mask (four levels), ii) Neuro-fuzzy classifier, and iii) the modified AMS. The following steps are adopted and the proposed method aims to enhance speech quality in noisy speech signals that results in efficient suppression of noise.

- Modified AMS features are extracted.
- Implementation on a Neuro-Fuzzy Classifier and training based on four classes (Masker class, Masker dominated, Target dominated class and Target class).
- In the enhancement phase, mask weights are assigned based on the predicted class of neuro-fuzzy classifier and the enhanced signal obtained by summing all the windowed and weighted signals.
- Evaluation metrics used are Perceptual Evaluation of Speech Quality (PESQ), Itakura–Saito distance (IS) and MARS based composite measures (Gibak Kim et al. 2009).
- A comparison with three different Neuro-Fuzzy classifiers (Sun CT & Jang JSR, 1998, Cetişli. B & Barkana. A, 2010, Cetişli. B, 2010) with the proposed technique (Gibak Kim, et al. 2009).

In the traditional techniques to suppress noise in speech, speech quality is improved rather than the speech intelligibility. Motivated by prior intelligibility studies of speech synthesizers, a technique is proposed that decomposes the input signal into TF units and makes decisions using the Neuro-Fuzzy classifier as to whether each TF unit is dominated by the target class, target-dominated class, masker-dominated class or the masker class. The technique consists of three phases i) Feature Extraction ii) Training phase and iii) Intelligibility Enhancement phase. Initially. The features are selected from the large speech corpus using the MAMS. Subsequently, features are trained with a Neuro-Fuzzy Classifier. In the enhancement phase, s the TF units of the noise-masked signal are classified into four classes such as target class, target-dominated class, masker class and masker-dominated class. Individual TF units of the noise-masked signal are multiplied with the corresponding weight of the class and the enhanced speech waveform is obtained. Figure 1 illustrates the block diagram of the proposed technique.

Feature Selection Module

In the proposed technique, the features of the speech signal are selected by Modified AMS. In AMS feature extraction, the signals are first sampled, bandpass filtered and subsequently rectified and seg-

Figure 1. Block diagram of the proposed technique

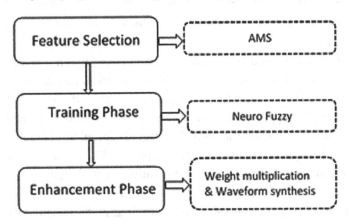

mented. The signals are then windowed, taken Fourier transform and multiplied with triangular functions and summed up to produce the feature vector (Gibak Kim et al., 2009). MAMS incorporating Discrete Cosine Transform rather than the Fourier Transform. Delta functions are added to improve the values. In feature selection from speech signals, relevant and important features of the input speech signal are selected to construct robust learning models.

The main steps in obtaining features through Modified AMS:

- Speech signal is sampled, quantized and pre-emphasized.
- Signals are band passed filtered into 25 band channels.
- The channel envelopes are rectified after being decimated by a factor of three.
- Decimated envelope is segmented into overlapping segments.
- The signals are windowed and DCT is applied to obtain a modulation spectrum.
- This modulation spectrum is multiplied with triangular functions and summed up to produce the feature vector.

The complete steps involved in the feature extraction phase are described below. The input to the feature extraction is the speech signal. Normally, the speech signal is a noisy signal which is a mixture of both the clean signal and the noise. The input signal is first sampled and quantized. A sampling of the sound wave results in the conversion of sound wave (continuous signal) to a sequence of samples (discrete signal). Let S(t) be the input speech signal and sampling be done at every T seconds and sampled signal S(n) be such that:

$$S(n) = S(nT); \; n=0,1,2,\ldots \tag{1}$$

Here, the sampling of the audio signal is done at 16 kHz and subsequently the sampled signal is then quantized. In quantization, a very large set of possible discrete values is approximated to a relatively small set of discrete integer values and here, 16-bit quantization is carried out and the improvement of the quantization is by incorporating the µ law.

The quantized signal is then pre-emphasized where the magnitudes of some frequencies are increased with respect to the magnitude of other lower frequencies, to improve the overall signal-to-noise ratio. It is achieved by minimizing attenuation distortion or saturation of recording media in subsequent parts of the system. It also filters out the lip radiation effect. This is achieved by the iterative scheme: $\bar{f}_n = f_n - \alpha f_{n-1}$ where α has a typical value of 0.95 and fn be the magnitude of the nth frequency.

The resultant signal is band passed filtered into 25 band channels. In a band-pass filter, the signals within the prescribed range of frequencies are passed while others are attenuated. That is, all the 25 band channels here will have signals lying in the range of frequencies defined for the respective channel. Each channel is defined by the upper limit frequency and the lower limit frequency. An envelope of each band is found out after the full-wave rectification. After rectification, it is decimated by a factor of three and is segmented into overlapping segments of 128 samples of 32 ms with an overlap of 64 samples.

The sampled signals are windowed, which is basically to get sharper peaks and to filter out the unnecessary components before taking the Cosine transform. Normally, a window function is a mathematical function that has a zero-value outside of the chosen interval. Hanning window of window size 25ms is used.

$$w(n) = 0.5\left[1 - \cos\left(\frac{2\Pi n}{N - 1}\right)\right] \tag{2}$$

where N represents the width of the samples, in the symmetrical window function and n is an integer, with values varying from $0<n<N-1$. Window functions reduce the artifacts in the spectrum. Figure 2 shows plots of the window function and the corresponding frequency response.

Figure 2. Window function and the corresponding frequency response

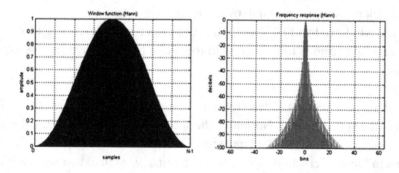

The window function vanishes outside the interval and the windowed signal is zero-padded. Discrete Cosine Transform is applied to the zero-padded signals. Here, the signal is transformed into a frequency domain signal decomposing the signal into its constituent frequencies.

Applying DCT,

$$X_K = \sum_{k=0}^{N-1} x_n \cdot \cos\left[\frac{\pi}{N}\left(n + \frac{1}{2}\right)k\right], where\ k = 0,...,N - 1 \tag{3}$$

The DCT computes the modulation spectrum in each of the 25 channels and each of the channels is then multiplied by fifteen triangular-shaped windows spaced uniformly across the 15.6–400 Hz range. Triangular shaped windows are defined by the equation:

$$w(n) = \frac{2}{N-1}\left(\frac{N-1}{2} - \left|n - \frac{N-1}{2}\right|\right)$$

(4)

where, N represents the width of the samples, in the symmetrical window function and n is an integer, with values varying from $0<n<N-1$. These are summed up to produce 15 modulation spectrum amplitudes and each of these represents the feature vector.

The feature vector is represented by $a_s(b,\tau)$ where τ represents the time slot and b represents the sub-band. To account for the variations in the time and the frequency domains, we include the delta functions to the features extracted.

The delta function for time is defined as,

$$\Delta a_T(b,\tau) = a_S(b,\tau) - a_S(b,\tau-1) \text{ for } \tau=2,\ldots,T$$

(5)

The frequency delta function is defined by,

$$\Delta a_B(b,\tau) = a_S(b,\tau) / a_S(b-1,\tau) \text{ for } b=2,\ldots,B.$$

(6)

When $\tau=1$, we can write the delta time function as

$$\Delta a_T(b,1) = a_S(b,2) - a_S(b,1)$$

and for $b=2$ we can write the frequency delta function as

$$\Delta a_B(1,\tau) = a_S(2,\tau) / a_S(1,\tau).$$

Considering the delta functions, we can write the overall feature vector as:

$$A_s(b,\tau) = [a_s(b,\tau), \Delta a_T(b,\tau), \Delta a_B(b,\tau)]$$

(7)

Here, in our case the number of sub-bands B is taken to be 25; $a_s(b,\tau)$, $\Delta aT_(b,\tau)$ and $\Delta aB_(b,\tau)$ are all of 15 dimension so the total dimension of the feature vector As(b,τ) is 45.

Training Module

In the proposed enhancement technique, a four-class Neuro-Fuzzy Classifier [30, 31, 32, 33] is used, where the four classes are classified as masker class, masker dominated class, target-dominated class and target class. The classes are represented as $\Lambda 1, \Lambda 2, \Lambda 3$, and $\Lambda 4$ respectively. The mask created is based on magnitude spectrum constraints rather than the local SNR criterion which results in better accuracy.

Consider the noisy speech spectrum $S(b, \tau)$ at the time slot τ and sub-band b. On multiplying the noisy spectrum with the gain function $G(b, \tau)$, we can get the estimate of the signal spectrum $\overline{X}(b, \tau)$ which is defined by:

$$\overline{X}(b, \tau) = G(b, \tau) . \mid S(b, \tau) \mid \tag{8}$$

Where Gain function $G(b, \tau)$ is computed using the equation:

$$G(b, \tau) = \sqrt{\frac{SNR_p(b, \tau)}{1 + SNR_p(b, \tau)}} \tag{9}$$

Where SNR_p is the priori signal to noise ratio which is based on equation (10)

$$SNR_p(b, \tau) = \frac{\alpha . \mid \overline{X}(b, \tau - 1) \mid^2}{\lambda_D(b, \tau - 1)} + (1 - \alpha) . \max \left[\frac{\mid S(b, \tau) \mid^2}{\lambda_D(b, \tau)} - 1, 0 \right] \tag{10}$$

Where $\alpha = 0.98$ is a smoothing constant and λD_i s the estimate of the background noise variance.

The estimated speech magnitude is compared with the true speech magnitude for each T-F unit and is assigned as Ω.

$$\Omega = \frac{\mid \overline{X}(b, \tau) \mid}{\mid S(b, \tau) \mid} \tag{11}$$

In the training stage, the noisy speech spectrum $S(b, \tau)$ at time slot τ and sub-band b can be classified into four classes as:

$$S(b, \tau) \in \begin{cases} \Lambda_1, for\ 0.00 \leq \Omega < 0.25 \\ \Lambda_2, for\ 0.25 \leq \Omega < 0.50 \\ \Lambda_3, for\ 0.50 \leq \Omega < 0.75 \\ \Lambda_4, for\ 0.75 \leq \Omega \leq 1.00 \end{cases} \tag{12}$$

Where, Λ_1 is the masker class, Λ_2 is the masker dominated class, Λ_3 is the target dominated class and Λ_4 is the target class.

Enhancement Module

The enhancement module consists of two stages. In the first stage, the masks of each T-F unit are first estimated using the Neuro-fuzzy classifier. Each T-F unit of the noisy speech signal is multiplied by the corresponding weight obtained from the estimated mask. In the second stage, the resultant signals are synthesized to produce enhanced speech waveforms. Figure 3 shows the block diagram of the waveform synthesizer.

Stage 1: Weight Assignment

For the enhancement phase, the modified feature vector is computed by the feature extraction process for the test signal. Then, the corresponding class of the TF units, Λ_1, Λ_2, Λ_3 and Λ_4 are obtained by the use of a trained neuro-fuzzy classifier. Based on the class label obtained from the neuro-fuzzy classifier, the corresponding weight is multiplied with the TF units. The predicted class produces the weight or the gain $G(b,\tau)$ of the mask given by:

$$G(b,\tau) = \begin{cases} 0.00, & \text{if the TF units belongs to class 1} \\ 0.33, & \text{if the TF units belongs to class 2} \\ 0.66, & \text{if the TF units belongs to class 3} \\ 1.00, & \text{if the TF units belongs to class 4} \end{cases} \qquad (13)$$

Figure 3. Block diagram of the waveform synthesizer

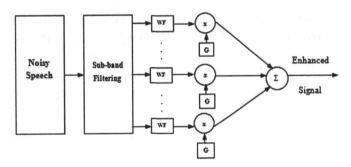

Stage 2: Waveform Synthesis

Figure 3 shows the process of waveform synthesis. Here WF is the window function and G is weight or the gain of the mask. Initially, the corrupted speech signal is filtered into the same number of bands that were used in the feature extraction stage. The output of each filter is time-reversed, passed through the filter, and reversed again, to avoid cross-talk distortions. The filtered waveforms are windowed and weighted by the mask $G(b,\tau)$. The raised cosine window is used for every 32 seconds with a 50% overlap between segments. Finally, the target signal is estimated by the summation of weighted responses.

RESULTS AND DISCUSSION

A detailed analysis of the method is made and a comparison with the existing methods prove the validity of the proposed method. Two databases are used for the evaluation of the proposed method. Noisy Speech Corpus (NOIZEUS) (Hu, Y. and Loizou, P, 2007) is used to facilitate the comparison of speech enhancement algorithms among the research groups. This database consists of 30 IEEE sentences corrupted by eight real-world noises at different levels of SNR. The sentences were recorded by three male and three female speakers in a sound-proof booth using the recording equipment of Tucker Davis Technologies. The IEEE database is preferred as it comprises phonetically balanced sentences with relatively low word-context predictability. Here, noise is added to the clean speech signal. A segment of noise of same length as the speech signal is taken from the noise recording. It is appropriately scaled to reach the desired SNR level and added to the filtered clean speech signal. The AURORA database includes suburban train noise, babble, car, exhibition hall, restaurant, street, airport and train-station noise.

Perceptual Evaluation of Speech Quality (PESQ), Itakura–Saito distance (IS) and Multivariate Adaptive Regression Splines (MARS) are the evaluation metrics (Yi Hu and Philipos C. L, 2008) that are used for evaluating the speech signals. PESQ is employed for automated assessment of speech quality. It is an objective measure to test the quality of voice. PESQ algorithm analyses the speech signal sample-by-sample after a temporal alignment of corresponding excerpts of reference and test signal. PESQ provides an end-to-end quality assessment. The PESQ score is computed as a linear combination of the average disturbance value D_{avg} and the average asymmetrical disturbance values A_{avg} and is given by the equation below (Antony. W. et al. 2000).

$$PESQ = b_0 + b_1 D_{avg} + b_2 A_{avg}, where\ b_0 = 4.50, b_1 = -0.10, b_2 = -0.0309 \tag{14}$$

Itakura–Saito distance (IS) measures the perceptual difference between an original spectrum and an approximation of that spectrum (Alan H. S. Chan & Sio-Iong Ao, 2008). If the original spectrum is $X(w)$ and the estimated is $\overline{X}(w)$, the distance D_{IS} is calculated by the formula given in the below equation;

$$D_{IS}(X(w), \overline{X}(w)) = \frac{1}{2\pi} \int_{-\pi}^{\pi} \left[\frac{X(w)}{\overline{X}(w)} - \log \frac{X(w)}{\overline{X}(w)} - 1 \right] dw \tag{15}$$

Multivariate Adaptive Regression Splines (MARS) is a non-parametric regression technique used for speech analysis. The MARS modeling technique is data driven and derives the best fitting function from the data. The basic idea of the MARS modeling is to use spline functions to locally fit the data in a region, and generates a global model by combining the data regions using basis functions. One of the features is that it allows interactions between the predictor (independent) variables so that a better fit can be found for the target (dependent) variable. MARS based composite measure (Yi Hu & Philipos C. L, 2008) is used for the evaluation.

Speech signals are taken from NOIZEUS (database 1) and AURORA (database 2) databases. PESQ, IS and MARS based composite measure are the evaluation metrics used for the analysis in various noise conditions at different levels of SNR. The performance of the proposed Neuro-fuzzy 4 classifier (NF4) is evaluated and compared with the performance of other techniques proposed earlier. Neuro-fuzzy 2 classifier (NF2) (B. Cetişli & A. Barkan, 2010), Neuro-fuzzy 3 (NF3) (Sun CT and Jang JSR, 1998) and Bayesian classifier (Gibak Kim et al. 2009) are the other techniques considered for the comparison. The various noises taken for the evaluation are from varying surroundings like Babble, Train, Car, Exhibition hall, Restaurant, Street from database 1 for varying signal powers 0, -5, -10, and -15 dB. Tables 1 to 6 summarize the results of the comparative analysis with database 1.

The proposed NF4 classifier performs better when compared to the other techniques. The evaluation metrics have given better results (refer tables 1 to table 6). PESQ and MARS values are best at noise level 0 dB and IS has the maximum value at noise level of -15 dB. Best PESQ score (1.768) and MARS score (3.690) for the proposed technique is obtained for Babble noise at 0 dB. Best IS for our proposed technique was obtained for train noise at -15dB having a value of 68.06. Overall best score (sum of the evaluation metrics) was obtained for the Exhibition Noise with a score of 167.34 considering all noise levels.

Table 1. Evaluation metrics for babble noise with database 1

Noise Added	NF4 (Proposed)			NF2			NF3			BAYESIAN		
	PESQ	IS	MARS	PESQ	IS	MARS	PESQ	IS	MARS	PESQ	IS	MARS
0 dB	1.770	7.658	3.690	0.861	7.516	3.629	1.028	6.912	3.674	1.327	12.27	3.501
-5 dB	0.946	29.11	3.333	1.110	15.99	3.464	0.897	15.34	3.471	1.494	36.88	3.255
-10 dB	0.856	33.59	3.288	0.841	32.62	3.298	0.823	30.41	3.20	1.415	83.65	2.788
-15 dB	0.858	40.94	3.215	0.796	42.71	3.197	0.814	35.18	3.272	0.8982	161.2	2.012

Table 2. Evaluation metrics for train noise with database 1

Noise Added	NF4 (Proposed)			NF2			NF3			BAYESIAN		
	PESQ	IS	MARS	PESQ	IS	MARS	PESQ	IS	MARS	PESQ	IS	MARS
0 dB	0.931	10.339	3.521	1.009	9.009	3.533	1.039	9.535	3.529	1.255	11.48	3.509
-5 dB	0.805	24.145	3.383	0.899	15.24	3.472	0.747	14.08	3.483	1.602	27.77	3.347
-10 dB	0.976	22.24	3.402	1.123	20.72	3.417	1.079	17.44	3.449	1.756	60.29	3.081
-15 dB	0.850	68.06	2.943	0.919	62.59	2.998	0.676	49.01	3.134	1.293	174.1	1.882

Table 3. Evaluation metrics for car noise with database 1

Noise Added	NF4 (Proposed)			NF2			NF3			BAYESIAN		
	PESQ	IS	MARS	PESQ	IS	MARS	PESQ	IS	MARS	PESQ	IS	MARS
0 dB	0.994	7.533	3.627	1.686	7.687	3.616	0.857	7.323	3.643	0.998	11.37	3.510
-5 dB	0.929	10.89	3.515	1.073	11.12	3.512	0.898	11.33	3.511	2.019	32.37	3.624
-10 dB	0.928	28.14	3.343	1.10	28.81	3.336	0.984	22.91	3.394	1.633	71.39	2.910
-15 dB	0.804	40.36	3.22	0.790	41.38	3.210	0.820	37.21	3.252	1.580	151.8	2.106

Table 4. Evaluation metrics for exhibition hall noise with database 1

Noise Added	NF4 (Proposed)			NF2			NF3			BAYESIAN		
	PESQ	IS	MARS	PESQ	IS	MARS	PESQ	IS	MARS	PESQ	IS	MARS
0 dB	1.051	7.859	3.602	1.001	7.878	3.604	1.064	7.589	3.623	1.827	11.68	3.638
-5 dB	1.011	50.51	3.118	0.929	16.98	3.454	0.911	17.34	3.451	1.756	45.51	3.229
-10 dB	0.919	29.26	3.331	0.946	27.07	3.353	0.878	29.48	3.331	1.822	76.42	2.986
-15 dB	0.793	62.89	2.995	0.788	58.17	3.042	0.839	50.12	3.122	1.318	181.3	1.810

Table 5. Evaluation Metrics for Restaurant noise with database 1

Noise Added	NF4 (Proposed)			NF2			NF3			BAYESIAN		
	PESQ	IS	MARS	PESQ	IS	MARS	PESQ	IS	MARS	PESQ	IS	MARS
0 dB	0.983	8.197	3.578	1.001	8.198	3.578	0.969	8.114	3.583	1.804	29.15	3.440
-5 dB	0.975	28.19	3.342	1.020	28.05	3.343	1.042	22.02	3.403	1.771	43.85	3.261
-10 dB	0.783	20.63	3.418	0.784	20.78	3.416	0.189	19.75	3.426	1.392	112.8	2.495
-15 dB	0.761	56.46	3.059	0.914	39.48	3.229	0.667	43.65	3.187	0.886	279.1	0.832

Table 6. Evaluation Metrics for Street noise with database 1

Noise Added	NF4 (Proposed)			NF2			NF3			BAYESIAN		
	PESQ	IS	MARS	PESQ	IS	MARS	PESQ	IS	MARS	PESQ	IS	MARS
0 dB	0.908	16.68	3.457	0.950	80667	3.542	0.969	8.080	3.586	1.911	15.61	3.683
-5 dB	0.924	18.98	3.434	0.869	19.18	3.432	0.891	18.65	3.437	1.253	28.91	3.334
-10 dB	0.897	15.98	3.434	0.983	17.06	3.453	0.848	12.63	3.185	0.917	177.8	1.854
-15 dB	0.813	60.46	3.019	0.875	60.25	3.021	0.759	43.83	3.185	1.38	107.3	2.550

The performance of the proposed NF4 classifier is evaluated and compared with the performance of other techniques using database 2. NF2, NF3 and Bayesian classifier are compared with the performance of NF4. Five categories of noises are taken for the evaluation. Tables 7 to 11 summarize the results of the comparative analysis with database 2.

The inference of comparative analysis using database 2 is given in the Tables 7 to 11. The performance of the proposed technique NF4 in comparison to NF2, NF3 and the Bayesian Classifier using the evaluation metrics considering five categories of noise with database 2 at different noise levels are discussed. NF4 has performed better than the other techniques for the evaluation metrics. PESQ and MARS values are best at noise level 0 dB and IS has the maximum value at noise level of -15 dB. Best PESQ score (2.204) and MARS score (3.947) for NF4 is obtained for Category 5 noise at 0 dB. Best IS value is obtained for Category 2 at 0 dB with a value of 94.03. Overall best score (sum of the evaluation metrics) was obtained for the Category 2 Noise with a score of 133.01 considering all noise levels. A combined analysis of NF4 from databases 1 and 2 are shown in Table 12.

Table 7. Evaluation metrics for category 1 with database 2

Noise Added	NF4 (Proposed)			NF2			NF3			BAYESIAN		
	PESQ	IS	MARS	PESQ	IS	MARS	PESQ	IS	MARS	PESQ	IS	MARS
0 dB	0.942	25.31	3.37	0.831	29.99	3.324	0.798	27.04	3.354	0.724	5.040	3.414
-10 dB	1.024	5.46	3.78	1.106	5.467	3.782	0.986	5.467	3.782	0.605	5.038	3.415
-15 dB	.713	5.814	3.756	1.030	5.637	3.770	1.031	5.627	3.770	0.678	4.926	3.423
-5 dB	1.150	5.623	3.771	1.609	5.647	3.769	1.093	5.632	3.770	0.389	5.018	3.416

Table 8. Evaluation metrics for category 2 with database 2

Noise Added	NF4 (Proposed)			NF2			NF3			BAYESIAN		
	PESQ	IS	MARS	PESQ	IS	MARS	PESQ	IS	MARS	PESQ	IS	MARS
0 dB	0.821	94.03	2.656	0.966	110.1	2.523	0.796	90.64	2.718	1.312	4.957	2.421
-10 dB	1.512	6.078	3.737	1.131	6.086	3.736	1.083	6.082	3.736	0.687	4.995	3.218
-15 dB	0.899	5.999	3.742	0.965	6.011	3.742	0.878	5.997	3.743	0.918	5.101	3.310
-5 dB	0.811	6.208	3.727	0.663	6.212	3.727	0.704	6.218	3.726	0.521	5.224	3.401

Table 9. Evaluation metrics for category 3 with database 2

Noise Added	NF4 (Proposed)			NF2			NF3			BAYESIAN		
	PESQ	IS	MARS	PESQ	IS	MARS	PESQ	IS	MARS	PESQ	IS	MARS
0 dB	0.797	40.32	3.221	0.866	43.26	3.191	0.727	41.03	3.214	0.828	8.257	3.173
-10 dB	0.819	7.696	3.615	1.540	7.667	3.617	1.546	7.701	3.615	1.352	8.175	3.579
-15 dB	1.084	7.721	3.613	1.048	7.662	3.621	1.048	7.622	3.619	2.107	8.287	3.582
-5 dB	1.013	7.698	3.615	1.016	7.709	3.614	1.016	7.709	3.613	1.021	8.069	3.587

Table 10. Evaluation metrics for category 4 with database 2

Noise Added	NF4 (Proposed)			NF2			NF3			BAYESIAN		
	PESQ	IS	MARS	PESQ	IS	MARS	PESQ	IS	MARS	PESQ	IS	MARS
0 dB	0.944	18.82	3.436	1.011	22.75	3.396	0.931	18.83	3.436	0.812	4.994	3.318
-10 dB	0.950	5.637	3.770	11.124	5.564	3.775	1.124	5.556	3.776	0.895	4.890	3.626
-15 dB	1.135	5.487	3.781	1.298	5.426	3.786	1.317	5.431	3.785	1.056	5.002	3.617
-5 dB	0.891	5.628	3.770	0.896	5.587	3.773	1.429	5.626	3.770	1.937	4.873	3.067

From Table 12, it is observed that the best PESQ score (at -5 dB) is obtained by category 5 noise (database 2) having PESQ value of 1.259; the best IS score (at -5 dB) is obtained by Exhibition noise (database 1) having IS value of 50.512; the best MARS score (at -5 dB) is obtained by category 1 noise (database 2) having MARS value of 3.771 and the overall best score (sum of the evaluation metrics) is obtained for the Exhibition Noise with a score of 54.641 considering -5dB noise level.

Table 11. Evaluation metrics for category 5 with database 2

Noise Added	NF4 (Proposed)			NF2			NF3			BAYESIAN		
	PESQ	IS	MARS	PESQ	IS	MARS	PESQ	IS	MARS	PESQ	IS	MARS
0 dB	2.204	7.384	3.947	0.919	15.66	3.472	1.019	14.96	3.474	1.753	5.878	3.808
-10 dB	1.138	6.275	3.722	1.133	6.282	3.721	1.113	6.275	3.722	1.689	5.852	3.704
-15 dB	1.084	6.346	3.716	1.095	6.349	3.716	1.088	6.350	3.716	1.693	5.834	3.705
-5 dB	1.259	6.186	3.728	1.178	6.172	3.730	1.259	6.187	3.728	1.470	5.966	3.705

Table 12. Evaluation metrics of neuro-fuzzy 4 classifier with various noises

Noise Taken at -5dB	Evaluation Metrics of Neuro-fuzzy 4 Classifier		
	PESQ	IS	MARS
Babble	0.946	29.10	3.332
Train	0.804	24.14	3.382
Car	0.929	10.89	3.515
Exhibition	1.011	50.512	3.118
Restaurant	0.974	28.18	3.342
Street	0.924	18.989	3.434
Category 1	1.150	5.623	3.771
Category 2	0.811	6.208	3.727
Category 3	1.013	7.698	3.615
Category 4	0.891	5.628	3.770
Category 5	1.259	6.186	3.728

CONCLUSION

In the proposed Neuro-fuzzy technique, enhancement of speech signals in noise using Modified AMS and Neuro-fuzzy 4 classifier is implemented. It consists of feature extraction phase, training phase and enhancement phase. Feature extraction phase involves extraction of Modified Amplitude Magnitude Spectrogram (MAMS). Subsequently, the Neuro-Fuzzy 4 classifier is used to classify the noisy speech. In the enhancement stage to improve the speech signal, the filtered waveforms are windowed and then weighted by the mask value and combined. Perceptual Evaluation of Speech Quality (PESQ), Itakura–Saito distance (IS) and MARS based composite measures are computed and the values are compared with that of the conventional techniques. The Neuro-fuzzy 4 classifier (NF4) is compared to Neuro-fuzzy 2 classifier (NF2), Neuro-fuzzy 3 (NF3) and Bayesian classifier. Based on the performance, it is concluded that the Neuro-fuzzy 4 classifier has shown a better performance with a mean value of 0.9738 as mean PESQ value, mean IS value of 17.558 and a mean Mars-based composite measure of 3.728, considering all noise categories at -5dB. The best score of the Neuro-fuzzy classifier for PESQ is 1.77, 94.03 for IS, and 3.947 for MARS based composite measures. The NF4 could be compared with the scores obtained by implementing a Deep Neural Network algorithm. Other datasets (dataset from University of Edinburgh, Centre for Speech Technology Research) can be also included for the comparison.

REFERENCES

Bahl, L. R., Brown, P. F., De Souza, P. V., & Mercer, R. L. (1993). Estimating Hidden Markov Model Parameters so as to maximize speech recognition Accuracy. *IEEE Transactions on Audio, Speech, and Language Processing, 1*(1), 77–83. doi:10.1109/89.221369

Ben Nasr, M., Saoud, S., & Cherif, A. (2013). Optimization of MLP using Genetic Algorithms Applied to Arabic Speech Recognition. *International Review on Computers and Software, 8*(2), 653–659.

Benzeghiba, M., De Mori, R., Deroo, O., Dupont, S., Erbes, T., Jouvet, D., ... Wellekens, C. (2007). Automatic Speech Recognition and Speech Variability: A review. *Speech Communication, 49*(10-11), 763–778. doi:10.1016/j.specom.2007.02.006

Cetişli, B. (2010). Development of an Adaptive Neuro-Fuzzy Classifier using Linguistic Hedges, 2010. *Expert Systems with Applications, 37*(8), 6093–6101. doi:10.1016/j.eswa.2010.02.108

Cetişli, B. (2010). The effect of linguistic hedges on feature selection. *Expert Systems with Applications, 37*(8), 6102–6108. doi:10.1016/j.eswa.2010.02.115

Cetişli, B., & Barkana, A. (2010). Speeding up the Scaled Conjugate Gradient Algorithm and its application in Neuro-Fuzzy classifier training. *Soft Computing, 14*(4), 365–378. doi:10.100700500-009-0410-8

Chan, A. H. S., & Ao, S.-I. (2008). *Advances in Industrial Engineering and Operations Research.* Springer. doi:10.1007/978-0-387-74905-1

Chi, T.-L., Liou, H.-C., & Yeh, Y. (2007). A Study of Web-Based Oral Activities enhanced by Automatic Speech Recognition for EFL College Learning. *Computer Assisted Language Learning, 20*(3), 209–233. doi:10.1080/09588220701489374

Chong, Gonina, & Keutzer. (2010). Efficient Automatic Speech Recognition on the GPU. *GPU Computing Gems*, 1-14.

Cooke, M., Green, P., Josifovski, L., & Vizinho, A. (2001). Robust Automatic Speech Recognition with Missing and Unreliable Acoustic Data. *Speech Communication, 34*(3), 267–285. doi:10.1016/S0167-6393(00)00034-0

Couvreur, L., & Couvreur, C. (2004). Blind Model Selection for Automatic Speech Recognition in Reverberant Environments. *Journal of VLSI Signal Processing Systems, 36*(3), 189–203. doi:10.1023/B:VLSI.0000015096.78139.82

Couvreur, L., Couvreur, C., & Ris, C. 2000. A Corpus-Based Approach for Robust ASR in Reverberant Environments. *Proceedings of International Conference on Spoken Language Processing (ICSLP), 1*, 397-400.

Droua-Hamdani, Selouani, Algiers, & Boudraa. (2010). Algerian Arabic Speech Database (ALGASD): Corpus Design and Automatic Speech Recognition Application. *Arabian Journal for Science and Engineering, 35*(2), 157–166.

Eisele, T., Haeb-Umbach, R., & Langmann, D. (1996). A Comparative Study of Linear Feature Transformation Techniques for Automatic Speech Recognition. *Proceedings of the Fourth International Conference on Spoken Language*, *1*, 252 - 255. 10.1109/ICSLP.1996.607092

El Ghazi, A., Daoui, C., Idrissi, N., Fakir, M., & Bouikhalene, B. (2011). Speech Recognition System Based on Hidden Markov Model Concerning the Moroccan Dialect DARIJA. *Global Journal of Computer Science and Technology*, *11*(15), 1–5.

Gaikwad, S. K., Gawali, B. W., & Yannawar, P. (2010). A Review on Speech Recognition Technique. *International Journal of Computers and Applications*, *10*(3), 16–24. doi:10.5120/1462-1976

Garg, A., & Sahu, O. P. (2019). A hybrid approach for speech enhancement using Bionic wavelet transform and Butterworth filter. *International Journal of Computers and Applications*, 1–11.

Gong, Y. (1995). Speech Recognition in Noisy Environments: A Survey. *Speech Communication*, *16*(3), 261–291. doi:10.1016/0167-6393(94)00059-J

Hu, Y., & Loizou, P. (2007). Subjective Evaluation and Comparison of Speech Enhancement Algorithms. *Speech Communication*, *49*(7-8), 588–601. doi:10.1016/j.specom.2006.12.006 PMID:18046463

Hu, Y., & Philipos, C. L. (2008). Evaluation of Objective Quality Measures for Speech Enhancement. *IEEE Transactions on Audio, Speech, and Language Processing*, *16*(1), 229–237. doi:10.1109/TASL.2007.911054

Huda, Hasan, Hassan, Kotwal, Islam, Hossain, & Muhammad. (2010). Inhibition/Enhancement Network Performance Evaluation for Noise Robust ASR. *International Review on Computers and Software*, *5*(5), 548–556.

Katagiri, S., & Lee, C.-H. (1993). A New hybrid algorithm for speech recognition based on HMM segmentation and learning Vector quantization. *IEEE Transactions on Audio, Speech, and Language Processing*, *1*(4), 21–430.

Kim, G., & Loizou, P. C. (2010). Improving Speech Intelligibility in Noise using a Binary Mask that is Based on Magnitude Spectrum Constraints. *IEEE Signal Processing Letters*, *17*(12), 1010–1013.

Kim, I.-S. (2006). Automatic Speech Recognition: Reliability and Pedagogical Implications for Teaching Pronunciation. *Journal of Educational Technology & Society*, *9*(1), 322–334.

Kim, Lu, Hu, & Loizou. (2009). An algorithm that improves Speech Intelligibility in Noise for Normal-Hearing Listeners. [PubMed]. *The Journal of the Acoustical Society of America*, *126*(3), 1486–1494. doi:10.1121/1.3184603

Nakamura, S., & Shikano, K. 1997. Room Acoustics and Reverberation: Impact on Hands-Free Recognition. *Proceedings of European Conference on Speech Communication and Technology*, *5*, 2419-2422.

Naz, & Rahim, & Suntie. (2011). Audio-Visual Speech Recognition Development Era; From Snakes to Neural Network: A Survey Based Study. *Canadian Journal on Artificial Intelligence. Machine Learning and Pattern Recognition*, *2*(1), 12–16.

Pan, Y., & Waibel, A. 2000. The Effects of Room Acoustics on MFCC Speech Parameter. *Proceedings of International Conference on Spoken Language Processing (ICSLP)*, *4*, 129-132.

Parchami, M., Zhu, W., Champagne, B., & Plourde, E. (2016). Recent Developments in Speech Enhancement in the Short-Time Fourier Transform Domain. IEEE Circuits and Systems Magazine, 16(3), 45-77. doi:10.1109/MCAS.2016.2583681

Patel & Rao. (2010). Speech Recognition using HMM with MFCC- an Analysis using Frequency Spectral Decomposition Technique. *International Journal (Toronto, Ont.)*, *1*(2), 101–110.

Paul, D., & Parekh, R. (2011). Automated Speech Recognition of Isolated Words Using Neural Networks. *International Journal of Engineering Science and Technology*, *3*(6), 4993–5000.

Rabiner, L.R., & Juang, B.H. (1993). Approaches to Automatic Speech Recognition by Machine. *Fundamentals of Speech Recognition*, 37-50.

Ram, R., & Mohanty, M. N. (2017). Deep Neural Network Based Speech Enhancement. Cognitive Informatics and Soft Computing. *Advances in Intelligent Systems and Computing*, *768*, 281–287. doi:10.1007/978-981-13-0617-4_27

Reddy, D. R. (2009). Speech Recognition by Machine: A Review. *Proceedings of the IEEE*, *64*(4), 501–531. doi:10.1109/PROC.1976.10158

Rix, Hollier, Hekstra, & Beerend. (2000). Perceptual Evaluation of Speech Quality (PESQ), and objective method for end-to-end speech quality assessment of narrowband telephone networks and speech codecs. ITU, ITU-T Rec.

Rojathai, S., & Venkatesulu, M. (2013). An Effective Tamil Speech Word Recognition Technique with Aid of MFCC and HMM (Hidden Markov Model). *International Review on Computers and Software*, *8*(2).

Samui, S., Chakrabarti, I., & Ghosh, S. K. (2019). Time-frequency masking based supervised speech enhancement framework using fuzzy deep belief network. *Applied Soft Computing*, *74*, 583–602. doi:10.1016/j.asoc.2018.10.031

Stuckless, R. (1994). Real-time transliteration of speech into print for hearing impaired students in regular classes. *American Annals of the Deaf*, *128*, 619–624. PMID:6227221

Sun, C. T., & Jang, J. S. R. (1998). A neuro-fuzzy classifier and its applications. *Proceedings* of *IEEE International Conference on Fuzzy Systems*, *1*, 94–98.

Young, S. (1996). A review of large-vocabulary continuous-speech recognition. *IEEE Signal Processing Magazine*, *13*(5), 45–56. doi:10.1109/79.536824

Zechner. (2011). Computing and Evaluating Syntactic Complexity Features for automated Scoring of Spontaneous Non-Native Speech. *Proceedings of the 49th Annual Meeting of The Association for Computational Linguistics*, 69(5), 722–731.

Chapter 10
Applications of Feature Engineering Techniques for Text Data

Shashwati Mishra

B.J.B. College (Autonomous), Bhubaneswar, India

Mrutyunjaya Panda

Utkal University, Vani Vihar, Bhubaneswar, India

ABSTRACT

Feature plays a very important role in the analysis and prediction of data as it carries the most valuable information about the data. This data may be in a structured format or in an unstructured format. Feature engineering process is used to extract features from these data. Selection of features is one of the crucial steps in the feature engineering process. This feature selection process can adopt four different approaches. On that basis, it can be classified into four basic categories, namely filter method, wrapper method, embedded method, and hybrid method. This chapter discusses about different techniques coming under these four categories along with the research work on feature selection.

INTRODUCTION

Feature engineering plays a very important role to prepare data for further processing activities. It is one of the vital steps in machine learning, as it helps in extracting appropriate features for predictive analysis (Nargesian et al., 2017). Machine learning algorithms are applied on data values, images, audio etc. for classification, prediction, retrieval and several types of analysis purposes. These algorithms can work if the inputs are in the form a set of feature vectors. So, the feature engineering process is very important and greatly affects the result of further computation and analysis. The feature engineering process involves the extraction of features from the object and selection of the relevant features from the set of extracted features. The final set of selected features is considered for further processing activities.

DOI: 10.4018/978-1-7998-6659-6.ch010

Performing the feature engineering manually, needs a lot of effort. The features selected in the manual process are also specific to the problem and the domain. Automated techniques use a statistical measure for feature selection (Garla & Brandt, 2012). Feature represents an important property, characteristic and attribute of data which is analysed to make some prediction. The data may be from a document or from an image or from a database. Feature engineering techniques help in extracting features from the data to improve the performance of machine learning algorithms. Text data can be structured or unstructured in nature. Structured text data are categorical having structured attributes. But documents contain unstructured data, where there is no specific ordering or arrangement of data. The words in a document vary from sentence to sentence. Word length and sentence length are also not fixed in a document. Words are arranged as per the syntax of the language so that a sentence becomes meaningful.

This unstructured natural language analysis has relevance in medical science to analyse medical text, in analysing public opinion on a particular topic, analysis of sentiment of the people, analysis of any social text etc. (Berry & Kogan, 2010; Aggarwal & Zhai, 2012; Struhl, 2015). J. Mishra (Misra, 2020) discussed about the life cycle of machine learning based solutions used to analyse text. Natural Language Processing Feature Specification Language has several meta elements. These are used by the feature extraction system to interpret the features.

Features from any natural language can be extracted at different levels such as, from a sentence or a group of sentences called paragraph or all the sentences in a document or all the text documents together. The level at which the features are extracted is specified by the analysis unit. The syntactic unit states the component of the linguistic features. It may be a word or a phrase or a N-gram or a regular expression or any combination of these components. Logical unit specifies the logical operators that is to be used between the components. These operators include AND, OR, AND NOT, OR NOT (Misra, 2020).

This chapter will discuss about the different feature engineering techniques for the analysis of such unstructured text data. The proposed chapter will have five sections followed by References. The chapter will first discuss about the need of feature engineering with specific importance to unstructured text data. The feature engineering process and different pre-processing stages will be discussed in section 2 followed by the different techniques of feature selection. The research work on text feature engineering using these techniques will be analysed in section 4. Section 5 will contain the concluding remarks.

FEATURE ENGINEERING PROCESS

Feature engineering process has a vital role in extraction and selection of appropriate features from the input data for further analysis and prediction. The feature engineering process involves deciding the type of features, creating the features, verifying the effectiveness of the features and accordingly improve or accept the features.

Machine learning algorithms are based on various mathematical, statistical and optimization principles. These techniques cannot be directly applied on unstructured text data. Therefore the unstructured text data must be converted to a structured format which will be easy for analysis. The preprocessing stage performs different activities like Tokenization, Noise removal etc..

Tokenization

The process of dividing the given textual input string into pieces is called tokenization. These individual pieces which comprise of keywords, symbols, phrases and other elements of a language are called tokens. Some symbols like punctuation marks are discarded in the process of tokenization.

Noise Removal

Text document contains some words and symbols which does not add much to further processing activities. Such extra tokens must be removed from the document to make further processing easier and error free. These may include:

- Different tags like HTML tags (Davydova, 2018).
- Stop words like articles, prepositions, pronouns etc. must be removed (Vijayarani et al., 2015).
- Accented characters are used particularly in English language, which are converted and standardized to ASCII characters (Davydova, 2018).
- Shortened versions of some words or phrases like don't, can't, you'll, it's, I'd etc. must be expanded to original form for obtaining a standardized text (Davydova, 2018).
- Non alphanumeric special symbols and characters should be removed from the text (Davydova, 2018).
- Stemming and lemmatization techniques can be applied to generate the base form of words in a document (Davydova, 2018).
- Extra whitespaces and repeated characters are also removed to make the text document noise free (Davydova, 2018).

Another important step of the feature engineering process is feature selection which can be of different types. Section 3 gives a detailed information about these feature selection techniques.

FEATURE SELECTION TECHNIQUES

Selection of appropriate features is one of the important pre-processing activities. The subsequent steps are applied on these selected features instead of the original input feature set. This makes the training process simple and faster. It also helps in easy interpretation and visualization. Selection of appropriate features also increases the accuracy of the computed results. Feature selection techniques can be categorized into four categories considering the technique used for feature selection. Those are filter method, wrapper methods, embedded method and hybrid method. Figure 1 represents this classification of feature selection methods and their further subdivisions.

Filter Methods

These methods adopt different statistical measures for feature selection. The selection of features are affected by their frequency count, their information content etc. The selection of features does not depend on any learning algorithm.

Figure 1. Classification of feature selection methods

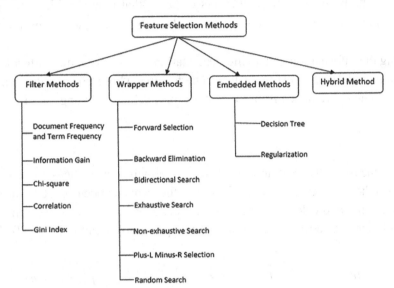

Document Frequency and Term Frequency

Frequency based feature selection methods calculates the number of times a term is present in the document or the number of documents containing the term. On that basis it is called as term frequency or document frequency respectively. N. Azam and J. Yao performed a comparative analysis of term and document frequency based methods of feature selection for text categorization. The comparison was made using Reuters 21,578 dataset under various feature sets. They observed that the term frequency based technique is better if the feature sets are small. Term frequency based technique also generate larger scatter of features among classes as compared to document frequency. They also proved to gather information in data faster (Azam & Yao, 2012).

Information Gain

Information gain selects a feature considering the information content of the feature (Al-Harbi, 2019). It considers the presence or absence of a term in a document to find the number of bits of information necessary for prediction (Li et al., 2009). Information gain can be calculated for a term by using the equation (1).

$$IG\left(term\right) = -\sum_{i=1}^{n} p\left(class_i\right)\log\left(p\left(class_i\right)\right) + p\left(term\right)\sum_{i=1}^{n} p(class_i \mid term)\log\left(p\left(class_i \mid term\right)\right)$$
$$+ p\left(\overline{term}\right)\sum_{i=1}^{n} p(class_i \mid \overline{term})\log\left(p\left(class_i \mid \overline{term}\right)\right)$$

Where, there is n number of classes for i=1,2,3,....n. $p(class_i)$ represents the probability of number of documents belonging to $class_i$. $p(term)$ indicates the probability of documents in which the term is present. $p(class_i|term)$ is the probability of documents of $class_i$ that contains the term. $p(class_i \mid \overline{term})$ represents the probability of documents belonging to $class_i$ that does not contain the term (Al-Harbi, 2019).

After computing the information gain using the equation (1), the computed information gain values are compared with a predefined threshold values. The features whose information gain values are less than this threshold value are removed from the feature space (Zheng & Feng, 2014).

Chi-Square Statistics

Chi-square statistics measures the expected and observed frequency differences for two events. In case of selecting the features these two events are occurrence of the term and occurrence of the class (Al-Harbi, 2019). This statistical method calculates the lack of independence between the term and category. If calculated value is 0, then the term and category are independent (Zheng & Feng, 2014).

$$\chi^2\left(term, class_i\right) = \frac{\left[p\left(term, class_i\right) p\left(\overline{term}, \overline{class_i}\right) - p\left(term, \overline{class_i}\right) p\left(\overline{term}, class_i\right)\right]^2}{p\left(term\right) p\left(\overline{term}\right) p\left(class_i\right) p\left(\overline{class_i}\right)}$$

where,

$p(term, class_i)$ is the probability of occurrences of a term in $class_i$,

$p(\overline{term}, \overline{class_i})$ is the probability of not-occurrences of the term and $class_i$ both,

$p\left(term, \overline{class_i}\right)$ is the probability of the term not belonging to $class_i$,

$p\left(\overline{term}, class_i\right)$ is the probability of not-occurrences of the term in $class_i$.

Suppose there are n classes, then (Zheng & Feng, 2014)

$$\chi^2\left(term\right) = \sum_{i=1}^{n} p\left(class_i\right) \log \chi^2\left(term, class_i\right)$$

Correlation

Correlation measure has value between -1 and +1 and used to evaluate the strength of bonding between features. Correlation between two sets of features x and y can be calculated as (Al-Harbi, 2019):

$$corel_{xy} = \frac{\sum_{i=1}^{n} x_i y_i - n\overline{xy}}{\left(n-1\right) sdv_x sdv_y}$$

where, n is the number of samples in each feature set, $\bar{x}$ and $\bar{y}$ represent the means of x and y respectively, sdv_x and sdv_y are the standard deviations of x and y respectively.

If the calculated correlation value is zero then the feature sets are not associated with each other. Positive correlation value indicates that with increase in the value of one feature set, value of other feature set also increases. In negative correlation increase in the value of one set, decreases the value of other (Al-Harbi, 2019).

Gini Index

Gini index finds the purity of features with respect to class for selecting the features. Purity is the discrimination level of the feature that distinguishes between the possible classes. The Gini index for a feature can be calculated as:

$$Gini\left(term_i\right) = \sum_{j=1}^{n} p(term_i \mid class_j)^2 \, p(class_j \mid term_i)^2$$

where, n is the number of classes, $p(term_i|class_j)$ is the probability of $term_i$ given $class_j$, $p(class_j|term_i)$ is the probability of $class_j$ given $term_i$ (Al-Harbi, 2019).

Drawbacks of Traditional Models

Traditional methods of feature engineering process based on the Bag of Words model. The bag of words model in the simplest way of representing the unstructured information as numeric vectors. Each dimension of this vector represents the frequency of occurrence of a word in the document. It simple creates a bag of the words present in the document and does not consider the ordering of these words in the original text. It also disregards the grammar in the original text. The dimension of the vector depends on the number of unique words present in the document. If a single word is considered then that is called a unigram or 1-gram, for two words bi-gram, for three words tri-grams etc. N-gram represents the word token comprising of n continuous and sequential words from a document. TF-IDF (Term Frequency – Inverse Document Frequency) method finds the importance of a term in a given document. Two statistical techniques term frequency and inverse document frequency are used for this purpose. Term frequency is the number of times a term is present in a document. Information provided by a particular word is measured by inverse document frequency, which searches for the presence or absence of a word in all documents. This can be calculated by dividing the total number of documents by the number of documents containing that word and then taking the logarithm of the quotient. TF-IDF is the multiplication of TF and IDF. Techniques like cosine similarity, Euclidean distance, Manhattan distance are used to generate features from the vectors obtained using TF-IDF technique.

These methods are very effective for feature selection and extraction. But these feature engineering methods does not consider the structure of the word, order of the words, their semantics etc. These information are consider by more advanced models to find word embedding. Bag of words model counts the frequency of words in a document does not consider the relationship among the words. This gives rise to a poor quality model for feature selection.

Wrapper Methods

These methods examine the impact of selected features on the performance of the model and accordingly improves the set of selected features. Since the features appropriateness is verified using those in training the model, the selection process become more refined. This helps in selection of better features than those extracted using any statistical technique. Such methods try to generate optimal result by considering the interaction among the words in a corpus. These methods first searches for a feature subset and train a model using these set of features. The training result is evaluated and the same process of selection and training is repeated. This process will continue until best subset of features are obtained that gives the best accuracy (Charfaoui, n.d.). Wrapper methods select a subset of features and train a model using that feature set. The error rate is examined to improve the set of features. So, the wrapper methods can adopt different searching techniques to improve the set of features (Xu, 2018).

Forward Feature Selection

This selection process starts with an empty feature set. The features that improve the model are gradually added to the set in an iterative manner. This process continues until the there is an improvement in the performance of the model (Charfaoui, n.d.).

Backward Feature Elimination

This works just opposite to the forward selection method. Initially all features are selected and gradually removed from the model in an iterative manner. This removal of features will continue until there is an improvement in the model performance (Charfaoui, n.d.).

Bidirectional Search

This refers to the search process that occurs both in forward and backward direction simultaneously. The search proceeds in both directions and finally one unique optimal solution is generated (Charfaoui, n.d.).

Exhaustive Search

Like brute force approach, it tries all possible feature combinations. The feature sets for which optimal result is obtained is selected for further processing activities (Charfaoui, n.d.). These techniques searches the whole state space and tests all possible combinations of features. So, these techniques require more memory space and time for execution. These methods are rarely used due to their high time complexity. Breadth First Search (BFS) is an example of such search techniques (Xu, 2018).

Non-Exhaustive Search

Methods like Branch and Bound search come into this category. These methods reduces the time complexity by reducing the search space. Such methods cut off the branches where there is no chance of getting a better solution than the current solution (Xu, 2018).

Plus-L Minus-R Selection (LRS)

This technique of feature selection combines the idea from forward selection and backward elimination. It can execute either starting from an empty set or considering the whole set of features. In the first approach the algorithm starts from an empty set, selects L features in each iteration and removes R features which are irrelevant. Another way is to start from the whole set of features, eliminate R features in each iteration and then add L features to improve the optimality of the result. The output of this approach is affected by the selection of the values of L and R (Xu, 2018).

Random Search

These searching methods randomly select a feature subset on which other algorithms can be applied to generate optimal result. The results obtained using these techniques are affected by random selection of features. So, in this case the same result is difficult to produce again (Xu, 2018).

These wrapper methods train a model to verify the effectiveness of features. So these methods are more expensive and complex than frequency based methods. But wrapper methods can select the best set of features for a specific type of model.

Embedded Methods

Unlike wrapper methods, embedded methods selects the features during training phase (Xu, 2018). Since the feature selection process is inside the training model, these techniques are called embedded methods. The learning algorithm is present in the training model.

Like wrapper methods, embedded methods also consider the interaction among features. Wrapper methods are also faster like filter methods. But the accuracy of embedded methods are better than the filter methods.

Decision Tree Learning

This is one of the simplest and popular embedded feature selection approach (Xu, 2018). This is based on the concept of supervised learning algorithm. ID3, C 4.5, CART are commonly used decision tree learning algorithms. It splits the dataset into small subsets based on various conditions and creates a tree like structure. The division of the dataset to create a tree structure depends on the satisfaction of conditions. That is why the technique is called decision tree method. In each iteration of the algorithm features are selected and the tree is further divided into next level. This process will continue until the sample subset at each node of the last level of the decision tree belongs to the same class.

Regularization

This method perform some changes in the learning algorithm in order to avoid overfitting. Regularization adds a penalty term to regularize the function value. This penalty is added to the function coefficients which in turn controls the fluctuation in the function value. Regularization helps in designing a robust and generalized model. In linear models three types of regularization can be used namely, L1 regularization or lasso regression, L2 regularization or ridge regression and L1/L2 regularization or elastic nets (Charfaoui, n.d.).

Hybrid Method

Another method of feature selection is the hybrid method which uses the ideas from both filter and wrapper method. This helps in taking the advantages of both filter and wrapper methods. By combining the different methods it tries to generate the best feature set. The advantages of these methods are that as compared to wrapper methods these are easier to compute. Hybrid methods are robust, flexible and give better accuracy as compared to the others.

Table 1. Advantages and disadvantages of feature selection techniques

Methods	Advantages	Disadvantages
Filter	Less expensive, Faster as there is no training phase, simple, independent of the classifier, computationally complexity is less	Independent of the model, lacks interaction among classifiers, slower
Wrapper	Model-oriented, performance is good, considers feature dependencies	Computationally intensive, Slower than filter method, higher chance of overfitting
Embedded	Feature selection is a part of learning, considers classifier interaction, computational complexity is better	Computationally demanding, dependent on classifier
Hybrid	Use the advantages of other methods, Flexible and robust for high dimensional data, Computational complexity is better than wrapper, better performance than filter	Depends on the combination of different feature selection techniques, results are affected by the selection of classifiers

LITERATURE REVIEW

M. Labani et al. (Labani et al., 2018) proposed a feature selection method called MRDC (Multivariate Relative Discrimination Criterion) for classifying text. This filter method uses the idea of minimum redundancy and maximum relevancy for feature selection. Document frequency is calculated for each term and importance of each term is also estimated. A correlation metric is also used to obtain the redundant features (Labani et al., 2018). S. D. Sarkar and S. Goswami performed an empirical study on selecting features using filter methods for text classification. Chi-square statistics, information gain, mutual information and symmetrical uncertainty methods were used for feature selection (Sarkar & Goswami, 2013). MOR (Multi-class Odds Ratio) and CDM (Class Discriminating Measure) were also used for feature selection. Naïve Bayesian classifier was applied on the selected features for classification (Chen et al., 2009). X. Tang et al. considered interactions among the features for feature selection. Their proposed approach helps in detecting the interactions among higher–order features by using two through five way interactions among features (Tang et al., 2019). Considering the good exploration capacity of PSO (Particle Swarm Optimization) algorithm, Y. Zhang et al. suggested an algorithm called FBPSO (Filter-based Bare-bone Particle Swarm Optimization). This proposed technique was tested on biological data, image data and also on text data. The technique uses two filter-based approaches: one based on average mutual information which helps in reducing the search space by eliminating the weekly relevant and irrelevant features; another is based on feature redundancy which is applied to improve the exploitation capability of the swarm (Zhang et al., 2019). A semantic-based technique of feature selection was developed for spam filtering. This technique uses semantic ontology for grouping words into topics and build feature vectors from them (Méndez et al., 2019).

H. Chantar et al. applied wrapper feature selection technique using an enhanced binary grey wolf optimizer (GWO) for Arabic text classification (Chantar et al., 2019). Wrapper selection methods are also sued for diabetes prediction (Fahmiin & Lim, 2019). M.H. Aghdam et al. (Aghdam et al., 2009) applied ant colony optimization for text features selection. Particle Swarm Optimization for selecting features and RBF (Radial Basis Function) network as classifier were used for Arabic text categorization (Zahran & Kanaan, 2009).

J. Zhang et al. proposed an embedded multi-label features selection technique with manifold regularization (Zhang et al., 2019). A hierarchical feature selection technique was also suggested with subtree based graph regularization (Tuo et al., 2019). W. Zheng et al. proposed an unsupervised feature selection method using self-paced learning regularization. This regularization is added to feature selection to reduce the effect of outliers (Zheng et al., 2020). Y. Peng et al. (Peng et al., 2009) developed a text categorization algorithm using lazy feature selection (Peng et al., 2009). Multi-label clinical records are classified using EEFS (Ensemble Embedded Feature Selection) method (Guo et al., 2016).

J. Lee et al. suggested a method of feature selection combining the ideas of filter and wrapper methods. This hybrid method considers Label Frequency Difference (LFD) feature filter. This feature filter along with the evolutionary feature wrapper were used for feature selection (Lee et al., 2019). An improvement in the existing versions of Ant Colony Optimization was proposed combining both the wrapper and filter method. In this approach filter method is used for evaluating the subset instead of wrapper method. This helps in reducing the complexity of the computation (Ghosh et al., 2019). A two-step feature selection method followed by the use of standard classifiers was suggested for text classification. Filter method based chi-square technique is used in the first step of feature selection for reducing the dimensionality of features. In the next step wrapper correlation based technique is applied to select most relevant features from the reduced set of features. Combining the advantages of filter and wrapper methods this technique helps in reducing the running time of the whole process and also increases the accuracy of classification (Adeleke et al., 2019). F. Z. Kermani et al. suggested a hybrid method for classification of textual information. First information gain is used for feature selection. After using this ranking-based filtering technique, in the next step subset selection based filter approach is used for feature selection. In this second step class dependent assumption and an embedded wrapper method principles are considered for designing the global Point-wise Mutual Information (PMI)-based feature selection method

(Kermani et al., 2019). Hybrid methods of feature selection are also applied for sentiment classification (Ansari et al., 2019). S. Wang et al. (Wang et al., 2007) used hybrid method of feature selection for Chinese text sentiment classification. The proposed hybrid method uses category distinguishing ability of words and information gain for feature selection (Wang et al., 2007). Hybrid features are also helpful for detecting phishing emails. L. Ma et al. (Ma et al., 2009) developed a method to detect phishing emails. The method uses information gain and a recursive learning process to select hybrid features (Ma et al., 2009). Combining the artificial bee colony optimization and differential evolution a hybrid feature selection method was proposed to select features for classification purpose. It was observed that this hybrid approach select better features than pure artificial bee colony optimization and differential evolution (Zorarpacı & Özel, 2016). A hybrid model of feature selection was developed using genetic algorithm and ant colony optimization for electricity load prediction (Zorarpacı & Özel, 2016).

CONCLUSION

This chapter discusses about the different steps of feature engineering process along with the various pre-processing steps. Selection and extraction of suitable features is the main stage of feature engineering as it greatly affects the succeeding steps. Different feature selection techniques along with their pros and cons are discussed in this chapter. The application of these techniques in text feature selection are also reviewed. The discussed methods of feature selection are also applicable for all types of data like structured data, unstructured data, linear data, nonlinear data etc. The analysis and discussion on these methods will be very helpful for further research on feature selection.

REFERENCES

Adeleke, A., Samsudin, N. A., Othman, Z. A., & Khalid, S. A. (2019). A two-step feature selection method for quranic text classification. *Indones. J. Electr. Eng. Comput. Sci*, *16*(2), 730–736. doi:10.11591/ijeecs.v16.i2.pp730-736

Aggarwal, C. C., & Zhai, C. (Eds.). (2012). *Mining text data*. Springer Science & Business Media. doi:10.1007/978-1-4614-3223-4

Aghdam, M. H., Ghasem-Aghaee, N., & Basiri, M. E. (2009). Text feature selection using ant colony optimization. *Expert Systems with Applications*, *36*(3), 6843–6853. doi:10.1016/j.eswa.2008.08.022

Al-Harbi, O. (2019). *A Comparative Study of Feature Selection Methods for Dialectal Arabic Sentiment Classification Using Support Vector Machine*. arXiv preprint arXiv:1902.06242

Ansari, G., Ahmad, T., & Doja, M. N. (2019). Hybrid Filter–Wrapper Feature Selection Method for Sentiment Classification. *Arabian Journal for Science and Engineering*, *44*(11), 9191–9208. doi:10.100713369-019-04064-6

Azam, N., & Yao, J. (2012). Comparison of term frequency and document frequency based feature selection metrics in text categorization. *Expert Systems with Applications*, *39*(5), 4760–4768. doi:10.1016/j.eswa.2011.09.160

Berry, M. W., & Kogan, J. (Eds.). (2010). *Text mining: applications and theory.* John Wiley & Sons. doi:10.1002/9780470689646

Chantar, H., Mafarja, M., Alsawalqah, H., Heidari, A. A., Aljarah, I., & Faris, H. (2019). Feature selection using binary grey wolf optimizer with elite-based crossover for Arabic text classification. *Neural Computing & Applications*, 1–20.

Chen, J., Huang, H., Tian, S., & Qu, Y. (2009). Feature selection for text classification with Naïve Bayes. *Expert Systems with Applications*, *36*(3), 5432–5435. doi:10.1016/j.eswa.2008.06.054

Fahmiin, M. A., & Lim, T. H. (2019, December). Evaluating the Effectiveness of Wrapper Feature Selection Methods with Artificial Neural Network Classifier for Diabetes Prediction. In *International Conference on Testbeds and Research Infrastructures* (pp. 3-17). Springer, Cham.

Garla, V. N., & Brandt, C. (2012). Ontology-guided feature engineering for clinical text classification. *Journal of Biomedical Informatics*, *45*(5), 992–998. doi:10.1016/j.jbi.2012.04.010 PMID:22580178

Ghosh, M., Guha, R., Sarkar, R., & Abraham, A. (2019). A wrapper-filter feature selection technique based on ant colony optimization. *Neural Computing & Applications*, 1–19.

Guo, Y., Chung, F., & Li, G. (2016, December). An ensemble embedded feature selection method for multi-label clinical text classification. In *2016 IEEE International Conference on Bioinformatics and Biomedicine (BIBM)* (pp. 823-826). IEEE.

Kermani, F. Z., Eslami, E., & Sadeghi, F. (2019). Global Filter–Wrapper method based on class-dependent correlation for text classification. *Engineering Applications of Artificial Intelligence*, *85*, 619–633. doi:10.1016/j.engappai.2019.07.003

Labani, M., Moradi, P., Ahmadizar, F., & Jalili, M. (2018). A novel multivariate filter method for feature selection in text classification problems. *Engineering Applications of Artificial Intelligence*, *70*, 25–37. doi:10.1016/j.engappai.2017.12.014

Lee, J., Yu, I., Park, J., & Kim, D. W. (2019). Memetic feature selection for multilabel text categorization using label frequency difference. *Information Sciences*, *485*, 263–280. doi:10.1016/j.ins.2019.02.021

Li, S., Xia, R., Zong, C., & Huang, C. R. (2009, August). A framework of feature selection methods for text categorization. In *Proceedings of the Joint Conference of the 47th Annual Meeting of the ACL and the 4th International Joint Conference on Natural Language Processing of the AFNLP: Volume 2-Volume 2* (pp. 692-700). Association for Computational Linguistics. 10.3115/1690219.1690243

Ma, L., Ofoghi, B., Watters, P., & Brown, S. (2009, July). Detecting phishing emails using hybrid features. In 2009 Symposia and Workshops on Ubiquitous, Autonomic and Trusted Computing (pp. 493-497). IEEE. doi:10.1109/UIC-ATC.2009.103

Méndez, J. R., Cotos-Yañez, T. R., & Ruano-Ordás, D. (2019). A new semantic-based feature selection method for spam filtering. *Applied Soft Computing*, *76*, 89–104. doi:10.1016/j.asoc.2018.12.008

Misra, J. (2020). *autoNLP: NLP Feature Recommendations for Text Analytics Applications.* arXiv preprint arXiv:2002.03056

Nargesian, F., Samulowitz, H., Khurana, U., Khalil, E. B., & Turaga, D. S. (2017, August). *Learning Feature Engineering for Classification*. IJCAI.

Peng, Y., Xuefeng, Z., Jianyong, Z., & Yumhong, X. (2009). Lazy learner text categorization algorithm based on embedded feature selection. *Journal of Systems Engineering and Electronics, 20*(3), 651–659.

Sarkar, S. D., & Goswami, S. (2013). Empirical study on filter based feature selection methods for text classification. *International Journal of Computers and Applications, 81*(6).

Sheikhan, M., & Mohammadi, N. (2012). Neural-based electricity load forecasting using hybrid of GA and ACO for feature selection. *Neural Computing & Applications, 21*(8), 1961–1970. doi:10.100700521-011-0599-1

Struhl, S. (2015). *Practical text analytics: Interpreting text and unstructured data for business intelligence*. Kogan Page Publishers.

Tang, X., Dai, Y., & Xiang, Y. (2019). Feature selection based on feature interactions with application to text categorization. *Expert Systems with Applications, 120*, 207–216. doi:10.1016/j.eswa.2018.11.018

Tuo, Q., Zhao, H., & Hu, Q. (2019). Hierarchical feature selection with subtree based graph regularization. *Knowledge-Based Systems, 163*, 996–1008. doi:10.1016/j.knosys.2018.10.023

Vijayarani, S., Ilamathi, M. J., & Nithya, M. (2015). Preprocessing techniques for text mining-an overview. *International Journal of Computer Science & Communication Networks, 5*(1), 7–16.

Wang, S., Wei, Y., Li, D., Zhang, W., & Li, W. (2007, August). A hybrid method of feature selection for Chinese text sentiment classification. In *Fourth International Conference on Fuzzy Systems and Knowledge Discovery (FSKD 2007)* (Vol. 3, pp. 435-439). IEEE. 10.1109/FSKD.2007.49

Zahran, B. M., & Kanaan, G. (2009). *Text feature selection using particle swarm optimization algorithm 1*. Academic Press.

Zhang, J., Luo, Z., Li, C., Zhou, C., & Li, S. (2019). Manifold regularized discriminative feature selection for multi-label learning. *Pattern Recognition, 95*, 136–150. doi:10.1016/j.patcog.2019.06.003

Zhang, Y., Li, H. G., Wang, Q., & Peng, C. (2019). A filter-based bare-bone particle swarm optimization algorithm for unsupervised feature selection. *Applied Intelligence, 49*(8), 2889–2898. doi:10.100710489-019-01420-9

Zheng, W., & Feng, G. (2014). Feature Selection Method Based on Improved Document Frequency. *Telkomnika, 12*(4), 905. doi:10.12928/telkomnika.v12i4.536

Zheng, W., Zhu, X., Wen, G., Zhu, Y., Yu, H., & Gan, J. (2020). Unsupervised feature selection by self-paced learning regularization. *Pattern Recognition Letters, 132*, 4–11. doi:10.1016/j.patrec.2018.06.029

Zorarpacı, E., & Özel, S. A. (2016). A hybrid approach of differential evolution and artificial bee colony for feature selection. *Expert Systems with Applications, 62*, 91–103. doi:10.1016/j.eswa.2016.06.004

Chapter 11
Deep Learning for Feature Engineering–Based Improved Weather Prediction:
A Predictive Modeling

Partha Sarathi Mishra
https://orcid.org/0000-0002-5129-3339
North Orissa University, India

Debabrata Nandi
North Orissa University, India

ABSTRACT

Weather prediction has gained a point of attraction for many researchers of variant research communities. The emerging deep learning techniques have motivated many researches to explore hidden hierarchical pattern in the great mass of weather dataset for weather prediction. In this chapter, four different categories of computationally efficient deep learning models—CNN, LSTM, CNN-LSTM, and ConvLSTM—have been critically examined for improved weather prediction. Here, emphasis has been given on supervised learning techniques for model development by considering the importance of feature engineering. Feature engineering plays a vital role in reducing dimension, decreasing model complexity as well as handling the noise and corrupted data. Using daily maximum temperature, this chapter investigates the performance of different deep learning models for improved predictions. The results obtained from different experiments conducted ensures that the feature engineering based deep learning study for the purpose of predictive modeling using time series data is really an encouraging approach.

DOI: 10.4018/978-1-7998-6659-6.ch011

INTRODUCTION

The task of classification in pattern recognition (Dehuri et al. (2011), data mining (Panda et al. (2015)), and big data analytics (Acharjya et al. (2015); Mishra et al. (2016)) has gained attention of many researchers for developing a robust and accurate model to predict unseen data. In all the above spheres, the accuracy of the model depends on the quality of data being used. In every view of the machine learning techniques, some input data is supplied to get certain output. The input data supplied involves features, which are in the form of structured columns. These features with certain specific features are generally asked by the algorithms to run more efficiently. Hence, the feature engineering plays a crucial role in the machine learning environment. In current scenario, many of the data, scientists spend 60% of their time in cleaning and organizing data. As per survey in Forbes, the rest of the time is spent in building training sets (3%), a dataset collection (19%), and mining data for patterns (9%), Refining algorithms (4%), and others (5%). The missing value is one of the most common problems that we come across while preparing the data for efficient modeling using machine learning algorithms. It affects the machine learning models to a great extent. Here, where the feature engineering stands.

Machine learning is the organized study of algorithms and systems that increase their knowledge or performance with experience. A large number of classification methods (Wu, 2007; Bennette, 2014; Dehuri & Cho, 2010) as well as prediction methods (Mishra & Dehuri, 2012; 2014, 2016; Mishra, 2018) have already been developed by different researchers as mentioned. Figure 1 below describes how the machine learning algorithm works for a given address problem. Here, the model addresses the task; learning algorithms to solve the problem which leads to the development process. In summary, we can say that machine learning deal with the use of an exact feature in the process of building an exact model to accomplish exact tasks.

Figure 1. Machine learning model using features

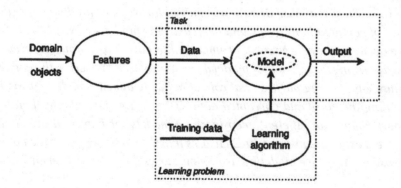

Weather prediction has gained a point of attraction for many researchers of variant research communities. The emerging deep learning techniques have motivated many researches to explore hidden hierarchical pattern in the great mass of weather dataset for weather prediction. It is very important, because it decides the future climate change of a locality and provides a baseline for publishing the new findings on environmental principles and technology. Many of our daily activities and businesses also depend on weather conditions. Unpredictable weather conditions may also lead to hazards as well as property loss.

These losses can be minimized if it is predicted too earlier. Many researchers have worked on weather prediction earlier using Artificial Neural Networks (ANN), Support Vector Machines (SVM), General Circulation Models (GCM), and clustering strategies etc. The successful applications of deep learning in various areas of research domains by the researchers have motivated to build a faster model for the purpose of weather prediction using the time series data. Though the deep learning methods are often developed for time series forecasting problems and perform worse than the other forecasting methods, still then working on hybrid models with CNN or other variations cannot be ignored. The objective of this chapter is to explore the potential of deep learning methods for the purpose of weather prediction using time series data.

Related Work

In the past, a lot of efforts have been made for weather prediction using statistical modeling, including machine learning techniques with fruitful results. The study by Chen and Hwang, (2000) has proposed a fuzzy time series model for temperature prediction based on the historical data. Maqsood et al. (2004) have also shown that ensemble of artificial neural networks (ANNs) successfully learns weather patterns. Liu et al. (2014) have studied deep neural network (DNN) for weather forecasting using the large volume of the weather data and have concluded that new obtained features can improve the performance of classical computational intelligence models. The intelligent predictive system using ANN for the purpose of weather prediction has also been studied by Baboo and Shereef, (2010). Salman et al. (2015) have also studied the different deep learning methods for weather prediction and have concluded that the recurrent neural network can be applied in the prediction of rainfall with adequate accuracy. Fente and Kumar Singh, (2018) have used the LSTM technique with the different weather parameters and have concluded that recurrent neural network based LSTM method provides substantial results with high accuracy among the other weather forecasting techniques. Suksri and Kimpan, (2016) have studied the weather forecasting method using artificial neural network trained by fireworks algorithm and have concluded that the performance of the model provides the acceptable results. Grover et al. (2015) have discussed about the data-intensive challenges via a hybrid approach that combines discriminatively trained predictive models with a deep neural network that models the joint statistics of set of weather related variables and have concluded that the model provides the promising results using real world meteorological data. Scher & Messori, (2019) have discussed about circulation models (GCMs) PUMA and PLASIM as a simplified reality on which deep neural networks is trained and have found that using the

neural networks to reproduce the climate of general circulation models including a seasonal cycle remains is challenging in contrast to earlier promising results on a model without seasonal cycle. Fan et al. (2019) have also studied deep learning-based feature engineering methods for improved building energy prediction and have concluded that the research results help to automate and improve the predictive modeling process while bridging the knowledge gaps between deep learning and building professionals. Therefore, we believe that this effort can make a springboard for the researchers who are specifically working in deep learning techniques for purpose of predictive modeling.

The rest of the chapter is organized as follows: In Section 2, we have discussed background materials along with the different feature engineering techniques used for weather prediction modeling. Section 3 provides descriptions about the different deep learning methods along with step-by-step process of model development. In section 4 we have presented the experimental studies and result interpretations. Section 5 concludes the chapter.

PRELIMINARIES

Regression Problem

In the modeling or simulation of a given occurring phenomena (regression analysis), the engineering analysis is required. This area comes with their unique characteristics in terms of objectives to achieve, data sources, and post-calibration implementation, requiring adequate approaches for a successful model development.

Regression Analysis

The regression analysis includes any technique or algorithm used for mapping or linking several variables among them. The focus is to develop a relationship among one or several dependent variables (outputs) with one or more independent variables (inputs). This relationship in machine learning algorithms is similar in form to what have been seen for classical data-driven models e.g. linear or polynomial equations, ARIMA, ARMA, Quantile Regression, to cite some of them. Therefore, a common property for the regression analysis is that the input-output mapping is expressed in the form of a mathematical expression. Nevertheless, for more sophisticated machine learning algorithms, their mathematical representation is quite complex for most of the cases (including initial data transformation) with the corresponding difficulty to interpret the components of the algorithm directly. This is one of the reasons why these machines were also called "black box algorithms".

The regression analysis can involve simulation, forecasting, rule extraction, processes automation, etc. This analysis can also be used to understand the importance of certain inputs related to the output variables, and the forms of these relationships.

In regression problems we want to model a continuous dependent variable from a number of independent variables. For example, a general linear regression problem can be explained by assuming some dependent variable Y_i which is influenced by inputs or independent variables $x_{i1}, x_{i2}, ...x_{iq}$. This relation can be expressed by a regression model:

$$Y_i = \beta_1 X_{i1} + \beta_2 X_{i2} + ... + \beta_q X_{iq} + \varepsilon \tag{1}$$

Where $\beta 1, \beta 2, ..., \beta q,$ fixed regression parameters and ε are is a random error or noise parameter. It is important to mention that machine learning approaches are nonlinear regression models in which they use parametric techniques that assume a functional form that can approximate a large number of complex functions by using non-linear transformation of a large number of parameters (Ticlavilca et al. 2011).

Data-Intensive Models

A data-Intensive model is based on the analysis of the data about a specific system. The main concept of data-intensive model is to find relationships between the system state variables (input and output) without explicit knowledge of the physical behavior of the system (Solomatine et al. 2008). Parish and Duraisamy, (2016) have also discussed the data-intensive predictive modeling using field inversion and machine learning in the field of computational physics.

Features: The Pillars of the Machine Learning

In data mining, Feature engineering is the process of using domain knowledge to extract features from raw data. Features are considered as the pillars of the machine learning. These determine the achievement of a machine learning application. Feature is a kind of parameter that can easily perform on any instance. Mathematically, they are functions that map from instance space to some set of feature values called as domain of the feature. Since measurements are often numerical, most common feature domain is a set of real numbers. Feature plays a vital role in model development process not because of model is defined in term of feature but because of one feature leading to univariate model. It is used in logical model to zoom in a particular area of instance space. It is also used in supervise learning. These features can be used to improve the performance accuracy of machine learning algorithms. Data does not always come with convenient features, and sometimes we have to renovate the features. Due to this reason machine learning processes are considered as iterative processes. The feature can be rightly justified if model performs satisfactorily; otherwise an insight into it must be given to improve. Some of the feature engineering techniques available in data sciences are: i) Imputation, ii) Handling Outliers, iii) Binning iv) Log Transform, v) One-Hot Encoding vi) Grouping Operations, vii) Feature Split, viii) Scaling, and ix) Extracting Date.

Data Imputation

Missing values are one of the significant problems that arise in the preparation of the input dataset for machine learning. The cause of the missing values is due to the human error, dataflow interruptions, privacy concerns, and so on. These missing values affect the performance of machine learning models. It is also observed that most of advanced machine learning algorithms do not accept the missing values dataset. So, error is generated. A new method of reinforcement programming missing values data imputation has been covered by Rachmawan and Barakbah (2015) to deal with incomplete data. The different imputation methods such as mode, Expectation-Maximization, and k-nearest neighbors have been used by García-Laencina et al. (2015). The class mean imputation (CMI) method based on the k-NN hot deck can be used for continuous and nominal missing data have been discussed by Song and Sheppard (2007). Folguera et al. (2015) have described the Self-organizing-map (SOM) based method of data imputation under the concept of distance object. Farhangfar et al. (2008) have discussed other methods of imputation using mean, hot deck, Naive-Bayes method. Batista and Monard (2003) have used k-NN method for missing data imputation. By concentrating on above cited literatures, we are motivated to use stochastic regression imputation as a feature engineering technique in our model development process which tries to find out the missing values from other related variables in the same dataset with some residual value by the process of regression. Here, also accountability of extrapolation as well as interpolation has been considered. The imputation mechanism is shown in Figure 2. The discussed mechanism is statistically valid if proper imputation method is considered.

Imputation is considered to be more superior than reducing in feature engineering because it conserves the size of the dataset. Sometimes it is very essential to use the median of the considered attributes for the purpose of the missing values. Hence, two different categories of imputations techniques such as numerical as well as categorical are used in the feature engineering.

Figure 2. Imputation mechanism for machine learning

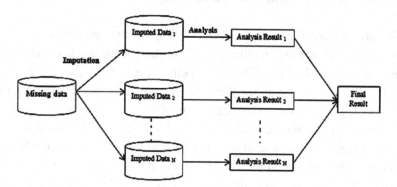

Outliers Handling

This type of feature engineering is also very crucial for the purpose of machine learning. There are many kinds of statistical approaches are found which are open to make faults, whereas envisioning the outliers give a chance to take a choice with high accuracy. This is achieved using standard deviation, and percentiles. Another type of outlier handling is there to Cap instead of reducing which leads to keeping size of the dataset more considerable for the performance of the model.

Binning

This type of feature engineering technique is used on both categorical and numerical data. The objective of using the binning is to make the model robust and prevent from over fitting. The trade-offs between the over fitting and performance are the main issues of the binning. This type of feature is redundant to some of the algorithms except some of the exceptional cases of over fitting.

Log Transform

It is one of the commonly used mathematical transformations found in feature engineering. It is more beneficial to the skewed data. It also diminishes the influence of outliers due to normalization of magnitude differences and makes the model more robust in nature. One of the import factors to be considered here is to take only the positive values, otherwise errors are generated. So, a tip is to add 1 to your data before log transform to get the positive value. It can be done using $Log(x+1)$.

One-Hot Encoding

It is one of the common encoding methods used in machine learning. This technique modifies categorical data to a numerical format and empowers to cluster categorical data without misplacing any evidence. Mainly, binary values such as 0 or 1 are used to establish the relationship between assembled and encoded column for conversion of categorical data to numerical form. Boxes 1 and 2 explain one hot encoding technique based on Town column.

Box 1.

User	Town
1	Balasore
2	Cuttack
1	Cuttack
3	Bhubaneswar
2	Bhubaneswar
1	Bhubaneswar
1	Balasore

Box 2.

User	Bhubaneswar	Cuttack
1	0	0
2	0	1
1	0	1
3	1	0
2	1	0
1	1	0
1	0	0

Grouping Operations

This technique is mainly used for the purpose of deciding aggregate functions of features. It is more appropriate for numerical features and is more problematical for categorical features. For the purpose of categorical grouping we have to choose highest frequency, pivot table, and group by function after applying one-hot encoding technique. But for the purpose of the numerical grouping mean and sum functions are most appropriate. Here, aggregate functions are used instead of binary numbers for values between clustered and encoded columns. The pivot table shown in Boxes 3 and 4 explains grouping operations using group by users.

Box 4.

User	Bhubaneswar	Cuttack	Balasore
1	3	1	4
2	4	2	0
3	1	0	0

Box 3.

User	Town	Appointment
1	Balasore	1
2	Cuttack	2
1	Cuttack	1
3	Bhubaneswar	1
2	Bhubaneswar	4
1	Bhubaneswar	3
1	Balasore	3

Splitting Features

It is one of the useful features for machine learning where dataset uses string column. It allows understanding string values by making bin and grouping them. It also improves the performance of model by uncovering prospective evidence. Though it is a good choice still there is no specific splitting technique is found. It is determined by the characteristics of the column.

Scaling

This technique helps continuous feature to become identical in terms of range. The algorithm based on distance such as k-nearest neighbors (k-NN) need to be scaled continuously. Basically, two variety of scaling techniques are used such as: i) Normalization, ii) Standardization. The normalization technique scales all values within range between 0 and 1. Equation 2 below represents normalization.

$$X_{norm} = \frac{X - X_{min}}{X_{max} - X_{min}} \tag{2}$$

Similarly, Standardization is represented by the equation 3 as given below:

$$z = \frac{x - \mu}{\sigma} \tag{3}$$

Where, μ represents the mean and σ represents the standard deviation.

Date Extraction

This is also an import technique used for the purpose of date extraction for finding weekday, weekend, and holiday etc. The date column is transformed into day, month and year by this technique for machine learning algorithms.

Need for Data Processing

Most of the machine learning algorithm makes assumption about data. So it is an important step in the process of data mining for best representing the structure of the problem. In this chapter, we have used three pre-processing techniques like rescaling, standardization and normalization for getting better results. Here, all values of the attributes have been rescaled within the range of 0 and 1. The same techniques are also used by regression method and neural networks. The algorithms which use distance measures like k-Nearest Neighbours (Elsalamony, 2014; Patel and Upadhaya, 2012) also follow the same principle. In this chapter we have given the importance to min-max scaling method for data processing (shown in Equation 2).

WEATHER PREDICTION USING DEEP LEARNING INJECTION

Deep learning has become popular now-a-days due to their intelligence, efficient learning, accuracy and robustness in model building (Mosavi et al. (2019)). It performs both feature extraction and model building simultaneously. It has already expanded its applications in various scientific and engineering domains. Health informatics, energy, urban informatics, safety, security, hydrological systems modeling, weather prediction modeling, economic, bioinformatics, and computational mechanics have been among the early application domains of deep learning. Survey on the machine learning and data-driven methods have indicated that deep learning, along with the ensemble and hybrid machine learning methods are the future of data science(Asadi et al.(2019); Choubin et al.(2019); Dehghani et al. (2019); Mosavi et al. (2018a); Mosavi et al. (2018b); Mohammadzadeh et al.(2019); Karballaeezadeh et al.(2019)).

The complex mappings from inputs to outputs and multiple inputs to outputs is only supported and automatically learned by the deep learning neural networks. These networks are dominant structures that offer a lot of assurance for time-series prediction, mostly on problems with complex-nonlinear dependencies, multivalent inputs, and multi-step forecasting.

Deep Learning Methods

Deep learning methods are fast evolving for higher performance. Convolutional neural network (CNN), Recurrent neural network (RNN), Denoising autoencoder (DAE), Deep belief networks (DBNs), Long Short-Term Memory (LSTM) are the most popular deep learning methods have been widely used. So we are motivated to use different learning methods for the purpose of weather prediction using time series data and to critically examine their performances in model building. In this section, the description of each method is described along with the notable applications.

Convolutional Neural Network (CNN)

CNN is one of the most known architectures of deep learning methods. The capability of CNN is to study and spontaneously extract features from raw input data. Basically, CNNs are designed for two dimensional image data, although they can be used for one-dimensional data such as sequences of text and time series. The CNN reads across a sequence of lag observations and learns to extract features that are relevant for making a prediction when applied on one-dimensional data. This method is generally employed for image processing applications. CNN concentrates on most salient elements which were the basic intention behind its development. It contains three types of layers with different convolutional, pooling, and fully connected layers (Fig. 3). In each CNN, there are two stages for training process, the feed-forward stage, and the back-propagation stage. The most common CNN architectures are ZFNet (Zeiler & Fergus, 2014), GoogLeNet(Szeged et al. (2015)), VGGNet (Simonyan & Zisserman,2014), AlexNet (Krizhevsky et al.(2012)), ResNet (He et al.(2016)).

The significant feature of CNN model is to alter processing units [...]. Such variety of processing units can produce an effective representation of local salience of the signals. The deep architecture then allows multiple layers of these processing units to be stacked and characterize the signals to be in different scales. It is a decent practice to identify manually and remove logical structures from time series data which makes the problem easier. But, overall competency of the networks recommends that this is not a prerequisite for an expert model. The CNN architecture differs from a "plain" multilayer perceptron

Figure 3. CNN architecture

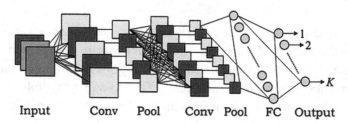

(MLP) network from its usage of convolutional layers, pooling, and non-linearity such as *tanh, sigmoid,* and Rectified Linear Unit (ReLU) activation function (Equation 5).

$$\mathrm{Re}\,LU(x) = \max(0,x) \tag{4}$$

Long Short-Term Memory (LSTM)

LSTM is a recurrent neural network (RNN) method (Architecture is shown in Fig.4) which benefits feedback connections to be used as a general purpose computer. This method can be used for both sequences and patterns recognition and image processing applications. It consists of gated memory cells that can assimilate information over longer time scales (as compared to simply using recurrent connections in a neural network). In general, LSTM contains three central units, including input, output, and forget gates. LSTM can control on deciding when to let the input enter the neuron and to remember what was computed in the previous time step. One of the main strength of the LSTM method is that it decides all these based on the current input itself. Fig. 5 presents the architecture of the LSTM method.

Figure 4. RNN architecture

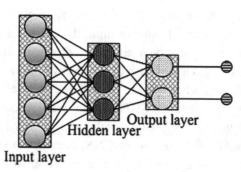

One more advantage of using LSTM is that it can learn automatically when to forget the memory for a particular sequence. The specific formula derivation of LSTM is illustrated through Equations (6)-(15):

$$sigmoid(x) = \frac{1}{1 + e^{-x}} \tag{5}$$

$$z^{-t} = W_z x^t + R_z y^{t-1} + b_z \tag{6}$$

$$z^t = \tanh(z^{-t}) \tag{7}$$

$$i^{-t} = W_i x^t + R_i y^{t-1} + p_i \Theta c^{t-1} + b_i \tag{8}$$

$$i^t = \text{sigmoid}(i^{-t}) \tag{9}$$

$$f^{-t} = W_f x^t + R_f y^{t-1} + p_f \Theta c^{t-1} + b_f \tag{10}$$

$$f^t = \text{sigmoid}(f^{-t}) \tag{11}$$

$$c^t = z^t \Theta i^t + c^{t-1} \Theta f^t \tag{12}$$

$$o^{-t} = W_o x^t + R_o y^{t-1} + p_o \Theta c^{t-1} + b_o \tag{13}$$

$$o^t = \text{sigmoid}(o^{-t}) \tag{14}$$

$$y^t = \tanh(c^t) \Theta o^t \tag{15}$$

Where, W_z, W_i, W_f and W_o are the input weights; R_z, R_i, R_f and R_o are the recurrent weights; p_i, p_f, p_o are the peephole weights; b_z, b_i, b_f and b_o are the bias weights; z^t is the block input gate; f^t is the forget gate; c^t is the memory cell; o^t is the output gate; y^t is the block output; and Θ represents point-wise multiplication. The CNN or LSTM can use back-propagation to adjust the parameters of the model during the process of training in order to reach at parameter optimization. LSTMs have recently been seen to be powerful in supervised sequence processing tasks such as speech recognition (Graves and Jaitly, 2014) and machine translation (Bahdanau et al. (2015)).

CNN-LSTM

It is seen that the CNN model is capable of automatically learning and extracting features from the raw sequence data without scaling. This capability can be combined with the LSTM where a CNN model is applied to sub-sequences of input data. The combined results together form a time series of extracted features which can be interpreted by an LSTM model. This combination of a CNN model with LSTM model is used to read multiple subsequences over time is called a CNN-LSTM model. Fig. 6 below shows architecture of a CNN-LSTM model which speaks that, 1D convolutional layer has followed a max pooling layer and the output is flattened to feed into LSTM layers. Here, two hidden LSTM layers have followed a dense layer to provide the output. In this type of model, the date is first reshaped and rescaled to fit three-dimensional input. Here, Rectified Linear Unit (ReLU), has been used as the activation function for better convergence and to avoid the problem of gradient disappearance.

Figure 5. LSTM architecture
(Greff et al. (2017))

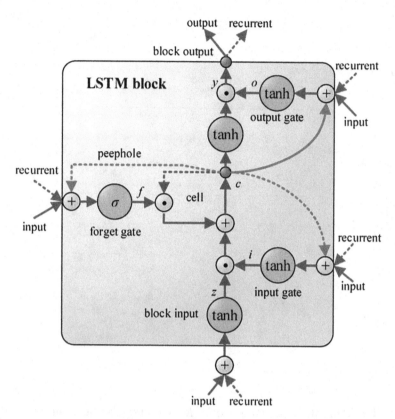

ConvLSTM

To read a part of the input sequence, a convolutional operation can be performed within each LSTM unit. This implies instead of reading a sequence one step at a time, the LSTM will read a block or subsequence of observations at a time using convolutional process like CNN does. This quite different to first reading an extracting features using a LSTM and interpreting the result with a LSTM. Here it performs the CNN operation at each time step as part of the LSTM. Hence, this type of model is called a Convolutional LSTM or ConvLSTM in short. Fig 7 below shows the architecture of a ConvLSTM cell. Just like the LSTM, It is also a recurrent layer. Here, convolution operations change the internal matrix multiplications to self. So the input dimension is converted to 3D vector instead of 1D vector with features when the data flows through the ConvLSTM cells.

Flow Diagram of Deep Learning Model

Figure 8 below shows the complete path of evaluation for proposed deep learning methods. The intuition behind preprocessing the dataset is to make it compatible for proposed learning methods. The original dataset is normalized using min-max scalar (Equation4) after being check for missing values. Then the normalized data is being divided into two parts: one for training data and other for testing data. To keep

Figure 6. CNN-LSTM architecture

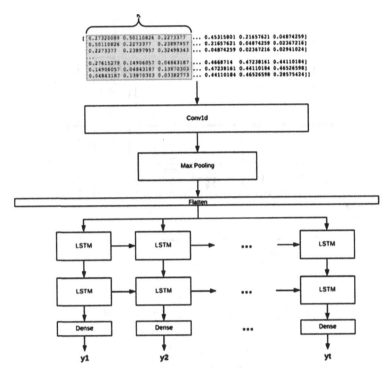

the fairness of performance evaluation, the training data is being restricted for training use only. Each time the training data is inputted to deep learning model, a loss value is generated, accordingly optimizer uses the back-propagation learning method to adjust the parameters of the model. After the completion of training process, the testing data is fed into the deep learning model for comparison of actual and predicted values to gauge the performance of the model.

EXPERIMENTAL DETAILS

Even though the proposed methods is primarily intended for predictions of datasets with large number of records and a moderate number of inputs, it can be also used very well on more conventional datasets. To exhibit this fact we evaluated our proposed flow diagram using a dataset consist of daily maximum air temperatures of Baripada, Odisha. We collected daily maximum air temperature in each day values starting from 1st January 1979 to 31st July 2014 for a period of thirty six years which amounted to be 12928 data points (shown in figure 9).

In order to get the best results from machine learning algorithms, we have performed data visualization in Python using Pandas. Figure 10, Figure 11, Figure 12, Figure 13, and Figure 14 below shows the different visualization in form of histogram, density plot, box and whisker plot, correlation matrix plot and scatter matrix plot respectively.

Figure 7. A ConvLSTM cell

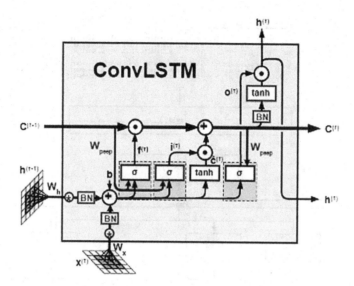

Figure 8. System flow diagram of the proposed deep learning models

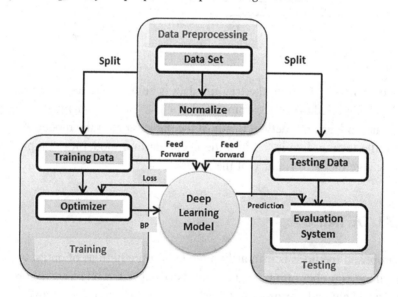

Environments

In order to evaluate the performance of the proposed deep learning methods for improved weather prediction, simulation experiments were carried out on a personal computer having Intel Core(TM) i3 CPU @ 2.30GHz x 4, 16GB of DDR3 RAM, and NVIDIA GeForce GTX 960M 4GB DDR5 GPU in a 64-bit Operating System. The comparison of standard CNN, LSTM, CNN-LSTM deep learning models is discussed based on the simulation results implemented in Python 3.7 version using Keras deep learning library which helps us a lot to customize the network.

Figure 9. Graph showing daily maximum temperatures of the day

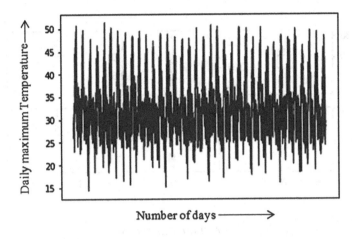

Figure 10. Graph showing number of observations in each bin

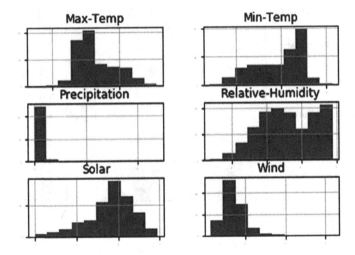

Figure 11. Graph showing distribution each attribute with a smooth curve over bin

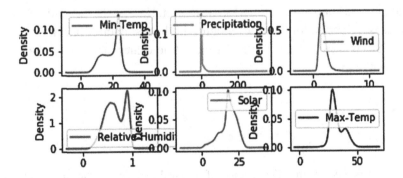

Figure 12. Graph showing spread of the data and dots outside of the whiskers show candidate outlier values

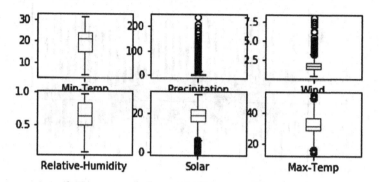

Figure 13. Graph showing correlations between the attributes

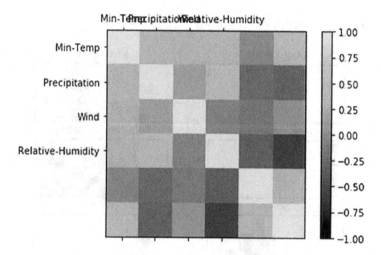

Parameters

For our experiment, we have split the dataset into train and test sets. The first 10342 observations were considered for training and 2586 observations for the test set. Here, walk-forward validation is considered because model makes a forecast for each observation in the test dataset one at a time. The Root Mean Squared Error (RMSE) is considered for comparison of true values in test set and error calculated using Equation 16 as shown below.

$$RMSE = \sqrt{\frac{1}{n}\sum_{i=1}^{n}(\hat{Y}_i - Y_i)^2}$$

(16)

where, $\hat{Y}_i$ = vector of n predictions, Y_i = vector of true values. To handle the overfitting we have used dropout layer after each of our network component. Then taking different model specific hyper-parameters(shown in Table 1, Table 2, Table 3, Table 4) our experiment is conducted.

Figure 14. Graph showing relationship between two variables as dots in two dimensions, one axis for each attribute.

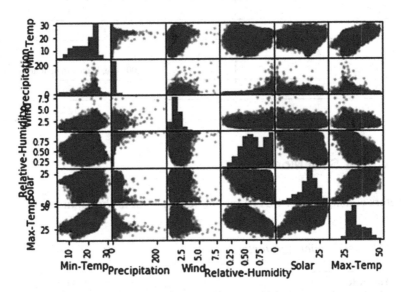

Parameter for CNN-Model

The hyper-parameters considered for CNN model deveopment is shown in Table 1.

Table 1. CNN model hyper-parameters

Parameter	Value
Input vector(Size)	432 (36 years i.e 36 x12)
Input channels(in number)	7
Feature maps numbers	10-200
Size of the Filter	256
Size of the pooling	1x3
Activation Function	ReLU (Rectified linear unit)
Learning rate	0.03
Weight decay	0.00005
Momentum	0.1-0.9
Dropout Probability	0.5
Mini batches size	1000 (i.e, batch gradient descent)
Maximum epoch	5000

Parameter for LSTM Model

The hyper-parameters considered for LSTM model deveopment is shown in Table 2.

Table 2. LSTM model hyper-parameters

Parameter	Value
Input vector(Size)	432 (36 years i.e 36 x12)
Number of nodes	50
Mini batches size	1000 (i.e, batch gradient descent)
Maximum epoch	5000
Number of differences	12

Parameter for CNN-LSTM Model

The hyper-parameters considered for LSTM model deveopment is shown in Table 3.

Table 3. CNN- LSTM model hyper-parameters

Parameter	Value
Input vector(Size)	432 (36 years i.e 36 x12)
Number of sequence	36
Number of time steps	12
Number of Filters	64
Number of Kernels	3
Number of nodes	100
Number of Epochs	5000
Mini batches size	1000 (i.e, batch gradient descent)

Parameter for ConvLSTM Model

The hyper-parameters considered for ConvLSTM model deveopment is shown in Table 4.

Table 4. ConvLSTM model hyper-parameters

Parameter	Value
Input vector(Size)	432 (36 years i.e 36 x12)
Number of sequence	36
Number of time steps	12
Number of Filters	256
Number of Kernels	3
Number of nodes	100
Number of Epochs	5000
Mini batches size	1000 (i.e, batch gradient descent)

Simulation Results

The experiments have been performed to study the performance of different deep learning models like CNN, LSTM, CNN-LSTM and ConvLSTM for improved weather prediction and results obtained is shown in Table 5, Figure 15 and Figure 16 respectively.

Figure 15. Graph showing comparison of different models

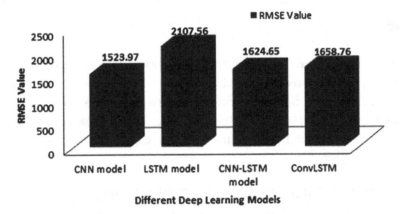

Figure 16. Boxplots showing performance of different deep learning models

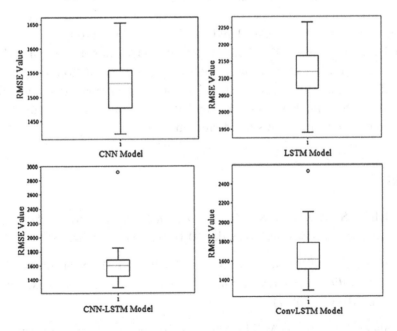

Table 5. RMSE values for different deep learning models

Mode Name	RMSE Value
CNN model	1523.97
LSTM model	2107.56
CNN-LSTM model	1624.65
ConvLSTM	1658.76

DISCUSSIONS

From the Table 5, it clear that we discovered one Convolutional neural network with three recurrent neural network architectures for predictive modeling. It is found that the CNN method is a better deep learning approach than the other three recurrent neural network models such as LSTM, CNN-LSTM, and ConvLSTM for weather prediction. But at the same time the performance of the CNN-LSTM model among other two recurrent network model cannot be neglected.

CONCLUSION AND FUTURE RESEARCH DIRECTIONS

This chapter investigates experimentally four different types of deep learning models using the feature engineering techniques. The models are considered due to the ability of direct use on raw dataset. After performing several experiments using the hyper-parameters, it is concluded that CNN deep learning model provides promising results for considered weather prediction problem. Meanwhile, the results of other three models like LSTM, CNN-LSTM, and ConvLSTM cannot be ignored. Finally, it is concluded that the use of different deep learning models for weather prediction using normalized dataset are well-intentioned of further study. The results of this study need more attentions and improvements for further validation of these models. Future research direction suggests the study of grid search deep learning with additional number of layers in different models.

REFERENCES

Acharjya, D. P., Dehuri, S., & Sanyal, S. (2015). *Computational Intelligence for Big Data Analysis: Frontier Advances and Applications*. Springer. doi:10.1007/978-3-319-16598-1

Asadi, E., Isazadeh, M., Samadianfard, S., Ramli, M. F., Mosavi, A., Shamshirband, S., & Chau, K. (2019). *Groundwater quality assessment for drinking and agricultural purposes in Tabriz aquifer*. doi:10.20944/preprints201907.0339.v1

Baboo, S. S., & Shereef, I. (2010). An efficient weather forecasting system using artificial neural network. *International Journal of Environmental Sciences and Development*, 321–326. doi:10.7763/IJESD.2010.V1.63

Bahdanau, D., Cho, K., & Bengio, Y. (2015).Neural machine translation by jointly learning to align and translate. *Proceedings of International Conference on Learning Representations*.

Batista, G. E., & Monard, M. C. (2003). An analysis of four missing data treatment methods for supervised learning. *Applied Artificial Intelligence, 17*(5-6), 519–533. doi:10.1080/713827181

Bennette, W. D. (2014). *Instance Selection for Model-Based Classifiers*. Graduate Thesis and Dissertations, Iowa State University.

Chen, S.M., & Hwang, J.R. (2000). Temperature prediction using fuzzy time series. *Systems, Man, and Cybernetics, Part B: Cybernetics, IEEE Transactions*, 263-275.

Choubin, B., Borji, M., Mosavi, A., Sajedi-Hosseini, F., Singh, V. P., & Shamshirband, S. (2019). Snow avalanche hazard prediction using machine learning methods. *Journal of Hydrology (Amsterdam), 577*, 123929. doi:10.1016/j.jhydrol.2019.123929

Dehghani, M., Riahi-Madvar, H., Hooshyaripor, F., Mosavi, A., Shamshirband, S., Zavadskas, E., & Chau, K. (2019). Prediction of hydropower generation using grey wolf optimization adaptive neuro-fuzzy inference system. *Energies, 12*(2), 289. doi:10.3390/en12020289

Dehuri, S., & Cho, S. B. (2010). Evolutionarily optimized features in functional link neural network for classification. *Expert Systems with Applications, 37*(6), 4379–4391. doi:10.1016/j.eswa.2009.11.090

Dehuri, S., Ghosh, S., & Cho, S. B. (2011). *Integration of Swarm Intelligence and Artificial Neural Network*. World Scientific. doi:10.1142/7375

Elsalamony, H. A. (2014). Bank direct marketing analysis of data mining techniques. *International Journal of Computers and Applications, 85*(7), 12–22. doi:10.5120/14852-3218

Fan, C., Sun, Y., Zhao, Y., Song, M., & Wang, J. (2019). Deep learning-based feature engineering methods for improved building energy prediction. *Applied Energy, 240*, 35–45. doi:10.1016/j.apenergy.2019.02.052

Farhangfar, A., Lukasz, K., & Dy, J. (2008). Impact of imputation of missing values on classification error for discrete data. *Pattern Recognition, 41*(12), 3692–3705. doi:10.1016/j.patcog.2008.05.019

Fente, D. N., & Kumar Singh, D. (2018). Weather forecasting using artificial neural network. *2018 Second International Conference on Inventive Communication and Computational Technologies (ICICCT)*. doi:10.1109/icicct.2018.8473167

Folguera, L., Zupan, J., Cicerone, D., & Magallanes, J. F. (2015). Self-organizing maps for imputation of missing data in incomplete data matrices. *Chemometrics and Intelligent Laboratory Systems, 143*, 146–151. doi:10.1016/j.chemolab.2015.03.002

García-Laencina, P. J., Abreu, P. H., Abreu, M. H., & Afonoso, N. (2015). Missing data imputation on the 5-year survival prediction of breast cancer patients with unknown discrete values. *Computers in Biology and Medicine, 59*, 125–133. doi:10.1016/j.compbiomed.2015.02.006 PMID:25725446

Graves, A., & Jaitly, N. (2014).Towards end-to-end speech recognition with recurrent neural networks. *Proceedings of the 31st International Conference on Machine Learning*, 1764-1772.

Greff, K., Srivastava, R. K., Koutnik, J., Steunebrink, B. R., & Schmidhuber, J. (2017). LSTM: A search space Odyssey. *IEEE Transactions on Neural Networks and Learning Systems, 28*(10), 2222–2232. doi:10.1109/TNNLS.2016.2582924 PMID:27411231

Grover, A., Kapoor, A., & Horvitz, E. (2015). A Deep Hybrid Model for Weather Forecasting. *Proceedings of the 21th ACM SIGKDD International Conference on Knowledge Discovery and Data Mining (KDD 2015)*, 379-386. 10.1145/2783258.2783275

He, K., Zhang, X., Ren, S., & Sun, J. (2016). Deep residual learning for image recognition. *2016 IEEE Conference on Computer Vision and Pattern Recognition (CVPR)*. 10.1109/CVPR.2016.90

Irachmawan, E. W., & Barakbah, A. R. (2015).Optimization of missing value imputation using reinforcement programming. In *Proceedings of International Electronics Symposium*, 128–133.

Karballaeezadeh, N., Mohammadzadeh, S. D., Shamshirband, S., Hajikhodaverdikhan, P., Mosavi, A., & Chau, K. (2019). Prediction of remaining service life of pavement using an optimized support vector machine (case study of Semnan–firuzkuh road). *Engineering Applications of Computational Fluid Mechanics*, *13*(1), 188–198. doi:10.1080/19942060.2018.1563829

Krizhevsky, A., Sutskever, I., & Hinton, G. E. (2012). Imagenet classification with deep convolutional neural networks. *Advances in Neural Information Processing Systems*.

Liu, J. N., Hu, Y., He, Y., Chan, P. W., & Lai, L. (2015). Deep neural network modeling for big data weather forecasting. *Studies in Big Data*, 389-408. doi:10.1007/978-3-319-08254-7_19

Maqsood, I., Khan, M. R., & Abraham, A. (2004). An ensemble of neural networks for weather forecasting. *Neural Computing & Applications*, 112–122.

Mishra, B. S. P., Dehuri, S., & Euiwhan, K. (2016). *Techniques and Environments for Big Data Analysis: Parallel, Cloud, and Grid Computing*. Springer. doi:10.1007/978-3-319-27520-8

Mishra, P. S. (2018). Optimization of the Radial Basis Function Neural Networks Using Genetic Algorithm for Stock Index Prediction. *International Journal on Computer Science and Engineering*, *6*(6), 43–51.

Mishra, P. S., & Dehuri, S. (2012). Potential indictors for stock index prediction: A Perspective. *International Journal of Electronic Finance*, *6*(2), 157–183. doi:10.1504/IJEF.2012.048465

Mishra, P. S., & Dehuri, S. (2014). Potential Indicators Based Neural Networks for Cash Forecasting of an ATM. *International Journal of Information Systems and Social Change*, *5*(4), 41–57. doi:10.4018/ijissc.2014100103

Mishra, P. S., & Dehuri, S. (2016). Higher Order Neural Network for Financial Modeling and Simulations. In M. Zhang (Ed.), *Applied Artificial Higher Order Neural Networks for Control and Recognition* (pp. 440–466). IGI-Global. doi:10.4018/978-1-5225-0063-6.ch018

Mohammadzadeh, S. D., Kazemi, S., Mosavi, A., Nasseralshariati, E., & Tah, J. H. (2019). Prediction of compression index of fine-grained soils using a gene expression programming model. *Infrastructures*, *4*(2), 26. doi:10.3390/infrastructures4020026

Mosavi, A., Ardabili, S., & Várkonyi-Kóczy, A. (2019). *List of deep learning models*. doi:10.20944/preprints201908.0152.v1

Mosavi, A., & Edalatifar, M. (2018b). A hybrid neuro-fuzzy algorithm for prediction of reference evapotranspiration. *Recent Advances in Technology Research and Education*, 235-243. doi:10.1007/978-3-319-99834-3_31

Mosavi, A., Ozturk, P., & Chau, K. (2018a). Flood prediction using machine learning models: Literature review. *Water (Basel)*, *10*(11), 1536. doi:10.3390/w10111536

Panda, M.,Dehuri, S., & Patra, M.R. (2015). *Modern Approaches of Data Mining: Theory and Practice*. Alpha Science International, Ltd.

Parish, E. J., & Duraisamy, K. (2016). A paradigm for data-driven predictive modeling using field inversion and machine learning. *Journal of Computational Physics*, *305*, 758–774. doi:10.1016/j.jcp.2015.11.012

Patel, N., & Upadhyay, S. (2012). Study of various decision tree pruning methods with their empirical comparison in weka. *International Journal of Computers and Applications*, *60*(12).

Salman, A. G., Kanigoro, B., & Heryadi, Y. (2015). Weather forecasting using deep learning techniques. *2015 International Conference on Advanced Computer Science and Information Systems (ICACSIS)*. 10.1109/ICACSIS.2015.7415154

Scher, S., & Messori, G. (2019). Weather and climate forecasting with neural networks: Using general circulation models (GCMs) with different complexity as a study ground. *Geoscientific Model Development*, *12*(7), 2797–2809. doi:10.5194/gmd-12-2797-2019

Simonyan, K., & Zisserman, A. (2014). *Very deep convolutional networks for large-scale image recognition*. arXiv preprint arXiv:1409.1556

Solomatine, D. P., & Ostfeld, A. (2008). A. Data-driven modelling: Some past experiences and new approaches. *Journal of Hydroinformatics*, *10*(1), 3–22. doi:10.2166/hydro.2008.015

Song, Q., & Shepperd, M. (2007). A new imputation method for small software project data sets. *Journal of Systems and Software*, *80*(1), 51–62. doi:10.1016/j.jss.2006.05.003

Suksri, S., & Kimpan, W. (2016). Neural network training model for weather forecasting using fireworks algorithm. *2016 International Computer Science and Engineering Conference (ICSEC)*. 10.1109/ICSEC.2016.7859952

Szegedy, C., Liu, W., Jia, Y., Sermanet, P., Reed, S., & Anguelov, D., ... Rabinovich, A. (2015). Going deeper with convolutions. *2015 IEEE Conference on Computer Vision and Pattern Recognition (CVPR)*. doi:10.1109/cvpr.2015.7298594

Ticlavilca, A. M., & McKee, M. (2011). Multivariate Bayesian regression approach to forecast releases from a system of multiple reservoirs. *Water Resources Management*, *25*(2), 523–543. doi:10.100711269-010-9712-y

Wu, X. L. (2007). Consistent feature selection reduction about classification data set. *Jisuanji Gongcheng yu Yingyong*, *42*(18), 174–176.

Zeiler, M. D., & Fergus, R. (2014). Visualizing and understanding Convolutional networks. *Computer Vision – ECCV 2014*, 818-833. doi:10.1007/978-3-319-10590-1_53

Chapter 12
Computationally Efficient and Effective Machine Learning Model Using Time Series Data in Different Prediction Problems

Dwiti Krishna Bebarta

ⓘ https://orcid.org/0000-0001-9860-3448

Gayatri Vidya Parishad College of Engineering for Women, India

Birendra Biswal

Gayatri Vidya Parishad College of Engineering (Autonomous), India

ABSTRACT

Automated feature engineering is to build predictive models that are capable of transforming raw data into features, that is, creation of new features from existing ones on various datasets to create meaningful features and examining their effect on planned model performances on various parameters like accuracy, efficiency, and prevent data leakage. So the challenges for experts are to plan computationally efficient and effective machine, learning-based predictive models. This chapter will provide an imminent to the important intelligent techniques that could be utilized to enhance predictive analytics by using an advanced form of the predictive model. A computationally efficient and effective machine learning model using functional link artificial neural network (FLANN) is discussed to design for predicting the business needs with a high degree of accuracy for the traders or investors. The performance of the models using FLANN is encouraging when scientifically analyzed the experimental results of the model using different statistical analyses.

DOI: 10.4018/978-1-7998-6659-6.ch012

INTRODUCTION

A feature is a computable property of any given datasets which is appeared as columns. Each feature, or column, represents a quantifiable piece of data that can be used for analysis based on needs. With processes like feature selection and feature engineering, the quality of the dataset can be improved to solve many real-world problems specifically business-related problems. The benefits of performing feature selection in a selected database before model designing reduces overfitting improve accuracy and reduces training time. In a similar context, the benefits of using the feature engineering process are to build better and faster predictive models for the analysts to transform the raw data into useful and meaningful features for better representations of any unseen data in a given problem. Introduction to automated feature engineering using machine learning will save time, build better predictive models, create meaningful features, and prevent data leakage. It requires expert knowledge i.e. applied machine learning is known as feature engineering to develop a better, efficient, and robust predictive model. Forecasting is an integral part of the planning and decision-making process for companies to survive in this modern and competitive world. Unlike past, business depends on the brand, and companies are limited so forecasting was not too important. Looking at the present scenarios where sentiment is not at all applicable the organizations need to make an accurate forecast on their future products to sustain in the market. According to literature forecasting can be defined:

"Forecasting is predicting, projecting, or estimating some future event or condition which is outside an organization's control and provides a basis for managerial planning"(Herbig et al., 1994).

"Forecasting is generally used to predict or describe what will happen (for example to sales demand, cash flow, or employment levels) given a set of circumstances or assumptions" (Waddell D., et.al, 1994)

Forecasting methods can be divided into three basic categories:

1. Quantitative or Statistical
2. Qualitative or Judgmental
3. Time Horizon

Quantitative or Statistical Method is based on mathematical models, past data, and other related features for forecasting the future. Qualitative or Judgmental method is based on opinions from experts, knowledge, and skills when there is no past data available. Time Horizon forecasts are based on a time span of the future it covers in terms of long-term, medium-term and short-term forecasts. Quantitative or Statistical Method is mainly applied in practice since they are objective and the availability of facts sufficiently in the present digitized world. Moreover, it could bring good results for the company with a significant change in economic effect. There are different techniques of forecasting in Quantitative methods such as Business Barometers, Time Series Analysis, Extrapolation, Regression Analysis, Econometric Models, and Input & Output Analysis.

The arrival of machine learning, big data, and cloud computing technologies has created exhilarating new ways for engineers to build a remunerative career helps to solve real-world challenges in different prediction problems and benefits companies to make better decisions. The use of automated feature engineering in machine learning solves many predictions problems in different domains such as stock market forecasting, currency exchange forecasting, electricity load forecasting and many more areas that involve a time component is named as time series forecasting. There are several types of models constructed using a special kind artificial neural network that makes predictions according to the data of previous times. Prediction of time series data is based on the evolution of a sequence taken at successive equally spaced points in time are known as discrete-time data such as daily closing price in the stock market, electricity price forecasting in the energy market, electricity load time-series data on hourly, radon time series data for earthquake forecasting studies, heights of ocean tides, etc. The discrete-time data is split into two parts where the first part is named as a training data set and the second part is as the test data set is used to predict the index. Automating feature engineering in machine learning solves many prediction problems and also uses different error metrics as a process of validating the model accuracy. Thus, numerous models have been illustrated with more precise predictions for organizations to improve business. The time-series data are more complicated than the other statistical data due to the long term trends, cyclical variations, seasonal variations, and irregular movements. Predicting such highly fluctuating and irregular data is usually subject to large errors. So developing more realistic models for predicting financial time series data to extract meaningful statistics from it more effectively and accurately is of great interest in financial data mining research. A considerable amount of studies has been done in the field of forecasting that includes hybrid combinations of soft computing technology and data mining analysis applied to time-series data. Traditionally, the linear statistical models like autoregressive moving average (ARMA) or ARIMA (Contreras et al., 2003; Flores et al., 2012; Valenzuelab et al., 2008) used for time-series forecasting are simple but suffer from several shortcomings due to the nonlinearity of data. Hence researchers have developed more efficient and accurate soft computing methods like ANN (Andrade de Oliveira & Nobre, 2011; Chen et al., 2003), Fuzzy Logic, Support Vector Machine, Rough Set theory, etc. in the field of forecasting. The benefits of using Artificial Neural Network (ANN) in different domains of prediction problems are:

1. Prior knowledge can be incorporated
2. Allows adaptive adjustment to the model
3. Non-linear description of the problems
4. Can handle a large number and variety of input variables

Later researchers introduced different hybrid models to get improved results by integrating ANN with several other linear methods such as autoregressive integrated moving average (ARIMA) (Khandelwal et al., 2015), ETS-ANN model (Panigrahi & Behera, 2017), Neuron-Fuzzy networks (Chien et al., 2010), etc. These ANN or hybrid models are a powerful tool in their application field of forecasting non-linear time-series data involves large computational complexity during training and testing. These networks are not efficient because of the multiple hidden layers between the input layer, and an output layer. To minimize computational cost and better prediction than the neural network, the intelligent functional link single-layer artificial neural network (FLANN) proposed by Pao and Takefji (1992) (Pao & Takefji, 1992) and is used in many application domains for developing efficient predictive models. The functional expansion of the input to the network effectively increases the dimensionality of the input vector and hence the hyper-planes generated by the FLANN provide greater discrimination capability in the input pattern space. A number of research papers on forecasting in various domains using FLAAN architecture have been reported in recent times is explained in next section. These experiments have proven the ability of FLANN to give out satisfactory results to problems with highly non-linear and dynamic data.

Applications of FLANN Model

Many researchers applied FLANN model to different application domains like forecasting of stocks, currency exchange, energy market, biomedical engineering, earthquake, etc. Majhi et al. (2005) described how functional neural network is used to predict the values of S&P 500 index of New York stock exchange (Majhi et al., 2005). Cheng-Hung et al. (2008) presents a functional-link-based neurofuzzy network (FLNFN) structure for nonlinear system control (Chen et al., 2008). Panda et al. (2009) (Majhi et al., 2009) introduced a functional link artificial neural network (FLANN) model using trigonometric polynomial function for short (one day) as well as long term (one month, two months) prediction of stock price of leading stock market indices: DJIA and S&P 500. Dehuri et al. (2010) (Dehuri & Cho, 2010) proposed a hybrid genetic based functional link artificial neural network (HFLANN) with simultaneous optimization of input features for the purpose of solving the problem of classification in data mining. Nanda et al., 2011 presented Functional link-based neural network models (Nanda & Tripathy, 2011) to predict opencast mining machineries noise. Bebarta et al., 2012, presented different forecasting functional link artificial neural network (FLANN) models (Bebarta, Biswal, & Dash, 2012) to investigate and compare various time series stock data. Dash et al (2016) and Bebarta et al. (2017) introduced hybrid functional link neural network trained by evolutionary unscented Kalman (Dash et al., 2016) and H-infinity (Hamdi et al., 2016) filter respectively for mining and forecasting electricity prices in energy market. Manel Hamdi et al., (2011) proposed a trigonometric functional link artificial neural network (FLANN) model (Bebarta et al., 2017) using backpropagation rule to predict the next day's spot price of US crude oil. Presently researchers are publishing several kinds of functional link artificial neural network models such as bilinear functional link artificial neural network filter for nonlinear active noise control and its stability condition (Le et al., 2018), Functional link artificial neural network filter based on the q-gradient for nonlinear active noise control (Yin et al., 2018), A new Exponentially Expanded Robust Random Vector Functional Link Network based MPPT model for Local Energy Management of PV-Battery Energy Storage Integrated Microgrid (Priyadarshini et al., 2020), Effective fault diagnosis and distance calculation for photovoltaic-based DC microgrid using adaptive EWT and kernel random vector functional link network (Naik et al., 2020), etc. in the diversity field of applications. Bebarta et al. (2012) presented several functional link artificial neural network models (Bebarta, Rout, Biswal et al, 2012) using different polynomial functions to get the patterns for predicting different Indian stock indices like IBM, BSE, Oracle, & RIL stock data. In this paper, more than a few functional link artificial neural networks presented for forecasting stock indices. The novel architecture of functional link artificial neural network model with working principle of different methods is provided to get the best model out of all designed model with an increase in accuracy of prediction and decrease in training time. The result of various methods shows under the study to be more accurate with respect to the relative mean square. All the tests are carried out using different Indian stock indices of RIL, DWSG, & IBM time series data of around 4000 records used for training and testing the model. The detailed work carried out in this paper explained in the below sections.

FLAAN Architecture

The functional link artificial neural network (FLANN) models are single-layer artificial neural network (ANN) possessing higher rate of convergence and lesser computational load than those of multi-layer perceptron (MLP) architectures. The application of FLANN architecture first introduced by J C Patra

(Patra & Pal, 1995) was capable of forming arbitrarily complex decision regions by generating nonlinear decision boundaries. The generalized FLANN architecture depicted below in figure-1 is a single-layer ANN structure possessing higher rate of convergence and lesser computational load than the Multilayer Perceptron (MLP) structure since no hidden layers are present. The functional expansion block (FEB) makes use of a functional model comprising of orthogonal basis functions to enhance the dimension of the input pattern space. For example, considering a two-dimensional input pattern $X = [x_1, x_2, ..., x_n]^T$. The enhanced pattern is obtained by using any one of the functions mentioned below is $X^* = [x0, E_1(x_1), ..., Ep(x_1), E1(x_2), ..., Ep(x_2), ..., E1(x_n), ..., Ep(x_n)]$ which is used by the network for the prediction purpose. The BP algorithm, which is used to train the network, becomes very simple because of absence of any hidden layer.

Figure 1. FLANN Architecture

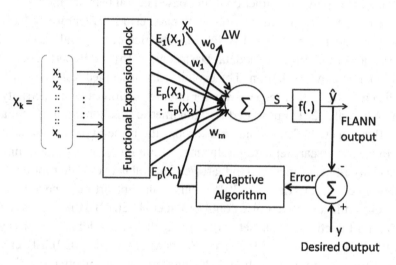

Functional Expansion Block (FEB)

Functional expansion block is introduced in place of the hidden layer as compared with basic ANN architecture for enhancement of the input patterns by using orthogonal polynomials such as Laguerre Chebyshev, Legendre, Trigonometric, Hermite, etc functions. The input pattern $X=\{x_1, x_2, x_3, ..., x_n\}$ applied to the FLANN architecture is enhanced using orthogonal polynomials. Let each element of the input pattern is functionally expanded using any one function mentioned. Assume that an element $x_i(k)$ is to be expanded between $1 \leq k \leq p$, where p is an integer to be chosen between 1 and 10 based on the need of result by suitably using lower and higher order polynomial equations.

Power Polynomial Function

A polynomial series called Power Polynomial Function may be used in FLANNs to enhance the input pattern the following equation may be used. The element in the given input pattern x_i can be enhanced as mentioned in eq. (1)

$$Pe_k = (x_i)^k \ where \ 1 \le k \le p \tag{1}$$

For instance, the given pattern $X = (x_1, x_2, x_3)$ can be enhanced with the use of FEB generates a large number of terms as the dimension of X increases to $(x_1, x_2, x_3, x_1^2, x_2^2, x_3^2, \ldots\ldots, x_1^p, x_2^p, x_3^p)$.

Laguerre Polynomial Function

The lower and higher order of Laguerre Polynomials obtained from the solution of the Laguerre differential equation is given in eq. (2 and 3) for an element x_i in the input pattern is as follows.

$$
\begin{aligned}
Le_1(x_i) &= 1 - x_i \\
Le_2(x_i) &= 0.5x_i^2 - 2x_i + 1 \\
Le_3(x_i) &= -x_i^3 / 6 + 3x_i^2 / 2 - 3x_i + 1 \\
Le_4(x_i) &= x_i^4 / 24 - 2x_i^3 / 3 + 3x_i^2 - 4x_i + 1 \\
Le_5(x_i) &= -x_i^5 / 120 + 5x_i^4 / 24 - 5x_i^3 / 3 + 5x_i^2 - 5x_i + 1
\end{aligned}
\tag{2}
$$

The recursive formula to generate higher order Laguerre polynomials is given in eq. (3)

$$Le_{r+1}(x_i) = 1 / (r+1) * ((2r+1)Le_r(x_i) - rLe_{r-1}(x_i)) \tag{3}$$

Legendre Polynomial Function

The lower and higher order of Legendre Polynomials is given in eq. (4 and 5) for an element x_i in the input pattern is as follows.

$$
\begin{aligned}
Le_1(x_i) &= x_i, & Le_2(x_i) &= \frac{(3x_i^2 - 1)}{2} \\
Le_3(x_i) &= \frac{(5x_i^3 - 3x_i)}{2}, & Le_4(x_i) &= \frac{(35x_i^4 - 30x_i^2 + 3)}{8} \\
Le_5(x_i) &= \frac{(63x_i^5 - 70x_i^3 + 15x_i)}{8}, & Le_6(x_i) &= \frac{(231x_i^6 - 315x_i^4 + 105x_i^2 - 5)}{16}
\end{aligned}
\tag{4}
$$

The recursive formula to generate higher order Legendre polynomial is given in eq. (5)

$$Le_{r+1}(x_i) = 1 / (r+1) * ((2r+1) * x_i * Le_r(x_i) - rLe_{r-1}(x_i)) \tag{5}$$

Chebyshev Polynomial Function

The lower and higher order of Chebyshev Polynomials used is given in eq. 6 and 7 to enhance an element x_i in the input pattern is as follows.

$$
\begin{aligned}
&Ce_1(x_i) = x_i, && Ce_2(x_i) = 2x_i^2 - 1 \\
&Ce_3(x_i) = 4x_i^3 - 3x_i, && Ce_4(x_i) = 8x_i^4 - 8x_i^2 + 1 \\
&Ce_5(x_i) = 16x_i^5 - 20x_i^3 + 5x_i, && Ce_6(x_i) = 32x_i^6 - 48x_i^4 + 18x_i^2 - 1
\end{aligned} \tag{6}
$$

The recursive formula to generate higher order Chebyshev polynomial is given in eq. (7)

$$
Ce_{r+1}(x_i) = 2 * x * Ce_r(x_i) - Ce_{r-1}(x_i) \tag{7}
$$

Trigonometric Function

Each x_i in input pattern is expanded using trigonometric functions as mentioned in eq. 8.

$$
\begin{aligned}
&Te_1(x_i) = \cos \prod x_i, && Te_2(x_i) = \sin \prod x_i \\
&Te_3(x_i) = \cos 2 \prod x_i, && Te_4(x_i) = \sin 2 \prod x_i \\
&Te_5(x_i) = \cos 3 \prod x_i, && Te_6(x_i) = \sin 3 \prod x_i
\end{aligned} \tag{8}
$$

$$\cdots\cdots\cdots\cdots\cdots\cdots\cdots\cdots$$

$$
Te_p(x_i) = \cos p \prod x_i, \quad Te_p(x_i) = \sin p \prod x_i
$$

Hermite Polynomial Function

The Hermite Polynomials used is given in eq. 09 to enhance an element x_i in the input pattern is as follows.

$$
\begin{aligned}
&He_1(x_i) = 2x_i, && He_2(x_i) = 4x_i^2 - 2 \\
&He_3(x_i) = 8x_i^3 - 12x_i, && He_4(x_i) = 16x_i^4 - 48x_i^2 + 12 \\
&He_5(x_i) = 32x_i^5 - 160x_i^3 + 120x_i, && He_6(x_i) = 64x_i^6 - 480x_i^4 + 720x_i^2 - 120
\end{aligned} \tag{9}
$$

Learning of FLANN Model

The expanded output pattern from the given input pattern is derived by applying a combination of lower and higher order polynomials mentioned above.

The enhanced pattern i.e. the output of FEB is

$$
X_e = \{X_0, E_1(x_1), \ldots, E_p(x_1), \ldots E_1(x_n), \ldots, E_p(x_n)\}
$$

The weight vector used as connection strentgth to all enhanced output pattern derived from FEB. the weight vector for the FLANN model is

$$W = \{W_0, W_1, W_2, \ldots, W_t\}$$

Where t is the total number of functional elements

All the elements in weight vector W were initialized to random numbers and are initialized between -1.0 to +1.0.

Weighted sum is derived as given in eq. (10) using enhanced output pattern and weight vector

$$S = X_e^T * W \tag{10}$$

The weighted sum of the enhanced input pattern is given as input to the activation function given in eq. (11) which is the output of the FLANN model.

$$\widehat{y} = F(S) \tag{11}$$

There are different types of activation functions can be used as part of the learning process of the model.

Let y be the desired output for which $\widehat{y}$ is the FLANN output is calculated for a given input pattern. Learning process of the FLANN model involves updating the weights in order to minimize the error of the system. Error is always considered as a cost function and the gradient descent algorithm is used to reduce the cost function. For k^{th} iteration, the error of the system is determined as given in eq. (12).

$$E_k = \frac{1}{2}(y_k - \widehat{y}_k)^2 = \frac{1}{2}e_k^2 \tag{12}$$

Where y_k and $\widehat{y}_k$ are the desired and the estimated output of FLANN model at k^{th} itertation. The goal of the learning algorithm is to minimize the error E_k and to convergent the error towards acceptable error value the weight vector is to be updated with every iteration given in eq. (13).

$$w_{k+1} = w_k + \nabla w_k \tag{13}$$

Activation Function

The neural network uses activation functions as a part of the learning process in the field of machine learning to determine the output. An activation function not only determines the output of the FLANN model but also the computational efficiency of the training and accuracy of the model. Another major effect of using an Activation function is the ability to converge and the convergence speed of error in the training process to reach quickly towards the desired output.

There are three types of activation functions. They are

1.   Binary Step Function

2.   Linear Activation Function
3.   Non-Linear Activation Functions

The computationally efficient FLANN models use non-linear activation functions for learning and modeling complex data, such as images, video, audio, and data sets which are non-linear or have high dimensionality. There are several non-linear activation functions mentioned below.

1.   Sigmoid/Logistic Activation Function: $f(x) = \dfrac{1}{1 + e^{-x}}$

2.   TanH / Hyperbolic Tangent: $f(x)= \mathrm{Tan}H(x)$

3.   ReLU (Rectified Linear Unit): $f(x)= \max(x,0)$ where z is a natural number

4.   Softmax: $f(x_j) = \dfrac{error\ in\ element\ x_j}{\sum_{j=1}^{K} error\ in\ element\ x_j}$ $where\ K\ is\ no.\ of\ output\ units$

Example: $\begin{pmatrix} 1.2 \\ 0.9 \\ 0.4 \end{pmatrix} \xrightarrow{Softmax\ f(x)} \begin{pmatrix} 0.48 \\ 0.36 \\ 0.16 \end{pmatrix}$

Feature of this Softmax activation function is it normalizes the outputs for each class between 0 and 1, like a Sigmaoid activation function but it divides each output such that the total sum of the outputs is equal to 1 as explained in above example.

Learning Algorithms

The learning process in FLANN architecture is just like in a neural network. There are many different types of learning algorithms with different characteristics and performance in terms of numerical precision, memory requirements, and processing speed. The learning process can be seen as a global optimization problem where the weight vector elements including bias must be adjusted in such a way that the estimated value of FLANN model will be minimized. There are several popular optimization techniques available for learning the model are;

1.   Gradient descent learning algorithm
2.   Stochastic descent learning algorithm

EXPERIMENTAL STUDY

Proposed Forecasting Methods

In this paper, the proposed FLANN model which uses the variety of polynomial basis functions such as Power series, Laguerre Polynomials, Legendre Polynomials, and Chebyshev Polynomials enhance the input pattern using a functional expansion block (FEB). The learning process of the model involves updating of the weights [W] using the backpropagation (BP) algorithm.

Data Collection and Feature Extraction

The real stock price data of Reliance Industries Limited (RIL), International Business Machines Corp. (IBM), and Dow Jones U.S. Small-Cap Growth (DWSG) considered for the study. More than 3000 of data patterns of trading days collected which consist of the opening price, highest price, lowest price, closing price, and total volume of the stocks traded for the day. The models which are designed to forecast are replicated to predict the closing price of the index on each day of the forecasting period. The considered data set is divided into two parts. The first data set is called the training data set consists of 2000 days trading data on closing price and the second data set is used for testing consists of 250 days trading data which is next to the end of 2000 days used for training. The third data set is used for testing again to demonstrate the result analysis consists of 10 days of trading data next to 250 days testing data on the real closing price. The model is trained and tested on real data selected above. The purpose of training the model is to make the model expert in learning the data capable of forecasting and the testing is to validate the planned FLANN model. The Mean Absolute Error (MAE) in eq. (14), Mean Absolute Percentage Error (MAPE) in eq. (15), Root Mean Square Error (RMSE) in eq. (16) used for validating the FLANN model.

$$MAE = \frac{\sum_{j=1}^{N}[abs(e)]}{N} \tag{14}$$

$$MAPE = \frac{1}{N}\sum_{j=1}^{N}[abs(e) / y_t] \times 100 \tag{15}$$

$$RMSE = \sqrt{\frac{1}{N}\sum_{j=1}^{N}[abs(e)]^2} \tag{16}$$

Where, y_t is target output, $e = y_t - y$ and y is network response, N is the number of input pattern used for testing.

Experiment Results and Discussion

The simulation results carried out using MATLAB software for the FLANN based forecasting model using different polynomial functions. The testing results and discussion of all outcomes using IBM, RIL, and DWSG real data are graphically represented in figure 2, 3, 4, and 5. To summarize and analysis the tabular data is presented in table 1, 2, 3, 4, and 5 for better understanding of the forecasting data.

The results are mentioned below is carried out using the FLANN model with Chebyshev polynomial basis function. The tabular data is showing the 10 days of real data and the corresponding forecasted data with average error to know the correctness of the model.

Figure 2. Testing result of IBM on real data

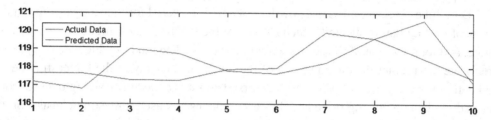

A common figure is given below to showcase the results taken from RIL real data using variety of polynomial functions along with a comparison table for better understanding of the FLANN model.

Figure 3. Testing result of RIL on real data

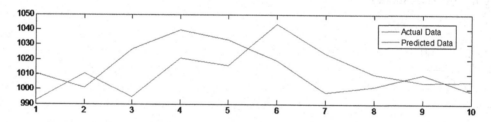

Bebarta et al. (2015) presented a comparative analysis of proposed PFLARNN model (Bebarta et al., 2015) with several other ANN models. This analysis is based on the result of MAPE error during testing of IBM data is given in table-VI.

Figure 4. Testing result of DWSG on real data

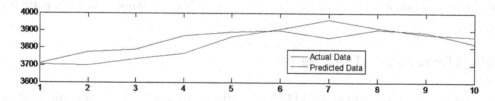

Tables 1, 2, 3, 4, 5, and 6 summarize the results for stock market forecasting by the proposed model. The table 1, 2, and 3, it can be seen that the proposed FLANN model with the use three different stock data IBM, RIL, and DWSG provided average percentage error of 0.748662, 1.636512, and 1.146273 respectively. In table 4, the results of forecasting value are provided which is calculated by using the model with different polynomial functions. Table 5 suggests that the results of average percentage error among all used polynomial functions. From the simulation studies, it was observed that the average percentage error of FLANN model with the use of Power series polynomial function in FEB was lower than the other polynomial functions used in the proposed model. Comparatively, the experimental results of the PFLRANN model perform better than the typical ANN structures in terms of MAPE performance evaluation measure used in the our study (Bebarta et al., 2015) as mentioned in table 6.

Table 1. Daily forecasting error and average error using IBM real data

Day	Actual Value	Forecast Value	% Error	% Avg. Error
24-Jul-09	117.64	117.1913	0.382873	
27-Jul-09	117.63	116.8118	0.700428	
28-Jul-09	117.28	119.0163	1.458863	
29-Jul-09	117.26	118.7424	1.2484	
30-Jul-09	117.86	117.7898	0.059592	0.748662
31-Jul-09	117.93	117.6308	0.254335	
3-Aug-09	119.92	118.2735	1.392138	
4-Aug-09	119.6	119.6241	0.020112	
5-Aug-09	118.47	120.5822	1.751677	
6-Aug-09	117.38	117.1618	0.218196	

Table 2. Daily Forecasting error and average error using RIL real data

Day	Actual Value	Forecast Value	% Error	% Avg. Error
15-Sep-10	1010.45	992.644	1.793795	
16-Sep-10	1000.9	1010.509	0.950862	
17-Sep-10	1026.75	994.7764	3.214146	
20-Sep-10	1039.7	1020.885	1.843053	
21-Sep-10	1032.9	1015.909	1.672457	1.636512
22-Sep-10	1019.25	1043.609	2.334144	
23-Sep-10	997.7	1023.719	2.541602	
24-Sep-10	1001.65	1009.805	0.807571	
27-Sep-10	1009.55	1004.318	0.520956	
28-Sep-10	998.25	1005.151	0.686534	

Table 3. Daily forecasting error and average error using DWSG real data

Day	Actual Value	Forecast Value	% Error	% Avg. Error
1-Nov-10	3708.865	3703.53	0.144059	
2-Nov-10	3773.496	3699.147	2.009902	
3-Nov-10	3787.981	3733.514	1.458857	
4-Nov-10	3869.099	3765.806	2.742898	
5-Nov-10	3890.779	3863.692	0.701048	
8-Nov-10	3899.907	3908.009	0.207328	1.146273
9-Nov-10	3858.018	3960.801	2.595022	
10-Nov-10	3902.678	3914.314	0.297267	
11-Nov-10	3888.233	3876.747	0.296281	
12-Nov-10	3823.037	3862.046	1.010065	

Table 4. 10 days of forecasting data on RIL with target data

Date	Target Data	Forecast Data (Chebyshev)	Forecast Data (Laguerre)	Forecast Data (Legendre)	Forecast Data (Power
15/09/10	1010.45	992.644	1002.89	970.06	993.91
16/09/10	1000.90	1010.509	1021.66	1016.95	1003.69
17/09/10	1026.75	994.7764	1021.42	977.91	1006.65
20/09/10	1039.70	1020.885	1040.52	1037.70	1016.94
21/09/10	1032.90	1015.909	1060.79	1042.47	1032.94
22/09/10	1019.25	1043.609	1059.91	1016.56	1033.46
23/09/10	997.70	1023.719	1045.81	993.94	1023.76
24/09/10	1001.65	1009.805	1021.89	963.25	1008.11
27/09/10	1009.55	1004.318	1017.40	991.16	1002.62
28/09/10	998.25	1005.151	1025.83	1002.91	1008.01

Table 5. Performance comparison on % avg. error for 10 days of RIL data

Duration	% Avg. Error for 10 Days 15/09/2010 to 28/09/2010			
	Chebyshev	Laguerre	Legendre	Power Series
15/09/2010 to 28/09/2010	1.636512	1.9893	1.8796	1.2394

CONCLUSION

In this chapter the FLANN model which can be considered as computationally efficient and effective machine learning model uses time series data for different prediction problems. The proposed and novel architecture is most simple and reliable than the other machine learning conventional networks due to lesser computational load because the absence of hidden layers and composed of a single layer. In fact, the most critical issue is the definition of the optimal architecture of an ANN. FLANN is the most reliable forecasting approach not only in terms of accuracy but also in terms of ability to reduce the computational load and accuracy as suggested by different published articles in reputed journals. Since FLANN gives the encouraging results the researchers published many articles using FLANN models in the field of prediction. It includes (i) real-life benchmark classification problems with highly non-linear boundaries; (ii) mapping the input features with various other polynomials; (iii) the stability and convergence analysis of the proposed method; and (iv) the use evolutionary methods of optimal FLANN using Differential Evolution Algorithm, Firefly Algorithm, Particle Swarm Optimization, and Genetic Algorithm. FLANN is also designed with innovative combinations to create hybrid FLANN models such as ARMA-functional link (ARMAFLNN) neural network, Polynomial Functional link Artificial Recurrent Neural Network (PFLARNN), Self Recurrent Functional Link Fuzzy Neural Network, etc published in various research articles. Many articles published till date as mentioned in reference section suggests that this low complexity FLANN based forecasting models used in many fields such as for stock market, exchange rate prediction, energy load, energy price, crude oil price, of Machinery Noise in Opencast Mines, etc.

Table 6. MAPE errors during testing IBM data set using different ANN models and PFLARNN model

Days Ahead Forecasting	MLP	ANFIS	WNN	RBFNN	PFLARNN
1	1.766	1.7212	1.743	1.562	1.382
3	2.371	2.176	2.132	1.897	1.764
5	2.834	2.316	2.659	2.005	2.083
7	3.181	2.995	3.125	2.394	2.409
15	4.613	3.946	4.232	3.096	3.142

Figure 5. 10 days of forecasting on RIL real data

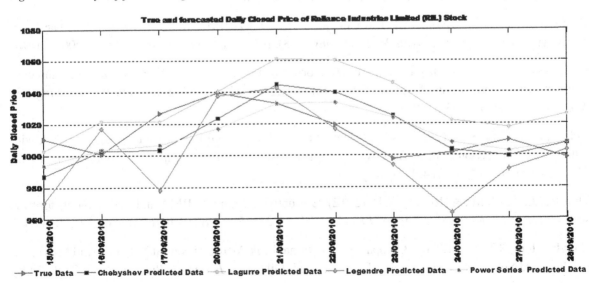

REFERENCES

Andrade de Oliveira, F., & Nobre, C. N. (2011). The Use of Artificial Neural Networks in the Analysis and Prediction of Stock Prices. *IEEE International Conference on Systems, Man and Cybernetics (SMC)*, 2151-2155. 10.1109/ICSMC.2011.6083990

Bebarta, D.K., Bisoi, R., & Dash, P.K. (2017). Mining of electricity prices in energy markets using a hybrid linear ARMA and nonlinear functional link neural network trained by evolutionary unscented H-infinity filter. *International Journal of Information and Decision Sciences, 9*(1), 1-26.

Bebarta, D. K., Biswal, B., & Dash, P. K. (2012). Comparative study of stock market forecasting using different functional link artificial neural networks. *International Journal of Data Analysis Techniques and Strategies, 4*(4), 398–427. doi:10.1504/IJDATS.2012.050407

Bebarta, D. K., Biswal, B., & Dash, P. K. (2015). Polynomial Based Functional Link Artificial Recurrent Neural Network adaptive System for predicting Indian Stocks. *International Journal of Computational Intelligence Systems, 8*(6), 1004–1016. doi:10.1080/18756891.2015.1099910

Bebarta, D. K., Rout, A. K., Biswal, B., & Dash, P. K. (2012). Forecasting and classification of Indian stocks using different polynomial functional link artificial neural networks. *India Conference (INDICON), 2012 Annual IEEE*, 178-182. 10.1109/INDCON.2012.6420611

Chen, A. S., Leung, M. T., & Daouk, H. (2003). Application of Neural Networks to an emerging financial market: Forecasting and trading the Taiwan Stock Index. *Computers & Operations Research on Elsevier, Vol, 30*(6), 901–923. doi:10.1016/S0305-0548(02)00037-0

Chen, C. H., Lin, C. J., & Lin, C. T. (2008). A functional-link based neurofuzzy network for nonlinear system control. *IEEE Transactions on Fuzzy Systems, 16*(5), 1362–1378. doi:10.1109/TFUZZ.2008.924334

Chien, S.-C., Wang, T.-Y., & Lin, S.-L. (2010, March). Application of neuro-fuzzy networks to forecast innovation performance – The example of Taiwanese manufacturing industry. *Expert Systems with Applications, 37*(2), 1086–1095. doi:10.1016/j.eswa.2009.06.107

Contreras, J., Rosario, E., Nogales, F. J., & Conejo, A. J. (2003). ARIMA Models to Predict Next-Day Electricity Prices. *IEEE Transactions on Power Systems, 18*(3), 1014–1020. doi:10.1109/TPWRS.2002.804943

Dash, S.K., Bisoi, R., & Dash, P.K. (2016). A hybrid functional link dynamic neural network and evolutionary unscented Kalman filter for short-term electricity price forecasting. *Neural Computing and Applications, 27*(7), 2123-2140.

Dehuri, S., & Cho, S. B. (2010). A hybrid genetic based functional link artificial neural network with a statistical comparison of classifiers over multiple datasets. *Neural Computing & Applications, 19*(2), 317–328. doi:10.100700521-009-0310-y

Flores, J. J., Graff, M., & Rodriguez, H. (2012). Evaluative design of ARMA and ANN models for time series forecasting. *Renewable Energy, Elsevier, Vol, 44*, 225–230. doi:10.1016/j.renene.2012.01.084

Hamdi, Aloui, & Nanda. (2016). Comparing Functional Link Artificial Neural Network And Multilayer Feedforward Neural Network Model To Forecast Crude Oil Prices. *Economic Bulletin, 36*(4), 2430–2442.

Herbig, Milewicz, Day, & Golden. (1994). Comparing Forecasting Behaviour between Industrial-Product Firms and Customer-Product Firms. *Proceedings of the 1994 Academy of Marketing Science (AMS) Annual Conference.*

Khandelwal, I., Adhikari, R., & Verma, G. (2015). Time Series Forecasting Using Hybrid ARIMA and ANN Models Based on DWT Decomposition. *Procedia Computer Science, 48,* 173-179.

Le, D. C., Zhang, J., & Pang, Y. (2018). A bilinear functional link artificial neural network filter for nonlinear active noise control and its stability condition. *Applied Acoustics, 132,* 19–25. doi:10.1016/j. apacoust.2017.10.023

Majhi, B., Hasan, S., & Mowafak, F. (2005). FLANN based forecasting of S&P 500 index. *Information Technology Journal, 4*(3), 289–292. doi:10.3923/itj.2005.289.292

Majhi, R., Panda, G., & Sahoo, G. (2009). Development and performance evaluation of FLANN based model for forecasting stock market. *Expert Systems with Applications, 36*(3), 6800–6808.

Naik, J., Dhar, S., & Dash, P. K. (2020). Effective fault diagnosis and distance calculation for photovoltaic-based DC microgrid using adaptive EWT and kernel random vector functional link network. *IET Generation, Transmission & Distribution, 14*(4), 690–703. doi:10.1049/iet-gtd.2019.1338

Nanda, S. K., & Tripathy, D. P. (2011). Application of Functional Link Artificial Neural Network for Prediction of Machinery Noise in Opencast Mines. *Advances in Fuzzy Systems.* doi:10.1155/2011/831261Vol

Panigrahi, S., & Behera, H. S. (2017). A hybrid ETS–ANN model for time series forecasting. *Engineering Applications of Artificial Intelligence, 66,* 49-59.

Pao, Y. H., & Takefji, Y. (1992). *Functional-Link Net Computing.* IEEE Computer Journal.

Patra, J. C., & Pal, R. N. (1995). Functional link artificial neural network-based adaptive channel equalization of nonlinear channels with QAM signal. *Proceedings of the IEEE International Conference on Systems, Man and Cybernetics, 3,* 2081–2086. 10.1109/ICSMC.1995.538086

Priyadarshini, L., Dash, P. K., & Dhar, S. (2020). A new Exponentially Expanded Robust Random Vector Functional Link Network based MPPT model for Local Energy Management of PV-Battery Energy Storage Integrated Microgrid (Vol. 91). Academic Press.

Valenzuelab, Rojas, Guillen, Herrera, Pomares, Marquez, & Pasadas. (2008). Soft-computing techniques and ARMA model for time series prediction. *Neural Computing, 71,* 519-537.

Yin, K., Zhao, H., & Lu, L. (2018). Functional link artificial neural network filter based on the q-gradient for nonlinear active noise control. *Journal of Sound and Vibration, 435,* 205–217. doi:10.1016/j. jsv.2018.08.015

Chapter 13
Machine Learning and Convolution Neural Network Approaches to Plant Leaf Recognition

Rajesh K. V. N.

Department of Computer Science and Systems Engineering, Andhra University College of Engineering (Autonomous), Andhra University, Visakhapatnam, India

Lalitha Bhaskari D.
ⓘ https://orcid.org/0000-0002-7773-7567

Department of Computer Science and Systems Engineering, Andhra University College of Engineering (Autonomous), Andhra University, Visakhapatnam, India

ABSTRACT

Plants are very important for the existence of human life. The total number of plant species is nearing 400 thousand as of date. With such a huge number of plant species, there is a need for intelligent systems for plant species recognition. The leaf is one of the most important and prominent parts of a plant and is available throughout the year. Leaf plays a major role in the identification of plants. Plant leaf recognition (PLR) is the process of automatically recognizing the plant species based on the image of the plant leaf. Many researchers have worked in this area of PLR using image processing, feature extraction, machine learning, and convolution neural network techniques. As a part of this chapter, the authors review several such latest methods of PLR and present the work done by various authors in the past five years in this area. The authors propose a generalized architecture for PLR based on this study and describe the major steps in PLR in detail. The authors then present a brief summary of the work that they are doing in this area of PLR for Ayurvedic plants.

DOI: 10.4018/978-1-7998-6659-6.ch013

INTRODUCTION

Plants constitute the most important part of the earth's ecology. Many plants and their products are the primary sources of food for other living species including Humans. Many plant extracts and products are being used as medicines. The ancient Indian system of medicine is known as Ayurveda and makes extensive use of Indian medicinal plant products for curing various diseases. Plants help in preventing global warming by consuming carbon dioxide for photosynthesis. Forest and thick vegetation result in rains. Recognition of plant species is important to be able to take full advantage of the benefits provided by the respective species. Given the huge number of plant species, the recognition of plant species requires knowledge and expertise. An expert botanist has the skill to recognize plant species based on morphological characteristics. Manual techniques to recognize plants are time-consuming and demands expert knowledge. Each plant can be identified using leaves, stem, petals, flowers, and seeds. Leaves of the plant play a dominant role in the identification of plants because of their availability in all seasons. Also, leaves of one plant species are discriminable from the leaves of other plant species. Classification of the plant species based on leaf images has become an active area of research. Due to advances in image processing and artificial intelligence techniques, it is possible to solve the complex problem of PLR. PLR is a multiclass classification problem that can be solved using digital image processing, machine learning and convolution neural network techniques.

BACKGROUND

This section reviews some of the PLR literature published between the year 2016 and the year 2020. The summary of the reviews is presented in Table I.

(Kala, J. R. et al., 2016) presented an approach for plant leaf recognition and classification using leaf shape feature called the sinuosity coefficients. Sinuosity coefficient is a new feature proposed by the authors and is a vector of sinuosity measures. Sinuosity measure represents the degree of meandering of a curve and characterizes a particular shape. The authors have used a subset of leaf images from the Flavia leaf images database for the purpose of experimentation. They have used 25 leaves each per four different species of plants. Multilayer Perceptron (MLP) classifier, K-Nearest Neighbor (KNN), and Naive Bayes classifiers were used to classify the images. A classification rate of 92%, 91%, and 94% was achieved respectively using MLP, KNN, and Naive Bayes classifier.

(Chaki, J., 2017, pp. 1992-2002) proposed a plant species recognition system using shape features of digital images of leaves. The author developed Shape Feature Selection Template (SFST) for the collection of shape features of the leaf. The aspect ratio of leaf images was taken into consideration for shape feature selection. Six combinations of aspect ratios were developed for the classification of leaf image into six types (Square, Very Wide, Wide, Medium, Narrow, and Very Narrow). The modules involved in this implementation are Pre-processing Module (PP), Simple Shape Module (SS), and classification. Visual features of a leaf are represented from the feature vectors generated from the shape module. Neuro-fuzzy controller (NFC) and Neural Network (NN) were used for the purpose of classification. A dataset of 1160 leaf images belonging to 58 classes was created from plantscan dataset and Flavia leaf dataset. This custom dataset was used for experimentation. An accuracy of 94% was achieved using this approach.

(Salve, P. et al., 2018) developed a multimodal plant identification system. The authors used five features (Vein features, HOG features, Geometric features, Spectral Signatures and the fusion of all aforementioned features) in their research work. Support Vector Machine (SVM) classifier, K-Nearest Neighbor (KNN) classifier and Distance classifier was used for the purpose of classification. A custom dataset of 600 images belonging to 60 plant species were used in this research work. An accuracy of 98.03% was achieved by using this approach.

(Mansur, P., 2018, pp. 30-36) designed a Plant Leaf Recognition (PLR) system using the kernel ensemble approach. The steps involved in this approach are pre-processing, creation of feature database and ensemble classification. Color normalization and bicubic interpolation were used in the pre-processing stage for the purpose of normalization and resizing of plant leaf images. Feature database was formed using a combination of 4th order color moments and nine energy maps of LAWS. Support Vector Machine (SVM) classifier with kernel ensemble classification was used for the purpose of classification. The author used the Folio leaf database for the purpose of experimentation. A recognition rate of 90.63% was achieved using this approach.

(Turkoglu, M., & Hanbay, D., 2019) proposed a leaf recognition system. The steps involved in this method are image Pre-processing, leaf divide and rotation, feature extraction, data normalization, and classification. The features were separately acquired from each piece of the leaf after dividing the leaf image into two and four pieces. A feature vector that describes the entire leaf image was generated by combining these features. Feature extraction was done using Color Features, Fourier Descriptors, Vein Features, and GLCM method. Extreme Learning Machines (ELM) classifier was used for the purpose of classification. Flavia leaf dataset was used for the experiment. An accuracy of 99.10% was achieved using this method.

(Oktaviani, O. et al., 2019) developed a plant identification system based on leaf shapes. The steps involved in this implementation are image Pre-processing, feature extraction, and leaf image identification. The authors used 16 basic leaf shapes based on 5 geometric features and 7 digital morphological features of leaves in this work. Multiclass Support vector machine (SVM) was used for the purpose of classification. The authors used three publicly available leaf datasets named Flavia, Folio, and Swedish leaf dataset for the purpose of research. 2540 leaf images belonging to 56 plant species were used for this experiment. An accuracy of 98.48% was achieved using this method.

(Pan, S. et al., 2019) developed a leaf classification and recognition method using hash learning. A subset of leaves was picked from Flavia Dataset for this research work. 14 types of leaves with 50-72 samples per each type was used in this work. The pre-processing stage consisted of steps like Low-pass filtering, Flood filling, Grayscale conversion, opening-and-closing operations, Binary Conversion and outline/contour image extraction. Eight shape/geometric features which have rotation, translation and affine invariance, were extracted out of the contour image. They are Aspect Ratio, Rectangularity, Circularity, Perimeter Convexity, Area Convexity, Sphericity, Form Factor and Eccentricity. Optimal Thresholds were calculated for each of these eight features. A simple hash mapping function was then applied to each of these features for the leaves. If the feature value was greater than the respective optimal threshold value, then the hash code was taken as 1 else it was taken as 0. The hash codes calculated for the eight geometric features were concatenated into a single hash code for the respective leaf. The similarity measure for the leaf images was calculated based on these hash codes. The type of leaf was determined based on this similarity measure. Average recognition accuracy of 80.5% was achieved using this method.

(Hamid, L. E., & Al-Haddad, S. A. R., 2019) proposed a Plant Leaf Classification system using automated leaf alignment and partial shape feature extraction. The pre-processing stage consisted of Grayscale conversion, Binary Conversion and automatic horizontal leaf alignment according to its main vein. The processed image was then divided into 4 equal horizontal quartiles and 4 equal vertical quartiles. 6 Horizontal features and 6 vertical features were calculated based on area and perimeter of the respective horizontal quartiles and vertical quartiles. One feature vector was then created by combining the extracted features. The prediction of the leaf class was done by applying the K-Nearest Neighbor (KNN) classifier on the feature vector. The Quartile Features were combined with Hu's Moment Invariants, using k-fold cross-validation technique. Maximum accuracy of 94.12% was achieved in this work.

(Fu, B. et al., 2019) proposed a Leaf Feature-based Plant recognition system. This work concentrates on the case where the background is complicated. In many other leaf recognition related research works, the input leaf images are created by plucking the leaves and photographing them against a plain background. The first step in this work is the removal of Non-green background. Image is transformed from RGB color space into a different vector space and then the Otsu thresholding method is applied for non-green background removal. Leaf segmentation is done using a watershed segmentation algorithm based on the iterative opening and closing reconstruction. The shape and texture features are extracted from the leaf. The color feature is not considered since there can be a seasonal variation of leaf color. Texture descriptor named Local Binary Pattern (LBP) is extracted and Block LBP algorithm is applied. Locally Linear Embedding Algorithm is applied for dimensionality reduction of Block LBP feature. For the shape features, the Fourier descriptors which describe the contour feature of the leaf are extracted. An integrated feature is generated by combining the mentioned texture and shape features. The classification is done on the integrated features using the SVM classifier. Recognition rates of up to 91.71% are achieved using this approach.

(Islam, M. M. et al., 2019) used Convolutional Neural Network (CNN) for the classification of plants based on leaf images. The initial steps in their work are image dataset collection and image dataset preparation. The image dataset preparation included whitening the leaf image background, image cropping, image resizing and minmax normalization. For the purpose of classification, multilayered CNN model consisting of input layer, 5 convolution layers, 4 max-pooling layers, flattening layer, dense layer, dropout layer and an output layer are used. ADAM optimizer is used for optimization. ReLU activation function is used in the hidden layers and the softmax function is used in the output layer. Validation accuracy of 95.86% and training accuracy of 96.54% was achieved using this CNN model.

(Wang, X. et al., 2020) presented a leaf image-based plant identification system. To start with, the color leaf image is converted to a gray level image. Elliptical half Gabor wavelet which highlights the shape, venation and main texture in leaf images, is used to convolute the gray level image. Line responses for 12 orientations are extracted. Maximum Gap Local Line Direction Pattern (MGLLDP) is extracted from the line responses. Directional Normalization of MGLLDPs is carried out. The histogram of the normalized MGLLDPs is calculated to make it less sensitive to scale change. This histogram is considered as the counting-based local structure descriptor. Classification is done using the SVM classifier. Testing was done on Swedish leaf database, Flavia leaf database and ICL leaf database. Maximum accuracies of 98.40%, 97.83% and 97.37% were achieved using this method when testing was done on the respective leaf databases.

(Sabzi, S. et al., 2020) proposed an automatic leaf classification system. The pre-processing stage consists of leaf image segmentation, binary conversion and improvement of the binary image using Matlab imclose function. In the feature extraction stage, 285 features consisting of various texture features, shape features and color features are extracted. Out of these 285 features, highly discriminative features are selected using a hybrid artificial neural network–differential evolution (ANN–DE) and hybrid artificial neural network–genetic algorithm (ANN–GA) methods. Finally, for leaf classification, three classifiers named hybrid artificial neural network–ant bee colony (ANN–ABC), hybrid artificial neural network–biogeography based optimization (ANN–BBO) and Fisher's linear discriminant analysis (LDA) are used. Mean correct classification rates (CCR) of 94.04%, 89.23%, and 93.99% were achieved using the respective classifiers.

Table 1. Comparison of some of the PLR literature published between year 2016 and year 2020

Authors and Year	Title	Methodology	Datasets Used	Accuracy
(Kala, J. R. et al., 2016)	Sinuosity Coefficients for Leaf Shape Characterisation	Features used: Sinuosity Coefficients Classification Methods used: Multilayer Perceptron(MLP), K-Nearest Neighbour (KNN) and Naive Bayes classifiers	Flavia dataset – A subset of 100 leaves belonging to four species were used	92.00% (MLP Classifier) 91.00% (KNN) 94.00% (Naive Bayes)
(Chaki, J., 2017, pp. 1992-2002)	Template based Shape Feature Selection for Plant Leaf Classification	Features used: Shape Feature Selection Template Classification Methods used: Neuro-Fuzzy Controller (NFC) and Neural Network(NN)	Custom Dataset (1160 leaf images belonging to 58 classes) created from plantscan dataset and Flavia leaf dataset	94.00%
(Salve, P. et al., 2018)	Multimodal plant recognition through hybrid feature fusion technique using imaging and non-imaging hyper-spectral data	Features used: Vein features, HOG features, Geometric features, Spectral Signatures and the fusion of all aforementioned features Classification Methods used: Support Vector Machine (SVM) classifier, K-Nearest Neighbor (KNN) classifier and Distance classifier	Custom dataset of 600 images belonging to 60 plant species	98.03%
(Mansur, P., 2018, pp. 30-36)	Plant leaf recognition system using kernel ensemble approach	Pre-processing method used: Color normalization and bicubic interpolation Features used: 4th order color moments and nine energy maps of LAWS Classification Methods used: Support Vector Machine (SVM) classifier with kernel ensemble classification	Folio database (640 leaf images belonging to 32 different species)	90.63%
(Turkoglu, M., & Hanbay, D., 2019)	Recognition of plant leaves: An approach with hybrid features produced by dividing leaf images into two and four parts	Features used: Color features, Vein features, Fourier Descriptors (FD) and Gray-Level Co-occurrence Matrix (GLCM) Classification Methods used: Extreme Learning Machines (ELM) classifier	Flavia Dataset (1907 leaf images belonging to 32 different species)	99.10%
(Oktaviani, O. et al., 2019)	Combination of Chain Code and Leaf Morphology Approach for Plant Identification	Features used: 16 basic leaf shapes based on 5 geometric features and 7 digital morphological features of leaves Classification Methods used: Multiclass Support Vector Machine (SVM)	Flavia, Folio and Swedish leaf dataset (2540 leaf images belonging to 56 plant species)	98.48%
(Pan, S. et al., 2019)	Leaf Contour Recognition Using Hash Learning	Pre-processing method used: Low-pass filtering, Flood filling, Grayscale conversion, opening-and-closing operations, Binary Conversion and outline/contour image extraction Features used: Eight geometric/shape features named Aspect Ratio, Rectangularity, Circularity, Perimeter Convexity, Area Convexity, Sphericity, Form Factor and Eccentricity of the contour image Classification Methods used: Leaf type was determined based on the similarity of hash codes which were calculated from the Eight geometric/shape features of the respective leaf	Subset of leaves picked from Flavia Dataset (14 types of leaves with 50-72 samples from each type)	80.50%

continues on following page

Table 1. Continued

Authors and Year	Title	Methodology	Datasets Used	Accuracy
(Hamid, L. E., & Al-Haddad, S. A. R., 2019)	Automated Leaf Alignment and Partial Shape Feature Extraction for Plant Leaf Classification	Pre-processing method used: Grayscale conversion, Binary Conversion and Automatic horizontal leaf alignment Features used: 6 Horizontal features and 6 vertical features calculated based on area and perimeter of 4 equal horizontal quartiles and 4 equal vertical quartiles, Hu's Moment Invariants Classification Methods used: K-Nearest Neighbor (KNN) classifier	Flavia Dataset (1907 leaf images belonging to 32 different species)	94.12%
(Fu, B. et al., 2019)	Recognition of Plants with Complicated Background by Leaf Features	Pre-processing method used: Non-green background removal, Leaf segmentation using watershed segmentation algorithm based on iterative opening and closing reconstruction Features used: Texture descriptor named Local Binary Pattern (LBP) with Block LBP algorithm applied on it. Locally Linear Embedding Algorithm then applied for dimensionality reduction, Fourier descriptors extracted for shape features Classification Methods used: Support Vector Machine (SVM)	Custom Leaf Image Dataset (from Wuhan Botanical Gardens) belonging to Fifty Species (consisting of 20 training samples and 10 testing samples per species)	91.71%
(Islam, M. M. et al., 2019)	PataNET: A Convolutional Neural Networks to Identify Plant from Leaf Images	Pre-processing method used: whitening the leaf image background, image cropping, image resizing and minmax normalization Features used: As a part of CNN, features are extracted using convolution operations in the form of feature maps, the discriminating features are learnt in the training process Classification Methods used: Multilayered CNN	Custom Leaf Image Dataset consisting of 3600 leaf images belonging to 6 species (600 leaf images per species)	96.54% (training accuracy), 95.86% (validation accuracy)
(Wang, X. et al., 2020)	Leaf Recognition Based on Elliptical Half Gabor and Maximum Gap Local Line Direction Pattern	Pre-processing method used: gray level image conversion Features used: Line responses for 12 orientations extracted from leaf image using Elliptical half Gabor wavelet, the histogram of the normalized MGLLDPs is finally calculated. Classification Methods used: Support Vector Machine (SVM)	Swedish, Flavia and ICL leaf image databases	98.40% (Swedish leaf database) 97.83% (Flavia leaf database) 97.37% (ICL leaf database)
(Sabzi, S. et al., 2020)	A Computer Vision System for the Automatic Classification of Five Varieties of Tree Leaf Images	Pre-processing method used: leaf image segmentation, binary conversion and improvement of binary image using Matlab imclose function Features used: 285 features consisting of various texture features, shape features and color features are extracted. Out of these, highly discriminative features are selected using ANN–DE and ANN–GA methods Classification Methods used: ANN–ABC classifier, ANN–BBO classifier and LDA classifier	Custom Leaf Image Dataset consisting of 516 leaf images belonging to 5 species	94.04% (ANN–ABC) 89.23% (ANN–BBO) 93.99% (LDA)

GENERALIZED ARCHITECTURE FOR PLR

Based on the literature study of PLR done in this chapter, a common generalized architecture for PLR as shown in Figure 1 is proposed. The literature review done in this chapter has shown various variations of this generalized architecture by various researchers.

Figure 1. Generalized architecture for PLR

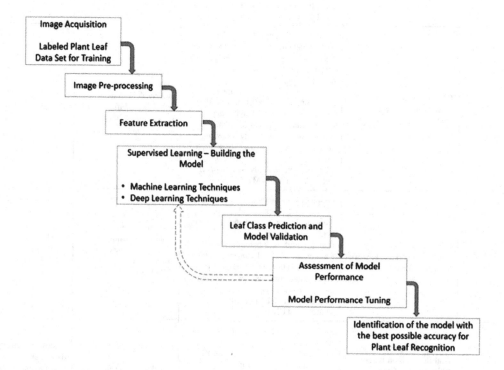

To get started with the PLR exercise, image acquisition is the first step. A properly labeled set of plant leaf images is needed for the purpose of training and validating the PLR model. The next step is Image Pre-processing. Rescaling the images to a common size is one example of Image Pre-processing. Leaves are recognized as belonging to a particular species due to different features like Shape, Color, Texture and Venation. So feature extraction is one of the most important steps which generates the inputs required for the creation of the PLR model. For PLR model creation, machine learning techniques or CNN techniques may be used. In the machine learning approach to PLR, feature extraction is explicitly done. In the CNN Approach, the discriminating features are learned in the convolution layers as a part of training the CNN model. PLR is a supervised learning-based classification problem. The model is trained using the leaf images, the extracted features, and the respective known leaf species names. Machine learning techniques take the leaf features and the respective leaf names as input. CNN techniques take the leaf images and the respective image labels as input. On completion of the model training, the model validation is done using the validation data set. The model is used to predict the leaf names of images in the validation data set. The predicted leaf names are compared with the actual leaf names of the validation data set. This information is used to assess the performance of the model using metrics like accuracy, precision, and recall. Also, the training performance metrics are compared with the validation performance metrics to uncover issues such as overfitting. Based on the study of the performance metrics, parameters associated with the model may be tuned or the architecture may be altered if needed. Then the process of training, validation, and assessment may be repeated until the best model with the best possible accuracy is identified.

IMAGE ACQUISTION

The first step in getting started with building a PLR model is to have a leaf image dataset. Leaf Image Dataset is required for training and thus creating machine learning models or CNN models for plant leaf recognition. There are two ways of getting a leaf image dataset:

- Build a custom leaf image dataset
- Use a publicly available leaf image dataset

Building a custom leaf image dataset is a time-taking and a tedious process. Especially, if the CNN route is taken, the number of leaf images required to build a robust PLR model is large. As per the research work done by the authors for PLR for six Ayurvedic plants, 600 training leaf images per species were required for achieving recognition rates above 98%. The leaf images can be photographed against a plain background or they can be photographed in their original natural environment setting. Photographing against a plain background is the preferred method since there is control on the quality of the leaf images. If leaves are photographed with natural background, then the leaf image part needs to be segmented out during the pre-processing stage. The issues faced while photographing leaves against a plain background are that the leaves need to be plucked and taken to a place where there is proper lighting and no wind and there are proper arrangements for photographing the leaf. This is always not possible since leaves of some species wither and wrap quickly when plucked. In such cases, the leaf images need to be photographed at the site immediately after plucking. This is problematic many a time due to the environmental conditions prevailing at the site which may not be conducive for taking photographs of the leaves.

Some researchers working in the area of PLR hence prefer using publicly available plant leaf image datasets. Table 2 lists some of such leaf datasets which can be downloaded and used for PLR experiments.

IMAGE PRE-PROCESSING

The next step in PLR is usually Image Pre-Processing. Pre-processing of the raw images of leaves is required in many cases so that the images become amenable to subsequent steps like feature extraction and image classification. Some of the pre-processing operations used in PLR are custom leaf alignment, grayscale conversion, binary conversion, opening and closing operations, contour image generation, leaf image segmentation, background removal, noise removal, image cropping, filtering, flood filling, normalization and rescaling.

Table 2. Details of some of the publicly available plant leaf datasets

Dataset Name	Number of Species	Number of Leaf Images	Download URL
Flavia	32 China plant species	1907 leaf images	https://sourceforge.net/projects/flavia/files/Leaf%20Image%20Dataset/1.0/Leaves.tar.bz2/download
Swedish leaf dataset	15 Swedish tree species	1125 leaf images	http://www.cvl.isy.liu.se/en/research/datasets/swedish-leaf/.
Leafsnap dataset	185 Northeastern United States tree species	23,147 high-quality lab images and 7719 field images	http://leafsnap.com/dataset/
Middle European Woody Plants	153 species	9745 images	http://zoi.utia.cas.cz/node/662

FEATURE EXTRACTION

The inputs for a model to differentiate the leaf image of one plant species from leaf image of another plant species are the features of the respective leaves. Selection of leaf image features and feature extraction are hence key to the success of PLR. The features can be classified as basic features, handcrafted features and learned features.

Explicit extraction of features is required in Machine Learning techniques of PLR since the feature values are the inputs to the classifiers. In PLR based on CNN techniques, the discriminative features are learned by the CNN itself during the training process.

In the Machine Learning approach to PLR, the basic and handcrafted features chosen for classification should be discriminative. Discriminability is the key aspect for differentiating the leaf image of one species from another. Also, the chosen features should not be susceptible to position, scale, direction, rotation, translation and affine variance. The main types of features used in the machine learning approach to PLR are Shape Features, Texture Features, Color Features and Venation Features.

Shape Features

The shape of the leaf is an important clue in identifying the species of the respective plant. Basic Shape Features of the leaves and their derived handcrafted features are the most important features used as input to classifiers in the machine learning approach to PLR. The shape descriptors may be broadly classified as contour-based and region-based. Contour based shape descriptors describe the shape of a leaf based on the contour of the leaf whereas region-based shape descriptors describe shape features based on the whole region of the leaf. Diameter, major axis length, minor axis length, area, perimeter, centroid are the basic geometric properties associated with a leaf shape. Some of the derived handcrafted shape features are Aspect Ratio, Centroid contour features, Circularity, Convexity, Eccentricity, Elongatedness, Form Factor, Fourier Descriptors, Hu's moment Invariants, Irregularity factor, Quartile Features, Rectangularity, Roundness factor, SIFT (Scale-invariant feature transform), Solidity, Sphericity and Zerkine Moment Invariants.

Texture Features

Texture as a term signifies the feel, appearance or consistency of a surface. Terms such as smoothness or roughness are used for surface texture. The surface of the leaf is used to characterize the texture of the leaf. Texture feature too is one of the important features useful for leaf image classification. Gabor filters (GF), Fractal Dimensions (FracDim), and Gray Level Co-occurrence Matrix (GCLM) are the most commonly used texture descriptors for leaf analysis. Other texture feature descriptors and methods used in PLR are Autocorrelation function, Contrast, Discrete Wave Transforms, Entropy, First-Order Statistics (FOS), Histogram Fourier (HF), Homogeneity, Local Binary Patterns (LBP) and Markov random field (MRF).

Color Features

Color plays a very important role in identifying the leaves. Color spaces such as red-green-blue (RGB), hue-saturation-value (HSV), and hue-saturation-intensity (HSI) are useful for defining the color properties of a leaf. Various color descriptors used for leaf recognition are color moments (CM), color histograms (CH), color coherence vector and color correlogram. One point that needs to be kept in mind while using Color Feature in PLR is that there is seasonal variation in the color of leaves.

Leaf Venation Features

Leaf venation is another important feature to identify plant species. The structure of the leaves is defined by the veins and is unique to a plant species. Leaf veins patterns found on the surface of the leaf can be used in leaf identification.

DIMENSIONALITY REDUCTION

A large number of shape, texture, color and leaf venation features can be used to describe a leaf image. There is a need to identify highly discriminative features and thus reduce the number of features before using them as input for classifiers. Some of the Dimensionality reduction techniques used in PLR are Principal Component Analysis (PCA), Locally Linear Embedding (LLE) and Linear Discriminant Analysis (LDA).

CLASSIFIERS

In multiclass classification problems in machine learning, classifiers are trained on the known relationships between the input data and respective classes. The trained classifiers are then used to predict the class for new observations or inputs. In the machine learning approach to PLR, the training dataset consists of plant leaf images and the respective plant species names. The classifiers are trained using the features extracted from the processed plant leaf images in the training dataset and the respective plant leaf species names. Some of the classifiers used in machine learning based approach to PLR are Artificial Neural Network (ANN), Decision Tree Classifier, Moving Median Center Hypersphere Classifier, Naive Bayes

Classifier, Nearest Neighbor Classifier, Probabilistic Neural Network (PNN), Random Forest Classifier and Support Vector Machine (SVM).

CONVOLUTION NEURAL NETWORK

This is a more automated approach to plant leaf image classification which requires very less pre-processing and does not require any explicit handcrafted feature extraction. The CNN model architecture consists of multiple layers like the input layer, convolution layers, pooling layers, flattening layer, fully connected dense layers, dropout layers and an output layer. The plant leaf image pixel information is fed through the input layer. Convolution layers act as filters that extract features from the input images and generate feature maps. To summarize the features and reduce the dimension of the feature maps, pooling layers are used. Though Max Pooling operations are frequently used in CNN, there are other pooling operations like Average Pooling and Global Pooling too. The flattening layer is added between the convolution layers and the fully connected dense layers. It converts the output data from the convolution layer into a 1-dimesional array so that it can be input to a fully connected dense layer. The building blocks for dense layers are artificial neurons which are mathematical functions that calculate the weighted aggregates of inputs. Since neural networks are used to solve problems which involve data which is not linearly separable, non-linearity is introduced using activation functions like Sigmoid, Relu and Tanh. Dropout layers too may be introduced for the purpose of preventing overfitting. They prevent the neural network from memorizing the training data. After one or more hidden dense layers, the final layer is the output layer. This layer is used to predict the plant leaf class. The functions used in the output layer are sigmoid or softmax function. For a binary classification problem, the sigmoid function is sufficient. Since PLR is a multiclass classification problem, softmax function is used. During the training process, the training leaf image data is processed by the chosen CNN model and the leaf species name is predicted. This is compared with the actual leaf species name. The difference between the true value and the predicted value is calculated using the loss function. This information is used to refine the network for better prediction. One full round of processing of complete training set by the CNN during training is known as an epoch. Due to the concepts of Gradient Descent and Backpropagation used during the training of CNN, there is a progressive decrease in loss and a progressive increase in accuracy with the number of epochs. During the training process, the CNN itself internally learns the features which help it in distinguishing images of one leaf species from another. That is why these features are known as learned features. The training is stopped when sufficient accuracy of prediction is achieved and no further significant improvement in accuracy with further epochs is observed. The CNN architecture described in this section is a simple sequential model. Much more complex and deep CNN architectures may also be designed and used as required.

CNN FOR RECOGNITION OF AYURVEDIC PLANTS

From ancient times of Indian civilization, Ayurveda has played a vital role in curing diseases. Active ingredients of ayurvedic medicines are extracts of medicinal plants. The authors are presently working on the usage of CNN for recognizing Ayurvedic plants based on the respective leaf images. The Authors created a custom dataset of images of leaves belonging to six Ayurvedic Plant species named

Tabernaemontana Divaricata, Syzygium Cumini, Hibiscus rosa sinensis, Ficus Religiosa, Eucalyptus and Catharanthus Roseus. 5400 leaves were photographed individually against a white background using a common smartphone camera. 900 leaf images were photographed per each of the chosen plant species to create a balanced plant leaf image dataset. Fig.2 shows one sample leaf image per each of the species of the mentioned custom Ayurvedic plant leaf image dataset. For each plant species, 600 leaf images were used for training and 150 leaf images were used for validation. 150 leaf images were kept separate per each species, for testing after identification of the best PLR model. The only pre-processing done was to rescale the images to 150 pixel X 150 pixel. Multilayer CNN as depicted in Fig.3 was designed by the authors for Ayurvedic Plant Leaf Recognition. The CNN consisted of an input layer, 3 convolution layers, 3 max-pooling layers, 1 flattening layer, 1 dense layer, 1 dropout layer and 1 output layer. The layers were arranged in the order depicted in Fig.3. ReLU activation function was used for the hidden dense layer and the Softmax function was used for the output layer. The loss function used in this CNN model is categorical cross-entropy. The optimization function used in this work is Adam. The evaluation metric used in this work is the Accuracy metric. The accuracy metric is defined as the percentage ratio of the number of correctly predicted leaf images to the total number of leaf images. The accuracy metric is sufficient for evaluation since the image dataset is balanced. Keras library and Python was used for implementing this CNN in Google Colab environment. The training was done until 200 epochs. A novel approach was used to identify the best model. At the end of each epoch, the model with parameter weights was saved using the checkpointing capability of Keras. After completion of 200 epochs, each of the saved models was used for prediction against the training dataset and the validation dataset. A high threshold value of 99% accuracy was chosen. The model for which the training accuracy as well as validation accuracy, was above 99% threshold value and the difference between the training and validation accuracy was the least, was chosen as the best model. Table III shows the training, validation and test accuracy achieved using the best model. It can be seen that a test accuracy of 98.33% was achieved using this method.

Table 3. Summary of CNN approach used by Authors for Ayurvedic PLR

Image Dataset	Balanced custom image dataset consisting of 5400 leaf images belonging to six ayurvedic plant species		
Pre-processing	Rescaling of all images to 150 pixel X 150 pixel		
PLR Approach	Multilayer CNN as depicted in Fig.3		
Activation Functions	ReLU function for hidden dense layer and softmax function for output layer		
Optimizer	Adam		
Loss Function	Categorical cross-entropy		
Environment	Python and Keras on Google Colab		
Evaluation Metrics	Accuracy		
Training Accuracy	Validation Accuracy		Test Accuracy
100%	100%		98.33%

Figure 2. Samples of Custom Ayurvedic Plant Leaf Image dataset, one sample leaf image per each plant species.

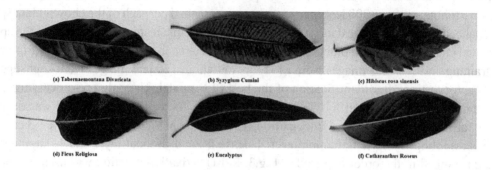

Figure 3. CNN model for Ayurvedic Plant Leaf Recognition

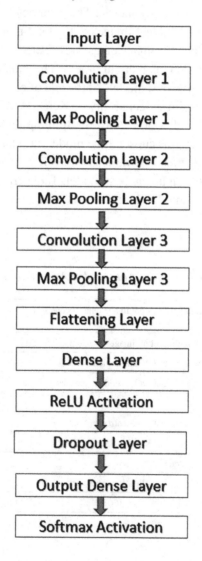

CONCLUSION

In this chapter, the machine learning and CNN approaches to Plant Leaf Recognition (PLR) has been discussed in detail. The authors have reviewed the work done in the past 5 years by various researchers in the area of PLR. A generalized architecture for PLR has been presented by the authors. It consists of image acquisition, image pre-processing, feature extraction, supervised learning and development of PLR models by training using machine-learning or CNN techniques, assessment of the model and identification of the best model. Authors have presented their research work and results on the recognition of Ayurvedic plants based on the respective plant leaf images. The authors presented a CNN based novel approach for best model identification which resulted in test accuracy of 98.33% on the custom Ayurvedic plant leaf dataset. In the context of PLR, it is seen that machine learning and CNN approaches have their own advantages and disadvantages. The machine learning approach needs handcrafted feature extraction for training the classifier for PLR. The accuracy that can be achieved using this approach depends on the handcrafted features that are chosen. On the other hand, the CNN approach learns the distinguishing features on its own, through the training process. CNN approach needs a larger dataset and more powerful hardware compared to the machine learning approach, to develop the PLR model.

REFERENCES

Chaki, J. (2017). Template based shape feature selection for plant leaf classification. *IACSIT International Journal of Engineering and Technology*, *9*(3), 1992–2002. doi:10.21817/ijet/2017/v9i3/1709030122

Fu, B., Mao, M., Zhao, X., Shan, Z., Yang, Z., He, L., & Wang, Z. (2019, March). Recognition of Plants with Complicated Background by Leaf Features. *Journal of Physics: Conference Series*, *1176*(3), 032053. doi:10.1088/1742-6596/1176/3/032053

Hamid, L. E., & Al-Haddad, S. A. R. (2019). Automated Leaf Alignment and Partial Shape Feature Extraction for Plant Leaf Classification. *ELCVIA. Electronic Letters on Computer Vision and Image Analysis*, *18*(1), 37. doi:10.5565/rev/elcvia.1143

Islam, M. M., Rabby, A. S. A., Arfin, M. H. R., & Hossain, S. A. (2019, July). PataNET: A Convolutional Neural Networks to Identify Plant from Leaf Images. In *2019 10th International Conference on Computing, Communication and Networking Technologies (ICCCNT)* (pp. 1-6). IEEE. 10.1109/ICCCNT45670.2019.8944667

Kala, J. R., Viriri, S., & Moodley, D. (2016). Sinuosity coefficients for leaf shape characterisation. In *Advances in Nature and Biologically Inspired Computing* (pp. 141–150). Cham: Springer. doi:10.1007/978-3-319-27400-3_13

Mansur, P. (2018). Plant leaf recognition system using kernel ensemble approach. *International Journal of Advances in Signal and Image Sciences*, *4*(1), 30–36. doi:10.29284/IJASIS.4.1.2018.30-36

Oktaviani, O., Madenda, S., Rodiah, R., Susetianingtias, D. T., Fitrianingsih, D. A., & Arianty, R. (2019). *Combination of Chain Code and Leaf Morphology Approach for Plant Identification*. Academic Press.

Pan, S., Li, T., & Yin, Y. (2019). Leaf Contour Recognition Using Hash Learning. *Academic Journal of Computing & Information Science, 2*(3).

Sabzi, S., Pourdarbani, R., & Arribas, J. I. (2020). A Computer Vision System for the Automatic Classification of Five Varieties of Tree Leaf Images. *Computers, 9*(1), 6. doi:10.3390/computers9010006

Salve, P., Yannawar, P., & Sardesai, M. (2018). Multimodal plant recognition through hybrid feature fusion technique using imaging and non-imaging hyper-spectral data. *Journal of King Saud University-Computer and Information Sciences.*

Turkoglu, M., & Hanbay, D. (2019). Recognition of plant leaves: An approach with hybrid features produced by dividing leaf images into two and four parts. *Applied Mathematics and Computation, 352*, 1–14. doi:10.1016/j.amc.2019.01.054

Wang, X., Du, W., Guo, F., & Hu, S. (2020). *Leaf Recognition Based on Elliptical Half Gabor and Maximum Gap Local Line Direction Pattern.* Academic Press.

Chapter 14
Reciprocation of Indian States on Trade Relation

Rabindranath Jana
Indian Statistical Institute, Kolkata, India

P. Vdhyarani
Sri Parasakthi College for Women, India

R. Maruthakutti
M. S. University, India

ABSTRACT

In the past few years, it is being observed that there is a wake-up call for creating one economic India, one market place with free movement of goods and people. Again, for creating one economic India, the needs of creating one economic India, it needs to preserve sovereignty for the Indian states. However, it is very pertinent to ask how much internal integration India has achieved through trade between states within India. Under such brief backdrop, the author has tried, as an initial attempt, to apply social network analysis (SNA) for studying empirically reciprocation/cohesiveness of Indian states using the data on inter-firm and intra-firm trade flows between states for the financial year 2015-2016. On the basis of reciprocity counts for weighted social networks on inter-states trade relation, the standardized reciprocity measures have been adopted for the chapter. The outcomes of the chapter seem to offer important implications for understanding cooperation and integration on inter-states trade interactions and to exhibit the equilibrium and circularity of inter-state trade flows.

INTRODUCTION

The trade concept has been originated since long ago along with human civilization and communication and is believed to have taken place throughout much of recorded human history. In the prehistoric age, trading was the main facility of people and people bartered goods from each other before the innovation of the modern day currency. Trade was thought of as goods exchange economy and hence it is the

DOI: 10.4018/978-1-7998-6659-6.ch014

transfer of ownership of goods from one person / entity to another. Such transfer was made by getting something in exchange from the buyer. Trade is sometimes loosely called commerce or financial transaction or barter. A market is nothing but a network that allows trade. Modern traders generally negotiate through a medium of exchange, such as money. Trade exists for man, due to specialization and division of labour, in which most people concentrate on a small aspect of production, trading for other products. In a society, trade is required for man due to specialization and division of labour, in which most people concentrate on a small aspect of production, trading for other products. Trade occurs between regions / entities, because different regions have a comparative advantage in the production of some tradable commodity. As such, trade at market prices between locations, benefits both locations.

In India, the idea of federalism and its economic importance are not new. It is argued that federalism and ensuing decentralization of power empower the local governments and consumers to have better information. Hence, they can make better decisions and planning (Hayek, 1945). Competition among States leads to more efficient resource allocation (Tiebout, 1956). Besides the gain from the efficiencies of resource allocation, however, is the additional prospect of creating a common market enabling all constituencies to utilize their respective comparative advantages in a geographical area otherwise separated by jurisdictional boundaries (Bagchi, 2002). In that sense, trade among States remains a vital element in utilizing the gains from decentralization and specialization. In India, in particular, gains from specialization are massive.

Trade and its effects on the Indian economy have been an important issue in the history ofIndian economy (e.g. Chand and Sen, 2002; Krishna and Mitra, 1998; Topalova and Khandelwal, 2011; Topalova, 2007). After the liberalization of Indian economy in 1991, the country has undergone massive structural changes and focused increasingly on principles of privatization and liberalization. Consequently, at present, international trade accounts for almost 38 per cent of India's GDP (World Bank, 2014) and the country ranks among the 12th largest traders in the world with total trade rising at more than 20 per cent per annum (World Bank, 2014).

While there are several studies with a lot of discussions about the success or failure or lack in India's international trade, very little work has been done to study the internal trade in India. India is a conglomeration of States having a variety of climatic, socio-economic, and ethno-cultural diversity. Though there is immense size and large diversity of local economies, the States have much potential for trade. Therefore, attempt for understanding how trade between the States in India, called internal trade, is running will be an important exercise What is known, however, is that internal trade in India is plagued by assortment of restrictions related to diversity in controls, and lack of uniformity in standards and taxing structures, and therefore, considerable room for improvement exists to improve facilitation of trade among various States in India itself (Behera, 2006).

It is now well accepted that barriers to trade are just one component of the factors that determine trade. The traditional gravity model says that "interaction between large economic clusters is stronger than that between smaller ones, and nearby clusters attract each other more than far-off ones" (Van Bergeijk and Brakman, 2010). More recently, literature has moved away from traditional size and distance models to include other non-economic determinants such as socio-cultural and linguistic similarities (Campbell, 2010), institutional and political differences (Möhlmann et al., 2009), differences in productivity and technological development, among others.

For the past few years, it has been observed that there is a wake-up call for creating one economic India, one market place for the free, unimpeded movement of goods and people. As in the report of the Economic Survey2016-2017, a cautious reading of the Constitution and the Constitutional Assembly debates in India intimates uncertainty; a less cautious reading indicates that the needs of creating one economic India were actually subordinated to imperatives of preserving sovereignty for the Indian states. However, when international integration is under siege and when India is on the cusp of implementing transformational reforms to create "One India, One Market, One Tax," via the Goods and Services Tax (GST), it is very pertinent to ask how much internal integration India has achieved through trade between states within India that would serve as a baseline to measure changes.

Under such brief backdrop, the author has tried, as an initial attempt, to apply social network analysis (SNA) for studying empirically reciprocation/cohesiveness of Indian states using the data on inter-firm and intra-firm trade flows between states for the financial year 2015-2016 as published in the report of the Economic Survey 2016-2017. On the basis of reciprocity counts for weighted (weight being trade value in Rupees crores) social networks on trade relation among the states, the standardized reciprocity measures (indicating cohesiveness, mutual cooperation and integration, solidarity etc. among the states through trade) have been adopted for the study. The outcomes of the study seem to offer important implications for understanding cooperation and integration on trade interactions among the states and to exhibit the balance / equilibrium and circularity of internal trade flows inside the country.

METHODOLOGY

Social network analysis (SNA) has been an important research tool for studying the connectedness in the world system. According to Breiger (1981), it is called "a natural wedding" between world-system / dependency theory and a general strategy for the analysis of the intertwining of multiple networks. The affiliation between network analysis and world-system/dependency perspectives is both theoretical and methodological. Theoretically, both approaches execute the priority of relational structures with individual attributes. Network analysts believe that characteristics of social units arise out of structural or relational processes (Wasserman & Faust 1994; Wellman 1988). World-system/dependency researchers(Chase-Dunn & Grimes 1995; Wallerstein 1974) argue that the development of a country largely depends on its structural position and relations with the other countries engaged in international exchange. Moreover, as studied by Wasserman & Faust (1994), methodologically, relations defined by linkages among inter-acting units are a fundamental component of network theories and analyses. It should also be noted that the world system is often defined as "a set of nested and overlapping interaction networks that link all units of social analysis" (Chase-Dunn & Grimes 1995).

Some sociologists have undertaken the network analysis approach for examining the world system (Breiger 1981; Smith & White 1992; Snyder & Kick 1979; Steiber 1979). They have noted a relationship between economic development and network position. Using block-model analyses, Snyder and Kick (1979) has found strong evidence for a core semi-periphery/periphery structure in the world system. Moreover, the structural position of a country in the system was found to have significant effects on economic growth (change in GNP per capita) of the country. In addition to identifying membership in strata, previous studies also address the number of strata existing in the world system (Steiber 1979); the configurations of asymmetrical trade between strata and change in the positions of particular countries in the system (Smith & White 1992); and the existence of a single core (Breiger 1981).

Globalization has often been described as an increased interconnection and interdependence between countries in terms of scope and intensity. Limiting our attention to its economic aspect, globalization is nothing but worldwide participation in economic exchange. Neoclassical economists tend to study trade as mutual benefit for developed and developing countries alike, whereas world-system theorists see trade as unequal exchange (Emmanuel 1972) - that is, the transfer of economic surplus from the periphery to the core. From the world-system point of view, globalization widens the gap between developed and developing countries (Klak 1998). If trade is positively related to development, as neoclassical economists argue, then less developed countries would increase their trade ties with other countries more rapidly than would developed countries that already have extensive trade ties. As a result, the structure of the world trade network would become less centralized over time. On the other hand, as argued by world-system / dependency theorists, if world trade is characterized by unequal exchange, then export from a core to a periphery country would be less reciprocated. As a result, the relational structure of the world tradewould be more centralized or remain constant over time.

From the beginning of human history, geographical proximity has been a primary condition for inter-societal commodity exchange, because distance becomes a barrier to trade. The appeal of regionalism is interesting, as technological advances in transportation and communication have significantly neutralized the negativity of geographical distance as a barrier. As global integration is intensified, it increases vulnerability to the performance of the world economy. In turn, this greater vulnerability forces countries to generate regional integrations to secure long term economic development and stability. Another possible attraction of regionalism is that the impact of interdependence provokes more towards regional integration, whereas the benefits from global integration are generally more remote and uncertain as compared with its immediate costs. Again, regional integration, by reducing tariff and nontariff barriers, even at a regional or sub-regional level, is bound to facilitate the phenomena of trade liberalization.

Indeed, both the theories on globalization/regionalization and world-system/dependency enlighten a perspective that a comprehensive understanding about the complexities of global society can no longer be achieved from an analytical focus on a single society. An image of increased interconnectedness and interdependence at either the global or regional level is observed from day to day. In Indian context, in one way, the states are interconnected and interdependent through inter-firm and intra-firm trade between the states. This emphasis on interconnectedness/interdependence among the Indian states renders social network analysis which is very relevant in studying economic integration/cohesiveness/reciprocation among the states of India.

Data and Methods

For the present study, the secondary data, as in Chapter 11 of the Report on Economic Survey 2016-17 in India, published by the Directorate General of Commercial Intelligence and Statistics (DGCIS) which is the only official source of internal trade data in India. The data are of two kinds — Inter-firm and Intra-firm estimated trade values (in Rupees Crores) between the states. The trade values are not exhaustive and its reasons are narrated in the Report. In each of both inter-firm and intra-firm trade values, the study has covered 20 states/union territories as in the report and they are presented here in Table 1 and Table 2 respectively. It should be taken care of the fact that the set of states for inter-firm trade is not same as that for intra-firm trade. Then we have rearranged the data set for each case as needed for social network analysis. The word state to be used later in the text will mean state or union territory.

Then if there is inter-firm/intra-firm export trade value form i-th state to j-th state, then there will be a directed tie from the i-th state to j-th state with its weight being the export trade value from the i-th state to j-th state. Thus, a weighted social network can be constructed among the states. Again, this weighted social network can also be represented mathematically by an adjacency matrix X of order N x

N, where diagonal cells are zero, N is the number of states, and the (i,j)-th cell value is a non-negative integer x_{ij}, the export value from the i-th state to j-th state. It implies that when x_{ij} becomes zero (i.e., when the weight of tie from the i-th state to j-th state is zero), then there is no export trade from the i-th state to j-th state. So, as in Jana and Bagchi (2015),

$$d_i = \sum_{j=1}^{N} x_{ij} = x_{io} = \text{i-th row sum of the matrix}$$

= export value from the i-th state to the other states
= out-degree of the i-th state, indicating export gravity of the i-th state as source state;

$$e_j = \sum_{i=1}^{N} x_{ij} = x_{oj} = \text{j-th column sum of the matrix}$$

= import value to the j-th state from the other states
= in-degree of the j-th state, indicating import capacity of the j-th state as destination state;

$$m = \sum_{i=1}^{N}\sum_{j=1}^{N} X_{ij} = X_{OO} = \text{grand total}$$

= total trade values among the states; and

$$s_O = \sum_{i<j}\sum \min(X_{ij}, X_{ji})$$

= total reciprocity count among the states, indicating cohesiveness, mutual cooperation and integration, solidarity among the states through trade, where the minimum of export value (X_{ij}) from the i-th state to the j-th state and import value (X_{ji}) from the j-th state to the i-th state, denoted by min(X_{ij}, X_{ji}), is defined as the reciprocity count between i-th and j-th states in the sense that there is a trade exchange between the two states at this minimum trade value.

Now, as exemplified by Rao and Rao (1992), for the study, we have considered the standardized measures of reciprocity (under several conditions) indicating the depth of overall mutual cooperation and integration socially and economically among the states through trade processes; measures of balance indicating the degree of reducing the trade disparities among the states; and lower and upper limits of circularity reflecting the idea about how the economy is rotating across the states through the trades. These measures are given below.

Measures of Reciprocity

ASSUMPTION-1: when only N is given.
Then the standardised reciprocity measure is

s_1: Here it is not applicable, because there is no upper bound for the weight of each tie.

ASSUMPTION-2: when N and m are given

The standardised reciprocity measure is

$$s_2 = \frac{s_0}{\left[\dfrac{m}{2}\right]} \times 100.$$

ASSUMPTION-3: when N and out-degrees are given

The standardised reciprocity measure is

$$s_3 = \frac{s_0}{\displaystyle\sum_{i(\neq i_0)=1}^{N} d_i} \times 100,$$

if there exists a row (i_0, say) of which row total is greater than m/2.

$$= \frac{s_0}{\left[\dfrac{m}{2}\right]} \times 100, \text{otherwise.}$$

ASSUMPTION-4: when both out-degrees and in-degrees are given

Define f_i = Minimum of d_i and e_i for i = 1, 2, ..., N.

The standardised reciprocity measure (approximate) is

$$s_4 \approx \frac{2 \times s_0}{\displaystyle\sum_{i=1}^{N} f_i} \times 100.$$

Measures of Balance

$$b_1 = \frac{\displaystyle\sum_{i=1}^{N} f_i}{m} \times 100,$$

and

$$b_2 = \frac{\dfrac{\sum\limits_{i=1}^{N} f_i}{2} - Q}{K - Q} \times 100,$$

where Q = Minimum of $f_1, f_2, ..., f_N$; and

$$K = \sum_{i(\neq i_0)=1}^{N} d_i, ,$$

if there exists a row (i_0, say) of which row total is greater than m/2 as in assumption-3.

= [m/2], otherwise.

Limits of Circularity

As the procedure to obtain the value of measure of circularity (C) considered for the study is very complex and quite difficult to find out its exact value, the lower and upper limits of the measure will be as $s_2 < C < b_2$.

RESULTS AND DISCUSSIONS

The data on internal trades of both inter-firm and intra-firm as considered above for the study have been depicted in Table 1 and Table 2 respectively along with the calculations required for finding various measures as mentioned above. The Table 3 shows the values of various measures for each of the two cases inter-firm and intra-firm trades between the states. From Table 3, it is observed that none of the measures of reciprocity in all trade processes is less than 50%. It indicates that in each case there is at least 50% mutual cooperation and integration socially and economically among the states through the two internal trade phenomena. Again, the reciprocity measures for inter-firm trade ($s_2 = s_3 = 67.80\%$ and $s_4 = 85.45\%$) are a little higher than intra-firm trade ($s_2 = s_3 = 52.34\%$ and $s_4 = 83.42\%$). Does it show whether inter-firm trade creates more economic integration/ cooperation among the states than intra-firm trade ? From the values of balance measures, all are above 60% for each case and hence it may be said that there is a high degree of reducing the trade disparities among the states or a greater level of trade balancing economy among the states. Also, this tendency for inter-firm trade ($b_1 = 79.34\%$ and $b_2 = 79.29\%$) is larger than intra-firm trade ($b_1 = 62.73\%$ and $b_2 = 62.74\%$). Besides, the lower limits of circularity measures for inter-firm and intra-firm trades are 67.80% and 52.34% respectively and the upper limits of the same measures for the two trades are 79.29% and 62.74% respectively. This reflects the fact of obtaining an overall idea about how the trade economy is rotating across the states or flow of trade economy from one state to another at the minimum and maximum levels.

Table 1. Inter-firm trade (in Rs. Crores) among the 20 states in India as per Economic Survey 2016-2017 with necessary calculations

State	Himachal Pradesh	Uttara-khand	Uttar Pradesh	Haryana	Madhya Pradesh	Chhat-tisgarh	Delhi	Assam	Bihar	Odisha	Jharkhand	West Bengal	Andhra Pradesh	Karnataka	Kerala	Tamil Nadu	Rajasthan	Gujarat	Goa	Maharashtra	Row Sum (d_i)	f_i = Min (d_i,c_i)	Sum of Min (Xij, Xji), i<j
Himachal Pradesh		2410	1228	1560	1630	243	2388	23	555	302	137	919	1060	1368	309	481	1491	1571	54	3295	21024	21024	19278
Uttarakhand	2655		3191	1786	3146	1185	5646	145	1958	1265	1214	3083	2890	4007	972	1497	2910	3498	188	8691	49927	49927	40781
Uttar Pradesh	3488	26900		4873	5983	1385	5848	162	2141	1450	968	4133	3225	4037	1514	1859	5569	8521	271	10849	93176	49445	38430
Haryana	8227	14124	6380		7049	2374	9469	871	3137	2898	1882	7390	8665	11534	6764	4761	15965	15327	969	25267	153053	37553	29334
Madhya Pradesh	1008	2650	3006	726		3101	2086	55	1047	1288	724	8540	3252	2267	697	2201	7227	6843	1057	11181	58956	58956	42780
Chhatisgarh	330	505	743	347	5923		646	150	342	2659	852	1635	5556	2421	412	687	2866	4265	120	11062	41521	41521	24868
Delhi	6642	16912	8791	6729	2684	1511		195	1265	1377	416	2885	2642	4519	2195	1628	7089	9898	216	8203	85797	49154	21668
Assam	21	75	266	158	541	236	188		608	169	96	1777	212	203	22	33	157	695	0	602	6659	4492	2467
Bihar	32	110	267	15	136	96	59	12		85	464	417	38	42	3	67	85	44	0	121	2693	2093	1366
Odisha	174	1337	933	311	2090	6832	347	187	1574		2172	9359	4301	2426	357	575	940	2385	34	7294	43628	43628	26558
Jharkhand	421	1750	2733	1183	1174	1657	518	48	4670	1796		10930	1388	1347	297	472	1316	1029	35	2092	34856	25466	13517
West Bengal	807	1783	1516	911	4066	4929	1399	951	7006	8442	6632		4550	2995	1219	2194	2181	6667	129	9716	68093	68093	28853
Andhra Pradesh	1794	2092	1728	692	4514	2897	1138	161	1187	6901	726	4664		18941	5291	10614	9769	6345	1276	25071	165801	105801	66550
Karnataka	1158	3430	2218	1782	8229	2042	2117	223	967	3332	1535	5686	20777		13589	19300	3465	9828	3403	32519	135600	135600	70749
Kerala	160	261	208	89	326	73	338	5	72	221	82	421	1383	3820		3559	183	1041	90	2830	15162	15162	7703
Tamil Nadu	1490	3846	2136	1414	7923	3146	2879	331	1136	4385	1991	6520	26217	40075	19856		4984	14463	1126	40113	184031	82860	32932
Rajasthan	2113	7714	3149	2776	4868	1014	3368	231	2020	1531	1102	5058	3644	3501	1778	2231		33743	308	11307	91456	91456	44243
Gujarat	4378	11717	6464	8105	22534	4799	3871	279	1536	6487	1457	9664	19679	12882	10618	11643	35627		4945	82044	258729	212558	82760
Goa	106	177	108	90	386	69	266	14	85	121	59	405	552	1817	678	265	285	716		2756	8955	8955	2756
Maharashtra	7137	22679	4380	4006	23634	7783	6583	449	3629	5438	2957	11409	30734	40253	12336	18793	10215	85679	7038		305132	295013	0
Col. Sum (c_i)	42141	120472	49445	37553	106836	45372	49154	4492	34935	50147	25466	94895	140765	158455	78907	82860	112324	212558	21259	295013	m = 1763049	Sum of f_i = 1398757	S_0 = 597593

Table 2. Intra-firm trade (in Rs. Crores) among the 20 states in India as per Economic Survey 2016-2017 with necessary calculations

From \ To	Punjab	Chandigarh	Uttar Pradesh	Madhya Pradesh	Chhattisgarh	Delhi	Odisha	Jharkhand	West Bengal	Andhra Pradesh	Karnataka	Kerala	Tamil Nadu	Puducherry	Rajasthan	Gujarat	Daman and Diu	Goa	Maharashtra	Dadra and Nagar Haveli	Col. Sum (e_j)
Punjab	—	4	1	0	0	0	0	0	0	0	1	0	2	0	0	0	0	0	0	0	8
Chandigarh	605	—	72	13	1	171	134	0	37	14	48	1	25	2	46	72	0	5	145	10	1401
Uttar Pradesh	1032	2	—	1374	278	3189	446	519	797	511	256	8	644	103	861	3670	11	58	1177	155	15091
Madhya Pradesh	2214	15	6440	—	769	4085	653	1554	1987	2669	2365	482	4672	236	2470	99736	127	845	25693	4203	161215
Chhattisgarh	868	2	1684	2346	—	851	2684	897	2086	5760	516	110	848	52	451	5040	37	158	7930	133	32453
Delhi	2288	151	13809	753	191	—	124	529	1576	599	1267	149	2772	126	3376	4461	44	223	7144	225	39807
Odisha	638	4	1265	423	1144	551	—	1302	6188	5865	456	113	999	94	152	629	28	168	2477	74	22570
Jharkhand	604	4	1202	459	2386	633	3340	—	8108	946	187	90	888	53	222	298	19	65	1450	25	20979
West Bengal	3450	8	6896	2289	2867	3718	10142	11807	—	6099	2842	389	7889	571	1375	5671	343	563	15009	430	82358
Andhra Pradesh	3704	12	4765	2544	1105	3051	2949	1720	6772	—	13997	13229	27506	1317	963	10346	211	1386	23173	1052	119802
Karnataka	7748	64	6764	2688	1529	4381	1309	1285	3107	21273	—	5593	25173	2026	1887	9954	260	2992	23814	734	122581
Kerala	1162	11	2344	1394	696	1087	997	140	1364	7312	9133	—	26102	1600	384	2937	29	930	7762	236	65620
Tamil Nadu	1193	68	1780	870	650	1746	606	1413	1495	7072	7725	3405	—	2672	543	3578	64	579	8429	1213	45101
Puducherry	11	1	60	20	1	48	8	3	454	1301	563	725	6693	—	3	305	17	33	529	90	10865
Rajasthan	4342	78	12272	2701	963	10019	994	2148	1464	1891	2250	196	4050	236	—	8406	89	597	7415	2896	63007
Gujarat	390	8	1272	4144	740	1524	1712	1674	1210	4816	2763	468	5848	354	501	—	1332	790	36044	4295	69885
Daman and Diu	19	0	54	31	0	1	1	0	58	18	61	6	67	163	9	2008	—	7	1854	245	4602
Goa	172	2	1066	177	69	171	83	2	1248	415	1429	481	481	26	162	1135	18	—	4390	8	11535
Maharashtra	12724	318	13211	14664	4402	11260	4538	10176	9604	23665	27107	2013	23638	1643	3747	101038	2556	6818	—	5334	278456
Dadra and Nagar Haveli	3	0	328	847	1	53	1024	2	582	156	45	27	14232	28	10	11615	307	23	5449	—	34732
Row Sum (d_i)	43167	752	75285	37737	17792	46539	31744	35171	48137	90382	73011	27485	152529	11302	17162	270899	5492	16240	179884	21358	m = 1202068
f_i= Min (d_i, c_i)	8	752	15091	37737	17792	39807	22570	20979	48137	90382	73011	27485	45101	10865	17162	69885	4602	11535	179884	21358	Sum of fi = 754143
Sum of Min (Xij, Xji), i<j	8	467	11616	33005	12363	18307	15038	12196	24519	59223	43880	7321	16980	908	4429	42461	2106	4398	5334	0	s0 = 314559

m/2 = 601034
Min(fi) = 8

Table 3. Values of different measures of reciprocity, balance and circularity

Trade	Measures of Reciprocity (in %)				Measures of Balance (in %)		Lower & Upper Limits of Circularity Measure (c)
	s_1	s_2	s_3	s_4	b_1	b_2	
Inter-firm	Not Applicable	67.80%	67.80%	85.45%	79.34%	79.29%	67.80, 79.29
Intra-firm	Not Applicable	52.34%	52.34%	83.42%	62.73%	62.74%	52.34,62.74

m/2 = 1763049/2 = 881524.5 (for Inter-firm) and 1202068/2 = 601034 (for Intra-firm)

=> no d_i's is greater than m/2 in either cases and hence $s_2 = s_3$ for each case.

Again the export-import data of both inter-firm and intra-firm have been presented by weighted digraphs (Figures 1 & 2) in the Appendix, where trade volume (in rupees crore) of export-import have been considered as weight of the corresponding directed tie from one state to another state. Similarly, for understanding the reciprocation among the states graphically, two weighted graphs (Figures 3 & 4 in the Appendix) of inter-firm and intra-firm have been depicted, where reciprocity count (in rupees crore) between two states is considered as weight of the corresponding undirected tie between the states. Since all the figures become congested, they do not say more from structural point of view. It needs further graphical analysis at in-depth level, like graph partition method for understanding whether there is any regionalisation on inter-state trade interaction in the country; centrality measures on both out-degree and in-degree (i.e., export and import volume respectively) for finding out dominating states in export and import and so on. These are left for future study.

Here, the network analysis approach has been undertaken on relations through trade and not on the attributes of the states/firms. The results of the analysis call for a deeper analysis of the underlying state attributes and firms' attributes. The study can also be extended by considering longitudinal trade data of all states for understanding pattern and trend. So the approach adopted here can be improved by using traditional analytical tools, particularly structural equation modelling, gravity modelling, regression modelling and multi-level linear hierarchical modelling. Then the upgraded interdisciplinary approach will provide the field with better and more comprehensive conclusions, accompanied by powerful outcomes offered by the field of network analysis.The study will be useful to the policy makers at state level or broader level by extending the study in case of India or beyond. Besides, the study is an indicative illustration in the sense that the approach may be applied to know how several countries are mutually interacted/participated on exports and imports for global/regional economic integration.

REFERENCES

Bagchi, A. (2002). Enforcing the Constitution' S Common Market Mandate: Time to Invoke Article 307. *Economic and Political Weekly, 37*(24), 2303–2305.

Behera, T. (2006). *India's Internal Trade: A Review of Interstate Movement of Major Commodities.* Indian Trade Journal.

Brieger, R. L. (1981). Structure of Economic interdependence among Nations. In P. M. Blau & R. K. Merton (Eds.), *Continuities in Structural Inquiry* (pp. 353–30). Sage Publications.

Campbell, D. L. (2010). *History, Culture, and Trade: A Dynamic Gravity Approach*. Academic Press.

Chand, S., & Sen, K. (2002). Trade Liberalization and Productivity Growth: Evidence from Indian Manufacturing. *Review of Development Economics*, *6*(1), 120–132. doi:10.1111/1467-9361.00145

Chase-Dunn, C., & Grimes, P. (1995). World-System Analysis. *Annual Review of Sociology*, *21*(1), 387–417. doi:10.1146/annurev.so.21.080195.002131

Emmanuel, A. (1972). *Unequal Exchange: A Study of the Imperialism of Trade*. New LeftBooks.

Hayek, F. (1945). The Use of Knowledge in Society. *The American Economic Review*, *1*(35), 519–530.

Jana, R., & Bagchi, S. B. (2015). Distributional Aspects of Some Statistics in Weighted Social Networks. *The Journal of Mathematical Sociology*, *39*(1), 1–28. doi:10.1080/0022250X.2013.866671

Klak, T. (1998). *Globalization and Neoliberalism: The Caribbean Context*. Rowman&Littlefield.

Krishna & Mitra. (1998). Trade Liberalization, Market Discipline and Productivity Growth: New Evidence from India. *The Journal of Development Studies*, *56*(2), 447–462.

Möhlmann, L. F., Ederveen, S., de Groot, H. L. F., & Linders, G. M. (2009). *Intangible Barriers to International Trade: A Sectoral Approach*. Tinbergen Institute Discussion Paper.

Rao, A. R., & Rao, S. B. (1992). *Measuring Reciprocity in Weighted Social Networks. Academic Press*.

Smith, D. A., & White, D. R. (1992). Structure and Dynamics of the Global Economy: Network Analysis of International Trade, 1965-1980. *Social Forces*, *70*(4), 857–893. doi:10.2307/2580193

Snyder, D., & Kick, E. (1979). Structural Position in the World System and Economic Growth, 1955-1970: A Multiple Network Approach. *American Journal of Sociology*, *84*, 1096–1123. doi:10.1086/226902

Steiber, S. (1979). The World System and World Trade: An Empirical Explanation ofConceptual Conflicts. *The Sociological Quarterly*, *20*(1), 23–36. doi:10.1111/j.1533-8525.1979.tb02182.x

Tiebout, C. (1956). A Pure Theory of Local Expenditures. *Journal of Political Economy*, *64*(5), 416–424. doi:10.1086/257839

Topalova, P. (2007). *Trade Liberalization, Poverty and Inequality: Evidence from Indian Districts. Globalization and Poverty*. http://www.nber.org/chapters/c0110.pdf

Van Bergeijk, P. A. G., & Brakman, S. (2010). Introduction: The Comeback of the Gravity Model. In P. A. G. Van Bergeijk & S. Brakman (Eds.), *The Gravity Model in International Trade: Advances and Applications* (pp. 1–28). Cambridge: Cambridge University Press. doi:10.1017/CBO9780511762109.001

Wallerstein, I. (1974). *The Modern World System*. Academic Press.

Wasserman, S., & Faust, K. (1994). *Social Network Analysis: MethodsApplications*. Cambridge University Press. doi:10.1017/CBO9780511815478

Wellman, B. (1988). Structural Analysis: From Method and Metaphor to TheorySubstance. In B. Wellm & S. D. Berkowitz (Eds.), *Social Structures: A Network Approach* (pp. 19–61). Cambridge University Press.

APPENDIX

Figure 1. Inter-firm trade weighted digraph with trade volume (in Rs. crores) as weight

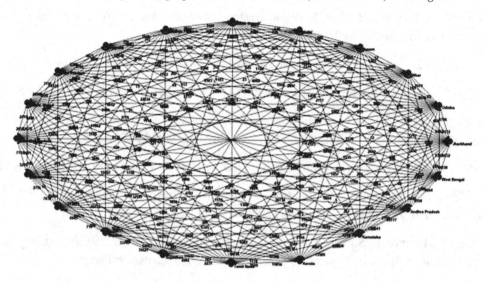

Figure 2. Intra-firm trade weighted digraph with trade volume (in Rs. crore) as weight

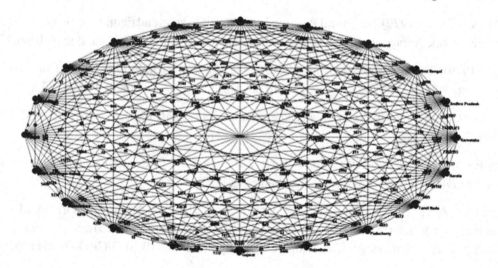

Figure 3. Inter-firm trade weighted graph with trade reciprocity count (in Rs. crore) as weight

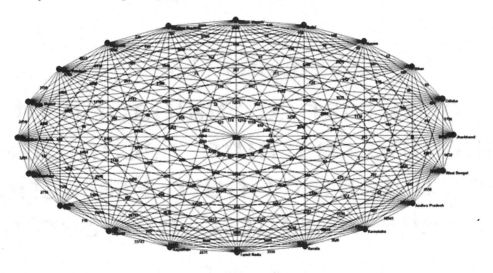

Figure 4. Intra-firm trade weighted graph with trade reciprocity count (in Rs. crore) as weight

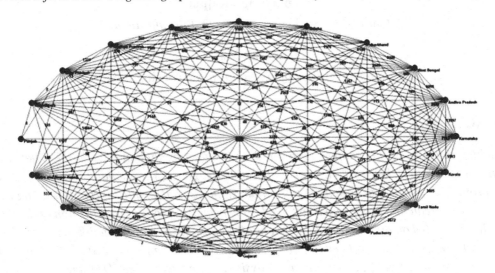

Chapter 15
Performance Evaluation of Machine Learning Techniques for Customer Churn Prediction in Telecommunication Sector

Babita Majhi
Guru Ghasidas Viswavidyalaya, Bilaspur, India

Sachin Singh Rajput
Guru Ghasidas Vishwavidyalaya, Bilaspur, India

Ritanjali Majhi
National Institute of Technology, Karnataka, India

ABSTRACT

The principle objective of this chapter is to build up a churn prediction model which helps telecom administrators to foresee clients who are no doubt liable to agitate. Many studies affirmed that AI innovation is profoundly effective to anticipate this circumstance as it is applied through training from past information. The prediction procedure is involved three primary stages: normalization of the data, then feature selection based on information gain, and finally, classification utilizing different AI methods, for example, back propagation neural network (BPNNM), naïve Bayesian, k-nearest neighborhood (KNN), support vector machine (SVM), discriminant analysis (DA), decision tree (DT), and extreme learning machine (ELM). It is shown from simulation study that out of these seven methods SVM with polynomial based kernel is coming about 91.33% of precision where ELM is at the primary situation with 92.10% of exactness and MLANN-based CCP model is at third rank with 90.4% of accuracy. Similar observation is noted for 10-fold cross validation also.

DOI: 10.4018/978-1-7998-6659-6.ch015

INTRODUCTION

Modeling of customer churn prediction(CCP) has been used in various sectors like different products, commodities, finance, social network, telecommunication, airlines, online gaming and banking(Athanassopoulos, 2000). The CCP models are developed to find out those customers whose probability or chances of churning or leaving the organization is high. It helps the organizations to focus seriously on those customers with some retention strategy. Hence it helps the enterprise to use efficiently its limited marketing budgets. Retention of consumers is highly profitable to companies because of three reasons: (1) finding out new customers is more costly than retaining existing customers(Athanassopoulos, 2000). (2) old customers are more loyal, do not attracted by other marketing competitors, require less budget to serve, and in the other hand they generate revenue for the organization through viral marketing (Farquad et. al., 2014), and (3) churn of customers means loss to organization due to reduction in sales(Ganesh et.al., 2000) . Therefore, most of the companies are now interested in retention of old customers than attracting new customers (Amin et. al., 2016). However, identification of active churners out of a large samples of customer base is a hectic job. For this reason, enterprises are now a days using predictive churn models to make their position in the competitive market.

Recently, (Höppner et. al, 2018) has proposed a expected maximum profit measure for customer churn (EMPC) using decision tree technique. Authors are employing social network analytics to predict customer churn in the telecommunication industry(Óskarsdóttira, et. al. 2017; Mitrovi et. al., 2019). The concept of classifier's certainty estimation using distance factor is presented for CCP in (Amin et. al., 2018). A predictive churn model by using big data has reported in (Shirazi et.al., 2018). ProfLogit, a classifier uses genetic algorithm during training step to maximize the EMPC has suggested in (Stripling et. al, 2018). Three new profit-driven strategies for CCP using support vector machine (SVM) is given in (Maldonado et. al. 2019).

Presently, organizations in the telecommunication sectors (TCS) have adequate data about their consumers where data mining can be applied. This enables the machine learning group to develop various predictive models to handle the CCP in TCS (Amin et.al., 2016). Prediction of churn is a binary classification problem. Using the historical data of the customers the ML models can be trained so that it can able to tell whether a new customer will churn or not. This motivates the authors to develop models using various ML techniques. The main objective of this paper is to study the performance of different machine learning techniques for the churn prediction of telecommunication data. The chapter has used Support Vector Machine (SVM), Multilayer Artificial Neural Network (MLANN), Decision tree (DT), Discriminant Analysis (DA), Naïve Bayesian classifier and Extreme Learning Machine(ELM) for developing CCP models and done the comparison between these models to find out the best model.

Rest of the chapter is organized as follows: Section 2 deals with brief description about each of the machine learning techniques used in this study. Development of a churn prediction model using multilayer artificial neural network is described in Section 3. Data collection and simulation study is given in Section 4. Discussion on results is outlined in the Section 5. Finally conclusion of the chapter is presented in Section 6.

Methodology Used

The churn prediction model is a binary classification model. Means there is only two classes whether the customer will churn (represented as 1) or not churn(represented as 0). For this binary classification purpose, the entire dataset is divided into training set and testing set. The training set is used to train or develop the classifier using the error correction method and then the classifier is validated using the testing samples. In this chapter classifiers like Support Vector Machine (SVM), Multilayer Artificial Neural Network (MLANN), Decision tree (DT), Discriminant Analysis (DA), Naïve Bayesian classifier and Extreme Learning Machine(ELM) are used. A brief description of the individual classifiers is as follows:

Multilayer Artificial Neural Network (MLANN)

Multilayer artificial neural network (ANN) is a nonlinear structure that mimics the conduct of biological brain. It includes a couple of interconnected layers and wide variety of processing elements known as neurons in every layer. Generally ANN consists of three layers: input layer, hidden layer and output layer. In churn prediction model development of a hard and fast of input neurons are defined which can be activated by way of the inputs of the training set. After elevated with weight values the inputs are transformed by way of a activation function. The outputs of these neurons are then exceeded to other neurons and the procedure is repeated until the desired result is obtained. Learning of the MLANN takes place by means of updating the weights between the neurons the usage of BP (Haykin, 2016) algorithm.

Support Vector Machine (SVM)

SVM is a supervised technique (Han and Kamber, 2012) used more often than not for classification and regression analysis. When few records points are given belong to two groups and we want to realize to which group a new record will belong. Then it's miles a linear classification problem. SVM considers each information factors as N dimensional vector and try and separate it by way of drawing N-1 quantity of traces or hyperplanes. The hyperplane having most margin from nearest statistics point of both classes is chosen and called maximum marginal hyperplane (MMH). For nonlinear type the SVM makes clustering or agencies of the information factors and tries to restoration a new statistics factor to one in all these businesses and for this reason does the category. Kernel capabilities are used for nonlinear class of information factors. The SVMs are employing Gaussian Radial Basis, Sigmoid and Polynomial characteristic as kernels. Its primary set of rules is based totally on structural Risk minimization principle (SRM). Here the error rate of a learning device is considered to be bounded by the sum of the training error rate and a term relying on the Vapnik Chervonenkis dimension(Mitra and Acharya, 2004).

Decision Tree (DT) Classifier

The decision tree(DT) (Höppner et.al.,2018) is a supervised and parametric method typically used for classification and regression. Based at the training records features it creates simple selection rules. The tree hence received is employed to predict the goal magnificence of checking out set. Every tuple of the training set contains quite a number of features and a category label. Each attribute within the training pattern corresponds to one node in the decision tree and every leaf node represents a class label. The mastering system divides the samples set into subsets iteratively at the attributes or till there is no further records gain. The information gain (IG) of a discrete random variable Y with probability mass function P(Y) is

$$I(Y) = -\log_2 P(Y) \tag{1}$$

Entropy is a measure of uncertainty in case of a random variable. It helps to pick out the attribute with maximum IG for further division decreasing the uncertainty at that instant. The entropy of the random variable is given as

$$H(Y) = E[I(Y)] = E[-\log_2 P(Y)] = -\sum_i \log_2 P(y_i) \tag{2}$$

Discriminant Analysis(DA)

Discriminant analysis (DA) (Dornaika et. al., 2020) is a statistical approach which is used for classification when the dependent variable is categorical and independent variables are interval in nature. Categorical variable means the variable divided into different categories or classes or groups. DA develops discriminate functions which can be are linear combos of independent variables that may discriminate properly among the dependent variables or target classes as given in (4).

$$DF = w_1 Y_1 + w_2 Y_2 + w_3 Y_3 + ... + w_n Y_n + c \tag{3}$$

where

DF = discriminate function
w = the discriminant coefficient or weight for that independent variable
Y = respondent's score for that independent variable
c = a constant

The weight values of the variable are selected in such as manner that it may maximize the class differences. It is a parametric technique to decide which weightings of quantitative variable nice discriminate between or more than two group of cases. The maximum quantity of functions is either the variety of predictors or the wide variety of groups minus one.

(E) K-Nearest neighbor: K-nearest neighbors(K-NN) (Han and Kamber, 2012) is a simple non-parametric algorithm that holds all training tuples and wait till it gets a checking out tuple, hence referred to as a lazy learner. On getting a new tuple for classification it classifies the new tuple primarily based on a distance measure. Here Euclidean distance is used as the space measure. A tuple is classified via majority vote of its neighbors. The tuple is assigned to the class that is most common among its K nearest neighbors measured by way of a distance function. When K = 1, then the new tuple is definitely assigned to the class of its nearest neighbor.

Extreme Learning Machine (ELM)

Extreme learning machine (Huang, 2006) is a feed forward network with single hidden layer whose hidden layer neurons and the enter weights are randomly selected. The output weights are determined by the use of Moore-Penrose pseudoinverse method so that the output of the network is equal to the goal or desired value. The network is strong and faster because of its low computation. It completely overcomes the hassle of how to do tuning of learning rate, a way to pick wide variety of epochs and tuning of hidden layer that are widespread problems in other conventional neural network techniques. The algorithm is as follows:

1. Let P is the training set,

$$P = \left\{ \left(x_i, y_i \right), x_i \in R^n, y_i \in R^m, i = 1, 2, 3......N \right\}.$$

Activation function is represented as $f(x)$ and number of hidden neurons is NH. Randomly assign the input weights w_i and baises b_i, $i=$ 1 to NH.

2. Compute H, the output matrix of hidden layer.
3. Compute the output weight

$$\beta = H^{-1}Y, where\, Y = [y_1, y_2, ...y_N]^T$$

and H^{-1} is the Moore–Penrose generalized inverse of matrix H.

Development of Customer Churn Prediction (CCP) Model

Churn prediction is normally consisting of four main phases: Data collection, Preprocessing, Feature selection and Classification. Fig. 1 shows the various steps followed in the development of the CCP model. First the data are collected. After normalization of the data the features are selected using Information Gain(IG) feature selection method.

Figure 1. Steps in development of churn prediction model

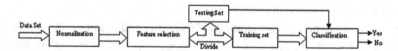

Information Gain Feature Selection

Entropy is generally used inside the facts concept degree, which characterizes the purity of an arbitrary series of examples. It's far in the basis of the IG characteristic ranking strategies. The entropy degree is taken into consideration as a degree of device's unpredictability. The entropy of Y is

$$H(Y) = -\sum_{y \in Y} p(y) \log_2(p(y)) \tag{4}$$

wherein $p(y)$ is the marginal possibility density characteristic for the random variable Y. If the discovered values of Y within the training data set S are partitioned in step with the values of a second function X, and the entropy of Y with appreciate to the partitions induced via X is less than the entropy of Y previous to partitioning, then there is a dating among capabilities Y and X. Then the entropy of Y after looking X is

$$H(Y \ / \ X) = -\sum_{x \in X} p(x) \sum_{y \in Y} p(y \ / \ x) \log_2(p(y \ / \ x)) \qquad (5)$$

wherein $p(y/x)$ is possibility of y given x. Given the entropy as a criterion of impurity in a dataset S, we are capable of outline a degree reflecting extra statistics approximately Y furnished by way of X that represents the quantity by manner of which the entropy of Y decreases. This diploma is known as IG. It is given via

$$IG = H(Y) - H(Y/X) = H(X) - H(X/Y) \qquad (6)$$

IG is a symmetrical degree. The information obtained about Y after watching X is same to the facts obtained about X after looking at Y. A weakness of the IG criterion is that it is miles biased in opt for of functions with more values even if they are not extra informative.

1. **Classification:** An adaptive classifier is designed to predict the churn status of the customers. Fig. 2(a) represents the classifier for churn prediction. For this purpose the chapter has used MLANN, SVM, DT, DA, K-NN, Naïve Bayesian and ELM techniques.

Figure 2. Churn prediction model

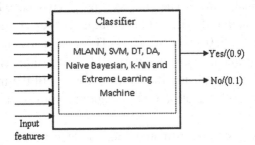

Development of a classifier consists of two phases: 1. Training phase and testing phase. During the training phase the classifier is trained using the past data. Once the classifier is ready then its performance is tested during testing phase. There are various methods of doing this such as holdout method, k-fold cross validation and leave-one-out method etc.

Holdout Method: In this method, the information is randomly divided into two: Training and Test/Validation set. Then the model is trained with the training dataset and examine the model on the Test/Validation dataset. Typically the training dataset is greater than the testing dataset. Typical ratios used for splitting the information set include 60:40, 80:20 etc. In our case we have taken the ratio of 80:20.

The development of a MLANN churn prediction model using holdout method is described below. Figure 3 shows the structure of a feed forward multilayer neural network model with one input, two hidden and one output layers.

Figure 3. Structure of a multilayer neural network model

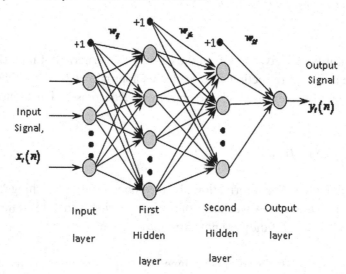

Here a 9:5:1 structure is used as a classifier. The nine input features of training set (2333 tuples) are applied to the feed forward neural network sequentially. The inputs are weighted and summed together at each neuron of the hidden layer. These intermediate outputs are then passed through the activation functions, 'tanh' to give the final outputs. The process is repeated at each layer of the network until the final output at output layer is obtained. The obtained output is then compared with 0.9 if the features belong to 'Yes' class otherwise with 0.1 for 'No' class. This completes one iteration and the iteration is repeated 5000 times. The experiment is repeated until all training samples are applied. The connecting weights and bias weights are updated using the BP algorithm until the mean squared error (MSE) is minimized. The MSE value for each iteration is stored and the convergence characteristics is obtained and shown in the Figure 4.

Once the training process is over the churn prediction model is tested using the testing features(1000 tuples) and accuracy of the classifier is calculated using (7). Similarly the other classifiers are developed using their respective techniques as described in Section II. Same way the k-fold cross validation method can also be used. The details of it are as follows:

k-Fold Cross Validation: Cross-validation is broadly speaking used in applied machine learning to estimate the talent of a system learning model on unseen records. That is, to apply a limited pattern to be able to estimate how the version is anticipated to perform in general while used to make predictions on statistics now not used at some point of the training of the model. The well known system is as follows

1. Shuffle the dataset randomly.
2. Split the dataset into k equal subsets.(k =10 in our case)
3. For every unique subset:

Figure 4. Convergence characteristics of MLANN model

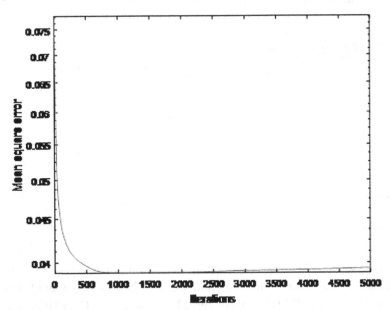

a. Take the subset as a hold out or take a look at records set
b. Take the remaining subsets as a training set
c. Fit a model on the training set and evaluate it on the take a look at set
d. Retain the assessment score and discard the version
4. Summarize the skill of the model using the pattern of version assessment scores

Performance Measures

To examine the class results, the quantity of True Positive (TP), True Negative (TN), False Positive (FP) and False Negative (FN) are counted. The FN price surely belongs to Positive P however is wrongly classified as Negative N, Similarly, FP price is certainly a part of N but wrongly categorized as P. Confusion matrix is a performance dimension for studying classification problem where output may be two or greater classes. It is a table with four exclusive mixtures of predicted and actual values in case of a binary classification problem as shown below in Table 1. The diagonal elements of the below given matrix, TP and TN show the amount of correct prediction for P and N classes respectively.

Table 1. Example of confusion matrix

Actual Values	Predicted Values	
	Positive(P)	Negative(N)
Positive (P)	TP	FP
Negative(N)	FN	TN

The percentage of classification accuracy is calculated as

$$\text{Percentage of Accuracy} = \frac{TP + TN}{P + N} \times 100 \qquad (7)$$

where

TP= true positive

TN = true negative

P= Total positive tuples

N= Total negative tuples

Simulation Study

This chapter uses a data set of 3333 unique customers of telecommunication sector collected from (bigml. com) where 2850customers are Non-churn (No) and 483 are Churn (Yes). Out of this 2333 data (80%) randomly used for training where 85.16% are No and 14.8% are Yes and rest 1000 data are used for testing of the model where 86.3% are No and 13.7% are Yes. The Matlab 2016 is used for the simulation study. The customer churn prediction process is comprised of three main stages: (i)normalization of the data (ii) feature selection and (iii) classification. In this study z-score normalization is used to normalize the data. Feature selection is an important and essential step in order to reduce the computational cost. If the number of features are more then unnecessarily they will increase the computational complexity and computation time. Out of the all features only nine features or attributes are selected based on their high information gain. The nine features are selected referring to (Amin et. al., 2016). Alternatively, these attributes are contributing more in the decision making in comparison to other features. The details of the attributes are given in Table 2. Referring to Figure 2 finally classification is done using various machine learning techniques such as MLANN, SVM, Naïve Bayesian, KNN, DA, DT and ELM. The different parameters used in simulation for the classifiers are given in Table 3. Once the classifiers are ready the testing of the models are done using the testing samples. The confusion matrices for best three models are shown in Table 4. Along with the hold out method, 10-fold cross validation is also carried out and the accuracy obtained are shown in the Table 5.

RESULTS AND DISCUSSION

It is exhibited from Table 5 that out of seven different techniques used for customer churn prediction ELM is giving the best prediction accuracy of 92.10% followed by SVM with polynomial kernel and MLANN with accuracy of 91.33% and 90.4% respectively in holdout method. The ELM is a single hidden layer neural network model which is faster in computation as compared to the MLANN model. Also the ELM is not using BP algorithm to update its weight which is the advantage of it. The minimum accuracy of 85.54% is obtained by using DA method. Rest of the methods are also performing average with an accuracy greater than 85.54%. Same is the observation incase of the 10-fold cross validation with accuracy of 92.09%, 91.37% and 90.64% for ELM, SVM(Polynomial) and MLANN models. On the basis of their performance the models can be ranked and suggested for practical use in telecommunication industries for CCP. The rank of ELM based prediction model is one. The SVM with polynomial kernel is at number two and the third rank is occupied by MLANN based CCP model.

CONCLUSION

The customer churn prediction is an important research topic for various business organizations as churn of their consumers have direct impact on the revenue of the enterprise. In recent past various machine learning algorithms are used by the researchers to find out a CCP model which will help the managers to know apriori about the probably customers whole are likely to churn. This chapter has collected 3333 telecom data and develop CCP models using seven different ML techniques. First the data are normalized, then feature selection is done to reduce the number of features based on maximum information gain. Finally classification is carried out. Out of all seven methods used ELM based prediction model outperformed all other models with an accuracy of 92.10%. The SVM with polynomial kernel based model is in second rank with accuracy of 91.33% and MLANN is at 3rd position with 90.4% of accuracy. Similar observation is noted for the 10-fold cross validation method. In future the CCP models can also be developed using convolution neural network, deep learning and other recent technology.

Table 2. Selected attributes on the basis of their Information gain

Sl. No.	Name of Attribute	Description	Different Counts	Minimum Value	Maximum Value
1	Voicemail_Message	Number of voice mail messages done by the customer	46	0	51
2	Day_minutes	Total number of minutes that a customer has used in daytime	1667	0	350.8
3	Day_charges	Call charges for total day time	1667	0	59.64
4	Evening_minutes	Total number of minutes that a customer has used at evening time	1611	0	363.7
5	Evening_charges	Call charges for total evening time	1440	0	30.91
6	International_minutes	Total number of minutes used during international calls	162	0	20
7	International_calls	Total number of calls used as international calls	21	0	20
8	International_charges	Charges for total amount of international calls	162	0	5.4
9	Customer_service_calls	Total number of calls made by a customer to customer service	10	0	9

(Amin et. al., 2016)

Table 3. Parameters of the classifiers used in simulation

Sl. No.	Technique Used	Parameters
1	MLANN	9:5:1 structure Learning parameter mu=0.001 Total no. of iterations:5000 No. of independent run=20
2	SVM	Kernel: RBF, Polynomial, Linear
3	K-NN	K=5, Euclidean distance
4	DA	Linear Discriminant
5	DT	----
6	Naïve Bayesian	Distribution: Normal
7	ELM	No. of neurons =100 in hidden layer

Table 4a. Confusion Matrices obtained for hold out method during testing: ELM based classifier

Actual Values	Predicted Values	
	Yes	No
137 (Yes)	127	10
863(No)	69	794
Total = 1000		

Table 4b. Confusion Matrices obtained for hold out method during testing: SVM(Polynomial) based classifier

Actual Values	Predicted Values	
	Yes	No
137 (Yes)	124	13
863(No)	74	789
Total = 1000		

Table 4c. Confusion Matrices obtained for hold out method during testing: ELM based classifier

Actual Values	Predicted Values	
	Yes	No
137 (Yes)	124	13
863(No)	83	780
Total = 1000		

Table 5. Comparison of accuracy obtained by different prediction models

Sl. No.	Type of Churn Prediction Models	Accuracy Obtained Using Holdout Method	Accuracy Obtained Using 10-Fold Cross Validation Method	Rank of Models
1.	MLANN	**90.4%**	**90.64%**	**3**
2.	SVM(Linear)	85.90%	85.94%	8
	SVM(RBF kernel)	88.93%	88.97%	6
	SVM(Polynomial kernel)	**91.33%**	**91.37%**	**2**
3.	KNN	89.80%	89.82%	4
4	DA	85.54%	85.65%	9
5	Naïve Bayesian	87.73%	87.83%	7
6	DT	89.47%	89.60%	5
7	ELM	**92.10%**	**92.09%**	**1**

REFERENCES

Amin, A., Al-Obeidat, F., Shah, B., Adnan, A., Loo, J., & Anwar, S. (2018). Customer churn prediction in telecommunication industry using data certainty. *Journal of Business Research*, *94*, 290–301. doi:10.1016/j.jbusres.2018.03.003

Amin, A., Anwar, S., Adnan, A., Nawaz, M., Alawfi, K., Hussain, A., & Huang, K. (2016). Customer Churn Prediction in Telecommunication Sector using Rough Set Approach. *Neurocomputing*. doi:10.1016/j.neucom.2016.12.009

Amin, A. & Singh, S. (1998). Recognition of handwritten-printed Chinese characters using decision trees/machine learning C4.5 system. *Pattern recognition and Applications, 1*, 130-141.

Athanassopoulos, A. D. (2000). Customer satisfaction cues to support market segmentation and explain 634 switching behavior. *Journal of Business Research*, *47*(3), 191–207. doi:10.1016/S0148-2963(98)00060-5

Dornaika, F., & Khoder, A. (2020). Linear embedding by joint robust Discriminant Analysis and Interclass Sparsity. *Neural Networks*, *127*, 141–159. doi:10.1016/j.neunet.2020.04.018 PMID:32361379

Farquad, M., Ravi, V., & Raju, S. B. (2014). Churn prediction using comprehensible support vector machine: An analytical crm application. *Applied Soft Computing*, *19*, 31–40. doi:10.1016/j.asoc.2014.01.031

Ganesh, J., Arnold, M. J., & Reynolds, K. E. (2000). Understanding the customer base of service providers: An examination of the differences between switchers and stayers. *Journal of Marketing*, *64*(3), 65–87. doi:10.1509/jmkg.64.3.65.18028

Han & Kamber. (2012). *Data Mining, Concepts and techniques* (3rd ed.). Elsevier.

Haykin, S. (2016). *Neural networks and learning machines* (3rd ed.). Pearson Education.

Höppner, S., Stripling, E., Baesens, B., Broucke, S. V., & Verdonck, T. (2018). Profit driven decision trees for churn prediction. *European Journal of Operational Research*. doi:10.1016/j.ejor.2018.11.072

Huang, G. B., Zhu, Q. Y., & Siew, C. K. (2006). Extreme learning machine: Theory and applications. *Neurocomputing, 70*(1-3), 489–501. doi:10.1016/j.neucom.2005.12.126

Maldonado, S., L'opez, J., & Vairetti, C. (2019). Profit-based churn prediction based on Minimax Probability Machines. *European Journal of Operational Research*. doi:10.1016/j.ejor.2019.12.007

Mitra, S. & Acharya, T. (2004). *Data Mining Multimedia, Soft computing and Bioinformatics*. John Wiley & Sons, Inc.

Mitrovi, S., Baesens, B., & Lemahieu, W. (2019). tcc2vec: RFM-informed representation learning on call graphs for churn prediction. *Information Sciences*. doi:10.1016/j.ins.2019.02.044

Óskarsdóttira, M., Bravob, C., Verbekec, W., Sarrauted, C., Baesensa, B., & Vanthienena, J. (2017). Social Network Analytics for Churn Prediction in Telco: Model Building, Evaluation and Network Architecture. *Expert Systems with Applications*. doi:10.1016/j.eswa.2017.05.028

Shirazi, F., & Mohammadi, M. A big data analytics model for customer churn prediction in the retiree segment. *International Journal of Information Management*. doi:10.1016/j.ijinfomgt.2018.10.005

Stripling, E., Broucke, S. V., Antonio, K., Baesens, B., & Snoeck, M. (2018). Profit maximizing logistic model for customer churn prediction using genetic algorithms. *Swarm and Evolutionary Computation, 40*, 116–130. doi:10.1016/j.swevo.2017.10.010

Chapter 16
Efficient Software Reliability Prediction With Evolutionary Virtual Data Position Exploration

Ajit Kumar Behera

Department of Computer Science and Application, Utkal University, India & Silicon Institute of Technology, Bhubaneswar, India

Mrutyunjaya Panda

Department of Computer Science and Application, Utkal University, India

ABSTRACT

Determining appropriate software reliability prediction technique is a challenging task for the software development process. So, it is essential for software engineers to develop good quality software product. Though several prediction models are in use for small size data, the estimation of the reliability of software system is crucial. Inadequate data may lead sub-optimal solution. This chapter proposes a technique of increasing training dataset by generating virtual data points original data. For improving the prediction of cumulative failure time in software, multilayer perceptron (MLP)-based virtual data positions (DEVDP) exploration techniques have been proposed. The parameters of the network are optimized by evolutionary algorithm differential evolution (DE). For validation of the model in presence of virtual data point (VDP), eight failure datasets from different sources has been used. The results obtained from the simulation studies indicate that proposed DEVDP exploration technique outperformed traditional models.

INTRODUCTION

The problem of software reliability forecasting is an interesting and challenging activity for software industry, researchers including stakeholders. Unreliable software may cause system failures, subsequently which causes economic loss, loss of life, customer's dissatisfaction. So, it is indispensible for software

DOI: 10.4018/978-1-7998-6659-6.ch016

engineers to emerge good quality software product. Software reliability generally measured as likelihood of failure free operation in particular instant under specified condition. For software failure prediction, the existing software reliability model is classified as parametric and non-parametric models. Usually, parametric models depend on some basic assumptions like development process, failure behavior, and development organization of software. Due to model inconsistency in parametric model, non-parametric are quite popular that are based on failure history of software rather than basic assumptions. The fundamental approach of non-parametric model is to predict future behavior based on past failure data. Normally, non-parametric models employs NN, SVM, fuzzy inference system (FIS), genetic algorithm (GA) for software reliability prediction (Musa, 2004; Amin et al., 2013; Rana et al., 2014). For predicting software reliability, software practitioner and researchers have applied many ANN based hybrid techniques found that these models have better prediction capability than parametric models (Lakshmanan et al., 2015). The parameters of ANN are trained using back propagation method (Jaiswal et al., 2018; Wang et al., 2018). Using back propagation algorithm many non-linear problems are solved, but it ensnared with local minima and suffers slow convergence rate.

Several other training methods such as differential evolution (DE), chemical reaction optimization (CRO), particle swarm optimization (PSO), harmonic search (HM), bat inspired algorithm (BA), bee colony optimization (BCO) have been developed over the last two decades (Kaswan et al., 2015). Malhotra and Negi (2015) designed a software reliability growth framework where the parameters are optimized by PSO. Roy et al. (2015) used a neuro-genetic model, where the parameters of ANN are globally optimized by GA. For improving the predictive capability, Behera et al. (2019) designed a single layer FLANN model with CRO and found better performance than traditional models. Kapil Juneja proposed a neuro-fuzzy frame work to identify the software faults in a project (Juneja, 2019). This generates a footpath for selecting an optimization method that needs less learning parameters without negotiating the prediction capability. DE has been used to solve many problems like data mining, stock marketing, classification, and neural network training.

Though NN models are better than traditional models, it requires enough data for proper training. For generalization of the NN model it requires sufficient data for training. Inadequate data may lead sub-optimal solution. Practically, adequate training pattern is always not available in all situations. Particularly in case of software testing the researchers may not get sufficient failure data. Also there may not be close relationship exists between the failure data because of the hidden defects in software. Recently some research has been attempted for increasing the training pattern by supporting some stochastic and evolutionary approach for prediction problem. In this chapter virtual data exploration method for enriching training data points is suggested. Besides existing data points, exploration of close data points improves the prediction accuracy remarkably. To enhance the learning capacity of ANN model on small size sample, many alternative methods appear, such as semi-supervised learning, active learning and support vector machine. Nowadays, the virtual sample generation approach is one of importance concept improve the generalization ability of NN learning on small size data. A virtual data position (VDP) is a probable value between two consecutive data points. The main focus is to enhance the predictive capability of the model by enriching the training patterns through evolutionary technique (Nayak et al. 2019). In this approach VDPs are estimated by an evolutionary method DE. Then the accumulated data is used in DE based MLP model for prediction of cumulative failures in software.

The foremost features of this chapter are outlined as:

1. For enriching the data set DEVDP approach is used.

2. ANN-DE model is presented for prediction of cumulative failure time where successive failure times are taken as input and cumulative failure time will be the output in the proposed framework.
3. The presented method is used on multiple data and found to be a better predictive approach that provides increased prediction accuracy.

The remainder of this chapter organized as in the following sections. Section 2 describes basic of software reliability prediction. Section 3 describes differential evolution algorithm in details. The proposed software reliability prediction methodology is discussed in Section 4. The existing VDP exploration scheme and DEVDP exploration method is discussed in Section 5. The simulation results and detail analysis are conferred in Section 6. Finally, Section 7 concludes the chapter followed references.

Basics of Software Reliability Prediction

In software industry, it is essential to develop reliable software with certain quality, within budget and time constraints. Insufficient knowledge about the nature of software makes very difficult to quantify certain level of reliability. Software reliability quantifies software failures, so it is desirable to have reliable software that is employed to forecast failures data. Usually software reliability assessment involves two activities namely, estimation and prediction. Software reliability estimation refers to current reliability assessment by means of the failure data during system testing. Software reliability prediction refers future failure forecasting based on recent and past failure data. In both cases, the reliability techniques are used on the collected data and assessment of reliability is carried out using statistical inference method. Software reliability models have been successfully employed for estimation and prediction of software failures that illustrates the software failure behavior.

Prediction of time between failures and cumulative failures time assist software engineers to decide the release time of software product. It is expected that, initially there is a high rate of failures per time unit and a low rate of failures at the end, after correcting the errors. After testing the software for certain period of time, if the number of failures is found stable then software practitioner stops testing and release the software product. The delivery time of the software will be decided by a long mean time to failure. This chapter presents a novel hybrid model to predict the cumulative failure time in software.

Differential Evolution Algorithm (DEA)

Differential Evolution (DE) is a meta-heuristic optimization technique that operates on real valued vectors (Dash et al., 2015). The basic operators of GA such as crossover, mutation, and selection are used in DE. However the solution vector is found on the weighted difference between two randomly chosen vectors of the recent population. During the evolving process DE uses some specific parameters like size of the population n_p, crossover probability Cr, and scaling parameter f_m. The objective function is described as:

$$Obj = \frac{1}{N} \sum_{k=1}^{N} \left(d(k) - y(k) \right)^2 \qquad (1)$$

where, N is the number of training patterns, d(k) is the anticipated value y(k) is the real value.

Algorithm: Differential Evolution (DE)

1. INITIALIZATION: *Generate a population of* n_p $x_i^{(k)} = \left\langle x_{i1}^{(k)}, x_{i2}^{(k)}, ..., x_{id}^{(k)} \right\rangle$

2. Do

3. *For every individual population i*

4. MUTATION: *Induce a donor vector as* $dv_i^{(k+1)} = x_{r1}^{(k)} + m_f * \left(x_{r2}^{(k)} - x_{r3}^{(k)} \right)$,

where m_f *is the mutation factor, the indices* r_1, r_2 *and* r_3 *are selected randomly such as* $r_1 r_2 r_3 \neq i$.

5. CROSSOVER: *Generate a trial vector as*

$$tv_{ij}^{(k+1)} = \begin{cases} dv_{ij}^{(k+1)} \; if \, (rand \leq c_r) \; or \; (i = rand(1,2,..,d)) \\ x_{ij}^{(k)} \; if \, (rand > c_r) \; and \, (i \neq rand(1,2,..,d)) \end{cases}$$

6. SELECTION: *Evaluate the trial vector as*

$$x_i^{(k+1)} = \begin{cases} tv_i^{(k+1)} \; if \; f(x_i^{(k+1)}) \leq f(x_i^{(k)}) \\ x_i^{(k)} \qquad otherwise. \end{cases}$$

7. End For

8. While (*Termination Criterion Met*)

MODEL AND METHODOLOGIES

An intelligent system is proposed here for prediction of cumulative failure time in software. An MLP is used as the base model and for tuning of the parameters, differential evolution has been adopted. The framework of the DE based ANN model is described in Fig. 1.

Figure 1. DE based MLP forecasting model

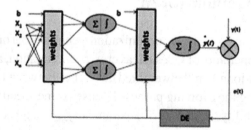

In the evolutionary ANN model, multiple delayed input and single output architecture has been adopted here. In this modeling, up to the kth cumulative failure time $\left\langle x_1, x_2, ..., x_k \right\rangle$ is taken as input to forecast x_{k+1} cumulative failure time.

For each neuron j in the hidden layer the output z is computed as:

$$z_j = f\left(B_j + \sum_{i=1}^{k} v_{ij} * X_i\right) \tag{1}$$

where, X_i is the input vector, v_{ij} is the synaptic weight between and $f(\bullet)$ is the activation function used to address non-linearity nature of software process. For single output y is calculated using linear activation function as:

$$\hat{y} = f\left(B_0 + \sum_{j=1}^{m} W_j * z_i\right) \tag{2}$$

where, W_j is connecting weight between hidden neuron and output neuron, B_0 signifies the output bias.

The predicted value of the cumulative failure time is compared with actual value to generate error signal. The MLP model is trained on the basis of populated error. The optimal weights and bias of MLP are adjusted by DE to minimize the error signal which subsequently minimizes the cumulative failures time. The algorithm of ANN-DE training for estimating the cumulative software failures is described below:

Algorithm: ANN-DE Training

```
1.         Initialize  a set of individual search space
2.         Setting Training and Test data, i.e selecting cumulative failure
times as input
3.         Normalization of  data
/*Training phase */
4.         While (termination criteria not met)
For every individual of the population
                           Compute the weighted sum at hidden unit
Compute the estimated output and error signal
Compute the fitness value from the error signal
                   End for
                   Apply DE
                   Update the search space
         End while
    /*Testing phase*/
5.         Setting the Testing input vector and optimal structure of  the model
6.         Repeat the steps 2-5 for patterns in the dataset.
7.         Calculate accuracy by computing the errors of the cumulative fail-
ures
```

The ANN-DE model is used to forecast the cumulative failure time in software where VDP method is adopted to enrich the existing data. These VDPs are calculated by DE termed as DEVDP and the network is trained by same model. The details of the DEVDP are discussed in section 5.

VDP Exploration Techniques

In general, the past software failure data is used forecast the future cumulative failure time. But the predictive performance of a model does not improve significantly for small size data set. It is observed that, virtual data can be generated between existing data position which subsequently helps in enhancing the prediction accuracy (Behera et al., 2019). Different methods were applied for exploration of virtual data points from the original data. Software reliability prediction has only one dependent variable without any explanatory variables, so a time series forecasting model is used. The cumulative failure time of software can be represented as time series $x_1, x_2, x_3, \ldots, x_t$, where x_i is accumulated failure time up to i^{th} failure. The objective of this process is to estimate the next cumulative failure time based on the current and past cumulative failure time which is represented by $X_t = f(x_{t-1}, x_{t-2}, \ldots, x_{t-p})$, where X_t is the cumulative failure time for the predicting model using the approximation function f. In this section the existing VDP techniques and proposed DEVDP techniques are discussed in details.

Existing VDP Exploration Techniques

Since general time series prediction model is used in software failure data, the training pattern of the neural network is represented as follows:

$$
\begin{array}{ccccccc}
x_1 & x_2 & \cdots & x_p & \vdots & x_{p+1} \\
x_2 & x_3 & \cdots & x_{p+1} & \vdots & x_{p+2} \\
\cdots & \cdots & \cdots & \cdots & \vdots & \cdots \\
x_{t-p} & x_{t-p+1} & \cdots & x_{t-1} & \vdots & x_t
\end{array}
$$

Where, n represents the total number data point. After introducing the virtual data to the existing failure data, the training examples is enriched over the data set are presented below.

$$
\begin{array}{ccccccc}
x_1 & x_{1.5} & x_2 & \cdots & x_p & \vdots & x_{p+1} \\
x_2 & x_{2.5} & x_3 & \cdots & x_{p+1} & \vdots & x_{p+2} \\
\cdots & \cdots & \cdots & \cdots & \cdots & \vdots & \cdots \\
x_{t-p} & x_{t-p+1} & x_{t-p+2} & \cdots & x_{t-p} & \vdots & x_t
\end{array}
$$

The next section describes the evolutionary based virtual data point exploration approach in details. Different interpolation approaches are used to generate virtual data positions from original failure data in software. There are three categories of VDP exploration schemes are described in literature namely: i) deterministic method, ii) stochastic method and iii) evolutionary method. In the proposed work an evolutionary method for exploration of virtual data position has been adopted, which is the novelty of this work.

Differential Evolution Based Virtual Data Position (DEVDP) Exploration and Forecasting

This section describes the detail process of virtual data generation by deferential evolution based neural network. For proper understanding of DEVDP approach, an example given below.

In general, without virtual points, the training data with length 3 is:

$$
\begin{array}{ccccc}
& X & & & Y \\
x_i & x_{i+1} & x_{i+2} & \vdots & x_{i+3} \\
x_{i+1} & x_{i+2} & x_{i+3} & \vdots & x_{i+4} \\
x_{i+2} & x_{i+3} & x_{i+4} & \vdots & x_{i+5}
\end{array}
$$

and the respective test data is

$$
\begin{array}{cccc}
X & & & Y \\
x_{i+3} & x_{i+4} & x_{i+5} & \vdots & x_{i+6}
\end{array}
$$

The VDPs are include into the training and testing patterns as follows:

$$
\begin{array}{ccccccc}
& & & X & & & Y \\
x_i & x_{i+0.5} & x_{i+1} & x_{i+1.5} & x_{i+2} & x_{i+2.5} & \vdots & x_{i+3} \\
x_{i+0.5} & x_{i+1} & x_{i+1.5} & x_{i+2} & x_{i+2.5} & x_{i+3} & \vdots & x_{i+3.5} \\
x_{i+1} & x_{i+1.5} & x_{i+2} & x_{i+2.5} & x_{i+3} & x_{i+3.5} & \vdots & x_{i+4} \\
x_{i+1.5} & x_{i+2} & x_{i+2.5} & x_{i+3} & x_{i+3.5} & x_{i+4} & \vdots & x_{i+4.5} \\
x_{i+2} & x_{i+2.5} & x_{i+3} & x_{i+3.5} & x_{i+4} & x_{i+4.5} & \vdots & x_{i+5}
\end{array}
$$

Data for exploration EVDP to be explored

$$
x_{i+2.5} \quad x_{i+3} \quad x_{i+3.5} \quad x_{i+4} \quad x_{i+4.5} \quad x_{i+5} \quad \vdots \quad x_{i+5.5}
$$

As explained above, the original data are supplied to the ANNDE model where it estimates the output. The artificial data thus generated is used as the virtual data for the subsequent training data. In the proposed model, for exploration of virtual data is used as well as for prediction of cumulative failures in software DEVDP technique is used. Here, VDP are calculated by the help of ANNDE. The actual output is presented, which is compared with estimated value to calculate the error value which is conserved for evaluating the performance of the proposed model.

Experimental Results

The proposed DEVDP scheme is used on eight data sets for performance evaluation. This section describes the data collection and processing, evaluation criteria and comparison results of the proposed method.

Data Collection and Preprocessing

For experimental work, eight failure data sets namely DS1, DS2, DS3, DS4, DS5, DS6, DS7, DS8 are used which is summarized in Table1 (Bisi & Goyol, 2015). The data sets are collected during system testing phase from various projects developed by different teams, skills, different environment and OS/Languages. Statistical models generally use these parameters for reliability estimation. As ANN has been focused during testing phase in this chapter, software failure data for reliability prediction are used. After creating the model the experimentation is conducted by distributing the data sets in 70:30 ratio for training and testing respectively. The MLP neural network is implemented using *MATLAB* 9.7 platform.

Table 1. Data sets used

Dataset Used	Errors Detected	Software Type
DS1	38	Military System
DS2	136	Real time Command and Control
DS3	46	On-line Data entry
DS4	27	Class Compiler Project
DS5	100	Tendem Computer Release
DS6	198	Electronic switching system
DS7	198	Wireless Network Product
DS8	198	Bug Tracking System

The predictive capability of the model is measured using MAPE and compared with NLE and ANN-PSO. The MAPE values of different datasets using DEVDP approach are shown in Table 2. MAPE values of DEVDP are found to be better than NLE and ANN-PSO for all datasets.

Evaluation Criteria

The impact of DEVDP on prediction of software failure is experimented using eight software datasets from different sources. For this experiment, vector of lagged variable has been used. To determine the performance measures, three performance measures have been used to estimate the prediction performance of the proposed method. They are mean absolute percentage error (MAPE), root mean square error (RMSE), relative root mean square error (RRMS).

$$MAPE = \frac{1}{n} \sum\nolimits_{i=1}^{n} abs\left((y_i' - y_i) / y_i \right) \tag{3}$$

$$RMSE = \sqrt{\frac{1}{n}\sum_{i=1}^{n}\left(y_i' - y_i\right)^2} \qquad (4)$$

$$RRMS = RMSE \bigg/ \frac{1}{n}\sum_{i=1}^{k} y_i \qquad (5)$$

where, y_i is the actual output and y_i' is the speculated output of ANN.

Comparison Results

In order to compare the performance of the proposed DEVDP approach with NLE and ANN-PSO, MAPE on DS-DS8 data sets is used which is shown in Table 2.

Table 2. Comparison of MAPE for different dataset

Data Set	NLE	ANN-PSO	DEVDP
DS1	6.52	5.72	5.18
DS2	9.08	6.54	5.74
DS3	3.83	2.51	2.12
DS4	6.31	4.75	3.95
DS5	7.89	3.45	2.88
DS6	1.49	1.45	1.33
DS7	3.19	1.57	1.26
DS8	5.18	4.18	3.55

The last three data sets (DS6, DS7, DS8) are used for prediction. The predictive ability of the proposed models in terms of RMSE and RRMS are shown in Table 3.

Table 3. Comparison of RMSE

Models	DS6		DS7		DS8	
	RMSE	RRMS	RMSE	RRMS	RMSE	RRMS
G-O	9.99	0.03	8.74	0.06	4.32	0.04
Yamada DSS	20.40	0.06	3.96	0.03	7.91	0.08
Goel NHPP	9.16	0.03	3.32	0.02	4.28	0.04
ANN-PSO	8.24	0.02	2.31	0.02	1.43	0.01
DEVDP	7.45	0.02	1.78	0.01	1.22	0.01

In case of ANN model, the performance of the model is heavily depends upon the amount of failure data used for training. As the training data increases in the DEVDP approach, the proposed technique has better RMSE and RRMS values than other models. As the RRMS value is less than 0.25 in our proposed DEVDP model is quite acceptable. The proposed DEVDP offers better RRMS for DS6, DS7, DS8 sets used for the performance evaluation.

CONCLUSION

Improving software reliability prediction accuracy with small size failure data is very important because the predictability of a model varies with the data sample. Different exploration techniques are used for generating virtual data that enhance the prediction accuracy. The DEVDP exploration techniques for generating artificial training samples have been used. Using the above method it could be able to record the intermediate data positions lead enhanced prediction capability of the model. For prediction of cumulative failure time, same DEVDP modeling approach is proposed. Differential evolution is used to optimize the MLP neural network. For this experiment eight different software reliability datasets are considered from different sources. The proposed model is assessed using three performance measures such as MAPE, RMSE and RRMS. From the performance metrics, it is established that proposed DEVDP exploration method reducing the prediction error to a substantial extent.

REFERENCES

Amin, A., Grunske, L., & Colman, A. (2013). An approach to software reliability prediction based on time series modeling. *Journal of Systems and Software*, *86*(7), 1923–1932. doi:10.1016/j.jss.2013.03.045

Behera, A. K., Nayak, S. C., Dash, C. S. K., Dehuri, S., & Panda, M. (2019). Improving software reliability prediction accuracy using CRO-based FLANN. In *Innovations in Computer Science and Engineering* (pp. 213–220). Singapore: Springer. doi:10.1007/978-981-10-8201-6_24

Behera, A. K., & Panda, M. (2019, December). Software Reliability Prediction with Ensemble Method and Virtual Data Point Incorporation. In *International Conference on Biologically Inspired Techniques in Many-Criteria Decision Making* (pp. 69-77). Springer.

Bisi, M., & Goyal, N. K. (2015, January). Predicting cumulative number of failures in software using an ANN-PSO based approach. In *2015 International Conference on Computational Intelligence and Networks* (pp. 9-14). IEEE. 10.1109/CINE.2015.12

Dash, C. S. K., Behera, A. K., Dehuri, S., Cho, S. B., & Wang, G. N. (2015). Towards crafting an improved functional link artificial neural network based on differential evolution and feature selection. *Informatica*, *39*(2).

Jaiswal, A., & Malhotra, R. (2018). Software reliability prediction using machine learning techniques. *International Journal of System Assurance Engineering and Management*, *9*(1), 230–244.

Juneja, K. (2019). A fuzzy-filtered neuro-fuzzy framework for software fault prediction for inter-version and inter-project evaluation. *Applied Soft Computing*, *77*, 696–713. doi:10.1016/j.asoc.2019.02.008

Kaswan, K. S., Choudhary, S., & Sharma, K. (2015). Software reliability modeling using soft computing techniques: Critical review. *Journal of Information Technology and Software Engineering*, *5*, 144.

Lakshmanan, I., & Ramasamy, S. (2015). An artificial neural-network approach to software reliability growth modeling. *Procedia Computer Science*, *57*, 695–702. doi:10.1016/j.procs.2015.07.450

Malhotra, R., & Negi, A. (2013). Reliability modeling using particle swarm optimization. *International Journal of System Assurance Engineering and Management*, *4*(3), 275–283.

Musa, J. D. (2004). *Software reliability engineering: more reliable software, faster and cheaper*. Tata McGraw-Hill Education.

Nayak, S. C., Misra, B. B., & Behera, H. S. (2019). Efficient financial time series prediction with evolutionary virtual data position exploration. *Neural Computing & Applications*, *31*(2), 1053–1074. doi:10.100700521-017-3061-1

Rana, R., Staron, M., Berger, C., Hansson, J., Nilsson, M., Törner, F., & Höglund, C. (2014). Selecting software reliability growth models and improving their predictive accuracy using historical projects data. *Journal of Systems and Software*, *98*, 59–78. doi:10.1016/j.jss.2014.08.033

Roy, P., Mahapatra, G. S., & Dey, K. N. (2015). Neuro-genetic approach on logistic model based software reliability prediction. *Expert Systems with Applications*, *42*(10), 4709–4718. doi:10.1016/j.eswa.2015.01.043

Wang, J., & Zhang, C. (2018). Software reliability prediction using a deep learning model based on the RNN encoder–decoder. *Reliability Engineering & System Safety*, *170*, 73–82. doi:10.1016/j.ress.2017.10.019

Chapter 17
Secure Chaotic Image Encryption Based on Multi-Point Row-Column-Crossover Operation

K. Abhimanyu Kumar Patro

National Institute of Technology, Raipur, India

Mukesh Drolia

National Institute of Technology, Raipur, India

Akash Deep Yadav

National Institute of Technology, Raipur, India

Bibhudendra Acharya

National Institute of Technology, Raipur, India

ABSTRACT

In this present era, where everything is getting digitalized, information or data in any form, important to an organization or individual, are at a greater risk of being attacked under acts, commonly known as cyber-attack. Hence, a proper and more efficient cryptosystem is the prime need of the hour to secure the data (especially the image data). This chapter proposes an efficient multi-point crossover operation-based chaotic image encryption system to secure images. The multi-point crossover operation is performed on both the rows and columns of bit-planes in the images. The improved one-dimensional chaotic maps are then used to perform pixel-permutation and diffusion operations. The main advantage of this technique is the use of multi-point crossover operation in bit-levels. The multi-point crossover operation not only increases the security of cipher images but also increases the key space of the algorithm. The outcomes and analyses of various parameters show the best performance of the algorithm in image encryption and different common attacks.

DOI: 10.4018/978-1-7998-6659-6.ch017

INTRODUCTION

In today's information age, the two parties communicate large amounts of multimedia information (particularly images). However, the rapid growth of emerging technologies and developments has made the securities of multimedia information quite vulnerable. Hence, it becomes very necessary to keep such information secure, which otherwise could result in a big loss. In the preliminary research method, scientists have developed numerous traditional image encryption techniques to encrypt images such as RSA, AES, and DES (Coppersmith, 1994; Pub, 2001). The traditional methods are not sufficiently effective for encrypting images, due to the large data requirement and the strong association of neighboring pixels in an image (Gao, Zhang, Liang, & Li, 2006; Samhita, Prasad, Patro, & Acharya, 2016). To address this issue, it is necessary to concentrate on methods that satisfy the need for diffusion and confusion in the encryption process (Zhang & Liu, 2011). Confusion is a cryptographic technique which is intended to increase plaintext vagueness. The technique ensures no indication of the plaintext is given in the ciphertext. The relation between ciphertext statistics and the value of the encryption key is retained as complex as possible in the confusion technique. The confusion can be achieved by using the complex method of permutation or scrambling depending on the key and the plaintext. On the other hand, diffusion is a cryptographic technique developed to enhance the plaintext redundancy in order to conceal the plaintext's statistical structure to protect efforts to reproduce the key.

Chaos-based encryption algorithms have gained much interest in recent years from a large number of researches. There are many essential attributes in chaos systems, such as non-periodicity, ergodicity, randomness, vulnerability to initial values. Despite of these features, the image encryption method based on the chaos principle is found to be more robust and appropriate for strong-security encryption (Guesmi, Farah, Kachouri, & Samet, 2016a, 2016b; Patro & Acharya, 2019a). In general, this method of encryption involves two stages: permutation and diffusion (Wang, Chen, & Wang, 2010; Zhang, Li, Wong, Shu, & Chen, 2012). With the support of chaotic maps, the location of the pixels is modified in the permutation step, where the pixel values are modified with the assistance of chaotic maps as in the diffusion step. Having both permutation and diffusion together is a must for high protection, and this was the research's effort when conducting encryption.

Basically, in the encryption of images, two types of chaotic maps are used like chaotic maps having high-dimensional and chaotic maps having one-dimensional (1D) (Liu, Sun, & Zhu, 2016; Patro, Acharya, & Nath, 2019b). In the encryption of images, 1D maps are appropriate to use because it have simplicity, high-efficiency, limited hardware resources requirement, etc., but they suffer from the problem of small key space (Özkaynak & Özer, 2016; Wang, Wang, Zhang, & Guo, 2017). To avoid this problem, the use of multiple 1D maps in image encryption is suggested. The combination of multiple 1D maps provide large key space to the algorithm. At present, most of the chaotic encryption algorithms are easy to be attacked by exhaustive attack (small key space); hence, the algorithm needs to be given large key space.

At the other hand, due to its simple implementation the genetic algorithm has gained popularity and interest in many recent researches. It is always found to give satisfactory outcomes with high fitness and improved security to images and data (Wang & Xu, 2014). The genetic crossover operation could be one-point, two-point or multi-point as per the requirement upon implementation. Though it has many advantages but it has its own limitations such as it does not go well when large number elements get exposed to mutation and also it increases the search size exponentially. Even though it has limitations, it is still one of the most used image encryption technique.

Based on the above discussions, the objectives of this chapter are as follows.

- **High-Security Encryption:** Chaotic system based image encryption provides reliable and high-security encryption.
- **Permutation and Diffusion:** Combination of permutation and diffusion provides more security to the encryption algorithm.
- **One-Dimensional Chaotic Maps:** The several features of 1D maps make the algorithm software and hardware efficient.
- **Large Key Space:** Multiple 1D maps give the algorithm sufficient key space to withstand brute-force attack.
- **Improved Security:** The multi-point genetic crossover operation provides satisfactory outcomes and improved security to images.

BACKGROUND

1D chaotic maps make the encryption algorithm efficient both in software and hardware implementation. On the other hand, multiples of 1D maps not only make the algorithm effective but also serve as high resistance to brute-force attack. The higher the key space, the stronger is the resistance to brute-force attack. Besides this, the use of the algorithm's combined permutation and diffusion operations makes it more secure. Many researchers have been used multiple 1D maps in image encryptions to perform the combined permutation and diffusion operations.

El-Latif et al. (2012) discussed a multiple 1D map based image encryption scheme in their research. The multiple 1D maps used in their research are Sine, Cubic, Tent, and Logistic. In this scheme, the multiple chaotic systems along with the cryptographic primitive operations increase key space and security of the algorithm. The security includes almost ideal value of entropy, weak correlation of adjacent pixels in cipher images, fairly uniform distribution of grayscale values in cipher images. But chaotic maps used in this algorithm have limited data range [0,1].

So, to improve the chaotic properties, Wu et al. (2015) discussed a color image encryption approach in their research using DNA and multiple improved 1D maps. In this algorithm, three new improved 1D maps such as Tent-Sine system (TSS), Logistic-Tent system (LTS), and Logistic-Sine system (LSS) are used to perform the permutation-diffusion operation. These are the combination of three seed maps such as Tent, Sine, and Logistic map. This algorithm provides high security but the use of DNA decreases the encryption speed of the algorithm. In DNA, the added processes like DNA-decoding and encoding decrease the encryption speed of the algorithm.

Ahmad et al. (2017) discussed a hash function scheme in their research. In this scheme, the multiple 1D maps such as Logistic, Tent, Skew-Tent, Cubic, Chirikov, and Baker are used to generate efficient hash functions. The chaotic maps used in this research also have limited data range [0,1].

MAIN FOCUS OF THE CHAPTER

Multiple Improved One-dimensional Chaotic Maps

1D maps used to encrypt images have restricted chaotic range and non-uniform output sequence distribution. So, improved 1D maps are required in image encryptions to perform permutation and diffusion operations. LSS, LTS, and TSS are the improved 1D maps, which have chaotic range in [0,4] and uniform distribution of output sequence [0,1]. This chapter also uses improved 1D maps such as LSS and TSS in image encryption technique.

Multi-point Genetic Crossover Operation

Multi-point genetic crossover operation gives satisfactory outcomes with improved security to images. It also provides high key space to the algorithm. Due to these properties, in this chapter, the proposed algorithm uses multi-point crossover operations to perform row and column permutations.

PRELIMINARIES OF THE CHAPTER

Tent-Sine System (TSS)

Through combining two different 1D chaotic maps like Sine and Tent, the TSS map is derived from this. The resulting 1D chaotic system with improved function of distribution of uniform density variants is claimed to show outstanding chaotic features. Independently, there is no uniform distribution of the 1D chaotic maps like Sine and Tent but their combined effect illustrates a simplistic, strongly stable system. Hence, in this chapter, the proposed algorithm uses the TSS map to perform encryption operation. It is described as (Zhou, Bao, & Chen, 2014)

$$
Z_{n+1} = \begin{cases} \left(\left(4 - r_a\right) \sin \dfrac{\pi Z_n}{4} + \dfrac{r_a Z_n}{2} \right) \bmod 1 & Z_i < 0.5 \\[4mm] \left(\left(4 - r_a\right) \sin \dfrac{\pi Z_n}{4} + \dfrac{r_a \left(1 - Z_n\right)}{2} \right) \bmod 1 & Z_i \geq 0.5 \end{cases}. \tag{1}
$$

where, the parameter $r_a \in (0,4]$.

Logistic-Sine System (LSS)

Similar to TSS map, the combination of Logistic and Sine map results in a simple and an improved uniform distribution of variant density function and strong chaotic properties. Hence, in this chapter, the proposed algorithm also uses the LSS map along with TSS map to perform encryption operation. The LSS map is described as (Zhou, Bao, & Chen, 2014)

$$Z_{n+1} = \left[\left(4 - r_a \right) sin \frac{\pi Z_n}{4} + r_a Z_n \left(1 - Z_n \right) \right] mod\, 1\,. \tag{2}$$

where, the parameter $r_a \in (0,4]$.

Crossover Operation

Crossover operation is also called as recombination operation. It is a genetic operation, which is used to generate new offspring by combining the genetic information of parents. In this algorithm, the crossover operation is used to generate new bit-planes by combining the bit information of two given bit-planes. Basically, the crossover operation is performed between two points, where as in this algorithm; the crossover operation is in multi-points. The multi-point crossover operation totally shuffles the bit values in bit-planes and generates new bit-planes. *Figure 1* shows the performance of crossover operation in two-points.

Figure 1. Crossover operation in two-points

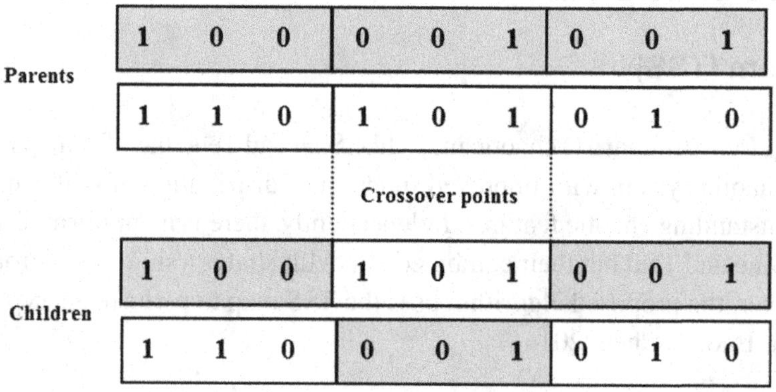

Secure Hash Algorithm (SHA)

SHA has come up against the growing 21st century cyber attacks. The SHA-256 algorithm (Member of SHA-2 family) establishes a unique fixed-size 256-bit hash. Hash function is a simple criterion which cannot be turned back into the inputs and thus useful for applications including password logins, secure key protection, digital signatures, etc. Throughout this chapter, the algorithm's keys are generated with SHA-256.

METHOD FOR IMAGE ENCRYPTION AND DECRYPTION

Image Encryption

Figure 2 shows the image encryption system. It is divided into following subsections.

1. Binary Bit-plane Decomposition
2. Random Points Generation
3. Multi-point Row-crossover Operation
4. Multi-point Column-crossover Operation
5. Bit-plane Combination
6. Hash-key Generation
7. Secret Key Generation of TSS Map
8. Pixel-shuffling Operation
9. Secret Key Generation of LSS Map
10. Pixel-diffusion (Bit-XOR) Operation

Each of the subsections is described below.

Step 1: Let *A* is the grayscale image as an input to the algorithm.
Step 2: Calculate size of *A* using the following code.

```
[M,N]=size(A);
```

Here, *N* and *M*, respectively, are the number of *A* columns and rows. The Matlab function "size". calculates the size of an image.

Binary Bit-plane Decomposition

Step 3: Using the following codes produce eight *A* bit-planes.

```
PN8=bitget(A,1);
PN7=bitget(A,2);
PN6=bitget(a,3);
PN5=bitget(a,4);
PN4=bitget(a,5);
PN3=bitget(a,6);
PN2=bitget(a,7);
PN1=bitget(a,8);
```

Here, *PN*1 to *PN*8 are the eight bit-planes of *A*, generated by the function "bitget". In this bit-planes, *PN*8 and *PN*1 are the MSB and LSB bit-planes, respectively.

Step 4: Copy all the bit-values of bit-planes *PN*1 to *PN*8 into *PN*11 to *PN*88, respectively.

Figure 2. Image encryption system

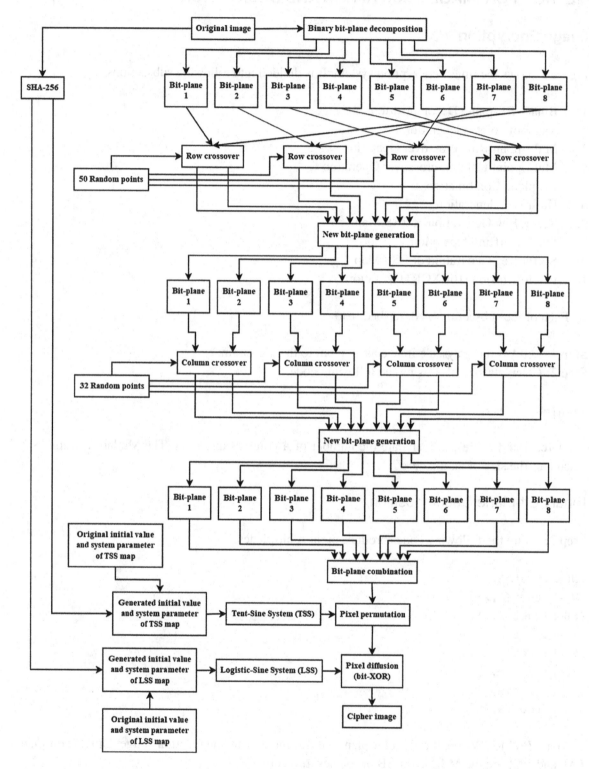

Random Points Generation

Step 5: Generate 50 random points for row-crossover operation and 32 random points for column-crossover operation. Code to generate random points is as given below.

```
zz=randi(N-5,1,50);
yy=randi(M-5,1,32)
```

Here, *zz* and *yy* are the arrays containing 50 and 32 random points, respectively. The function "randi" finds uniformly distributed pseudorandom integers.

Step 6: Sort the random points of arrays *zz* and *yy*. Let the sorted arrays are denoted as *z* and *y* of *zz* and *yy*, respectively.

Multi-Point Row-crossover Operation

Step 7: Perform multi-point (50-point) row-crossover operation between the bit-planes *PN*1 and *PN*8, *PN*2 and *PN*7, *PN*3 and *PN*6, *PN*4 and *PN*5. Code to perform row-crossover operation of first two points $z(1)$ and $z(2)$ are as given below.

```
for l=1:M
 for k=1:z(1)
 PN1(l,k)=PN88(l,k);
 PN8(l,k)=PN11(l,k);
 PN2(l,k)=PN77(l,k);
 PN7(l,k)=PN22(l,k);
 PN3(l,k)=PN66(l,k);
 PN6(l,k)=PN33(l,k);
 PN4(l,k)=PN55(l,k);
 PN5(l,k)=PN44(l,k);
 end
end
for l=1:M
 for k=z(1)+1:z(2)
 PN1(l,k)=PN88((M+1)-l,k);
 PN8(l,k)=PN11((M+1)-l,k);
 PN2(l,k)=PN77((M+1)-l,k);
 PN7(l,k)=PN22((M+1)-l,k);
 PN3(l,k)=PN66((M+1)-l,k);
 PN6(l,k)=PN33((M+1)-l,k);
 PN4(l,k)=PN55((M+1)-l,k);
 PN5(l,k)=PN44((M+1)-l,k);
 end
end
```

In the above code, for each crossover operation, first $z(1)$ pixels of lth row of *PN*1 bit-plane are crossover with $z(1)$ pixels of lth row of *PN*8 bit-plane. Similarly, for $z(1)$ pixels, *PN*2 is crossover with *PN*7, *PN*3 is crossover with *PN*6, and *PN*4 is crossover with *PN*5. Next, $z(2)$ pixels of lth row of *PN*1 bit-plane are crossover with $z(2)$ pixels of $((M+1)-l)^{th}$ row of *PN*8 bit-plane, similarly, for $z(2)$ pixels, *PN*2 is crossover with *PN*7, *PN*3 is crossover with *PN*6, and *PN*4 is crossover with *PN*5. The same operation is carried out for the rest 48 points.

Step 8: Copy all the bit-values of bit-planes *PN*1 to *PN*8 into *PN*111 to *PN*888, respectively.

Multi-Point Column-Crossover Operation

Step 9: After multi-point row-crossover operation, perform multi-point (32-point) column-crossover operation between the bit-planes *PN*1 and *PN*2, *PN*3 and *PN*4, *PN*5 and *PN*6, *PN*7 and *PN*8. Code to perform column-crossover operation between two points $y(1)$ and $y(2)$ is as given below.

```
for k=1:N
 for l=y(1):y(2)
 PN1(l,k)=PN222(l,k);
 PN2(l,k)=PN111(l,k);
 PN3(l,k)=PN444(l,k);
 PN4(l,k)=PN333(l,k);
 PN5(l,k)=PN666(l,k);
 PN6(l,k)=PN555(l,k);
 PN7(l,k)=PN888(l,k);
 PN8(l,k)=PN777(l,k);
 end
end
```

In this code, for each column-crossover operation, $y(1): y(2)$ pixels of kth column of *PN*1 bit-plane are crossover with $y(1): y(2)$ pixels of kth column of *PN*2 bit-plane. Similarly, for $y(1): y(2)$ pixels, *PN*3 is crossover with *PN*4, *PN*5 is crossover with *PN*6, and *PN*7 is crossover with *PN*8. The same process is repeated for

$$y\big(3\big): y\big(4\big), y\big(5\big): y\big(6\big), \cdots\cdots, y\big(31\big): y\big(32\big)\,\text{pixels.}$$

Bit-Plane Combination

Step 10: After performing multi-point column-crossover operation, combine all the bit-planes *PN*1 to *PN*8 to generate the bit-plane combined image *AA*. Code to perform bit-plane combination operation is as given below.

```
for l=1:M
 for k=1:N
```

```
AA(l,k)=(PN1(l,k)*2^7)+(PN2(l,k)*2^6)+(PN3(l,k)*2^5)+(PN4(l,k)* 2^4)+(PN5(l,k
)*2^3)+(PN6(l,k)*2^2)+(PN7(l,k)*2)+ (PN8(l,k));
 end
end
```

Step 11: Place all the pixels of the image *AA* in a single row. Let the reshaped image is denoted as *AA*1. The code for placement of pixels in a single row is as given below.

```
AA1=reshape(AA,1,M*N);
```

The function "reshape" shapes the size of the image.

Hash-key Generation

Step 12: Generate 256-bit hash values of image *A* using hash algorithm SHA-256. The 256-bit hash values are represented as

$$hb = hb_1, hb_2, hb_3, \cdots\cdots, hb_{255}, hb_{256}$$

Step 13: Generate 32-decimal hash values from 256-bit hash values by combining eight bits for each decimal hash value. It is represented as

$$hd = hd_1, hd_2, hd_3, \cdots\cdots, hd_{31}, hd_{32}$$

Secret Key Generation of TSS Map

Step 14: Generate TSS map based keys by,

$$\begin{cases} s1 = s + \left(\left(mod\left(\left(hd_1 + hd_2 + \cdots + hd_8 \right), 256 \right) \times 10^{-2} \right) / 2^9 \right) \\ r1 = r + \left(\left(mod\left(\left(hd_9 + hd_{10} + \cdots + hd_{16} \right), 256 \right) \times 10^{-2} \right) / 2^9 \right) \end{cases} \tag{3}$$

In the equation (3), *s* and *s*1 are the known and produced initial values of TSS map, respectively. *r* and *r*1 are the known and produced system parameters of TSS map, respectively.

Pixel-Shuffling Operation

Step 15: Iterate Eq.(1) *M*×*N* times to generate TSS map based chaotic sequence. Let the iterated sequence is denoted as *tss*. Code to generate the iterated sequence is as given below.

```
tss(1)=mod(((r1*(1-s1))/2+(((4-r1)*sin(3.14*s1))/4)),1);
for l=2:M*N
```

```
if(tss(l-1)>=0.5)
tss(l)=mod((((r1*(1-tss(l-1))))/2+(((4-r1)*sin(3.14*tss(l-1)))/4)),1);
else
tss(l)=mod((((r1*tss(l-1))/2+(((4-r1)*sin(3.14*tss(l-1)))/4)),1);
end
end
```

Step 16: Sort the iterated sequence *tss* in ascending order. Let *tsssort* is the sorted iterated sequence and *tssindex* is their corresponding indexed sequence. Code to generate the sorted iterated sequence and their corresponding indexed sequence is as given below.

```
[tsssort,tssindex]=sort(tss);
```

In the above code, the function "sort" sorts the array elements either in ascending order or in descending order.

Step 17: Shuffle the pixels of the reshaped one-row image *AA*1 by *tss*index. Let *AA*11 is the pixel scrambled image. Code to perform pixel-shuffling operation is as given below.

```
for l=1:M*N
 AA11(l)=AA1(tssindex(l));
end
```

Step 18: Reshape the image into the original size of the image *M×N*. Let the reshaped image is denoted as *RA*1.

Secret Key Generation of LSS Map

Step 19: Generate LSS map based keys by,

$$
\begin{cases}
ss1 = ss + \left(\left(mod\left(\left(hd_{17} + hd_{18} + \cdots + hd_{24} \right), 256 \right) \times 10^{-2} \right) / 2^9 \right) \\
rr1 = rr + \left(\left(mod\left(\left(hd_{25} + hd_{26} + \cdots + hd_{32} \right), 256 \right) \times 10^{-2} \right) / 2^9 \right)
\end{cases}
\tag{4}
$$

In the equation (4), *ss* and *ss*1 are the known and produced initial values of LSS map, respectively. *rr* and *rr*1 are the known and produced system parameters of LSS map, respectively.

Pixel-Diffusion Operation

Step 20: Iterate Eq.(2) *M×N* times to generate LSS map based chaotic sequence. Let the iterated sequence is denoted as *lss*. Code to generate the iterated sequence is as given below.

```
lss(1)=mod((rr1*ss1*(1-ss1)+(((4-rr1)*sin(3.14*ss1))/4)),1);
for l=2:M*N
 lss(p)=mod((rr1*lss(l-1)*(1-lss(l-1))+(((4-rr1)*sin(3.14*lss(l-1)))/ 4)),1);
end
```

Step 21: Reshape the iterated sequence *lss* of size $(1 \times (M \times N))$ into a size $(M \times N)$. Let *lss*1 is the reshaped iterated sequence.

Step 22: Perform pre-processing operation of the iterated sequence *lss*1. Code to perform pre-processing operation is as given below.

```
lss1=mod(fix(lss1*10^6),256);
```

Here, the modulo operation is performed by the function "mod" and the round value operation towards zero is performed by the function "fix".

Step 23: Perform pixel-diffusion (bit-XOR) operation between the corresponding pixels of pixel-shuffled image *RA*1 (output of **Step 18**) and *lss*1 (output of **Step 22**). Codes to perform pixel-diffusion operation are as given below.

```
for l=1:M
 for k=1:N
 C(l,k)=bitxor(lss1(l,k),AA1(l,k));
 end
end
```

In the above code, the function "bitxor" performs bit-wise XOR operation. *C* is the cipher image generated by bit-XOR operation.

Image Decryption

Figure 3 shows the image decryption system. It is divided into following subsections.

1. Secret Key Generation of LSS Map
2. Reverse Pixel-diffusion (Bit-XOR) Operation
3. Secret Key Generation of TSS Map
4. Reverse Pixel-shuffling Operation
5. Binary Bit-plane Decomposition
6. Multi-point Column-crossover Operation
7. Multi-point Row-crossover Operation
8. Bit-plane Combination

Figure 3. Image decryption system

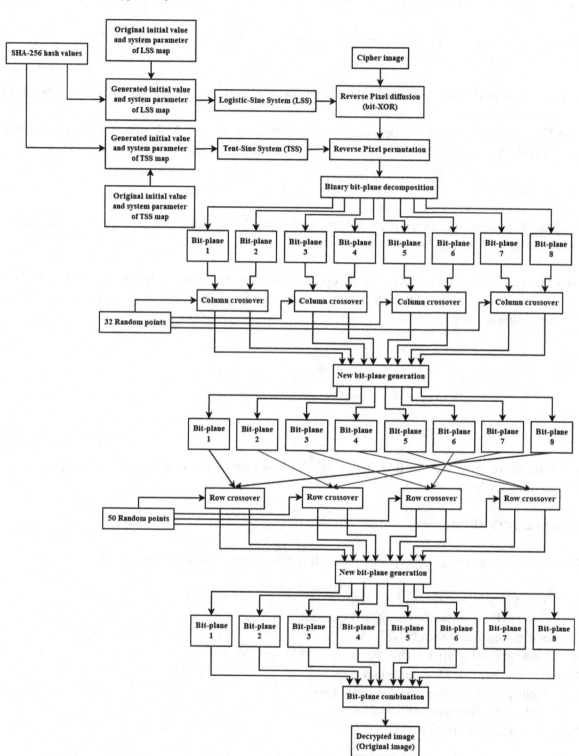

Each of the subsections is described as below.

Step 1: Receiver side receives the cipher image C, original initial values and system parameters of LSS and TSS map, 50 random points for row-crossover operation, 32 random points for column-crossover operation, and hash values of 256-bits.

Step 2: Calculate cipher image size C. Let it is denoted as ($M \times N$).

Step 3: Generate 32-decimal hash values from 256-bit hash values by combining eight bits for each decimal hash value. It is represented as

$$rhd = rhd_1, rhd_2, rhd_3, \cdots\cdots, rhd_{31}, rhd_{32}$$

Secret Key Generation of LSS Map

Step 4: Generate LSS map based keys by,

$$\begin{cases} rss1 = rss + \left(\left(mod\left(\left(rhd_{17} + rhd_{18} + \cdots + rhd_{24} \right), 256 \right) \times 10^{-2} \right) / 2^9 \right) \\ rrr1 = rrr + \left(\left(mod\left(\left(rhd_{25} + rhd_{26} + \cdots + rhd_{32} \right), 256 \right) \times 10^{-2} \right) / 2^9 \right) \end{cases} \tag{5}$$

In the above equation, rss and $rssi1$ are the known and produced initial values of LSS map, respectively. rrr and $rrr1$ are the known and produced system parameters of LSS map, respectively.

Reverse Pixel-Diffusion Operation

Step 5: Iterate Eq.(2) $M \times N$ times to generate LSS map based chaotic sequence. Let $rlss$ is the iterated sequence.

Step 6: Reshape the iterated sequence $rlss$ of size $(1 \times (M \times N))$ into a size $(M \times N)$. Let $rlss1$ is the reshaped iterated sequence.

Step 7: Perform pre-processing operation of the iterated sequence $rlss1$. Code to perform pre-processing operation is as given below.

```
rlss1=mod(fix(rlss1*10^6),256);
```

Step 8: Perform reverse pixel-diffusion (bit-XOR) operation between the cipher image C and $rlssi1$. Code to perform reverse pixel-diffusion operation is as given below.

```
for l=1:M
 for k=1:N
 C1(l,k)=bitxor(rlss1(l,k),C(l,k));
 end
end
```

$C1$ is the pixel-diffused image generated by bit-XOR operation.

Step 9: Place all the pixels of the image $C1$ in a single row. Let the reshaped image is denoted as $CC1$. The code for placement of pixels in a single row is as given below.

```
CC1=reshape(C1,1,M*N);
```

Secret Key Generation of TSS Map

Step 10: Generate TSS map based keys by,

$$
\begin{cases}
rs1 = rs + \left(\left(mod\left(\left(rhd_1 + rhd_2 + \cdots + rhd_8 \right), 256 \right) \times 10^{-2} \right) / 2^9 \right) \\
rr1 = rr + \left(\left(mod\left(\left(rhd_9 + rhd_{10} + \cdots + rhd_{16} \right), 256 \right) \times 10^{-2} \right) / 2^9 \right)
\end{cases}
\tag{6}
$$

In the equation (6), rs and $rs1$ are the known and produced initial values of TSS map, respectively. rr and $rr1$ are the known and produced system parameters of TSS map, respectively.

Reverse Pixel-Shuffling Operation

Step 11: Iterate equation (1) $M \times N$ times to generate TSS map based chaotic sequence. Let $rtss$ is the iterated sequence. Code to generate the iterated sequence is as given below.

```
rtss(1)=mod(((rr1*(1-rs1))/2+(((4-rr1)*sin(3.14*rs1))/4)),1);
for l=2:M*N
 if(rtss(l-1)>=0.5)
 rtss(l)=mod(((rr1*(1-rtss(l-1)))/2+(((4-rr1)*sin(3.14*rtss(l-1)))/ 4)),1);
 else
rtss(l)=mod(((rr1*rtss(l-1))/2+(((4-rr1)*sin(3.14*rtss(l-1)))/ 4)),1);
 end
end
```

Step 12: Sort the iterated sequence $rtss$ in ascending order. Let $rtsssort$ is the sorted iterated sequence and $rtssindex$ is their corresponding indexed sequence. Code to generate the sorted iterated sequence and their corresponding indexed sequence is as given below.

```
[rtsssort,rtssindex]=sort(rtss);
```

Step 13: Reverse shuffle the pixels of the reshaped one-row image $CC1$ by $rtss$index. Let $CC11$ is reverse pixel scrambled image. Code to perform reverse pixel-shuffling operation is as given below.

```
for l=1:M*N
 CCC11(rtssindex(l))=CC11(l);
end
```

Step 14: Reshape the image into the original size of the image $M \times N$. Let the reshaped image is denoted as *CCC*111.

Binary Bit-Plane Decomposition

Step 15: Generate bit-planes of *CCC*111 using the following codes.

```
RPN8=bitget(CCC111,1);
RPN7=bitget(CCC111,2);
RPN6=bitget(CCC111,3);
RPN5=bitget(CCC111,4);
RPN4=bitget(CCC111,5);
RPN3=bitget(CCC111,6);
RPN2=bitget(CCC111,7);
RPN1=bitget(CCC111,8);
```

Here,

*RPN*8, *RPN*7, *RPN*6, *RPN*5, *RPN*4, *RPN*3, *RPN*2, *RPN*1

are the eight bit-planes of the image *CCC*111.

Step 16: Reshape all the bit-planes

*RPN*8, *RPN*7, *RPN*6, *RPN*5, *RPN*4, *RPN*3, *RPN*2, *RPN*1

and copy the bit-values of bit-planes into

*RPN*88, *RPN*77, *RPN*66, *RPN*55, *RPN*44, *RPN*33, *RPN*22, *RPN*11.

Code to perform these operations is as follows.

```
RPN1=reshape(RPN1,M,N);RPN11=RPN1;
RPN2=reshape(RPN2,M,N);RPN22=RPN2;
RPN3=reshape(RPN3,M,N);RPN33=RPN3;
RPN4=reshape(RPN4,M,N);RPN44=RPN4;
RPN5=reshape(RPN5,M,N);RPN55=RPN5;
RPN6=reshape(RPN6,M,N);RPN66=RPN6;
RPN7=reshape(RPN7,M,N);RPN77=RPN7;
RPN8=reshape(RPN8,M,N);RPN88=RPN8;
```

Multi-Point Column-crossover Operation

Step 17: Sort the collected random points in the receiver side. Let the array of sorted 50 random points and 32 random points are denoted as rz and ry, respectively.

Step 18: Perform multi-point (32-point) column-crossover operation between the bit-planes $RPN1$ and $RPN2$, $RPN3$ and $RPN4$, $RPN5$ and $RPN6$, $RPN7$ and $RPN8$. Code to perform column-crossover operation between two points $ry(1)$ and $ry(2)$ is as given below.

```
for k=1:N
 for l=ry(1):ry(2)
 RPN1(l,k)=RPN22(l,k);
 RPN2(l,k)=RPN11(l,k);
 RPN3(l,k)=RPN44(l,k);
 RPN4(l,k)=RPN33(l,k);
 RPN5(l,k)=RPN66(l,k);
 RPN6(l,k)=RPN55(l,k);
 RPN7(l,k)=RPN88(l,k);
 RPN8(l,k)=RPN77(l,k);
 end
end
```

In the above code, for each column-crossover operation, $ry(1)$: $ry(2)$ pixels of kth column of $RPN1$ bit-plane are crossover with $ry(1)$: $ry(2)$ pixels of kth column of $RPN2$ bit-plane. Similarly, for $ry(1)$: $ry(2)$ pixels, $RPN3$ is crossover with $RPN4$, $RPN5$ is crossover with $RPN6$, and $RPN7$ is crossover with $RPN8$. The same process is repeated for

$$ry\left(3\right):ry\left(4\right), ry\left(5\right):ry\left(6\right), \cdots\cdots, ry\left(31\right):ry\left(32\right)\, \text{pixels.}$$

Step 19: Copy all the bit-values of bit-planes

$RPN8, RPN7, RPN6, RPN5, RPN4, RPN3, RPN2, RPN1$

into

$RPN888, RPN777, RPN666, RPN555, RPN444, RPN333, RPN222, RPN111,$

respectively.

Multi-Point Row-Crossover Operation

Step 20: Perform multi-point (50-point) row-crossover operation between the bit-planes $RPN1$ and $RPN2$, $RPN3$ and $RPN4$, $RPN5$ and $RPN6$, $RPN7$ and $RPN8$. Code to perform row-crossover operation of first two points $rz(1)$ and $rz(2)$ is as given below.

```
for l=1:M
 for k=1:rz(1)
 RPN1(l,k)=RPN888(l,k);
 RPN8(l,k)=RPN111(l,k);
 RPN2(l,k)=RPN777(l,k);
 RPN7(l,k)=RPN222(l,k);
 RPN3(l,k)=RPN666(l,k);
 RPN6(l,k)=RPN333(l,k);
 RPN4(l,k)=RPN555(l,k);
 RPN5(l,k)=RPN444(l,k);
 end
end
for l=1:M
 for k=rz(1)+1:rz(2)
 RPN1(l,k)=RPN888((M+1)-l,k);
 RPN8(l,k)=RPN111((M+1)-l,k);
 RPN2(l,k)=RPN777((M+1)-l,k);
 RPN7(l,k)=RPN222((M+1)-l,k);
 RPN3(l,k)=RPN666((M+1)-l,k);
 RPN6(l,k)=RPN333((M+1)-l,k);
 RPN4(l,k)=RPN555((M+1)-l,k);
 RPN5(l,k)=RPN444((M+1)-l,k);
 end
end
```

In the above code, for each crossover operation, first $rz(1)$ pixels of lth row of *RPN1* bit-plane are crossover with $rz(1)$ pixels of lth row of *RPN8* bit-plane. Similarly, for $rz(1)$ pixels, *RPN2* is crossover with *RPN7*, *RPN3* is crossover with *RPN6*, and *RPN4* is crossover with *RPN5*. Next, $rz(2)$ pixels of lth row of *PN1* bit-plane are crossover with $rz(2)$ pixels of $((M+1)-l)^{th}$ row of *RPN8* bit-plane. Similarly, for $rz(2)$ pixels, *RPN2* is crossover with *RPN7*, *RPN3* is crossover with *RPN6*, and *RPN4* is crossover with *RPN5*. The same operation is carried out for the rest 48 points.

Bit-Plane Combination

Step 21: After performing multi-point row-crossover operation, combine all the bit-planes

RPN8, RPN7, RPN6, RPN5, RPN4, RPN3, RPN2, RPN1

to generate the bit-plane combined image *D*. Code to perform bit-plane combination operation is as given below.

```
for l=1:M
 for k=1:N
 D(l,k)= (RPN1(l,k)*2^7)+(RPN2(l,k)*2^6)+(RPN3(l,k)*2^5)+(RPN4 (l,k)*2^4)+(RPN
```

```
5(l,k)*2^3)+(RPN6(l,k)*2^2)+(RPN7(l,k)*2) +(RPN8(l,k));
 end
end
```

The bit-plane combined image *D* is called as the decrypted image.

SIMULATION RESULTS AND SECURITY ANALYSIS

Computer simulation of the proposed algorithm is carried out on three different size grayscale images such as "Boat.tiff" of size (512×512), "Lena.tif" of size (256×256), and "Textures.tiff" of size (1024×1024). The simulation is conducted on a PC with a processor of 3.40 GHz and RAM of 8 GB using MATLAB R2012a. All images of grayscale are collected from "USC-SIPI image database" (USC-SIPI image database, n.d.). The TSS and LSS map based keys are listed in *Table 1*. The outputs from the simulation are shown in *Figure 4*. Here, *Figure 4 (c, f, i), (b, e, h),* and *(a, d, g)* respectively shows the decrypted, encrypted, and original grayscale images. The encrypted images seem like noisy output of the original image in this simulation result. This indicates the good encryption outcomes of the proposed scheme. Similarly, by observing the decrypted images, it is found the results of decrypted and original images similar. This proves that the proposed decryption algorithm decrypts the cipher images correctly using the correct secret keys.

The security analysis is as follows.

Figure 4. Computer simulation outputs: (a, b, c) "Lena", (d, e, f) "Boat", and (g, h, i) "Textures" images

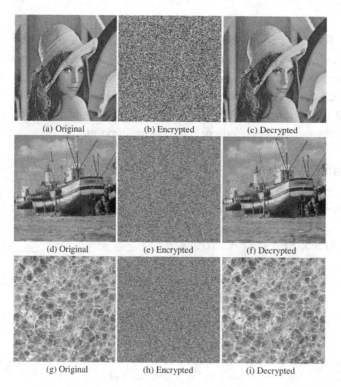

Table 1. Chaotic map based key values

Chaotic Maps	Key Values
TSS map	Initial value: s= 0.6502648155198965 System parameter: r= 3.956747643593481
LSS map	Initial value: ss= 0.678452956678329 System parameter: rr= 3.999854736274398

Key Space Analysis

Key space is the set of all keys used to perform the encryption and decryption process in an algorithm (Patro, Banerjee, & Acharya, 2017). The key space for an effective algorithm must be greater than 2^{128} to withstand brute-force attack (Kulsoom, Xiao, & Abbas, 2016). Keys used in this algorithm are

- 50 random values in row-crossover operation
- 32 random values in column-crossover operation
- TSS and LSS map based key values
- Hash values of 256-bits

Table 2 shows the mechanism by which the proposed algorithm calculates the total key space. The 50 random values and the 32 random values occupy the memory space of 50 bytes ($\approx$ 400 bits) and 32 bytes ($\approx$ 256 bits), respectively. Hence, the key space for 50 random points and 32 random points are 2^{400} and 2^{256}, respectively. For each of the individual keys of the chaotic maps (TSS and LSS), the algorithm uses a key space of 10^{15} (Floating-point Working Group, n.d.). Therefore, chaotic map based key space is $10^{30} \times 10^{30} = 10^{60} \approx 2.4891 \times 2^{198}$. In addition, for the "Secure Hash Algorithm SHA-256", the proposed methodology uses a key space of 2^{128}. Therefore, the overall key space is 2.4891×2^{982}.

Table 2. Total key space of the suggested methodology

Particulars	Keys	Key Space
Random points	50 random points	2^{400}
	32 random points	2^{256}
Hash key	256-bit hash key	2^{128}
Chaotic maps	Tent-Sine System (TSS) map (Initial value: s and System parameter: r)	$10^{30} \approx 1.5777 \times 2^{99}$
	Logistic-Sine System (LSS) map (Initial value: ss and System parameter: rr)	$10^{30} \approx 1.5777 \times 2^{99}$
Total key space		2.4891×2^{982}

Statistical Attack Analysis

Three different measures are used for statistical attack such as Histogram analysis, histogram variance analysis, and correlation analysis. Each of them is described below.

Histogram Analysis

Histogram analysis is the study of the statistical attack by graphical visualization. It is the graphical representation of the frequency distribution indicating the occurrences of the different valued pixels. The two requirements for histogram analysis are (Wang & Zhang, 2016; Patro, Acharya, & Nath, 2019a),

- Cipher image and original image histograms must vary substantially from one another.
- The gray pixel values for the cipher image must be distributed uniformly.

Figure 5. Histogram outputs: (a, b) "Lena", (c, d) "Boat", (e, f) "Textures"

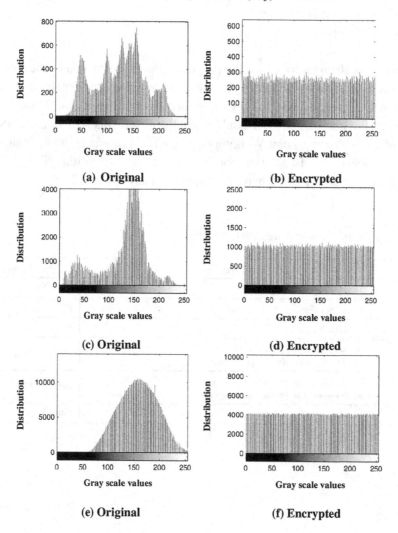

Figure 5 shows the histogram plots of "Lena", "Boat", and "Textures" image in which *Figure 5 (a, c, e)* and *(b, d, f)* shows the histogram plots of original and cipher images, respectively. In the histogram plots the cipher images are found to be completely different from the original images. The uniform distribution of gray pixel values is also found in the histograms of cipher images. It indicates the high resistance of the proposed algorithm to a statistical attack.

Histogram Variance Analysis

Histogram variance is the quantitative method of statistical attack analysis. It involves the calculation of pixel gray values that are uniform in cipher images. The lower the histogram variance value, the higher is the uniformity of the pixel grayscale. The histogram variance is expressed as,

$$var\left(Z\right) = \frac{1}{p^2}\sum_{i=1}^{p}\sum_{j=1}^{p}\frac{\left(z_i - z_j\right)^2}{2} \qquad (7)$$

where,

p is the grayscale value,
z_j and z_i are the pixel quantities in the grayscale values j and i respectively, and $\{z_j z_i\} \in Z$.

Table 3 shows the histogram variance of several test images. In the table, the third and fourth column shows the histogram variance of original and encrypted images, respectively. By observing the third column and fourth column variance results, it is realized that the third column results are larger than the results of fourth column. It means that the cipher images are completely different from the original images. In the table, it is also observed a small value of variance of encrypted images, which indicates the high grayscale uniformity of pixel values in cipher images.

Correlation Analysis

Analysis of correlation tests the interaction of neighboring pixels within images. The correlation of neighboring pixels in cipher and original images is very low and high, respectively. For high association of adjacent pixels the correlation value is closer to +1 and the correlation value is nearer to 0 for low association of adjacent pixels (Patro & Acharya, 2018). The association of neighboring pixels should be very low, or close to 0, in a successful encryption algorithm. 5000-pairs of adjacent pixels are chosen randomly in this algorithm to conduct the correlation analysis. The association of adjacent pixels is checked by,

$$corr_{pq} = \frac{\frac{1}{M}\sum_{i=1}^{M}\left(p_i - E\left(p\right)\right)\left(q_i - E\left(q\right)\right)}{\sqrt{\frac{1}{M}\sum_{i=1}^{M}\left(p_i - E\left(p\right)\right)^2} \times \sqrt{\frac{1}{M}\sum_{i=1}^{M}\left(q_i - E\left(q\right)\right)^2}} \qquad (8)$$

where,

p,q - Gray level pixel values of adjacent pixels,
M - Total number of selected pixels,
$E(p)$, $E(q)$ - Mean value of p and q, respectively, and
$corr_{pq}$ - Correlation between p and q.

Table 3. Histogram variance of various test images

Test Images	Sizes	Original Images	Encrypted Images
Cameraman	256×256	110970	226.1094
Lena	256×256	38951	263.9141
Tree	256×256	66010	267.2266
Airplane	512×512	2871100	1083.3
Baboon	512×512	749430	1062.9
Boat	512×512	1535900	1145.6
Elaine	512×512	562670	969.7891
House	512×512	1347800	1051.4
Lake	512×512	719620	961.6875
Lena	512×512	633400	1027.1
Peppers	512×512	480660	1140.9
Aerials	1024×1024	35580000	4299.4
Textures	1024×1024	14971000	4155.0

The mean $E(p)$ and $E(q)$ are expressed as:

$$E\left(p\right) = \frac{1}{M}\sum_{i=1}^{M} p_i \tag{9}$$

and

$$E\left(q\right) = \frac{1}{M}\sum_{i=1}^{M} q_i \tag{10}$$

Table 4 and *Table 5* shows the correlation analysis result of various test images. *Table 4* represents only original image, where as *Table 5* represents the encrypted image. It is quite clear from *Table 4* and *Table 5* that in the horizontal, vertical, and diagonal directions, the adjacent pixel correlation values are close to 0 for the cipher images and close to 1 for the original images. *Figure 6* and *Figure 7* shows the correlation plot of "Lena", "Boat", and "Textures" images. *Figure 6* represents the original image and *Figure 7* represents the encrypted image. In the correlation plot, the strong correlation of neighboring pixels (linear distribution of pixels) is seen in the original images, whereas in encrypted images weak correlation of neighboring pixels (uniform distribution of pixels) is observed. As per the definition, the correlation coefficients among the adjacent pixels of encrypted images in any direction should be as small as possible for a good encryption algorithm; hence it is resistant to statistical attack.

Table 4. Correlation analysis results of various original images

Test Images	Sizes	Original Images		
		Horizontal	Vertical	Diagonal
Cameraman	256×256	0.9355	0.9588	0.9210
Lena	256×256	0.8991	0.9487	0.8808
Tree	256×256	0.9682	0.9448	0.9337
Airplane	512×512	0.9672	0.9676	0.9362
Baboon	512×512	0.8668	0.7611	0.7177
Boat	512×512	0.9412	0.9700	0.9218
Elaine	512×512	0.9745	0.9712	0.9676
House	512×512	0.9535	0.9551	0.9202
Lake	512×512	0.9755	0.9695	0.9570
Lena	512×512	0.9727	0.9843	0.9625
Peppers	512×512	0.9734	0.9788	0.9662
Aerials	1024×1024	0.7704	0.7687	0.7200
Textures	1024×1024	0.9414	0.9399	0.9166

Table 5. Correlation analysis results of various encrypted images

Test Images	Sizes	Encrypted Images		
		Horizontal	Vertical	Diagonal
Cameraman	256×256	0.0049	0.0017	0.0013
Lena	256×256	0.0017	-0.0024	0.0016
Tree	256×256	0.0029	-0.0025	-0.0002
Airplane	512×512	-0.0039	0.0012	-0.0035
Baboon	512×512	-0.0041	-0.0003	-0.0023
Boat	512×512	-0.0028	0.0025	-0.0043
Elaine	512×512	-0.0018	0.0038	0.0031
House	512×512	-0.0007	0.0027	-0.0026
Lake	512×512	0.0046	-0.0058	-0.0068
Lena	512×512	-0.0003	-0.0019	0.0003
Peppers	512×512	0.0019	0.0036	0.0020
Aerials	1024×1024	0.0017	-0.0032	0.0016
Textures	1024×1024	0.0018	0.0006	0.0022

Figure 6. Correlation plot of original images: (a, b, c) "Lena", (d, e, f) "Boat", (g, h, i) "Textures"

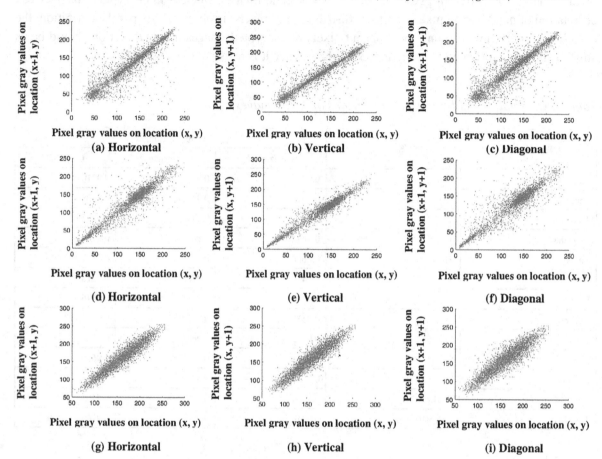

(a) Horizontal   **(b) Vertical**   **(c) Diagonal**

(d) Horizontal   **(e) Vertical**   **(f) Diagonal**

(g) Horizontal   **(h) Vertical**   **(i) Diagonal**

Differential Attack Analysis

The fundamental goal of all encryption approaches is that the original image will vary considerably from the cipher image. Number of Pixel Change Rate (NPCR) and Unified Average Changing Intensity (UACI) are the two measures used to quantify the difference between original and cipher image (Patro, Raghuvanshi, & Acharya, 2019). The NPCR and UACI are measured by,

$$NPCR_g = \frac{\sum_{i,j} D_g(i,j)}{M_g \times N_g} \times 100 \tag{11}$$

$$UACI_g = \frac{1}{M_g \times N_g} \left[\sum_{i,j} \frac{\left| C_{g1}(i,j) - C_{g2}(i,j) \right|}{255} \right] \times 100 \tag{12}$$

where,

$M_g \times N_g$ - The image size,

$NPCR_g$ and $UACI_g$ - NPCR and UACI of 256-grayscale image, respectively,

$C_{g1}(i,j)$ - Original cipher image,

$C_{g2}(i,j)$ – Cipher image after changing one pixel in plain image, and

$D_g(i,j)$ can be defined by

$$D_g\left(i,j\right) = \begin{cases} 0 & if\, C_{g1}\left(i,j\right) = C_{g2}\left(i,j\right) \\ 1 & if\, C_{g1}\left(i,j\right) \ne C_{g2}\left(i,j\right) \end{cases} \tag{13}$$

Figure 7. Correlation plot of encrypted images: (a, b, c) "Lena", (d, e, f) "Boat", (g, h, i) "Textures"

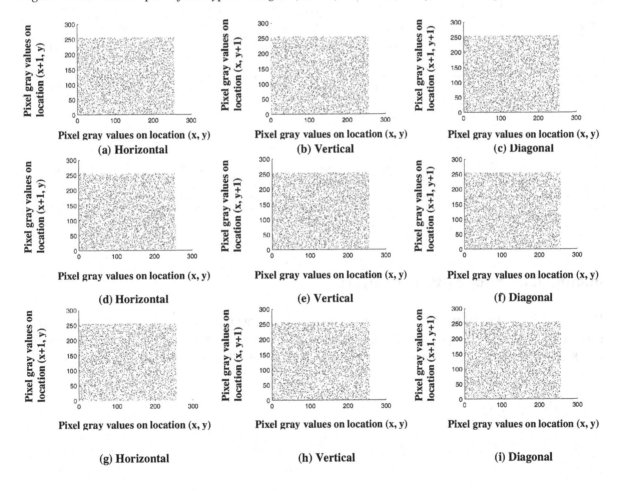

The NPCR and UACI values are expected to be 99.6094% and 33.4635%, respectively, for an image (Gupta, Thawait, Patro, & Acharya, 2016). The algorithm is stronger for differential attack, if the NPCR and UACI values are higher than their predicted values. The average (Avg.), maximum (Max.), and minimum (Min.) NPCR and UACI results of different test images are shown in *Table 6*. All three NPCR and UACI values (Min., Max., and Avg.) are determined by changing 100 pixel values randomly in the original image. From *Table 6* it is clear that the average NPCR and UACI values for all test images are larger than their ideal values, making it reliable to provide adequate protection to withstand differential attack.

Table 6. NPCR and UACI results of various test images using the proposed cryptosystem

Test Images	Sizes	NPCR (%)			UACI (%)		
		Min.	Max.	Avg.	Min.	Max.	Avg.
Cameraman	256×256	99.5453	99.6567	99.6126	33.2573	33.7013	33.4678
Lena	256×256	99.5575	99.6643	99.6123	33.2672	33.7192	33.4896
Tree	256×256	99.5285	99.6552	99.6098	33.2132	33.6909	33.4671
Airplane	512×512	99.5827	99.6414	99.6100	33.3247	33.6643	33.4661
Baboon	512×512	99.5804	99.6326	99.6111	33.3525	33.6494	33.4666
Boat	512×512	99.5785	99.6403	99.6097	33.3361	33.6473	33.4659
Elaine	512×512	99.5861	99.6399	99.6117	33.3818	33.5767	33.4693
House	512×512	99.5850	99.6326	99.6094	33.3318	33.5854	33.4679
Lake	512×512	99.5831	99.6407	99.6134	33.3708	33.5911	33.4757
Lena	512×512	99.5750	99.6387	99.6099	33.3829	33.6195	33.4803
Peppers	512×512	99.5808	99.6403	99.6095	33.3537	33.5995	33.4650
Aerials	1024×1024	99.5930	99.6240	99.6100	33.4085	33.5847	33.4641
Textures	1024×1024	99.5985	99.6243	99.6111	33.4077	33.6135	33.4679

Information Entropy Attack Analysis

Entropy is simply measuring pixel randomness in an image. Data protection is dependent on the higher entropy value of cipher images. Ideally, an image with 256 grayscale entropy is 8. The nearest the value is to 8, the higher the pixel randomness (Patro & Acharya, 2019b). The pixel randomness is measured by,

$$H\left(n\right)=\sum_{i=1}^{2^m-1}p\left(n_i\right)log_2\frac{1}{p\left(n_i\right)} \tag{14}$$

where,

n - The information source,
$H(n)$ - Entropy of information source n,

$p(n_i)$ - Probability of the symbol n_i, and

m - Number of bits to represent each of the pixel gray values.

Table 7 provides the results of the entropy from different test images. In the table, the third and fourth column entropy results represent the original and cipher images, respectively. It is obvious from the table that the entropy of all encrypted test images is closer to the ideal value, which indicates the higher pixel randomness in cipher images. It implies that the suggested scheme firmly resists the attack against entropy.

Table 7. Information entropy results of various test images

Test Images	Sizes	Original Images	Encrypted Images
Cameraman	256×256	7.0097	7.9975
Lena	256×256	7.4750	7.9971
Tree	256×256	7.3103	7.9970
Airplane	512×512	6.7025	7.9993
Baboon	512×512	7.3583	7.9993
Boat	512×512	7.1914	7.9992
Elaine	512×512	7.5060	7.9993
House	512×512	7.2334	7.9993
Lake	512×512	7.4842	7.9993
Lena	512×512	7.4451	7.9993
Peppers	512×512	7.5937	7.9992
Aerials	1024×1024	6.5754	7.9998
Textures	1024×1024	7.2281	7.9998

Mean Square Error (MSE) and Peak Signal-to-Noise Ratio (PSNR) Analysis

MSE and PSNR are the security parameters, which differentiates the original and encrypted image and vice versa. Higher value of MSE and smaller value of PSNR represents the huge difference of original and encrypted image. Similarly, MSE zero value and PSNR infinite value mean similarity between original and decrypted image. MSE and PSNR are calculated as

$$MSE_{OE} = \frac{1}{M_g \times N_g} \sum_{i=1}^{M_g} \sum_{j=1}^{N_g} \left(O_{ij} - E_{ij} \right)^2 \tag{15}$$

$$MSE_{OD} = \frac{1}{M_g \times N_g} \sum_{i=1}^{M_g} \sum_{j=1}^{N_g} \left(O_{ij} - D_{ij} \right)^2 \tag{16}$$

$$PSNR_{OE} = 20 \log_{10} \frac{P_{max}}{\sqrt{MSE_{OE}}} \qquad (17)$$

$$PSNR_{OD} = 20 \log_{10} \frac{P_{max}}{\sqrt{MSE_{OD}}} \qquad (18)$$

where,

O,E,D – Original, encrypted, and decrypted images, respectively,

$M_g \times N_g$ - Size of the image in which M_g is the height and N_g is the width of the image,

P_{max} - Peak pixel value of the image,

MSE_{OE} - MSE between original and encrypted image,

MSE_{OD} - MSE between original and decrypted image,

$PSNR_{OE}$ - PSNR between original and encrypted image, and

$PSNR_{OD}$ - PSNR between original and decrypted image.

The results for PSNR and MSE are reported in *Table 8*. It is observed in the table that between the original and cipher images there is low PSNR value and high MSE value. It is also observed in the table that between the original and decrypted images there is infinite PSNR value and zero MSE value. It shows that the cipher images vary significantly from the original images and also shows that the decrypted images are identical to the original images.

Table 8. MSE and PSNR results of various test images

Test Images	Sizes	MSE		PSNR	
		MSE_{OE}	MSE_{OD}	$PSNR_{OE}$	$PSNR_{OD}$
Cameraman	256×256	9414.9	0	8.3926	∞
Lena	256×256	7831.4	0	9.1924	∞
Tree	256×256	9951.8	0	8.1518	∞
Airplane	512×512	10291.0	0	8.0062	∞
Baboon	512×512	7238.6	0	9.5343	∞
Boat	512×512	7632.4	0	9.3042	∞
Elaine	512×512	7654.7	0	9.2915	∞
House	512×512	8920.8	0	8.6268	∞
Lake	512×512	9800.7	0	8.2182	∞
Lena	512×512	7781.9	0	9.2199	∞
Peppers	512×512	8428.4	0	8.8734	∞
Aerials	1024×1024	6754.4	0	9.8349	∞
Textures	1024×1024	7774.6	0	9.2240	∞

Key Sensitivity Analysis

Key sensitivity analysis reveals how it affects the encryption system by simply adjusting the key value at 10^{-15} position. The keys to the algorithm should be highly sensitive enough to resist brute-force attack. *Figure 8*, *Figure 9* and *Figure 10* shows the results of key sensitivity of "Lena", "Boat", and "Textures" image, respectively. In *Figure 8, 9,* and *10*, the sub-figure *(a)* is the original cipher image, sub-figures *(b), (d), (f),* and *(h)* are the changed cipher images by changing keys *s,r,ss,* and *rr* in 10^{-15} positions, respectively, and sub-figures *(c), (e), (g),* and *(i)* are the corresponding difference images of original cipher images and changed cipher images. It is observed from the difference images that there is a large difference between the changed cipher image and the original cipher image. It indicates how high the keys are sensitive to the suggested algorithm.

The key sensitivity analysis results are shown in *Table 9* and *Table 10* using the NPCR and UACI. *Table 9* is the key sensitivity of TSS map based keys, where as *Table 10* represents the key sensitivity of LSS map based keys. If the NPCR and UACI are higher than 90% and 30%, the algorithm is highly sensitive to the keys, respectively. By looking at both tables, it is found that the NPCR and UACI values are higher than 90% and 30% respectively for all the test images. This proves that all the keys in the proposed algorithm are highly sensitive.

Figure 8. Key sensitivity results of "Lena" image: (a) Cipher image using original keys, (b, d, f, h) Cipher images using changed keys, (c, e, g, i) Difference images

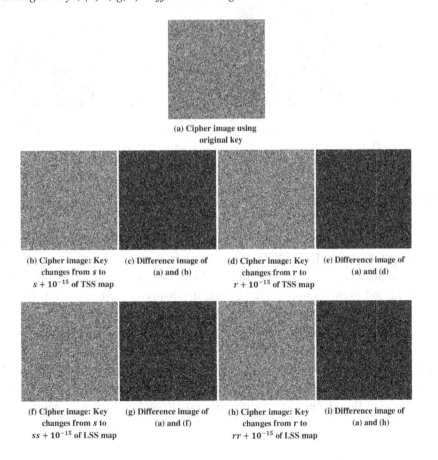

Figure 9. Key sensitivity results of "Boat" image: (a) Cipher image using original keys, (b, d, f, h) Cipher images using changed keys, (c, e, g, i) Difference images

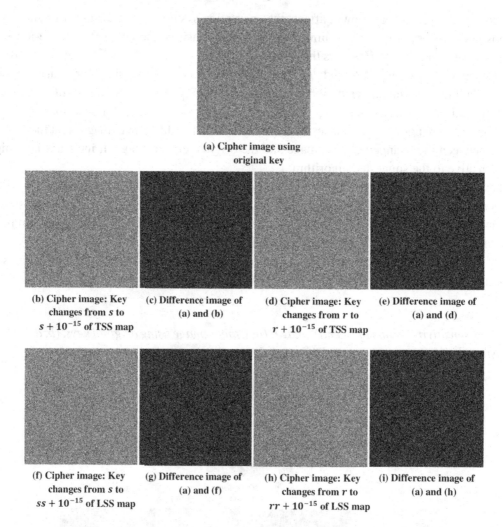

(a) Cipher image using original key

(b) Cipher image: Key changes from s to $s + 10^{-15}$ of TSS map

(c) Difference image of (a) and (b)

(d) Cipher image: Key changes from r to $r + 10^{-15}$ of TSS map

(e) Difference image of (a) and (d)

(f) Cipher image: Key changes from s to $ss + 10^{-15}$ of LSS map

(g) Difference image of (a) and (f)

(h) Cipher image: Key changes from r to $rr + 10^{-15}$ of LSS map

(i) Difference image of (a) and (h)

Plaintext Sensitivity Analysis

Plaintext, also referred to as un-ciphered text, is used as an input to the encryption algorithm. Hence its security is highly important. The plaintext sensitivity is performed in this algorithm by changing the value of only one pixel in one of the positions and keeping the values of the other pixels the same. *Figure 11*, *Figure 12* and *Figure 13* shows the plaintext sensitivity analysis results of "Lena", "Boat", and "Textures" image, respectively. In *Figure 11, 12,* and *13*, the sub-figure *(a)* is the original cipher image, sub-figures *(b), (d), (f),* and *(h)* are the changed cipher images by changing pixel positions at (17, 39), (50, 91), (128, 128), and (190, 232), respectively, and sub-figures *(c), (e), (g),* and *(i)* are the corresponding difference images between original cipher images and changed cipher images. It is found from the difference images that the modified cipher image is substantially different from the original cipher image. This shows that the proposed algorithm is extremely reactive to plaintext.

Figure 10. Key sensitivity results of "Textures" image: (a) Cipher image using original keys, (b, d, f, h) Cipher images using changed keys, (c, e, g, i) Difference images

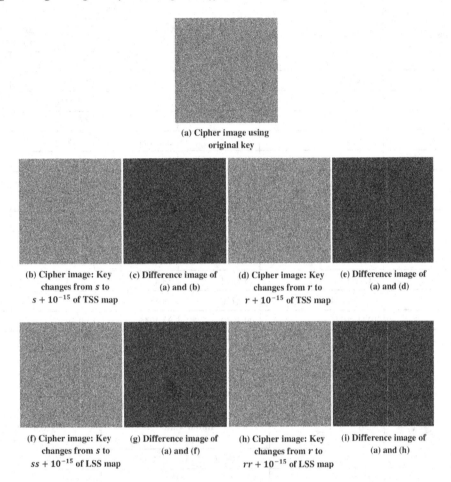

(a) Cipher image using
original key

(b) Cipher image: Key changes from s to $s + 10^{-15}$ of TSS map

(c) Difference image of (a) and (b)

(d) Cipher image: Key changes from r to $r + 10^{-15}$ of TSS map

(e) Difference image of (a) and (d)

(f) Cipher image: Key changes from s to $ss + 10^{-15}$ of LSS map

(g) Difference image of (a) and (f)

(h) Cipher image: Key changes from r to $rr + 10^{-15}$ of LSS map

(i) Difference image of (a) and (h)

The results of the plaintext sensitivity are reported using the NPCR and UACI in *Table 11*. It is realized in the table that the NPCR and UACI values are higher than 90% and 30% respectively for all the cipher images. It shows the high plaintext sensitivity of the proposed algorithm.

Occlusion Attack Analysis

There is a risk that the encrypted data may be corrupted during exchange of messages from transmitter to recipient due to unsecured network. The corrupted data is known as occluded data. In this algorithm, for occlusion analysis, 1/16th, 1/8th, 1/4th, and 1/2th occlusion parts of cipher images are taken. *Figure 14*, *Figure 15*, and *Figure 16* shows the occlusion attack analysis results of "Lena", "Boat", and "Textures" image. It is seen in the results that the decrypted images show distortions but the images are still visible by occlusion of up to 50%. It is therefore inferred that the suggested method of image encryption will withstand an occlusion attack of up to 50%.

Table 9. Key sensitivity results (NPCR and UACI) of TSS map based keys

Test Images	Sizes	TSS Map			
		Initial Value: s to $s+10^{-15}$		System Parameter: r to $r+10^{-15}$	
		NPCR	UACI	NPCR	UACI
Cameraman	256×256	99.2432	33.5701	99.1943	33.5495
Lena	256×256	99.4583	33.6943	99.3546	33.5032
Tree	256×256	99.3362	33.3739	99.4278	33.2639
Airplane	512×512	98.8781	33.4144	98.9002	33.4643
Baboon	512×512	99.3202	33.4222	99.3645	33.4422
Boat	512×512	99.3717	33.4792	99.3271	33.3977
Elaine	512×512	99.4305	33.5067	99.4347	33.4555
House	512×512	99.2172	33.4568	99.1928	33.5045
Lake	512×512	99.4900	33.4458	99.4446	33.5431
Lena	512×512	99.4499	33.4558	99.4637	33.5218
Peppers	512×512	99.4614	33.4652	99.4492	33.4056
Aerials	1024×1024	99.2720	33.4511	99.2608	33.4537
Textures	1024×1024	99.4049	33.4945	99.3950	33.4365

Table 10. Key sensitivity results (NPCR and UACI) of LSS map based keys

Test Images	Sizes	LSS Map			
		Initial Value: ss to $ss+10^{-15}$		System Parameter: rr to $rr+10^{-15}$	
		NPCR	UACI	NPCR	UACI
Cameraman	256×256	99.5758	33.2832	99.5804	33.4188
Lena	256×256	99.5667	33.4285	99.6216	33.5050
Tree	256×256	99.6246	33.4843	99.5575	33.5312
Airplane	512×512	99.5926	33.4711	99.6098	33.4535
Baboon	512×512	99.6101	33.4256	99.6162	33.4347
Boat	512×512	99.5907	33.4456	99.6277	33.5033
Elaine	512×512	99.6048	33.4293	99.5899	33.4358
House	512×512	99.6071	33.4788	99.6239	33.3949
Lake	512×512	99.5911	33.3443	99.6086	33.4351
Lena	512×512	99.6117	33.4232	99.6048	33.5203
Peppers	512×512	99.6044	33.4398	99.6429	33.5040
Aerials	1024×1024	99.6075	33.4546	99.5963	33.4152
Textures	1024×1024	99.6027	33.4528	99.6158	33.4334

Figure 11. Plaintext sensitivity results of "Lena" image: (a) Original cipher image, (b, d, f, h) Cipher images by changing pixels in different positions, (c, e, g, i) Difference images

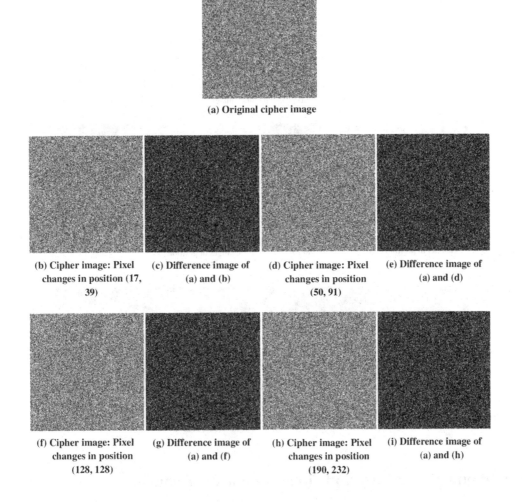

(a) Original cipher image

(b) Cipher image: Pixel changes in position (17, 39)

(c) Difference image of (a) and (b)

(d) Cipher image: Pixel changes in position (50, 91)

(e) Difference image of (a) and (d)

(f) Cipher image: Pixel changes in position (128, 128)

(g) Difference image of (a) and (f)

(h) Cipher image: Pixel changes in position (190, 232)

(i) Difference image of (a) and (h)

Chosen-Plaintext Attack (CPA) and Known-Plaintext Attack (KPA) Analysis

Essentially, CPA and KPA have cracked many image encryption algorithms. The proposed scheme generates keys from the values given for the key parameters and the plain image hash values. Therefore the key values always change as the plain images change. Several chaotic sequences are generated for different key values, and different cipher images are also obtained. Consequently, attackers cannot acquire cipher images by choosing other plain images known to them. This means both Chosen-plaintext Attack and Known-plaintext Attack are not possible in the proposed algorithm.

Figure 12. Plaintext sensitivity results of "Boat" image: (a) Original cipher image, (b, d, f, h) Cipher images by changing pixels in different positions, (c, e, g, i) Difference images

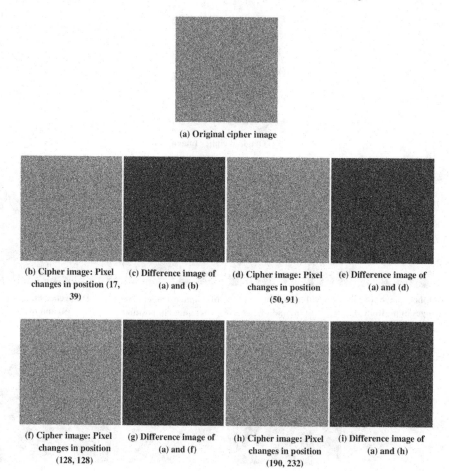

(a) Original cipher image

(b) Cipher image: Pixel changes in position (17, 39)

(c) Difference image of (a) and (b)

(d) Cipher image: Pixel changes in position (50, 91)

(e) Difference image of (a) and (d)

(f) Cipher image: Pixel changes in position (128, 128)

(g) Difference image of (a) and (f)

(h) Cipher image: Pixel changes in position (190, 232)

(i) Difference image of (a) and (h)

Computational Complexity and Time-Complexity Analysis

The permutation-diffusion operation and the process of producing chaotic sequences are the three main time-consuming parts of any chaotic map based algorithm to encrypt an image. Chaotic maps TSS and LSS are used for generating chaotic sequences in this algorithm. Multi-point row-crossover and multi-point column-crossover operations are performed to shuffle the bits of bit-planes. The TSS map based pixel-permutation process is executed to scramble the pixels. Finally, the LSS map based diffusion process is executed through bit-XOR operation. In this algorithm, a grayscale image ($M{\times}N$) is used to encrypt and decrypt images.

In the generation of chaotic sequences, the computational complexities are $O(M{\times}N)$ and $O(M{\times}N)$ for TSS and LSS maps, respectively. So the total complexity of the computation is $O(2MN)$. In the permutation operation, the computational complexities are $O(50M)$ and $O(16N)$ for 50-point row-crossover and 32-point column-crossover operation, respectively. For the combined row-column crossover operation, the computational complexity is $O(50M+16N)$. Since, the crossover operation is in between eight bit-planes, hence, the total complexity of the computation is

Figure 13. Plaintext sensitivity results of "Textures" image: (a) Original cipher image, (b, d, f, h) Cipher images by changing pixels in different positions, (c, e, g, i) Difference images

(a) Original cipher image

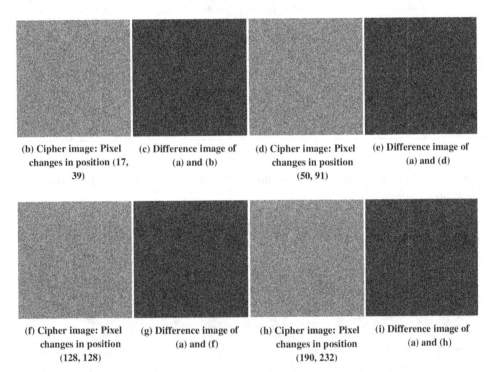

| **(b) Cipher image: Pixel changes in position (17, 39)** | **(c) Difference image of (a) and (b)** | **(d) Cipher image: Pixel changes in position (50, 91)** | **(e) Difference image of (a) and (d)** |

| **(f) Cipher image: Pixel changes in position (128, 128)** | **(g) Difference image of (a) and (f)** | **(h) Cipher image: Pixel changes in position (190, 232)** | **(i) Difference image of (a) and (h)** |

$O(8(50M + 16N)) = O(400M + 128N)$.

The computational complexity for pixel-permutation is $O(M{\times}N)$. In the diffusion operation, the complexity of performing $M{\times}N{\times}8$ bits XOR operation is $O(8MN)$.

Therefore, to perform encryption operation, the complexity of the computation is

$O(2MN + 50M + 16N + MN + 8MN) = O(11MN + 50M + 16N) \approx O(M \times N)$.

Since this algorithm performs one stage of permutation-diffusion and one stage of chaotic sequence generation, the total time complexity is therefore $O(M{\times}N)$.

Table 11. Plaintext sensitivity results (NPCR and UACI) of the proposed cryptosystem

Test Images	(17,39)		(50,91)		(128,128)		(190,232)	
	NPCR	UACI	NPCR	UACI	NPCR	UACI	NPCR	UACI
Cameraman	99.6063	33.4872	99.5865	33.5099	99.6109	33.4405	99.6216	33.4538
Lena (256×256)	99.6155	33.4208	99.5911	33.5665	99.6155	33.4384	99.6475	33.3671
Tree	99.5987	33.4574	99.6765	33.5006	99.6063	33.6238	99.6185	33.4540
Airplane	99.6098	33.4283	99.6262	33.4295	99.6078	33.4189	99.5975	33.4684
Baboon	99.5995	33.4401	99.6113	33.4663	99.6136	33.4777	99.6159	33.4349
Boat	99.6044	33.4037	99.6033	33.4191	99.6185	33.4081	99.6323	33.4367
Elaine	99.5850	33.4971	99.6078	33.4340	99.6239	33.5061	99.6262	33.4518
House	99.5838	33.4683	99.6284	33.4815	99.5964	33.4706	99.6109	33.3789
Lake	99.6304	33.5370	99.6170	33.4206	99.6109	33.5433	99.6212	33.4682
Lena (512×512)	99.5834	33.5117	99.5857	33.4767	99.5811	33.4783	99.6204	33.5163
Peppers	99.5953	33.4473	99.5899	33.4891	99.6098	33.3590	99.6128	33.4897
Aerials	99.6213	33.4628	99.6069	33.4657	99.6003	33.4862	99.5953	33.5012
Textures	99.6021	33.4456	99.6170	33.4167	99.6002	33.4373	99.6133	33.3946

Figure 14. Occlusion attack results of "Lena" image: (a, c, e, g) Occluded cipher images, (b, d, f, h) Occluded decrypted images

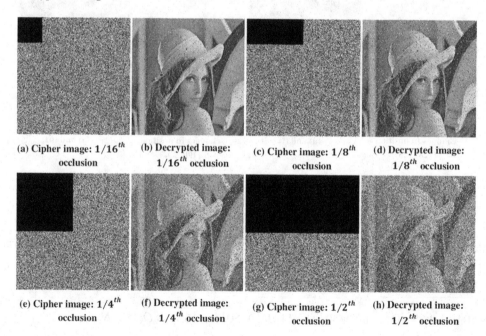

(a) Cipher image: $1/16^{th}$ occlusion (b) Decrypted image: $1/16^{th}$ occlusion (c) Cipher image: $1/8^{th}$ occlusion (d) Decrypted image: $1/8^{th}$ occlusion

(e) Cipher image: $1/4^{th}$ occlusion (f) Decrypted image: $1/4^{th}$ occlusion (g) Cipher image: $1/2^{th}$ occlusion (h) Decrypted image: $1/2^{th}$ occlusion

Figure 15. Occlusion attack results of "Boat" image: (a, c, e, g) Occluded cipher images, (b, d, f, h) Occluded decrypted images

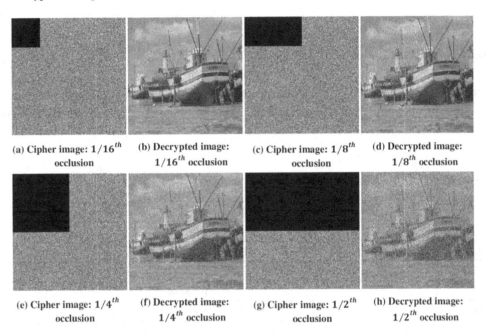

(a) Cipher image: $1/16^{th}$ occlusion

(b) Decrypted image: $1/16^{th}$ occlusion

(c) Cipher image: $1/8^{th}$ occlusion

(d) Decrypted image: $1/8^{th}$ occlusion

(e) Cipher image: $1/4^{th}$ occlusion

(f) Decrypted image: $1/4^{th}$ occlusion

(g) Cipher image: $1/2^{th}$ occlusion

(h) Decrypted image: $1/2^{th}$ occlusion

Figure 16. Occlusion attack results of "Textures" image: (a, c, e, g) Occluded cipher images, (b, d, f, h) Occluded decrypted images

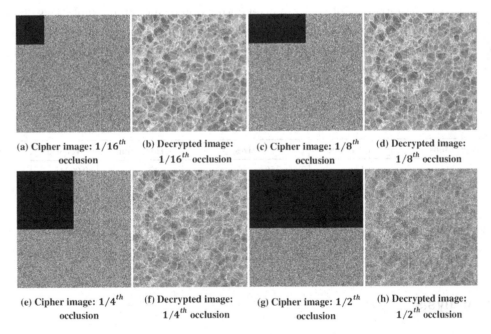

(a) Cipher image: $1/16^{th}$ occlusion

(b) Decrypted image: $1/16^{th}$ occlusion

(c) Cipher image: $1/8^{th}$ occlusion

(d) Decrypted image: $1/8^{th}$ occlusion

(e) Cipher image: $1/4^{th}$ occlusion

(f) Decrypted image: $1/4^{th}$ occlusion

(g) Cipher image: $1/2^{th}$ occlusion

(h) Decrypted image: $1/2^{th}$ occlusion

SECURITY COMPARISON ANALYSIS

The following are comparisons of different image encryption methods based on various measured criteria.

Key Space Analysis

Table 12 presents the comparison of key space results. The table shows that the proposed algorithm has larger key space than the other reported algorithms. This shows the greater brute-force attack resistivity of the proposed scheme.

Table 12. Comparison of key space results

Algorithms	Key Space
Proposed	2.4891×2^{982}
El-Latif et al. (2012)	$>2^{349}$
Wu et al. (2015)	$\geq 10^{90} \approx 2^{299}$
Ye et al. (2018)	$10^{56} \approx 1.0195 \times 2^{186}$
Luo et al. (2019)	Approx. 2^{532}

Correlation Analysis

Table 13 presents the comparison of adjacent pixel correlation results. In the table, it is observed that the correlation values of encrypted "Lena" image along diagonal, vertical, and horizontal directions are nearer to zero for all the algorithms including the proposed algorithm. It shows the algorithm proposed is highly resistant to statistical attack.

Table 13. Comparison of adjacent pixel correlation results of encrypted "Lena" image

Algorithms	Images	Sizes	Horizontal	Vertical	Diagonal
Proposed	Lena	256×256	0.0017	-0.0024	0.0016
	Lena	512×512	-0.0003	-0.0019	0.0003
El-Latif et al. (2012)	Lena	512×512	0.0003	0.0024	0.0015
Wu et al. (2015)	Lena	256×256	-0.0084	0.0004	-0.0015
Luo et al. (2019)	Lena	256×256	0.0006	0.0006	-0.0003

Entropy Analysis

Table 14 presents the comparison of information entropy results. In the table it is observed that for all algorithms including the proposed algorithm, the entropy values of the encrypted "Lena" image are closer to the ideal value 8. It shows the algorithm proposed is highly resistant to entropy attack.

Table 14. Comparison of information entropy results of encrypted "Lena" image

Algorithms	Images	Sizes	Encrypted Images
Proposed	Lena	256×256	7.9971
	Lena	512×512	7.9993
El-Latif et al. (2012)	Lena	512×512	7.9997
Ye et al. (2018)	Lena	256×256	7.997067
Luo et al. (2019)	Lena	256×256	7.9974

FUTURE RESEARCH DIRECTIONS

In future, researchers can use multi-point crossover operation to encrypt multiple color images. Multiple color image encryption is a research direction towards the big data security. Researchers can use mutation operation along with crossover operation to improve the security in image encryption.

CONCLUSION

In the proposed algorithm, a multi-point row and column crossover-operation is employed for the initial confusion process. 50 and 32 randomly generated points are used in the multi-point crossover operation. SHA-256 is used to generate initial values and system parameters for 1D chaotic maps such as Tent-Sine system and Logistic-Sine system. These maps help in diffusion and shuffling process. The strong key space and high security make the encryption algorithm strong enough to withstand any attack. The desired entropy and correlation coefficients as obtained in security analysis add to the reliability of the proposed encryption algorithm.

REFERENCES

Ahmad, M., Khurana, S., Singh, S., & AlSharari, H. D. (2017). A simple secure hash function scheme using multiple chaotic maps. *3D Research*, *8*(2), 13.

Coppersmith, D. (1994). The Data Encryption Standard (DES) and its strength against attacks. *IBM Journal of Research and Development*, *38*(3), 243–250. doi:10.1147/rd.383.0243

El-Latif, A. A. A., Li, L., Zhang, T., Wang, N., Song, X., & Niu, X. (2012). Digital image encryption scheme based on multiple chaotic systems. *Sensing and Imaging: An International Journal*, *13*(2), 67–88. doi:10.100711220-012-0071-z

Floating-point Working Group. (1985). *IEEE Standard for Binary Floating-Point Arithmetic. ANSI* (pp. 754–1985). IEEE Std.

Gao, H., Zhang, Y., Liang, S., & Li, D. (2006). A new chaotic algorithm for image encryption. *Chaos, Solitons, and Fractals*, *29*(2), 393–399. doi:10.1016/j.chaos.2005.08.110

Guesmi, R., Farah, M. A. B., Kachouri, A., & Samet, M. (2016a). A novel chaos-based image encryption using DNA sequence operation and Secure Hash Algorithm SHA-2. *Nonlinear Dynamics*, *83*(3), 1123–1136. doi:10.100711071-015-2392-7

Guesmi, R., Farah, M. A. B., Kachouri, A., & Samet, M. (2016b). Hash key-based image encryption using crossover operator and chaos. *Multimedia Tools and Applications*, *75*(8), 4753–4769. doi:10.100711042-015-2501-0

Gupta, A., Thawait, R., Patro, K. A. K., & Acharya, B. (2016). A novel image encryption based on bit-shuffled improved tent map. *Int J Control Theory Appl*, *9*(34), 1–16.

Kulsoom, A., Xiao, D., & Abbas, S. A. (2016). An efficient and noise resistive selective image encryption scheme for gray images based on chaotic maps and DNA complementary rules. *Multimedia Tools and Applications*, *75*(1), 1–23. doi:10.100711042-014-2221-x

Liu, W., Sun, K., & Zhu, C. (2016). A fast image encryption algorithm based on chaotic map. *Optics and Lasers in Engineering*, *84*, 26–36. doi:10.1016/j.optlaseng.2016.03.019

Luo, Y., Yu, J., Lai, W., & Liu, L. (2019). A novel chaotic image encryption algorithm based on improved baker map and logistic map. *Multimedia Tools and Applications*, 1–21.

Özkaynak, F., & Özer, A. B. (2016). Cryptanalysis of a new image encryption algorithm based on chaos. *Optik (Stuttgart)*, *127*(13), 5190–5192. doi:10.1016/j.ijleo.2016.03.018

Patro, K. A. K., & Acharya, B. (2018). Secure multi–level permutation operation based multiple colour image encryption. *Journal of Information Security and Applications, 40*, 111-133.

Patro, K. A. K., & Acharya, B. (2019a). A Simple, Secure, and Time-Efficient Bit-Plane Operated Bit-Level Image Encryption Scheme Using 1-D Chaotic Maps. In *Innovations in Soft Computing and Information Technology* (pp. 261–278). Singapore: Springer. doi:10.1007/978-981-13-3185-5_23

Patro, K. A. K., & Acharya, B. (2019b). An efficient colour image encryption scheme based on 1-D chaotic maps. *Journal of Information Security and Applications*, *46*, 23–41. doi:10.1016/j.jisa.2019.02.006

Patro, K. A. K., Acharya, B., & Nath, V. (2019a). Secure, Lossless, and Noise-resistive Image Encryption using Chaos, Hyper-chaos, and DNA Sequence Operation. *IETE Technical Review*, 1–23.

Patro, K. A. K., Acharya, B., & Nath, V. (2019b). Secure multilevel permutation-diffusion based image encryption using chaotic and hyper-chaotic maps. *Microsystem Technologies*, 1–15.

Patro, K. A. K., Banerjee, A., & Acharya, B. (2017, October). A simple, secure and time efficient multi-way rotational permutation and diffusion based image encryption by using multiple 1-D chaotic maps. In *International Conference on Next Generation Computing Technologies* (pp. 396-418). Springer.

Patro, K. A. K., Raghuvanshi, A. S., & Acharya, B. (2019). A Parallel Bit-Plane Operation Based Chaotic Image Encryption Scheme. In *Proceedings of the Third International Conference on Microelectronics, Computing and Communication Systems* (pp. 143-154). Springer.

Pub, N. F. 197: Advanced Encryption Standard (AES), Federal Information Processing Standards Publication 197, US Department of Commerce/NIST, November 26, 2001. Available from the NIST website.

Samhita, P., Prasad, P., Patro, K. A. K., & Acharya, B. (2016). A secure chaos-based image encryption and decryption using crossover and mutation operator. *International Journal of Control Theory and Applications*, *9*(34), 17–28.

USC-SIPI image database for research in image processing, image analysis, and machine vision. (n.d.). Retrieved from http://sipi.usc.edu/database/

Wang, X., Wang, S., Zhang, Y., & Guo, K. (2017). A novel image encryption algorithm based on chaotic shuffling method. *Information Security Journal: A Global Perspective*, *26*(1), 7-16.

Wang, X., & Xu, D. (2014). Image encryption using genetic operators and intertwining logistic map. *Nonlinear Dynamics*, *78*(4), 2975–2984. doi:10.100711071-014-1639-z

Wang, X., & Zhang, H. L. (2016). A novel image encryption algorithm based on genetic recombination and hyper-chaotic systems. *Nonlinear Dynamics*, *83*(1-2), 333–346. doi:10.100711071-015-2330-8

Wang, X. Y., Chen, F., & Wang, T. (2010). A new compound mode of confusion and diffusion for block encryption of image based on chaos. *Communications in Nonlinear Science and Numerical Simulation*, *15*(9), 2479–2485. doi:10.1016/j.cnsns.2009.10.001

Wu, X., Kan, H., & Kurths, J. (2015). A new color image encryption scheme based on DNA sequences and multiple improved 1D chaotic maps. *Applied Soft Computing*, *37*, 24–39. doi:10.1016/j.asoc.2015.08.008

Ye, G., Pan, C., Huang, X., & Mei, Q. (2018). An efficient pixel-level chaotic image encryption algorithm. *Nonlinear Dynamics*, *94*(1), 745–756. doi:10.100711071-018-4391-y

Zhang, G., & Liu, Q. (2011). A novel image encryption method based on total shuffling scheme. *Optics Communications*, *284*(12), 2775–2780. doi:10.1016/j.optcom.2011.02.039

Zhang, L. Y., Li, C., Wong, K. W., Shu, S., & Chen, G. (2012). Cryptanalyzing a chaos-based image encryption algorithm using alternate structure. *Journal of Systems and Software*, *85*(9), 2077–2085. doi:10.1016/j.jss.2012.04.002

Zhou, Y., Bao, L., & Chen, C. P. (2014). A new 1D chaotic system for image encryption. *Signal Processing*, *97*, 172–182. doi:10.1016/j.sigpro.2013.10.034

ADDITIONAL READING

Firdous, A., ur Rehman, A., & Missen, M. M. S. (2019). A highly efficient color image encryption based on linear transformation using chaos theory and SHA-2. *Multimedia Tools and Applications*, 1–27.

Kumar, J., & Nirmala, S. (2018). Random Selection of Crossover Operation with Mutation for Image Encryption—A New Approach. In *Advanced Computing and Communication Technologies* (pp. 63–72). Singapore: Springer. doi:10.1007/978-981-10-4603-2_7

Liu, H., Zhao, B., & Huang, L. (2019). A novel quantum image encryption algorithm based on crossover operation and mutation operation. *Multimedia Tools and Applications*, 1–19.

Mondal, B., Kumar, P., & Singh, S. (2018). A chaotic permutation and diffusion based image encryption algorithm for secure communications. *Multimedia Tools and Applications*, *77*(23), 31177–31198. doi:10.100711042-018-6214-z

Mozaffari, S. (2018). Parallel image encryption with bitplane decomposition and genetic algorithm. *Multimedia Tools and Applications*, *77*(19), 25799–25819. doi:10.100711042-018-5817-8

Pareek, N. K., & Patidar, V. (2016). Medical image protection using genetic algorithm operations. *Soft Computing*, *20*(2), 763–772. doi:10.100700500-014-1539-7

Ravichandran, D., Praveenkumar, P., Rayappan, J. B. B., & Amirtharajan, R. (2016). Chaos based crossover and mutation for securing DICOM image. *Computers in Biology and Medicine*, *72*, 170–184. doi:10.1016/j.compbiomed.2016.03.020 PMID:27046666

KEY TERMS AND DEFINITIONS

Chaos: A state of disorder or simply confusion.

Chaotic Maps: Study of dynamical systems. It is a differential equation describing the dynamical systems.

Cryptography: Secret writing of information. It is a method of converting an intelligible message into an unintelligible message.

Decryption: Unreadable encrypted data into readable form. It is the process of converting the protected encrypted data into readable form so that authorized users can read or understand it.

Diffusion: Changing the value of data elements. It is the method of changing the original data elements so that it is completely different than the original one.

Encryption: Readable data into unreadable form. It is the process of converting data into unreadable form so that unauthorized users cannot read or understand it.

Image Security: Securing image data in storage and transmission.

Permutation: Shuffling of data elements. It is the method of shuffling the data so that it is unreadable or noise-like structure.

Chapter 18
Machine Automation Making Cyber–Policy Violator More Resilient:
A Proportionate Study

Gyana Ranjana Panigrahi

🆔 https://orcid.org/0000-0003-2173-2545

Sambalpur University, India

Nalini Kanta Barpanda

Sambalpur University, India

Madhumita Panda

Gangadhar Meher University, India

ABSTRACT

Cybersecurity is of global importance. Nearly all association suffer from an active cyber-attack. However, there is a lack of making cyber policy violator more resilient for analysts in proportionately analyzing security incidents. Now the question: Is there any proper technique of implementations for assisting automated decision to the analyst using a comparison study feature selection method? The authors take multi-criteria decision-making methods for comparison. Here the authors use CICDDoS2019 datasets consisting of Windows benign and the most vanguard for shared bouts. Hill-climbing algorithm may be incorporated to select best features. The time-based pragmatic data can be extracted from the mainsheet for classification as distributed cyber-policy violator or legitimate benign using decision tree (DT) with analytical hierarchy process (AHP) (DT-AHP), support vector machine (SVM) with technique for order of preference by similarity to ideal solution (SVM-TOPSIS) and mixed model of k-nearest neighbor (KNN AHP-TOPSIS) algorithms.

DOI: 10.4018/978-1-7998-6659-6.ch018

INTRODUCTION

Cybersecurity is unparalleled and where significant problems that most of us face in today's digital world. These bring it to a significant place in exploration. The availability, confidentiality and integrity of statistics must have provided. This action can be portrayed as intrusive if one of them is threatened by an individual or else one. The cyber-policy violator may classify through passive and active bouts. Passive bouts can screen and examine web congestion and basing on espionage. However, disrupting and blocking of the web may render through active bouts with its normal behaviour. Machine automation can do by applying feature extraction to the data through manual or various algorithms. The extraction of data automatically involves Machine learning. It is a study of investigation in the fields of quantitative analysis, synthetic intelligence and information technology and can refer to as extrapolative analysis or statistical training. The uses and approaches of machine learning in today's world becoming highly acceptable and prevalent. This learning of machines has categorized through managed and unmanaged algorithms. Here, in this proposal, DT-AHP, SVM-TOPSIS and KNN AHP-TOPSIS managed systems have used for making cyber-policy violator more resilient. Machine automation is highly essential because for processing the intellectual applications like decisions of if, else and to adjust implicit user inputs.

Rest of the section then organized as portion two focused on literature review and its corresponding discussion on cyber-policy violator. Portion three emphasis on taken resources and approaches. Portion four presents investigational outcomes and their routine calculations proportionately. Lastly, the result and our future work placed in portion five.

LITERATURE REVIEW

It offers a dataset-driven windows benign feature engineering method called Hill-climbing algorithm, explaining the learning of machine automation and its representations through standing topographies grounded on comprehensive status. Pope et al. (2018) have proposed that it is a bit difficult infect time killing process and implementations through manual investigation even ridiculously costlier. These are also restricting the capability to respond to novel challenger methods. Potluri et al. (2017) have anticipated that it is more right by using a ranking-based hierarchical network to accomplish top routine calculation for cyber-policy violator and its finding regardless of enhanced precisions through amalgam architecture. The feature can evade the downsides of the distinct feature extraction by giving precisions out of the existing practices. Zhu et al. (2019) have proposed ReasonSmith data-driven with automatic feature engineering explaining machine learning representations for malware finding through both qualitative and quantitative data based on their global ranking. Kosmidis et al. (2017) have proposed improved feature extraction with processing patterns with the study of different appearances of malware binaries to protect against various bouts. Fraley et al. (2017) have proposed a cyber defensing mechanism by finding and high pointing unconventional malwares using machine learning schemes for the specialists. Kesavan et al. (2019) have worked on the conventional optimization delinquent of sensors nodes deployment using the problems of NP-hard class which may help to regulate the precise localization. They have used hybrid Cuckoo Search using a hill-climbing process which delivers distributed localization for obtaining next level improvisation. At last, it helps by confirming through a solution by a value of the threshold for IoT. Chandra et al. (2019) have proposed a cross prototypical and given an idea about lessening the dimension of features from the dataset utilizing filter-based feature assortment. They have detected several classes of bouts taking KDD99 dataset using K-means grouping, successive nominal optimization and machine learning techniques for their first exercise and compiling of the model. They have taken a comparison method between two models utilizing several conventional systems of measurement. It provides protuberant development in the form of correctness in comparison to k-means SVM prototypical. Wang et al. (2020) have given some idea like in communal systems, and account inconsistencies are often revealed in two forms: communal automaton accounts and risk accounts. One Intruders usually create a group of robotic accounts instructions to emulate the actions of ordinary users from a program. There are various causes of spreading malicious information by attracting uncommon users through feature selections. The technique of spreading malicious information by interconnecting different users from various locations can produce countless logging subscriptions and abhorrence within less span of time duration. Though the torrent of accounts that have excluded from policy operatives, still intruders can gain access to re-create similar accounts to distribute malicious information. Authors have used the info-quality gain relation for providing measurable care using AHP to enlighten correctness in addition to calculate the weightiness of the feature dataset. Ullah et al. (2020) have given the idea about uncontrolled evolution of IoT devices provides coaches with a great surface for promoting more useless cyber-attacks. Intended to consume IoT network resources in the network with poor prowler activity. Newer detection methods and systems require a well-designed set of data for IoT systems. First, they study the impossibility of many elements of expression in the application. Second, they proposed a new data set specifically from IoTID20. Third, they have provided substantial rate of topography model which helps by conforming their masses. Again, authors have suggested a publishing process of cataloguing taking the help of generated data set. Gniewkowski et al. (2020) have anticipated detecting the DDoS attacks from past data depending on managed & unmanaged culture using DARPA 1998 and 99 datasets. Mohammadi et al. (2019) have offered an algorithm based on IDS signature assortment (JSON) and grouping approaches by means of filter and covering techniques (FGLCC and CFA). DT has taken as core order for an anticipated scheme. For routine corroboration, the taken method implemented on KDD Cup 99 on huge data groups. Akinsola et al. (2019) they have proposed methods for the selection of different algorithms and their models using Multi-Criteria Decision making (MCDM) delinquent encompasses through one or more principle. For better assortment and result, they have taken seven unique cataloguing algorithms ten routine principles using Fuzzy-based Analytical Hierarchical Process (F-AHP) & Technique or Order of Preference by Similarity to Ideal Solution (TOPSIS) prototypical. Arabameri et al. (2019) have proposed a sturdy statistical model using MCDM which give us the idea to filter our essential features from the dataset. Where they even used the hybrid model like AHP and TOPSIS to get the optimum result from a big data set. The core aims of the study are to assess the routine of TOPSIS and VIKOR using spatial distribution MCDM comparison predicting method among two statistical methods. Nino-Adan et al. (2019) have given the idea about regularization approaches. Especially these approaches extensively used for transmuting the features from the given data set. Here they have exhibited three individual realistic approaches Regularization-Standard (Reg-St), Minimum-Maximum (MM) and Middle Absolute Deviation (MAD). A comprehensive study of the transmuted signatures, choices and impact on the arbitrary distance have been concluded with the result about clustering using each signature entity can obtain through best regularization standard. Hence, they have processed a two-phase approach for regularization and control managed feature calculation. All these approaches based on the coefficient of Pearson correlation and forest feature based on random estimation methods. However, they have chosen and preferred five best features using a two-phased anticipated method in terms of correctness, outclasses and k-means routine regularization which can be used and helps us with our work. Wittstruck et al. (2012) have aimed to evolve one integrated MCDM approach which provisions reutilizing associates. They have acknowledged some prevailing restrictions related to their design and integration using AHP-TOPSIS model. They describe further related to MCDM their jeopardy and compliance administration giving the underpinning of integrity, standards and values successfully. Again, in their study, they have not focused on various factors having the characteristics from interrelationships. They have not focused and studied to indicate interdependencies which play an important role in the feature selection process. Santos et al. (2018) they have also worked on MCDM approach to help physicians to select the adequate classifiers to yield excellent outcomes from their routine calculations using naïve Bayes, SMO, KNN, Bayesnet & C 4.5. They have taken five routine pointers for each classifier as precision, actual rate, accuracy, the curve of ROC and f1-measure. They have presented the results as SMO, C 4.5 and Naïve Bayes respectively occupying maximum ranking through grading of classifiers basing on the said approaches. Gu et al. (2019) suggested that it must, therefore, be proposed dramatically how to identify bouts related to DDoS from congested data network. Recently, prevailing oversight has several restrictions, including controlled ML schemes which requires traffic of data. But uncontrolled learning algorithms can rather diminutively rate of recognition with higher degree of false positive cases. These concerns can address by representing semi-supervised K-mean scheme of detection. Precisely, results have presented a Hadoop-based fusion feature assortment process for finding the most well-organized entities which offers density-based clustering scheme for solving problem related to in and out periphery. Three conclusions they have proposed the first is a feature selection scheme TOPSIS could be deployed for evaluation element. Second, upgraded selection algorithm can be select not only for primary cluster centers basing on the presence of density effective of outsider nodes but also from maximum concentration point. Third, the proposed recognition method exceeds the recognition criteria performance and placement. Kanimozhi et al. (2019) what the idea have presented is that their proposed system is one of the classifications of botnet attacks that pose severe risk for the fiscal sector and service areas. Projected scheme was formed taking the upgraded AI to an open cyberspace resistance data set (CSE-CIC-IDS 2018), was most recent broadcasting data locater set in 2018 by the Canadian Institute AWS (Amazon Web Services) Cybersecurity (CIC). It is a form of featured botnet artificial intelligence system of attack detection which was sturdier, more precise and specific. Their innovative system can apply to the n number of machines under predictable network traffic examination. The planned scheme has extended for detecting everything that it sets for remaining attack sections from the realistic data that could include all actual and existing bouts. The frame has used the AI Scikit for learning and its optimization based on the central processing unit. Panigrahi et al. (2018) have anticipated that Canadian Institute of IDS cyber security has proposed a important data set called CICIDS 2017 presenting about the newest risks and entities for regular performance. It attracts many scholars for consideration because this signifies a threat that has not been addressed by older datasets. Experimental research on CCIDSS 2017 has shown that the dataset has some major flaws. These problems are enough to make any common IDS detection engine biased. They have discovered the thorough features of the CCIDS 2017 dataset and summaries its underlying problems. Lastly, it presents a composite dataset for better cataloguing and documentation of future intrusion detection engines. Researchers have already proposed various intrusion detection models, claiming that the exactness is 98% + along with very inadequate false apprehensions under 1%. This high degree of exactness has engrossed scholars along with MNCs for capitalizing cash to provide effective incentives for users. However, only a few models are adopted by the industries to mature real-world IDs. To find out why, authors look at the latest short-term IDS models, its training sets and schemes for production of universal datasets. Sapre et al. (2019) have given the real scenario that intrusion-based IoT attacks have augmented significantly; hence sophisticated intrusion detection systems (IDS) are required. Much of the current IDS are machine automated that means here the core concentration will be on the received quality of the data that is fidelity of IoT based grid network. Reportedly, as far as authors could realize and consider there are two commonly IDS based datasets can be accepted, they are KDDCup99 and NSL-KDD. Their core projection to make a rigorous assessment on both the datasets. What the authors have done they have evaluated the routine of different MLS systems that can be qualified by looking to an arrangement of larger metrics. The authors have worked and concluded that among the two numbers of datasets the NSL-KDD having higher quality rate of exactness in comparison to KDDCup99. Kyatham et al. (2020), they have suggested the probability parameter of the proposed method is used as the key for two machine learning models one for combine factor and another for new detecting attacks model. In this method, it has said that the decision can only be final when the particularity of model and sample must be explicit. Hence, calculations can make using the assurance that the decision is correct probability parameters and indicates how the probability parameter chances will be right. Thus, the collection of both the models are manufactured by considering as, if prototypical 1 is not confirmed explicitly then result must not be taken into account hence the warranty of prototypical 2 can be checked. If confirmed then, the decision of 1 will be final for 2 prototypical and vice versa. At end, the action of final prototypical can encouraged. Out of two models that the authors have created but can qualified from two unalike datasets, the first uses the NSL-KDD then the second use the datasets from the Canadian Cyber Security Institute. They have proposed a new hyper-parameter where the presence of two is related to the probability parameter with the machine learning model. Nehinbe et al. (2020) have intricately illuminated related to various hurdles and barebones that allied with DDoS data sets. The authors they have chosen the language of C++ programming to validate the possible data sets empirically. From the result it is clear that, the useful DDoS data sets may secure to the researchers by integrating various datasets to one. Uramová et al. (2018) have proposed and the aim is to develop a method for creating a habit set of data so that there are normal network traffic and traffic including a variety of attacks. The data set can be used for testing the network group identification method used by the research team for which he works in the information network department. They have started with a thorough study of the available data sets, which can be an important source of information for creating a custom to recognize datasets and the weaknesses of these datasets. They define the application path, test, and description optimization of possible solutions. The author's information about the design of appropriate infrastructure and uses the system for data sets Creation. Abdulrahman et al. (2020) have examined a reliable data set that is supportable standards and BSD open access is CICIDS-2017 which has comprised of windows benign along with DDoS bout system streams. They have proposed a model which helps in regard of performance estimation of whole ML algorithms with network congestion feature sets by designating finest feature to sense the solid classes of attacks. Authors goal is to save the IP address of destination for the detection of an invader using the misuse detection scheme. Sallam et al. (2020) what they have anticipated is the complexity is involved in the identification of Distributed Daniel of Service (DDOS) processes that reduce the overall performance of the system. As a result, it can lead to inefficiency or failure Internet. The authors indicate that the attack databases are classified into a group of different groups by classifying them as the most aggressive type of attack. Prominent entities which can describe the contour of individual bout, together with penetrating congested features. AdaBoost, DT, Random Forest, KNN and Naïve Bayes are taken for ordering apiece of their attacker's contour properties. DDoS bouts can be taken for all selected Classifier. The main reason behind the feature selection method to increase system appreciation rate. Their characteristics that have included as a function is to be displayed as more accurate features of the excluded operation due to its durability profile properties that attack the target (e.g. DDoS), and may not be significantly aggressive at all for those type of attack in a falling state. For example, the number of samples that included in the function should not overlapped with the functions that are excluded from the terms of DDoS attack detection. Rajasinghe et al. (2018) what they have intended to propose a key task which is project and administration of Network Intrusion Detection (IDS) systems that are limited data sets used for IDS training and its impact on system performance. If the training data set is not updated or the required features are missing, this will affect the effectiveness of IDS. To win, to meet this challenge, they have offered an extremely customizable package ability to create network access data tags subject to demand. Tends to the ability to adapt features, it adopts two ways of entering and exiting data. An input method real-time data is collected by running selected package network nodes, and the other is downloading raw PCAP files other data providers. The output would be either raw PCAP with selected features per package or processed data set custom features related to both individual package features and the overall driving behaviour over a while. Power this software compared to a similar product purpose and significant innovation and proposed possibilities defined system. The authors suggest a package that creates on-demand data sets that can work on the selected network and ability for users to fully modify the data set according to their needs. The data set formed by the projected package context contains not only a raw PCAP file for each package but also a managed data set file in CSV or JSON format that can easily feed into a machine learning tool. The package will also be available with the MIT license so that the research communal will be able to create many new and relevant datasets by adapting every aspect of the dataset. Ferrag et al. (2020), they have proposed an innovative intrusion detection system (IDS) called RDTIDS, for Internet-of-Things (IoT) networks. RDTIDS that syndicates unlike cataloguing methods based on the concept of decision trees and rules, e.g. REP trees, JRip procedures and more. In particular, both methods first and second take the data set as the input selection and categorize it to network traffic as a bout/malware. The third classifier uses features other than the original data set at the output of the first and second category as inputs. Obtained experimental results to prove superiority by analyzing suggested identifiers using CICIDS2017 datasets and BoT-IoT datasets in terms of accurateness, uncovering rate, false alarm rate and existing overhead scheme. Authors said that the data unevenness is one of the details that reduce the efficiency of the Machine Learning processes in cataloguing. The reason may through first, as a simple fact of intentional task used in most sorting tasks is not enough when faced with data sorting imbalance and the second originates from the circulation of classes in the majority class from minority areas are more likely to be invaded. Capacity and classification errors increase, and vice versa. Usually, due to incorrect classification, this can classify an attack as a general behaviour or as another attack in the same or different category. Saputra et al. (2018) the authors suggest data mining IDS as an alternative to abusive IDS and anomaly-based IDS to detect botnet activity. Authors designed a new method that improves the usefulness of IDS in detecting botnets. Their method names two statistical methods in the feature selection process, the low variance filter and the Pearson correlation filter. To prove that their method can increase the performance of data mining IDS, we use exactness and computation time as strictures. A reference entry data set (ISCX2017) has used to evaluate their work. Thus, the author reduced the number of attributes processed by the IDS method from 77 to 15, while the attribute computation time reduced from 71 seconds to 5.6 seconds. This may help us to implement in our work. Authors have studied and implemented a hybrid data mining penetration detection to detect botnet movement on the ongoing network system. Decision tree algorithm has taken as oversight data mining process because it can handle a lot the information flows throughout the network. Authors have proposed a processing priority development for expanding the fidelity of the feature set with a new method in the integrated feature selection stage which helps them to combine two statistical methods, low variance filter and Interaction filter. Increases the efficiency of these methods IDS, especially when determining botnet activity. Lastly, it has proposed that a set of properties is related to time Connection plays a powerful role in perceiving botnet activity. Rios et al. (2019), what they have anticipated as to use of automatic-based ML techniques to identify networks penetration is an important problem in cybersecurity. Different designed to help identify machine learning models malicious intentions of network users. Here authors have deployed two deep learning repetitive neural networks with the variable number of hidden layers: Long Short-Term Memory (LSTM) and Gated Repeat the unit (GRU). Authors have conducted a recently proposed evaluation on Broad Learning System (BLS) and its strictures. The models have trained and tested using the Border Gateway Protocol (BGP) dataset Which includes routing records collected by Reseaux IP Europeans (RIPE) and BCNET, as well as NLS-KDD datasets Network connection registration. Algorithmic comparisons have made with correctness and score F1. Here the use of LSTM and GRU makes the study more viable as authors have found to implement using deep neural networks variable in the hidden layer. Here the routine assessment has done using a radial base function (RBF) mapped of daisy-chained functions to grow hosts and extensive learning. The deep neural networks, BLS and successive combinations of mapped features and its magnifications can be achieved through nodes using a comparative performance and shorter training time due to their wide and deep topographies. BLS the models have a small number of hidden levels and adjustments weight using pseudo-center instead of back extension. They dynamically inform the weight in increasing cases learning from hidden layers. It did its best from the weight due to the extra data scores for large data sets such as NSL-KDD. Growing time properties have mapped as well as the number of extension nodes matching teams resulted in better performance as required extra memory and training time.

In addition to the methods of convention and learning IDS systems, it has been categorized into four different types to deal with information technology, as shown in Figure 1.

Figure 1. Cataloguing of IDS

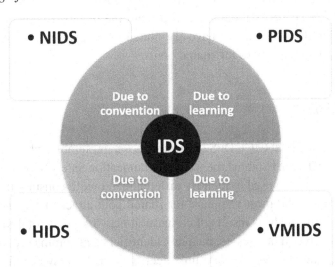

Network IDS (NIDS)

A self-governing stage which classifies it by examining network congestion and tracking can make through several hosts. It can gain access to web traffic using networking devices that have used for socket mirroring or tapping network. Here in this approach sensors are positioned at congest points to track the network, every so often at the restricted area (Demilitarized zones-DMZ) between cross-sectional points of routing. Then the detention of congested traffic that tracked through sensors and can evaluate each packet for the presence of malicious activity in the traffic using some popular tools like snort.

Host-based IDS (HIDS)

Here the host takes the help of an agent to detect impositions through system logs, program calls and by access control modifications. Generally, here sensors are comprised of an application agent. These are sometimes system-specific using custom tools and techniques like Splunk and Apache. It is a form of an essential application for tracing various doubtful activity in a computer or network system, whereby there are many chances of including impositions through external or internal attackers.

Perimeter IDS (PIDS)

First of all, here it helps to detect and clamp the location of imposition. Once this identifies then tries upon the perimeter boundaries of numerous organizations fitted by the help of either most advanced optical carrier or electronic interface technology. When the impositions detected and considered by the system, then it triggers the alarm immediately.

VM-based IDS (VMIDS)

Here the process of detection is being monitored through the virtual machine. This virtual machine monitoring helps to deploy IDS which is the recent emerging technology under progress. It is an integral part of the detection system, which has the power to screen complete system actions. Here, authors have used the most updated CICDDoS2019 dataset and present the results by comparing, unlike machine learning systems. The details of the dataset have elaborated in the dataset section, which comprised of windows benign and the most vanguard for shared bouts.

DATASET AND SCHEME

Here, the most restructured dataset CICDDoS2019 have chosen preferably, which is the common dataset of the collaborative body between Establishment of Communication Safety (CSE) along with the Institute of Canadian Cybersecurity (CIC) used to identify different bandwidth consumption attacks and mostly DDoS. Windows benign and the most vanguard for shared bout attacks have encompassed in CICD-DoS2019 which includes the analysis results of congestion network using total forward, and backward IP packets, sender and receiver IP addresses, data link identifiers and comma separated values (CSV). It contains various records and features like data link identifiers, sockets (switched or permanent) virtual

Table 1. Samples and records of CICDDoS2019

Sender IP	Sender DLCI	Receiver DLCI	Streaming Duration	Tot. Fwd. IP Packets	Tot. Bwd IP Packets	Sockets
192.168.17.21	44987	80	417	4	4	SVC*
192.168.17.21	43134	57	5817	12	16	SVC
192.168.17.26	41543	443	27654	25	29	SVC
192.168.17.21	44423	443	54987	5	5	SVC
192.168.17.28	43675	53	156276	58	63	SVC

*SVC-Switched Virtual Circuit

circuits, conventions, sender IP, receiver IP and streaming duration. Samples and records have shown in Table 1. The entire process took three days for sample collection through various DDoS attacks containing Windows benign congestion.

DDoS Bout Finding Approaches

To accomplish the task here, three distinguished groups of detection can use for DDoS attacks they are

Detection Phase One: Detection is depending on the controlled and managed culture.
Detection Phase Two: We are depending on unmanaged or semi-managed culture.
Detection Phase Three: Finding depending on time series incongruity uncovering culture.

Impeccably these classifications cannot be distinguishable; however, these approaches permit us to understand in a better way that those have used in the problem from the dataset.

Detection Phase One: Depending on a controlled and managed culture.

The most straightforward instance of controlled and managed culture is KNN with AHP-TOPSIS the hybrid model. Timewise different researchers have used this to categorize various status of network (current, before and after the attacks) rather than the congestion of the network itself. The authors used entropy CICDDoS2019 dataset features.

Detection Phase Two: Depending on unmanaged or semi-managed culture.

Various DDoS bout uncovering approaches have depended on unmanaged or semi-managed culture. The training data have managed to divide into two different groups where one has selected for regulating network congestion, and second is for incongruities. This approach permits to improve the distribution that not having the form of sphere segment in routing.

Detection Phase Three: Depending on time series incongruity uncovering culture.

Hill-climbing is one of the extensively used approach depending on time series incongruity uncovering culture. Because the network congestion can reckon as a series of values concerning time and for that reason, it can be applied. Incongruity in the form of a possible bout is a state where the projected value varies from the real value. This can be tested only through the flooding of TCP & UDP packets.

Further realization of the problem can apprehend in a better way through recalling the process of DDoS logging attacks:

Process One: Communicating (L3-Layer) devices.

Networking or Internetworking devices like switch or router can stop from functioning through remote attack bouts.

Process Two: Operating System Level.

Attacks due to the application fault of the corresponding protocol from the OS.

Process Three: Application Intensive level.

Mistakes and faults from the user application layer like ill-defined delimiters and memory (caches or buffers) overflow. And others like

- flooding of data packets that means broadcasting torrent of data to a single device concurrently.
- manipulation due to convention feature bouts like 'synchronization of broadcasting bouts'.

METHODOLOGY

To get the result carefully and accurately, Decision Tree, SVM and KNN managed algorithms can take to organize logs by Windows benign or distributed cyber-policy violator. Machine learning can achieve by merging with AHP, TOPSIS & AHP-TOPSIS as multi-criteria decision-making methods. Then obtained test data can take to measure the precision of learning algorithms. The process of cataloguing is essential for the finest feature selection. Nevertheless, when the higher degree proportion of features including all descriptions have selected, then it extends the duration of accomplishment time, which itself is not a preferable classification choice. Furthermore, hence the most advanced controlled technique which therefore can select as Hill-Climbing algorithm for feature selection. This algorithm helps in reducing the higher degree proportion by finding the most excellent features. As nominated q features $W \in P^{dxn}$ test data reduces to $Y \in P^{mxn}$. Then the Hill-Climbing can be estimated by equation number (1) as

$$F\left(P\right) = tvr\left\{\left(\overline{Ds}\right)\left(\overline{Do} + \zeta j\right)^{-1}\right\}$$

(1)

Where, ζ a parameter of positive regularization, $\overline{Ds}$ Sandwiched-class dispersed matrix, $\overline{Do}$ overall dispersed matrix. Assume i^{th} is the whole dataset correspondent feature using mean and standard deviation, then Hill-Climb of ith feature can be computed in equation number (2) as

$$F\left(Y^i\right) = \frac{\sum_{l=1}^{c} M_k \left(\eta_k^i - \eta^i\right)^2}{\left(\rho^j\right)^2} \tag{2}$$

The high priority features can carefully choose for individual Hill-Climb calculation where it holds sub-dataset of reduced one of the high-rank features from the original set. Comparative accuracy using multi-criteria decision-making method can achieve through appending hierarchy of analytical process (AHP) with decision tree (DT) algorithm. It is the process of clustering algorithm where it can obtain repeatedly using DT-AHP by segregating the test data into relevant clusters further and further, until matching all cluster essentials with its corresponding class label. Some of the patterned systems like support vector machine (SVM) which have skeleton using statistical learning, rounded optimization and operational risk minimization. More often these can be used as a direct or indirect resolver in the field of classification and design recognition problems. When the authors are in search of higher degree optimum feature selection out of the entire dataset, they can take the help of TOPSIS multi-criteria comparison method (SVM-TOPSIS). It may take for solving out the large-scale decision-making problems from various alternatives. SVM-TOPSIS indeed a solution to achieve machine automation to make the tools more resilient. As far as concern another developed classification algorithm k nearest neighbours (KNN) can be deployed for determining closest k value between available to the new problems looking to the similarity measurement of classifications. Value can calculate by fixing the value of the closest K by calculating the arbitrary distance between the target to the other. Afterwards, distances can order by calculating the minimum distance for determining the closest neighbours. However, the problem is to collect and select the closest one out of the large scale. Hence, the authors have taken the hybrid implementation of AHP-TOPSIS integration (KNN AHP-TOPSIS) for making the proportionate model. The proposed flowchart, as shown in Figure 2. The entire model has divided into two parts necessarily first initial set (training) of data for ninety percentages and second input (Test) data for ten per cent.

Each feature and its effect can determine through Hill-Climbing algorithm by creating its respective weight vector classification. Having a maximum weight subset of training data can be attained under k features. The concept of ambiguous sets is well recognized since the eighties of the past century. Therefore, uncertain set model is an arm and extension of the traditional set, where the (many-valued logic) inclusive variables may bear any values in between 0 and 1. Over and above, the theory is very much useful in schemes like multifaceted dependences, multi-dimensional, graded and with inner response rings. Usually, multi-criteria decision-making methods for comparison can apply in circumstances where measurable computational methods can disclose the defects on the source of routine assessment may erroneous to the proposed designs. Now the technical issues can be used to resolve by various multi-criteria decision-making methods to acquire an optimized result (not necessarily technical) through comparison.

Figure 2. Proposed flowchart

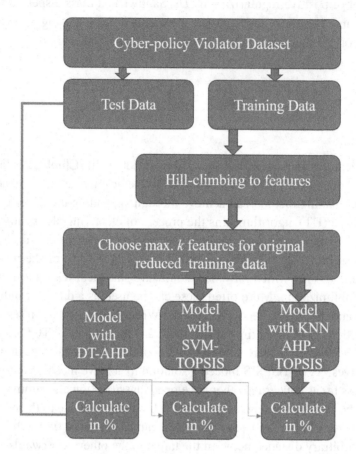

PROPOSED RESULTS

Hill-climbing algorithm may be incorporated to select the best features. The time-based pragmatic data can be extracted from the mainsheet for classification as distributed cyber-policy violator or legitimate benign using DT-AHP, SVM-TOPSIS and mixed model KNN AHP-TOPSIS systems. Here the authors have used various DDoS attacks containing Windows benign congestion for training learning algorithms. A diversity index has used for normalized information gain in DT-AHP, then a linear data separable kernel used for SVM-TOPSIS and an identical label as the neighbouring value used for the training set in KNN AHP-TOPSIS algorithm.

For testing purpose, the authors have taken the most robust ten statistical features out of eighty to meet the need of the current experiment, and the rates of accuracy then calculated respectively. The average results for learning approaches have tested and calculated against a hundred iterations. The ideal feature number is forty for SVM-TOPSIS and DT-AHP. As the KNN AHP-TOPSIS contains more feature so more chance of facing interferences which may diminish the accuracy as in the form of the correctness of feature cut break as given in Figure 3.

Figure 3. Correctness of feature cut break

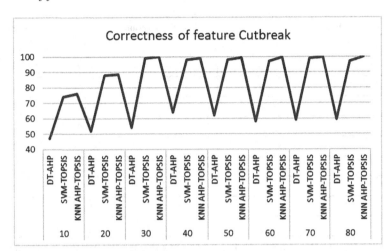

It has seen that features with 40 show the rate of ninety-nine per cent of accuracy, but ninety-seven per cent accuracy achieved through 80 features. Though the size of statistical features reduced from 80 to 40 still, DT-AHP did not show any further variation in the rate of accuracy that it further remains with ninety-nine per cent. Above and beyond to the set of rules, a different system of measurements has used for the routine assessment using eighty and forty features in binary taxonomies, as shown in Table 2.

Table 2. Classifier Assessment Result

Set of Rules	DT-AHP		SVM-TOPSIS		KNN AHP-TOPSIS	
Features size	80	40	80	40	80	40
Correctness	0.9997	0.9997	0.7854	0.7334	0.9685	0.9996
Recall set	0.9997	0.9997	0.8167	0.7145	0.9778	0.9988
Precision set	0.9997	0.9997	0.6745	0.6547	0.9756	0.9977
F1-Score (HM)	0.9997	0.9997	0.7388	0.6831	0.9766	0.9982

Table 2. shows the different system of measurements where KNN AHP-TOPSIS did improved outcomes with forty features and remain the same for DT-AHP approach. However, the selection of 80 and 40 features did not fulfil for SVM-TOPSIS approach. Lastly, to distinguish different cyber-attacks, the Hill-Climbing algorithm can be used for machine automation.

This algorithm gives the most practical list of ten features (Looking to their position of importance) listed in Table 3. for making cyber-policy violator more resilient using 'Mean interval of front Packet' feature tag. This is the high priority important feature which helps to detect any intrusion. The table also shows the way of congestion reporting capability in the form of FECN, BECN & DE.

Table 3. The list of ten best feature tags for intrusion detection

Feature Tag	Priority Position	Congestion Reporting Capability
'Mean interval of front packet'	1	FECN*
'Avg size front porch'	2	FECN
'Max interval of front Packet'	3	FECN
'BWD IAT Std'	4	BECN*
'Total_fpackets'	5	FECN
'Sflow_bbytes'	6	BECN
'FWD IAT Std'	7	FECN
'Packet Length Variance'	8	DE*
'AVG Bwd Segment Size'	9	BECN
'Active Max'	10	DE

*FECN - Frontward Explicit Cramming Net, *BECN - Backward Explicit Cramming Net, *DE-Discard Eligibility

CONCLUSION AND FUTURE WORK

At last, the proposal may present the routine quantities of DT-AHP, SVM-TOPSIS and KNN AHP-TOPSIS basing on CICDDoS2019 dataset proportionately. Outcomes show that DT-AHP algorithm made similar significances for both 100 and 40 features. Whereas SVM-TOPSIS precision is falling, while the precision of KNN AHP-TOPSIS is increasing when feature number reduces from 100 to 40. A regular practice that has acquainted within this study can become workable and implementable for some other study also. The result of this chapter may benefit to the data benefactors, specialists, detectives then law suiters for presiding counter to the invaders.

Our future planning is to run all the dataset of various attacks side by side using Splunk by means of deep learning skills to exercise and assess the feature sets for upcoming exertion.

REFERENCES

Abdulrahman, A. A., & Ibrahem, M. K. (2018). Evaluation of DDoS attacks Detection in a New Intrusion Dataset Based on Classification Algorithms. *Iraqi Journal of Information & Communications Technology*, *1*(3), 49–55. doi:10.31987/ijict.1.3.40

Akinsola, J. E. T., Kuyoro, S. O., Awodele, O., & Kasali, F. A. (2019). Performance Evaluation of Supervised Machine Learning Algorithms Using Multi-Criteria Decision Making Techniques. In *International Conference on Information Technology in Education and Development (ITED) Proceedings* (pp. 17-34). Academic Press.

Arabameri, A., Rezaei, K., Cerdà, A., Conoscenti, C., & Kalantari, Z. (2019). A comparison of statistical methods and multi-criteria decision making to map flood hazard susceptibility in Northern Iran. *The Science of the Total Environment*, *660*, 443–458. doi:10.1016/j.scitotenv.2019.01.021 PMID:30640112

Chandra, A., Khatri, S. K., & Simon, R. (2019, February). Filter-based attribute selection approach for intrusion detection using k-means clustering and sequential minimal optimization techniq. In *2019 Amity International Conference on Artificial Intelligence (AICAI)* (pp. 740-745). IEEE. 10.1109/AICAI.2019.8701373

dos Santos, F. D. M. R., de Oliveira Almeida, F. G., Martins, A. C. P. R., Reis, A. C. B., & Holanda, M. (2018, September). Ranking Machine Learning Classifiers Using Multicriteria Approach. In *2018 11th International Conference on the Quality of Information and Communications Technology (QUATIC)* (pp. 168-174). IEEE.

Ferrag, M. A., Maglaras, L., Ahmim, A., Derdour, M., & Janicke, H. (2020). RDTIDS: Rules and Decision Tree-Based Intrusion Detection System for Internet-of-Things Networks. *Future Internet*, *12*(3), 44. doi:10.3390/fi12030044

Fraley, J. B., & Cannady, J. (2017, March). The promise of machine learning in cybersecurity. In SoutheastCon 2017 (pp. 1-6). IEEE. doi:10.1109/SECON.2017.7925283

Gniewkowski, M. (2020, June). An Overview of DoS and DDoS Attack Detection Techniques. In *International Conference on Dependability and Complex Systems* (pp. 233-241). Springer.

Gu, Y., Li, K., Guo, Z., & Wang, Y. (2019). Semi-supervised K-means DDoS detection method using hybrid feature selection algorithm. *IEEE Access: Practical Innovations, Open Solutions*, *7*, 64351–64365. doi:10.1109/ACCESS.2019.2917532

Kanimozhi, V., & Jacob, T. P. (2019, April). Artificial intelligence-based network intrusion detection with hyper-parameter optimization tuning on the realistic cyber dataset CSE-CIC-IDS2018 using cloud computing. In *2019 International Conference on Communication and Signal Processing (ICCSP)* (pp. 0033-0036). IEEE. 10.1109/ICCSP.2019.8698029

Kesavan, S. P., Sivaraj, K., Palanisamy, A., & Murugasamy, R. (2019). Distributed Localization Algorithm Using Hybrid Cuckoo Search with Hill Climbing (CS-HC) Algorithm for Internet of Things. *International Journal of Psychosocial Rehabilitation*, *23*(4).

Kosmidis, K., & Kalloniatis, C. (2017, September). Machine learning and images for malware detection and classification. In *Proceedings of the 21st Pan-Hellenic Conference on Informatics* (pp. 1-6). 10.1145/3139367.3139400

Kyatham, A. S., Nichal, M. A., & Deore, B. S. (2020, March). A Novel Approach for Network Intrusion Detection using Probability Parameter to Ensemble Machine Learning Models. In *2020 Fourth International Conference on Computing Methodologies and Communication (ICCMC)* (pp. 608-613). IEEE. 10.1109/ICCMC48092.2020.ICCMC-000113

Li, Z., Rios, A. L. G., Xu, G., & Trajković, L. (2019, May). Machine learning techniques for classifying network anomalies and intrusions. In 2019 IEEE international symposium on circuits and systems (ISCAS) (pp. 1-5). IEEE. doi:10.1109/ISCAS.2019.8702583

. Mohammadi, S., Mirvaziri, H., Ghazizadeh-Ahsaee, M., & Karimipour, H. (2019). Cyber intrusion detection by combined feature selection algorithm. *Journal of Information Security and Applications*, *44*, 80-88.

Nehinbe, J. O., & Onyeabor, U. S. (2020). An exhaustive study of DDOS attacks and DDOS datasets. *International Journal of Internet Technology and Secured Transactions, 10*(3), 268–285. doi:10.1504/IJITST.2020.107075

Niño-Adan, I., Landa-Torres, I., Portillo, E., & Manjarres, D. (2019, May). Analysis and Application of Normalization Methods with Supervised Feature Weighting to Improve K-means Accuracy. In *International Workshop on Soft Computing Models in Industrial and Environmental Applications* (pp. 14-24). Springer.

. Panigrahi, R., & Borah, S. (2018). A detailed analysis of CICIDS2017 dataset for designing Intrusion Detection Systems. *International Journal of Engineering & Technology, 7*(3.24), 479-482.

Pope, A. S., Morning, R., Tauritz, D. R., & Kent, A. D. (2018, July). Automated design of network security metrics. In *Proceedings of the Genetic and Evolutionary Computation Conference Companion* (pp. 1680-1687). 10.1145/3205651.3208266

Potluri, S., Henry, N. F., & Diedrich, C. (2017, September). Evaluation of hybrid deep learning techniques for ensuring security in networked control systems. In *2017 22nd IEEE International Conference on Emerging Technologies and Factory Automation (ETFA)* (pp. 1-8). IEEE. 10.1109/ETFA.2017.8247662

Rajasinghe, N., Samarabandu, J., & Wang, X. (2018, May). INSecS-DCS: a highly customizable network intrusion dataset creation framework. In *2018 IEEE Canadian Conference on Electrical & Computer Engineering (CCECE)* (pp. 1-4). IEEE. 10.1109/CCECE.2018.8447661

Sallam, A. A., Kabir, M. N., Alginahi, Y. M., Jamal, A., & Esmeel, T. K. (2020, February). IDS for Improving DDoS Attack Recognition Based on Attack Profiles and Network Traffic Features. In *2020 16th IEEE International Colloquium on Signal Processing & Its Applications (CSPA)* (pp. 255-260). IEEE.

Sapre, S., Ahmadi, P., & Islam, K. (2019). *A Robust Comparison of the KDDCup99 and NSL-KDD IoT Network Intrusion Detection Datasets Through Various Machine Learning Algorithms.* arXiv preprint arXiv:1912.13204

Saputra, F. A., Masputra, M. F., Syarif, I., & Ramli, K. (2018, September). Botnet Detection in Network System Through Hybrid Low Variance Filter, Correlation Filter and Supervised Mining Process. In *2018 Thirteenth International Conference on Digital Information Management (ICDIM)* (pp. 112-117). IEEE. 10.1109/ICDIM.2018.8847076

Ullah, I., & Mahmoud, Q. H. (2020, May). A Scheme for Generating a Dataset for Anomalous Activity Detection in IoT Networks. In *Canadian Conference on Artificial Intelligence* (pp. 508-520). Springer.

Uramová, J., Segeč, P., Moravčík, M., Papán, J., Kontšek, M., & Hrabovský, J. (2018, November). Infrastructure for generating new IDS dataset. In *2018 16th International Conference on Emerging eLearning Technologies and Applications (ICETA)* (pp. 603-610). IEEE. 10.1109/ICETA.2018.8572201

Wang, X., Tang, H., Zheng, K., & Tao, Y. (2020). Detection of compromised accounts for online social networks based on a supervised analytical hierarchy process. *IET Information Security, 14*(4), 401–409. doi:10.1049/iet-ifs.2018.5286

Wittstruck, D., & Teuteberg, F. (2012). Integrating the concept of sustainability into the partner selection process: A fuzzy-AHP-TOPSIS approach. *International Journal of Logistics Systems and Management*, *12*(2), 195–226. doi:10.1504/IJLSM.2012.047221

Yin, C., Zhu, Y., Fei, J., & He, X. (2017). A deep learning approach for intrusion detection using recurrent neural networks. *IEEE Access: Practical Innovations, Open Solutions*, *5*, 21954–21961. doi:10.1109/ACCESS.2017.2762418

KEY TERMS AND DEFINITIONS

AHP: Generally, analytic hierarchy process (AHP) method is using in multifaceted surroundings for machine automation to deal with multi-criteria programming where it is difficult to find out the selected alternatives out of listed feature sets.

CICDDoS2019: It is an authorized set of assessment features introduced by Canadian Institute for Cybersecurity which are the ultimate remedies for all existing DDoS inadequacies.

DT: Decision tree (DT) is like a hub and stub chain model for decision care schemes including their imaginable significances, occurrence of coincidental consequences, cost of properties and efficacy.

Intrusion Detection: It is an uncovering scheme of hardware devices or software program for analyzing host to its corresponding network and policy violator. It helps us to gather the data of malicious or violated actions centrally in well-defined manner.

KNN: K-nearest neighbors the only outfit scheme of machine automation for the process of reversion and sorting insufficiencies. It itself uses the data of its scheme and come up with a newer feature set of facts basing on the actions of resemblance. Finally, sorting will be done through majority votes of its neighbors.

Machine Learning: Learning and study of CPU algorithms through automation which improvises its actions from its own knowledges. More or less it is the subcategory of AI system.

SVM: Basically, it is more popular computerized learning replicas can find in managed ML system related to knowledge-based schemes. It can examine data for sorting and retrogressive processes for automated systems.

TOPSIS: It is an upfront kind of candid MCDM method that is 'technique of order preference similarity to the ideal solution'. It's a process of finding results between an idyllic to an anti-idyllic resolution by equating the arbitrary detachment of one substitute to another.

Compilation of References

AAD. (n.d.). *Melanoma: Signs and symptoms.* https://www.aad.org/public/diseases/skin-cancer/melanoma

Abbes, W., & Sellami, D. (2016, November). High-level features for automatic skin lesions neural network based classification. In *2016 International Image Processing, Applications and Systems (IPAS)* (pp. 1-7). IEEE.

Abdulhay, E., Arunkumar, N., Kumaravelu, N., & Vellaiappan, E. (2018). Gait and tremor investigation using machine learning techniques for the diagnosis of Parkinson disease. *Future Generation Computer Systems, 83*, 366–373. doi:10.1016/j.future.2018.02.009

Abdulkarem, M., Samsudin, K., Rokhani, F. Z., & Rasid, A. (2020). Wireless sensor network for structural health monitoring: A contemporary review of technologies, challenges, and future direction. *Structural Health Monitoring, 19*(3), 693–735. doi:10.1177/1475921719854528

Abdulrahman, A. A., & Ibrahem, M. K. (2018). Evaluation of DDoS attacks Detection in a New Intrusion Dataset Based on Classification Algorithms. *Iraqi Journal of Information & Communications Technology, 1*(3), 49–55. doi:10.31987/ijict.1.3.40

Aberg, P., Nicander, I., Hansson, J., Geladi, P., Holmgren, U., & Ollmar, S. (2004). Skin cancer identification using multifrequency electrical impedance-a potential screening tool. *IEEE Transactions on Biomedical Engineering, 51*(12), 2097–2102. doi:10.1109/TBME.2004.836523 PMID:15605856

Abuzaghleh, O., Faezipour, M., & Barkana, B. D. (2015, May). A comparison of feature sets for an automated skin lesion analysis system for melanoma early detection and prevention. In *2015 Long Island Systems, Applications and Technology* (pp. 1-6). IEEE.

Acharjya, D. P., Dehuri, S., & Sanyal, S. (2015). *Computational Intelligence for Big Data Analysis: Frontier Advances and Applications.* Springer. doi:10.1007/978-3-319-16598-1

Adeleke, A., Samsudin, N. A., Othman, Z. A., & Khalid, S. A. (2019). A two-step feature selection method for quranic text classification. *Indones. J. Electr. Eng. Comput. Sci, 16*(2), 730–736. doi:10.11591/ijeecs.v16.i2.pp730-736

Afza, F., Khan, M. A., Sharif, M., & Rehman, A. (2019). Microscopic skin laceration segmentation and classification: A framework of statistical normal distribution and optimal feature selection. *Microscopy Research and Technique, 82*(9), 1471–1488. doi:10.1002/jemt.23301 PMID:31168871

Aggarwal, C. C., & Zhai, C. (Eds.). (2012). *Mining text data.* Springer Science & Business Media. doi:10.1007/978-1-4614-3223-4

Aghdam, M. H., Ghasem-Aghaee, N., & Basiri, M. E. (2009). Text feature selection using ant colony optimization. *Expert Systems with Applications, 36*(3), 6843–6853. doi:10.1016/j.eswa.2008.08.022

Ahlrichs, C., Samà, A., Lawo, M., Cabestany, J., Rodríguez-Martín, D., Pérez-López, C., ... Rodríguez-Molinero, A. (2016). Detecting freezing of gait with a tri- axial accelerometer in Parkinson's disease patients. *Medical & Biological Engineering & Computing*, *54*(1), 223–233. doi:10.100711517-015-1395-3 PMID:26429349

Ahmad, M., Khurana, S., Singh, S., & AlSharari, H. D. (2017). A simple secure hash function scheme using multiple chaotic maps. *3D Research*, *8*(2), 13.

Ahmed, K., Sachindra, D. A., Shahid, S., Iqbal, Z., Nawaz, N., & Khan, N. (2020). Multi-model ensemble predictions of precipitation and temperature using machine learning algorithms. *Atmospheric Research*, *236*. doi:10.1016/j.atmosres.2019.104806

Ahn, J., Park, J., Park, D., Paek, J., & Ko, J. (2018). Convolutional neural network-based classification system design with compressed wireless sensor network images. *PLoS One*, *13*(5), e0196251. doi:10.1371/journal.pone.0196251 PMID:29738564

Akinsola, J. E. T., Kuyoro, S. O., Awodele, O., & Kasali, F. A. (2019). Performance Evaluation of Supervised Machine Learning Algorithms Using Multi-Criteria Decision Making Techniques. In *International Conference on Information Technology in Education and Development (ITED) Proceedings* (pp. 17-34). Academic Press.

Alcantarilla, P. F., Bergasa, L. M., & Davison, A. J. (2013). Gauge-SURF descriptors. *Image and Vision Computing*, *31*(1), 103–116. doi:10.1016/j.imavis.2012.11.001

Al-Harbi, O. (2019). *A Comparative Study of Feature Selection Methods for Dialectal Arabic Sentiment Classification Using Support Vector Machine.* arXiv preprint arXiv:1902.06242

Alkawaz, M. H., Sulong, G., Saba, T., & Rehman, A. (2018). Detection of copy-move image forgery based on discrete cosine transform. *Neural Computing & Applications*, *30*(1), 183–192. doi:10.100700521-016-2663-3

Alshazly, H., Linse, C., Barth, E., & Martinetz, T. (2019). Handcrafted versus CNN features for ear recognition. *Symmetry*, *11*(12), 1493. doi:10.3390ym11121493

Amalina, F., Feizollah, A., Anuar, N., & Gani, A. (2016). Evaluation of machine learning classifiers for mobile malware detection. *Soft Computing*, *20*(1), 343–357. doi:10.100700500-014-1511-6

Amin, A. & Singh, S. (1998). Recognition of handwritten-printed Chinese characters using decision trees/machine learning C4.5 system. *Pattern recognition and Applications, 1*, 130-141.

Amin, A., Al-Obeidat, F., Shah, B., Adnan, A., Loo, J., & Anwar, S. (2018). Customer churn prediction in telecommunication industry using data certainty. *Journal of Business Research*, *94*, 290–301. doi:10.1016/j.jbusres.2018.03.003

Amin, A., Anwar, S., Adnan, A., Nawaz, M., Alawfi, K., Hussain, A., & Huang, K. (2016). Customer Churn Prediction in Telecommunication Sector using Rough Set Approach. *Neurocomputing*. doi:10.1016/j.neucom.2016.12.009

Amin, A., Grunske, L., & Colman, A. (2013). An approach to software reliability prediction based on time series modeling. *Journal of Systems and Software*, *86*(7), 1923–1932. doi:10.1016/j.jss.2013.03.045

Anandhi, A., Srinivas, V. V., Kumar, D. N., & Nanjundiah, R. S. (2009). Role of predictors in downscaling surface temperature to river basin in India for IPCC SRES scenarios using support vector machine. *International Journal of Climatology*, *29*(4), 583–603. doi:10.1002/joc.1719

Anantha, M., Moss, R. H., & Stoecker, W. V. (2004). Detection of pigment network in dermatoscopy images using texture analysis. *Computerized Medical Imaging and Graphics*, *28*(5), 225–234. doi:10.1016/j.compmedimag.2004.04.002 PMID:15249068

Andrade de Oliveira, F., & Nobre, C. N. (2011). The Use of Artificial Neural Networks in the Analysis and Prediction of Stock Prices. *IEEE International Conference on Systems, Man and Cybernetics (SMC)*, 2151-2155. 10.1109/ICSMC.2011.6083990

Andrade, E. L., Blunsden, S., & Fisher, R. B. (2006, August). Modelling crowd scenes for event detection. In *18th international conference on pattern recognition (ICPR'06)* (Vol. 1, pp. 175-178). IEEE. 10.1109/ICPR.2006.806

Ang, J. C., Mirzal, A., Haron, H., & Hamed, H. N. A. (2016). Supervised, unsupervised, and semi-supervised feature selection: A review on gene selection. *IEEE/ACM Transactions on Computational Biology and Bioinformatics*, *13*(5), 971–989. doi:10.1109/TCBB.2015.2478454 PMID:26390495

Ansari, G., Ahmad, T., & Doja, M. N. (2019). Hybrid Filter–Wrapper Feature Selection Method for Sentiment Classification. *Arabian Journal for Science and Engineering*, *44*(11), 9191–9208. doi:10.100713369-019-04064-6

Arabameri, A., Rezaei, K., Cerdà, A., Conoscenti, C., & Kalantari, Z. (2019). A comparison of statistical methods and multi-criteria decision making to map flood hazard susceptibility in Northern Iran. *The Science of the Total Environment*, *660*, 443–458. doi:10.1016/j.scitotenv.2019.01.021 PMID:30640112

Araujo, T., Aresta, G., Castro, E., Rouco, J., Aguiar, P., Eloy, C., ... Campilho, A. (2017). Classification of breast cancer histology images using convolutional neural networks. *PLoS One*, *12*(6), e0177544. doi:10.1371/journal.pone.0177544

Argenziano & Giorgy. (2002). Interactive Atlas of Dermoscopy. Dermoscopy Tutorial: Vascular Structures. EDRA Medical Publishing & New Media.

Argenziano, G., Fabbrocini, G., Carli, P., De Giorgi, V., Sammarco, E., & Delfino, M. (1998). Epiluminescence microscopy for the diagnosis of doubtful melanocytic skin lesions: Comparison of the ABCD rule of dermatoscopy and a new 7-point checklist based on pattern analysis. *Archives of Dermatology*, *134*(12), 1563–1570. doi:10.1001/archderm.134.12.1563 PMID:9875194

Asadi, E., Isazadeh, M., Samadianfard, S., Ramli, M. F., Mosavi, A., Shamshirband, S., & Chau, K. (2019). *Groundwater quality assessment for drinking and agricultural purposes in Tabriz aquifer*. doi:10.20944/preprints201907.0339.v1

Ashour, A. S., Attar, A. E., Dey, N., & Abd Elnaby, M. M., & Abd elkader, H. A. A., (2018). Patient- dependent freezing of gait detection using signals from multi-accelerometer sensors in Parkinson's disease. *9th Cairo International Biomedical Engineering Conference (CIBEC)*, 171-174. 10.1109/CIBEC.2018.8641809

Astorino, A., Fuduli, A., Gaudioso, M., & Vocaturo, E. (2019). Multiple instance learning algorithm for medical image classification. *SEBD, 2400*.

Astorino, A., Fuduli, A., Gaudioso, M., & Vocaturo, E. (2019, June). Multiple Instance Learning algorithm for medical image classification. In CEUR Workshop Proceedings (Vol. 2400). Academic Press.

Astorino, A., Fuduli, A., Veltri, P., & Vocaturo, E. (2017, November). On a recent algorithm for multiple instance learning. Preliminary applications in image classification. In *2017 IEEE international conference on bioinformatics and biomedicine (BIBM)* (pp. 1615-1619). IEEE.

Astorino, A., Fuduli, A., Gaudioso, M., & Vocaturo, E. (2018, June). A multiple instance learning algorithm for color images classification. In *Proceedings of the 22nd International Database Engineering & Applications Symposium* (pp. 262-266). 10.1145/3216122.3216144

Astorino, A., Fuduli, A., Veltri, P., & Vocaturo, E. (2020). Melanoma detection by means of multiple instance learning. *Interdisciplinary Sciences, Computational Life Sciences*, *12*(1), 24–31. doi:10.100712539-019-00341-y PMID:31292853

Astrid, R., Mohieddine, J., & Dirk, S. (2015). A brief review and a first application of time- frequency-based analysis methods for monitoring of strip rolling mills. *Journal of Process Control, 35*, 65–79. doi:10.1016/j.jprocont.2015.08.010

Athanassopoulos, A. D. (2000). Customer satisfaction cues to support market segmentation and explain 634 switching behavior. *Journal of Business Research, 47*(3), 191–207. doi:10.1016/S0148-2963(98)00060-5

Azam, N., & Yao, J. (2012). Comparison of term frequency and document frequency based feature selection metrics in text categorization. *Expert Systems with Applications, 39*(5), 4760–4768. doi:10.1016/j.eswa.2011.09.160

Bächlin, M., Plotnik, M., Roggen, D., Maidan, I., Hausdorff, J. M., Giladi, N., & Tröster, G. (2010). Wearable assistant for Parkinson's disease patients with the freezing of gait symptom. *IEEE Transactions on Information Technology in Biomedicine, 14*(2), 436–446. doi:10.1109/TITB.2009.2036165 PMID:19906597

Baboo, S. S., & Shereef, I. (2010). An efficient weather forecasting system using artificial neural network. *International Journal of Environmental Sciences and Development*, 321–326. doi:10.7763/IJESD.2010.V1.63

Bagchi, A. (2002). Enforcing the Constitution' S Common Market Mandate: Time to Invoke Article 307. *Economic and Political Weekly, 37*(24), 2303–2305.

Bahdanau, D., Cho, K., & Bengio, Y. (2015).Neural machine translation by jointly learning to align and translate. *Proceedings of International Conference on Learning Representations*.

Bahl, L. R., Brown, P. F., De Souza, P. V., & Mercer, R. L. (1993). Estimating Hidden Markov Model Parameters so as to maximize speech recognition Accuracy. *IEEE Transactions on Audio, Speech, and Language Processing, 1*(1), 77–83. doi:10.1109/89.221369

Balan, P. S., & Sunny, L. E. (2018). Survey on Feature Extraction Techniques in Image Processing. [IJRASET]. *International Journal for Research in Applied Science and Engineering Technology, 6*(3).

Barata, C., Celebi, M. E., & Marques, J. S. (2018). A survey of feature extraction in dermoscopy image analysis of skin cancer. *IEEE Journal of Biomedical and Health Informatics, 23*(3), 1096–1109. doi:10.1109/JBHI.2018.2845939 PMID:29994234

Barata, C., Marques, J. S., & Rozeira, J. (2012). A system for the detection of pigment network in dermoscopy images using directional filters. *IEEE Transactions on Biomedical Engineering, 59*(10), 2744–2754. doi:10.1109/TBME.2012.2209423 PMID:22829364

Barata, C., Ruela, M., Mendonça, T., & Marques, J. S. (2014). A bag-of-features approach for the classification of melanomas in dermoscopy images: The role of color and texture descriptors. In *Computer vision techniques for the diagnosis of skin cancer* (pp. 49–69). Berlin: Springer. doi:10.1007/978-3-642-39608-3_3

Batista, G. E., & Monard, M. C. (2003). An analysis of four missing data treatment methods for supervised learning. *Applied Artificial Intelligence, 17*(5-6), 519–533. doi:10.1080/713827181

Bay, H., Tuytelaars, T., & Van Gool, L. (2006). SURF: Speeded up robust features. Lecture Notes in Computer Science, 3951, 404-417.

Bebarta, D. K., Rout, A. K., Biswal, B., & Dash, P. K. (2012). Forecasting and classification of Indian stocks using different polynomial functional link artificial neural networks. *India Conference (INDICON), 2012 Annual IEEE*, 178-182. 10.1109/INDCON.2012.6420611

Bebarta, D.K., Bisoi, R., & Dash, P.K. (2017). Mining of electricity prices in energy markets using a hybrid linear ARMA and nonlinear functional link neural network trained by evolutionary unscented H-infinity filter. *International Journal of Information and Decision Sciences, 9*(1), 1-26.

Bebarta, D. K., Biswal, B., & Dash, P. K. (2012). Comparative study of stock market forecasting using different functional link artificial neural networks. *International Journal of Data Analysis Techniques and Strategies*, *4*(4), 398–427. doi:10.1504/IJDATS.2012.050407

Bebarta, D. K., Biswal, B., & Dash, P. K. (2015). Polynomial Based Functional Link Artificial Recurrent Neural Network adaptive System for predicting Indian Stocks. *International Journal of Computational Intelligence Systems*, *8*(6), 1004–1016. doi:10.1080/18756891.2015.1099910

Behera, A. K., Nayak, S. C., Dash, C. S. K., Dehuri, S., & Panda, M. (2019). Improving software reliability prediction accuracy using CRO-based FLANN. In *Innovations in Computer Science and Engineering* (pp. 213–220). Singapore: Springer. doi:10.1007/978-981-10-8201-6_24

Behera, A. K., & Panda, M. (2019, December). Software Reliability Prediction with Ensemble Method and Virtual Data Point Incorporation. In *International Conference on Biologically Inspired Techniques in Many-Criteria Decision Making* (pp. 69-77). Springer.

Behera, T. (2006). *India's Internal Trade: A Review of Interstate Movement of Major Commodities*. Indian Trade Journal.

Ben Nasr, M., Saoud, S., & Cherif, A. (2013). Optimization of MLP using Genetic Algorithms Applied to Arabic Speech Recognition. *International Review on Computers and Software*, *8*(2), 653–659.

Benestad, R. E., Hanssen-Bauer, I., & Førland, E. J. (2007). An evaluation of statistical models for downscaling precipitation and their ability to capture long-term trends. *International Journal of Climatology*, *27*(5), 649–665. doi:10.1002/joc.1421

Bengio, Y., Courville, A., & Vincent, P. (2013). Representation learning: A review and new perspectives. *IEEE Transactions on Pattern Analysis and Machine Intelligence*, *35*(8), 1798–1828. doi:10.1109/TPAMI.2013.50

Bennasar, Hicks, & Setchi. (2015). Feature selection using Joint Mutual Information Maximisation. *Expert Systems With Applications*.

Bennette, W. D. (2014). *Instance Selection for Model-Based Classifiers*. Graduate Thesis and Dissertations, Iowa State University.

Benzebouchi, N. E., Azizi, N., & Ayadi, K. (2019). A computer-aided diagnosis system for breast cancer using deep convolutional neural networks. In *Computational Intelligence in Data Mining* (pp. 583–593). Singapore: Springer. doi:10.1007/978-981-10-8055-5_52

Benzeghiba, M., De Mori, R., Deroo, O., Dupont, S., Erbes, T., Jouvet, D., ... Wellekens, C. (2007). Automatic Speech Recognition and Speech Variability: A review. *Speech Communication*, *49*(10-11), 763–778. doi:10.1016/j.specom.2007.02.006

Berry, M. W., & Kogan, J. (Eds.). (2010). *Text mining: applications and theory*. John Wiley & Sons. doi:10.1002/9780470689646

Betta, G., Di Leo, G., Fabbrocini, G., Paolillo, A., & Scalvenzi, M. (2005, May). Automated Application of the "7-point checklist" Diagnosis Method for Skin Lesions: Estimation of Chromatic and Shape Parameters. In *2005 IEEE Instrumentation and Measurement Technology Conference Proceedings* (Vol. 3, pp. 1818-1822). IEEE. 10.1109/IMTC.2005.1604486

Bhardwaj, A., Bhattacherjee, S., Chavan, A., Deshpande, A., Elmore, A. J., Madden, S., & Parameswaran, A. G. (2014). *Datahub: Collaborative data science & dataset version management at scale*. arXiv preprint arXiv:1409.0798

Bishop, G., & Welch, G. (2001). An introduction to the kalman filter. *Proc of SIGGRAPH, Course*, *8*(27599-23175), 41.

Bisi, M., & Goyal, N. K. (2015, January). Predicting cumulative number of failures in software using an ANN-PSO based approach. In *2015 International Conference on Computational Intelligence and Networks* (pp. 9-14). IEEE. 10.1109/CINE.2015.12

Biswas, S., Bordoloi, M., & Purkayastha, B. (2017). Review on feature selection and classification using neuro-fuzzy approaches. *International Journal of Applied Evolutionary Computation, 7*(4), 28–44. doi:10.4018/IJAEC.2016100102

Bolandi, H., Lajnef, N., Jiao, P., Barri, K., Hasni, H., & Alavi, A. H. (2019). A novel data reduction approach for structural health monitoring systems. *Sensors (Basel), 19*(22), 4823. doi:10.339019224823 PMID:31698686

Bolón-Canedo, V., Sánchez-Maroño, N., & Alonso-Betanzos, A. (2015). (2015). Recent advances and emerging challenges of feature selection in the context of Big Data. *Knowledge-Based Systems, 86*, 33–45. doi:10.1016/j.knosys.2015.05.014

Boualem, B. (2015). *Time-frequency signal analysis and processing: A comprehensive reference.* Academic Press.

Box, G. E., & Cox, D. R. (1964). An analysis of transformations. *Journal of the Royal Statistical Society. Series B. Methodological, 26*(2), 211–243. doi:10.1111/j.2517-6161.1964.tb00553.x

Bray, F., Ferlay, J., Soerjomataram, I., Siegel, R. L., Torre, L. A., & Jemal, A. (2018). Global cancer statistics 2018: GLOBOCAN estimates of incidence and mortality worldwide for 36 cancers in 185 countries. *CA: a Cancer Journal for Clinicians, 68*(6), 394–424. doi:10.3322/caac.21492 PMID:30207593

Brieger, R. L. (1981). Structure of Economic interdependence among Nations. In P. M. Blau & R. K. Merton (Eds.), *Continuities in Structural Inquiry* (pp. 353–30). Sage Publications.

Broomhead, D. (1988). Multivariable functional interpolation and adaptive networks. *Complex Systems, 2*, 321–355.

Bruna, J., & Mallat, S. (2013). Invariant scattering convolution networks. *IEEE Transactions on Pattern Analysis and Machine Intelligence, 35*(8), 1872–1886. doi:10.1109/TPAMI.2012.230

Campbell, D. L. (2010). *History, Culture, and Trade: A Dynamic Gravity Approach.* Academic Press.

Cannon, A. J., & Whitfield, P. H. (2002). Downscaling recent streamflow conditions in British Columbia, Canada using ensemble neural network models. *Journal of Hydrology (Amsterdam), 259*(1–4), 136–151. doi:10.1016/S0022-1694(01)00581-9

Capecci, M., Pepa, L., Verdini, F., & Ceravolo, M. (2016). A smartphone-based architecture to detect and quantify freezing of gait in Parkinson's disease. Gait & amp. *Posture, 50*, 28–33. doi:10.1016/j.gaitpost.2016.08.018 PMID:27567449

Celebi, M. E., Wen, Q., Iyatomi, H., Shimizu, K., Zhou, H., & Schaefer, G. (2015). A state-of-the-art survey on lesion border detection in dermoscopy images. *Dermoscopy Image Analysis, 10*, 97-129.

Celebi, M. E., Iyatomi, H., Stoecker, W. V., Moss, R. H., Rabinovitz, H. S., Argenziano, G., & Soyer, H. P. (2008). Automatic detection of blue-white veil and related structures in dermoscopy images. *Computerized Medical Imaging and Graphics, 32*(8), 670–677. doi:10.1016/j.compmedimag.2008.08.003 PMID:18804955

Celebi, M. E., Kingravi, H. A., Uddin, B., Iyatomi, H., Aslandogan, Y. A., Stoecker, W. V., & Moss, R. H. (2007). A methodological approach to the classification of dermoscopy images. *Computerized Medical Imaging and Graphics, 31*(6), 362–373. doi:10.1016/j.compmedimag.2007.01.003 PMID:17387001

Celebi, M. E., Mendonca, T., & Marques, J. S. (Eds.). (2015). *Dermoscopy image analysis* (Vol. 10). CRC Press. doi:10.1201/b19107

Cetişli, B. (2010). Development of an Adaptive Neuro-Fuzzy Classifier using Linguistic Hedges, 2010. *Expert Systems with Applications, 37*(8), 6093–6101. doi:10.1016/j.eswa.2010.02.108

Cetişli, B. (2010). The effect of linguistic hedges on feature selection. *Expert Systems with Applications*, *37*(8), 6102–6108. doi:10.1016/j.eswa.2010.02.115

Cetişli, B., & Barkana, A. (2010). Speeding up the Scaled Conjugate Gradient Algorithm and its application in Neuro-Fuzzy classifier training. *Soft Computing*, *14*(4), 365–378. doi:10.100700500-009-0410-8

Chaki, J. (2017). Template based shape feature selection for plant leaf classification. *IACSIT International Journal of Engineering and Technology*, *9*(3), 1992–2002. doi:10.21817/ijet/2017/v9i3/1709030122

Chakraborty, S., Aich, S., & Kim, H. (2020). 3D textural, morphological and statistical analysis of voxel of interests in 3T MRI scans for the detection of Parkinson's disease using artificial neural networks. *Multidisciplinary Digital Publishing Institute*, *8*(1), 34. PMID:32046073

Chakraborty, S., & Das, S. (2018). Simultaneous variable weighting and determining the number of clusters—A weighted Gaussian means algorithm. *Statistics & Probability Letters*, *137*, 148–156. doi:10.1016/j.spl.2018.01.015

Challa, K., Pagolu, V., Panda, G., & Majhi, B. (2016). An improved approach for prediction of Parkinson's disease using machine learning techniques. *International Conference on Signal Processing, Communication, Power and Embedded System (SCOPES)*, 1446-1451. 10.1109/SCOPES.2016.7955679

Chan, A. H. S., & Ao, S.-I. (2008). *Advances in Industrial Engineering and Operations Research*. Springer. doi:10.1007/978-0-387-74905-1

Chandniha, S. K., & Kansal, M. L. (2016). Rainfall estimation using multiple linear regression based statistical downscaling for Piperiya watershed in Chhattisgarh. *Journal of Agrometeorology*, *18*(1), 106–112.

Chandra, A., Khatri, S. K., & Simon, R. (2019, February). Filter-based attribute selection approach for intrusion detection using k-means clustering and sequential minimal optimization techniq. In *2019 Amity International Conference on Artificial Intelligence (AICAI)* (pp. 740-745). IEEE. 10.1109/AICAI.2019.8701373

Chandrashekar, G., & Sahin, F. (2017). A survey on feature selection methods. *Computers & Electrical Engineering*, *40*(1), 16–28. doi:10.1016/j.compeleceng.2013.11.024

Chand, S., & Sen, K. (2002). Trade Liberalization and Productivity Growth: Evidence from Indian Manufacturing. *Review of Development Economics*, *6*(1), 120–132. doi:10.1111/1467-9361.00145

Chantar, H., Mafarja, M., Alsawalqah, H., Heidari, A. A., Aljarah, I., & Faris, H. (2019). Feature selection using binary grey wolf optimizer with elite-based crossover for Arabic text classification. *Neural Computing & Applications*, 1–20.

Chase-Dunn, C., & Grimes, P. (1995). World-System Analysis. *Annual Review of Sociology*, *21*(1), 387–417. doi:10.1146/annurev.so.21.080195.002131

Chatterjee, S., Dey, D., & Munshi, S. (2018). Optimal selection of features using wavelet fractal descriptors and automatic correlation bias reduction for classifying skin lesions. *Biomedical Signal Processing and Control*, *40*, 252–262. doi:10.1016/j.bspc.2017.09.028

Cha, Y., Choi, W., & Büyüköztürk, O. (2017). Deep learning-based crack damage detection using convolutional neural networks. *Computer-Aided Civil and Infrastructure Engineering*, *32*(5), 361–378. doi:10.1111/mice.12263

Chebi, H., & Acheli, D. (2015, December). Dynamic detection of anomalies in crowd's behavior analysis. In *2015 4th International Conference on Electrical Engineering (ICEE)* (pp. 1-5). IEEE. 10.1109/INTEE.2015.7416735

Chebi, H., Acheli, D., & Kesraoui, M. (2017, October). Intelligent Detection Without Modeling of Behavior Unusual by Fuzzy Logic. In *International Conference on Model and Data Engineering* (pp. 300-307). Springer. 10.1007/978-3-319-66854-3_23

Chebi, H., Acheli, D., & Kesraoui, M. (2018). Crowd events recognition in a video without threshold value setting. *International Journal of Applied Pattern Recognition, 5*(2), 101–118. doi:10.1504/IJAPR.2018.092518

Chebi, H., Tabet-Derraz, H., Sayah, R., Meroufel, A., Acheli, D., Benaissa, A., & Meraihi, Y. (2020). Intelligence and Adaptive Global Algorithm Detection of Crowd Behavior. *International Journal of Computer Vision and Image Processing, 10*(1), 24–41. doi:10.4018/IJCVIP.2020010102

Chen, S.M., & Hwang, J.R. (2000). Temperature prediction using fuzzy time series. *Systems, Man, and Cybernetics, Part B: Cybernetics, IEEE Transactions,* 263-275.

Chen, A. S., Leung, M. T., & Daouk, H. (2003). Application of Neural Networks to an emerging financial market: Forecasting and trading the Taiwan Stock Index. *Computers & Operations Research on Elsevier, Vol, 30*(6), 901–923. doi:10.1016/S0305-0548(02)00037-0

Chen, C. H., Lin, C. J., & Lin, C. T. (2008). A functional-link based neurofuzzy network for nonlinear system control. *IEEE Transactions on Fuzzy Systems, 16*(5), 1362–1378. doi:10.1109/TFUZZ.2008.924334

Chen, D. Y., & Huang, P. C. (2011). Motion-based unusual event detection in human crowds. *Journal of Visual Communication and Image Representation, 22*(2), 178–186. doi:10.1016/j.jvcir.2010.12.004

Cheng, C. S., Li, G., Li, Q., & Auld, H. (2008). Statistical downscaling of hourly and daily climate scenarios for various meteorological variables in South-central Canada. *Theoretical and Applied Climatology, 91*(1–4), 129–147. doi:10.100700704-007-0302-8

Cheng, J., Yang, W., Huang, M., Huang, W., Jiang, J., Zhou, Y., ... Chen, W. (2016). Retrieval of brain tumors by adaptive spatial pooling and fisher vector representation. *PLoS One, 11*(6), e0157112. doi:10.1371/journal.pone.0157112 PMID:27273091

Chen, H., Guo, J., Xiong, W., Guo, S., & Xu, C.-Y. (2010). Downscaling GCMs using the Smooth Support Vector Machine method to predict daily precipitation in the Hanjiang Basin. *Advances in Atmospheric Sciences, 27*(2), 274–284. doi:10.100700376-009-8071-1

Chen, H., Xu, C. Y., & Guo, S. (2012). Comparison and evaluation of multiple GCMs, statistical downscaling and hydrological models in the study of climate change impacts on runoff. *Journal of Hydrology (Amsterdam), 434–435,* 36–45. doi:10.1016/j.jhydrol.2012.02.040

Chen, J., Huang, H., Tian, S., & Qu, Y. (2009). Feature selection for text classification with Naïve Bayes. *Expert Systems with Applications, 36*(3), 5432–5435. doi:10.1016/j.eswa.2008.06.054

Chen, S. T., Yu, P. S., & Tang, Y. H. (2010). Statistical downscaling of daily precipitation using support vector machines and multivariate analysis. *Journal of Hydrology (Amsterdam), 385*(1–4), 13–22. doi:10.1016/j.jhydrol.2010.01.021

Cheplygina, V., de Bruijne, M., & Pluim, J. P. (2019). Not-so-supervised: A survey of semi-supervised, multi-instance, and transfer learning in medical image analysis. *Medical Image Analysis, 54,* 280–296.

Chhikara, R.R., Sharma, P., & Singh, L. (n.d.). A hybrid feature selection approach based on improved PSO and filter approaches for image steganalysis. *Int J Mach Learn Cybern,* 1–12.

Chien, S.-C., Wang, T.-Y., & Lin, S.-L. (2010, March). Application of neuro-fuzzy networks to forecast innovation performance – The example of Taiwanese manufacturing industry. *Expert Systems with Applications, 37*(2), 1086–1095. doi:10.1016/j.eswa.2009.06.107

Chi, T.-L., Liou, H.-C., & Yeh, Y. (2007). A Study of Web-Based Oral Activities enhanced by Automatic Speech Recognition for EFL College Learning. *Computer Assisted Language Learning, 20*(3), 209–233. doi:10.1080/09588220701489374

Chong, Gonina, & Keutzer. (2010). Efficient Automatic Speech Recognition on the GPU. *GPU Computing Gems*, 1-14.

Choubin, B., Borji, M., Mosavi, A., Sajedi-Hosseini, F., Singh, V. P., & Shamshirband, S. (2019). Snow avalanche hazard prediction using machine learning methods. *Journal of Hydrology (Amsterdam), 577*, 123929. doi:10.1016/j.jhydrol.2019.123929

Claridge, E., Cotton, S., Hall, P., & Moncrieff, M. (2003). From colour to tissue histology: Physics-based interpretation of images of pigmented skin lesions. *Medical Image Analysis, 7*(4), 489–502. doi:10.1016/S1361-8415(03)00033-1 PMID:14561553

Clausi, D. A., & Deng, H. (2005). Design-based texture feature fusion using Gabor filters and co-occurrence probabilities. *IEEE Transactions on Image Processing, 14*(7), 925–936. doi:10.1109/TIP.2005.849319 PMID:16028556

Coates, A., Ng, A., & Lee, H. (2011, June). An analysis of single-layer networks in unsupervised feature learning. In *Proceedings of the fourteenth international conference on artificial intelligence and statistics* (pp. 215-223). Academic Press.

Contreras, J., Rosario, E., Nogales, F. J., & Conejo, A. J. (2003). ARIMA Models to Predict Next-Day Electricity Prices. *IEEE Transactions on Power Systems, 18*(3), 1014–1020. doi:10.1109/TPWRS.2002.804943

Cooke, M., Green, P., Josifovski, L., & Vizinho, A. (2001). Robust Automatic Speech Recognition with Missing and Unreliable Acoustic Data. *Speech Communication, 34*(3), 267–285. doi:10.1016/S0167-6393(00)00034-0

Coppersmith, D. (1994). The Data Encryption Standard (DES) and its strength against attacks. *IBM Journal of Research and Development, 38*(3), 243–250. doi:10.1147/rd.383.0243

Courant, R., & Hilbert, D. (2008). *Methods of Mathematical Physics. In Methods of Mathematical Physics* (Vol. 2, pp. 1–830). Wiley Blackwell. doi:10.1002/9783527617234

Couvreur, L., & Couvreur, C. (2004). Blind Model Selection for Automatic Speech Recognition in Reverberant Environments. *Journal of VLSI Signal Processing Systems, 36*(3), 189–203. doi:10.1023/B:VLSI.0000015096.78139.82

Couvreur, L., Couvreur, C., & Ris, C. 2000. A Corpus-Based Approach for Robust ASR in Reverberant Environments. *Proceedings of International Conference on Spoken Language Processing (ICSLP), 1*, 397-400.

Cudek, P., Paja, W., & Wrzesień, M. (2011). Automatic system for classification of melanocytic skin lesions based on images recognition. In *Man-Machine Interactions 2* (pp. 189–196). Berlin: Springer. doi:10.1007/978-3-642-23169-8_21

Cui, J., Xie, J., Liu, T., Guo, X., & Chen, Z. (2014). Corners detection on finger vein images using the improved Harris algorithm. *Optik (Stuttgart), 125*(17), 4668–4671. doi:10.1016/j.ijleo.2014.05.026

Dash, C. S. K., Behera, A. K., Dehuri, S., Cho, S. B., & Wang, G. N. (2015). Towards crafting an improved functional link artificial neural network based on differential evolution and feature selection. *Informatica, 39*(2).

Dash, S.K., Bisoi, R., & Dash, P.K. (2016). A hybrid functional link dynamic neural network and evolutionary unscented Kalman filter for short-term electricity price forecasting. *Neural Computing and Applications, 27*(7), 2123-2140.

Dataset. (2009). *Unusual crowd activity dataset of University of Minnesota*. Available from http://mha.cs.umn.edu/movies/crowdactivity-all.avi

de Almeida, I. R., & Jung, C. R. (2013, August). Change detection in human crowds. In *2013 XXVI Conference on Graphics, Patterns and Images* (pp. 63-69). IEEE. 10.1109/SIBGRAPI.2013.18

De Sousa, S. P. (2018). *Real-time detection of FOG episodes in patients with Parkinson's disease* (PhD Dissertation). Engineering Faculty, The University of Porto, Porto, Portugal.

Deepak, S., & Ameer, P. M. (2019). Brain tumor classification using deep CNN features via transfer learning. *Computers in Biology and Medicine*, *111*, 103345. doi:10.1016/j.compbiomed.2019.103345 PMID:31279167

Dehghani, M., Riahi-Madvar, H., Hooshyaripor, F., Mosavi, A., Shamshirband, S., Zavadskas, E., & Chau, K. (2019). Prediction of hydropower generation using grey wolf optimization adaptive neuro-fuzzy inference system. *Energies*, *12*(2), 289. doi:10.3390/en12020289

Dehuri, S., & Cho, S. B. (2010). A hybrid genetic based functional link artificial neural network with a statistical comparison of classifiers over multiple datasets. *Neural Computing & Applications*, *19*(2), 317–328. doi:10.100700521-009-0310-y

Dehuri, S., & Cho, S. B. (2010). Evolutionarily optimized features in functional link neural network for classification. *Expert Systems with Applications*, *37*(6), 4379–4391. doi:10.1016/j.eswa.2009.11.090

Dehuri, S., Ghosh, S., & Cho, S. B. (2011). *Integration of Swarm Intelligence and Artificial Neural Network*. World Scientific. doi:10.1142/7375

Dessì, N., & Pes, B. (2015). Similarity of feature selection methods: An empirical study across data intensive classification tasks. *Expert Systems with Applications*.

Devi, T. M., Ramani, G., & Arockiaraj, S. X. (2018, March). Mr brain tumor classification and segmentation via wavelets. In *2018 International Conference on Wireless Communications, Signal Processing and Networking (WiSPNET)* (pp. 1-4). IEEE. 10.1109/WiSPNET.2018.8538643

Di Leo, G., Fabbrocini, G., Paolillo, A., Rescigno, O., & Sommella, P. (2009, March). Towards an automatic diagnosis system for skin lesions: estimation of blue-whitish veil and regression structures. In *2009 6th International Multi-Conference on Systems, Signals and Devices* (pp. 1-6). IEEE.

Dibike, Y. B., & Coulibaly, P. (2005). Hydrologic impact of climate change in the Saguenay watershed: Comparison of downscaling methods and hydrologic models. *Journal of Hydrology (Amsterdam)*, *307*(1–4), 145–163. doi:10.1016/j.jhydrol.2004.10.012

Dolianitis, C., Kelly, J., Wolfe, R., & Simpson, P. (2005). Comparative performance of 4 dermoscopic algorithms by nonexperts for the diagnosis of melanocytic lesions. *Archives of Dermatology*, *141*(8), 1008–1014. doi:10.1001/archderm.141.8.1008 PMID:16103330

Dong, G., & Liu, H. (Eds.). (2018). *Feature engineering for machine learning and data analytics*. CRC Press.

Dorafshan, S., Thomas, R., & Maguire, M. (2018a). Comparison of deep convolutional neural networks and edge detectors for image-based crack detection in concrete. *Construction & Building Materials*, *186*, 1031–1045. doi:10.1016/j.conbuildmat.2018.08.011

Dorafshan, S., Thomas, R., & Maguire, M. (2018b). SDNET2018: An annotated image dataset for non-contact concrete crack detection using deep convolutional neural networks. *Data in Brief*, *21*, 1664–1668. doi:10.1016/j.dib.2018.11.015 PMID:30505897

Dornaika, F., & Khoder, A. (2020). Linear embedding by joint robust Discriminant Analysis and Inter-class Sparsity. *Neural Networks*, *127*, 141–159. doi:10.1016/j.neunet.2020.04.018 PMID:32361379

Dorvash, S., Pakzad, S., & Cheng, L. (2013). An iterative modal identification algorithm for structural health monitoring using wireless sensor networks. *Earthquake Spectra*, *29*(2), 339–365. doi:10.1193/1.4000133

dos Santos, F. D. M. R., de Oliveira Almeida, F. G., Martins, A. C. P. R., Reis, A. C. B., & Holanda, M. (2018, September). Ranking Machine Learning Classifiers Using Multicriteria Approach. In *2018 11th International Conference on the Quality of Information and Communications Technology (QUATIC)* (pp. 168-174). IEEE.

Dougherty, J., Kohavi, R., & Sahami, M. (1995). Supervised and unsupervised discretization of continuous features. In Machine learning proceedings 1995 (pp. 194-202). doi:10.1016/B978-1-55860-377-6.50032-3

Droua-Hamdani, Selouani, Algiers, & Boudraa. (2010). Algerian Arabic Speech Database (ALGASD): Corpus Design and Automatic Speech Recognition Application. *Arabian Journal for Science and Engineering*, *35*(2), 157–166.

Dua, T., Cumbrera, M., Mathers, C., & Saxena, S. (2006). Neurological disorders public health challenges. World Health Organization (WHO).

Dua, T., Janca, A., Kale, R., Montero, F., Muscetta, A., & Peden, M. (2006). Neurological disorders public health challenges. World Health Organization (WHO).

Duhan, D., & Pandey, A. (2015). Statistical downscaling of temperature using three techniques in the Tons River basin in Central India. *Theoretical and Applied Climatology*, *121*(3–4), 605–622. doi:10.100700704-014-1253-5

Duron, L., Balvay, D., Perre, S. V., Bouchouicha, A., Savatovsky, J., Sadik, J. C., ... Lecler, A. (2019). Gray-level discretization impacts reproducible MRI radiomics texture features. *PLoS One*, *14*(3).

Du, S., Ma, Y., Li, S., & Ma, Y. (2017). Robust unsupervised feature selection via matrix factorization. *Neurocomputing*, *241*, 115–127.

Eisele, T., Haeb-Umbach, R., & Langmann, D. (1996). A Comparative Study of Linear Feature Transformation Techniques for Automatic Speech Recognition. *Proceedings of the Fourth International Conference on Spoken Language*, *1*, 252 - 255. 10.1109/ICSLP.1996.607092

El Attar, A., Ashour, A. S., Dey, N., Abdelkader, H. A., Abd Elnaby M. M., & Fuqian, S., (2018). Hybrid DWT-FFT features for detecting freezing of gait in Parkinson's disease. *ITITS*, 117-126.

El Ghazi, A., Daoui, C., Idrissi, N., Fakir, M., & Bouikhalene, B. (2011). Speech Recognition System Based on Hidden Markov Model Concerning the Moroccan Dialect DARIJA. *Global Journal of Computer Science and Technology*, *11*(15), 1–5.

El-Bendary, N., Tan, Q., Pivot, F., & Lam, A. (2013). Fall detection and prevention for the elderly: A review of trends and challenges. *International Journal on Smart Sensing and Intelligent Systems*, *6*(3). doi:10.21307/ijssis-2017-588

El-Bendary, N., Zawbaa, H., Hassanien, A., & Snasel, V. (2011). PCA-based home videos annotation system. *International Journal of Reasoning-based Intelligent Systems*, *3*(2), 71–79. doi:10.1504/IJRIS.2011.042202

Elhariri, E., El-Bendary, N., & Taie, S. (2019). Performance analysis of using feature fusion for crack detection in images of historical buildings. *11th International Conference on Management of Digital EcoSystems, MEDES 2019* (pp. 308-315). New York, NY: Association for Computing Machinery, Inc. 10.1145/3297662.3365800

Elhariri, E., El-Bendary, N., & Taie, S. (2020). Using hybrid filter-wrapper feature selection with multi-objective improved-salp optimization for crack severity recognition. *IEEE Access: Practical Innovations, Open Solutions*, *8*, 84290–84315. doi:10.1109/ACCESS.2020.2991968

El-Latif, A. A. A., Li, L., Zhang, T., Wang, N., Song, X., & Niu, X. (2012). Digital image encryption scheme based on multiple chaotic systems. *Sensing and Imaging: An International Journal, 13*(2), 67–88. doi:10.100711220-012-0071-z

Elsalamony, H. A. (2014). Bank direct marketing analysis of data mining techniques. *International Journal of Computers and Applications, 85*(7), 12–22. doi:10.5120/14852-3218

Emmanuel, A. (1972). *Unequal Exchange: A Study of the Imperialism of Trade.* New LeftBooks.

Fahmiin, M. A., & Lim, T. H. (2019, December). Evaluating the Effectiveness of Wrapper Feature Selection Methods with Artificial Neural Network Classifier for Diabetes Prediction. In *International Conference on Testbeds and Research Infrastructures* (pp. 3-17). Springer, Cham.

Faisal, A. I., Majumder, S., Mondal, T., Cowan, D., Naseh, S., & Deen, M. J. (2019). Monitoring methods of human body joints: State-of-the-art and research challenges. *Sensors (Basel), 19*(11), 2629. doi:10.339019112629 PMID:31185629

Fan, C., Sun, Y., Zhao, Y., Song, M., & Wang, J. (2019). Deep learning-based feature engineering methods for improved building energy prediction. *Applied Energy, 240*, 35–45. doi:10.1016/j.apenergy.2019.02.052

Fang, K., Liu, C., & Teng, J. (2018). Cluster-based optimal wireless sensor deployment for structural health monitoring. *Structural Health Monitoring, 17*(2), 266–278. doi:10.1177/1475921717689967

Farhangfar, A., Lukasz, K., & Dy, J. (2008). Impact of imputation of missing values on classification error for discrete data. *Pattern Recognition, 41*(12), 3692–3705. doi:10.1016/j.patcog.2008.05.019

Farquad, M., Ravi, V., & Raju, S. B. (2014). Churn prediction using comprehensible support vector machine: An analytical crm application. *Applied Soft Computing, 19*, 31–40. doi:10.1016/j.asoc.2014.01.031

Fatemeh, N., Horst, S., Udayan, K., Elias, B. K., & Deepak, T. (2017). Learning feature engineering for classification. In *Proceedings of the 26th International Joint Conference on Artificial Intelligence* (pp. 2529-2535). Melbourne, Australia: AAAI Press.

Fente, D. N., & Kumar Singh, D. (2018). Weather forecasting using artificial neural network. *2018 Second International Conference on Inventive Communication and Computational Technologies (ICICCT).* doi:10.1109/icicct.2018.8473167

Ferrag, M. A., Maglaras, L., Ahmim, A., Derdour, M., & Janicke, H. (2020). RDTIDS: Rules and Decision Tree-Based Intrusion Detection System for Internet-of-Things Networks. *Future Internet, 12*(3), 44. doi:10.3390/fi12030044

Fleming, M. G., Steger, C., Zhang, J., Gao, J., Cognetta, A. B., & Dyer, C. R. (1998). Techniques for a structural analysis of dermatoscopic imagery. *Computerized Medical Imaging and Graphics, 22*(5), 375–389. doi:10.1016/S0895-6111(98)00048-2 PMID:9890182

Floating-point Working Group. (1985). *IEEE Standard for Binary Floating-Point Arithmetic.* ANSI (pp. 754–1985). IEEE Std.

Flores, J. J., Graff, M., & Rodriguez, H. (2012). Evaluative design of ARMA and ANN models for time series forecasting. *Renewable Energy, Elsevier, Vol, 44*, 225–230. doi:10.1016/j.renene.2012.01.084

Folguera, L., Zupan, J., Cicerone, D., & Magallanes, J. F. (2015). Self-organizing maps for imputation of missing data in incomplete data matrices. *Chemometrics and Intelligent Laboratory Systems, 143*, 146–151. doi:10.1016/j.chemolab.2015.03.002

Fradi, H., & Dugelay, J. L. (2015). Towards crowd density-aware video surveillance applications. *Information Fusion, 24*, 3–15. doi:10.1016/j.inffus.2014.09.005

Fraley, J. B., & Cannady, J. (2017, March). The promise of machine learning in cybersecurity. In SoutheastCon 2017 (pp. 1-6). IEEE. doi:10.1109/SECON.2017.7925283

Fu, B., Mao, M., Zhao, X., Shan, Z., Yang, Z., He, L., & Wang, Z. (2019, March). Recognition of Plants with Complicated Background by Leaf Features. *Journal of Physics: Conference Series, 1176*(3), 032053. doi:10.1088/1742-6596/1176/3/032053

Fuduli, A., Veltri, P., Vocaturo, E., & Zumpano, E. (2019). Melanoma detection using color and texture features in computer vision systems. Advances in Science. *Technology and Engineering Systems Journal, 4*(5), 16–22. doi:10.25046/aj040502

Funk, N. (2003). A study of the Kalman filter applied to visual tracking. *University of Alberta, Project for CMPUT, 652*(6).

Gabriel, P. F., Verly, J. G., Piater, J. H., & Genon, A. (2003, September). The state of the art in multiple object tracking under occlusion in video sequences. In Advanced Concepts for Intelligent Vision Systems (pp. 166-173). Academic Press.

Gaikwad, S. K., Gawali, B. W., & Yannawar, P. (2010). A Review on Speech Recognition Technique. *International Journal of Computers and Applications, 10*(3), 16–24. doi:10.5120/1462-1976

Ganesh, J., Arnold, M. J., & Reynolds, K. E. (2000). Understanding the customer base of service providers: An examination of the differences between switchers and stayers. *Journal of Marketing, 64*(3), 65–87. doi:10.1509/jmkg.64.3.65.18028

Gao, J., Hauptmann, A. G., Bharucha, A., & Wactlar, H. D. (2004, August). Dining activity analysis using a hidden markov model. In *Proceedings of the 17th International Conference on Pattern Recognition, 2004. ICPR 2004* (Vol. 2, pp. 915-918). IEEE.

Gao, H., Zhang, Y., Liang, S., & Li, D. (2006). A new chaotic algorithm for image encryption. *Chaos, Solitons, and Fractals, 29*(2), 393–399. doi:10.1016/j.chaos.2005.08.110

García-Laencina, P. J., Abreu, P. H., Abreu, M. H., & Afonoso, N. (2015). Missing data imputation on the 5-year survival prediction of breast cancer patients with unknown discrete values. *Computers in Biology and Medicine, 59*, 125–133. doi:10.1016/j.compbiomed.2015.02.006 PMID:25725446

Garg, A., & Sahu, O. P. (2019). A hybrid approach for speech enhancement using Bionic wavelet transform and Butterworth filter. *International Journal of Computers and Applications*, 1–11.

Garla, V. N., & Brandt, C. (2012). Ontology-guided feature engineering for clinical text classification. *Journal of Biomedical Informatics, 45*(5), 992–998. doi:10.1016/j.jbi.2012.04.010 PMID:22580178

Gaudioso, M., Giallombardo, G., Miglionico, G., & Vocaturo, E. (2019). Classification in the multiple instance learning framework via spherical separation. *Soft Computing*, 1–7.

Ghosh, N., & Banerjee, I. (2019). IoT-based freezing of gait detection using grey relational analysis. Elsevier. doi:10.1016/j.iot.2019.100068

Ghosh, M., Guha, R., Sarkar, R., & Abraham, A. (2019). A wrapper-filter feature selection technique based on ant colony optimization. *Neural Computing & Applications*, 1–19.

Ghosh, S., & Mujumdar, P. P. (2008). Statistical downscaling of GCM simulations to streamflow using relevance vector machine. *Advances in Water Resources, 31*(1), 132–146. doi:10.1016/j.advwatres.2007.07.005

Giuffrida, R., Conforti, C., Di Meo, N., Deinlein, T., Guida, S., & Zalaudek, I. (2020). Use of noninvasive imaging in the management of skin cancer. *Current Opinion in Oncology, 32*(2), 98–105. doi:10.1097/CCO.0000000000000611 PMID:31850969

Gniewkowski, M. (2020, June). An Overview of DoS and DDoS Attack Detection Techniques. In *International Conference on Dependability and Complex Systems* (pp. 233-241). Springer.

Gomez, D. D., Butakoff, C., Ersboll, B. K., & Stoecker, W. (2007). Independent histogram pursuit for segmentation of skin lesions. *IEEE Transactions on Biomedical Engineering, 55*(1), 157–161. doi:10.1109/TBME.2007.910651 PMID:18232357

Gong, Y. (1995). Speech Recognition in Noisy Environments: A Survey. *Speech Communication, 16*(3), 261–291. doi:10.1016/0167-6393(94)00059-J

Goyal, M. K., & Ojha, C. S. P. (2012). Downscaling of surface temperature for lake catchment in an arid region in India using linear multiple regression and neural networks. *International Journal of Climatology, 32*(4), 552–566. doi:10.1002/joc.2286

Grana, C., Pellacani, G., Cucchiara, R., & Seidenari, S. (2003). A new algorithm for border description of polarized light surface microscopic images of pigmented skin lesions. *IEEE Transactions on Medical Imaging, 22*(8), 959–964. doi:10.1109/TMI.2003.815901 PMID:12906250

Graves, A., & Jaitly, N. (2014).Towards end-to-end speech recognition with recurrent neural networks. *Proceedings of the 31st International Conference on Machine Learning*, 1764-1772.

Greenspan, H., Van Ginneken, B., & Summers, R. M. (2016). Guest editorial deep learning in medical imaging: Overview and future promise of an exciting new technique. *IEEE Transactions on Medical Imaging, 35*(5), 1153–1159. doi:10.1109/TMI.2016.2553401

Greff, K., Srivastava, R. K., Koutnik, J., Steunebrink, B. R., & Schmidhuber, J. (2017). LSTM: A search space Odyssey. *IEEE Transactions on Neural Networks and Learning Systems, 28*(10), 2222–2232. doi:10.1109/TNNLS.2016.2582924 PMID:27411231

Grover, A., Kapoor, A., & Horvitz, E. (2015). A Deep Hybrid Model for Weather Forecasting. *Proceedings of the 21th ACM SIGKDD International Conference on Knowledge Discovery and Data Mining (KDD 2015)*, 379-386. 10.1145/2783258.2783275

Guesmi, R., Farah, M. A. B., Kachouri, A., & Samet, M. (2016a). A novel chaos-based image encryption using DNA sequence operation and Secure Hash Algorithm SHA-2. *Nonlinear Dynamics, 83*(3), 1123–1136. doi:10.100711071-015-2392-7

Guesmi, R., Farah, M. A. B., Kachouri, A., & Samet, M. (2016b). Hash key-based image encryption using crossover operator and chaos. *Multimedia Tools and Applications, 75*(8), 4753–4769. doi:10.100711042-015-2501-0

Guo, Y., Chung, F., & Li, G. (2016, December). An ensemble embedded feature selection method for multi-label clinical text classification. In *2016 IEEE International Conference on Bioinformatics and Biomedicine (BIBM)* (pp. 823-826). IEEE.

Gupta, A., Thawait, R., Patro, K. A. K., & Acharya, B. (2016). A novel image encryption based on bit-shuffled improved tent map. *Int J Control Theory Appl, 9*(34), 1–16.

Gu, Y., Li, K., Guo, Z., & Wang, Y. (2019). Semi-supervised K-means DDoS detection method using hybrid feature selection algorithm. *IEEE Access: Practical Innovations, Open Solutions, 7*, 64351–64365. doi:10.1109/ACCESS.2019.2917532

Guyon, I., Gunn, S., Nikravesh, M., & Zadeh, L. A. (Eds.). (2008). *Feature extraction: foundations and applications* (Vol. 207). Springer.

Hamdi, Aloui, & Nanda. (2016). Comparing Functional Link Artificial Neural Network And Multilayer Feedforward Neural Network Model To Forecast Crude Oil Prices. *Economic Bulletin, 36*(4), 2430–2442.

Hamid, L. E., & Al-Haddad, S. A. R. (2019). Automated Leaf Alignment and Partial Shape Feature Extraction for Plant Leaf Classification. *ELCVIA. Electronic Letters on Computer Vision and Image Analysis*, *18*(1), 37. doi:10.5565/rev/elcvia.1143

Hammami, M., Bechikh, S., Hung, C., & Ben Said, L. (2019). 6 1). A Multi-objective hybrid filter-wrapper evolutionary approach for feature selection. *Memetic Computing*, *11*(2), 193–208. doi:10.100712293-018-0269-2

Han & Kamber. (2012). *Data Mining, Concepts and techniques* (3rd ed.). Elsevier.

Hancer, E. (2018) A diferential evolution approach for simultaneous clustering and feature selection. *International conference on artifcial intelligence and data processing*, 1–7.

Hancer, E. (2020). A new multi-objective diferential evolution approach for simultaneous clustering and feature selection. *Engineering Applications of Artificial Intelligence*, *87*, 103307. doi:10.1016/j.engappai.2019.103307

Hancer, E., Xue, B., & Zhang, M. (2018). Differential evolution for filter feature selection based on information theory and feature ranking. *Knowledge-Based Systems*, *140*, 103–119. doi:10.1016/j.knosys.2017.10.028

Hancer, E., Xue, B., & Zhang, M. (2020). A survey on feature selection approaches for clustering. *Artificial Intelligence Review*, *53*(6), 4519–4545. doi:10.100710462-019-09800-w

Han, J., Pei, J., & Kamber, M. (2011). *Data mining: concepts and techniques*. Elsevier.

Hayek, F. (1945). The Use of Knowledge in Society. *The American Economic Review*, *1*(35), 519–530.

Haykin, S. (1999). *Neural Networks: A Comprehensive Foundation (3rd Edition). The Knowledge Engineering Review* (Vol. 13, p. S0269888998214044). Prentice-Hall, Inc. Retrieved from http://www.journals.cambridge.org/abstract_S0269888998214044

Haykin, S. (2016). *Neural networks and learning machines* (3rd ed.). Pearson Education.

Heaton, J. (2016, March). An empirical analysis of feature engineering for predictive modeling. In SoutheastCon 2016 (pp. 1-6). IEEE. doi:10.1109/SECON.2016.7506650

He, K., Zhang, X., Ren, S., & Sun, J. (2016). Deep residual learning for image recognition. *2016 IEEE Conference on Computer Vision and Pattern Recognition (CVPR)*. 10.1109/CVPR.2016.90

Hemanth, D. J., Anitha, J., Naaji, A., Geman, O., Popescu, D. E., & Hoang Son, L. (2018). A modified deep convolutional neural network for abnormal brain image classification. *IEEE Access: Practical Innovations, Open Solutions*, *7*, 4275–4283. doi:10.1109/ACCESS.2018.2885639

Henning, J. S., Dusza, S. W., Wang, S. Q., Marghoob, A. A., Rabinovitz, H. S., Polsky, D., & Kopf, A. W. (2007). The CASH (color, architecture, symmetry, and homogeneity) algorithm for dermoscopy. *Journal of the American Academy of Dermatology*, *56*(1), 45–52. doi:10.1016/j.jaad.2006.09.003 PMID:17190620

Herbig, Milewicz, Day, & Golden. (1994). Comparing Forecasting Behaviour between Industrial-Product Firms and Customer-Product Firms. *Proceedings of the 1994 Academy of Marketing Science (AMS) Annual Conference*.

Hira & Gillies. (2015). *A Review of Feature Selection and Feature Extraction Methods Applied on Microarray Data*. Hindawi Publishing Corporation Advances in Bioinformatics. . doi:10.1155/2015/198363

Höppner, S., Stripling, E., Baesens, B., Broucke, S. V., & Verdonck, T. (2018). Profit driven decision trees for churn prediction. *European Journal of Operational Research*. doi:10.1016/j.ejor.2018.11.072

Horain, P., & Bomb, M. (2002, December). 3D model based gesture acquisition using a single camera. In *Sixth IEEE Workshop on Applications of Computer Vision, 2002.(WACV 2002). Proceedings* (pp. 158-162). IEEE.

Hu, Y., Zhao, C., & Wang, H. (2010). Automatic pavement crack detection using texture and shape descriptors. *IETE Technical Review, 27*(5), 398-405.

Huang, G. B., Zhu, Q. Y., & Siew, C. K. (2006). Extreme learning machine: Theory and applications. *Neurocomputing, 70*(1-3), 489–501. doi:10.1016/j.neucom.2005.12.126

Huang, J., Cai, Y., & Xu, X. (2007). A hybrid genetic algorithm for feature selection wrapper based on mutual information. *Pattern Recognition Letters, 28*(13), 1825–1844. doi:10.1016/j.patrec.2007.05.011

Huda, Hasan, Hassan, Kotwal, Islam, Hossain, & Muhammad. (2010). Inhibition/Enhancement Network Performance Evaluation for Noise Robust ASR. *International Review on Computers and Software, 5*(5), 548–556.

Huth, R. (1999). Statistical downscaling in central Europe: Evaluation of methods and potential predictors. *Climate Research, 13*(2), 91–101. doi:10.3354/cr013091

Huth, R. (2002). Statistical downscaling of daily temperature in central Europe. *Journal of Climate, 15*(13), 1731–1742. doi:10.1175/1520-0442(2002)015<1731:SDODTI>2.0.CO;2

Huth, R. (2004). Sensitivity of local daily temperature change estimates to the selection of downscaling models and predictors. *Journal of Climate, 17*(3), 640–652. doi:10.1175/1520-0442(2004)017<0640:SOLDTC>2.0.CO;2

Hu, Y., & Loizou, P. (2007). Subjective Evaluation and Comparison of Speech Enhancement Algorithms. *Speech Communication, 49*(7-8), 588–601. doi:10.1016/j.specom.2006.12.006 PMID:18046463

Hu, Y., & Philipos, C. L. (2008). Evaluation of Objective Quality Measures for Speech Enhancement. *IEEE Transactions on Audio, Speech, and Language Processing, 16*(1), 229–237. doi:10.1109/TASL.2007.911054

International Agency for Research on Cancer. (2019). *Global cancer observatory.* World Health Organization. http://gco. iarc. fr

IPCC. (1996). Intergovernmental Panel on Climate Change (IPCC), 1996. Report of the Twelfth Season of the Intergovernmental Panel on Climate Change, Mexico City.

IPCC. (2007). The physical science basis. Summary for policymakers. Contribution of working group I to the fourth assessment report. The Intergovernmental Panel on Climate Change. *Climatic Change.*

Irachmawan, E. W., & Barakbah, A. R. (2015).Optimization of missing value imputation using reinforcement programming. In *Proceedings of International Electronics Symposium*, 128–133.

Isard, M., & Blake, A. (1998). Condensation—Conditional density propagation for visual tracking. *International Journal of Computer Vision, 29*(1), 5–28. doi:10.1023/A:1008078328650

Islam, M. M., Rabby, A. S. A., Arfin, M. H. R., & Hossain, S. A. (2019, July). PataNET: A Convolutional Neural Networks to Identify Plant from Leaf Images. In *2019 10th International Conference on Computing, Communication and Networking Technologies (ICCCNT)* (pp. 1-6). IEEE. 10.1109/ICCCNT45670.2019.8944667

Jain, S., & Pise, N. (2015). Computer aided melanoma skin cancer detection using image processing. *Procedia Computer Science, 48*, 735–740. doi:10.1016/j.procs.2015.04.209

Jaiswal, A., & Malhotra, R. (2018). Software reliability prediction using machine learning techniques. *International Journal of System Assurance Engineering and Management, 9*(1), 230–244.

Jana, R., & Bagchi, S. B. (2015). Distributional Aspects of Some Statistics in Weighted Social Networks. *The Journal of Mathematical Sociology*, *39*(1), 1–28. doi:10.1080/0022250X.2013.866671

Jang, K., Kim, N., & An, Y.-K. (2019). Deep learning–based autonomous concrete crack evaluation through hybrid image scanning. *Structural Health Monitoring*, *18*(5-6), 1722–1737. doi:10.1177/1475921718821719

Jaworek-Korjakowska, J., & Kłeczek, P. (2016). Automatic classification of specific melanocytic lesions using artificial intelligence. *BioMed Research International*. PMID:26885520

Jiang, Y., Cukic, B., & Menzies, T. (2008, July). Can data transformation help in the detection of fault-prone modules? In *Proceedings of the 2008 workshop on Defects in large software systems* (pp. 16-20). 10.1145/1390817.1390822

Ji, J., Bai, T., Zhou, C., Ma, C., & Wang, Z. (2013). An improved k-prototypes clustering algorithm for mixed numeric and categorical data. *Neurocomputing*, *120*, 590–596. doi:10.1016/j.neucom.2013.04.011

Jin, C., & Yang, C. (2011). Integrating hierarchical feature selection and classifier training for multi-label image annotation. In *Proceedings of the 34th international ACM SIGIR conference on Research and development in Information Retrieval*, (pp. 515–524). ACM 10.1145/2009916.2009987

Ji, Q., & Yang, X. (2002). Real-time eye, gaze, and face pose tracking for monitoring driver vigilance. *Real-Time Imaging*, *8*(5), 357–377. doi:10.1006/rtim.2002.0279

Juneja, K. (2019). A fuzzy-filtered neuro-fuzzy framework for software fault prediction for inter-version and inter-project evaluation. *Applied Soft Computing*, *77*, 696–713. doi:10.1016/j.asoc.2019.02.008

Kabir, S. (2010). Imaging-based detection of AAR induced map-crack damage in concrete structure. *NDT & E International*, *43*(6), 461–469. doi:10.1016/j.ndteint.2010.04.007

Kala, J. R., Viriri, S., & Moodley, D. (2016). Sinuosity coefficients for leaf shape characterisation. In *Advances in Nature and Biologically Inspired Computing* (pp. 141–150). Cham: Springer. doi:10.1007/978-3-319-27400-3_13

Kanimozhi, V., & Jacob, T. P. (2019, April). Artificial intelligence-based network intrusion detection with hyper-parameter optimization tuning on the realistic cyber dataset CSE-CIC-IDS2018 using cloud computing. In *2019 International Conference on Communication and Signal Processing (ICCSP)* (pp. 0033-0036). IEEE. 10.1109/ICCSP.2019.8698029

Karaddi, S. H., Babu, A., & Reddy, R. K. (2018), Detection of Brain Tumor Using Otsu-Region Based Method of Segmentation. *Proc. 2nd Int. Conf. Comput. Methodol. Commun. ICCMC 2018*, 128–134. 10.1109/ICCMC.2018.8488013

Karan, B., Sahu, S., & Mahto, K. (2020). Parkinson disease prediction using intrinsic mode function based features from speech signal. *Biocybernetics and Biomedical Engineering*, *40*(1), 249–264. doi:10.1016/j.bbe.2019.05.005

Karballaeezadeh, N., Mohammadzadeh, S. D., Shamshirband, S., Hajikhodaverdikhan, P., Mosavi, A., & Chau, K. (2019). Prediction of remaining service life of pavement using an optimized support vector machine (case study of Semnan–firuzkuh road). *Engineering Applications of Computational Fluid Mechanics*, *13*(1), 188–198. doi:10.1080/19942060.2018.1563829

Karpathy, A., & Fei-Fei, L. (2015). Deep visual-semantic alignments for generating image descriptions. In *Proceedings of the IEEE conference on computer vision and pattern recognition* (pp. 3128-3137). 10.1109/CVPR.2015.7298932

Kasmi, R., & Mokrani, K. (2016). Classification of malignant melanoma and benign skin lesions: Implementation of automatic ABCD rule. *IET Image Processing*, *10*(6), 448–455. doi:10.1049/iet-ipr.2015.0385

Kaswan, K. S., Choudhary, S., & Sharma, K. (2015). Software reliability modeling using soft computing techniques: Critical review. *Journal of Information Technology and Software Engineering*, *5*, 144.

Katagiri, S., & Lee, C.-H. (1993). A New hybrid algorithm for speech recognition based on HMM segmentation and learning Vector quantization. *IEEE Transactions on Audio, Speech, and Language Processing, 1*(4), 21–430.

Keerthi, S. S., & Lin, C. J. (2003). Asymptotic behaviors of support vector machines with gaussian kernel. *Neural Computation, 15*(7), 1667–1689. doi:10.1162/089976603321891855 PMID:12816571

Kendall, A., Grimes, M., & Cipolla, R. (2015). Posenet: A convolutional network for real-time 6-dof camera relocalization. *Proceedings of the IEEE international conference on computer vision*, 2938–2946.

Kermani, F. Z., Eslami, E., & Sadeghi, F. (2019). Global Filter–Wrapper method based on class-dependent correlation for text classification. *Engineering Applications of Artificial Intelligence, 85*, 619–633. doi:10.1016/j.engappai.2019.07.003

Kesavan, S. P., Sivaraj, K., Palanisamy, A., & Murugasamy, R. (2019). Distributed Localization Algorithm Using Hybrid Cuckoo Search with Hill Climbing (CS-HC) Algorithm for Internet of Things. *International Journal of Psychosocial Rehabilitation, 23*(4).

Khandelwal, I., Adhikari, R., & Verma, G. (2015). Time Series Forecasting Using Hybrid ARIMA and ANN Models Based on DWT Decomposition. *Procedia Computer Science, 48*, 173-179.

Khan, M. A., Sharif, M., Javed, M. Y., Akram, T., Yasmin, M., & Saba, T. (2017). License number plate recognition system using entropy-based features selection approach with SVM. *IET Image Processing, 12*(2), 200–209. doi:10.1049/iet-ipr.2017.0368

Khiabani, F. B., Ramezankhani, A., Azizi, F., Hadaegh, F., Steyerberg, E. W., & Khalili, D. (2015). A tutorial on variable selection for clinical prediction models: Feature selection methods in data-mining could improve the results. *Journal of Clinical Epidemiology*. doi:10.1016/j.jclinepi.2015.10.002

Khurana, U., Turaga, D., Samulowitz, H., & Parthasrathy, S. (2016, December). Cognito: Automated feature engineering for supervised learning. In *2016 IEEE 16th International Conference on Data Mining Workshops (ICDMW)* (pp. 1304-1307). IEEE.

Kim, G., & Loizou, P. C. (2010). Improving Speech Intelligibility in Noise using a Binary Mask that is Based on Magnitude Spectrum Constraints. *IEEE Signal Processing Letters, 17*(12), 1010–1013.

Kim, H., Ahn, E., Shin, M., & Sim, S.-H. (2019). Crack and noncrack classification from concrete surface images using machine learning. *Structural Health Monitoring, 18*(3), 725–738. doi:10.1177/1475921718768747

Kim, I.-S. (2006). Automatic Speech Recognition: Reliability and Pedagogical Implications for Teaching Pronunciation. *Journal of Educational Technology & Society, 9*(1), 322–334.

Kim, Lu, Hu, & Loizou. (2009). An algorithm that improves Speech Intelligibility in Noise for Normal-Hearing Listeners. [PubMed]. *The Journal of the Acoustical Society of America, 126*(3), 1486–1494. doi:10.1121/1.3184603

Kim, S., & Kim, H. S. (2008). Neural networks and genetic algorithm approach for nonlinear evaporation and evapotranspiration modeling. *Journal of Hydrology (Amsterdam), 351*(3–4), 299–317. doi:10.1016/j.jhydrol.2007.12.014

Klak, T. (1998). *Globalization and Neoliberalism: The Caribbean Context*. Rowman&Littlefield.

Kosmidis, K., & Kalloniatis, C. (2017, September). Machine learning and images for malware detection and classification. In *Proceedings of the 21st Pan-Hellenic Conference on Informatics* (pp. 1-6). 10.1145/3139367.3139400

Kostopoulou, E., Giannakopoulos, C., Anagnostopoulou, C., Tolika, K., Maheras, P., Vafiadis, M., & Founda, D. (2007). Simulating maximum and minimum temperature over Greece: A comparison of three downscaling techniques. *Theoretical and Applied Climatology, 90*(1–2), 65–82. doi:10.100700704-006-0269-x

Krasanakis, E., Spyromitros-Xioufis, E., Papadopoulos, S., & Kompatsiaris, Y. (2018, April). Adaptive sensitive re-weighting to mitigate bias in fairness-aware classification. In *Proceedings of the 2018 World Wide Web Conference* (pp. 853-862). 10.1145/3178876.3186133

Krig, S., & Krig, S. (2014). Interest point detector and feature descriptor survey. In Computer Vision Metrics (pp. 217-282). Apress. doi:10.1007/978-1-4302-5930-5_6

Krishna & Mitra. (1998). Trade Liberalization, Market Discipline and Productivity Growth: New Evidence from India. *The Journal of Development Studies, 56*(2), 447–462.

Krizhevsky, A., Sutskever, I., & Hinton, G. E. (2012). Imagenet classification with deep convolutional neural networks. In Advances in neural information processing systems (pp. 1097-1105). Academic Press.

Krizhevsky, A., Sutskever, I., & Hinton, G. E. (2012). Imagenet classification with deep convolutional neural networks. *Advances in Neural Information Processing Systems.*

Kuhn, M., & Johnson, K. (2019). *Feature engineering and selection: A practical approach for predictive models.* CRC Press. doi:10.1201/9781315108230

Kulsoom, A., Xiao, D., & Abbas, S. A. (2016). An efficient and noise resistive selective image encryption scheme for gray images based on chaotic maps and DNA complementary rules. *Multimedia Tools and Applications, 75*(1), 1–23. doi:10.100711042-014-2221-x

Kumar, A. (2016). Machine learning based approaches for prediction of Parkinson's disease. *Machine Learning and Applications: An International Journal, 3*(2), 33–39. doi:10.5121/mlaij.2016.3203

Kumar, A., & Sharma, M. P. (2017). Estimation of green house gas emissions from Koteshwar hydropower reservoir, India. *Environmental Monitoring and Assessment, 189*(5). doi:10.100710661-017-5958-7 PMID:28451962

Kumar, P. S., & Chatteijee, S. (2016, December). Computer aided diagnostic for cancer detection using MRI images of brain (Brain tumor detection and classification system). In *2016 IEEE Annual India Conference (INDICON)* (pp. 1-6). IEEE. 10.1109/INDICON.2016.7838875

Kyatham, A. S., Nichal, M. A., & Deore, B. S. (2020, March). A Novel Approach for Network Intrusion Detection using Probability Parameter to Ensemble Machine Learning Models. In *2020 Fourth International Conference on Computing Methodologies and Communication (ICCMC)* (pp. 608-613). IEEE. 10.1109/ICCMC48092.2020.ICCMC-000113

Labani, M., Moradi, P., Ahmadizar, F., & Jalili, M. (2018). A novel multivariate filter method for feature selection in text classification problems. *Engineering Applications of Artificial Intelligence, 70*, 25–37. doi:10.1016/j.engappai.2017.12.014

Lakshmanan, I., & Ramasamy, S. (2015). An artificial neural-network approach to software reliability growth modeling. *Procedia Computer Science, 57*, 695–702. doi:10.1016/j.procs.2015.07.450

Lal Kansal, M., Chandniha, S. K., & Tyagi, A. (2015). Distance based water sustainability assessment using SPI for the state of Chhattisgarh in India. In *World Environmental and Water Resources Congress 2015: Floods, Droughts, and Ecosystems - Proceedings of the 2015 World Environmental and Water Resources Congress* (pp. 2300–2319). American Society of Civil Engineers (ASCE). https://doi.org/10.1061/9780784479162.227

Landman, W. A., Mason, S. J., Tyson, P. D., & Tennant, W. J. (2001). Statistical downscaling of GCM simulations to streamflow. *Journal of Hydrology (Amsterdam), 252*(1–4), 221–236. doi:10.1016/S0022-1694(01)00457-7

Le, D. C., Zhang, J., & Pang, Y. (2018). A bilinear functional link artificial neural network filter for nonlinear active noise control and its stability condition. *Applied Acoustics, 132*, 19–25. doi:10.1016/j.apacoust.2017.10.023

Lee, T. K., & Atkins, M. S. (2000, June). New approach to measure border irregularity for melanocytic lesions. In Medical Imaging 2000: Image Processing (Vol. 3979, pp. 668-675). International Society for Optics and Photonics.

Lee, J., Yu, I., Park, J., & Kim, D. W. (2019). Memetic feature selection for multilabel text categorization using label frequency difference. *Information Sciences*, *485*, 263–280. doi:10.1016/j.ins.2019.02.021

Lee, P. Y., Loh, W. P., & Chin, J. F. (2017). feature selection for multimedia: A state of the art. *Image and Vision Computing*, *67*, 29–42. doi:10.1016/j.imavis.2017.09.004

Lee, T., Ng, V., Gallagher, R., Coldman, A., & McLean, D. (1997). Dullrazor®: A software approach to hair removal from images. *Computers in Biology and Medicine*, *27*(6), 533–543. doi:10.1016/S0010-4825(97)00020-6 PMID:9437554

Lensen, A., Xue, B., & Zhang, M. (2017). Using particle swarm optimisation and the silhouette metric to estimate the number of clusters, select features, and perform clustering. In G. Squillero & K. Sim (Eds.), *Applications of evolutionary computation* (pp. 538–554). Berlin: Springer. doi:10.1007/978-3-319-55849-3_35

Li, Z., Rios, A. L. G., Xu, G., & Trajković, L. (2019, May). Machine learning techniques for classifying network anomalies and intrusions. In 2019 IEEE international symposium on circuits and systems (ISCAS) (pp. 1-5). IEEE. doi:10.1109/ISCAS.2019.8702583

Lin, H., & Lin, C. (2003). A study on sigmoid kernels for SVM and the training of non-PSD kernels by SMO-type methods. *Neural Computation*, (2): 1–32. https://doi.org/10.1.1.14.6709

Li, S., Xia, R., Zong, C., & Huang, C. R. (2009, August). A framework of feature selection methods for text categorization. In *Proceedings of the Joint Conference of the 47th Annual Meeting of the ACL and the 4th International Joint Conference on Natural Language Processing of the AFNLP: Volume 2-Volume 2* (pp. 692-700). Association for Computational Linguistics. 10.3115/1690219.1690243

Li, T., Meng, Z., Ni, B., Shen, J., & Wang, M. (2016). Robust geometric p-norm feature pooling for image classification and action recognition. *Image and Vision Computing*, *55*(Part 2), 64–76. doi:10.1016/j.imavis.2016.04.002

Liu, J. N., Hu, Y., He, Y., Chan, P. W., & Lai, L. (2015). Deep neural network modeling for big data weather forecasting. *Studies in Big Data*, 389-408. doi:10.1007/978-3-319-08254-7_19

Liu, W., Sun, K., & Zhu, C. (2016). A fast image encryption algorithm based on chaotic map. *Optics and Lasers in Engineering*, *84*, 26–36. doi:10.1016/j.optlaseng.2016.03.019

Li, Y., Liu, W., Li, X., Huang, Q., & Li, X. (2014). GA-SIFT: A new scale invariant feature transform for multispectral image using geometric algebra. *Information Sciences*, *281*, 559–572. doi:10.1016/j.ins.2013.12.022

Loane, M. A., Gore, H. E., Corbett, R., Steele, K., Mathews, C., Bloomer, S. E., ... Wootton, R. (1997). Effect of camera performance on diagnostic accuracy: Preliminary results from the Northern Ireland arms of the UK Multicentre Teledermatology Trial. *Journal of Telemedicine and Telecare*, *3*(2), 83–88. doi:10.1258/1357633971930913 PMID:9206278

Lorenzo, P. R., Nalepa, J., Bobek-Billewicz, B., Wawrzyniak, P., Mrukwa, G., Kawulok, M., ... Hayball, M. P. (2019). Segmenting brain tumors from FLAIR MRI using fully convolutional neural networks. *Computer Methods and Programs in Biomedicine*, *176*, 135–148. doi:10.1016/j.cmpb.2019.05.006 PMID:31200901

Luo, Y., Yu, J., Lai, W., & Liu, L. (2019). A novel chaotic image encryption algorithm based on improved baker map and logistic map. *Multimedia Tools and Applications*, 1–21.

Ma, L., Ofoghi, B., Watters, P., & Brown, S. (2009, July). Detecting phishing emails using hybrid features. In 2009 Symposia and Workshops on Ubiquitous, Autonomic and Trusted Computing (pp. 493-497). IEEE. doi:10.1109/UIC-ATC.2009.103

Machhale, K., Nandpuru, H. B., Kapur, V., & Kosta, L. (2015, May). MRI brain cancer classification using hybrid classifier (SVM-KNN). In *2015 International Conference on Industrial Instrumentation and Control (ICIC)* (pp. 60-65). IEEE.

Madooei, A., Drew, M. S., Sadeghi, M., & Atkins, M. S. (2013, September). Automatic detection of blue-white veil by discrete colour matching in dermoscopy images. In *International Conference on Medical Image Computing and Computer-Assisted Intervention* (pp. 453-460). Springer. 10.1007/978-3-642-40760-4_57

Maeda, H., Sekimoto, Y., Seto, T., Kashiyama, T., & Omata, H. (2018). Road damage detection and classification using deep neural networks with smartphone images. *Computer-Aided Civil and Infrastructure Engineering, 33*(12), 1127–1141. doi:10.1111/mice.12387

Maglogiannis, I., & Doukas, C. N. (2009). Overview of advanced computer vision systems for skin lesions characterization. *IEEE Transactions on Information Technology in Biomedicine, 13*(5), 721–733. doi:10.1109/TITB.2009.2017529 PMID:19304487

Maglogiannis, I., Pavlopoulos, S., & Koutsouris, D. (2005). An integrated computer supported acquisition, handling, and characterization system for pigmented skin lesions in dermatological images. *IEEE Transactions on Information Technology in Biomedicine, 9*(1), 86–98. doi:10.1109/TITB.2004.837859 PMID:15787011

Maheras, P., Tolika, K., Anagnostopoulou, C., Vafiadis, M., Patrikas, I., & Flocas, H. (2004). On the relationships between circulation types and changes in rainfall variability in Greece. *International Journal of Climatology, 24*(13), 1695–1712. doi:10.1002/joc.1088

Mahesh, & Subramanyam, M. (2012). Automatic image mosaic system using steerable Harris corner detector. *2012 International Conference on Machine Vision and Image Processing, MVIP 2012*, 87-91.

Maier, T., Kulichova, D., Schotten, K., Astrid, R., Ruzicka, T., Berking, C., & Udrea, A. (2015). Accuracy of a smartphone application using fractal image analysis of pigmented moles compared to clinical diagnosis and histological result. *Journal of the European Academy of Dermatology and Venereology, 29*(4), 663–667. doi:10.1111/jdv.12648 PMID:25087492

Majhi, R., Panda, G., & Sahoo, G. (2009). Development and performance evaluation of FLANN based model for forecasting stock market. *Expert Systems with Applications, 36*(3), 6800–6808.

Majhi, B., Hasan, S., & Mowafak, F. (2005). FLANN based forecasting of S&P 500 index. *Information Technology Journal, 4*(3), 289–292. doi:10.3923/itj.2005.289.292

Maldonado, S., L'opez, J., & Vairetti, C. (2019). Profit-based churn prediction based on Minimax Probability Machines. *European Journal of Operational Research*. doi:10.1016/j.ejor.2019.12.007

Malhotra, R., & Negi, A. (2013). Reliability modeling using particle swarm optimization. *International Journal of System Assurance Engineering and Management, 4*(3), 275–283.

Malinski, L., & Smolka, B. (2016). Fast averaging peer group filter for the impulsive noise removal in color images. *Journal of Real-Time Image Processing, 11*(3), 427–444. doi:10.100711554-015-0500-z

Manikandan, G., & Abirami, S. (2018). A survey on feature selection and extraction techniques for high-dimensional microarray datasets. *Knowledge Computing in Specific Domains, 2*, 311–333.

Mansur, P. (2018). Plant leaf recognition system using kernel ensemble approach. *International Journal of Advances in Signal and Image Sciences, 4*(1), 30–36. doi:10.29284/IJASIS.4.1.2018.30-36

Maqsood, I., Khan, M. R., & Abraham, A. (2004). An ensemble of neural networks for weather forecasting. *Neural Computing & Applications*, 112–122.

Mathes, T., & Piater, J. H. (2006, September). Robust non-rigid object tracking using point distribution manifolds. In *Joint Pattern Recognition Symposium* (pp. 515-524). Springer. 10.1007/11861898_52

Mathew, A. R., & Anto, P. B. (2017, July). Tumor detection and classification of MRI brain image using wavelet transform and SVM. In *2017 International Conference on Signal Processing and Communication (ICSPC)* (pp. 75-78). IEEE. 10.1109/CSPC.2017.8305810

Mathew, A. R., Anto, P. B., & Thara, N. K. (2017, July). Brain tumor segmentation and classification using DWT, Gabour wavelet and GLCM. In *2017 International Conference on Intelligent Computing, Instrumentation and Control Technologies (ICICICT)* (pp. 1744-1750). IEEE. 10.1109/ICICICT1.2017.8342834

Ma, Z., & Tavares, J. M. R. (2017). Effective features to classify skin lesions in dermoscopic images. *Expert Systems with Applications*, *84*, 92–101. doi:10.1016/j.eswa.2017.05.003

Mazilu, S., Calatroni, A., Gazit, E., Roggen, D., Hausdorff, J. M., & Ro¨ster, G. T. (2013) Feature learning for detection and prediction of freezing of gait in Parkinson's disease. In *Proceedings: The International Workshop of Machine Learning and Data Mining in Pattern Recognition*. Springer. 10.1007/978-3-642-39712-7_11

Mazilu, S., Blanke, U., Calatroni, A., Gazit, E., Hausdorff, J., & Tro¨ster, G. (2016). The role of wrist- mounted inertial sensors in detecting gait freeze episodes in Parkinson's disease. *Pervasive and Mobile Computing*, *33*, 1–16. doi:10.1016/j.pmcj.2015.12.007

Mazzetta, I., Zampogna, A., Suppa, A., Gumiero, A., Pessione, M., & Irrera, F. (2019). Wearable sensors system for an improved analysis of freezing of gait in Parkinson's disease using electromyography and inertial signals. *Sensors (Basel)*, *19*(4), 948. doi:10.339019040948 PMID:30813411

McKenna, S. J., Jabri, S., Duric, Z., Rosenfeld, A., & Wechsler, H. (2000). Tracking groups of people. *Computer Vision and Image Understanding*, *80*(1), 42–56. doi:10.1006/cviu.2000.0870

Mehran, R., Oyama, A., & Shah, M. (2009, June). Abnormal crowd behavior detection using social force model. In *2009 IEEE Conference on Computer Vision and Pattern Recognition* (pp. 935-942). IEEE. 10.1109/CVPR.2009.5206641

Méndez, J. R., Cotos-Yañez, T. R., & Ruano-Ordás, D. (2019). A new semantic-based feature selection method for spam filtering. *Applied Soft Computing*, *76*, 89–104. doi:10.1016/j.asoc.2018.12.008

Mendonça, T., Ferreira, P. M., Marques, J. S., Marcal, A. R., & Rozeira, J. (2013, July). PH 2-A dermoscopic image database for research and benchmarking. In *2013 35th annual international conference of the IEEE engineering in medicine and biology society (EMBC)* (pp. 5437-5440). IEEE.

Menzies, S. W., Ingvar, C., & McCarthy, W. H. (1996). A sensitivity and specificity analysis of the surface microscopy features of invasive melanoma. *Melanoma Research*, *6*(1), 55–62. doi:10.1097/00008390-199602000-00008 PMID:8640071

Mishra, B. S. P., Dehuri, S., & Euiwhan, K. (2016). *Techniques and Environments for Big Data Analysis: Parallel, Cloud, and Grid Computing*. Springer. doi:10.1007/978-3-319-27520-8

Mishra, P. K., Khare, D., Mondal, A., & Kundu, S. (2014). *Multiple Linear Regression Based Statistical Downscaling of Daily Precipitation in a Canal Command. In Climate Change and Biodiversity* (pp. 73–83). Tokyo: Springer. doi:10.1007/978-4-431-54838-6_6

Mishra, P. S. (2018). Optimization of the Radial Basis Function Neural Networks Using Genetic Algorithm for Stock Index Prediction. *International Journal on Computer Science and Engineering*, *6*(6), 43–51.

Mishra, P. S., & Dehuri, S. (2012). Potential indictors for stock index prediction: A Perspective. *International Journal of Electronic Finance*, *6*(2), 157–183. doi:10.1504/IJEF.2012.048465

Mishra, P. S., & Dehuri, S. (2014). Potential Indicators Based Neural Networks for Cash Forecasting of an ATM. *International Journal of Information Systems and Social Change, 5*(4), 41–57. doi:10.4018/ijissc.2014100103

Mishra, P. S., & Dehuri, S. (2016). Higher Order Neural Network for Financial Modeling and Simulations. In M. Zhang (Ed.), *Applied Artificial Higher Order Neural Networks for Control and Recognition* (pp. 440–466). IGI-Global. doi:10.4018/978-1-5225-0063-6.ch018

Misra, J. (2020). *autoNLP: NLP Feature Recommendations for Text Analytics Applications.* arXiv preprint arXiv:2002.03056

Mitra, S. & Acharya, T. (2004). *Data Mining Multimedia, Soft computing and Bioinformatics.* John Wiley & Sons, Inc.

Mitrovi, S., Baesens, B., & Lemahieu, W. (2019). tcc2vec: RFM-informed representation learning on call graphs for churn prediction. *Information Sciences.* doi:10.1016/j.ins.2019.02.044

Mohammadzadeh, S. D., Kazemi, S., Mosavi, A., Nasseralshariati, E., & Tah, J. H. (2019). Prediction of compression index of fine-grained soils using a gene expression programming model. *Infrastructures, 4*(2), 26. doi:10.3390/infrastructures4020026

Mohanaiah, P., Sathyanarayana, P., & GuruKumar, L. (2013). Image texture feature extraction using GLCM approach. *International Journal of Scientific and Research Publications, 3*(5), 1.

Möhlmann, L. F., Ederveen, S., de Groot, H. L. F., & Linders, G. M. (2009). *Intangible Barriers to International Trade: A Sectoral Approach.* Tinbergen Institute Discussion Paper.

Moolayil, J. (2019). An Introduction to Deep Learning and Keras. In *Learn Keras for Deep Neural Networks* (pp. 1–16). Berkeley, CA: Apress. doi:10.1007/978-1-4842-4240-7_1

Mosavi, A., & Edalatifar, M. (2018b). A hybrid neuro-fuzzy algorithm for prediction of reference evapotranspiration. *Recent Advances in Technology Research and Education,* 235-243. doi:10.1007/978-3-319-99834-3_31

Mosavi, A., Ardabili, S., & Várkonyi-Kóczy, A. (2019). *List of deep learning models.* doi:10.20944/preprints201908.0152.v1

Mosavi, A., Ozturk, P., & Chau, K. (2018a). Flood prediction using machine learning models: Literature review. *Water (Basel), 10*(11), 1536. doi:10.3390/w10111536

Moussa, R., Gerges, F., Salem, C., Akiki, R., Falou, O., & Azar, D. (2016, October). Computer-aided detection of Melanoma using geometric features. In *2016 3rd Middle East Conference on Biomedical Engineering (MECBME)* (pp. 125-128). IEEE. 10.1109/MECBME.2016.7745423

Murphy, B. F., & Timbal, B. (2008). A review of recent climate variability and climate change in Southeastern Australia. *International Journal of Climatology,* (28): 859–879. doi:10.1002/joc.1627

Musa, J. D. (2004). *Software reliability engineering: more reliable software, faster and cheaper.* Tata McGraw-Hill Education.

Naik, J., Dhar, S., & Dash, P. K. (2020). Effective fault diagnosis and distance calculation for photovoltaic-based DC microgrid using adaptive EWT and kernel random vector functional link network. *IET Generation, Transmission & Distribution, 14*(4), 690–703. doi:10.1049/iet-gtd.2019.1338

Najafi, M. R., Moradkhani, H., & Jung, I. W. (2011). Assessing the uncertainties of hydrologic model selection in climate change impact studies. *Hydrological Processes, 25*(18), 2814–2826. doi:10.1002/hyp.8043

Nakamura, S., & Shikano, K. 1997. Room Acoustics and Reverberation: Impact on Hands-Free Recognition. *Proceedings of European Conference on Speech Communication and Technology, 5,* 2419-2422.

Nakariyakul, S., & Casasent, D. P. (2008, August). Improved forward floating selection algorithm for feature subset selection. In *2008 International Conference on Wavelet Analysis and Pattern Recognition* (Vol. 2, pp. 793-798). IEEE 10.1109/ICWAPR.2008.4635885

Nanda, S. K., & Tripathy, D. P. (2011). Application of Functional Link Artificial Neural Network for Prediction of Machinery Noise in Opencast Mines. Advances in Fuzzy Systems. doi:10.1155/2011/831261Vol

Nanni, L., Ghidoni, S., & Brahnam, S. (2017). Handcrafted vs. non-handcrafted features for computer vision classification. *Pattern Recognition*, *71*, 158–172. doi:10.1016/j.patcog.2017.05.025

Nargesian, F., Samulowitz, H., Khurana, U., Khalil, E. B., & Turaga, D. S. (2017, August). *Learning Feature Engineering for Classification* (pp. 2529–2535). IJCAI.

Nash, J. E., & Sutcliffe, J. V. (1970). River flow forecasting through conceptual models part I - A discussion of principles. *Journal of Hydrology (Amsterdam)*, *10*(3), 282–290. doi:10.1016/0022-1694(70)90255-6

Nasir, M., Attique Khan, M., Sharif, M., Lali, I. U., Saba, T., & Iqbal, T. (2018). An improved strategy for skin lesion detection and classification using uniform segmentation and feature selection based approach. *Microscopy Research and Technique*, *81*(6), 528–543. doi:10.1002/jemt.23009 PMID:29464868

Nathanson, L. (Ed.). (2012). *Basic and clinical aspects of malignant melanoma* (Vol. 35). Springer Science & Business Media.

Nayak, S. C., Misra, B. B., & Behera, H. S. (2019). Efficient financial time series prediction with evolutionary virtual data position exploration. *Neural Computing & Applications*, *31*(2), 1053–1074. doi:10.100700521-017-3061-1

Naz, & Rahim, & Suntie. (2011). Audio-Visual Speech Recognition Development Era; From Snakes to Neural Network: A Survey Based Study. *Canadian Journal on Artificial Intelligence. Machine Learning and Pattern Recognition*, *2*(1), 12–16.

Nehinbe, J. O., & Onyeabor, U. S. (2020). An exhaustive study of DDOS attacks and DDOS datasets. *International Journal of Internet Technology and Secured Transactions*, *10*(3), 268–285. doi:10.1504/IJITST.2020.107075

Nilashi, M. (2016). Accuracy improvement for predicting Parkinson's disease progression. Scientific Reports. *Nature*, *6*, 34181. PMID:27686748

Niño-Adan, I., Landa-Torres, I., Portillo, E., & Manjarres, D. (2019, May). Analysis and Application of Normalization Methods with Supervised Feature Weighting to Improve K-means Accuracy. In *International Workshop on Soft Computing Models in Industrial and Environmental Applications* (pp. 14-24). Springer.

O'Sullivan, B., & Wooldridge, M. (2015). *Artificial intelligence foundations theory and applications. Feature selection for high dimensional data*. Springer.

Ojha, C. S. P. (2013). Downscaling of Precipitation for Lake Catchment in Arid Region in India using Linear Multiple Regression and Neural Networks. *The Open Hydrology Journal*, *4*(1), 122–136. doi:10.2174/1874378101004010122

Oktaviani, O., Madenda, S., Rodiah, R., Susetianingtias, D. T., Fitrianingsih, D. A., & Arianty, R. (2019). *Combination of Chain Code and Leaf Morphology Approach for Plant Identification*. Academic Press.

Oliveira, R. B., Pereira, A. S., & Tavares, J. M. R. (2019). Computational diagnosis of skin lesions from dermoscopic images using combined features. *Neural Computing & Applications*, *31*(10), 6091–6111. doi:10.100700521-018-3439-8

Óskarsdóttira, M., Bravob, C., Verbekec, W., Sarrauted, C., Baesensa, B., & Vanthienena, J. (2017). Social Network Analytics for Churn Prediction in Telco: Model Building, Evaluation and Network Architecture. *Expert Systems with Applications*. doi:10.1016/j.eswa.2017.05.028

Özkaynak, F., & Özer, A. B. (2016). Cryptanalysis of a new image encryption algorithm based on chaos. *Optik (Stuttgart)*, *127*(13), 5190–5192. doi:10.1016/j.ijleo.2016.03.018

Padlia, M., & Sharma, J. (2019). Fractional Sobel filter based brain tumor detection and segmentation using statistical features and SVM. In *Nanoelectronics, circuits and communication systems* (pp. 161–175). Singapore: Springer. doi:10.1007/978-981-13-0776-8_15

Pan, S., Li, T., & Yin, Y. (2019). Leaf Contour Recognition Using Hash Learning. *Academic Journal of Computing & Information Science, 2*(3).

Panda, B., & Panda, C. S. (2019). *A Review on Brain Tumor Classification Methodologies*. Academic Press.

Panda, M.,Dehuri, S., & Patra, M.R. (2015). *Modern Approaches of Data Mining: Theory and Practice*. Alpha Science International, Ltd.

Panigrahi, S., & Behera, H. S. (2017). A hybrid ETS–ANN model for time series forecasting. *Engineering Applications of Artificial Intelligence, 66*, 49-59.

Pan, Y., & Waibel, A. 2000. The Effects of Room Acoustics on MFCC Speech Parameter. *Proceedings of International Conference on Spoken Language Processing (ICSLP), 4*, 129-132.

Pao, Y. H., & Takefji, Y. (1992). *Functional-Link Net Computing*. IEEE Computer Journal.

Parchami, M., Zhu, W., Champagne, B., & Plourde, E. (2016). Recent Developments in Speech Enhancement in the Short-Time Fourier Transform Domain. IEEE Circuits and Systems Magazine, 16(3), 45-77. doi:10.1109/MCAS.2016.2583681

Parish, E. J., & Duraisamy, K. (2016). A paradigm for data-driven predictive modeling using field inversion and machine learning. *Journal of Computational Physics, 305*, 758–774. doi:10.1016/j.jcp.2015.11.012

Patel & Rao. (2010). Speech Recognition using HMM with MFCC- an Analysis using Frequency Spectral Decomposition Technique. *International Journal (Toronto, Ont.), 1*(2), 101–110.

Patel, N., & Upadhyay, S. (2012). Study of various decision tree pruning methods with their empirical comparison in weka. *International Journal of Computers and Applications, 60*(12).

Patra, J. C., & Pal, R. N. (1995). Functional link artificial neural network-based adaptive channel equalization of nonlinear channels with QAM signal. *Proceedings of the IEEE International Conference on Systems, Man and Cybernetics, 3*, 2081–2086. 10.1109/ICSMC.1995.538086

Patro, K. A. K., & Acharya, B. (2018). Secure multi–level permutation operation based multiple colour image encryption. *Journal of Information Security and Applications, 40*, 111-133.

Patro, K. A. K., & Acharya, B. (2019a). A Simple, Secure, and Time-Efficient Bit-Plane Operated Bit-Level Image Encryption Scheme Using 1-D Chaotic Maps. In *Innovations in Soft Computing and Information Technology* (pp. 261–278). Singapore: Springer. doi:10.1007/978-981-13-3185-5_23

Patro, K. A. K., & Acharya, B. (2019b). An efficient colour image encryption scheme based on 1-D chaotic maps. *Journal of Information Security and Applications, 46*, 23–41. doi:10.1016/j.jisa.2019.02.006

Patro, K. A. K., Acharya, B., & Nath, V. (2019a). Secure, Lossless, and Noise-resistive Image Encryption using Chaos, Hyper-chaos, and DNA Sequence Operation. *IETE Technical Review*, 1–23.

Patro, K. A. K., Acharya, B., & Nath, V. (2019b). Secure multilevel permutation-diffusion based image encryption using chaotic and hyper-chaotic maps. *Microsystem Technologies*, 1–15.

Patro, K. A. K., Banerjee, A., & Acharya, B. (2017, October). A simple, secure and time efficient multi-way rotational permutation and diffusion based image encryption by using multiple 1-D chaotic maps. In *International Conference on Next Generation Computing Technologies* (pp. 396-418). Springer.

Patro, K. A. K., Raghuvanshi, A. S., & Acharya, B. (2019). A Parallel Bit-Plane Operation Based Chaotic Image Encryption Scheme. In *Proceedings of the Third International Conference on Microelectronics, Computing and Communication Systems* (pp. 143-154). Springer.

Paul, D., & Parekh, R. (2011). Automated Speech Recognition of Isolated Words Using Neural Networks. *International Journal of Engineering Science and Technology, 3*(6), 4993–5000.

Peng, Y., Wu, Z., & Jiang, J. (2010). A novel feature selection approach for biomedical data classification. *Journal of Biomedical Informatics, 43*(1), 15–23. doi:10.1016/j.jbi.2009.07.008

Peng, Y., Xuefeng, Z., Jianyong, Z., & Yumhong, X. (2009). Lazy learner text categorization algorithm based on embedded feature selection. *Journal of Systems Engineering and Electronics, 20*(3), 651–659.

Pennisi, A., Bloisi, D. D., Nardi, D., Giampetruzzi, A. R., Mondino, C., & Facchiano, A. (2016). Skin lesion image segmentation using Delaunay Triangulation for melanoma detection. *Computerized Medical Imaging and Graphics, 52*, 89–103. doi:10.1016/j.compmedimag.2016.05.002 PMID:27215953

Phinyomark, A., Hu, H., Phukpattaranont, P., & Limsakul, C. (2012). Application of linear discriminant analysis in dimensionality reduction for hand motion classification. *Measurement Science Review, 12*(3), 82–89. doi:10.2478/v10048-012-0015-8

Polat, K. (2019). Freezing of gait (FoG) detection using logistic regression in Parkinson's disease from acceleration signals. Scientific Meeting on Electrical-Electronics & Biomedical Engineering and Computer Science (EBBT), 1-4.

Pope, A. S., Morning, R., Tauritz, D. R., & Kent, A. D. (2018, July). Automated design of network security metrics. In *Proceedings of the Genetic and Evolutionary Computation Conference Companion* (pp. 1680-1687). 10.1145/3205651.3208266

Potluri, S., Henry, N. F., & Diedrich, C. (2017, September). Evaluation of hybrid deep learning techniques for ensuring security in networked control systems. In *2017 22nd IEEE International Conference on Emerging Technologies and Factory Automation (ETFA)* (pp. 1-8). IEEE. 10.1109/ETFA.2017.8247662

Prakash, J., & Singh, P. K. (2019). Gravitational search algorithm and k-means for simultaneous feature selection and data clustering: A multi-objective approach. *Soft Computing, 23*(6), 2083–2100. doi:10.100700500-017-2923-x

Praveen, G. B., & Agrawal, A. (2016, March). Multi stage classification and segmentation of brain tumor. In *2016 3rd International Conference on Computing for Sustainable Global Development (INDIACom)* (pp. 1628-1632). IEEE.

Priyadarshini, L., Dash, P. K., & Dhar, S. (2020). A new Exponentially Expanded Robust Random Vector Functional Link Network based MPPT model for Local Energy Management of PV-Battery Energy Storage Integrated Microgrid (Vol. 91). Academic Press.

Psaty, E. L., & Halpern, A. C. (2009). Current and emerging technologies in melanoma diagnosis: The state of the art. *Clinics in Dermatology, 27*(1), 35–45. doi:10.1016/j.clindermatol.2008.09.004 PMID:19095152

Pub, N. F. 197: Advanced Encryption Standard (AES), Federal Information Processing Standards Publication 197, US Department of Commerce/NIST, November 26, 2001. Available from the NIST website.

Qian, M., & Zhai, C. (2013). Robust unsupervised feature selection. In: Proceedings of the twenty-third international joint conference on artifcial intelligence. *IJCAI (United States), 13*, 1621–1627.

Quellec, G., Cazuguel, G., Cochener, B., & Lamard, M. (2017). Multiple-instance learning for medical image and video analysis. *IEEE Reviews in Biomedical Engineering*, *10*, 213–234.

Qu, Z., Lin, S.-P., Ju, F.-R., & Liu, L. (2015). The improved algorithm of fast panorama stitching for image sequence and reducing the distortion errors. *Mathematical Problems in Engineering*, 2015.

Rabaud, V., & Belongie, S. (2006, June). Counting crowded moving objects. In *2006 IEEE Computer Society Conference on Computer Vision and Pattern Recognition (CVPR'06)* (Vol. 1, pp. 705-711). IEEE.

Rabiner, L.R., & Juang, B.H. (1993). Approaches to Automatic Speech Recognition by Machine. *Fundamentals of Speech Recognition*, 37-50.

Raffel, M., Willert, C. E., Wereley, S. T., Kompenhans, J., Willert, S., Wereley, S. T., & Kompenhans, J. (2007). Particle Image Velocimetry: A Practical Guide. In Particle Image Velocimetry (Vol. 2, p. 448). Springer. https://doi.org/doi:10.1097/JTO.0b013e3182370e69

Raftery, A. E., & Dean, N. (2006). Variable selection for model-based clustering. *Journal of the American Statistical Association*, *101*(473), 168–178. doi:10.1198/016214506000000113

Rajasinghe, N., Samarabandu, J., & Wang, X. (2018, May). INSecS-DCS: a highly customizable network intrusion dataset creation framework. In *2018 IEEE Canadian Conference on Electrical & Computer Engineering (CCECE)* (pp. 1-4). IEEE. 10.1109/CCECE.2018.8447661

Ram, R., & Mohanty, M. N. (2017). Deep Neural Network Based Speech Enhancement. Cognitive Informatics and Soft Computing. *Advances in Intelligent Systems and Computing*, *768*, 281–287. doi:10.1007/978-981-13-0617-4_27

Rana, R., Staron, M., Berger, C., Hansson, J., Nilsson, M., Törner, F., & Höglund, C. (2014). Selecting software reliability growth models and improving their predictive accuracy using historical projects data. *Journal of Systems and Software*, *98*, 59–78. doi:10.1016/j.jss.2014.08.033

Rao, A. R., & Rao, S. B. (1992). *Measuring Reciprocity in Weighted Social Networks. Academic Press.*

Rastgoo, M., Garcia, R., Morel, O., & Marzani, F. (2015). Automatic differentiation of melanoma from dysplastic nevi. *Computerized Medical Imaging and Graphics*, *43*, 44–52. doi:10.1016/j.compmedimag.2015.02.011 PMID:25797605

Reddy, D. R. (2009). Speech Recognition by Machine: A Review. *Proceedings of the IEEE*, *64*(4), 501–531. doi:10.1109/PROC.1976.10158

Rezvanian, S., & Lockhart, T. E. (2016). Towards real-time detection of freezing of gait using wavelet transform on wireless accelerometer data. *Sensors (Basel)*, *16*(4), 475. doi:10.339016040475 PMID:27049389

Rindi, G., Klimstra, D. S., Abedi-Ardekani, B., Asa, S. L., Bosman, F. T., Brambilla, E., ... Fernandez-Cuesta, L. (2018). A common classification framework for neuroendocrine neoplasms: An International Agency for Research on Cancer (IARC) and World Health Organization (WHO) expert consensus proposal. *Modern Pathology*, *31*(12), 1770–1786. doi:10.103841379-018-0110-y PMID:30140036

Rix, Hollier, Hekstra, & Beerend. (2000). Perceptual Evaluation of Speech Quality (PESQ), and objective method for end-to-end speech quality assessment of narrowband telephone networks and speech codecs. ITU, ITU-T Rec.

Rodrıguez-Martın, D., Sama, A., Pérez-López, C., Catala, A., Moreno Arostegui, J. M., Cabestany, J., ... Rodríguez-Molinero, A. (2017). Home detection of freezing of gait using support vector machines through a single waist- worn triaxial accelerometer. *PLoS One*, *12*(2), e0171764. doi:10.1371/journal.pone.0171764 PMID:28199357

Roh, Y., Heo, G., & Whang, S. E. (2019). A survey on data collection for machine learning: A big data-ai integration perspective. *IEEE Transactions on Knowledge and Data Engineering*, 1. doi:10.1109/TKDE.2019.2946162

Rojathai, S., & Venkatesulu, M. (2013). An Effective Tamil Speech Word Recognition Technique with Aid of MFCC and HMM (Hidden Markov Model). *International Review on Computers and Software*, 8(2).

Roy, P., Mahapatra, G. S., & Dey, K. N. (2015). Neuro-genetic approach on logistic model based software reliability prediction. *Expert Systems with Applications*, 42(10), 4709–4718. doi:10.1016/j.eswa.2015.01.043

Ruder, S., Peters, M. E., Swayamdipta, S., & Wolf, T. (2019, June). Transfer learning in natural language processing. In *Proceedings of the 2019 Conference of the North American Chapter of the Association for Computational Linguistics: Tutorials* (pp. 15-18). Academic Press.

Ruela, M., Barata, C., Marques, J. S., & Rozeira, J. (2017). A system for the detection of melanomas in dermoscopy images using shape and symmetry features. *Computer Methods in Biomechanics and Biomedical Engineering. Imaging & Visualization*, 5(2), 127–137. doi:10.1080/21681163.2015.1029080

Sabzi, S., Pourdarbani, R., & Arribas, J. I. (2020). A Computer Vision System for the Automatic Classification of Five Varieties of Tree Leaf Images. *Computers*, 9(1), 6. doi:10.3390/computers9010006

Sachindra, D. A., Ahmed, K., Rashid, M. M., Shahid, S., & Perera, B. J. C. (2018). Statistical downscaling of precipitation using machine learning techniques. *Atmospheric Research*, 212, 240–258. doi:10.1016/j.atmosres.2018.05.022

Sachindra, D. A., Huang, F., Barton, A., & Perera, B. J. C. (2013). Least square support vector and multi-linear regression for statistically downscaling general circulation model outputs to catchment streamflows. *International Journal of Climatology*, 33(5), 1087–1106. doi:10.1002/joc.3493

Sadeghi, M., Lee, T. K., McLean, D., Lui, H., & Atkins, M. S. (2013). Detection and analysis of irregular streaks in dermoscopic images of skin lesions. *IEEE Transactions on Medical Imaging*, 32(5), 849–861. doi:10.1109/TMI.2013.2239307 PMID:23335664

Sallam, A. A., Kabir, M. N., Alginahi, Y. M., Jamal, A., & Esmeel, T. K. (2020, February). IDS for Improving DDoS Attack Recognition Based on Attack Profiles and Network Traffic Features. In *2020 16th IEEE International Colloquium on Signal Processing & Its Applications (CSPA)* (pp. 255-260). IEEE.

Salman, A. G., Kanigoro, B., & Heryadi, Y. (2015). Weather forecasting using deep learning techniques. *2015 International Conference on Advanced Computer Science and Information Systems (ICACSIS)*. 10.1109/ICACSIS.2015.7415154

Salve, P., Yannawar, P., & Sardesai, M. (2018). Multimodal plant recognition through hybrid feature fusion technique using imaging and non-imaging hyper-spectral data. *Journal of King Saud University-Computer and Information Sciences*.

Samadi, S., Carbone, G. J., Mahdavi, M., Sharifi, F., & Bihamta, M. R. (2013). Statistical Downscaling of River Runoff in a Semi Arid Catchment. *Water Resources Management*, 27(1), 117–136. doi:10.100711269-012-0170-6

Samanta, A. K., & Khan, A. A. (2018, February). Computer aided diagnostic system for automatic detection of brain tumor through MRI using clustering based segmentation technique and SVM classifier. In *International Conference on Advanced Machine Learning Technologies and Applications* (pp. 343-351). Springer. 10.1007/978-3-319-74690-6_34

Samhita, P., Prasad, P., Patro, K. A. K., & Acharya, B. (2016). A secure chaos-based image encryption and decryption using crossover and mutation operator. *International Journal of Control Theory and Applications*, 9(34), 17–28.

Samui, S., Chakrabarti, I., & Ghosh, S. K. (2019). Time-frequency masking based supervised speech enhancement framework using fuzzy deep belief network. *Applied Soft Computing*, 74, 583–602. doi:10.1016/j.asoc.2018.10.031

Sapre, S., Ahmadi, P., & Islam, K. (2019). *A Robust Comparison of the KDDCup99 and NSL-KDD IoT Network Intrusion Detection Datasets Through Various Machine Learning Algorithms.* arXiv preprint arXiv:1912.13204

Saputra, F. A., Masputra, M. F., Syarif, I., & Ramli, K. (2018, September). Botnet Detection in Network System Through Hybrid Low Variance Filter, Correlation Filter and Supervised Mining Process. In *2018 Thirteenth International Conference on Digital Information Management (ICDIM)* (pp. 112-117). IEEE. 10.1109/ICDIM.2018.8847076

Sarkar, S. D., & Goswami, S. (2013). Empirical study on filter based feature selection methods for text classification. *International Journal of Computers and Applications, 81*(6).

Sawatsky, A. P., Rosenman, D. J., Merry, S. P., & McDonald, F. S. (2010, August). Eight years of the Mayo International Health Program: What an international elective adds to resident education. *Mayo Clinic Proceedings, 85*(8), 734–741. doi:10.4065/mcp.2010.0107 PMID:20675512

Scher, S., & Messori, G. (2019). Weather and climate forecasting with neural networks: Using general circulation models (GCMs) with different complexity as a study ground. *Geoscientific Model Development, 12*(7), 2797–2809. doi:10.5194/gmd-12-2797-2019

Schindewolf, T., Schiffner, R., Stolz, W., Albert, R., Abmayr, W., & Harms, H. (1994). Evaluation of different image acquisition techniques for a computer vision system in the diagnosis of malignant melanoma. *Journal of the American Academy of Dermatology, 31*(1), 33–41. doi:10.1016/S0190-9622(94)70132-6 PMID:8021369

Schmid, P. (1999). Segmentation of digitized dermatoscopic images by two-dimensional color clustering. *IEEE Transactions on Medical Imaging, 18*(2), 164–171. doi:10.1109/42.759124 PMID:10232673

Schmitz, M., Soderland, S., Bart, R., & Etzioni, O. (2012, July). Open language learning for information extraction. In *Proceedings of the 2012 Joint Conference on Empirical Methods in Natural Language Processing and Computational Natural Language Learning* (pp. 523-534). Academic Press.

Schoof, J. T., Pryor, S. C., & Robeson, S. M. (2007). Downscaling daily maximum and minimum temperatures in the midwestern USA: A hybrid empirical approach. *International Journal of Climatology, 27*(4), 439–454. doi:10.1002/joc.1412

Scott, S., & Matwin, S. (1999). Feature engineering for text classification. In *ICML* (Vol. 99, pp. 379–388). Citeseer.

Seetha, J., & Raja, S. S. (2018). Brain tumor classification using convolutional neural networks. *Biomedical & Pharmacology Journal, 11*(3), 1457–1461. doi:10.13005/bpj/1511

Senturk, Z. (2020). Early diagnosis of Parkinson's disease using machine learning algorithms. *Medical Hypotheses, 138*, 109603. doi:10.1016/j.mehy.2020.109603 PMID:32028195

Serajeh, R., Faez, K., & Ghahnavieh, A. E. (2013, March). Robust multiple human tracking using particle swarm optimization and the Kalman filter on full occlusion conditions. In *2013 First Iranian Conference on Pattern Recognition and Image Analysis (PRIA)* (pp. 1-4). IEEE. 10.1109/PRIA.2013.6528450

Shah, S., Iqbal, K., & Riaz, A. (2018). Constrained optimization-based extreme learning machines with bagging for freezing of gait detection. *Big Data and Cognitive Computing, 2*(4), 31. doi:10.3390/bdcc2040031

Shao, L., Zhu, F., & Li, X. (2014). Transfer learning for visual categorization: A survey. *IEEE Transactions on Neural Networks and Learning Systems, 26*(5), 1019–1034. doi:10.1109/TNNLS.2014.2330900 PMID:25014970

Sharif, M., Khan, M. A., Akram, T., Javed, M. Y., Saba, T., & Rehman, A. (2017). A framework of human detection and action recognition based on uniform segmentation and combination of Euclidean distance and joint entropy-based features selection. *EURASIP Journal on Image and Video Processing, 2017*(1), 89. doi:10.118613640-017-0236-8

Sheha, M. A., Sharwy, A., & Mabrouk, M. S. (2014, December). Pigmented skin lesion diagnosis using geometric and chromatic features. In *2014 Cairo International Biomedical Engineering Conference (CIBEC)* (pp. 115-120). IEEE. 10.1109/CIBEC.2014.7020931

Sheikhan, M., & Mohammadi, N. (2012). Neural-based electricity load forecasting using hybrid of GA and ACO for feature selection. *Neural Computing & Applications*, *21*(8), 1961–1970. doi:10.100700521-011-0599-1

Shin, H. C., Roth, H. R., Gao, M., Lu, L., Xu, Z., Nogues, I., ... Summers, R. M. (2016). Deep convolutional neural networks for computer-aided detection: CNN architectures, dataset characteristics and transfer learning. *IEEE Transactions on Medical Imaging*, *35*(5), 1285–1298. doi:10.1109/TMI.2016.2528162 PMID:26886976

Shi, P., Yang, T., Zhang, K., Tang, Q., Yu, Z., & Zhou, X. (2016). Large-scale climate patterns and precipitation in an arid endorheic region: Linkage and underlying mechanism. *Environmental Research Letters*, *11*(4). doi:10.1088/1748-9326/11/4/044006

Shirazi, F., & Mohammadi, M. A big data analytics model for customer churn prediction in the retiree segment. *International Journal of Information Management*. doi:10.1016/j.ijinfomgt.2018.10.005

Shoieb, D. A., Youssef, S. M., & Aly, W. M. (2016). Computer-aided model for skin diagnosis using deep learning. *Journal of Image and Graphics*, *4*(2), 122–129. doi:10.18178/joig.4.2.122-129

Shu, M. (2019). *Deep learning for image classification on very small datasets using transfer learning*. Academic Press.

Sigurdsson, S., Philipsen, P. A., Hansen, L. K., Larsen, J., Gniadecka, M., & Wulf, H. C. (2004). Detection of skin cancer by classification of Raman spectra. *IEEE Transactions on Biomedical Engineering*, *51*(10), 1784–1793. doi:10.1109/TBME.2004.831538 PMID:15490825

Silva, W., & Lucena, D. (2018). Concrete cracks detection based on deep learning image classification. *Proceedings*, *2*(8), 489. doi:10.3390/ICEM18-05387

Simonyan, K., & Zisserman, A. (2014). *Very deep convolutional networks for large-scale image recognition*. arXiv preprint arXiv:1409.1556

Singh, A. (2015, February). Detection of brain tumor in MRI images, using combination of fuzzy c-means and SVM. In *2015 2nd International Conference on Signal Processing and Integrated Networks (SPIN)* (pp. 98-102). IEEE.

Singh, G., & Ansari, M. A. (2016, August). Efficient detection of brain tumor from MRIs using K-means segmentation and normalized histogram. In *2016 1st India International Conference on Information Processing (IICIP)* (pp. 1-6). IEEE.

Singh, S., Stevenson, J. H., & McGurty, D. (2001). An evaluation of Polaroid photographic imaging for cutaneous-lesion referrals to an outpatient clinic: A pilot study. *British Journal of Plastic Surgery*, *54*(2), 140–143. doi:10.1054/bjps.2000.3507 PMID:11207125

Smith, D. A., & White, D. R. (1992). Structure and Dynamics of the Global Economy: Network Analysis of International Trade, 1965-1980. *Social Forces*, *70*(4), 857–893. doi:10.2307/2580193

Snyder, D., & Kick, E. (1979). Structural Position in the World System and Economic Growth, 1955-1970: A Multiple Network Approach. *American Journal of Sociology*, *84*, 1096–1123. doi:10.1086/226902

Solomatine, D. P., & Ostfeld, A. (2008). A. Data-driven modelling: Some past experiences and new approaches. *Journal of Hydroinformatics*, *10*(1), 3–22. doi:10.2166/hydro.2008.015

Sonavane, R., & Sonar, P. (2016, December). Classification and segmentation of brain tumor using Adaboost classifier. In *2016 International Conference on Global Trends in Signal Processing, Information Computing and Communication (ICGTSPICC)* (pp. 396-403). IEEE. 10.1109/ICGTSPICC.2016.7955334

Song, L., Smola, A., Gretton, A., Borgwardt, K., & Bedo, J. (2007). Supervised feature selection via dependence estimation. *Proceedings of the 24th International Conference on Machine Learning*, 823-830.

Song, Q., & Shepperd, M. (2007). A new imputation method for small software project data sets. *Journal of Systems and Software*, *80*(1), 51–62. doi:10.1016/j.jss.2006.05.003

Song, W., Jia, G., Zhu, H., Jia, D., & Gao, L. (2020). Automated pavement crack damage detection using deep multiscale convolutional features. *Journal of Advanced Transportation*.

Stanley, R. J., Stoecker, W. V., & Moss, R. H. (2007). A relative color approach to color discrimination for malignant melanoma detection in dermoscopy images. *Skin Research and Technology*, *13*(1), 62–72. doi:10.1111/j.1600-0846.2007.00192.x PMID:17250534

Staroszczyk, T., Osowski, S., & Markiewicz, T. (2012). Comparative Analysis of Feature Selection Methods for Blood Cell Recognition in Leukemia. *Proceedings of the 8th International Conference on Machine Learning and Data Mining in Pattern Recognition, MLDM 2012*, 467-481. 10.1007/978-3-642-31537-4_37

Steiber, S. (1979). The World System and World Trade: An Empirical Explanation ofConceptual Conflicts. *The Sociological Quarterly*, *20*(1), 23–36. doi:10.1111/j.1533-8525.1979.tb02182.x

Stoecker, W. V., Gupta, K., Stanley, R. J., Moss, R. H., & Shrestha, B. (2005). Detection of asymmetric blotches (asymmetric structureless areas) in dermoscopy images of malignant melanoma using relative color. *Skin Research and Technology*, *11*(3), 179–184. doi:10.1111/j.1600-0846.2005.00117.x PMID:15998328

Stripling, E., Broucke, S. V., Antonio, K., Baesens, B., & Snoeck, M. (2018). Profit maximizing logistic model for customer churn prediction using genetic algorithms. *Swarm and Evolutionary Computation*, *40*, 116–130. doi:10.1016/j.swevo.2017.10.010

Struhl, S. (2015). *Practical text analytics: Interpreting text and unstructured data for business intelligence*. Kogan Page Publishers.

Stuckless, R. (1994). Real-time transliteration of speech into print for hearing impaired students in regular classes. *American Annals of the Deaf*, *128*, 619–624. PMID:6227221

Sujatha, J., & Rajagopalan, S. (2017). Performance evaluation of machine learning algorithms in the classification of parkinson disease using voice attributes. *International Journal of Applied Engineering Research*, *12*(21), 10669–10675.

Suksri, S., & Kimpan, W. (2016). Neural network training model for weather forecasting using fireworks algorithm. *2016 International Computer Science and Engineering Conference (ICSEC)*. 10.1109/ICSEC.2016.7859952

Sun, C. T., & Jang, J. S. R. (1998). A neuro-fuzzy classifier and its applications. *Proceedings of IEEE International Conference on Fuzzy Systems*, *1*, 94–98.

Sun, L., Shang, Z., Xia, Y., Bhowmick, S., & Nagarajaiah, S. (2020). Review of bridge structural health monitoring aided by big data and artificial intelligence: From condition assessment to damage detection. *Journal of Structural Engineering (United States)*, *146*(5).

Suppa, A., Kita, A., Leodori, G., Zampogna, A., Nicolini, E., Lorenzi, P., ... Irrera, F. (2017). l-DOPA and freezing of gait in Parkinson's disease: Objective assessment through a wearable wireless system. *Frontiers in Neurology*, *8*, 406. doi:10.3389/fneur.2017.00406 PMID:28855889

Suykens, J. A. K., & Vandewalle, J. (1999). Least squares support vector machine classifiers. *Neural Processing Letters*, *9*(3), 293–300. doi:10.1023/A:1018628609742

Suykens, J. A. K., Vandewalle, J., & De Moor, B. (2001). Optimal control by least squares support vector machines. *Neural Networks*, *14*(1), 23–35. doi:10.1016/S0893-6080(00)00077-0 PMID:11213211

Sveinbjornsdottir, S. (2016). The clinical symptoms of Parkinson's disease. *Journal of Neurochemistry*, *139*, 318–324. doi:10.1111/jnc.13691 PMID:27401947

Szegedy, C., Liu, W., Jia, Y., Sermanet, P., Reed, S., & Anguelov, D., … Rabinovich, A. (2015). Going deeper with convolutions. *2015 IEEE Conference on Computer Vision and Pattern Recognition (CVPR)*. doi:10.1109/cvpr.2015.7298594

Tafti, A. D., & Mirsadeghi, E. (2012, November). A novel adaptive recursive median filter in image noise reduction based on using the entropy. In *2012 IEEE International Conference on Control System, Computing and Engineering* (pp. 520-523). IEEE. 10.1109/ICCSCE.2012.6487201

Tahafchi, P., Molina, R., Roper, J., Sowalsky, K., Hass, C. J., Gunduz, A., … Judy, J. W. (2017). Freezing-of-gait detection using temporal, spatial, and physiological features with a support- vector-machine classifier. *39th Annual International Conference of the IEEE Engineering in Medicine and Biology Society (EMBC)*, 2867-2870.

Talo, M., Baloglu, U. B., Yıldırım, Ö., & Acharya, U. R. (2019). Application of deep transfer learning for automated brain abnormality classification using MR images. *Cognitive Systems Research*, *54*, 176–188. doi:10.1016/j.cogsys.2018.12.007

Tanaka, T., Torii, S., Kabuta, I., Shimizu, K., & Tanaka, M. (2008). Pattern classification of nevus with texture analysis. *IEEJ Transactions on Electrical and Electronic Engineering*, *3*(1), 143–150. doi:10.1002/tee.20246

Tang, Alelyani, & Liu. (2016). Feature selection for classification: A Review. *Egyptian Informatics J*. doi:10.1016/j.eij.2018.03.002

Tang, J., Alelyani, S., & Liu, H. (2014). *Feature selection for classification: a review*. Data Classification Algorithm Applications.

Tang, J., Alelyani, S., & Liu, H. (2014). Feature Selection for Classification: A Review. In C. C. Aggarwal (Ed.), *Data Classification: Algorithms and Applications* (pp. 37–64). CRC Press.

Tang, X., Dai, Y., & Xiang, Y. (2019). Feature selection based on feature interactions with application to text categorization. *Expert Systems with Applications*, *120*, 207–216. doi:10.1016/j.eswa.2018.11.018

Ticlavilca, A. M., & McKee, M. (2011). Multivariate Bayesian regression approach to forecast releases from a system of multiple reservoirs. *Water Resources Management*, *25*(2), 523–543. doi:10.100711269-010-9712-y

Tiebout, C. (1956). A Pure Theory of Local Expenditures. *Journal of Political Economy*, *64*(5), 416–424. doi:10.1086/257839

Tisseuil, C., Vrac, M., Lek, S., & Wade, A. J. (2010). Statistical downscaling of river flows. *Journal of Hydrology (Amsterdam)*, *385*(1–4), 279–291. doi:10.1016/j.jhydrol.2010.02.030

Tolika, K., Maheras, P., Flocas, H. A., & Arseni-Papadimitriou, A. (2006). An evaluation of a general circulation model (GCM) and the NCEP-NCAR reanalysis data for winter precipitation in Greece. *International Journal of Climatology*, *26*(7), 935–955. doi:10.1002/joc.1290

Tommaso, P., & Helmut, L. (2011). Does the Box-Cox transformation help in forecasting macroeconomic time series? Academic Press.

Tomozeiu, R., Cacciamani, C., Pavan, V., Morgillo, A., & Busuioc, A. (2007). Climate change scenarios for surface temperature in Emilia-Romagna (Italy) obtained using statistical downscaling models. *Theoretical and Applied Climatology*, *90*(1–2), 25–47. doi:10.100700704-006-0275-z

Tong, J., Zhao, Y., Zhang, P., Chen, L., & Jiang, L. (2019). MRI brain tumor segmentation based on texture features and kernel sparse coding. *Biomedical Signal Processing and Control*, *47*, 387–392. doi:10.1016/j.bspc.2018.06.001

Topalova, P. (2007). *Trade Liberalization, Poverty and Inequality: Evidence from Indian Districts. Globalization and Poverty*. http://www.nber.org/chapters/c0110.pdf

Trigo, R. M., & Palutikof, J. P. (2001). Precipitation scenarios over Iberia: A comparison between direct GCM output and different downscaling techniques. *Journal of Climate*, *14*(23), 4422–4446. doi:10.1175/1520-0442(2001)014<4422:PSOIAC>2.0.CO;2

Tripathi, S., Srinivas, V. V., & Nanjundiah, R. S. (2006). Downscaling of precipitation for climate change scenarios: A support vector machine approach. *Journal of Hydrology (Amsterdam)*, *330*(3–4), 621–640. doi:10.1016/j.jhydrol.2006.04.030

Trivedi, S. (2016). A study of machine learning classifiers for spam detection. In *Proceedings: The 4th International Symposium on Computational and Business Intelligence, ISCBI*, 176-180. 10.1109/ISCBI.2016.7743279

Tuo, Q., Zhao, H., & Hu, Q. (2019). Hierarchical feature selection with subtree based graph regularization. *Knowledge-Based Systems*, *163*, 996–1008. doi:10.1016/j.knosys.2018.10.023

Turkoglu, M., & Hanbay, D. (2019). Recognition of plant leaves: An approach with hybrid features produced by dividing leaf images into two and four parts. *Applied Mathematics and Computation*, *352*, 1–14. doi:10.1016/j.amc.2019.01.054

Tuv, E., Borisov, A., Runger, G., & Torkkola, K. (2009). Feature selection with ensembles, artificial variables, and redundancy elimination. *Journal of Machine Learning Research*, *10*, 1341–1366.

Ullah, I., & Mahmoud, Q. H. (2020, May). A Scheme for Generating a Dataset for Anomalous Activity Detection in IoT Networks. In *Canadian Conference on Artificial Intelligence* (pp. 508-520). Springer.

Umbaugh, S. E., Moss, R. H., & Stoecker, W. V. (1991). Applying artificial intelligence to the identification of variegated coloring in skin tumors. *IEEE Engineering in Medicine and Biology Magazine*, *10*(4), 57–62. doi:10.1109/51.107171 PMID:18238392

Uramová, J., Scgeč, P., Moravčík, M., Papán, J., Kontšek, M., & Hrabovský, J. (2018, November). Infrastructure for generating new IDS dataset. In *2018 16th International Conference on Emerging eLearning Technologies and Applications (ICETA)* (pp. 603-610). IEEE. 10.1109/ICETA.2018.8572201

USC-SIPI image database for research in image processing, image analysis, and machine vision. (n.d.). Retrieved from http://sipi.usc.edu/database/

Valenzuelab, Rojas, Guillen, Herrera, Pomares, Marquez, & Pasadas. (2008). Soft-computing techniques and ARMA model for time series prediction. *Neural Computing*, *71*, 519-537.

Van Bergeijk, P. A. G., & Brakman, S. (2010). Introduction: The Comeback of the Gravity Model. In P. A. G. Van Bergeijk & S. Brakman (Eds.), *The Gravity Model in International Trade: Advances and Applications* (pp. 1–28). Cambridge: Cambridge University Press. doi:10.1017/CBO9780511762109.001

Vandal, T., Kodra, E., & Ganguly, A. R. (2019). Intercomparison of machine learning methods for statistical downscaling: The case of daily and extreme precipitation. *Theoretical and Applied Climatology*, *137*(1–2), 557–570. doi:10.100700704-018-2613-3

Vedaldi, A., & Lenc, K. (2015, October). Matconvnet: Convolutional neural networks for matlab. In *Proceedings of the 23rd ACM international conference on Multimedia* (pp. 689-692). 10.1145/2733373.2807412

Vidyarthi, A., & Mittal, N. (2015, December). Performance analysis of Gabor-Wavelet based features in classification of high grade malignant brain tumors. In *2015 39th National Systems Conference (NSC)* (pp. 1-6). IEEE. 10.1109/NATSYS.2015.7489135

Vijayarani, S., Ilamathi, M. J., & Nithya, M. (2015). Preprocessing techniques for text mining-an overview. *International Journal of Computer Science & Communication Networks, 5*(1), 7–16.

Vocaturo, E., & Veltri, P. (2017). On the use of Networks in Biomedicine. *FNC/MobiSPC, 2017,* 498-503.

Vocaturo, E., & Zumpano, E. (2020). A Multiple Instance Learning Solution for Automatic Detection of Dysplastic Nevi. *Proceedings of the 28th Italian Symposium on Advanced Database Systems, Villasimius (Sud Sardegna).*

Vocaturo, E., Perna, D., & Zumpano, E. (2019a, November). Machine Learning Techniques for Automated Melanoma Detection. In *2019 IEEE International Conference on Bioinformatics and Biomedicine (BIBM)* (pp. 2310-2317). IEEE. 10.1109/BIBM47256.2019.8983165

Vocaturo, E., & Zumpano, E. (2019, November). Dangerousness of dysplastic nevi: a Multiple Instance Learning Solution for Early Diagnosis. In *2019 IEEE International Conference on Bioinformatics and Biomedicine (BIBM)* (pp. 2318-2323). IEEE. 10.1109/BIBM47256.2019.8983056

Vocaturo, E., Zumpano, E., & Veltri, P. (2018, December). Image pre-processing in computer vision systems for melanoma detection. In *2018 IEEE International Conference on Bioinformatics and Biomedicine (BIBM)* (pp. 2117-2124). IEEE. 10.1109/BIBM.2018.8621507

Vocaturo, E., Zumpano, E., & Veltri, P. (2019b, June). On the Usefulness of Pre-Processing Step in Melanoma Detection Using Multiple Instance Learning. In *International Conference on Flexible Query Answering Systems* (pp. 374-382). Springer. 10.1007/978-3-030-27629-4_34

Wallerstein, I. (1974). *The Modern World System.* Academic Press.

Wang, X., Du, W., Guo, F., & Hu, S. (2020). *Leaf Recognition Based on Elliptical Half Gabor and Maximum Gap Local Line Direction Pattern.* Academic Press.

Wang, X., Wang, S., Zhang, Y., & Guo, K. (2017). A novel image encryption algorithm based on chaotic shuffling method. *Information Security Journal: A Global Perspective, 26*(1), 7-16.

Wang, B., Zhao, W., Gao, P., Zhang, Y., & Wang, Z. (2018). Crack damage detection method via multiple visual features and efficient multi-task learning model. *Sensors (Basel), 18*(6), 1796. doi:10.339018061796 PMID:29865256

Wang, H., Jing, X., & Niu, B. (2017). A discrete bacterial algorithm for feature selection in classifcation of microarray gene expression cancer data. *Knowledge-Based Systems, 126,* 8–19. doi:10.1016/j.knosys.2017.04.004

Wang, J., & Zhang, C. (2018). Software reliability prediction using a deep learning model based on the RNN encoder–decoder. *Reliability Engineering & System Safety, 170,* 73–82. doi:10.1016/j.ress.2017.10.019

Wang, L., Wang, C., & Chen, Y. A. (2018). Fast three-dimensional display method for time- frequency spectrogram used in embedded fault diagnosis devices. *Applied Sciences, 8*(10), 1930. doi:10.3390/app8101930

Wang, S., Wei, Y., Li, D., Zhang, W., & Li, W. (2007, August). A hybrid method of feature selection for Chinese text sentiment classification. In *Fourth International Conference on Fuzzy Systems and Knowledge Discovery (FSKD 2007)* (Vol. 3, pp. 435-439). IEEE. 10.1109/FSKD.2007.49

Wang, X. Y., Chen, F., & Wang, T. (2010). A new compound mode of confusion and diffusion for block encryption of image based on chaos. *Communications in Nonlinear Science and Numerical Simulation, 15*(9), 2479–2485. doi:10.1016/j.cnsns.2009.10.001

Wang, X., & Paliwal, K. K. (2003). Feature extraction and dimensionality reduction algorithms and their applications in vowel recognition. *Pattern Recognition, 36*(10), 2429–2439. doi:10.1016/S0031-3203(03)00044-X

Wang, X., Tang, H., Zheng, K., & Tao, Y. (2020). Detection of compromised accounts for online social networks based on a supervised analytical hierarchy process. *IET Information Security, 14*(4), 401–409. doi:10.1049/iet-ifs.2018.5286

Wang, X., & Xu, D. (2014). Image encryption using genetic operators and intertwining logistic map. *Nonlinear Dynamics, 78*(4), 2975–2984. doi:10.100711071-014-1639-z

Wang, X., & Zhang, H. L. (2016). A novel image encryption algorithm based on genetic recombination and hyper-chaotic systems. *Nonlinear Dynamics, 83*(1-2), 333–346. doi:10.100711071-015-2330-8

Wasserman, S., & Faust, K. (1994). *Social Network Analysis: MethodsApplications*. Cambridge University Press. doi:10.1017/CBO9780511815478

Wellman, B. (1988). Structural Analysis: From Method and Metaphor to TheorySubstance. In B. Wellm & S. D. Berkowitz (Eds.), *Social Structures: A Network Approach* (pp. 19–61). Cambridge University Press.

Wetterhall, F., Halldin, S., & Xu, C. Y. (2005). Statistical precipitation downscaling in central Sweden with the analogue method. *Journal of Hydrology (Amsterdam), 306*(1–4), 174–190. doi:10.1016/j.jhydrol.2004.09.008

Wighton, P., Lee, T. K., & Atkins, M. S. (2008, March). Dermascopic hair disocclusion using inpainting. In Medical Imaging 2008: Image Processing (Vol. 6914, p. 691427). International Society for Optics and Photonics. doi:10.1117/12.770776

Wilby, R. L., Charles, S. P., Zorita, E., Timbal, B., Whetton, P., & Mearns, L. O. (2004). *Guidelines for use of climate scenarios developed from statistical downscaling methods. In IPCC Data Distribution Centre Report* (p. 27). Norwich, UK: UEA.

Wilby, R. L., Dawson, C. W., & Barrow, E. M. (2002). SDSM - A decision support tool for the assessment of regional climate change impacts. *Environmental Modelling & Software, 17*(2), 145–157. doi:10.10161364-8152(01)00060-3

Wittstruck, D., & Teuteberg, F. (2012). Integrating the concept of sustainability into the partner selection process: A fuzzy-AHP-TOPSIS approach. *International Journal of Logistics Systems and Management, 12*(2), 195–226. doi:10.1504/IJLSM.2012.047221

Woo, S., & Lee, C. (2018). Incremental feature extraction based on decision boundaries. *Pattern Recognition, 77*, 65–74. doi:10.1016/j.patcog.2017.12.010

Worden, K. (2010). Structural health monitoring using pattern recognition. In *New Trends in Vibration Based Structural Health Monitoring* (pp. 183–246). Vienna: Springer. doi:10.1007/978-3-7091-0399-9_5

Worden, K., & Dulieu-Barton, J. M. (2004). An overview of intelligent fault detection in systems and structures. *Structural Health Monitoring, 3*(1), 85–98. doi:10.1177/1475921704041866

Wu, X. L. (2007). Consistent feature selection reduction about classification data set. *Jisuanji Gongcheng yu Yingyong, 42*(18), 174–176.

Wu, X., Kan, H., & Kurths, J. (2015). A new color image encryption scheme based on DNA sequences and multiple improved 1D chaotic maps. *Applied Soft Computing, 37*, 24–39. doi:10.1016/j.asoc.2015.08.008

Xu, C., He, J., Zhang, X., Wang, C., & Duan, S. (2017). Detection of freezing of gait using template- matching-based approaches. *Journal of Sensors*, 1–8.

Xu, H., Su, X., Wang, Y., Cai, H., Cui, K., & Chen, X. (2019). Automatic bridge crack detection using a convolutional neural network. *Applied Sciences*, 9(14), 2867. doi:10.3390/app9142867

Xu, R., Chen, N., Chen, Y., & Chen, Z. (2020). Downscaling and Projection of Multi-CMIP5 Precipitation Using Machine Learning Methods in the Upper Han River Basin. *Advances in Meteorology, 2020*. doi:10.1155/2020/8680436

Yang, T., Cui, T., Xu, C. Y., Ciais, P., & Shi, P. (2017). Development of a new IHA method for impact assessment of climate change on flow regime. *Global and Planetary Change*, *156*, 68–79. doi:10.1016/j.gloplacha.2017.07.006

Yang, T., Pan, Q., Li, J., & Li, S. Z. (2005, June). Real-time multiple objects tracking with occlusion handling in dynamic scenes. In *2005 IEEE Computer Society Conference on Computer Vision and Pattern Recognition (CVPR'05)* (Vol. 1, pp. 970-975). IEEE. 10.1109/CVPR.2005.292

Yang, T., Shao, Q., Hao, Z. C., Chen, X., Zhang, Z., Xu, C. Y., & Sun, L. (2010). Regional frequency analysis and spatio-temporal pattern characterization of rainfall extremes in the Pearl River Basin, China. *Journal of Hydrology (Amsterdam)*, *380*(3–4), 386–405. doi:10.1016/j.jhydrol.2009.11.013

Yang, T., Wang, C., Chen, Y., Chen, X., & Yu, Z. (2015). Climate change and water storage variability over an arid endorheic region. *Journal of Hydrology (Amsterdam)*, *529*(P1), 330–339. doi:10.1016/j.jhydrol.2015.07.051

Yan, R., Chen, X., & Mukhopadhyay, S. C. (2017). Advanced signal processing for structural health monitoring. In *Structural Health Monitoring* (pp. 1–11). Cham: Springer. doi:10.1007/978-3-319-56126-4_1

Ye, G., Pan, C., Huang, X., & Mei, Q. (2018). An efficient pixel-level chaotic image encryption algorithm. *Nonlinear Dynamics*, *94*(1), 745–756. doi:10.100711071-018-4391-y

Ye, X. W., Dong, C. Z., & Liu, T. (2016). A review of machine vision-based structural health monitoring: Methodologies and applications. *Journal of Sensors*.

Yin, C., Zhu, Y., Fei, J., & He, X. (2017). A deep learning approach for intrusion detection using recurrent neural networks. *IEEE Access: Practical Innovations, Open Solutions*, *5*, 21954–21961. doi:10.1109/ACCESS.2017.2762418

Yin, K., Zhao, H., & Lu, L. (2018). Functional link artificial neural network filter based on the q-gradient for nonlinear active noise control. *Journal of Sound and Vibration*, *435*, 205–217. doi:10.1016/j.jsv.2018.08.015

Young, S. (1996). A review of large-vocabulary continuous-speech recognition. *IEEE Signal Processing Magazine*, *13*(5), 45–56. doi:10.1109/79.536824

Zahavy, T., Ben-Zrihem, N., & Mannor, S. (2016). Graying the black box: Understanding dqns. *International Conference on Machine Learning*, 1899–1908.

Zahran, B. M., & Kanaan, G. (2009). *Text feature selection using particle swarm optimization algorithm 1*. Academic Press.

Zechner. (2011). Computing and Evaluating Syntactic Complexity Features for automated Scoring of Spontaneous Non-Native Speech. *Proceedings of the 49th Annual Meeting of The Association for Computational Linguistics*, 69(5), 722–731.

Zeiler, M. D., & Fergus, R. (2014). Visualizing and understanding Convolutional networks. *Computer Vision – ECCV 2014*, 818-833. doi:10.1007/978-3-319-10590-1_53

Zhang, B., & Govindaraju, R. S. (2000). Prediction of watershed runoff using Bayesian concepts and modular neural networks. *Water Resources Research*, *36*(3), 753–762. doi:10.1029/1999WR900264

Zhang, G., & Liu, Q. (2011). A novel image encryption method based on total shuffling scheme. *Optics Communications, 284*(12), 2775–2780. doi:10.1016/j.optcom.2011.02.039

Zhang, J., Luo, Z., Li, C., Zhou, C., & Li, S. (2019). Manifold regularized discriminative feature selection for multi-label learning. *Pattern Recognition, 95,* 136–150. doi:10.1016/j.patcog.2019.06.003

Zhang, K., Cheng, H., & Zhang, B. (2018). Unified approach to pavement crack and sealed crack detection using pre-classification based on transfer learning. *Journal of Computing in Civil Engineering, 32*(2), 04018001. doi:10.1061/(ASCE)CP.1943-5487.0000736

Zhang, L. Y., Li, C., Wong, K. W., Shu, S., & Chen, G. (2012). Cryptanalyzing a chaos-based image encryption algorithm using alternate structure. *Journal of Systems and Software, 85*(9), 2077–2085. doi:10.1016/j.jss.2012.04.002

Zhang, Y., Gong, D., Gao, X., Tian, T., & Sun, X. (2020). Binary differential evolution with self-learning for multi-objective feature selection. *Information Sciences, 507,* 67–85. doi:10.1016/j.ins.2019.08.040

Zhang, Y., Li, H. G., Wang, Q., & Peng, C. (2019). A filter-based bare-bone particle swarm optimization algorithm for unsupervised feature selection. *Applied Intelligence, 49*(8), 2889–2898. doi:10.100710489-019-01420-9

Zheng, A., & Casari, A. (2018). *Feature engineering for machine learning: principles and techniques for data scientists.* Academic Press.

Zheng, W., & Feng, G. (2014). Feature Selection Method Based on Improved Document Frequency. *Telkomnika, 12*(4), 905. doi:10.12928/telkomnika.v12i4.536

Zheng, W., Zhu, X., Wen, G., Zhu, Y., Yu, H., & Gan, J. (2020). Unsupervised feature selection by self-paced learning regularization. *Pattern Recognition Letters, 132,* 4–11. doi:10.1016/j.patrec.2018.06.029

Zhou, G.-D., & Yi, T.-H. (2013). The nonuniform node configuration of wireless sensor networks for long-span bridge health monitoring. *International Journal of Distributed Sensor Networks.*

Zhou, H., Schaefer, G., Sadka, A. H., & Celebi, M. E. (2009). Anisotropic mean shift based fuzzy c-means segmentation of dermoscopy images. *IEEE Journal of Selected Topics in Signal Processing, 3*(1), 26–34. doi:10.1109/JSTSP.2008.2010631

Zhou, Y., Bao, L., & Chen, C. P. (2014). A new 1D chaotic system for image encryption. *Signal Processing, 97,* 172–182. doi:10.1016/j.sigpro.2013.10.034

Zhu, Q. H., & Yang, Y. B. (2018). Discriminative embedded unsupervised feature selection. *Pattern Recognition Letters, 112,* 219–225. doi:10.1016/j.patrec.2018.07.018

Zorarpacı, E., & Özel, S. A. (2016). A hybrid approach of differential evolution and artificial bee colony for feature selection. *Expert Systems with Applications, 62,* 91–103. doi:10.1016/j.eswa.2016.06.004

Zumpano, E., Iaquinta, P., Caroprese, L., Dattola, F., Tradigo, G., Veltri, P., & Vocaturo, E. (2018, December). Simpatico 3d: A medical information system for diagnostic procedures. In *2018 IEEE International Conference on Bioinformatics and Biomedicine (BIBM)* (pp. 2125-2128). IEEE. 10.1109/BIBM.2018.8621090

About the Contributors

Mrutyunjaya Panda is currently working as Reader in the P.G. Department of Computer Science and Applications, Utkal University, Vani Vihar, Bhubaneswar, Odisha, India. He has published about 75 papers in international and national journals and conferences. He has also published 10 book chapters, edited books in Springer and authored text books on: soft computing techniques and modern approaches of data mining; to his credit. His active areas of research include data mining, intrusion detection, social networking, wireless sensor networks, image processing, information retrieval, and sentiment analysis.

* * *

Bibhudendra Acharya received the M. Tech. and Ph.D. degree in Electronics and Telecommunication from National Institute of Technology, Rourkela, India. He is currently an Assistant Professor in the Electronics and Communication Engineering Department, National Institute of Technology Raipur, Chhattisgarh, India. His research interests include Cryptography and Network Security, Microcontroller and Embedded system, Signal Processing, Mobile Communication. He has more than 100 research publications in National/ International Journals and conferences.

Nalini Kanta Barpanda received the B.E. in Electrical Engineering from Utkal University and M. Tech. degrees in Electronics & Communication Engineering from BP University of Technology respectively. He got his Ph.D. in the field of Computer Science & Engineering from Sambalpur University. He is now working as Reader and Head, P.G Department of Electronics, Sambalpur University, Burla, Odisha, India. His research area includes Performance analysis of Computer Interconnection Networks, Wireless Sensor Network & IOT.

Dwiti Krishna Bebarta is presently working as Associate Professor and HoD in the Department of Information Technology, GVP College of Engineering for Women, Vishakhapatnam. Dr. Bebarta has received his UG degree in electronic and communication engineering from The Institution of Engineers (India) in 1996, M. Tech. in Computer Science from Utkal University in 2002, and a Ph.D. degree in Computer Science and Engineering from Siksha 'O' Anusandhan University, Bhubaneswar, Odisha, India in 2016. He has published more than 20 journal and conference research articles with various reputed publishers. His area of research interest lies in Data Mining, Soft Computing, Image Processing, and Cryptography. He is a Life Member of the Indian Society for Technical Education (ISTE). ORCID id: https://orcid.org/0000-0001-9860-3448.

Ajit Kumar Behera is working as an Asst. Professor in MCA Department, Silicon Institute of Technology, Patia, Bhubaneswar, Odisha. Currently he is pursuing his PhD in Utkal University, Vani Vihar, Bhubaneswar, Odisha, India. His research interests are software reliability, Neural Networks and soft computing techniques.

Birendra Biswal received an M.E. degree in engineering from the University College of Engineering Burla, Sambalpur, India, in 2001. He received his Ph.D. from Biju Patnaik University of Technology (BPUT), Rourkela, India in the year 2009. He is currently working as a Professor of Electronics and Communication Engineering at GVP College of Engineering (A), Andhra Pradesh, India. His major research work focuses on biomedical signal & image processing for a variety of medical imaging applications. He has published scholarly articles in several international journals like IEEE, IET, and Elsevier with high impact factor. He is currently working on Diabetic Retinopathy, Hypertensive Retinopathy, and Prostate Cancer to develop novel algorithms for the detection and classification of diseases under the "Centre for Medical Imaging (CMI)" lab at GVP College of Engineering (A), India.

Bhanu Chander, a Research scholar at Pondicherry University, India. Graduated from Acharya Nagarjuna University, A.P, in the year of 2013. A post-graduate degree from Central University of Rajasthan, Rajasthan in the year of 2016. Presently his main interesting areas include Wireless Sensor Networks, Machine Learning, Deep Learning, Neural networks, Cryptography, and Computer networks.

Hocine Chebi: born on April 26, in Tazmalt (W: Bejaïa), Algiers. He obtained his baccalaureate in Electrical Engineering in 2007 from the technical school of Mekla (W: Tizi-ouzou), Algiers. He then obtained his State Engineer degree in Control of Industrial Processesing in June 2013, from the faculty of hydrocarbons and chemistry (FHC) at the university of Boumerdès, Algiers. He then went on to obtain a Magister in Electrical engineering/automatic option controls and order in 2015 at the polytechnic Military academy (EMP) of Bordj El Bahri, Algiers. He enrolled in the Faculty of hydrocarbons and chemistry (FHC) at the University of Boumerdès, for a PhD in Automation and Industrial Informatics since December 2015. His field of research is directed towards the vision by computer, and the detection of anomalies.

Lalitha Dhavala is a Professor in Department of computer science & Systems Engineering in Andhra University College of Engineering(A), Andhra Pradesh, Visakhapatnam, India. she has received her Ph.D from JNT University Hyderabad in 2009. 9 PhDs were awarded under her guidance and she is presently guiding more than 20 research scholars. Her research interests include Deep Learning, Cryptography & Network Security, Stenography & Digital Watermarking, Pattern Recognition, Image Processing, Cyber Crime & Digital Forensics.

Mukesh Drolia received the B.Tech. degree in Electronics and Telecommunication Engineering from the National Institute of Technology, Raipur, Chhattisgarh, India. In B.Tech., his project work is on Image Encryption Techniques

Nashwa El-Bendary received the Ph.D. degree in information technology from the Faculty of Computers and Information, Cairo University, Egypt, in 2008. She is a Professor with the College of Computing and Information Technology, Arab Academy for Science, Technology, and Maritime Transport (AASTMT). She has authored more than 80 articles published in indexed international journals and conferences. She also participated in several international research projects. Her research interests include image and signal processing, machine learning, pattern recognition, and Internet of Things. Dr. El-Bendary was a recipient of the UNESCO-ALECSO Award for Creativity and Technical Innovation for Young Researchers, in 2014, and The L'Oréal-UNESCO For Women in Science Fellowship, in 2015. Also, she is an Editorial Board Member of the Applied Soft Computing Journal, Elsevier and an IEEE Senior Member.

Esraa Elhariri received the B.Sc. degree in computer science from the Faculty of Computers and Information (FCI), Fayoum University, Egypt, in 2010, and the M.Sc. degree from FCI-Cairo University, Egypt, in 2015. Her M.Sc. topic was about content-based image retrieval for agricultural crops. She is currently pursuing the Ph.D. degree with FCI-Fayoum University. While her Ph.D. topic is about IOT-based technique for historical and cultural heritage preservation. She is currently a Lecturer Assistant with the Faculty of Computers and Information, Fayoum University. She is also the Deputy Director of Alumni Follow-Up Unit. She has published several articles in international journals and peer-reviewed international conference proceedings along with a book chapter. Her research interests include machine learning, image and signal processing, bio-inspired optimization, wireless sensors network cloud computing security, and the IoT.

Hadeer Elziaat received the bachelor degree in Java Mobile Application, Computer Science department from Future University in Egypt, in 2013. She is currently pursuing the master degree in Deep learning and Signal processing at Arab Academy for science and Technology, Egypt, 2016. From 2009 till now, she is a Teaching Assistance at Future University in Egypt.

Rabindranath Jana is presently doing research, teaching and training in Indian Statistical Institute, Kolkata as an Associate Scientist-'B'. His research experience in social sciences, especially in social networks and its analysis is more than 25 years. He has published several research articles in various peer-reviewed journals. He has participated and presented research paper in national and international conferences/ seminars/ workshops. Currently, he is doing research on different sociological issues (like migration, trade, health etc.) using social network analysis approaches.

Judith Justin, Professor & Head of Department of Biomedical Instrumentation Engineering at School of Engineering, Avinashilingam Institute of Home Science and Higher Education, Coimbatore, graduated in Instrumentation and Control Engineering from Government College of Technology, Coimbatore, India. She post-graduated in Biomedical Engineering from Indian Institute of Technology, Madras, India and obtained her doctorate in Information and Communication Engineering from Anna University, Chennai, India. Her research interests are in the field of Bio-signal & Image Processing, Wearable Sensors and Medical Instrumentation. Her research publications include more than 40 in peer-reviewed journals, book chapters and conference proceedings. She has gained many research funds from government funding agencies. She serves as a subject expert in Biomedical Engineering and a doctoral committee member for research scholars.

Rajesh K. completed his M.Tech in Computer Science and Technology from Andhra University in 2010. He is currently pursuing his Ph.D in Department of Computer Science and Engineering, College of Engineering, Andhra University, Visakhapatnam. He is a member of Computer Society of India. His research interests include Deep Learning, Computer Vision, Business Intelligence, Location Intelligence, Artificial Intelligence and Big Data and he has published papers in the respective areas.

Babita Majhi did her Ph.D. in 2009 from National Institute of Technology Rourkela, Odisha and Post Doctoral research work at the University of Sheffield, UK (Dec.2011-Dec. 2012) under the prestigious BOYSCAST Fellowship of DST, Govt. of India. She is presently working as an Asst. Professor in the department of Computer Science and Information Technology, Guru Ghasidas Vishwavidyalaya, Central University, Bilaspur, India. She has guided 06 Ph.D., 08 M.Tech. theses in the field of adaptive signal processing, bioinformatics, data mining, computational finance and Machine Learning and 70 MCA/MSc theses. She has published 128 research papers in various referred International journals and conferences. Her total number of citations are 1506 with h-index:19 and i10index:35. She is a senior member of IEEE. Her research interests are Adaptive Signal Processing, Machine Learning, Computational Finance, Distributed Signal Processing and Data Mining.

Ritanjali Majhi is an Associate professor at School of Management, National Institute of Technology Karnataka, Surathkal. She has expertise in the field of Green Marketing, Big data Analysis, Consumer decision making, Time series Prediction, Artificial intelligence and soft and evolutionary application to Management, Marketing effectiveness metrics, E-Marketing, and Marketing Analytics. She has more than 15years experience of research with publication in high impact factor journals and has worked on research project funded by Indian government. She has guided 02 Ph.D. and 50 Master theses. She has published 98 research papers in various referred International journals and conferences. Her total number of citations are 517 with h-index: 10. She has reviewed many reputed journals. She is in the Board of Studies members of Many prestigious institutions.

R. Maruthakutti is teaching Sociology and doing research for more than 25 years. Currently he is Professor, Department of Sociology, Manonmaniam Sundaranar University, Tirunelveli, Tamil Nadu. He has carried out very important and creditable research on working class families, mainstream and transitional societies including tribal societies, gender issues and gerontology. Equipped with the network framework, he has mapped out the social network of senior citizens and their overall support system. He has presented research papers at international forums including World Congress of Gerontology, Adelaide (1997), Rio de Janerio (2005), DICGF conference, Taiwan (2013) and World Congress of Sociology, Durban (2006), Yakohama, Japan (2014). He has also presented 18 papers in the national level conferences. Further, he has 21 publications in refereed journals. He has guided eleven Ph.D. and six M.Phil. students. He has been awarded three major research projects from World Bank assisted FREEP, UGC and ICSSR and also submitted three minor research projects. To his credit, he earned Commonwealth Fellowship and visited University of Wales, Bangor, UK during 2002-2003. He has done collaborative research with Swansea University, UK on the issues involving institutionalization of the elderly.

Partha Sarathi Mishra is an Assistant Professor in the Department of Computer Science at North Orissa University, Baripada, Odisha, India. He received his Master degree in Computer Applications from North Orissa University, M. Tech degree in Computer Science from Fakir Mohan University, and Ph.D. degree in Computer Science and Information Technology from North Orissa University respectively. He also received his Master degree in Personnel Management & Industrial Relation (PM&IR) from

North Orissa University. His research interests include Neural Networks, High Order Neural networks, Evolutionary Algorithms and creation of computational intelligent systems that incorporate robustness, adaptation and creativity in their approaches for solving computationally intensive financial problems. He has already published more than twenty research papers in reputed journals and referred conferences, and has published three books for undergraduate and post graduate students.

Shashwati Mishra is currently working as an Assistant Professor in the Department of Computer Science, B.J.B.(A.) College, Bhubaneswar, Khordha, Odisha, India. She has 9 years of teaching experience.

Ramadan Moawad obtained his B.Sc from Military Technical Collage in Electric Engineering and M.Sc degree from Military Technical College in Computer Engineering. He obtained his PhD from ENSAE college, France in Software Engineering. He joined Future University in 2011 and currently working as Vice- Dean of FCIT and Head Department of Computer Science.

Sudhir Kumar Mohapatra is an Associate Professor in Department of Software Engineering, Addis Ababa Science & Technology University, Ethiopia. He has completed Ph.D. from SOA University, India in Software Testing. He has published several research papers in peer reviewed international journals and conferences. He is also reviewers in international journals of high repute.

Debabrata Nandi is an Assistant Professor in the Department of Remote sensing and GIS, North Orissa University, Baripada, Odisha. He received his M.Sc. and Ph.D degree from North Orissa University Baripada. He has 10 years of teaching and research experience in different aspects of Remote Sensing & GIS field. He has published 35 research papers in national and international journals of repute in the area of geosciences. He has also published three text book as Per CBCS syllabus "Remote sensing & Cartography", Hydrogeology of hard rock Terrain: A Geospatial Approach, Fundamental of Remote Sensing & GIS, and Two Edited book one is Geospatial Technology & Environmental Management and Application of Space Technology in Natural Resource Management.

Madhumita Panda completed her Ph.D. in Computer Science from Sambalpur University. She has publications in many national, International journals and Conferences. Her research areas include Wireless Sensor Networks, Security and Business Process Re-engineering. She was working as an Assistant Professor in Department of Computer Science, Sambalpur University. Currently she is working as an Associate Professor in the School of Computer Science, Gangadhar Meher University (GMU), Amruta Vihar, Sambalpur, Odisha, India.

Manorama Patnaik is a Ph.D. Research Scholar from the Department of Computer Science and Engineering, Birla Institute of Technolgy, Mesra, Ranchi. She has completed her Master of Computer Application from Berhampur University, Odisha. Her area of Research includes the Internet of Things, wireless network security, Data Science, Machine learning and Body sensor Area Network.

K. Abhimanyu Kumar Patro received the M.Tech. degree in Electronics and Telecommunication Engineering from the National Institute of Science and Technology, Odisha, India, and a Ph.D. degree from the Department of Electronics and Telecommunication Engineering, National Institute of Technology Raipur, Chhattisgarh, India. He is currently serving as a Faculty in the Department of Electronics and Communication Engineering, National Institute of Technology Raipur, Chhattisgarh, India. His research interests include Cryptography and Network Security, Digital Image Processing, Digital Signal Processing. He has more than 25 research publications in National/International Journals and conferences.

Srinivas Prasad, Professr, CSE Dept, at GITAM University, AP, India. He has published many papers in reputed international journals and conferences. His current research interest includes software engineering, data mining and big data.

Sachin Singh Rajput is a 6th Semester student of MCA at CSIT Department of Guru Ghasidas Vishwavidyalaya, Central University, Bilaspur. His interests are data mining and machine learning.

Nilesh Kumar Sahu received his Masters Degree (Computer Science) from Birla Institute of Technology, Mesra (Ranchi), India in 2020 and his Bachelor's degree in Computer Science Engineering from Birla Institute of Technology, Mesra India in 2017. He is currently working as an Artificial Intelligence and Data Science at Crimsons Angle Pvt. Ltd. (Startup). His areas of interest include Machine Learning, Deep Learning, Data Science, Artificial Intelligence, Data Analyst, Mobile and Wireless Sensor Networks and Internet of Things.

Itu Snigdh received her Ph.D degree in 2016 in the area of Wireless sensor networks, Department of Electronics and Communication Engineering, B.I.T Mesra.She received her Masters Degree (Software Engineering) from B.I.T Mesra(Ranchi), India in 2002 and her Bachelor's degree in Electrical Engineering from B.I.T Sindri, India in 1996. She joined the Department of Computer Science and Engineering at BIT Mesra in 2003 and is currently working as an Assistant Professor. She has authored and coauthored a number of technical journal articles and conference papers. Her areas of interest include Software Engineering, Database Management Systems, Mobile and Wireless Sensor Networks.

Shereen A. Taie received the B.Sc. degree in computer science from the Faculty of Science, Cairo University, in 1996, and the M.S. and Ph.D. degrees in computer science from the Computer and Mathematics Department, Faculty of Science, Cairo University, in 2006 and 2012, respectively. She is currently theVice Dean for Students Affairs, Faculty of Computer and Information, Fayoum University, Egypt, where she is also an Associate Professor with the Computer Science Department, Faculty of Computers and Information, and the Head of Center of Electronic Courses Production.

R. Vanithamani is currently a Professor in the Department of Biomedical Instrumentation Engineering, School of Engineering at the Avinashilingam Institute for Home Science and Higher Education for Women, in Tamil Nadu, India. She received her B.E. Electronics and Communication Engineering from Bharathiar University, Tamil Nadu, India and her M.E. (Communication Systems) and Ph.D. in Information and Communication Engineering from Anna University, Chennai - India. Dr. Vanithamani published a number of papers in peer-reviewed journals and chapters in books. She also presented research papers at several national and international conferences including the International Conference IEEE TENCON 2011 at Bali, Indonesia and International Conference of the Sri Lanka Association for Artificial Intelligence -2018 at Srilanka. Her research interests include bio-signal processing and medical image analysis.

P. Vidhyarani is teaching Mathematics for more than a decade. Currently she is working as a Assistant Professor, Department of Mathematics at Sri Parasakthi College For Women, Courtallam, Tenkasi District, Tamil Nadu. She has published seven papers in National and International journals and proceedings. Her research interest includes Graph Theory, Algebra and Operations Research. She is a member of Academy of Discrete Mathematics and its Applications (ADMA).

Eugenio Vocaturo received a degree in management engineering (2002) at University of Calabria, a Master in Industrial Engineering Management (2006), a master in Finance issued by SDA Bocconi (2016) and a PhD degree in Information and Communication Technologies at the University of Calabria, Rende, Italy (2020). He has decades of experience as company director, production and logistics manager of business groups. He works at CNR-Nanotec and is currently a contract professor of Computer Science and assistant professor of the Process Mining course at the Department of Computer Science, Modeling, Electronics and Systems Engineering (DIMES) of University of Calabria. His current research interests include machine learning, optimization, issues related to classification problems applied to the medical context, emerging issues related to Cultural Heritage. He is a member of SIBIM (Italian Scientific Society of Biomedical Informatics) and of HL7 Italy (formed in 2003 as part of HL7 International), company responsible for the localization of health standards aiming at promoting the modernization of Italian health IT.

Akash Deep Yadav received the B.Tech. degree in Electronics and Telecommunication Engineering from the National Institute of Technology, Raipur, India. In B.Tech., his project work is on Image Encryption Techniques.

Ester Zumpano is an associate professor of computer engineering at the University of Calabria, Italy. She obtained her Ph.D. in computer and systems engineering in 2003. Her areas of research include health information systems, data integration, logic programming, view updating, distributed systems, artificial Intelligence, database management. She is member of the Steering Committee of the European Conference on Advances in Databases and Information Systems (ADBIS) Conference (2007 until now). She is program char at the CILC conference 2020; she has been program chair of the 22nd International Database Engineering & Applications Symposium -IDEAS 2018; program chair of the IEEE International Workshop on Artificial Intelligence Techniques for BioMedicine and HealthCare (AIBH) at BIBM 2018 and BIBM 2019; organizer and program chair of the special session "Machine Learning in Health" at the 18th IEEE International Conference on Machine Learning and Applications (IEEE ICMLA-2019). Editor of the of the Information Systems Special issue - Managing, Mining and Learning in the Legal Data Domain for the Information Science Journal; editor of the special issue on Application of Machine Learning Methods in Bio-medical Informatics for Mathematical Biosciences and Engineering journal; editor of the special issue Mathematical Theories in the Era of Big Data for the Mathematical Problems in Engineering Journal. She is author of over 100 publications including journal articles, conference papers and book chapters.

Index

Ensure Quality Research is Introduced to the Academic Community

Become an IGI Global Reviewer for Authored Book Projects

Premier Reference Source

Emerging GIS Applications for Emergency and Disaster Management

Premier Reference Source

Managerial Strategies and Green Solutions for Project Sustainability

Premier Reference Source

Comparative Approaches to Using R and Python for Statistical Data Analysis

Premier Reference Source

Solutions for High-Touch Communications in a High-Tech World

The overall success of an authored book project is dependent on quality and timely reviews.

In this competitive age of scholarly publishing, constructive and timely feedback significantly expedites the turnaround time of manuscripts from submission to acceptance, allowing the publication and discovery of forward-thinking research at a much more expeditious rate. Several IGI Global authored book projects are currently seeking highly-qualified experts in the field to fill vacancies on their respective editorial review boards:

Applications and Inquiries may be sent to:
development@igi-global.com

Applicants must have a doctorate (or an equivalent degree) as well as publishing and reviewing experience. Reviewers are asked to complete the open-ended evaluation questions with as much detail as possible in a timely, collegial, and constructive manner. All reviewers' tenures run for one-year terms on the editorial review boards and are expected to complete at least three reviews per term. Upon successful completion of this term, reviewers can be considered for an additional term.

If you have a colleague that may be interested in this opportunity,
we encourage you to share this information with them.

IGI Global's Transformative Open Access (OA) Model:
How to Turn Your University Library's Database Acquisitions Into a Source of OA Funding

In response to the OA movement and well in advance of Plan S, IGI Global, early last year, unveiled their OA Fee Waiver (Read & Publish) Initiative.

Under this initiative, librarians who invest in IGI Global's InfoSci-Books (5,300+ reference books) and/or InfoSci-Journals (185+ scholarly journals) databases will be able to subsidize their patron's OA article processing charges (APC) when their work is submitted and accepted (after the peer review process) into an IGI Global journal. *See website for details.

How Does it Work?

1. When a library subscribes or perpetually purchases IGI Global's InfoSci-Databases and/or their discipline/subject-focused subsets, IGI Global will match the library's investment with a fund of equal value to go toward subsidizing the OA article processing charges (APCs) for their patrons.

   Researchers: **Be sure to recommend the InfoSci-Books and InfoSci-Journals to take advantage of this initiative.**

2. When a student, faculty, or staff member submits a paper and it is accepted (following the peer review) into one of IGI Global's 185+ scholarly journals, the author will have the option to have their paper published under a traditional publishing model or as OA.

3. When the author chooses to have their paper published under OA, IGI Global will notify them of the OA Fee Waiver (Read and Publish) Initiative. If the author decides they would like to take advantage of this initiative, IGI Global will deduct the US$ 2,000 APC from the created fund.

4. This fund will be offered on an annual basis and will renew as the subscription is renewed for each year thereafter. IGI Global will manage the fund and award the APC waivers unless the librarian has a preference as to how the funds should be managed.

Hear From the Experts on This Initiative:

"I'm very happy to have been able to make one of my recent research contributions, "Visualizing the Social Media Conversations of a National Information Technology Professional Association" featured in the *International Journal of Human Capital and Information Technology Professionals*, freely available along with having access to the valuable resources found within IGI Global's InfoSci-Journals database."

– **Prof. Stuart Palmer**,
Deakin University, Australia

For More Information, Visit: www.igi-global.com/publish/contributor-resources/open-access/read-publish-model
or contact IGI Global's Database Team at eresources@igi-global.com.

Printed in the United States
By Bookmasters